Lecture Notes in Computer Science

Edited by G. Goos, J. Hartmanis, and J. van Leeuw

T0250581

Springer
Berlin
Heidelberg
New York
Barcelona
Hong Kong
London
Milan
Paris
Tokyo

Werner Damm   Ernst-Rüdiger Olderog (Eds.)

Formal Techniques in Real-Time and Fault-Tolerant Systems

7th International Symposium, FTRTFT 2002
Co-sponsored by IFIP WG 2.2
Oldenburg, Germany, September 9-12, 2002
Proceedings

 Springer

Series Editors

Gerhard Goos, Karlsruhe University, Germany
Juris Hartmanis, Cornell University, NY, USA
Jan van Leeuwen, Utrecht University, The Netherlands

Volume Editors

Werner Damm
Ernst-Rüdiger Olderog
Fachbereich Informatik, Universität Oldenburg
Ammerländer Herrstr. 114-118, 26129 Oldenburg, Germany
E-mail: {damm,olderog}@informatik.uni-oldenburg.de

Cataloging-in-Publication Data applied for

Die Deutsche Bibliothek - CIP-Einheitsaufnahme

Formal techniques in real time and fault tolerant systems : 7th
international symposium ; proceedings / FTRTFT 2002, Oldenburg, Germany,
September 9 - 12, 2002. Werner Damm ; Ernst-Rüdiger Olderog (ed.).
Co-sponsored by IFIP WG 2.2. - Berlin ; Heidelberg ; New York ; Barcelona ;
Hong Kong ; London ; Milan ; Paris ; Tokyo : Springer, 2002
   (Lecture notes in computer science ; Vol. 2469)
   ISBN 3-540-44165-4

CR Subject Classification (1998): D.3.1, F.3.1, C.1.m, C.3, B.3.4, B.1.3

ISSN 0302-9743
ISBN 3-540-44165-4 Springer-Verlag Berlin Heidelberg New York

Springer-Verlag Berlin Heidelberg New York
a member of BertelsmannSpringer Science+Business Media GmbH

http://www.springer.de

© Springer-Verlag Berlin Heidelberg 2002
Printed in Germany

Typesetting: Camera-ready by author, data conversion by Olgun Computergrafik
Printed on acid-free paper   SPIN: 10871306   06/3142   5 4 3 2 1 0

Preface

This volume contains the proceedings of FTRTFT 2002, the International Symposium on *Formal Techniques in Real-Time and Fault-Tolerant Systems*, held at the University of Oldenburg, Germany, 9–12 September 2002. This symposium was the seventh in a series of FTRTFT symposia devoted to problems and solutions in safe system design. The previous symposia took place in Warwick 1990, Nijmegen 1992, Lübeck 1994, Uppsala 1996, Lyngby 1998, and Pune 2000. Proceedings of these symposia were published as volumes 331, 571, 863, 1135, 1486, and 1926 in the LNCS series by Springer-Verlag. This year the symposium was co-sponsored by IFIP Working Group 2.2 on *Formal Description of Programming Concepts*.

The symposium presented advances in the development and use of formal techniques in the design of real-time, hybrid, fault-tolerant embedded systems, covering all stages from requirements analysis to hardware and/or software implementation. Particular emphasis was placed on UML-based development of real-time systems. Through invited presentations, links between the dependable systems and formal methods research communities were strengthened. With the increasing use of such formal techniques in industrial settings, the conference aimed at stimulating cross-fertilization between challenges in industrial usages of formal methods and advanced research.

In response to the call for papers, 39 submissions were received. Each submission was reviewed by four program committee members assisted by additional referees. At the end of the reviewing process, the program committee accepted 17 papers for presentation at the symposium.

These proceedings contain revised versions of the accepted papers addressing the following topics that constituted the sessions of the symposium:

- Synthesis and Scheduling
- Timed Automata
- Bounded Model Checking of Timed Systems
- Verification and Conformance Testing
- UML Models and Model Checking

The program of the symposium was enriched by two invited tutorials:

- J. McDermid, *Software Hazard and Safety Analysis*
- K.G. Larsen, *Advances in Real-Time Model Checking*

and by six invited lectures:

- G. Buttazzo, *Real-Time Operating Systems: Problems and Solutions*
- B.P. Douglass, *Real-Time UML*
- D. Kozen, *Efficient Code Certification for Open Firmware*
- A. Pnueli, *Applications of Formal Methods in Biology*

- J. Rushby, *An Overview of Formal Verification for the Time-Triggered Architecture*
- J. Sifakis, *Scheduler Modeling Based on the Controller Synthesis Paradigm*

These proceedings also contain two overview papers by the tutorial speakers and four papers and two abstracts by the other invited speakers.

Program Committee

The program committee of FTRTFT 2002 consisted of:

R. Alur, Pennsylvania	R. de Lemos, Kent
F.S. de Boer, Utrecht	O. Maler, Grenoble
M. Broy, München	E.-R. Olderog, Oldenburg (co-chair)
A. Burns, York	A. Pnueli, Rehovot
W. Damm, Oldenburg (co-chair)	A.P. Ravn, Aalborg
J. McDermid, York	W.P. de Roever, Kiel
T. Henzinger, Berkeley	J. Rushby, Stanford
B. Jonsson, Uppsala	D. Sangiorgi, Sophia-Antipolis
M. Joseph, Pune	J. Sifakis, Grenoble
K.G. Larsen, Aalborg	B. Steffen, Dortmund

Additional Referees

We are very grateful to the following persons who assisted in reviewing the submissions:

N. Audsley	J. Hooman	O. Niese	A. Sreenivas
E. Asarin	A. Hughes	T. Noll	M. Steffen
R. Banach	H. Hungar	D. von Oheimb	A. Tiwari
M. von der Beeck	A. de Groot	O. Rüthing	S. Tripakis
G. Behrmann	J. Knoop	G.K. Palshikar	R. Venkatesh
A. Bouajjani	M. Kyas	M. Périn	B. Victor
P. Bouyer	Y. Lakhnech	P. Pettersson	M. Vidyasagar
P. Braun	S. La Torre	C. Pierik	E. de Vink
M. Cerioli	P. Makowski	B. Schätz	R. Wiesniewski
D. Dams	N. Mitra	O. Slotosch	H. Wimmel
B. Dutertre	J.-F. Monin	O. Sokolsky	A. Wißpeintner
E. Fleury	L. Mounier	M. Sorea	W. Yi
M. Fränzle	M. Müller-Olm	K. Spies	S. Yovine

Steering Committee

The steering committee of the FTRTFT series of symposia consists of M. Joseph, Pune; A. Pnueli, Rehvot; H. Rischel, Lyngby; W.-P. de Roever, Kiel; J. Yytopil, Nijmegen.

Organizing Committee

A team of members of the Fachbereich Informatik, Universität Oldenburg, and the institute OFFIS helped us in organizing the FTRTFT 2002. We would like to thank Henning Dierks, Martin Fränzle, Andrea Göken, Jochen Hoenicke, Bernhard Josko, Michael Möller, Christiane Stückemann, and Heike Wehrheim for their continuing support.

Sponsors

FTRTFT 2002 received generous support from the following institutions:

- Fachbereich Informatik, Universität Oldenburg
- OFFIS, Oldenburg
- Deutsche Forschungsgemeinschaft, Bonn (DFG)
- European IST-Project OMEGA
- BMW AG, München
- DaimlerChrysler AG, Stuttgart

Finally, we wish you, the reader of these proceedings, many new insights from studying the subsequent papers.

July 2002   W. Damm and E.-R. Olderog

Table of Contents

V   Bounded Model Checking

VI   Verification and Conformance Testing

VII   UML Models and Model Checking

VIII   Timed Automata II

Author Index

Part I

Invited Tutorials

UPPAAL Implementation Secrets

Gerd Behrmann[2], Johan Bengtsson[1], Alexandre David[1], Kim G. Larsen[2],
Paul Pettersson[1], and Wang Yi[1]

[1] Department of Information Technology, Uppsala University, Sweden
{johanb,adavid,paupet,yi}@docs.uu.se.
[2] Basic Research in Computer Science, Aalborg University, Denmark
{behrmann,kgl}@cs.auc.dk.

Abstract. In this paper we present the continuous and on-going development of datastructures and algorithms underlying the verification engine of the tool UPPAAL. In particular, we review the datastructures of Difference Bounded Matrices, Minimal Constraint Representation and Clock Difference Diagrams used in symbolic state-space representation and -analysis for real-time systems.

In addition we report on distributed versions of the tool, and outline the design and experimental results for new internal datastructures to be used in the next generation of UPPAAL.

Finally, we mention work on complementing methods involving acceleration, abstraction and compositionality.

1 Introduction

UPPAAL [LPY97] is a tool for modeling, simulation and verification of real-time systems, developed jointly by BRICS at Aalborg University and the Department of Computer Systems at Uppsala University. The tool is appropriate for systems that can be modeled as a collection of non-deterministic processes with finite control structure and real-valued clocks, communicating through channels or shared variables. Typical application areas include real-time controllers and communication protocols.

Since the first release of UPPAAL in 1995, the tool has been under constant development by the teams in Aalborg and Uppsala. The tool has consistently gained in performance over the years, which may be ascribed both to the development of new datastructures and algorithms as well as constant optimizations of their actual implementations. By now (and since long) UPPAAL has reached a state, where it is mature for application on real industrial development of real-time systems as witnessed by a number of already carried out case-studies[1].

Tables 1 and 2 show the variations of time and space consumption for three different versions of UPPAAL applied to five examples from the literature: Fischer's mutual exclusion protocol with five processes [Lam87], Philips audio-control protocol with bus-collision detection [BGK+96], a Power-Down Controller [HLS99], a TDMA start-up algorithm with three nodes [LP97], and a

---

[1] See www.uppaal.com for detailed list.

W. Damm and E.-R. Olderog (Eds.): FTRTFT 2002, LNCS 2469, pp. 3–22, 2002.

Table 1. Time requirements (in seconds) for three different UPPAAL versions.

	1998	2000	DBM	Min	Ctrl	Act	PWL	State	2002
Fischer 5	126.30	13.50	4.79	6.02	3.98	2.13	3.83	12.66	0.19
Audio	-	2.23	1.50	1.79	1.45	0.50	1.57	2.28	0.45
Power Down	*	407.82	207.76	233.63	217.62	53.00	125.25	364.87	13.26
Collision Detection	128.64	17.40	7.75	8.50	7.43	7.94	7.04	19.16	6.92
TDMA	108.70	14.36	9.15	9.84	9.38	6.01	9.33	16.96	6.01

CSMA/CD protocol with eight nodes [BDM+98]. In the column "1998" and "2000" we give the run-time data of UPPAAL versions dated January 1998 and January 2000 respectively. In addition, we report the data of the current version dated June 2002. The numbers in column "DBM" were measured without any optimisations, "Min" with Minimal Constraints Representation, "Ctrl" with Control Structure Reduction [LPY95], "Act" with Active Clock Reduction [DT98], "PWL" with the Passed and Waiting List Unification, "State" with Compact Representation of States, and finally "2002" with the best combination of options available in the current version of UPPAAL. The different versions have been compiled with a recent version of gcc and were run on the same Sun Enterprise 450 computer equipped with four 400 MHz processors and 4 Gb or physical memory. In the diagrams we use "-" to indicate that the input model was not accepted due to compability issues, and "*" to indicate that the verification did not terminate within one hour. We notice that both the time and space performance has improved significantly over the years. For the previous period December 1996 to September 1998 a report on the run-time and space improvements may be found in [Pet99]. Similar diagrams for the time period November 1998 to Januari 2001 are reported in [ABB+01].

Despite this success improvement in performance, the state-explosion problem is a still a reality[2] which prevents the tool from ever[3] being able to provide fully automatic verification of arbitrarily large and complex systems. Thus, to truely scale up, automatic verification should be complemented by other methods. Such methods investigated in the context of UPPAAL include that of *acceleration* [HL02] and *abstractions* and *compositionality* [JLS00].

The outline of the paper is as follows: Section 2 summaries the definition of timed automata, the semantics, and the basic timed automaton reachability algorithm. In section 3 we present the three main symbolic datastructures applied in UPPAAL: Difference Bounded Matrices, Minimal Constraint Representation and Clock Difference Diagrams and in section 4 we review various schemes for compact representations for symbolic states. Section 5 introduces a new exloration algorithm based on a unification of Passed and Waiting list datastructures and Section 6 reviews our considerable effort in parallel and distributed reach-

---

[2] Model-checking is either EXPTIME- or PSPACE-complete depending on the expressiveness of the logic considered.

[3] unless we succeed in showing P=PSPACE

Table 2. Space requirements (in Mb) of for different UPPAAL versions.

	1998	2000	DBM	Min	Ctrl	Act	PWL	State	2002
Fischer 5	8.86	8.14	9.72	6.97	6.40	6.35	6.74	4.83	3.21
Audio	-	3.02	5.58	5.53	5.58	4.33	4.75	3.06	3.06
Power Down	*	218.90	162.18	161.17	132.75	44.32	18.58	117.73	8.99
Collision Detection	17.00	12.78	25.75	21.94	25.75	25.75	10.38	13.70	10.38
TDMA	8.42	8.00	11.29	8.09	11.29	11.29	4.82	6.58	4.82

ability checking. Section 7 presents recent work on acceleration techniques and section 8 reviews work on abstraction and compositionality. Finally, we conclude by stating what we consider open problems for future research.

2 Preliminaries

In this section we summaries the basic definition of timed automata, their concrete and symbolic semantics and the reachability algorithm underlying the currently distributed version of UPPAAL.

Definition 1 (Timed Automaton). *Let C be the set of clocks. Let $B(C)$ be the set of conjunctions over simple conditions on the forms $x \bowtie c$ and $x - y \bowtie c$, where $x, y \in C$, $\bowtie \in \{<, \leq, =, \geq, >\}$ and c is a natural number. A timed automaton over C is a tuple (L, l_0, E, g, r, I), where L is a set of locations, $l_0 \in L$ is the initial location, $E \in L \times L$ is a set of edges, $g : E \to B(C)$ assigns guards to edges, $r : E \to 2^C$ assigns clocks to be reset to edges, and $I : L \to B(C)$ assigns invariants to locations.*

Intuitively, a timed automaton is a graph annotated with conditions and resets of non-negative real valued clocks.

Definition 2 (TA Semantics). *A clock valuation is a function $u : C \to \mathbb{R}_{\geq 0}$ from the set of clocks to the non-negative reals. Let $\mathbb{R}^C$ be the set of all clock valuations. Let $u_0(x) = 0$ for all $x \in C$. We will abuse the notation by considering guards and invariants as sets of clock valuations.*

The semantics of a timed automaton (L, l_0, E, g, r, I) over C is defined as a transition system $(S, s_0, \to)$, where $S = L \times \mathbb{R}^C$ is the set of states, $s_0 = (l_0, u_0)$ is the initial state, and $\to \subseteq S \times S$ is the transition relation such that:

- $(l, u) \to (l, u + d)$ *if* $u \in I(l)$ *and* $u + d \in I(l)$
- $(l, u) \to (l', u')$ *if there exists* $e = (l, l') \in E$ *s.t.* $u \in g(e)$, $u' = [r(e) \mapsto 0]u$, *and* $u' \in I(l)$

where for $d \in \mathbb{R}$, $u + d$ maps each clock x in C to the value $u(x) + d$, and $[r \mapsto 0]u$ denotes the clock valuation which maps each clock in r to the value 0 and agrees with u over $C \setminus r$.

The semantics of timed automata results in an uncountable transition system. It is a well known-fact that there exists a exact finite state abstraction based on convex polyhedra in $\mathbb{R}^C$ called zones (a zone can be represented by a conjunction in $B(C)$). This abstraction leads to the following symbolic semantics.

Definition 3 (Symbolic TA Semantics). *Let* $Z_0 = \bigwedge_{x \in C} x \geq 0$ *be the initial zone. The symbolic semantics of a timed automaton* (L, l_0, E, g, r, I) *over* C *is defined as a transition system* $(S, s_0, \Rightarrow)$ *called the* simulation graph, *where* $S = L \times B(C)$ *is the set of symbolic states,* $s_0 = (l_0, Z_0 \wedge I(l_0))$ *is the initial state,* $\Rightarrow = \{(s, u) \in S \times S \mid \exists e, t : s \overset{e}{\Rightarrow} t \overset{\delta}{\Rightarrow} u\}$ *: is the transition relation, and:*

- $(l, Z) \overset{\delta}{\Rightarrow} (l, norm(M, (Z \wedge I(l))^\uparrow \wedge I(l)))$
- $(l, Z) \overset{e}{\Rightarrow} (l', r_e(g(e) \wedge Z \wedge I(l)) \wedge I(l'))$ *if* $e = (l, l') \in E$.

where $Z^\uparrow = \{u + d \mid u \in Z \wedge d \in \mathbb{R}_{\geq 0}\}$ *(the* future *operation), and* $r_e(Z) = \{[r(e) \mapsto 0]u \mid u \in Z\}$ *(the* reset *operation). The function* $norm : \mathbf{N} \times B(C) \to B(C)$ *normalises the clock constraints with respect to the maximum constant* M *of the timed automaton.*

The relation $\overset{\delta}{\Rightarrow}$ contains the delay transitions and $\overset{e}{\Rightarrow}$ the edge transitions. Given the symbolic semantics it is straight forward to construct the reachability algorithm, shown in Figure 1. The symbolic semantics can be extended to cover networks of communicating timed automata (resulting in a location vector to be used instead of a location), timed automata with data variables (resulting in the addition of a variable vector).

3   Symbolic Datastructures

To utilize the above symbolic semantics algorithmically, as for example in the reachability algorithm of Figure 1, it is important to design efficient data structures and algorithms for the representation and manipulation of clock constraints. In this section, we present three such datastructures: Diffence Bounded Matrices, Minimal Constraint Representation and Clock Difference Diagrams.

Difference Bounded Matrices

Difference Bounded Matrices (DBM, see [Bel57,Dil89]) is well–known data structure which offers a canonical representation for constraint systems. A DBM representation of a constraint system Z is simply a weighted, directed graph, where the vertices correspond to the clocks of C and an additional zero–vertex 0. The graph has an edge from x to y with weight m provided $x - y \leq m$ is a constraint of Z. Similarly, there is an edge from 0 to x (from x to 0) with weight m, whenever $x \leq m$ ($x \geq -m$) is a constraint of Z^4. As an example, consider the constraint system E over $\{x_0, x_1, x_2, x_3\}$ being a conjunction of the atomic constraints $x_0 - x_1 \leq 3$, $x_3 - x_0 \leq 5$, $x_3 - x_1 \leq 2$, $x_2 - x_3 \leq 2$, $x_2 - x_1 \leq 10$, and $x_1 - x_2 \leq -4$. The graph representing E is given in Figure 2 (a).

---

[4] We assume that Z has been simplified to contain at most one upper and lower bound for each clock and clock–difference.

```
W = {(l₀, Z₀ ∧ I(l₀))}
P = ∅
while W ≠ ∅ do
    (l, Z) = W.popstate()
    if testProperty(l, Z) then return true
    if ∀(l, Y) ∈ P : Z ⊄ Y then
        P = P ∪ {(l, Z)}
        ∀(l', Z') : (l, Z) ⇒ (l', Z') do
            if ∀(l', Y') ∈ W : Z' ⊄ Y' then
                W = W ∪ {(l', Z')}
            endif
        done
    endif
done
return false
```

Fig. 1. The timed automaton reachability algorithm, with P being the passed-list containing all explored symbolic states, and W being the waiting-list containing encountered symbolic states waiting to be explored. The function *testProperty* evaluates the state property that is being checked for satisfiability. The while loop is refered to as the exploration loop.

In general, the same set of clock assignments may be described by several constraint systems (and hence graphs). To test for inclusion between constraint systems Z and Z'[5], which we recall is essential for the termination of the reachability algorithm of Figure 1, it is advantageous, that Z is *closed under entailment* in the sense that no constraint of Z can be strengthened without reducing the solution set. In particular, for Z a closed constraint system, $Z \subseteq Z'$ holds if and only if for any constraint in Z' there is a constraint in Z at least as tight; i.e. whenever $(x - y \leq m) \in Z'$ then $(x - y \leq m') \in Z$ for some $m' \leq m$. Thus, closedness provides a canonical representation, as two closed constraint systems describe the same solution set precisely when they are identical. To close a constraint system Z simply amounts to derive the shortest–path closure for its graph and can thus be computed in time $\mathcal{O}(n^3)$, where n is the number of clocks of Z . The graph representation of the closure of the constraint system E from Figure 2 (a) is given in Figure 2 (b). The emptiness-check of a constraint system Z simply amounts to checking for negative–weight cycles in its graph representation. Finally, given a closed constraint system Z the operations $Z^\uparrow$ and $r(Z)$ may be performed in time $\mathcal{O}(n)$. For more detailed information on how to efficiently implement these and other operations on DBM's we refer the reader to [Ben02,Rok93].

Minimal Constraint Representation

For the reasons stated above a matrix representation of constraint systems in closed form is an attractive data structure, which has been successfully employed

---

[5] To be precise, it is the inclusion between the *solution sets* for Z and Z'.

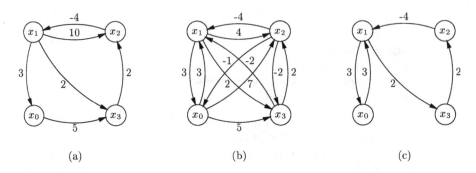

Fig. 2. Graph for E (a), its shortest–path closure (b), and shortest–path reduction (c).

by a number of real–time verification tools, e.g. UPPAAL [BLL⁺96] and KRO-
NOS [DY95]. As it gives an explicit (tightest) bound for the difference between
each pair of clocks (and each individual clock), its space–usage is of the order
$\mathcal{O}(n^2)$. However, in practice it often turns out that most of these bounds are redundant, and the reachability algorithm of Figure 1 is consequently hampered in
two ways by this representation. Firstly, the main–data structure P (the passed
list) will in many cases store all the reachable symbolic states of the automaton.
Thus, it is desirable, that when saving a symbolic state in the passed list, we
save a representation of the constraint–system with as few constraints as possible. Secondly, a constraint system Z added to the passedlist is subsequently
only used in checking inclusions of the form $Z' \subseteq Z$. Recalling the method for
inclusion–check from the previous section, we note that (given Z' is closed) the
time–complexity of the inclusion–check is linear in the number of constraints of
Z. Thus, again it is advantageous for Z to have as few constraints as possible.

In [LLPY97,LLPY02] we have presented an $\mathcal{O}(n^3)$ algorithm, which given
a constraint system constructs an equivalent reduced system with the minimal number of constraints. The reduced constraint system is canonical in the
sense that two constrain systems with the same solution set give rise to identical reduced systems. The algorithm is essentially a minimization algorithm for
weighted directed graphs. Given a weighted, directed graph with n vertices, it
constructs in time $\mathcal{O}(n^3)$ a reduced graph with the minimal number of edges
having the same shortest path closure as the original graph. Figure 2 (c) shows
the minimal graph of the graphs in Figure 2 (a) and (b), which is computed by
the algorithm.

The key to reduce a graph is obviously to remove *redundant edges*, i.e. edges
for which there exist alternative paths whose (accumulated) weight does not
exceed the weight of the edgesthemselves. E.g. in the graph of Figure 2 (a)
the edge (x_1, x_2) is clearly redundant as the accumulated weight of the path
$(x_1, x_3, (x_3, x_2)$ has a weight (4) not exceeding the weight of the edge itself
(10). Being redundant, the edge (x_1, x_2) may be removed without changing the
shortest-path closure (and hence the solution-set of the corresponding constraint
system). In this manner both the edges (x_1, x_2) and (x_2, x_3) of Figure 2 (b) are

found to be redundant. However, thought redundant, we cannot just remove the two edges as removal of one clearly requires the presence of the other. In fact, all edges between the vertices x_1, x_2 and x_3 are redundant, but obviously we cannot remove them all simultaneously without affecting the solution-set. The key explanation of this phenomena is that x_1, x_2 and x_3 constitute a zero-cycle. In fact, for zero-cycle free graphs simulataneous removal of redundant edges leads to a canonical shortest-path reduction form. For general graphs the reduction is based on a partitioning of the vertices according to membership of zero-cycles.

Our experimental results demonstrated significant space-reductions compared with traditional DBMimplmentation: on a number of benchmark and industrial examples the space saving was between 75% and 94%. Additionally, time-performance was improved.

Clock Difference Diagrams

Difference Bound Matrices (DBM's) as the standard representation for time zones in analysis of Timed Automata have a well-known shortcoming: they are not closed under set-union. This comes from the fact that a set represented by a DBM is convex, while the union of two convex sets is not necessarily convex.

Within the symbolic computation for the reachability analysis of UPPAAL, set-union however is a crucial operation which occurs in every symbolic step. The shortcoming of DBM's leads to a situation, where symbolic states which could be treated as one in theory have to be handled as a collection of several different symbolic states in practice. This leads to trade-offs in memory and time consumption, as more symbolic states have to be stored and visited during in the algorithm.

DBM's represent a zone as a conjunction of constraints on the differences between each pair of clocks of the timed automata (including a fictitious clock representing the value 0). The major idea of CDD's (Clock Difference Diagrams) is to store a zone as a decision tree of clock differences, generalizing the ideas of BDD's (Binary Decision Diagrams, see [Bry86]) and IDD's (Integer Decision Diagrams, see [ST98])

The nodes of the decision tree represent clock differences. Nodes on the same level of the tree represent the same clock difference. The order of the clock differences is fixed a-priori, all CDD's have to agree on the same ordering. The leaves of the decision tree are two nodes representing true and false, as in the case of BDD's.

Each node can have several outgoing edges. Edges are labeled with integral intervals: open, half-closed and closed intervals with integer values as the borders. A node representing the clock difference $X - Y$ together with an outgoing edge with interval I represents the constraint "$X - Y$ within I". The leafs represent the global constraints true and false respectively.

A path in a CDD from a node down to a leaf represents the set of clock values with fulfill the conjunction of constraints found along the path. Remember that a constraint is found from the pair node and outgoing edge. Paths going to false thus always represent the empty set, and thus only paths leading to the true

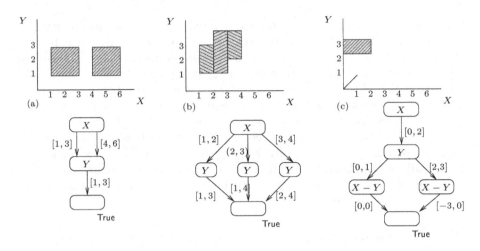

Fig. 3. Three example CDD's. Intervals not shown lead implicitly to False.

node need to be stored in the CDD. A CDD itself represents the set given by the union of all sets represented by the paths going from the root to the true node. From this clearly CDD's are closed under set-union. Figure 3 gives three examples of two-dimensional zones and their representation as CDDs. Note that the same zone can have different CDD representations.

All operations on DBM's can be lifted straightforward to CDD's. Care has to be taken when the canonical form of the DBM is involved in the operation, as there is no direct equivalent to the (unique) canonical form of DBM's for CDD's.

CDD's generalize IDD's, where the nodes represent clock values instead of clock differences. As clock differences, in contrast to clock values, are not independent of each other, operations on CDD's are much more elaborated than the same operations on IDD's. CDD's can be implemented space-efficient by using the standard BDD's technique of sharing common substructure. This sharing can also take place between different CDD's.

Experimental results have shown that using CDD's instead of DBM's can lead to space savings of up to 99%. However, in some cases a moderate increase in run time (up to 20%) has to be paid. This comes from the fact that operations involving the canonical form are much more complicated in the case of CDD's compared to DBM's. More on CDD's can be found in [LWYP99] and [BLP+99]. A similar datastructure is that of DDD's presented in [MLAH99a,MLAH99b].

4   Compact Representation of States

Symbolic states are the core objects of state space search and one of the key issues in implementing a verifier is how to represent them. In the earlier versions of UPPAAL each entity in a state (i.e. an element in the location vector, the value of an integer variable or a bound in the DBM) is mapped on a machine word.

The reason for this is simplicity and speed. However the number of possible values for each entity is usually small, and using a machine word for each of them is often a waste of space.

To conquer this problem two additional, more compact, state representations have been added. In both of them the discrete part of each state is encoded as a number, using a multiply and add scheme. This encoding is much like looking at the discrete part as a number, where each digit is an entity in the discrete state and the base varies with the number of different digits.

In the first packing scheme, the DBM is encoded using the same technique as the discrete part of the state. This gives a very space efficient but computationally expensive representation, where each state takes a minimum amount of memory but where a number of bignum division operations have to be performed to check inclusion between two DBMs.

In the second packing scheme, some of the space performance is sacrificed to allow a more efficient inclusion check. Here each bound in the DBM is encoded as a bit string long enough to represent all the possible values of this bound plus one *test bit*, i.e. if a bound can have 10 possible values then five bits are used to represent the bound. This allows cheap inclusion checking based on ideas of Paul and Simon [PS80] on comparing vectors using subtraction of long bit strings.

In experiments we have seen that the space performance of these representations are both substantially better than the traditional representation, with space savings of between 25% and 70%. As we expect, the performance of the first packing scheme, with an expensive inclusion check, is somewhat better, space-wise, than the packing scheme with the cheap inclusion check.

Considering the time performance for the packed state representations we have found that the price for using the encoding with expensive inclusion check is a slowdown of 2 − 12 times, while using the other encoding sometimes is even faster than the traditional representation. For more detailed information on this we refer the interested reader to [Ben02].

5   Passed and Waiting List Unification

The standard reachability algorithm currently applied in UPPAAL is based on two lists: the passed and the waiting lists. These lists are used in the exploration loop that pops states to be explored from the waiting list, explores them, and keeps track of already explored states with the passed list. The first algorithm of Figure 4 shows this algorithm based on two distinct lists.

We have unified these structures to a *PWList* and a queue. The queue has only references to states in PWList and is a trivial queue structure: it stores nothing by itself. The PWList acts semantically as a buffer that eliminates duplicate states, i.e. if the same state is added to the buffer several times it can only be retrieved once, even when the state was retrieved before the state is inserted a second time. To achieve this effect the PWList must keep a record of the states seen and thus it provides the functionality of both the passed list and the waiting list.

$W = \{(l_0, Z_0 \wedge I(l_0))\}$
$P = \varnothing$
while $W \neq \varnothing$ **do**
  $(l, Z) = W.popState()$
  if $testProperty(l, Z)$
  then return true
  if $\forall(l, Y) \in P : Z \not\subseteq Y$
  then
    $P = P \cup \{(l, Z)\}$
    $\forall(l', Z') : (l, Z) \Rightarrow (l', Z')$ **do**
      if $\forall(l', Y') \in W : Z' \not\subseteq Y'$
      then
        $W = W \cup \{(l', Z')\}$
      endif
    done
  endif
done
return false

$\rightarrow$

$Q = PW = \{(l_0, Z_0 \wedge I(l_0))\}$
while $Q \neq \varnothing$ **do**
  $(l, Z) = Q.popState()$
  if $testProperty(l, Z)$
  then return true
  $\forall(l', Z') : (l, Z) \Rightarrow (l', Z')$ **do**
    if $\forall(l', Y') \in PW : Z' \not\subseteq Y'$
    then
      $PW = PW \cup \{(l', Z')\}$
      $Q.append(l', Z')$
    endif
  done
done
return false

Fig. 4. Reachability algorithm with classical passed (P) and waiting (W) lists adapted to a the unified list (Q and PW).

Definition 4 (PWList). *Formally, a PWList can be described as a pair* (P, W) $\in 2^S \times 2^S$, *where* S *is the set of symbolic states, and the two functions put :* $2^S \times 2^S \times S \to 2^S \times 2^S$ *and get :* $2^S \times 2^S \to 2^S \times 2^S \times S$, *such that:*

– $put(P, W, (l, Z)) = (P \cup \{(l, Z)\}, W')$ *where*

$$W' = \begin{cases} W \cup \{(l, Z)\} & if\ (l, Z) \notin P \\ W & otherwise \end{cases}$$

– $get(P, W) = (P, W \setminus \{(l, Z)\}, (l, Z))$ *for some* $(l, Z) \in W$.

Here P and W play the role of the passed list and waiting list, respectively, but as we will see this definition provides room for alternative implementations. It is possible to loosen the elimination requirement such that some states can be returned several times while still ensuring termination, thus reducing the memory requirements [LLPY97].

The reachability algorithm can then be simplified as shows in Figure 4. The main difference with the former algorithm shows when a state is pushed to PWList: it is pushed conceptually to the passed and the waiting lists at the same time. States to be explored are considered already explored for the inclusion checking of new generated states. This greedy behaviour improves performance.

The reference implementation uses a hash table based on the discrete part of the states to find them. Every state entry has its symbolic part represented as a zone union (single linked list of zones). The queue is a simple linked list with references to the discrete and symbolic parts. Only one hash computation and one inclusion checking are necessary for every state inserted into this structure, compared to two with the former passed and waiting lists. Furthermore we gather states with a common discrete part. The former representation did not have this zone union structure. This zone union structure is particularly well-suited for other union representations of zones such as CDDs [BLP+99,LWYP99].

A number of options are realisable via different implementations of the PWList to approximate the representation of the state-space such as *bitstate hashing* [Hol87], or choose a particular order for state-space exploration such as *breadth first, depth first, best first* or *random* [BHV00,BFH+01]. The ordering is orthogonal to the storage structure and can be combined with any data representation.

This implementation is built on top of the storage structure that is in charge of storing raw data. The PWList uses *keys* as references to these data. This storage structure is orthogonal to a particular choice of data representation, in particular, algorithms aimed at reducing the memory footprint such as *convex hull approximation* [WT95] or *minimal constraint representation* [LLPY97] are possible implementations. We have implemented two variants of this storage, namely one with simple copy and the other one with data sharing.

Depending on the careful options given to UPPAAL our new implementation has been experimentally show to give improvements of up to 80% in memory and improves speed significantly. The memory gain is expected due to the showed sharing property of data. The speed gain (in spite of the overheads) comes from only having a single hash table and from the zone union structure: the discrete test is done only once, then comes only inclusion checks on all the zones in one union. This is showed by the results of the simple copy version. For more information we refer the interested reader to [DBLY].

6   Parallel and Distributed Reachability Checking

Parallel and distributed reachability analysis has become quite popular during recent years. Most work is based on the same explicit state exploration algorithm: The state space is partitioned over a number of nodes using a hash function. Each node is responsible for storing and exploring those states assigned to it by the hash function. The successors of a state are transfered to the owning nodes according to the hash function. Given that all nodes agree on the hash function to use and that the hash function maps states uniformly to the nodes, this results in a very effective distributed algorithm where both memory and CPU usage are distributed uniformly among all nodes.

In [BHV00] we reported on a version of UPPAAL using the variation in Figure 5 of the above algorithm on a parallel computer (thus providing efficient interprocess communication). The algorithm would only hash on the discrete part of a symbolic state such that states with the same discrete part would map to the same nodes, thus keeping the inclusion checking on the waiting list and passed list. Due to the symbolic nature of the reachability algorithm, the number of states explored depends on the search order. One noticeable side effect of the distribution was an altered search order which most of the time would increase

$W_A = \{(l_0, Z_0 \land I(l_0)) \mid h(l_0) = A\}$
$P_A = \varnothing$
while $\neg terminated$ **do**
   $(l, Z) = W_A.popState()$
   if $\forall(l, Y) \in P_A : Z \not\sqsubseteq Y$ **then**
     $P_A = P_A \cup \{(l, Z)\}$
     $\forall(l', Z') : (l, Z) \Rightarrow (l', Z')$ **do**
       $d = h(l', Z')$
       if $\forall(l', Y') \in W_d : Z' \not\sqsubseteq Y'$ **then**
         $W_d = W_d \cup \{(l', Z')\}$
       endif
     done
   endif
done

Fig. 5. The distributed timed automaton reachability algorithm parameterised on node A. The waiting list W and the passed list P is partitioned over the nodes using a function h. States are popped of the local waiting list and added to the local passed list. Successors are mapped to a destination node d.

the number of states explored. Replacing the waiting list with a priority queue always returning the state with the smallest distance to the initial state solved the problem.

More recently [Beh] we have ported the algorithm to a multi-threaded version and a version running on a Linux Beowulf Cluster using the new PWList structure. Surprisingly, initial experiments on the cluster showed severe load balancing problems, despite the fact that the hash function distributed states uniformly. The problem turned out to be that the exploration rate of each node depends on the load of the node[6] (due to the inclusion checking). Slight load variations will thus result in slight variations of the exploration rate of each node. A node with a high load will have a lower exploration rate, and thus the load rapidly becomes even higher. This is an unstable system. On the parallel machine used in [BHV00] this is not a problem for most input systems (probably due to the fast interprocess communication which reduces the load variations). Increasing the size of the hash table used for the waiting list and/or using the new PWList structure reduces this effect. Even with these modifications, some input systems cause load balancing problems, e.g. Fischer protocol for mutual exclusion. Most remaining load balancing problems can be eliminated by an explicit load balancing layer which uses a proportional controller that redirects states from nodes with a high load to nodes with a low load.

The multi-threaded version uses a different approach to ensure that all threads are equally balanced. All threads share the same PWList, or more precisely, the hash table underlying the PWList is shared but the list of states needed to be explored is thread local. Thus, if a thread inserts a state it will be retrieved by

---

[6] The load of a node is defined as the length of its waiting list.

the same thread. With this approach we avoid that the threads need to access the same queue. Each bucket in the hash table is protected by a semaphore. If the hash table has much more buckets than we have threads, then the risk of multiple simultaneous accesses is low. By default, each thread keeps all successors on the same thread (since the hash table is shared it does not matter to which thread a state is mapped). When the system is unbalanced some states are redirected to other threads. Experiments show that this results in very high locality.

Experiments with the parallel version are very encouraging, showing excellent speedups (in the range of 80-100% of optimal on a 4 processor machine). The distributed version is implemented using MPI[7] over TCP/IP over Fast Ethernet. This results in high processing overhead of communication causing low speedups in the range of 50-60% of optimal at 14 nodes. Future work will focus on combining the two approaches such that nodes located on the same physical machine can share the PWList. Also, experiments with alternatives to MPI over TCP/IP will be evaluated, such as VIA[8]. Finally, it is unclear if the sharing of sub-elements of a state introduced in the previous section will scale to the distributed case.

7   Accelerating Cycles

An important problem concerning symbolic model checking of timed automata, is encountered when the timed automata in a model use different *time scales*. This, for example, is often the case for models of reactive programs with their environment. Typically, the automata that model the reactive programs are based on microseconds whereas the automata of the environment function in the order of seconds. This difference can give rise to an unnecessary fragmentation of the symbolic state space. As a result, the time and memory consumption of the model check process increases.

The fragmentation problem has already been encountered and described by Hune and Iversen et al during the verification of LEGO Mindstorms programs using UPPAAL [Hun00,IKL+00]. The symbolic state space is severely fragmented by the busy-waiting behaviour of the control program automata. Other examples were the phenomena of fragmantation is likely to show up include reactive programs, and polling real-time systems, e.g., programmable logic controllers [Die99]. The validation of communication protocols will probably also suffer from the fragmentation problem when the context of the protocol is taken into account.

In [HL02] we have proposed an acceleration technique for a subset of timed automata, namely those that contain special cycles, that addresses the fragmentation problem. The technique consists of a syntactical adjustment that can easily be computed from the timed automaton itself. It is proven that the syntactical adjusment is exact with repsect to reachability properties, and it is

---

[7] The Message Passing Interface.
[8] The Virtual Interface Architecture.

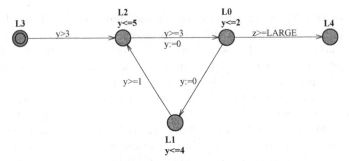

Fig. 6. Timed automaton P.

experimentally validated that the technique effectively speed-up the symbolic reachability analysis.

The timed automaton of figure 6 offers a simplified modeling of a control program combined with an environment. The cycle L0, L1, L2 corresponds to cyclic execution of a control program consisting of three atomic instructions with the invariants and guards on the clock y providing execution time information. Whenever the control cycle is in location L0, the enviroment (modelled by the clock z) is consulted potentially leading to an exit of the control cycle. The size of the threshold constant LARGE determines how slow the environment is relative to the execution time of control program instructions: the larger the constant the slower. Depending on the value of LARGE the cycle in automaton P must be executed a certain (large) number of times before the edge to location L4 is enabled. In a symbolic forward exploration the cycle must similarly be explored a large number of times with a fragmentation of the symbolic states involving location L0 as a consequence.

The acceleration technique proposed in [HL02] eliminates the fragmentation that is due to special cycles. The subset of cycles we can accelerate may use only a single clock y in the invariants, guards and resets. Though this might seem like a strong restriction, this kind of cycles often occur in control graphs of single-processor polling real-time systems. To be acceleratable all ingoing edges to the first location of the cycle C should reset the clock y. This guarantees that C has a *window* $[a, b]$, in the sense that any execution of C has accumulated delay between a and b, and, conversely, for any delay d between a and b any execution of C can be 'adjusted' to have accumulated delay d. Now, the acceleration of such a cycle C is given by addition of a simple unfolding of C, where the invariant of the (copy of the) intial location is removed. Figure 7 illustrates the result of adding the unfolded cycle to the model. Provided $3a \leq 2b$ it can be proved that in terms of rechability (of original locations) the two models are equivalent. Thus, the acceleration is *exact*. In case $(n + 1)b \leq na$ a similar result holds provided the cycle is unfolded n times. If moreover the clock y is reset on the first edge of C, all reachable states may be obtained by a *single* execution of the unfolded cycle. Consequently, a symbolic breadth-first analysis of the accelerated version of P in Figure 7 experimentally proves to be insensitive to the value of LARGE.

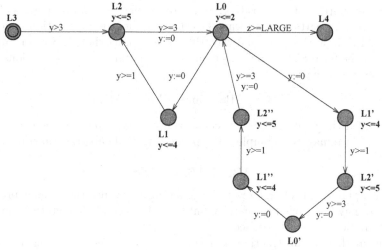

Fig. 7. The accelerated version of P.

In [HL02] and [Hen02] the proposed acceleration technique has been succesfully applied to analysis of models of LEGO Mindstorm byte code. In particular, the acceleration technique allowed UPPAAL to establish (at the byte code level) several properties of the Production Cell which could not otherwise be analysed.

8   Abstraction and Compositionality

Despite the vast improvement in performance of UPPAAL due to the development improved datastructures and algorithms, the state-explosion is a reality. Thus, in order for the application of a verification tools to truely scale up it is imperative that they are complemented by other methods.

One such method is that of *abstraction*. Assume that SYS is a model of some considered real-time system, and assume that we want some property φ to be established, i.e. SYS $\models \varphi$. Now, the model, SYS, may be too complex for our tools to settle this verification problem automatically (despite all of our algorithmic efforts). The goal of abstraction is to replace the problem with another, hopefully tractable problem ABS $\models \varphi$, where ABS is an abstraction of SYS being smaller in size and less complex. This method requires the user not only to supply the abstraction but also to argue that the abstraction is *safe* in the sense that all relevant properties established for ABS also hold for SYS; i.e. it should be established that SYS $\leq$ ABS, for some property-preserving relationship $\leq$ between models[9]. Unfortunately, this brings the problem of state-explosion right back in the picture because establishing SYS $\leq$ ABS may be as computationally difficult as the original verification problem SYS $\models \varphi$.

To alleviate the above problem, the method of abstraction may be combined with that of *compositionality*. Here, compositionality refers to principles

---

[9] i.e. $A \leq B$ and $B \models \phi$ should imply that $A \models \phi$.

allowing properties of composite systems to be inferred from properties of their components. In particular we want to establish the safe abstraction condition, $SYS \leq ABS$, in a compositional way, that is, assuming that SYS is a composite system of the form $SYS_1 \parallel SYS_2$, we may hope to find simple abstractions ABS_1 and ABS_2 such that:

$$SYS_1 \leq ABS_1 \quad \text{and} \quad SYS_2 \leq ABS_2$$

Provided the relation $\leq$ is a precongruence with respect to the composition operator $\parallel$, we may now complete the proof of the safe abstraction condition by establishing:

$$ABS_1 \parallel ABS_2 \leq ABS$$

This approach nicely factors the original problem into the smaller problems and, and may be applied recursively until problems small enough to be handled by automatic means are reached.

The method of abstraction and compositionality is an old-fashion recipe with roots going back to the original, foundational work on concurrency theory [Mil89,Hoa78,OG76,Jon83,CM88]. In [JLS00] we have instantiated the method to UPPAAL, where real-time systems are modelled as networks of timed automata communicating over (urgent) channels and shared discrete (e.g. integer) variables. A fundamental relationship between timed automata preserving safety properties — and hence useful in establishing safe abstraction properties — is that of timed simulation. However, in the presence of urgent communication and shared variables, this relationship fails to be a precongruence, and hence does not support compositionality. In [JLS00] we identify a notion of timed ready simulation supporting both abstraction and compositionality for UPPAAL models. In addition, a method for automatically *testing* for the existence of timed ready simulation between timed automata using reachability analysis is presented (see also [ABL98]). Thus UPPAAL itself may be applied for such tests. The usefulness of the developed method is demonstrated by application to the verification of an industrial design: a system for audio/video power control developed by the company Bang & Olufsen. The size of the full protocol model is of such complexity that UPPAAL immediately encounters the state-explosion problem in a direct verification. However by application of the compositionality result and testing theory we were able to carry through a verification of the full protocol model. In [SS01] a similar approach is applied to the verification of the IEEE 1394a Root contentin Protocol using UPPAAL.

9   Conclusion

In addition to the techniques described in the previous sections, UPPAAL offers a range of other verification options including active clock reduction and approximate analysis based on convex-hull, supertrace and hash compaction. We refer the reader to www.uppaal.com for information on this.

The long effort effort spend on developing and implementing efficient datastructures and algorithms for analysing timed systems has succesfully payed off in terms of tools mature for industrial real-time applications. However, there is still room and need for improvements. Below we give an incomplete list of what could be some of the main algorithmic challanges for future research in the area:

- Continued search for appropriate BDD-like datastructures allowing for efficient representation and analysis of real-timed systems. CDDs and DDDs may be seen as promising first attempts.
- Partial order reduction for timed systems, and more generally, methods for exploiting structure (e.g. hierarchicies) and (in)dependencies.
- Exploitation of symmetries to reduction explored and stored state-space.
- Extension of distributed and parallel reachability algorithm towards full TCTL model checking.
- Development of techniques allowing efficient use of disk (secondary memory) for storing explored state-spaces.
- Extension of acceleration technique to allow for more general cycles (e.g. involving more than one clock).
- Application of abstract interpretation in particular for dealing with models where the discrete part plays a major role (which is increasingly the case).

References

ABB+01. Tobias Amnell, Gerd Behrmann, Johan Bengtsson, Pedro R. D'Argenio, Alexandre David, Ansgar Fehnker, Thomas Hune, Bertrand Jeannet, Kim G. Larsen, M. Oliver Möller, Paul Pettersson, Carsten Weise, and Wang Yi. UPPAAL - Now, Next, and Future. In F. Cassez, C. Jard, B. Rozoy, and M. Ryan, editors, *Modelling and Verification of Parallel Processes*, number 2067 in Lecture Notes in Computer Science, pages 100–125. Springer–Verlag, 2001.

ABL98. Luca Aceto, Augusto Burgueno, and Kim G. Larsen. Model checking via reachability testing for timed automata. In Bernhard Steffen, editor, *Proc. 4th Int. Conference on Tools and Algorithms for the Construction and Analysis of Systems (TACAS'98)*, volume 1384 of *Lecture Notes in Computer Science*, pages 263–280. Springer, 1998.

BDM+98. Marius Bozga, Conrado Daws, Oded Maler, Alfredo Olivero, Stavros Tripakis, and Sergio Yovine. Kronos: A model-Checking Tool for Real-Time Systems. In *Proc. of the 10th Int. Conf. on Computer Aided Verification*, number 1427 in Lecture Notes in Computer Science, pages 546–550. Springer–Verlag, 1998.

Beh. Gerd Behrmann. A performance study of distributed timed automata reachability analysis. Submitted.

Bel57. Richard Bellman. *Dynamic Programming*. Princeton University Press, 1957.

Ben02. Johan Bengtsson. *Clocks, DBMs and STates in Timed Systems*. PhD thesis, Faculty of Science and Technology, Uppsala University, 2002.

BFH+01. Gerd Behrmann, Ansgar Fehnker, Thomas S. Hune, Kim Larsen, Paul Petterson, and Judi Romijn. Efficient guiding towards cost-optimality in uppaal. In *Proc. of TACAS'2001*, Lecture Notes in Computer Science. Springer–Verlag, 2001.

BGK⁺96.   Johan Bengtsson, W.O. David Griffioen, Kåre J. Kristoffersen, Kim G. Larsen, Fredrik Larsson, Paul Pettersson, and Wang Yi. Verification of an Audio Protocol with Bus Collision Using UPPAAL. In Rajeev Alur and Thomas A. Henzinger, editors, *Proc. of the 8th Int. Conf. on Computer Aided Verification*, number 1102 in Lecture Notes in Computer Science, pages 244–256. Springer–Verlag, July 1996.

BHV00.   Gerd Behrmann, Thomas Hune, and Frits Vaandrager. Distributed timed model checking - How the search order matters. In *Proc. of 12th International Conference on Computer Aided Verification*, Lecture Notes in Computer Science, Chicago, Juli 2000. Springer-Verlag.

BLL⁺96.   Johan Bengtsson, Kim G. Larsen, Fredrik Larsson, Paul Pettersson, and Wang Yi. UPPAAL in 1995. In *Proc. of the 2nd Workshop on Tools and Algorithms for the Construction and Analysis of Systems*, number 1055 in Lecture Notes in Computer Science, pages 431–434. Springer–Verlag, March 1996.

BLP⁺99.   Gerd Behrmann, Kim G. Larsen, Justin Pearson, Carsten Weise, and Wang Yi. Efficient Timed Reachability Analysis Using Clock Difference Diagrams. In *Proc. of the 11th Int. Conf. on Computer Aided Verification*, number 1633 in Lecture Notes in Computer Science. Springer–Verlag, 1999.

Bry86.   Randal E. Bryant. Graph-Based Algorithms for Boolean Function Manipulation. *IEEE Trans. on Computers*, 1986.

CM88.   K.M. Chandy and J. Misra. *Parallel Program Design: A Foundation*. Addison Wesley, 1988.

DBLY.   Alexandre David, Gerd Behrmann, Kim G. Larsen, and Wang Yi. The next generation of uppaal. Submitted.

Die99.   H. Dierks. *Specification and Verification of Polling Real-Time Systems*. PhD thesis, Carl von Ossietzky Universität Oldenburg, July 1999.

Dil89.   David Dill. Timing Assumptions and Verification of Finite-State Concurrent Systems. In J. Sifakis, editor, *Proc. of Automatic Verification Methods for Finite State Systems*, number 407 in Lecture Notes in Computer Science, pages 197–212. Springer–Verlag, 1989.

DT98.   Conrado Daws and Stavros Tripakis. Model checking of real-time reachability properties using abstractions. In Bernard Steffen, editor, *Proc. of the 4th Workshop on Tools and Algorithms for the Construction and Analysis of Systems*, number 1384 in Lecture Notes in Computer Science, pages 313–329. Springer–Verlag, 1998.

DY95.   C. Daws and S. Yovine. Two examples of verification of multirate timed automata with KRONOS. In *Proc. of the 16th IEEE Real-Time Systems Symposium*, pages 66–75. IEEE Computer Society Press, December 1995.

Hen02.   Martijn Hendriks. Devlopment of reactive programs using uppaal. Master's thesis, KUN, Nijmegen University, 2002.

HL02.   Martin Hndriks and Kim G. Larsen. Exact acceleration of real-time model checking. In *Theory and Practice of Timed Systems*, volume 65 of *Electronic Notes in Theoretical Computer Science*. Elsevier Science Publishers, 2002.

HLS99.   Klaus Havelund, Kim G. Larsen, and Arne Skou. Formal verification of a power controller using the real-time model checker UPPAAL. In *Proceedings of AMST 1999*, volume 1601 of *Lecture Notes in Computer Science*, pages 277–298, 1999.

Hoa78.   C.A.R. Hoare. Communicating Sequential Processes. *Communications of the ACM*, 21(8):666–677, 1978.
Hol87.   Gerard J. Holzmann. On limits and possibilities of automated protocol analysis. In *Proc. 7th IFIP WG 6.1 Int. Workshop on Protocol Specification, Testing, and Verification*, pages 137–161, 1987.
Hun00.   Thomas S. Hune. Modeling a language for embedded systems in timed automata. Technical Report RS-00-17, BRICS, Basic Research in computer Science, August 2000. 26 pp. Earlier version entitled *Modelling a Real-Time Language* appeared in FMICS99, pages 259–282.
IKL⁺00.   Torsten K. Iversen, Kåre J. Kristoffersen, Kim G. Larsen, Morten Laursen, Rune G. Madsen, Steffen K. Mortensen, Paul Pettersson, and Chris B. Thomasen. Model-Checking Real-Time Control Programs — Verifying LEGO Mindstorms Systems Using UPPAAL. In *Proc. of 12th Euromicro Conference on Real-Time Systems*, pages 147–155. IEEE Computer Society Press, June 2000.
JLS00.   Henrik Ejersbo Jensen, Kim G. Larsen, and Arne Skou. Scaling up Uppaal - automatic verification of real-time systems using compositionality and abstraction. In *Proceedings of FTRTFT 2000*, volume 1926 of *Lecture Notes in Computer Science*, pages 19–30, 2000.
Jon83.   C. Jones. Tentative steps toward a development method for interfering programs. *ACM Transactions on Programming Languages and Systems*, 5(4):596–620, 1983.
Lam87.   Leslie Lamport. A Fast Mutual Exclusion Algorithm. *ACM Trans. on Computer Systems*, 5(1):1–11, February 1987. Also appeared as SRC Research Report 7.
LLPY97.   Kim G. Larsen, Fredrik Larsson, Paul Pettersson, and Wang Yi. Efficient Verification of Real-Time Systems: Compact Data Structures and State-Space Reduction. In *Proc. of the 18th IEEE Real-Time Systems Symposium*, pages 14–24. IEEE Computer Society Press, December 1997.
LLPY02.   Kim G. Larsen, Fredrik Larsson, Paul Pettersson, and Wang Yi. Compact data structure and state-space reduction for model-checking real-time systems. *Real-Time Systems - the International Journal of Time-Critical Computing Systems*, 2002. To appear – accepted for publication.
LP97.   Henrik Lönn and Paul Pettersson. Formal Verification of a TDMA Protocol Startup Mechanism. In *Proc. of the Pacific Rim Int. Symp. on Fault-Tolerant Systems*, pages 235–242, December 1997.
LPY95.   Kim G. Larsen, Paul Pettersson, and Wang Yi. Compositional and Symbolic Model-Checking of Real-Time Systems. In *Proc. of the 16th IEEE Real-Time Systems Symposium*, pages 76–87. IEEE Computer Society Press, December 1995.
LPY97.   Kim G. Larsen, Paul Pettersson, and Wang Yi. UPPAAL in a Nutshell. *Int. Journal on Software Tools for Technology Transfer*, 1(1–2):134–152, October 1997.
LWYP99.   Kim G. Larsen, Carsten Weise, Wang Yi, and Justin Pearson. Clock Difference Diagrams. *Nordic Journal of Computing*, 6(3):271–298, 1999.
Mil89.   R. Milner. *Communication and Concurrency*. Prentice Hall, Englewood Cliffs, 1989.
MLAH99a.   J. Møller, J. Lichtenberg, H. R. Andersen, and H. Hulgaard. Difference decision diagrams. In *Proceedings 13th International Conference on Computer Science Logic*, volume 1683 of *Lecture Notes in Computer Science*, pages 111–125, Madrid, Spain, September 1999.

MLAH99b.   J. Møller, J. Lichtenberg, H. R. Andersen, and H. Hulgaard. Fully symbolic model checking of timed systems using difference decision diagrams.
In *Proceedings First International Workshop on Symbolic Model Checking*, volume 23-2 of *Electronic Notes in Theoretical Computer Science*,
Trento, Italy, July 1999.

OG76.   S. Owicki and D. Gries. An Axiomatic Proof Technique for Parallel
Programs I. *Acta Informatica*, 6(4):319–340, 1976.

Pet99.   Paul Pettersson. *Modelling and Analysis of Real-Time Systems Using
Timed Automata: Theory and Practice*. PhD thesis, Department of Computer Systems, Uppsala University, February 1999.

PS80.   Wolfgang J. Paul and Janos Simon. Decision Trees and Random
Access Machines. In *Logic and Algorithmic*, volume 30 of *Monogra-
phie de L'Enseignement Mathématique*, pages 331–340. L'Enseignement
Mathématique, Université de Genève, 1980.

Rok93.   Tomas Gerhard Rokicki. *Representing and Modeling Digital Circuits*.
PhD thesis, Stanford University, 1993.

SS01.   D.P.L. Simons and M.I.A. Stoelinga. Mechanical verification of the IEEE
1394a root contention protocol using Uppaal2k. *Springer International
Journal of Software Tools for Technology Transfer*, 2001.

ST98.   Karsten Strehl and Lothar Thiele. Symbolic Model Checking of Process Networks Using Interval Diagram Techniques. In *Proceedings of
the IEEE/ACM International Conference on Computer-Aided Design
(ICCAD-98)*, pages 686–692, 1998.

WT95.   Howard Wong-Toi. *Symbolic Approximations for Verifying Real-Time
Systems*. PhD thesis, Standford University, 1995.

Software Hazard and Safety Analysis

John McDermid

University of York,
Heslington,
York, YO10 5DD
UK

Abstract. Safety is a system property and software, of itself, cannot be
safe or unsafe. However software has a major influence on safety in many
modern systems, e.g. aircraft and engine controls, railway signalling, and
medical equipment.

The paper outlines the principles of system hazard and safety analysis,
and briefly describes work on adapting classical hazard and safety analysis techniques to apply to software. It then briefly discusses the role of
formal analysis in software hazard and safety assessment, indicating both
the state of practice and the aims of some ongoing research projects.

Note: this paper is provided to support a tutorial on software hazard and
safety analysis, and is not intended to be a definitive treatment of the
issues.

1   Introduction

Safety is concerned with protection of human life, the environment and property.
There is no such thing as absolute safety – all human endeavour has attendant
risks. However we say that a system is safe (enough) if the risk of causing damage
to life, the environment or property is acceptable. Normally we measure risk as
a combination of the probability of damage occurring and the extent of damage,
e.g. the number of lives which are expected to be lost. Acceptability of such
risks is a complex issue; ultimately it is a societal judgement. Discussion of
acceptability of risk is outside the scope of this paper.

Damage, as defined above, can arise in two basic ways – by uncontrolled or
unintended transfer of energy, and through failure to contain harmful materials,
e.g. toxins or radioactive sources (the purist might argue that this too is a failure
of energy containment). Software is not a harmful substance, nor does it have
high energy levels – thus it cannot be safe or unsafe of itself. However it is
used in many systems where it contributes to safety, e.g. through control over
hazardous physical processes [1]. We use the term *software hazard and safety
analysis* to refer to the process of assessing the contribution of software to safety
in its broader system context.

In essence there are four safety-relevant parts of a system development process:

W. Damm and E.-R. Olderog (Eds.): FTRTFT 2002, LNCS 2469, pp. 23–34, 2002.

- Identifying hazards and associated safety requirements;
- Designing the system to meet its safety requirements;
- Analysing the system to show that it meets its safety requirements;
- Demonstrating the safety of the system by producing a safety case.

We briefly give an overview of a typical safety process, then consider these process elements in turn.

2   Safety Processes and Software

Safety processes parallel and complement system development processes, being concerned with identifying and controlling ways in which systems may behave, or fail, so as to be unsafe. The processes are normally structured around the notion of a *hazard* – a circumstance which can lead to damage, e.g. the loss of braking on a car is a hazard. The early phases of the safety process are concerned with identifying hazards, and then determining the associated risk. If the risk is deemed unacceptable, then remedial design work must be undertaken – to make the hazard less likely to occur or to mitigate the consequences. The results of such analysis are often referred to as *derived safety requirements*, or DSRs.

Once hazard analysis has been undertaken, design and implementation can continue, with the aim of producing a system which meets all its requirements, including the DSRs. Whilst the above implies that there is a clean break between requirements and design, in practice there is a progressive shift in focus and often significant design iteration. Also there will inevitably be the need for trade-offs between different requirements, including DSRs, to meet overall project goals.

Once the design and implementation is complete, and as it is being integrated, analysis and testing is undertaken to show that the system meets its requirements, including DSRs. The analysis and test results provide evidence that the system is safe. However it is becoming increasingly common to provide a *safety case*, not just analysis results, for inspection by a third party, e.g. a certification agency. The safety case complements the evidence by providing the *arguments* which show why the evidence is (deemed) sufficient to demonstrate safety of the system.

In practice, processes are much more complex than implied above, but the essence of the activities is as described. Also, most real-world projects are governed by standards – of which there are many. References 2 to 6 are some of the more widely used standards in the defence and aerospace sector. Hermann [7] gives an overview of these, and many other, standards.

Most safety standards are concerned with how engineered systems can fail and can give rise to hazards. Software can only "fail" due to *systematic* causes, e.g. requirements or design errors, and the usual analysis processes do not apply. Instead, the community have taken the view that the best way to approach the issue is to have design processes which reduce the likelihood of introducing such flaws into software. Consequently many standards for the development of safety critical software have been written. References 8 to 10 are some of the better known standards in this area. However some standards cover both system and software issues: IEC 61508 [10] deals with system issues and the Australian Standard Def(Aust) 5679 [4] also addresses software issues. Generally these standards try to control software-related risk through the notion of *safety integrity levels*, or SILs.

Superficially these standards are very different but, on closer inspection, there are many areas of commonality, e.g. the concept of hazard, the intent to reduce risk, and so on. An attempt has been made to rationalise these different processes [11] and to show that there is significant commonality in these standards. However there is divergence in how they treat systematic issues, and this has led to a number of authors questioning the notion of SILs and the soundness of the guidance in the standards [12, 13]. We defer any further discussion of SILs to our treatment of safety cases.

3   Software Hazard Analysis and Derived Requirements

In considering software it is reasonable to assume that the early stages of the system safety process have identified hazards, and have determined those hazards to which software can contribute. We thus assume that the system safety process has identified *hazardous failure conditions* (HFCs) for the software which are conditions which are either sufficient in themselves, or sufficient in conjunction with other credible conditions, to give rise to a (system level) hazard.

Assuming also that there is a specification for the software in a system, we have two questions to answer:

- If the software functions as specified, does this give rise to any HFCs?
- Are there plausible failure modes of the software, or of the underlying computing hardware which are not contained by the software, which can give rise to HFCs?

Software hazard analysis amounts to answering these questions and determining consequential actions.

If specifications are informal then these questions can only be addressed through the use of human skill and judgement. The majority of techniques used at this stage of the process are informal, based on functional models of the system – the method perhaps most widely used in the aerospace sector is *functional failure analysis* (FFA) (see [6]). FFA uses three "guidewords" to prompt analysis:

- Function provided when not intended (commission);
- Function not provided when required (omission)
- Function provided incorrectly.

The analysis considers each function in turn and decides whether or not these *hypothetical* failure modes are credible and, if they are, what the consequences might be. For failure modes which are deemed credible, and where the consequences are severe, some remedial action will be identified. The remedial action may be for a specification change if the problem is "deep seated", or to produce

DSRs for system components, e.g. to detect and mitigate failures, perhaps by using alternative sensors or control algorithms.

This type of analysis is judgemental and error prone. Indeed it has been estimated that typical analyses only identify 80% of hazards (or high level causes of hazards). It is thus tempting to consider the use of formal methods so that the analysis can be made more certain.

If the specifications are in the form of state machines, and the HFCs can be formalised, then the first question above amounts to model checking. This is not the place for a survey of model-checking techniques, but references 14–16 give an idea of the state of the art in this area. Where specifications are not in the form of state machines it is less clear cut how to address the first question, see the discussion of research issues below.

Considering the second question amounts to applying the FFA guidewords, or a more precise interpretation thereof, to the specification to produce a "mutated" specification incorporating possible failure scenarios. Next we need to determine whether or not any HFCs can arise from the "mutated" specification. Typically we have transitions annotated with labels of the form:

$$e[c]/a$$

to be read "when event e occurs and condition c holds then (take the transition and) perform action a". Omission can be characterised as "a does not happen when event e occurs and condition c holds", and so on. The third guideword needs the most interpretation, as the notion of erroneous can be taken to mean inappropriate transitions taken, inappropriate actions, and so on. This gives rise to problems of combinatorial explosion, see the research issues below.

Analysis of the "transition mutations" shows that they reduce to a relatively small number of regular forms, all of which can be represented as additional transitions in the state machine (inevitably introducing non-determinism). Once more model checking can be used to see if HFCs can arise – although the computational cost is much higher. In fact it is possible to automate the generation of the mutated state machines, and then to determine which mutants, if any, give rise to the HFCs (Reference 17 describes the overall approach in the context of UML, although not the details of the automation.)

The results of this "hazard analysis" need some interpretation. First, some situations which are formally possible may be physically impossible, and must be discounted. Second, some may show deep flaws in the system concept, and thus must give rise to a change in the system specification. Third, the analysis may identify DSRs on parts of the design which are critical to avoiding the HFCs. Generally these will be simpler than full functional correctness, e.g. correct operation of an interlock, and will be the focus of more detailed design and analysis. These DSRs must be represented in a means which is compatible with the specification approach used; in our case we have chosen to use a form of rely-guarantee conditions [17].

The approach outlined above is intended to be generic, although we have appealed to work in York for more concrete illustrations of the ideas. Similar ideas can be found elsewhere, e.g. in Leveson's SpecTRM method [18].

4   Software Design and Implementation

There are two important aspects to software design and implementation – the software engineering process and the (software) safety process. Many academics advocate the use of refinement from (formal) specifications, and it might be thought that safety is an area where such processes ought to be used (indeed this is one of the requirements of DS 00-55). However using refinement is not so straightforward, as we now endeavour to explain.

The idea of program refinement [19] goes back over 30 years, and the idea has been extended into a formal framework, e.g. the seminal work of Carroll Morgan [20]. However it has become acknowledged that refinement has its difficulties and, for example, non-functional properties such as safety and security are not necessarily preserved through refinement, e.g. weakening a pre-condition may admit an unsafe behaviour which is not present in the more abstract specification. Problems with refinement have been known for some time [21]. More recently, acknowledgement of these problems has led to the introduction of the notion of retrenchment [22] which tries to find formally defensible ways of developing programs whilst breaking the standard rules of formal refinement. However we do not view retrenchment, in its current state, as being mature enough to apply to real systems. Instead we assume a more informal approach to developing programs has to be adopted, and thus turn our attention to the safety process.

The safety process has two main concerns:

- Flowing down DSRs to low level components;
- Assessing the design for additional potential contributions to HFCs, and hence deriving further DSRs.

The first of these is part of the normal "requirements flow down" in system development, except that our concern is only with DSRs. In system safety a more systematic approach is used. This is based on fault trees, and known as *preliminary system safety assessment* (PSSA) [6]. In the software case, the fault tree would be built from an HFC down to the level of failure modes of software components. The component level DSRs are (safety) properties which the component must guarantee for the system to behave safely. Unfortunately, the guidance in the system safety standards is inadequate for dealing with software based systems [23], and considerable judgement is needed for this part of the process. Perhaps the best description of the approach is in Leveson's SpecTRM [18].

The second safety concern requires us to consider ways in which any "extra" functionality introduced in producing the design may contribute to HFCs. In a way the problem is like that of hazard analysis except that, at this stage, it is possible to say much more about which types of failure mode are credible as much more is known about the design and implementation, e.g. the mapping of software to the computing hardware. Approaches like FFA are sometimes employed, but it is more common to use adaptations of HAZOP as this considers both causes and consequences of deviations from intended behaviour (Leveson uses the term "deviation analysis").

HAZOP is similar to FFA, in that it hypothesises failure modes, but the range of guidewords is much greater, including: early, late, too much, too little, etc. Adaptations of HAZOP to computer systems have sometimes simply accepted the normal HAZOP guidewords [24] (originally developed for the chemical industry) or sought to adapt them to computer systems and software [25]. In principle model checking could be applied in the same way as described at specification level – but too our knowledge this work has only ever been done manually, due to the complexity of the designs which need to be analysed.

In theory, new hazardous behaviours can be introduced at each level in the design decomposition, thus design analysis needs to be repeated at each level. Such analysis could be done, but it would be very onerous. Our experience is that the analysis tends to be done once at a level quite close to the code – where there is a simple refinement to the implementation. In other words, it is carried out a level where no more new potentially hazardous behaviours will be introduced in the development process.

Ultimately software has to be realised by implementation in a programming language, and the DSRs "flowed down" to the program – in the form of pre- and post-conditions. There is really only one commercial tool which supports such a use of formal annotations and formal analysis – the SPARK Examiner [26]. We discuss program level issues in more detail in the next section, but first consider some trends in software development which have an impact on the way software is developed and analysed.

The discussion above implicitly assumes that al programs are produced manually from a specification or, more likely, at the "bottom" of a hierarchy of specifications. This is probably true of the majority of current safety critical applications, but there are trends to the use of greater automation.

Current projects are considering, or using, design notations such as Matlab/Simulink [27] and employing such tools to generate code from the designs. This is somewhat in conflict with the use of classical formal verification approaches, as these tools do not usually include pre- and post-conditions in the code. In theory, if the code generators were trustworthy, this would not be an issue. However, these tools are continually evolving so it is difficult to be confident in their output – without further checks. This is perhaps mainly a research issue at present, but it will become more of an issue as code generation is more routinely used for generating critical code. This suggests the need for analysis techniques which are independent of the way in which the code is produced, and which do not require insertion of pre- and post-conditions in the code.

5   Software Safety Analysis

The aim of software safety analysis is to show that the software meets the DSRs, locally, and overall does not contribute (in unacceptable ways) to the HFCs. In principle this can be done using safety analysis techniques or using software engineering techniques. We believe that it is most appropriate to employ software engineering methods, but we start by considering safety analysis techniques as this gives a basis for explaining this point of view.

Researchers in software safety have adapted standard system safety techniques, e.g. fault trees and failure modes and effects analyses to software, but with mixed success. Perhaps the most fully developed approach is due to Leveson [28, 29] who pioneered the application of fault trees to software. In essence software fault-tree analysis is a modified form of wp-calculus, but focusing on causes of HFCs or violations of DSRs, not establishing partial correctness. Our experience, and that of others, is that software fault trees work well in particular circumstances, but are difficult to apply to large programs, without mechanical support for expression evaluation, etc. There is a growing view that the use of static code analysis and proof techniques is much more cost-effective, especially when tool supported. (we consider testing below.)

In the UK, Defence Standard 00-55 [9] requires the application of static code analysis to safety-critical software. The standard has probably not been applied in its entirety, but elements of it have been used on a number of projects. For example, static code analysis techniques have been applied retrospectively to the software on the C130J aircraft. All the code was developed to the requirements of DO178B. Some of the code was written in SPARK Ada [26], and hence used the SPARK tools. Other code in C, full Ada, etc. was analysed using Malpas [30]. The approach was initially to apply static analysis in a blanket way, but later this was refined to use a hazard directed approach, i.e. focusing on DSRs and HFCs.

There are limited publications on the work but there are some "snapshots" of the project, e.g. reference 31. To the author's knowledge about 550 kLoC of code has been analysed. Initially around 50 potentially safety critical code anomalies were found, but these were removed in later builds of the software (and the error correction suitably verified). Interestingly, the project found that informal familiarisation with code was by far the most effective and cost-effective way of finding faults – followed by full semantic analysis (i.e. proof). Simpler and cheap static analysis, e.g. information and data flow, found relatively few problems. This shows the capability of the technology, applied to software developed in conventional ways.

More recently, QinetiQ have been applying a rather different approach to software which has been derived from control law definitions, including Matlab models. The approach has been to use an intermediate language (Z) and to translate the specifications and code into a common form, and to verify equivalence. As the structure of the conjectures produced is very regular it is possible to use tactics to automate the analysis. The principles are discussed in reference 32, although this does not discuss practical applications in detail. At the time of writing, about 80% of a build of the EuroFighter flying control software had been analysed in this way, and QinetiQ aim to verify 100% of the next build – fully automatically. (Note: this provides much of the capability we identified at the end of section 4.) Interestingly, relatively few anomalies have been found, and there are questions about the cost-effectiveness of the approach, especially as the specifications being used as the basis for verification are very low level.

Note that this is concerned more with program-specification conformance than verification that the programs do not violate DSRs.

Other researchers have used model checking on specifications, to show that the software as specified (at a detailed level) does not contradict DSRs. This contrasts with the QinetiQ approach as it is abstracting from low-level specifications to system-level properties, not addressing specification-code correspondence. An example of the use of this approach on a model of an aircraft system is given in reference 33. Arguably this approach is more compelling than that used by QinetiQ as it is more naturally hazard directed. A potential limitation of this approach is that it does not address errors that might be introduced at program level. However, such issues are addressed by conventional verification activities – and the capacity to introduce new safety problems is very limited if there is a true refinement between the low level specification and the program.

As indicated above, although there needs to be a focus on safety, there is also a need to show that programs function as intended. There is no value in replicating such work in assessing safety. Thus we take it as read that testing is undertaken, both to show that the software behaves as expected on real hardware, and as part of the overall validation process. It is worth observing that many safety problems relate to requirements errors, not mistakes in coding. Thus testing has an important role in validating safety requirements. Indeed, it is common to do "fault injection testing" as may be difficult to validate fault detection and recovery specifications (including DSRs) any other way. There are other interesting testing issues but, given the remit of the tutorial, we have focused on the application of formal techniques to safety properties, and will not consider testing further.

So far we have focused on functional properties of programs, but we also need to consider non-functional issues, e.g. timing. With some classes of processor, timing properties are amenable to automated (formal) analysis [34]. However modern processors pose significant challenges for static timing analysis [35], and a combination of static analysis and testing must be used. Space precludes further discussion of non-functional properties of programs.

In general, the choice of suitable combinations of analysis techniques is a complex issue. Many of the software safety standards identify suitable (recommended) sets of techniques for developing and assessing software, although there is surprising divergence between the recommendations of different standards [11]. We briefly return to this point when discussing the software safety case.

6   Software Safety Cases

The notion of a safety case was introduced by Lord Cullen following the Piper Alpha disaster [36]. In essence a safety case consists of arguments why a system is believed to be safe enough to be operated. This argument is backed up by supporting evidence, e.g. test and other analysis results. In many situations a safety case report will be produced which contains the primary arguments, with the supporting evidence relegated to other documents or electronic media, due to their bulk.

In current industrial practice software safety is usually argued by appeal to a process, i.e. safety is asserted to arise from use of a process appropriate for a given SIL. For example, in DO178B, an accomplishment summary is produced that shows that key parts of the process have been followed; the requirements, e.g. for independent checks on activities, grow more stringent with the severity of the HFCs. There are growing doubts about the validity of the approach, for example the C130J analysis showed no noticeable correlation between SIL (DAL in DO178B terminology) and fault density. Some other concerns about use of SILs are set out in reference 13. One of the key concerns is that DO178B and other standards seem more to be governing quality, than safety, in that there is little focus on HFCs.

An alternative form of safety case would provide evidence that the software meets relevant DSRs and makes only acceptable contributions to HFCs. It is intended that the adaptation of classical safety analysis techniques to software, and the use of formal analysis on specifications/programs, can facilitate the production of such a safety case. However this is far from current practice. Further, although there is some informal acceptance of this approach to software safety cases the community is not in agreement as to what constitutes adequate software safety evidence. For example, how, if at all, should the software safety evidence vary with the criticality of the hazard? Some attempt is being made to develop a systematic approach to software safety arguments and evidence, see for example [36], but much remains to be done. This leads naturally to the identification of some research issues – to which we now turn.

7   Research Issues

There are research issues to be addressed at all stages in the safety process, not just for safety cases. Some of the more important issues are:

- How can formal approaches be used to explore the potentially hazardous failure behaviour of systems specified using techniques other than state charts? What are suitable requirements representations, and how can the hypothetical failure modes (omission, commission, etc.) be formalised and the analysis automated?
- What are appropriate HAZOP/FFA guidewords to apply to software designs? The work in reference 25 suggests one approach, but there are other possibilities and, by its very nature, a set of failure guidewords is hard to validate.
- How should non-functional properties of specifications be analysed – at all levels in the design process? Can formal analysis be extended to address application domain properties such as stability of control systems [38]?
- How can changes in designs and specifications be assessed efficiently?
- How can model-checking and other techniques be enhanced to deal with the challenges of "combinatorial explosion" that arise when considering failure behaviours as well as "intended" behaviour?

- What constitutes "sufficient" software safety evidence, and how should this vary with severity of hazard, acceptable probability of occurrence of the HFC, and so on?
- How can hazard and safety analysis techniques be applied to modern software engineering approaches such as object-oriented design? How can domain-specific tools such as Matlab be employed most effectively in a system safety process?
- What is an appropriate balance between automation and human involvement in the safety process [39]? Automation is essential to deal with problems of scale – but it is necessarily based on models, not reality. Humans are good at extrapolating beyond models; automata are not. How do we get the best of human and machine capabilities?

Addressing these research issues requires a combination of skills in software engineering, safety engineering, theory of computer science (especially in the area of optimising model checking, without making it unsound), tool development, and perhaps in certain application domains. Many of the challenges are also long-term, as the scale and complexity of systems and software being developed are growing faster than our ability to analyse them. This is an area where co-operation between diverse research groups is needed to make significant progress.

8   Conclusions

Software safety is an immature discipline – yet it is an important one due to the ever-growing reliance of modern, complex, systems on computers and software to function safely. For many years, hazard and safety analysis have been carried out informally and, despite the strictures of standards such as 00-55 in the UK, most practical software safety assessment has relied on testing and review. However things are now changing.

The capability of formal techniques, and the capacity of modern computers, means that it is becoming increasingly practical to apply automated analyses to realistic systems, as the C130J and EuroFighter examples show. However there remain many research challenges and it is clear that automation is not a panacea. One of the biggest issues that needs to be addressed is how to use automation to deal with problems of scale, whilst enabling human judgement to be applied at critical points in the process.

Acknowledgements

This work is funded in part by the Engineering and Physical Science Research Council (EPSRC) under grant GR/R70590/01.

References

1. Leveson, N.G., *Safeware: System Safety and Computers*, Addison Wesley, 1995.
2. US Department of Defense, *Military Standard 882C (Change Notice 1): System Safety Program Requirements*, 1996.
3. UK Ministry of Defence, *Defence Standard 00-56 Issue 2: Safety Management Requirements for Defence Systems*, 1996.
4. Australian Department of Defence, *Australian Defence Standard Def(Aust) 5679: Procurement of Computer-based Safety Critical Systems*, 1998.
5. Society of Automotive Engineers Inc, *Aerospace Recommended Practice (ARP) 4754: Certification Considerations for Highly-Integrated or Complex Aircraft Systems*, 1996.
6. Society of Automotive Engineers Inc, *Aerospace Recommended Practice (ARP) 4761: Guidelines and methods for conducting the safety assessment process on civil airborne systems and equipment*, 1996.
7. Hermann, D., *Software Safety and Reliability*, IEEE Computer Society Press, 1999.
8. RTCA and EUROCAE. *Software Considerations in Airborne Systems and Equipment Certification*, Radio Technical Commission for Aeronautics RTCA DO-17B/EUROCAE ED-12B, 1993
9. UK Ministry of Defence, *Defence Standard 00-55 Requirements of Safety Related Software in Defence Equipment*, 1997
10. IEC (International Electrotechnical Commission). *IEC-61508: Functional safety of electrical/electronic/ programmable electronic safety-related systems*, 1997.
11. Y Papadopoulos, Y., McDermid, J. A., *The Potential for a Generic Approach to the Certification of Safety-Critical Systems in the Transportation Sector*, Reliability Engineering and System Safety, Vol. 63, Issue 1, 1999.
12. Redmill, F. *Safety Integrity Levels – Theory and Problems*, in Lessons in System Safety, Proceedings of the Eighth Safety-Critical Systems Symposium, Springer Verlag, 2000.
13. McDermid, J. A., *Software Safety: Where's the Evidence?*, in Proc. 6th Australian Workshop on Industrial Experience with Safety systems and Software, Australian Computer Society, 2001.
14. Clarke, E.M., Grumberg, O., Peled, D.A., *Model Checking*, The MIT Press, 1999
15. Burch, J.R., Clarke, E.M., McMillan, K.L., Dill, D.L., Hwang, L.J., *Symbolic Model Checking: 10^{20} States and Beyond*, Information and Computation, Volume 98, Number 2, 1992.
16. Clarke, E., Grumberg, O., Somesh, J., Lu, Y., Veith, H., *Progress on the State Explosion Problem in Model Checking*, in Informatics: 10 years Back. 10 Years Ahead, Wilhelm, R. (Ed.), LNCS 2000, Springer Verlag, 2001.
17. Hawkins R. D., McDermid, J. A., *Performing Hazard and Safety Analysis of Object Oriented Systems*, in Proceedngs of ISSC, Denver, August 2002.
18. Leveson, N. G., *Safeware Engineering Corporation – SpecTRM*, http://www.safeware-eng.com/.
19. Wirth, N., *Program Development by Stepwise Refinement*, Communications of the ACM, Volume 14, Number 4, 1971.
20. Morgan, C. C., *Programming from Specifications*, Prentice Hall, 1994.
21. Neilsen, D. S., *From Z to C: Illustration of a Rigorous Proof Method*, DPhil Thesis, Oxford 1989.
22. Banach, R., Poppleton, M., *Sharp Retrenchment, Modulated Refinement, and Simulation*, Formal Aspects of Computing, 11, 498–540, 1999

23. S K Dawkins, S. K., Kelly, T. P., McDermid, J. A., Murdoch, J., Pumfrey, D. J., *Issues in the Conduct of PSSA*, In Proceedings of ISSC, Orlando, 1999

24. UK Ministry of Defence, *Defence Standard 00-58: HAZOP Studies on Systems Containing Programmable Electronics*, 1996.

25. McDermid, J. A., Pumfrey, D. J., *A Development of Hazard Analysis to aid Software Design*, in Proceedings of COMPASS'94, Gaithersburg, 1994.

26. Barnes, J. G., *High Integrity Ada: The SPARK Approach*, Addison Wesley, 1997.

27. http://www.mathworks.com/

28. Leveson, N. G., Harvey, P. R., *Software Fault Tree Analysis*, Journal of Systems and Software, 1983.

29. Leveson, N. G., Shimeall, T. J., *Safety Verification of Ada Programs using Software Fault Trees*, IEEE Software, 1991.

30. http://www.tagroup.co.uk/malpas.htm

31. Harrison, K. J., *Static Code Analysis on the C-130J Hercules Safety Critical Software*, Aerosystems International, 1999

32. O'Halloran, C., Smith, A., *Verification of Picture-Generated Code*, in Proceedings of the 14th IEEE Conference on Automated Software Engineering, 1999

33. Damm W., et al, *Formal Verification of an Avionics Application using Abstraction and Model Checking*, in Towards System Safety, F Redmill, F., Anderson, T. (Eds), Springer Verlag, 1999

34. Eccles, M. A., *STAMP Tool Assessment*, BAe-WSC-RP-R&D-0031, BAe Warton, 1995.

35. Bate, I. J., Conmy, P. M., McDermid, J. A., *Generating Evidence for Certification of Modern Processors for use in Safety-Critical Systems*, in Proceedings of the 5th International High Assurance Systems Engineering Symposium, Albuquerque, 2000.

36. Cullen, the Hon. Lord, *The Public Enquiry into the Piper Alpha Disaster*, HMSO, ISBN 0-10-113102, 1990.

37. Weaver, R. A., McDermid, J. A., Kelly, T. P., *Software Safety Arguments: Towards a Systematic Categorisation of Evidence*, in Proceedings of ISSC, Denver, August 2002.

38. Blow, J., Buttle, D., Galloway, A. J., *Differential Proof Contexts in SPARK*, submitted for publication, 2002.

39. Galloway, A. J., McDermid, J. A., Murdoch, J. M., Pumfrey D. J ., *Automation of System Safety Analysis: Possibilities and Pitfalls*, in Proceedings of ISSC, Denver, August 2002.

Part II

Invited Papers

Real-Time Operating Systems:
Problems and Novel Solutions

Giorgio Buttazzo

University of Pavia
buttazzo@unipv.it

Abstract. This work presents some methodologies for enhancing predictability in real-time computing systems, where explicit timing constraints have to be enforced on application processes. In order to provide an off-line guarantee of the critical timing constraints, deterministic and analyzable algorithms are required in all kernel mechanisms, especially involving scheduling, inter-task communication, synchronization and interrupt handling. This paper illustrates some problems that may arise in real-time concurrent applications and some solutions that can be adopted in the kernel to overcome those problems. In particular, task scheduling algorithms and resource management policies will be considered in detail, as they have great influence on system behavior. Finally, a novel approach will be introduced for handling transient overloads and execution overruns in soft real-time systems working in dynamic environments. These techniques provide efficient support to real-time multimedia systems.

1 Introduction

Often, people say that real-time systems must react fast to external events. Such a definition, however, is not precise, because processing speed does not provide any information on the actual capability of the system to react timely to events. In fact, the effect of controller actions in a system can only be evaluated when considering the dynamic characteristics of the controlled environment.

A more precise definition would say that a real-time system is a system in which performance depends not only on the correctness of the single controller actions, but also on the time at which actions are produced [24]. The main difference between a real-time task and a non real-time task is that a real-time task must complete within a given *deadline*. In other words, a deadline is the maximum time allowed for a computational process to finish its execution. In real-time applications, a result produced after its deadline is not only late, but can be dangerous. Depending on the consequences caused by a missed deadline, real-time activities can be classified in *hard* and *soft* tasks [23]. A real-time task is said to be *hard* if missing a deadline may have catastrophic consequences in the controlled system. A real-time task is said to be *soft* if missing a deadline causes a performance degradation, but does not jeopardize correct system behavior. An operating system able to manage hard tasks is called a *hard real-time system* [4][25].

In general, hard real-time systems have to handle both hard and soft activities. In a control application, typical hard tasks include sensory data acquisition, detection of critical conditions, motor actuation, and action planning. Typical soft tasks include

W. Damm and E.-R. Olderog (Eds.): FTRTFT 2002, LNCS 2469, pp. 37–51, 2002.

user command interpretation, keyboard input, message visualization, system status representation, and graphical activities. The great interest in real-time systems is motivated by the growing diffusion they have in our society in several application fields, including chemical and nuclear power plants, flight control systems, traffic monitoring systems, telecommunication systems, automotive devices, industrial automation, military systems, space missions, and robotic systems.

Despite this large application domain, most of today's real-time control systems are still designed using ad hoc techniques and heuristic approaches. Very often, control applications with stringent time constraints are implemented by writing large portions of code in assembly language, programming timers, writing low-level drivers for device handling, and manipulating task and interrupt priorities. Although the code produced by these techniques can be optimized to run very efficiently, this approach has several disadvantages. First of all, the implementation of large and complex applications in assembly language is much more difficult and time consuming than using high-level programming. Moreover, the efficiency of the code strongly depends on the programmer's ability. In addition, assembly code optimization makes a program more difficult to comprehend, complicating software maintenance. Finally, without the support of specific tools and methodologies for code and schedulability analysis, the verification of time constraints becomes practically impossible.

The major consequence of this state of affairs is that control software produced by empirical techniques can be highly unpredictable. If all critical time constraints cannot be verified a priori and the operating system does not include specific features for handling real-time tasks, the system apparently works well for a period of time, but may collapse in certain rare, but possible, situations. The consequences of a failure can sometimes be catastrophic and may injure people or cause serious damage to the environment. A trustworthy guarantee of system behavior under all possible operating conditions can only be achieved by adopting appropriate design methodologies and kernel mechanisms specifically developed for handling explicit timing constraints.

1.1   Achieving Predictability

The most important property of a real-time system is not high speed, but predictability. In a predictable system we should be able to determine in advance whether all the computational activities can be completed within their timing constraints. The deterministic behavior of a system typically depends on several factors, ranging from the hardware architecture to the operating system, up to the programming language used to write the application.

Architectural features that have major influence on task execution include interrupts, DMA, cache and pre-fetching mechanisms. Although such features improve the average performance of the processor, they introduce a non deterministic behavior in process execution, prolonging the worst-case response times. Other factors that significantly affect task execution are due to the internal mechanisms used in the operating system, such as the scheduling algorithm, the synchronization mechanisms, the memory management policy, and the method used to handle I/O devices. The programming language has also an important impact on predictability, through the constructs it provides to handle the timing requirements specified for computational activities.

2   Periodic Task Handling

Periodic activities represent the major computational load in a real-time control system. For example activities such as actuator regulation, signal acquisition, filtering, sensory data processing, action planning, and monitoring, need to be executed with a frequency derived from the application requirements.

A periodic task is characterized by an infinite sequence of *instances*, or *jobs*. Each job is characterized by a *request time* and a *deadline*. The request time $r(k)$ of the k-th job of a task represents the time at which the task becomes ready for execution for the k-th time. The interval of time between two consecutive request times is equal to the task period. The absolute deadline of the k-th job, denoted with $d(k)$, represents the time within which the job has to complete its execution, and $r(k) < d(k) \leq r(k+1)$.

2.1   Timeline Scheduling

Timeline Scheduling (TS), also known as a *cyclic executive*, is one of the most used approaches to handle periodic tasks in defense military systems and traffic control systems. The method consists in dividing the temporal axis into *slices* of equal length, in which one or more tasks can be allocated for execution, in such a way to respect the frequencies derived from the application requirements. A timer synchronizes the activation of the tasks at the beginning of each time slice. In order to illustrate this method, consider the following example, in which three tasks, A, B and C, need to be executed with a frequency of 40, 20 and 10 Hz, respectively. By analyzing the task periods, it is easy to verify that the optimal length for the time slice is 25 ms, which is the Greatest Common Divisor of the periods. Hence, to meet the required frequencies, task A needs to be executed every time slice, task B every two slices, and task C every four slices. A possible scheduling solution for this task set is illustrated in Figure 1.

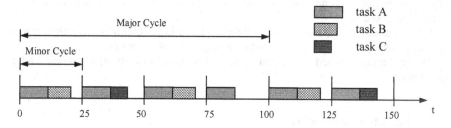

Fig. 1. Example of timeline scheduling

The duration of the time slice is also called a *Minor Cycle*, whereas the minimum period after which the schedule repeats itself is called a *Major Cycle*. In general, the major cycle is equal to the least common multiple of all the periods (in the example it is equal to 100 ms).

In order to guarantee a priori that a schedule is feasible on a particular processor, it is sufficient to know the task worst-case execution times and verify that the sum of the executions within each time slice is less than or equal to the minor cycle. In the example shown in Figure 1, if C_A, C_B and C_C denote the execution times of the tasks, it is sufficient to verify that

$$C_A + C_B \leq 25 \text{ ms}$$

$$C_A + C_C \leq 25 \text{ ms}$$

The major relevant advantage of timeline scheduling is its simplicity. The method can be implemented by programming a timer to interrupt with a period equal to the minor cycle and by writing a main program that calls the tasks in the order given in the major cycle, inserting a time synchronization point at the beginning of each minor cycle. Since the task sequence is not decided by a scheduling algorithm in the kernel, but it is triggered by the calls made by the main program, there are no context switches, so the runtime overhead is very low. Moreover, the sequence of tasks in the schedule is always the same, can be easily visualized, and it is not affected by jitter (i.e., task start times and response times are not subject to large variations).

In spite of these advantages, timeline scheduling has some problems. For example, it is very fragile during overload conditions. If a task does not terminate at the minor cycle boundary, we can either let it continue or abort it. In both cases, however, the system may enter in a risky situation. In fact, if we leave the failing task in execution, it can cause a domino effect on the other tasks, breaking the entire schedule (*timeline break*). On the other hand, if the failing task is aborted, the system may be left in an inconsistent state, jeopardizing correct system behavior.

Another big problem of the timeline scheduling technique is its sensitivity to application changes. If updating a task requires an increase of its computation time or its activation frequency, the entire scheduling sequence may need to be reconstructed from scratch. Considering the previous example, if task B is updated to B' and the code change is such that $C_A + C_{B'} > 25$ ms, then we have to divide B' in two or more pieces to be allocated in the available intervals of the timeline. Changing the task frequencies may cause even more radical changes in the schedule. For example, if the frequency of task B changes from 20 Hz to 25 Hz, the previous schedule is not valid any more, because the new Minor Cycle is equal to 10 ms and the new Major Cycle is equal to 200 ms.

Finally, another limitation of the timeline scheduling is that it is difficult to handle aperiodic activities efficiently without changing the task sequence.

The problems outlined above can be solved by using priority based scheduling algorithms.

2.2   Rate Monotonic (RM)

The *Rate-Monotonic* (RM) algorithm assigns each task a priority directly proportional to its activation frequency, so that tasks with shorter period have higher priority. Since a period is usually kept constant for a task, the RM algorithm implements a static priority assignment, in the sense that task priorities are decided at task creation and remain unchanged for the entire application run. RM is typically preemptive, although it can also be used in a non-preemptive mode.

In 1973, Liu and Layland [17] showed that RM is optimal among all static scheduling algorithms, in the sense that if a task set is not schedulable by RM, then the task set cannot be feasibly scheduled by any other fixed priority assignment. Another important result proved by the same authors is that a set $\Gamma = \{\tau_1, ..., \tau_n\}$ of n periodic tasks is schedulable by RM if

$$\sum_{i=1}^{n} \frac{C_i}{T_i} \leq n\left(2^{1/n} - 1\right)$$

where C_i and T_i represent the worst-case computation time and the period of task τ_i, respectively. The quantity

$$U = \sum_{i=1}^{n} \frac{C_i}{T_i}$$

represents the *processor utilization factor* and denotes the fraction of time used by the processor to execute the entire task set. Table 1 shows the values of $n(2^{1/n} - 1)$ for n from 1 to 10. As can be seen, the factor decreases with n and, for large n, it tends to the following limit value:

$$\lim_{n \to \infty} n\left(2^{1/n} - 1\right) = \ln 2 \cong 0.69$$

Table 1. Maximum processor utilization for the Rate Monotonic algorithm

n	$n(2^{1/n} - 1)$
1	1.000
2	0.828
3	0.780
4	0.757
5	0.743
6	0.735
7	0.729
8	0.724
9	0.721
10	0.718

We note that the Liu and Layland test only gives a sufficient condition for guaranteeing a feasible schedule under the RM algorithm. Hence, a task set can be schedulable by RM even though the utilization condition is not satisfied. Nevertheless, we can certainly state that a periodic task set cannot be feasibly scheduled by any algorithm if $U > 1$. A statistical study carried out by Lehoczky, Sha, and Ding [14] on randomly generated task sets showed that the utilization bound of the RM algorithm has an average value of 0.88, and becomes 1 for periodic tasks with harmonic period relations.

In spite of the limitation on the schedulability bound, which in most cases prevents the full processor utilization, the RM algorithm is widely used in real-time applications, manly for its simplicity. At the same time, being a static scheduling algorithm, it can be easily implemented on top of commercial operating systems, using a set of fixed priority levels. Moreover, in overload conditions, the highest priority tasks are less prone to missing their deadlines. For all these reasons, the Software Engineering Institute of Pittsburgh has prepared a sort of user guide for the design and analysis of real-time systems based on the RM algorithm [11].

Since the RM algorithm is optimal among all fixed priority assignments, the schedulability bound can only be improved through a dynamic priority assignment.

2.3   Earliest Deadline First (EDF)

The *Earliest Deadline First* (EDF) algorithm consists in selecting (among the ready tasks) the task with the earliest absolute deadline. The EDF algorithm is typically *preemptive*, in the sense that, a newly arrived task can preempt the running task if its absolute deadline is shorter.

If the operating system does not support explicit timing constraints, EDF (as RM) can be implemented on a priority-based kernel, where priorities are dynamically assigned to tasks. A task will receive the highest priority if its deadline is the earliest among those of the ready tasks, whereas it will receive the lowest priority if its deadline is the latest one. A task gets a priority which is inversely proportional to its absolute deadline.

The EDF algorithm is more general than RM, since it can be used to schedule both periodic and aperiodic task sets, because the selection of a task is based on the value of its absolute deadline, which can be defined for both types of tasks. Typically, a periodic task that completed its execution is suspended by the kernel until its next release, coincident with the end of the current period. Dertouzos [8] showed that EDF is optimal among all on line algorithms, while Liu and Layland [17] proved that a set $\Gamma = \{\tau_1, \tau_2, ..., \tau_n\}$ of n periodic tasks is schedulable by EDF *if and only if*

$$\sum_{i=1}^{n} \frac{C_i}{T_i} \leq 1$$

It is worth noting that the EDF schedulability condition is necessary and sufficient to guarantee a feasible schedule. This mean that, if it is not satisfied, no algorithm is able to produce a feasible schedule for that task set.

The dynamic priority assignment allows EDF to exploit the full processor, reaching up to 100% of the available processing time. When the task set has a processor utilization factor less than one, the residual fraction of time can be efficiently used to handle aperiodic requests activated by external events. In addition, compared with RM, EDF generates a lower number of context switches, thus causing less runtime overhead. On the other hand, RM is simpler to implement on a fixed priority kernel and is more predictable in overload situations, because higher priority tasks are less viable to miss their deadlines.

2.4   Tasks with Deadlines Less Than Periods

Using RM or EDF, a periodic task can be executed at any time during its period. The only guarantee provided by the schedulability test is that each task will be able to complete its execution before the next release time. In some real-time applications, however, there is the need for some periodic task to complete within an interval less than its period.

The *Deadline Monotonic* (DM) algorithm, proposed by Leung and Whitehead [16], extends RM to handle tasks with a relative deadline less than or equal to their period. According to DM, at each instant the processor is assigned to the task with the shortest relative deadline. In priority-based kernels, this is equivalent to assigning each task a priority $P_i \propto 1/D_i$ inversely proportional to its relative deadline.

With D_i fixed for each task, DM is classified as a static scheduling algorithm. In the recent years, several authors [2][10][14] independently proposed a necessary and sufficient test to verify the schedulability of a periodic task set. For example, the method proposed by Audsley et al. [2] consists in computing the worst-case response time R_i of each periodic task. It is derived by summing its computation time and the interference caused by tasks with higher priority:

$$ R_i = C_i + \sum_{k \in hp(i)} \left\lceil \frac{R_i}{T_k} \right\rceil C_k $$

where *hp(i)* denotes the set of tasks having priority higher than task i and $\lceil x \rceil$ denotes the ceiling of a rational number, i.e., the smaller integer greater than or equal to x. The equation above can be solved by an iterative approach, starting with $R_i^{(0)} = C_i$ and terminating when $R_i^{(s)} = R_i^{(s-1)}$. If $R_i^{(s)} > D_i$ for some task, then the task set cannot be feasibly scheduled by DM.

Under EDF, the schedulability analysis for periodic task sets with deadlines less than periods is based on the *processor demand criterion*, proposed by Baruah, Howell, and Rosier [3]. According to this method, a task set is schedulable by EDF if and only if, in every interval of length L (starting at time 0), the overall computational demand is no greater than the available processing time, that is, if and only if

$$ \forall L > 0 \quad \sum_{i=1}^{n} \left\lfloor \frac{L + T_i - D_i}{T_i} \right\rfloor C_i \leq L $$

This test is feasible, because L can only be checked for values equal to task deadlines no larger than the least common multiple of the periods.

3   Aperiodic Task Handling

Although in a real-time system most acquisition and control tasks are periodic, there exist computational activities that must be executed only at the occurrence of external events (typically signalled through interrupts), which may arrive at irregular times. When the system must handle aperiodic requests of computation, we have to balance two conflicting interests: on the one hand, we would like to serve an event as soon as possible to improve system responsiveness; on the other hand, we do not want to jeopardize the schedulability of periodic tasks.

If aperiodic activities are less critical than periodic tasks, then the objective of a scheduling algorithm should be to minimize their response time, while guaranteeing that all periodic tasks (although being delayed by the aperiodic service) complete their executions within their deadlines. If some aperiodic task has a hard deadline, we should try to guarantee its timely completion off-line. Such a guarantee can only be done by assuming that aperiodic requests, although arriving at irregular intervals, do not exceed a maximum given frequency, that is, they are separated by a *minimum interarrival time*. An aperiodic task characterized by a minimum interarrival time is called a *sporadic task*.

Let us consider an example in which an aperiodic job J_a of 3 units of time must be scheduled by RM along with two periodic tasks, having computation times $C_1 = 1$, $C_2 = 3$ and periods $T_1 = 4$, $T_2 = 6$, respectively. As shown in Figure 2, if the aperiodic request is serviced immediately (that is, with a priority higher than that assigned to periodic tasks), then task τ_2 will miss its deadline.

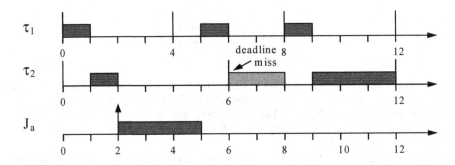

Fig. 2. Immediate service of an aperiodic task. Periodic tasks are scheduled by RM

The simplest technique for managing aperiodic activities while preserving the guarantee for periodic tasks is to schedule them in background. This means that an aperiodic task executes only when the processor is not busy with periodic tasks. The disadvantage of this solution is that, if the computational load due to periodic tasks is high, the residual time left for aperiodic execution can be insufficient for satisfying their deadlines.

Considering the same task set as before, Figure 3 illustrates how job J_a is handled by a background service.

The response time of aperiodic tasks can be improved by handling them through a periodic *server* dedicated to their execution. As any other periodic task, a server is characterized by a period T_s and an execution time C_s, called the server *capacity* (or *budget*).

In general, the server is scheduled using the algorithm adopted for periodic tasks and, once activated, it starts serving the pending aperiodic requests within the limit of its current capacity. The order of service of the aperiodic requests is independent of the scheduling algorithm used for the periodic tasks, and it can be a function of the arrival time, computation time or deadline.

During the last years, several aperiodic service algorithms have been proposed in the real-time literature, differing in performance and complexity. Among the fixed priority algorithms we mention the *Polling Server* and the *Deferrable Server* [13][27], the *Sporadic Server* [20], and the *Slack Stealer* [15]. Among those servers using dynamic priorities (which are more efficient on the average) we recall the *Dynamic Sporadic Server* [9][21], the *Total Bandwidth Server* [22], the *Tunable Bandwidth Server* [5], and the *Constant Bandwidth Server* [1].

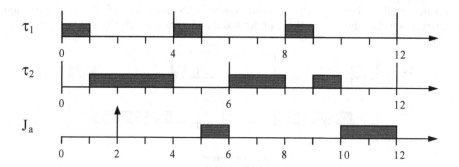

Fig. 3. Background service of an aperiodic task. Periodic tasks are scheduled by RM

In order to clarify the idea behind an aperiodic server, Figure 4 illustrates the schedule produced, under EDF, by a *Dynamic Deferrable Server* with capacity $C_s = 1$ and period $T_s = 4$. We note that, when the absolute deadline of the server is equal to the one of a periodic task, priority is given to the server in order to enhance aperiodic responsiveness. We also observe that the same task set would not be schedulable under a fixed priority system.

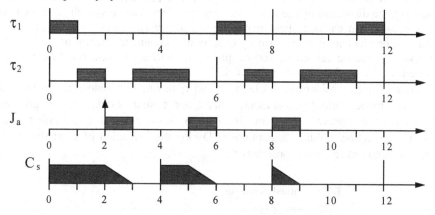

Fig. 4. Aperiodic service performed by a Dynamic Deferrable Server. Periodic tasks, including the server, are scheduled by EDF. C_s is the remaining budget available for J_a

Although the response time achieved by a server is less than that achieved through the background service, it is not the minimum possible. The minimum response time can be obtained with an optimal server (TB*) which assigns each aperiodic request the earliest possible deadline which still produces a feasible EDF schedule [5]. The schedule generated by the optimal TB* algorithm is illustrated in Figure 5, where the minimum response time for job J_a is equal to 5 units of time (obtained by assigning the job a deadline $d_a = 7$).

As for all the efficient solutions, the better performance is achieved at the price of a larger runtime overhead (due to the complexity of computing the minimum deadline). However, adopting a variant of the algorithm, called the *Tunable Bandwidth Server* [5], overhead cost and performance can be balanced in order to select the best service method for a given real-time system. An overview of the most common aperiodic service algorithms (both under fixed and dynamic priorities) can be found in [4].

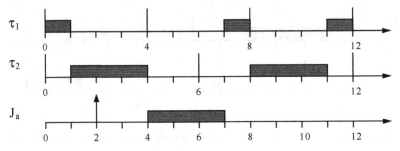

Fig. 5. Optimal aperiodic service under EDF

4   Protocols for Accessing Shared Resources

When two or more tasks interact through shared resources (e.g., shared memory buffers), the direct use of classical synchronization mechanisms, such as semaphores or monitors, can cause a phenomenon known as *priority inversion*: a high priority task can be blocked by a low priority task for an unbounded interval of time. Such a blocking condition can create serious problems in safety critical real-time systems, since it can cause deadlines to be missed.

For example, consider three tasks, τ_1, τ_2 and τ_3, having decreasing priority (τ_1 is the task with highest priority), and assume that τ_1 and τ_3 share a data structure protected by a binary semaphore S. As shown in Figure 6, suppose that at time t_1 task τ_3 enters its critical section, holding semaphore S. During the execution of τ_3, at time t_2, assume τ_1 becomes ready and preempts τ_3.

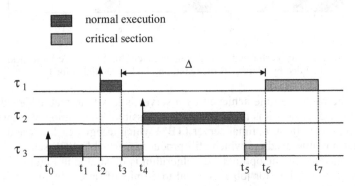

Fig. 6. Example of priority inversion

At time t_3, when τ_1 tries to access the shared resource, it is blocked on semaphore S, since the resource is used by τ_3. Since τ_1 is the highest priority task, we would expect it to be blocked for an interval no longer than the time needed by τ_3 to complete its critical section. Unfortunately, however, the maximum blocking time for τ_1 can become much larger. In fact, task τ_3, while holding the resource, can be preempted by medium priority tasks (like τ_2), which will prolong the blocking interval of τ_1 for their entire execution!

The situation illustrated in Figure 6 can be avoided by simply preventing preemption inside critical sections. This solution, however, is appropriate only for very short critical sections, because it could cause unnecessary delays for high priority tasks. For example, a low priority task inside a long critical section would prevent the execution of a high priority task, even though they do not share any resource.

A more efficient solution is to regulate the access to shared resource through the use of specific concurrency control protocols, designed to limit the priority inversion phenomenon.

4.1   Priority Inheritance Protocol

An elegant solution to the priority inversion phenomenon caused by mutual exclusion is offered by the *Priority Inheritance Protocol* (PIP) [19]. Here, the problem is solved by dynamically modifying the priorities of tasks that cause a blocking condition. In particular, when a task τ_a blocks on a shared resource, it transmits its priority to the task τ_b that is holding the resource. In this way, τ_b will execute its critical section with the priority of task τ_a. In general, τ_b *inherits* the highest priority among the tasks it blocks. Moreover, priority inheritance is transitive, thus if task τ_c blocks τ_b, which in turn blocks τ_a, then τ_c will inherit the priority of τ_a through τ_b.

Figure 7 illustrates how the schedule shown in Figure 6 is changed when resources are accessed using the Priority Inheritance Protocol. Until time t_3 the system evolution is the same as the one shown in Figure 6. At time t_3, the high priority task τ_1 blocks after attempting to enter the resource held by τ_3 (*direct blocking*). In this case, however, the protocol imposes that τ_3 inherits the maximum priority among the tasks blocked on that resource, thus it continues the execution of its critical section at the priority of τ_1. Under these conditions, at time t_4, task τ_2 is not able to preempt τ_3, hence it blocks until the resource is released (*push-through blocking*).

In other words, although τ_2 has a nominal priority greater than τ_3, it cannot execute, because τ_3 inherited the priority of τ_1. At time t_5, τ_3 exits its critical section, releases the semaphore and recovers its nominal priority. As a consequence, τ_1 can proceed until its completion, which occurs at time t_6. Only then τ_2 can start executing.

The Priority Inheritance Protocol has the following property [19]:

> Given a task τ, if n is the number of tasks with lower priority sharing a resource with a task with priority higher or equal to τ and m is the number of semaphores that could block τ, then τ can be blocked for at most the duration of *min(n,m)* critical sections.

Although the Priority Inheritance Protocol limits the priority inversion phenomenon, the maximum blocking time for high priority tasks can still be significant, due to possible chained blocking conditions. Moreover, *deadlock* can occur if semaphores are not properly used in nested critical sections.

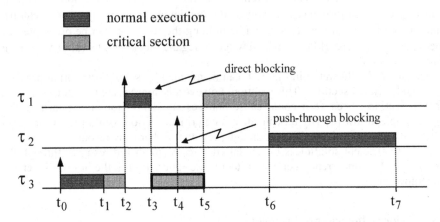

Fig. 7. Schedule produced using Priority Inheritance on the task set of Figure 6

The Priority Inheritance Protocol has the following property [19]:

> Given a task τ, if n is the number of tasks with lower priority sharing a resource with a task with priority higher or equal to τ and m is the number of semaphores that could block τ, then τ can be blocked for at most the duration of *min(n,m)* critical sections.

Although the Priority Inheritance Protocol limits the priority inversion phenomenon, the maximum blocking time for high priority tasks can still be significant, due to possible chained blocking conditions. Moreover, *deadlock* can occur if semaphores are not properly used in nested critical sections.

4.2   Priority Ceiling Protocol

The *Priority Ceiling Protocol* (PCP) [19] provides a better solution for the priority inversion phenomenon, also avoiding chained blocking and deadlock conditions.

The basic idea behind this protocol is to ensure that, whenever a task τ enters a critical section, its priority is the highest among those that can be inherited from all the lower priority tasks that are currently suspended in a critical section. If this condition is not satisfied, τ is blocked and the task that is blocking τ inherits τ's priority.

This idea is implemented by assigning each semaphore a *priority ceiling* equal to the highest priority of the tasks using that semaphore. Then, a task τ is allowed to enter a critical section only if its priority is strictly greater than all priority ceilings of the semaphores held by the other tasks. As for the Priority Inheritance Protocol, the inheritance mechanism is transitive.

The Priority Ceiling Protocol, besides avoiding chained blocking and deadlocks, has the property that each task can be blocked for at most the duration of a single critical section.

4.3   Schedulability Analysis

The importance of the protocols for accessing shared resources in a real-time system derives from the fact that they can bound the maximum blocking time experienced by a task. This is essential for analyzing the schedulability of a set of real-time tasks interacting through shared buffers or any other non-preemptable resource, e.g., a communication port or bus.

To verify the schedulability of task τ_i using the processor utilization approach, we need to consider the utilization factor of task τ_i, the interference caused by the higher priority tasks and the blocking time caused by lower priority tasks. If B_i is the maximum blocking time that can be experienced by task τ_i, then the sum of the utilization factors due to these three causes cannot exceed the least upper bound of the scheduling algorithm, that is:

$$\forall i = 1,...,n \qquad \frac{C_i}{T_i} + \sum_{k \in hp(i)} \frac{C_k}{T_k} + \frac{B_i}{T_i} \leq i\left(2^{1/i} - 1\right)$$

where $hp(i)$ denotes the set of tasks with priority higher than τ_i. The same test is valid for both the protocols described above, the only difference being the amount of blocking that each task may experience.

5   New Applications and Trends

In the last years, real-time system technology has been applied to several application domains, where computational activities have less stringent timing constraints and occasional deadline misses are typically tolerated. Examples of such systems include monitoring, multimedia systems, flight simulators and, in general, virtual reality games. In such applications, missing a deadline does not cause catastrophic effects on the system, but just a performance degradation. Hence, instead of requiring an absolute guarantee for the feasibility of the schedule, such systems demand an acceptable *Quality of Service* (QoS). It is worth observing that, since some timing constraints need to be handled anyway (although not critical), a non real-time operating system, such a Linux or Windows, is not appropriate: First of all, such systems do not provide temporal isolation among tasks, thus a sporadic peak load on a task may negatively affect the execution of other tasks in the system. Furthermore, the lack of concurrency control mechanisms which prevent priority inversion makes these systems unsuitable for guaranteeing a desired QoS level.

On the other hand, a hard real-time approach is also not well suited for supporting such applications, because resources would be wasted due to static allocation mechanisms and pessimistic design assumptions. Moreover, in many multimedia applications, tasks are characterized by highly variable execution times (consider, for instance, an mpeg player), thus providing precise estimations on task computation times is practically impossible, unless one uses overly pessimistic figures.

In order to provide efficient as well as predictable support for this type of real-time applications, several new approaches and scheduling methodologies have been proposed. They increase the flexibility and the adaptability of a system to on-line variations. For example, temporal protection mechanisms have been proposed to isolate task overruns and reduce reciprocal task interference [1][26]. Statistical analysis techniques have been introduced to provide a probabilistic guarantee aimed at improving system efficiency [1].

Other techniques have been devised to handle transient and permanent overload conditions in a controlled fashion, thus increasing the average computational load in the system. One method absorbs the overload by regularly aborting some jobs of a periodic task, without exceeding a maximum limit specified by the user through a QoS parameter describing the minimum number of jobs between two consecutive abortions [7][12]. Another technique handles overloads through a suitable variation of periods, managed to decreased the processor utilization up to a desired level [6].

6   Conclusions

This paper surveyed some kernel methodologies aimed at enhancing the efficiency and the predictability of real-time control applications. In particular, the paper presented some scheduling algorithms and analysis techniques for periodic and aperiodic task sets. Two concurrency control protocols have been described to access shared resources in mutual exclusion while avoiding the priority inversion phenomenon. Each technique has the property to be analyzable, so that an off-line guarantee can be provided for feasibility of the schedule within the timing constraints imposed by the application.

For soft real-time systems, such as multimedia systems or simulators, the hard real-time approach can be too rigid and inefficient, especially when the application tasks have highly variable computation times. In these cases, novel methodologies have been introduced to improve average resource exploitation. They are also able to guarantee a desired QoS level and control performance degradation during overload conditions.

In addition to research efforts aimed at providing solutions to more complex problems, a concrete increase in the reliability of future real-time systems can only be achieved if the mature methodologies are actually integrated in next generation operating systems and languages, defining new standards for the development of real-time applications. At the same time, programmers and software engineers need to be educated to the appropriate use of the available technologies.

References

1. Abeni, L., and G. Buttazzo: "Integrating Multimedia Applications in Hard Real-Time Systems", Proceedings of the *IEEE Real-Time Systems Symposium*, Madrid, Spain, December 1998.
2. Audsley, N. C., A. Burns, M. Richardson, and A. Wellings: "Hard Real-Time Scheduling: The Deadline Monotonic Approach", *IEEE Workshop on Real-Time Operating Systems*, 1992.
3. Baruah, S. K., R. R. Howell, and L. E. Rosier: "Algorithms and Complexity Concerning the Preemptive Scheduling of Periodic Real-Time Tasks on One Processor," *Real-Time Systems*, 2, 1990.
4. Buttazzo, G. C.: *HARD REAL-TIME COMPUTING SYSTEMS: Predictable Scheduling Algorithms and Applications*, Kluwer Academic Publishers, Boston, 1997.
5. Buttazzo, G. C. and F. Sensini: "Optimal Deadline Assignment for Scheduling Soft Aperiodic Tasks in Hard Real-Time Environments", *3rd IEEE International Conference on Engineering of Complex Computer Systems* (ICECCS), Como, Italy, September 1997.

6. Buttazzo, G. C., G. Lipari, and L. Abeni: "Elastic Task Model for Adaptive Rate Control", *Proceedings of the IEEE Real-Time Systems Symposium*, Madrid, Spain, December 1998.
7. Buttazzo, G. C., and M. Caccamo: "Minimizing Aperiodic Response Times in a Firm Real-Time Environment", *IEEE Transactions on Software Engineering*, Vol. 25, No. 1, pp. 22-32, January/February 1999.
8. Dertouzos, M. L.: "Control Robotics: the Procedural Control of Physical Processes", *Information Processing 74*, North-Holland Publishing Company, 1974.
9. Ghazalie, T. M. and T. P. Baker: "Aperiodic Servers In A Deadline Scheduling Environment". *The Journal of Real-Time Systems*, 1995.
10. M. Joseph and P. Pandya, "Finding Response Times in a Real-Time System," *The Computer Journal*, 29(5), pp. 390-395, 1986.
11. Klein, M.H., et al.: *A Practitioners' Handbook for Real-Time Analysis: Guide to Rate Monotonic Analysis for Real-Time Systems*. Boston, MA: Kluwer Academic Publishers, 1993.
12. Koren, G., and D. Shasha: "Skip-Over: Algorithms and Complexity for Overloaded Systems that Allow Skips", *IEEE Real-Time System Symposium*, December 1995.
13. Lehoczky, J. P., L. Sha, and J. K. Strosnider: "Enhanced Aperiodic Responsiveness in Hard Real-Time Environments", *IEEE Real-Time Systems Symposium*, pp. 261-270, San Jose, CA, December 1987.
14. Lehoczky, J. P., L. Sha, and Y. Ding: "The Rate-Monotonic Scheduling Algorithm: Exact Characterization and Average Case Behaviour", *IEEE Real-Time Systems Symposium*, pp. 166-171, 1989.
15. Lehoczky, J. P., and S. Ramos-Thuel: "An Optimal Algorithm for Scheduling Soft-Aperiodic Tasks in Fixed-Priority Preemptive Systems", *IEEE Real-Time Systems Symposium*, 1992.
16. Leung, J., and J. Whitehead: "On the Complexity of Fixed Priority Scheduling of Periodic Real-Time Tasks", *Performance Evaluation*, 2(4), pp. 237-250, 1982.
17. Liu, C. L., and J. W. Layland: "Scheduling Algoritms for Multiprogramming in a Hard-Real-Time Environment", *Journal of ACM*, Vol. 20, No. 1, January 1973.
18. Rajkumar, R.: *Synchronous Programming of Reactive Systems*, Kluwer Academic Publishing, 1991.
19. Sha, L., R. Rajkumar, and J. P. Lehoczky: "Priority Inheritance Protocols: An Approach to Real-Time Synchronization", *IEEE Transactions on Computers*, Vol. 39, No. 9, September 1990.
20. Sprunt, B., L. Sha, and J. Lehoczky: "Aperiodic Task Scheduling for Hard Real-Time System", *Journal of Real-Time Systems*, 1, pp. 27-60, June 1989.
21. Spuri, M., and G. C. Buttazzo: "Efficient Aperiodic Service under Earliest Deadline Scheduling", *15th IEEE Real-Time Systems Symposium*, San Juan, Puerto Rico, 1994.
22. Spuri, M., and G. C. Buttazzo: "Scheduling Aperiodic Tasks in Dynamic Priority Systems", *Journal of Real-Time Systems*, Vol. 10, No. 2, pp. 1-32, 1996.
23. Stankovic, J., and K. Ramamritham: *Tutorial on Hard Real-Time Systems*, IEEE Computer Society Press, 1988.
24. Stankovic, J.: "A Serious Problem for Next-Generation Systems", *IEEE Computer*, pp. 10-19, October 1988.
25. Stankovic, J., M. Spuri, M. Di Natale, G. Buttazzo: "Implications of Classical Scheduling Results for Real-Time Systems", *IEEE Computer*, Vol. 28, No. 6, pp. 16-25, June 1995.
26. Stoica, I., H-Abdel-Wahab, K. Jeffay, S. Baruah, J.E. Gehrke, and G. C. Plaxton: "A Proportional Share Resource Allocation Algorithm for Real-Time Timeshared Systems", *IEEE Real-Time Systems Symposium*, Dec. 1996
27. Strosnider, J. K., J. P. Lehoczky and L. Sha: "The Deferrable Server Algorithm for Enhanced Aperiodic Responsiveness in Hard Real-Time Environments", *IEEE Transactions on Computers*, Vol. 44, No. 1, pp. 73-91, January 1995.

Real-Time UML

Bruce Powel Douglass

I-Logix

Abstract. The UML (Unified Modeling Language) is a third-generation object-oriented modeling language recently accepted as a standard by the OMG (Object Management Group). The OMG is an association of over 800 leading technology companies that have banded together to promote standards in the object community. The UML standard draws on the last decade of intensive experience in object modeling, discarding features that didn't work and enhancing support for those that have proven their value. The UML has successfully been applied to the development of real-time and embedded systems in many different vertical markets from medical systems to avionics to military systems to office automation. The UML is clearly and demonstrably completely adequate to model and develop real-time systems without requiring extensions or modifications. By "Real-Time UML", I mean the application of the UML standard to the development of real-time and embedded systems, and focusing attention on those aspects of UML especially relevant to the areas of special concern for such systems.

1 Real-Time Issues

Real-time systems have all the problems of "normal" software systems, such as capturing requirements, designing functionality, proving correctness, and testing, plus several more: timeliness, concurrency, predictability, efficiency, distribution and communication, fault tolerance (and related issues of reliability and safety), and hardware interfacing. Standard structured methods don't deal explicitly with any of these issues. Is the UML any better? The answer, as it turns out, is "YES!" Let's deal with each of these issues in turn.

1.1 Timeliness

The timeliness of an action is most often modeled as the completion of the action with respect to a deadline. Deadlines may be "hard" or "soft". Missing a hard deadline constitutes a system failure of some kind, so great care must be taken to ensure that all such actions execute in a timely way. The important modeling concerns of timeliness are modeling execution time, deadlines, arrival patterns, synchronization patterns (see concurrency, below) and time sources.

Timeliness requirements may be addressed by first determining the end-to-end performance requirement of an event-response action sequence. These are normally determined during use case or context analysis. For example, a deadline

W. Damm and E.-R. Olderog (Eds.): FTRTFT 2002, LNCS 2469, pp. 53–70, 2002.

might exist from an external perspective: e.g. "when the actor VolumeControl sends an Increase command, the system shall respond within 10 ms +/- 2 ms." Both use case and context analysis view the system from a black-box perspective and serve as a means of capturing external requirements, such as overall performance and response times. Once the "box is opened" and classes are identified, a sequence diagram shows the objects (and operations) involved in handling the request and controlling the output response. Each operation in the sequence is given a portion of that budget such that the sum of all execution times for each operation in the sequence, including potential blocking, is less than or equal to the overall performance budget. These budgets may be captured as constraints associated with the class operations or captured graphically on sequence diagrams using timing constraint expressions.

Time sources themselves are modeling implicitly using the tm() operator defined for statecharts, which specifies the precondition for the transition is that a fixed period of time has elapsed. It is also simple to explicitly model OS and hardware timers as classes that propagate timeout events to client objects.

1.2 Concurrency

Concurrency is the simultaneous (or non-deterministic interleaved) execution of multiple sequential chains of actions. These chains may execute on one processor ("pseudoconcurrency") or multiple processors ("true concurrency"). The UML models concurrency by identifying a small set of "active" objects within a system. These active objects are the roots of the system's concurrent threads. Active objects are similar to Ada's task types but have all the power of normal classes as well. Idiomatically, it is common to construct a "task diagram" by simply including only the active objects on a single class diagram. Often, active objects are composite objects that tightly aggregate their component parts that, in turn, execute within the thread of their composite.

One of the issues with concurrent reactive systems is the arrival patterns of the initiating events. Two main categories are periodic and aperiodic. A periodic arrival pattern means that the thread is re-initiated on a fixed period, plus or minus a small variation (jitter). Such threads are commonly called periodic tasks. Aperiodic tasks don't occur with a regular period. Instead, they appear to occur (to the system, at least) randomly. For such systems to be schedulable, the frequency of occurrence of the initiating event must be bounded in time. One such bound is a minimum interarrival time, that is, a minimum time that must elapse between incoming events. A minimum interarrival bound is normally used when the response deadline is "hard". Another common aperiodic bound is an average event rate. This is used with so-called "soft" deadlines.

If concurrent threads were truly independent, life would be much less interesting. Fortunately (or unfortunately, depending on your outlook), threads must communicate and share resources. Communication in object systems takes place via messages. Messaging is a logical abstraction that includes a variety of rendezvous patterns, including synchronous function calls, asynchronous, waiting, timed, and balking. By far, the most common are synchronous function calls.

Objects in one thread directly call the methods of objects in another, effectively operating within the same thread of control. Asynchronous calls are supported by real-time operating systems by queuing a message from another thread and acting on it when it is convenient, but meanwhile the caller continues without waiting. A waiting rendezvous means that the calling task will wait indefinitely for the called task to become ready, while in a timed rendezvous the caller will wait for a specified length of time before aborting the synchronization attempt. Finally, a balking rendezvous means simply that if the called task is not immediately available, the caller will abort the attempt and take other actions.

Rendezvous are specified within object methods by stereotyping messages and events with a rendezvous pattern. Some common message stereotypes are identified in [4]. It is important to characterize the rendezvous patterns of cross-thread messaging in order to ensure deadlines will always be met.

Another common problem in concurrent systems is the robust sharing of resources. The common solutions involve the serialization of access through mutual exclusion semaphores or queues. In object systems, such access control may be done through the Guarded Call Pattern or other design pattern approaches [5]. This can be indicated using the pattern notation of the UML or by adding an {exclusion} constraint on the relevant operation.

1.3 Predictability

A key aspect of many real-time systems is their predictability. This is crucial for many safety-critical and high-reliability systems, such as nuclear power plants, avionics systems, and medical devices. Predictability refers to the assurance that a system will always meet its timeliness requirements. This can be determined in some cases by static mathematical analysis, such as Rate Monotonic Analysis (RMA) [3]. In other cases, it can be ensured by disallowing preemption and using simple control algorithms, such as cyclic executives. Using active objects to represent tasks and identifying the performance characteristics of the tasks allows a variety of scheduling algorithms to be used.

Most real-time systems must be efficient both in terms of their timeliness as well as memory requirements. Object oriented systems can be just as efficient as structured systems. Object-oriented analysis allows, but does not require, better abstraction and encapsulation control. As with all modeling concepts, object-oriented or otherwise, it is up to the designer to select the appropriate level of abstraction to ensure correctness and maintainability while still meeting system performance requirements.

1.4 Distributed Systems

For large distributed multiprocessor systems, software components can be constructed. Components are run-time executable structures created from object models. These can be mapped to processor nodes using deployment diagrams. Deployment diagrams consist primarily of nodes (processors and other devices) linked together via interconnects. Selecting appropriate distribution architectures is commonly done by considering the tradeoffs of processor load balancing, communications bottlenecks, run-time flexibility via symmetric multiprocessing, and so on.

As mentioned above, communication among objects is modeled using the message abstraction. Although many systems can make do with commercial off-the-shelf (COTS) protocols, embedded systems must frequently use custom protocols to optimize the use of system resources, available bandwidth, and system reliability. Protocols can be, and are, profitably developed as a set of layered classes with elaborate state behavior to handle connections, disconnections, retries, timeouts, and failure modes. Object modeling is an ideal means for capturing the semantic details of complex communications protocols.

1.5   Fault Tolerance and Safety

Many embedded systems have high availability requirements. Typical applications include fire control, avionics, nuclear power, life support, and medical systems. Many of these systems must not only be reliable, but they must also be safe; that is, if they do fail, they do so without causing injury or loss of life.

There are many approaches to the development of reliable and safe systems, but all involve architectural redundancy in some form [3]. The common approach to capturing and representing this redundancy is through the use of architectural design patterns [5]. For example, the Heterogeneous Redundancy Pattern [ibid] arranges components into multiple redundant channels that can be used in either majority-wins-all or a failure-switchover policies. The Monitor-Actuator Pattern separates out the system actuation from the monitoring to ensure that single point failures can be identified and appropriate corrective action taken. Once again, objects provide a clear means for capturing and representing appropriate design solutions.

1.6   Low-Level Hardware Interfacing

Finally, a hallmark of real-time systems is the low-level control of hardware. Objects can easily and effectively model hardware interfaces [4]. Once modeled as classes, they may be subclassed and applied in a variety of environments. Once the interface to a low-level hardware device, such as an A/D converter, is modeled, then multiple instances of this class can directly represent the physical devices attached and controlled by your system.

1.7   Modeling Real-Time Aspects of Systems

In the UML, a constraint is a user-defined well-formedness rule that applies to one or more model elements. Development engineers have approached the problems of modeling the real-time aspects of systems is to apply constraints to specify the properties. The recently adopted *UML^{TM} Profile for Schedulability,*

Performance, and Time Specification [2] (UPSPT) is an attempt to codify the standard ways that have been used now for several years of applying the UML to the problems of real-time and embedded systems. The profile really adds no new capabilities to the UML, but does standardize how certain aspects can be represented, facilitating model exchange.

Even though true profile, the UPSPT also provides metamodels for the various aspects related to schedulability, performance and time at least as a conceptual justification and explanation of the profile. The profile itself consists of a set of class stereotypes and various tagged values to specify various real-time properties. Since the tagged value identifiers are specified, this means that models can be exchanged among different kinds of tools for model entry, model analysis, code generation and so on.

1.8   Using the UML in a Design Process

The process described briefly below is the Rapid Object-Oriented Process for Embedded Systems (ROPES[1]). It has simultaneous three strong foci of concern:

- Architecture – which represents the large scale strategic decisions about the structure and behavior of the system as a whole
- Requirements – which capture both the functional and quality of service properties of the system required for correctness
- Models – which are used to represent the architecture and the requirements and ensure that they are consistent

The ROPES process is a spiral model, incrementally constructing the system throughout the development lifecycle. Figure 1 shows the primary process phases and their overall roles in product development.

Each spiral is divided into work phases, as shown in Figure 2, each of which has its own worker activities and artifacts.

Party Phase. This is also known as Process Planning Phase. The main activities here are

- Initial project planning (first iteration only)
- Review/assess/update
  - Schedule
  - Architecture
  - Development Process

The primary artifacts produced and modified during this phase are the project schedule, architectural documents (normally class and object diagrams), and development plans.

---

[1] The ROPES process is discussed in more detail in [3]

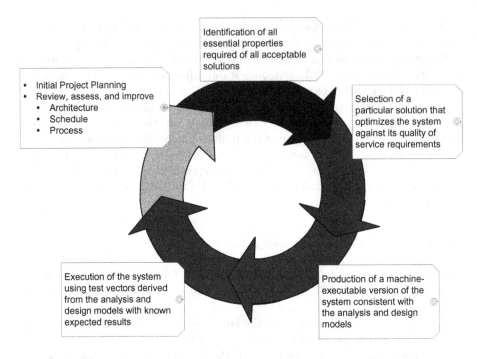

Fig. 1. Overview of Model-Driven Development

Analysis Phase. The analysis phase, as shown in Figure 1, is all about identifying the essential properties true of *all* possibly acceptable solutions. The main activities are

- Requirements analysis – both functional and quality of service requirements are captured as use cases, use case specifications (such as with statecharts), and use case scenarios).
- Systems Engineering – this work activity is used only on larger systems, especially ones in which software and hardware is co-developed. The primary work activities here include the identification of the high-level subsystem architecture (captured with subsystem (object) diagrams), the interfaces among those, and the breakdown of responsibilities among the different disciplines contributing to the system (e.g. electronic, mechanical, chemical, and software). The architecture is *tested* early via execution of the subsystem model of the elaborated use case scenarios. This ensures that the architecture is adequate to support the responsibilities of the system to implement the captured requirements.
- Object Analysis – this work activity primarily identifies the software objects required to realize the use cases. These are represented via class and object diagrams, for the structural aspects, elaborated sequence diagrams (for the collaborative behavior), and statecharts (for the behavior of the individual objects).

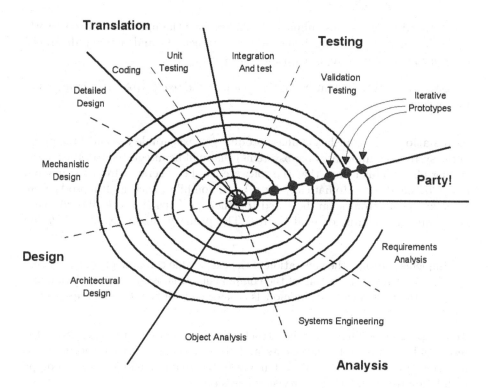

Fig. 2. ROPES Spiral (Detailed View)

Analysis is driven primarily by the functional requirements of the system.

Design Phase. The design phase picks a single solution that is consistent with the analysis model but is optimized or tuned for the particular product's optimality requirements. The design phase is all about optimization of the analysis model against all of the various quality of service requirements simultaneously. The primary subphases of design are:

- Architectqural Design – this subphase identifies the strategic design decisions that affect most or all of the system. There are 5 primary aspects of design which are identified in this phase captured using UML
  - Subsystem/component architecture
  - Concurrency architecture
  - Distribution architecture
  - Safety and reliability architecture
  - Deployment architecture
- Mechanistic Design – this subphase optimizes individual collaborations that realize the use cases, so the scope of the design decisions are limited to the set of object realizing a specific use case.

– Detailed Design – this subphase optimizes how the individual objects work, including their internal behavior with statecharts and activity diagrams, their internal data representation, and so on.

Design is driven primarily by the *quality of service* (QoS) requirements of the system.

Translation. The translation phase produces an executable version of the pieces of the system (components or subsystems) that will be integrated together in the testing phase. This means that the software can be generated from the models, either by hand, or automatically by a UML compiler, such as Rhapsody from I-Logix; the electronics can be wired together, perhaps as a breadboard, wire-wrap, first-cut boards, or final boards. The primary subphases of translation are

– Implementation – the generation of the executable components of the system
– Unit Testing – the testing of the components or subsystems in isolation and then the peer review of the models and/or code of the tested component

Testing. The testing phase constructs the incremental prototype from the tested subsystems and components and tests it to ensure that the design is met (integration testing) and that it meets the requirements of the prototype (validation testing). The primary subphases are

– Integration Testing – construction of the incremental prototype from the tested subsystems and components, testing the interfaces among these large pieces of the system
– Validation Testing – application of the test vectors derived from the requirements in the requirements analysis phase to ensure that the prototype of the system meets its requirements.

It should be noted that "prototype" as used here means "executable version of the system" and NOT "throw-away proof-of-concept". In early spirals, the prototype will not have all of the requirements implemented nor will the ones implemented necessarily all be done to the ultimately required degree of fidelity. But as the system matures over time, it becomes more and more complete and correct, until one of the prototypes is the final released system.

1.9   Requirements Capture with UML

Use cases are the means that the UML provides to organize requirements. A use case organizes a cohesive set of requirements around a single (named) system capability but does not imply anything about internal implementation. A use case is represented on a use case diagram as a named oval, as shown in Figure 3. In this case, the system is an elevator and the use cases are the primary capabilities of the elevator. The stick figures in Figure 3 are called *actors*, and represent

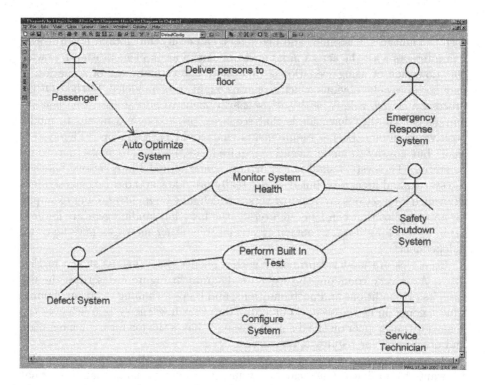

Fig. 3. Actors and Use Cases for an Elevator System

any object outside the scope of the system that interacts with the system in ways that we care about. The line connecting the actors to the use case means that that actor interacts in some interesting way with the system as the system executes that use case. You will notice in Figure 3, the association line connecting *Passenger* with *Auto Optimize System* is a directed line; this indicates that information flows in a single direction from the actor to the use case.

Use cases are named containers for more detailed requirements. What does "Monitor System Health" for the elevator system mean exactly? This use case internally contains more details about that it means. There are two primary means that the UML provides to what we call "detailing the requirements": namely, by example or by specification.

A common way to detail a use case is to provide a set of example scenarios. Each scenario captures a specific interaction of the use case (or, equivalently, the system executing the use case) with its associated actors. The use case is then detailed by providing a set of these scenarios, each scenario providing typical or exceptional cases of the use of that system capability. Scenarios capture 3 different kinds of requirements: messages or operations performed by the system, protocols of interaction between the system and its actors; and constraints on messages, operations, or protocols.

A good thing about modeling scenarios is that non-technical stakeholders, such as managers, customer, and marketers, can easily understand how the system interacts with the actors in its environment in an implementation-free way. One downside of using scenarios is that there is an infinite set of scenarios; it may not always be obvious which scenarios ought to be modeled. In the ROPES process, a simple rule is used: each scenario ought to add at least one new requirement. Another downside is that scenarios provide only a means to model positive requirements, i.e. requirements that could be stated as "The system shall" but no way to model negative requirements, i.e. requirements that would be stated "The system shall not" Further, scenario model interactions between the system and its actors, but does not really provide a standard means to identify which interactions are *required* versus which may be *incidental*. For example, for an autopilot that can land an aircraft, the fact that landing gear are lowered *prior* to touching down is obviously crucial, but other messages may be order independent[2].

Scenarios are modeled primarily with sequence diagrams, as shown in Figure 4. As is very common, the sequence diagram in Figure 4 describes the use case, its preconditions and postconditions, and keeps a running dialog explaining what's going on as the scenario unfolds. Note that how the system achieves the goals does not appear on the diagram, because that is the job for implementation and design, not for requirements capture.

This particular scenario shows what happens when P1 wants to go up and P2 wants to go down. Once can easily imagine many variants that show what happens when they both want to go up, what happens when the same request occurs several times, what happens when the cable breaks, and so on. Each of these different scenarios would be captured in a different sequence diagram, resulting in probably a dozen or so scenarios to elaborate what we mean by "Deliver Persons to Floor".

The other approach to detailing use cases is by *specification*. The UML provides statecharts and activity diagrams to specify what happens in all circumstances. Note that this is clearly different than sequence diagrams that show only a single example of actor-system interaction.

The statechart in Figure 5 specifies how the system responds to events. Most of the events come from the *Passenger* actor, of course, such as DownRequest, UpRequest, and FloorRequest. The actions specified on the statechart are the things that the system does in response to those incoming events, including sending messages back to the actors. For example, the GEN(Ack) action generates an acknowledgement that is sent back to the Passenger. The © symbols are conditional pseudostates and they represent branches taken based on the evaluation of guard conditions on out-going transitions, such as [Down Floor Request is queued].

The dashed lines represent concurrent regions of the statechart. Figure 5 has three such regions – one of which is responsible for the movement of the elevator,

---

[2] Most of the shortcomings of sequence diagrams are being addressed in the UML 2.0 specification.

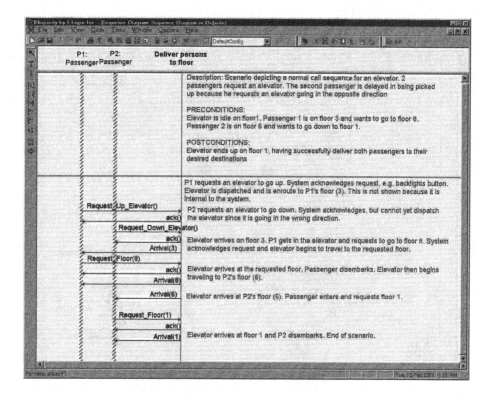

Fig. 4. Sequence Diagram

one responsible for handling incoming requests for an elevator going up or down, and one for handling requests to go to a specific floor once the passenger is in an elevator.

Because more people use the UML for systems design than for their requirements specification, it is actually more common to use statecharts and sequence diagrams to specify the behaviors of the internal structural pieces of the system. Nevertheless, they are useful for capturing, specifying, and illustrating requirements on the system as well.

1.10   Design Structure with UML

The UML is, at its core, an object oriented language based on the notion of objects and classes. An object is nothing more than one or more pieces of information tightly coupled together with operations that act on that information. An object occupies some particular location in memory for some specific period of time during the execution of the system. An object is an *instance* of a class. A class is nothing more than the specification of a set of objects. In the UML and other object-oriented languages, we design the structure of the system by identifying the objects, how they relate to each other, and their classes.

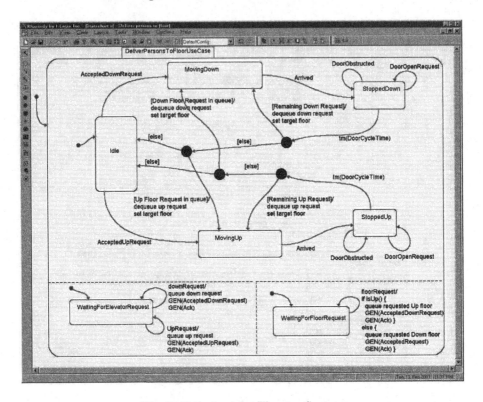

Fig. 5. Statechart for Elevator System

The UML is a graphical language, so diagrams are used to depict the object structure of the system. It is more common to show class diagrams, specifying the structure of collaborations of objects that will exist at run-time, rather than the object diagrams themselves. Such a class diagram for an embedded system is shown in Figure 6.

The rectangles are the structural elements of the system – either classes (roughly, the "types" of the objects) or specific objects that exist in the system during execution. It is easy to tell the difference: if the name is underlined or contains a colon (as in *UpButton* : *Button*), then it is an object; otherwise it is a class, which represents one or more objects at run-time. Classes are typically shown either as simple named rectangles (such as *backlight* in the figure), as rectangles containing other rectangles (such as *Elevator*), or as a rectangle with multiple partitions (such as *PositionSensor*), depending on what you want to show about the class in question. The containment of one class within another is one way to show the composition relationship among classes. The multiple partition box allows you to show some or all of the attributes (information known by objects of the class) and some or all of the operations (behaviors which may be requested by the class). In the case of *PositionSensor*, the class has an attribute called *position* which is of type *int*, and it shows a single operation *getPosition*

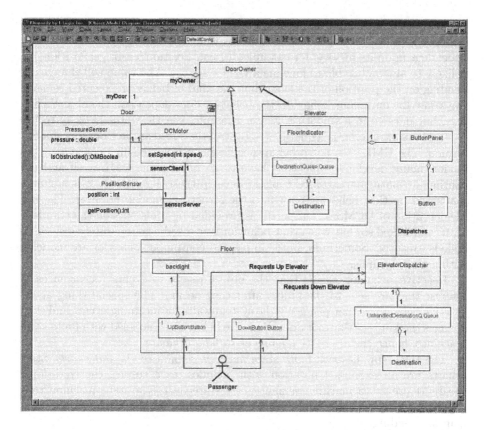

Fig. 6. Class Diagram for an Elevator System

which returns, unsurprisingly, an *int*. These different notations allow the designer to decide exactly how much he wishes to expose on any particular diagram. Note that *PositionSensor* may have additional attributes, such as perhaps a *calibrationConstant* and additional operations, such as *executeSelfTest()* but they are not shown on this diagram.

Most of the time, classes are shown on the diagram, but sometimes it is useful to show the named instances of those classes. For example, it is clear that the *Floor* object contains two objects of class *Button*, one called *upButton* and one called *downButton*. Both these objects are structurally the same and have the same set of operations since they are difference instances of the same class, but they serve different purposes in the executing system.

1.11   Design Behavior with UML

The other side of design, is of course, how the system *behaviors*, or acts over time. The UML provides ways of showing behavior of individual structural elements as well as how these elements behavior in the context of a collaboration.

A structural element may behavior in one of three ways: simply, continuously, or reactively. Simple behavior means that how the object behaves is not dependent upon its history; for example, if I call PositionSensor.getPosition() it is likely to always be able to give me a valid response. The value will change depending on the position of the Door, but the kind of behavior executed remains the same. In continuous behavior, the behavior does depend on the object's history, but does so in a smooth way. For example, the DCMotor is likely to use control laws or differential equations to control the speed of the Door in a smooth fashion. The UML does not provide specific means for modeling continuous behavior; many developers find they have to go beyond the UML itself and use continuous mathematics-based tools to develop these algorithms. It is a simple matter to tie that behavior back into the structural model, however. The implementation of DCMotot.setSpeed() is provided by tools outside the standard UML and linked so that when that behavior is invoked, the separately-generated code is executed. Sometimes, both simple and continuous behavior are modeled with activity graphs.

Reactive behavior means that the object reacts to events (occurrences of interest that are sent to the object after they occur). The special thing about reactive behavior is that primarily the system waits for incoming events and then changes the kinds of things it does. Reactive behavior is modeled with finite state machines, hence the alternative name of *stateful behavior*.

The UML supplies rich finite state machine semantics via *statecharts*. Statecharts are an expanded notation with includes, as a subset, the traditional Mealy-Moore state machine semantics. A statechart is a state machine that supports additional constructs over the more traditional Mealy-Moore state machines, including:

- Nested states
- Or-states (exclusive)
- And-states (concurrent)
- History
- Conditional pseudostates (branching)

The statechart in the figure shows how the door behaves. We can see actions are executed either on the transition between states (such as the two actions executed on the OpenedEvent transition from the Opening::SlidingOpen state to the Open state, or on the entry into the state itself, such as the execution of the setInterlock(OFF) in the Closing::DisconnectingDoors state. Actions may also be executed when an object leaves a state as well. The transition with a single rounded end is called an initial state connector or an initial pseudostate. It indicates which is the default state when the object comes into existence or enters a state with substates.

The general form for a transition is

Event name '[' guard ']' '/' action list

Where

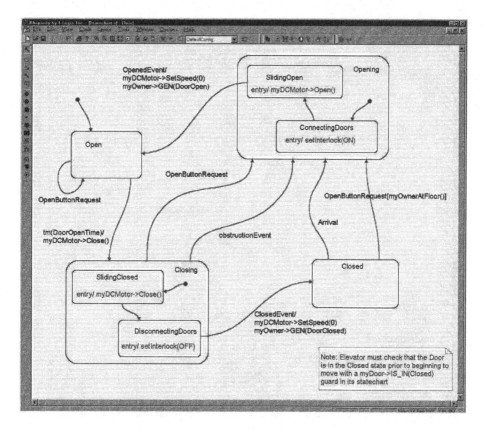

Fig. 7. Statechart for Door Class

- Event name is the name of the event received by the object that invokes the transition
- The guard is a Boolean expression. If present, the transition is only taken if the named event occurs and the guard evaluates to true
- The action list specifies a list of actions to be performed when the transition is taken. This can be primitive statements (such as ++x), operations on the object or other objects with which this object has an association, or the creation of an event (such as using the GEN() statement in the figure).

We can see how the Door processes the events that it receives. The Door starts off in the Open state. After a period of time (DoorOpenTime), a timeout fires and the Door transitions to its Closing State. The Closing state has two substates. The first (as indicated by the initial pseudostate) is the SlidingClosed State. While in this state, the Door commands the DCMotor to close the door. When that action is complete, the object transitions to the DisconnectingDoors state. If during the Closed state an obstruction is detected (as indicated by an event sent to the Door from the PressureSensor), then the Door transitions to the Opening State, and so on.

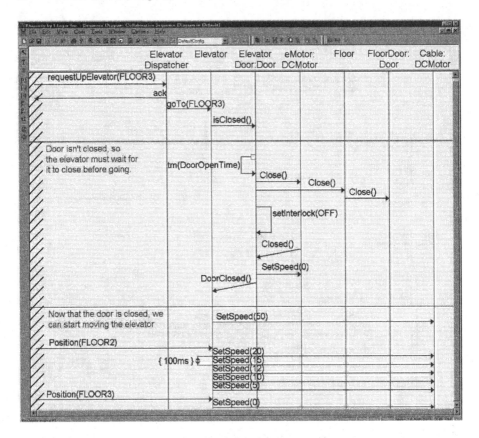

Fig. 8. Collaboration Sequence Diagram

Statecharts work very well for defining the behavior of reactive objects. But what if you want to understand how a set of objects work in collaboration? The UML provide sequence diagrams to show how object collaborate by sending message (calling operations) and events to each other.

Figure 8 shows an illustrative example of a sequence diagram. The vertical lines represent objects (not classes) during the execution of the system. The arrowed lines are messages (either calls to operations on objects or events sent to objects). The hatched area on the left is called a "collaboration boundary" and represents all objects in the universe other than those explicitly represented as instance lines on the diagram. Time flows down the page. It is easy to see how these objects work together to produce the desired system effect – picking up and delivering a person, upon request, from one floor to another. The scenario isn't complete, but nevertheless it shows most of the major elements of sequence diagrams: instance lines, messages, events, comments, and even a timing constraint (the number in curly braces is expressing the time between two message invocations). Although you can see very easily how the objects collaborate together, the internal behavior of individual objects is not readily apparent.

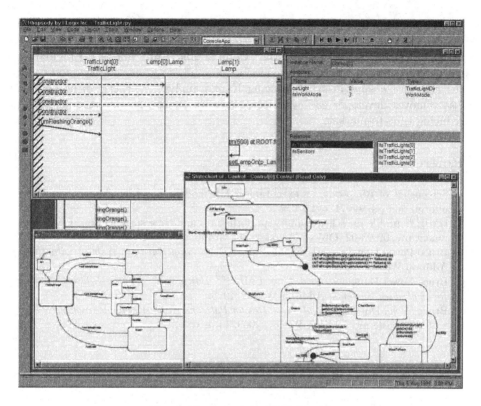

Fig. 9. Executing the UML Model

1.12   Executing UML Models

As one of the early pioneers of computers, Immanuel Kant, said in the 17th century, modeling has a fundamental problem which he called the "analytic-synthetic dichotomy". Simply put, is states "that which is real (i.e. running) cannot be known, and that which is known (i.e. modeled) cannot be real." In most modeling languages, that is more or less true, because the models only bear a vague resemblance to the executing system. With UML, however, the core of the behavioral model is based on statecharts, a well-understood executable technology. With the UML, it *is* possible to execute your models and to use them to synthesize your software (and potentially hardware as well).

It has been said that the best way not to have bugs in your delivered system is not to put them in the system in the first place. Since no ones knows *how* to do that yet, the next best thing is to remove them immediately after you put them in. How do you do that? Simple – you execute your model *early and often*.

A snapshot of an executing UML is shown in the last figure [1]. Statecharts are color coded to show the current state of the object, while a sequence diagram is dynamically drawn as the objects collaborate during the execution of the system. Additionally, the current values of the attributes can be shown.

The ability to execute even partial UML models means that we can test our models for correctness as early as possible and as often as we want with very little effort (other than pushing the "Compile and Run" button). Eliminating the need to manual write source code for the models means that the model and the code are *always* in synch, solving Kant's analytic-synthetic dichotomy. It also removes developer coding defects, thereby improving system quality and reducing time-to-market.

References

1. Screenshot of Rhapsody, an executable UML modeling and development tool. For information see `www.ilogix.com`.
2. UML^{TM} profile for schedulability, performance, and time specification. OMG document ptc/02-03-02, Object Management Group 2002.
3. Bruce Powel Douglass. *Doing hard time: Developing real-time systems with UML.* Addison Wesley, 1999.
4. Bruce Powel Douglass. *Real-Time UML 2nd Edition: Developing Efficient Objects for Embedded Systems.* Addison Wesley, 1999.
5. Bruce Powel Douglass. *Real-Time Design Patterns: Robust scalable architecture for real-time systems.* Addison Wesley, 2003. in press.

Eager Class Initialization for Java

Dexter Kozen[1] and Matt Stillerman[2]

[1] Computer Science Department, Cornell University, Ithaca, NY 14853-7501, USA
kozen@cs.cornell.edu
[2] ATC-NY, 33 Thornwood Drive, Ithaca, NY 14850-1250, USA
matt@atc-nycorp.com

Abstract. We describe a static analysis method on Java bytecode to determine class initialization dependencies. This method can be used for eager class loading and initialization. It catches many initialization circularities that are missed by the standard lazy implementation. Except for contrived examples, the computed initialization order gives the same results as standard lazy initialization.

1 Introduction

Class initialization refers to the computation and assignment of initial values specified by the programmer to the static fields of a class. It is not to be confused with *preparation*, which refers to the assignment of default values to each static field when the class is created—null to reference types, 0 to numeric types, etc.

Initialization is a notoriously thorny issue in Java semantics [3,5,10]. For example, consider the legal Java fragment in Fig. 1. What are the initial values

```
class A {
    static int a = B.b + 1;
}
class B {
    static int b = A.a + 1;
}
```

Fig. 1.

of A.a and B.b? The answer to this question is not determined by the fragment. They can be either A.a = 2 and B.b = 1 or vice versa, depending on the order in which the classes are loaded.

The standard Java lazy class loading and initialization method can detect such circular dependencies, but it does not treat them as errors, because in some cases they are useful. For example, the program of Fig. 2 contains a common Java idiom. The circularity in this example is a self-loop on the class Widget. The class initializer of Widget calls the instance initializer of Widget, which in turn accesses the static field nextSerialNumber. This is a "good" circularity.

W. Damm and E.-R. Olderog (Eds.): FTRTFT 2002, LNCS 2469, pp. 71–80, 2002.

```
class Widget {
    static int nextSerialNumber = 10000;
    int serialNumber;
    static Widget protoWidget = new Widget();

    Widget() {
        serialNumber = nextSerialNumber++;
    }
}
```

Fig. 2.

```
int serialNumber;
static Widget protoWidget = new Widget();
static int nextSerialNumber = 10000;
```

Fig. 3.

However, if we were to permute the declarations as in Fig. 3, it would be erroneous, because `nextSerialNumber` is accessed before it is initialized. The value of `protoWidget.serialNumber` will be 0, the default value of the static field `nextSerialNumber` supplied during class preparation, instead of the intended 10000. Although it is illegal for a static initializer to access a static field of the same class whose declaration occurs lexically later [9], the compiler check for this error is typically limited to direct access only. Indirect access, such as through the instance initializer in this example, escapes notice.

The guiding principle here is that static fields should be initialized before they are used. The fragment of Fig. 1 above violates this principle no matter what the initialization order, and any such circularity arising in practice is almost surely a programming error. Ideally, the initialization process should respect initialization dependencies and catch such erroneous circularities wherever possible. But because this principle is difficult to enforce without ruling out good circularities such as Fig. 2, Java compilers do little to enforce it.

Even in the absence of circular dependencies, lazy initialization may fail to initialize correctly. For example, in the fragment of Fig. 4, if A is loaded before B,

```
class A {
    static int a = 2;
    static int aa = B.b + 1;
}
class B {
    static int b = A.a + 1;
}
```

Fig. 4.

then the fields are initialized correctly, but not if they are loaded in the opposite order.

Lazy loading and initialization, in which classes are loaded and initialized at the time of their first active use, is the preferred strategy of the Java language designers. Other strategies are allowed in principle, but the Java virtual machine specification insists that any exceptions that would be thrown during loading and initialization are to be thrown at the same time as under the standard lazy implementation [9, p. 42]. Unfortunately, the runtime overhead imposed by this restriction would reduce the performance advantage gained by using an eager initialization strategy, besides being a pain to implement. Thus this restriction effectively rules out other strategies for standard Java implementations.

Nevertheless, an eager approach to class loading and initialization may be more appropriate for certain specialized applications. For example, in applications involving boot firmware, boot drivers for plug-in components, and embedded systems, platform independence and security are issues of major concern. The IEEE Open Firmware standard [7], based on Sun OpenBoot, specifies Forth as the language of choice for firmware implementation for reasons of platform independence. The Forth virtual machine is similar to the JVM in many ways, except that instructions are untyped, there is no support for objects, and there is no bytecode verification. But because security is a growing concern, and because the Open Firmware device tree architecture is naturally object-oriented, Java presents an attractive alternative.

Firmware runs in an extremely primitive environment with little or no operating system support or mediation. Boot device drivers run in privileged mode and have full access to the entire system, including other devices. In addition, embedded systems may be subject to real-time constraints. For these reasons, it is desirable to avoid the runtime overhead of lazy class loading and initialization.

Besides the obvious runtime performance advantages, there are other benefits to eager initialization:

- Errors are identified earlier.
- There is a clean description of class initialization semantics.
- Class initialization can be precompiled in JVM-to-native (just-in-time) compilation.

In this paper we describe an algorithm for determining a class initialization order that can be used for eager class loading and initialization. The algorithm runs at the bytecode level and computes a conservative estimate of the true dependency relation on static fields by static analysis of the call graph. Bad circularities, which are almost surely programming errors, are caught, whereas good circularities are allowed to pass. This distinction is defined formally in Section 2.

The key insight that allows us to distinguish good circularities from bad is that the instantiation of a class B in the static initializer of A does not automatically create an initialization dependency $A \Rightarrow B$ ("$\Rightarrow$" = "depends on" = "should be initialized after"). The creation of a new instance of B by itself is not the source of any dependencies. The only reason B might have to be initialized first is if the constructor B.<init>, or some method called by it directly or indirectly, references a static field of B. We can discover such a dependency by static analysis of the call graph.

This introduces a rather radical twist to the initialization process: during class initialization, we might actually end up instantiating a class before it is initialized, provided its constructor (or any method called directly or indirectly by the constructor) does not reference any static fields of the class.

Another radical departure from conventional wisdom is that there is no inherent dependency of subclasses on superclasses. The JVM specification requires that superclasses be initialized before their subclasses, but there is really no reason for this unless the static initializer of the subclass references, directly or indirectly, a static field of the superclass. Our static analysis will discover all such potential references.

Our method flags the examples of Figs. 1 and 4 above as errors, but allows Fig. 2 to pass. Currently our implementation allows Fig. 3 to pass, but it could be extended without much difficulty to catch errors of this form as well.

We conjecture that circularities such as Figs. 1, 3, and 4 are rare, and that when they do occur, they are almost surely unintended. Moreover, we conjecture that in virtually all practical instances, any class initialization order respecting the static dependencies computed by our algorithm will give the same initial values as the standard lazy method.

We have tested our first conjecture experimentally by running our algorithm on several publicly available Java class libraries (see Section 3), including the entire COLT distribution from CERN [4] and a portion of the JDK version 1.4 from Sun [8]. In no case did it report a bad circularity. It is possible to concoct pathological examples for which our algorithm erroneously reports a bad circularity where in fact there is none, but these are so contrived that we suspect they would be unlikely to arise in practice.

2   Algorithm

In this section we describe the implementation of our algorithm for determining the class initialization order.

The order is defined in terms of a dependency relation $\Rightarrow$ on classes. Roughly speaking, $A \Rightarrow B$ if it can be determined by static analysis that the execution of the static initializer of A could potentially read or write a static field of B. Thus if $A \Rightarrow B$, then B should be initialized before A. Note that this is independent of whether the initialization of A can create an instance of B.

We assume that all classes are locally available for static analysis and that all methods are available in bytecode form (i.e., no native methods). We distinguish between *system classes* (e.g., java.util.Hashtable) and *application classes*. Our algorithm does not analyze system classes, since no system class would normally know about application classes and thus would not reference their static fields. It can be proved formally that without explicit syntactic reference, system class initialization cannot directly or indirectly access any static field of an application class (this is false for general computation).

We describe $\Rightarrow$ as the transitive closure of the edge relation $\rightarrow$ of a particular directed graph whose vertices are classes and methods. The graph will be constructed dynamically. Let LC be the set of application classes, SC the set of system classes, and AM the set of static and instance methods of application classes. The relation $\rightarrow$ is defined to be the edge relation on $(LC \cup SC \cup AM) \times (LC \cup SC \cup AM)$ consisting of the following ordered pairs:

(i) If A is an application class and A has a class initializer A.<clinit>, then A $\rightarrow$ A.<clinit>.

(ii) If f is a static or instance method of an application class, and if f calls another static or instance method g, then f $\rightarrow$ g. Such a call must be of the form either invokestatic g, invokespecial g, invokeinterface g, or invokevirtual g. In addition, if g is an instance method invoked by invokevirtual g, and if g' is another method with the same name and descriptor in a subclass of the class in which g is defined, then f $\rightarrow$ g'.

(iii) If f is a static or instance method of an application class A, and if f contains an instruction getstatic B.a or putstatic B.a, which reads or writes the static field B.a, then f $\rightarrow$ B.

We are actually only interested in the restriction of $\Rightarrow$ to classes, since this will determine the class initialization order. Also, for efficiency, we do not construct the entire relation $\rightarrow$, but only the part reachable from the main class.

We start with an initial set of vertices consisting of

(a) all application classes accessible by some chain of references from the main class,

(b) all system classes accessible from the main class, and

(c) all <clinit> methods of the application classes in (a).

The classes in (a) are available from the constant pools of all loaded classes. Classes are loaded and prepared eagerly, and we assume that this has already been done. Any class whose name appears in the constant pool of any loaded class is also loaded. The initial set of edges is (i), the edges from the application classes to their own <clinit> methods.

We now describe the computation of the call graph. Initially, we push all <clinit> methods in (c) on a stack, then repeat the following until the stack is empty.

Pop the next method f off the stack. If we have already processed f, discard it and go on to the next. If we have not processed f yet, scan its code looking for all instructions that would cause an edge to be created. These can be instructions getstatic B.a or putstatic B.a that access a static field or a method invocation invoke... g. In the case of a getstatic B.a or putstatic B.a instruction, create a new edge f $\rightarrow$ B if it is not already present. In case of a method invocation invoke... g, create a new edge f $\rightarrow$ g and push g on the stack for subsequent processing. It may also be necessary to insert g as a new vertex in the graph if it does not already exist. In addition, if g is an instance method invoked by invokevirtual g, and if g' is another method with the same

name and descriptor in a subclass of the class in which g is defined, create a new
edge f $\rightarrow$ g′ and push g′ on the stack for subsequent processing. When done,
mark f as processed.

The reason for the special treatment of instance method invocations invokevirtual g is that g is not necessarily the method that is dispatched. It could
be g or any method that shadows it, i.e., a method with the same name and
descriptor as g declared in a subclass, depending on the runtime type of the
object. In general we may not know the runtime type of the object at the time
of initialization, so to be conservative, we insert edges to all such methods.

```
class B {
    static int g(A1 a) {
        return a.f();
    }
    static A3 a = new A3();
    static int b = g(a);
}
class A1 {
    static int e = 1;
    int f() {
        return e;
    }
}
class A2 extends A1 {
    static int e = 2;
    int f() {
        return e;
    }
}
class A3 extends A2 {}
```

Fig. 5.

Fig. 5 illustrates this situation. The correct initial value for B.b is 2, because
A2.f is dispatched in the call to a.f() in B.g, not A1.f. We must insert the edge
B.g $\rightarrow$ A2.f when we insert the edge B.g $\rightarrow$ A1.f to account for the dependency
of B.b on A2.e.

A dependency A $\Rightarrow$ B is thus induced by a chain of intermediate method
calls starting with A.<clinit> and ending with a getstatic or putstatic
instruction, and all computed dependencies A $\Rightarrow$ B are of this form. The number
of intermediate calls can be arbitrarily long. For example, if A.<clinit> calls f,
which calls g, which accesses the field B.a, then this entails a dependency A $\Rightarrow$ B.
However, note that it does not necessarily entail a dependency A $\Rightarrow$ C, where C
is the class of f or g.

A new B bytecode instruction appearing in A.<clinit> or any method called
directly or indirectly by A.<clinit> also does not by itself introduce a depen-

dency A ⇒ B. The purpose of the new B instruction is to tell the JVM to allocate and prepare a new instance of the class B, and no static fields are accessed in this process. However, a new B instruction would normally be followed by an explicit call to an initializer B.<init>, which can access static fields. But our algorithm will see the call to B.<init> and will push it on the stack for later processing.

Once the graph is created, we perform depth-first search and calculate the strongly connected components. This takes linear time [2]. Each component represents an equivalence class of methods and classes that are all reachable from each other under the dependence relation →.

In our current implementation, a *bad component* is taken to be a strongly connected component containing at least two classes. If A and B are two classes contained in a bad component, then there must be a cycle

$$A \rightarrow A.\texttt{<clinit>} \rightarrow f_2 \rightarrow \cdots \rightarrow f_n \rightarrow B \rightarrow B.\texttt{<clinit>} \rightarrow g_2 \rightarrow \cdots \rightarrow g_m \rightarrow A,$$

indicating that the initialization of A directly or indirectly accesses a static field of B and vice versa. Such bad components are flagged as errors.

If there are no bad components, then the relation ⇒ restricted to vertices $LC \cup SC$ is acyclic. In this case, any topological sort of the induced subgraph on $LC \cup SC$ can be used as a class initialization order. In our implementation, we just use the postorder number of the low vertex of each component computed during depth-first search.

In the absence of reported bad circularities, our eager initialization strategy and the standard lazy strategy should normally give the same initial values. This is because we conservatively trace all possible call chains, so if there is a true dependency of a static field A.a on another static field B.b, where A and B are distinct, both the lazy method and our method will see it and will initialize B.b first. Any call chain involving at least two distinct classes that would result in a field receiving its default value instead of its initial value in the lazy method will appear as a bad circularity in our method.

However, it would be difficult to formulate a complete set of conditions under which the eager and lazy strategies could be formally guaranteed to give the same initial values. One would have to rule out all possible ways in which a class initializer could directly or indirectly modify a static field of another class. Without this restriction, each class could identify itself in a common location as it is initialized, thereby recording the actual initialization order. Thus initial values would not be the same unless the initialization order were the same. To avoid this, one would have to rule out a variety of possible indirect channels: exceptions, concurrency, reflection, native methods, and file or console IO, for example.

3   Experimental Results

To provide evidence that bad circularities are rare in practice, we have analyzed several large publicly available Java class libraries in a variety of application areas. We found no bad circularities. Besides portions of the JDK version 1.4 [8], we have analyzed the complete distribution of each of the following libraries.

The COLT distribution from CERN [4] is an extensive toolkit for computational high energy physics. It provides packages for data analysis and display, linear algebra, matrix decomposition, statistical analysis, and Monte Carlo simulation, among others. The distribution consists of 836 class files.

GEO [6] is a class library and environment supporting the creation, manipulation, and display of 3D geometric objects. The distribution consists of 43 class files.

The ACME distribution [1] is a package with several general-purpose utilities, including extensions to the Java Windows Toolkit, PostScript-like graphics, a `printf()` facility, a cryptography package including implementations of DES, Blowfish, and secure hashing, an HTTP server, a multithreaded caching daemon, a netnews database backend, image processing software including PPM, JPEG, and GIF codecs and RGB image filters, and a simple chat system. The distribution consists of 180 class files.

4   Remarks and Conclusions

An interesting open problem is to formulate conditions under which, in the absence of reported bad circularities, the eager and lazy strategies would be guaranteed to give the same initial values. A formal statement and proof of this result might be based on a bytecode or source-level type system in the style of [5].

As illustrated in Fig. 4, the true dependency relation is between static fields, not classes. The relation $\Rightarrow$ between classes is only a coarse approximation. A finer-grained approximation $\Rightarrow$ between static fields could be computed and would give sharper results. But because the `<clinit>` methods are compiled to be executed atomically, we could not take advantage of this extra information without recompilation. Besides, our experimental results indicate that the class-level approximation is sufficient for all practical purposes.

As mentioned, for *class* initialization, there is no inherent dependency of subclasses on superclasses. Such a dependency exists only if a static field of a superclass is referenced directly or indirectly by the static initializer of the subclass. Static initializers are never invoked explicitly from bytecode, but only by the virtual machine. *Instance* initialization is another matter, however. The constructor `B.<init>` always contains an explicit call to the parent constructor `SuperclassOfB.<init>`. Thus if B is instantiated during the course of static initialization, our algorithm automatically traces the chain of calls to the parent constructors.

Acknowledgements

We thank Thomas J. Merritt, Greg Morrisett, and Andrew Myers for valuable ideas and discussions and Prashant Palsokar and Reba Schuller for their assistance with the implementation. This work was supported in part by the AFRL/Cornell Information Assurance Institute AFOSR grant F49620-00-1-0209, DARPA contracts DAAH01-01-C-R026 and DAAH01-02-C-R080, NSF grant CCR-0105586, and ONR Grant N00014-01-1-0968. The views and conclusions contained herein are those of the authors and do not necessarily represent the official policies or endorsements, either expressed or implied, of these organizations or the US Government.

References

1. ACME Java class library.
   http://www.acme.com/java/software/Package-Acme.html.
2. A. V. Aho, J. E. Hopcroft, and J. D. Ullman. *The Design and Analysis of Computer Algorithms*. Addison-Wesley, 1974.
3. Egon Börger and Wolfram Schulte. Initialization problems for Java. *Software Concepts and Tools*, 20(4), 1999.
4. COLT Java class library.
   http://tilde-hoschek.home.cern.ch/ hoschek/colt/V1.0.1/doc/overview-summary.html.
5. Stephen N. Freund and John C. Mitchell. A type system for object initialization in the Java bytecode language. *Trans. Programming Languages and Systems*, 21(6):1196–1250, 1999.
6. GEO Java class library. http://www.kcnet.com/ ameech/geo/.
7. IEEE Standard for Boot (Initialization Configuration) Firmware: Core Requirements and Practices, 1994. IEEE Standard 1275-1994.
8. Java development kit, version 1.4. http://www.java.sun.com/.
9. Tim Lindholm and Frank Yellin. *The Java Virtual Machine Specification*. Addison Wesley, 1996.
10. Martijn Warnier. Specification and verification of sequential Java programs. Master's thesis, Utrecht University, January 2002.

Appendix

The following sample run shows the output obtained on the fragment of Fig. 5 in the text above, along with the main class

```
class Pathologies {
    static public void main(String args[]) {
        System.out.println(B.b);
    }
}
```

The depth-first search tree is shown. After each vertex are listed its preorder and postorder numbers and low vertex, followed by a list of edges. The *low vertex* is the eldest reachable ancestor and serves as a canonical representative of the strongly connected component [2]. The nontrivial components (i.e., those with more than one member) are listed, and those with at least two classes are flagged as bad. In this example there are no bad components.

```
pathologies Sun Jul 22 09:49:24 EDT 2001
Loading class info...
Local classes loaded: 5
System classes: 3
Main class: Pathologies
Resolving references...
0 error(s)
Constructing class hierarchy...
Calculating dependencies...
Component analysis:
A1, A1.<clinit>()V
A2, A2.<clinit>()V
B.<clinit>()V, B
3 nontrivial component(s)
0 bad component(s)


pathologies Sun Jul 22 09:49:24 EDT 2001
A3.<init>()V: PRE=0 POST=2 LOW=A3.<init>()V
  A2.<init>()V TREE
A1.<init>()V: PRE=2 POST=0 LOW=A1.<init>()V
B.<clinit>()V: PRE=3 POST=11 LOW=B.<clinit>()V
  B.g(LA1;)I TREE
  B TREE
  A3.<init>()V CROSS
A2.<init>()V: PRE=1 POST=1 LOW=A2.<init>()V
  A1.<init>()V TREE
A1.<clinit>()V: PRE=7 POST=3 LOW=A1
  A1 BACK
A2.<clinit>()V: PRE=10 POST=6 LOW=A2
  A2 BACK
B: PRE=11 POST=10 LOW=B.<clinit>()V
  B.<clinit>()V BACK
A1: PRE=6 POST=4 LOW=A1
  A1.<clinit>()V TREE
A2.f()I: PRE=8 POST=8 LOW=A2.f()I
  A2 TREE
Pathologies: PRE=12 POST=12 LOW=Pathologies
A2: PRE=9 POST=7 LOW=A2
  A2.<clinit>()V TREE
A1.f()I: PRE=5 POST=5 LOW=A1.f()I
  A1 TREE
A3: PRE=13 POST=13 LOW=A3
B.g(LA1;)I: PRE=4 POST=9 LOW=B.g(LA1;)I
  A1.f()I TREE
  A2.f()I TREE
```

Applications of Formal Methods in Biology

Amir Pnueli

Department of Applied Mathematics and Computer Science
The Weizmann Institute of Science, Rehovot, Israel 76100
amir@wisdom.weizmann.ac.il

Abstract. From the first introduction of the notion of "Reactive Systems" and development of specification languages (such as Temporal Logic and Statecharts) and verification methods for this class of systems, it has been stated that this notion encompasses a wider class of systems than just programs or hardware designs, and should be applicable to other complex systems unrelated to computers. In a similar vein, the acronym UML talks about "modeling language" rather than "programming language", implying that the approach should be applicable to a more general class of systems than just computer-related.

While this claim of wider applicability has been always implied, it was never before seriously substantiated. In this talk, I will describe some recent attempts to apply the discipline of formal methods to the modeling, analysis, and prediction of biological systems. This corresponds to an emerging trend in Biology, according to which Biology in the 21st century will have to direct its attention towards understanding how component parts collaborate to create a whole system or organism. The transition from identifying building blocks (analysis) to integrating the parts into a whole (synthesis) will have to use mathematics and algorithmics. We need a language that is legible both to biologists and computers, and that is faithful to the logic of the biological system of interest.

In search for an appropriate rigorous approach to modeling biological systems, we examined formal modeling methods in computer science that were originally developed for specification, design, and analysis of reactive systems. We found that the visual formalism of statecharts can address this challenge, within the general framework of object-oriented modeling. This conclusion followed an initial study we carried out, in which we constructed a detailed executable model for T cell activation, and were able, using verification techniques to find and correct a flaw in the original model.

Following this preliminary study, we have now undertaken the more challenging project of applying and extending this methodology for constructing a detailed model of the developmental processes that lead to the formation of the egg-laying system in the nematode C. elegans. The model is built to capture in a natural yet rigorous and analyzable way the aspects of concurrency, multi scalar data, and hierarchical organization. This project involves a close collaboration with Naaman Kam, David Harel, and Irun Cohen from the department of Immunology at the Weizmann Institute.

W. Damm and E.-R. Olderog (Eds.): FTRTFT 2002, LNCS 2469, p. 81, 2002.

An Overview of Formal Verification
for the Time-Triggered Architecture*

John Rushby

Computer Science Laboratory
SRI International
333 Ravenswood Avenue
Menlo Park, CA 94025, USA
rushby@csl.sri.com

Abstract. We describe formal verification of some of the key algorithms in the Time-Triggered Architecture (TTA) for real-time safety-critical control applications. Some of these algorithms pose formidable challenges to current techniques and have been formally verified only in simplified form or under restricted fault assumptions. We describe what has been done and what remains to be done and indicate some directions that seem promising for the remaining cases and for increasing the automation that can be applied. We also describe the larger challenges posed by formal verification of the interaction of the constituent algorithms and of their emergent properties.

1 Introduction

The Time-Triggered Architecture (TTA) provides an infrastructure for safety-critical real-time control systems of the kind used in modern cars and airplanes. Concretely, it comprises an interlocking suite of distributed algorithms for functions such as clock synchronization and group membership, and their implementation in the form of TTA controllers, buses, and hubs. The suite of algorithms is known as TTP/C (an adjunct for non safety-critical applications is known as TTP/A) and was originally developed by Kopetz and colleagues at the Technical University of Vienna [25]; its current specification and commercial realization are by TTTech of Vienna [70]. More abstractly, TTA is part of a comprehensive approach to safety-critical real-time system design [22] that centers on time-triggered operation [23] and includes notions such as "temporal firewalls" [21] and "elementary" interfaces [24].

The algorithms of TTA are an exciting target for formal verification because they are individually challenging and they interact in interesting ways. To practitioners and developers of formal verification methods and their tools, these

* This research was supported by NASA Langley Research Center under Cooperative Agreement NCC-1-377 with Honeywell Incorporated, by DARPA through the US Air Force Rome Laboratory under Contract F30602-96-C-0291, by the National Science Foundation under Contract CCR-00-86096, and by the NextTTA project of the European Union.

W. Damm and E.-R. Olderog (Eds.): FTRTFT 2002, LNCS 2469, pp. 83–105, 2002.
© Springer-Verlag Berlin Heidelberg 2002

algorithms are excellent test cases—first, to be able to verify them at all, then to be able to verify them with sufficient automation that the techniques used can plausibly be transferred to nonspecialists for use in similar applications. For the developers and users of TTA, formal verification provides valuable assurance for its safety-critical claims, and explication of the assumptions on which these rest. As new versions of TTA and its implementations are developed, there is the additional opportunity to employ formal methods in the design loop.

TTA provides the functionality of a bus: host computers attach to TTA and are able to exchange messages with other hosts; in addition, TTA provides certain services to the hosts (e.g., an indication which other hosts have failed). Because it is used in safety-critical systems, TTA must be fault tolerant: that is, it must continue to provide its services to nonfaulty hosts in the presence of faulty hosts and in the presence of faults in its own components. In addition, the services that it provides to hosts are chosen to ease the design and construction of fault-tolerant applications (e.g., in an automobile brake-by-wire application, each wheel has a brake that is controlled by its own host computer; the services provided by TTA make it fairly simple to arrange a safe distributed algorithm in which each host can adjust the braking force applied to its wheel to compensate for the failure of one of the other brakes or its host).

Serious consideration of fault-tolerant systems requires careful identification of the fault containment units (components that fail independently), fault hypotheses (the kind, arrival rate, and total number of faults to be tolerated), and the type of fault tolerance to be provided (e.g., what constitutes acceptable behavior in the presence of faults: fault masking vs. fail silence, self stabilization, or never-give-up). The basic goal in verifying a fault-tolerant algorithm is to prove

fault hypotheses satisfied *implies* acceptable behavior.

Stochastic or other probabilistic and experimental methods must then establish that the probability of the fault hypotheses being satisfied is sufficiently large to satisfy the mission requirements.

In this short paper, it is not possible to provide much by way of background to the topics adumbrated above, nor to discuss the design choices in TTA, but a suitable introduction is available in a previous paper [50] (and in more detail in [51]). Neither is it possible, within the limitations of this paper, to describe in detail the formal verifications that have already been performed for certain TTA algorithms. Instead, my goal here is to provide an overview of these verifications, and some of their historical antecedents, focusing on the importance of the exact fault hypotheses that are considered for each algorithm and on the ways in which the different algorithms interact. I also indicate techniques that increase the amount of automation that can be used in these verifications, and suggest approaches that may be useful in tackling some of the challenges that still remain.

2   Clock Synchronization

As its full name indicates, the Time-Triggered Architecture uses the passage of time to schedule its activity and to coordinate its distributed components.

A fault tolerant distributed clock synchronization algorithm is therefore one of TTA's fundamental elements.

Host computers attach to TTA through an interface controller that implements the TTP/C protocol. I refer to the combination of a host and its TTA controller as a *node*. Each controller contains an oscillator from which it derives its local notion of time (i.e., a clock). Operation of TTA is driven by a global schedule, so it is important that the local clocks are always in close agreement. Drift in the oscillators causes the various local clocks to drift apart so periodically (several hundred times a second) they must be resynchronized. What makes this difficult is that some of the clocks may be faulty.

The clock synchronization algorithm used in TTA is a modification of the Welch-Lynch (also known as Lundelius-Lynch) algorithm [73], which itself can be understood as a particular case of the abstract algorithm described by Schneider [61]. Schneider's abstract algorithm operates as follows: periodically, the nodes decide that it is time to resynchronize their clocks, each node determines the skews between its own clock and those of other nodes, forms a *fault-tolerant average* of these values, and adjusts its own clock by that amount.

An intuitive explanation for the general approach is the following. After a resynchronization, all the nonfaulty clocks will be close together (this is the definition of synchronization); by the time that they next synchronize, the nonfaulty clocks may have drifted further apart, but the amount of drift is bounded (this is the definition of a good clock); the clocks can be brought back together by setting them to some value close to the middle of their spread. An "ordinary average" (e.g., the mean or median) over all clocks may be affected by wild readings from faulty clocks (which, under a *Byzantine* fault hypothesis, may provide different readings to different observers), so we need a "fault-tolerant average" that is insensitive to a certain number of readings from faulty clocks.

The Welch-Lynch algorithm is characterized by use of the *fault-tolerant midpoint* as its averaging function. If we have n clocks and the maximum number of simultaneous faults to be tolerated is k $(3k < n)$, then the fault-tolerant midpoint is the average of the $k + 1$'st and $n - k$'th clock skew readings, when these are arranged in order from smallest to largest. If there are at most k faulty clocks, then some reading from a nonfaulty clock must be at least as small as the $k + 1$'st reading, and the reading from another nonfaulty clock must be at least as great as the $n - k$'th; hence, the average of these two readings should be close to the middle of the spread of readings from good clocks.

The TTA algorithm is basically the Welch-Lynch algorithm specialized for $k = 1$ (i.e., it tolerates a single fault): that is, clocks are set to the average of the 2nd and $n - 1$'st clock readings (i.e., the second-smallest and second-largest). This algorithm works and tolerates a single arbitrary fault whenever $n \geq 4$. TTA does not use dedicated wires to communicate clock readings among the nodes attached to the network; instead, it exploits the fact that communication is time triggered according to a global schedule. When a node a receives a message from a node b, it notes the reading of its local clock and subtracts a fixed correction term to account for the network delay; the difference between this adjusted clock reading and the time for b's transmission that is indicated in the global schedule yields a's perception of the skew between clocks a and b.

Not all nodes in a TTA system need have accurate oscillators (they are expensive), so TTA's algorithm is modified from Welch-Lynch to use only the clock skews from nodes marked[1] as having accurate oscillators. Analysis and verification of this variant can be adapted straightforwardly from that of the basic algorithm. Unfortunately, TTA adds another complication.

For scalability, an implementation on the Welch-Lynch algorithm should use data structures that are independent of the number of nodes—i.e., it should not be necessary for each node to store the clock difference readings for all (accurate) clocks. Clearly, the second-smallest clock difference reading can be determined with just two registers (one to hold the smallest and another for the second-smallest reading seen so far), and the second-largest can be determined similarly, for a total of four registers per node. If TTA used this approach, verification of its clock synchronization algorithm would follow straightforwardly from that of Welch-Lynch. Instead, for reasons that are not described, TTA does not consider all the accurate clocks when choosing the second-smallest and second-largest, but just four of them.

The four clocks considered for synchronization are chosen as follows. First, TTA is able to tolerate more than a single fault by reconfiguring to exclude nodes that are detected to be faulty. This is accomplished by the group membership algorithm of TTA, which is discussed in the following section[2]. The four clocks considered for synchronization are chosen from the members of the current membership; it is therefore essential that group membership have the property that all nonfaulty nodes have the same members at all times. Next, each node maintains a queue of four clock readings[3]; whenever a message is received from a node that is in the current membership and that has the SYF field set, the clock difference reading is pushed on to the receiving node's queue (ejecting the oldest reading in the queue). Finally, when the current slot has the synchronization field (CS) set in the MEDL, each node runs the synchronization algorithm using the four clock readings stored in its queue.

Even glossing over some complexities (what goes on the queue when a message is not received correctly?), it is clear that formal verification of the TTA algorithm requires more than simply verifying a four-clocks version of the basic Welch-Lynch algorithm (e.g., the chosen clocks can change from one round to the next). However, verification of the basic algorithm should provide a foundation for the TTA case.

Formal verification of clock synchronization algorithms has quite a long history, beginning with Rushby and von Henke's verification [55] of the interactive convergence algorithm of Lamport and Melliar Smith [29]; this is similar to the

---

[1] By having the SYF field set in the MEDL (the global schedule known to all nodes).

[2] A node whose clock loses synchronization will suffer send and/or receive faults and will therefore be detected and excluded by the group membership algorithm.

[3] It is described as a push-down stack in the TTP/C specification [70], but this seems to be an error.

Welch-Lynch algorithm, except that the *egocentric mean* is used as the fault-tolerant average. Shankar [65] formally verified Schneider's abstract algorithm and its instantiation for interactive convergence. This formalization was subsequently improved by Miner (reducing the difficulty of the proof obligations needed to establish the correctness of specific instantiations), who also verified the Welch-Lynch instantiation [34]. All these verifications were undertaken with EHDM [56], a precursor to PVS [37]. The treatment developed by Miner was translated to PVS and generalized (to admit nonaveraging algorithms such as that of Srikanth and Toueg [68] that do not conform to Schneider's treatment) by Schweier and von Henke [64]. This treatment was then extended to the TTA algorithm by Pfeifer, Schweier and von Henke [41].

The TTA algorithm is intended to operate in networks where there are at least four good clocks, and it is able to mask any single fault in this circumstance. Pfeifer, Schweier and von Henke's verification establishes this property. Additional challenges still remain, however.

In keeping with the *never give up* philosophy that is appropriate for safety-critical applications, TTA should remain operational with less than four good clocks, though "the requirement to handle a Byzantine fault is waived" [70, page 85]. It would be valuable to characterize and formally verify the exact fault tolerance achieved in these cases. One approach to achieving this would be to undertake the verification in the context of a "hybrid" fault model such as that introduced for consensus by Thambidurai and Park [69]. In a pure Byzantine fault model, all faults are treated as arbitrary: nothing is assumed about the behavior of faulty components. A hybrid fault model introduces additional, constrained kinds of faults and the verification is extended to examine the behavior of the algorithm concerned under combinations of several faults of different kinds. Thambidurai and Park's model augments the Byzantine or *arbitrary* fault model with *manifest* and *symmetric* faults. A manifest fault is one that is consistently detectable by all nonfaulty nodes; a symmetric fault is unconstrained, except that it appears the same to all nonfaulty nodes. Rushby reinterpreted this fault model for clock synchronization and extended verification of the interactive convergence algorithm to this more elaborate fault model [45]. He showed that the interactive convergence algorithm with n nodes can withstand a arbitrary, s symmetric, and m manifest faults simultaneously, provided $n > 3a + 2s + m$. Thus, a three-clock system using this algorithm can withstand a symmetric fault or two manifest faults.

Rushby also extended this analysis to *link* faults, which can be considered as asymmetric and possibly intermittent manifest faults (i.e., node a may obtain a correct reading of node b's clock while node c obtains a detectably faulty reading). The fault tolerance of the algorithm is then $n > 3a + 2s + m + l$ where l is the maximum, over all pairs of nodes, of the number of nodes that have faulty links to one or other of the pair.

It would be interesting to extend formal verification of the TTA algorithm to this fault model. Not only would this enlarge the analysis to cases where fewer than three good clocks remain, but it could also provide a much simpler way to deal with the peculiarities of the TTA algorithm (i.e., its use of queues of just four clocks). Instead of explicitly modeling properties of the queues, we could, under a fault model that admits link faults, imagine that the queues are larger and contain clock difference readings from the full set of nodes, but that link faults reduce the number of valid readings actually present in each queue to four (this idea was suggested by Holger Pfeifer). A recent paper by Schmid [59] considers link faults for clock synchronization in a very general setting, and establishes bounds on fault tolerance for both the Welch-Lynch and Srikanth-Toueg algorithms and I believe this would be an excellent foundation for a comprehensive verification of the TTA algorithm.

All the formal verifications of clock synchronizations mentioned above are "brute force": they are essentially mechanized reproductions of proofs originally undertaken by hand. The proofs depend heavily on arithmetic reasoning and can be formalized at reasonable cost only with the aid of verification systems that provide effective mechanization for arithmetic, such as PVS. Even these systems, however, typically mechanize only linear arithmetic and require tediously many human-directed proof steps (or numerous intermediate lemmas) to verify the formulas that arise in clock synchronization. The new ICS decision procedures [14] developed for PVS include (incomplete) extensions to nonlinear products and it will be interesting to explore the extent to which such extensions simplify formal verification of clock synchronization algorithms[4]. Even if all the arithmetic reasoning were completely automated, current approaches to formal verification of clock synchronization algorithms still depend heavily on human insight and guidance. The problem is that the synchronization property is not inductive: it must be strengthened by the conjunction of several other properties to achieve a property that is inductive. These additional properties are intricate arithmetic statements whose invention seems to require considerable human insight. It would be interesting to see if modern methods for invariant discovery and strengthening [5, 6, 71] can generate some of these automatically, or if the need for them could be sidestepped using reachability analysis on linear hybrid automata.

All the verifications described above deal with the steady-state case; initial synchronization is quite a different challenge. Note that (re)initialization may be required during operation if the system suffers a massive failure (e.g., due to powerful electromagnetic effects), so it must be fast. The basic idea is that a node that detects no activity on the bus for some time will assume that initialization is required and it will broadcast a wakeup message: nodes that receive the message will synchronize to it. Of course, other nodes may make the same determination at about the same time and may send wakeup messages that collide with others. In these cases, nodes back off for (different) node-specific intervals and try again. However, it is difficult to detect collisions with perfect accuracy and simple algorithms can lead to existence of groups of nodes syn-

---

[4] It is not enough to mechanize real arithmetic on its own; it must be combined with inequalities, integer linear arithmetic, equality over uninterpreted function symbols and several other theories [46].

chronized within themselves but unaware of the existence of the other groups. All of these complications must be addressed in a context where some nodes are faulty and may not be following (indeed, may be actively disrupting) the intended algorithm. The latest version of TTA uses a star topology and the initialization algorithm is being revised to exploit some additional safeguards that the central guardian makes possible [38]. Verification of initialization algorithms is challenging because, as clearly explained in [38], the essential purpose of such an algorithm is to cause a transition between two models of computation: from asynchronous to synchronous. Formal explication of this issue, and verification of the TTA initialization algorithm, are worthwhile endeavors for the future.

3 Transmission Window Timing

Synchronized clocks and a global schedule ensure that nonfaulty nodes broadcast their messages in disjoint time slots: messages sent by nonfaulty nodes are guaranteed not to collide on the bus. A faulty node, however, could broadcast at any time—it could even broadcast constantly (the *babbling* failure mode). This fault is countered by use of a separate fault containment unit called a *guardian* that has independent knowledge of the time and the schedule: a message sent by one node will reach others only if the guardian agrees that it is indeed scheduled for that time.

Now, the sending node, the guardian, and each receiving node have synchronized clocks, but there must be some slack in the time window they assign to each slot so that good messages are not truncated or rejected due to clock skew within the bounds guaranteed by the synchronization algorithm. The design rules used in TTA are the following, where Π is the maximum clock skew between synchronized components.

- The receive window extends from the beginning of the slot to $4\,\Pi$ beyond its allotted duration.
- Transmission begins $2\,\Pi$ units after the beginning of the slot and should last no longer than the allotted duration.
- The bus guardian for a transmitter opens its window Π units after the beginning of the slot and closes it $3\,\Pi$ beyond its allotted duration.

These rules are intended to ensure the following requirements.

Agreement: If any nonfaulty node accepts a transmission, then all nonfaulty nodes do.

Validity: If any nonfaulty node transmits a message, then all nonfaulty nodes will accept the transmission.

Separation: messages sent by nonfaulty nodes or passed by nonfaulty guardians do not arrive before other components have finished the previous slot, nor after they have started the following one.

Formal specification and verification of these properties is a relatively straightforward exercise. Description of a formal treatment using PVS is available as a technical report [53].

4 Group Membership

The clock synchronization algorithm tolerates only a single (arbitrary) fault. Additional faults are tolerated by diagnosing the faulty node and reconfiguring to exclude it. This diagnosis and reconfiguration is performed by the *group membership* algorithm of TTA, which ensures that each TTA node has a record of which nodes are currently considered nonfaulty. In addition to supporting the internal fault tolerance of TTA, membership information is made available as a service to applications; this supports the construction of relatively simple, but correct, strategies for tolerating faults at the application level. For example, in an automobile brake-by-wire application, the node at each wheel can adjust its braking force to compensate for the failure (as indicated in the membership information) of the node or brake at another wheel. For such strategies to work, it is obviously necessary that the membership information should be reliable, and that the application state of nonmembers should be predictable (e.g., the brake is fully released).

Group membership is a distributed algorithm: each node maintains a private *membership* list, which records all the nodes that it believes to be nonfaulty. Reliability of the membership information is characterized by the following requirements.

Agreement: The membership lists of all nonfaulty nodes are the same.

Validity: The membership lists of all nonfaulty nodes contain all nonfaulty nodes and at most one faulty node (we cannot require immediate removal of faulty nodes because a fault must be manifested before it can be diagnosed).

These requirements can be satisfied only under restricted fault hypotheses. For example, validity cannot be satisfied if new faults arrive too rapidly, and it is provably impossible to diagnose an arbitrary-faulty node with certainty. When unable to maintain accurate membership, the best recourse is to maintain agreement, but sacrifice validity. This weakened requirement is called *clique avoidance*.

Two additional properties also are desirable in a group membership algorithm.

Self-diagnosis: faulty nodes eventually remove themselves from their own membership lists and fail silently (i.e., cease broadcasting).

Reintegration: it should be possible for excluded but recovered nodes to determine the current membership and be readmitted.

TTA operates as a broadcast bus (even though the recent versions are stars topologically); the global schedule executes as a repetitive series of *rounds*, and each node is allocated one or more broadcast slots in round. The fault hypothesis of the membership algorithm is a benign one: faults must arrive two or more rounds apart, and must be symmetric in their manifestations: either *all* or exactly *one* node may fail to receive a broadcast message (the former is called a *send* fault, the latter a *receive* fault). The membership requirements would be relatively easy to satisfy if each node were to attach a copy of its membership list to each message that it broadcasts. Unfortunately, since messages are typically very short, this would use rather a lot of bandwidth (and bandwidth was a precious commodity in early implementations of TTA), so the algorithm must operate with less explicit information and nodes must infer the state and membership of other nodes through indirect means. This operates as follows.

Each active TTA node maintains a membership list of those nodes (including itself) that it believes to be active and operating correctly. Each node listens for messages from other nodes and updates its membership list according to the information that it receives. The time-triggered nature of the protocol means that each node knows when to expect a message from another node, and it can therefore detect the absence of such a message. Each message carries a CRC checksum that encodes information about its sender's *C-State*, which includes its local membership list. To infer the local membership of the sender of a message, receivers must append their estimate of that membership (and other C-state information) to the message and then check whether the calculated CRC matches that sent with the message. It is not feasible (or reliable) to try all possible memberships, so receivers perform the check against just their own local membership, and one or two variants.

Transmission faults are detected as follows: each broadcaster listens for the message from its *first successor* (roughly speaking, this will be the next node to broadcast) to check whether it suffered a transmission fault: this will be indicated by its exclusion from the membership list of the message from its first successor. However, this indication is ambiguous: it could be the result of a transmission fault by the original broadcaster, or of a receive fault by the successor. Nodes use the local membership carried by the message from their *second successor* to resolve this ambiguity: a membership that excludes the original broadcaster but includes the first successor indicates a transmission fault by the original broadcaster, and one that includes the original broadcaster but excludes the first successor indicates a receive fault by the first successor.

Nodes that suffer receive faults could diagnose themselves in a similar way: their local membership lists will differ from those of nonfaulty nodes, so their next broadcast will be rejected by both their successors. However, the algorithm actually performs this diagnosis differently. Each node maintains *accept* and *reject* counters that are initialized to 1 and 0, respectively, following its own broadcast. Incoming messages that indicate a membership matching that of the receiver cause the receiver to increment its accept count; others (and missing messages) cause it to increment its reject count. Before broadcasting, each node compares its accept and reject counts and shuts down unless the former is greater than the latter.

Formal verification of this algorithm is difficult. We wish to prove that agreement and validity are invariants of the algorithm (i.e., they are true of all reachable states), but it is difficult to do this directly (because it is hard to characterize the reachable states). So, instead, we try to prove a stronger property: namely, that agreement and validity are *inductive* (that is, true of the initial states and preserved by all steps of the algorithm). The general problem with this approach to verification of safety properties of distributed algorithms is that natural statements of the properties of interest are seldom inductive. Instead, it is necessary to strengthen them by conjoining additional properties until they become inductive. The additional properties typically are discovered by examining failed proofs and require human insight.

Before details of the TTA group membership algorithm were known, Katz, Lincoln, and Rushby published a different algorithm for a similar problem, together with an informal proof of its correctness [20] (I will call this the "WDAG" algorithm). A flaw in this algorithm for the special case of three nodes was discovered independently by Shankar and by Creese and Roscoe [10] and considerable effort was expended in attempts to formally verify the corrected version. A suitable method was found by Rushby [49] who used it to formally verify the WDAG algorithm, but used a simplified algorithm (called the "CAV" algorithm) to explicate the method in [49]. The method is based on strengthening a putative safety property into a *disjunction* of "configurations" that can easily be proved to be inductive. Configurations can be constructed systematically and transitions among them have a natural diagrammatic representation that conveys insight into the operation of the algorithm. Pfeifer subsequently used this method to verify validity, agreement, and self-diagnosis for the full TTA membership algorithm [40] (verification of self-diagnosis is not described in the paper).

Although the method just described is systematic, it does require considerable human interaction and insight, so more automatic methods are desirable. All the group membership algorithms mentioned (CAV, WDAG, TTA) are n-process algorithms (so-called *parameterized systems*), so one attractive class of methods seeks to reduce the general case to some fixed configuration (say four processes) of an abstracted algorithm that can be model checked. Creese and Roscoe [10] report an investigation along these lines for the WDAG algorithm. The difficulty in such approaches is that proving that the abstracted algorithm is faithful to the original is often as hard as the direct proof.

An alternative is to *construct* the abstracted algorithm using automated theorem proving so that the result is guaranteed to be sound, but possibly too conservative. These methods are widely used for predicate [57] and data [9] abstraction (both methods are implemented in PVS using a generalization of the technique described in [58]), and have been applied to n-process examples [66]. The precision of an abstraction is determined by the guidance provided to the calculation (e.g., which predicates to abstract on) and by the power of the automated deduction methods that are employed[5]. The logic called WS1S is very attractive in this regard, because it is very expressive (it can represent arithmetic and set operations on integers) and it is decidable [12]. The method implemented in the PAX tool [3, 4] performs automated abstraction of parameterized specifications modeled in WS1S. Application of the tool to the CAV group membership protocol is described on the PAX web page at http:

---

[5] In this context, automated deduction methods are used in a *failure-tolerant* manner, so that if the methods fail to prove a true theorem, the resulting abstraction will be sound, but more conservative than necessary.

`//www.informatik.uni-kiel.de/ kba/pax/examples.html`. The abstraction yields a finite-state system that can be examined by model checking. I conjecture that extension of this method to the TTA algorithm may prove difficult because the counters used in that algorithm add an extra unbounded dimension.

The design of TTA (and particularly of the central guardian) is intended to minimize violations of the benign fault hypothesis of the group membership algorithm. But we cannot guarantee absence of such violations, so the membership algorithm is buttressed by a clique avoidance algorithm (it would better be called a clique elimination algorithm) that sacrifices validity but maintains agreement under weakened fault hypotheses. Clique avoidance is actually a subalgorithm of the membership algorithm: it comprises just the part that manages the accept and reject counters and that causes a node to shut down prior to a broadcast unless its accept count exceeds its reject count at that point. The clique avoidance algorithm can be analyzed either in isolation or, more accurately, in the presence of the rest of the membership algorithm (this is, the part that deals with the first and second successor).

Beyond benign fault hypothesis lie *asymmetric* faults (where more than one but less than all nodes fail to receive a broadcast correctly), and *multiple* faults, which are those that arrive less than two rounds apart. These hypotheses all concern loss of messages; additional hypotheses include *processor* faults, where nodes fail to follow the algorithm, and *transient* faults, where nodes have their state corrupted (e.g., by high-intensity radiation) but otherwise follow the algorithm correctly.

Bauer and Paulitsch, who introduced the clique avoidance algorithm, give an informal proof [2] that it tolerates a single asymmetric fault. Their analysis includes the effects of the rest of the membership algorithm. Bouajjani and Merceron [7] prove that the clique avoidance algorithm, considered in isolation, tolerates multiple asymmetric faults; they also describe an abstraction for the n-node, k-faults parameterized case that yields a counter automaton. Reachability is decidable for this class of systems, and experiments are reported with two automated verifiers for the $k = 1$ case.

For transient faults, I conjecture that the most appropriate framework for analysis is that of self-stabilization [63]. An algorithm is said to be *self-stabilizing* if it converges to a stable "good" state starting from an arbitrary initial state. The arbitrary initial state can be one caused by an electromagnetic upset (e.g., that changes the values of the accepts and reject counters), or by other faults outside the benign faulty hypotheses.

An attractive treatment of self-stabilization is provided by the "Detectors and Correctors" theory of Arora and Kulkarni. The full theory [1,28] is comprehensive and more than is needed for my purposes, so I present a simplified and slightly modified version that adapts the important insights of the original formulation to the problem at hand.

We assume some "base" algorithm M whose purpose is to maintain an invariant S: that is, if the (distributed) system starts in a state satisfying the predicate S, then execution of M will maintain that property. In our case, M is the TTA group membership algorithm, and S is the conjunction of the agreement and validity properties. M corresponds to what Arora and Kulkarni call the "fault-intolerant" program, but in our context it is actually a fault-tolerant algorithm in its own right. This aspect of the system's operation can be specified by the Hoare formula

$$\{S\} \ M\|F \ \{S\}$$

where F is a "fault injector" that characterizes the fault hypothesis of the base algorithm and $M\|F$ denotes the concurrent execution of M and F.

Now, a transient fault can take the system to some state not satisfying S, and at this point our hope is that a "corrector" algorithm C will take over and somehow cause the system to converge to a state satisfying S, where the base algorithm can take over again. We can represent this by the following formula

$$C \models \Diamond S$$

where $\Diamond$ is the *eventually* modality of temporal logic.

In our case, C is the TTA clique avoidance algorithm. So far we have treated M and C separately but, as noted previously, they must actually run concurrently, so we really require

$$\{S\} \ C\|M\|F \ \{S\}$$

and

$$C\|M\|F \models \Diamond S.$$

The presence of F in the last of these represents the fact that although the disturbance that took the system to an arbitrary state is assumed to have passed when convergence begins, the standard, benign fault hypothesis still applies.

To ensure the first of these formulas, we need that C does not interfere with M—that is, that $C\|M$ behaves the same as M (and hence $C\|M\|F$ behaves the same as $M\|F$). A very direct way to ensure this is for C actually to be a subalgorithm of M—for then $C\|M$ *is* the same as M. As we have already seen later, this is the case in TTA, where the clique avoidance algorithm is just a part of the membership algorithm.

A slight additional complication is that the corrector may not be able to restore the system to the ideal condition characterized by S, but only to some "safe" approximation to it, characterized by S'. This is the case in TTA, where clique avoidance sacrifices validity. Our formulas therefore become the following.

$$\{S\} \ C\|M\|F \ \{S\} \tag{1}$$

$$\{S'\} \ C\|M\|F \ \{S' \vee S\}, \text{ and } S \supset S' \tag{2}$$

and

$$C\|M\|F \models \Diamond S'. \tag{3}$$

The challenge is formally to verify these three formulas. Concretely, (1) is accomplished for TTA by Pfeifer's verification [40] (and potentially, in more automated form, by extensions to the approaches of [3, 7]), (2) should require little more than an adjustment to those proofs, and the hard case is (3). Bouajjani and Merceron's analysis [7] can be seen as establishing

$$C \models \Diamond S'$$

for the restricted case where the arbitrary initial state is one produced by the occurrence of multiple, possibly asymmetric faults in message transmission or reception. The general case must consider the possibility that the initial state is produced by some outside disturbance that sets the counters and flags of the algorithm to arbitrary values (I have formally verified this case for a simplified algorithm), and must also consider the presence of M and F. Formal verification of this general case is an interesting challenge for the future. Kulkarni [27, 28] has formally specified and verified the general detectors and correctors theory in PVS, and this provides a useful framework in which to develop the argument. A separate topic is to examine the consequences of giving up validity in order to maintain agreement under the clique avoidance algorithm. Under the never give up philosophy, it is reasonable to sacrifice one property rather than lose all coordination when the standard fault hypothesis is violated, but some useful insight may be gained through an attempt to formally characterize the possible behaviors in these cases.

Reintegration has so far been absent from the discussion. A node that diagnoses a problem in its own operation will drop out of the membership, perform diagnostic tests and, if these are satisfactory (indicating that the original fault was a transient event), attempt to reintegrate itself into the running system. This requires that the node first (re)synchronizes its clock to the running system, then acquires the current membership, and then "speaks up" at its next slot in the schedule. There are several difficult cases in this scenario: for example, a broadcast by a node a may be missed by a node b whose membership is used to initialize a reintegrating node c; rejection of its message by b and c then causes the good node a to shut down. Formal examination of reintegration scenarios is another interesting challenge for the future.

5   Interaction of Clock Synchronization and Group Membership

Previous sections considered clock synchronization and group membership in isolation but noted that, in reality, they interact: synchronization depends on membership to eliminate nodes diagnosed as faulty, while membership depends on synchronization to create the time-triggered round structure on which its operation depends. Mutual dependence of components on the correct operation of each other is generally formalized in terms of assume-guarantee reasoning, first introduced by Chandy and Misra [35] and Jones [19]. The idea is to show that component X_1 guarantees certain properties P_1 on the assumption that component X_2 delivers certain properties P_2, and *vice versa* for X_2, and then claim that the composition of X_1 and X_2 guarantees P_1 and P_2 unconditionally. This kind of reasoning appears—and indeed is—circular in that X_1 depends on X_2 and *vice versa*. The circularity can lead to unsoundness and there has been much research on the formulation of rules for assume-guarantee reasoning that are both sound and useful. Different rules may be compared according to the kinds of system models and specification they support, the extent to which they lend themselves to mechanized analysis, and the extent to which they are preserved under refinement (i.e., the circumstances under which X_1 can be replaced by an implementation that may do more than X_1).

Closer examination of the circular dependency in TTA reveals that it is not circular if the temporal evolution of the system is taken into consideration: clock synchronization in round t depends on group membership in round $t-1$, which in turn depends on clock synchronization in round $t-2$ and so on. McMillan [33] has introduced an assume-guarantee rule that seems appropriate to this case. McMillan's rule can be expressed as follows, where H is a "helper" property (which can be simply *true*), $\Box$ is the "always" modality of Linear Temporal Logic (LTL), and $p \rhd q$ ("p constrains q") means that if p is always true up to time t, then q holds at time $t+1$ (i.e., p fails before q), where we interpret time as rounds.

$$\frac{\langle H \rangle X_1 \langle P_2 \rhd P_1 \rangle \qquad \langle H \rangle X_2 \langle P_1 \rhd P_2 \rangle}{\langle H \rangle \quad X_1 \| X_2 \quad \langle \Box (P_1 \wedge P_2) \rangle} \tag{4}$$

Notice that $p \rhd q$ can be written as the LTL formula $\neg(p \, \mathsf{U} \, \neg q)$, where U is the LTL "until" operator. This means that the antecedent formulas can be established by LTL model checking if the transition relations for X_1 and X_2 are finite.

I believe the soundness of the circular interaction between the clock synchronization and group membership algorithms of TTA can be formally verified using McMillan's rule. To carry this out, we need to import the proof rule (4) into the verification framework employed—and for this we probably need to embed the semantics of the rule into the specification language concerned. McMillan's presentation of the rule only sketches the argument for its soundness; a more formal treatment is given by Namjoshi and Trefler [36], but it is not easy reading and does not convey the basic intuition. Rushby [52] presents an embedding of LTL in the PVS specification language and formally verifies the soundness of the rule. The specification and proof are surprisingly short and provide a good demonstration of the power and convenience of the PVS language and prover.

Using this foundation to verify the interaction between the clock synchronization and group membership algorithms of TTA remains a challenge for the future. Observe that such an application of assume-guarantee reasoning has rather an unusual character: conventionally, the components in assume-guarantee reasoning are viewed as separate, peer processes, whereas here they are distributed algorithms the form part of a protocol hierarchy (with membership above synchronization).

6   Emergent Properties

Clock synchronization, transmission window timing, and group membership are important and useful properties, but what makes TTA useful are not the individual properties of its constituent algorithms, but the emergent properties that come about through their combination. These emergent properties are understood by the designers and advocates of TTA, but they have not been articulated formally in ways that are fully satisfactory, and I consider this the most important and interesting of the tasks that remain in the formal analysis of TTA.

I consider the three "top level" properties of TTA to be the time-triggered model of computation, support for application-independent fault tolerance, and partitioning. The time-triggered model of computation can be construed narrowly or broadly. Narrowly, it is a variant on the notion of synchronous system [31]: these are distributed computer systems where there are known upper bounds on the time that it takes nonfaulty processors to perform certain operations, and on the time that it takes for a message sent by one nonfaulty processor to be received by another. The existence of these bounds simplifies the development of fault-tolerant systems because nonfaulty processes executing a common algorithm can use the passage of time to predict each others' progress, and the absence of expected messages can be detected. This property contrasts with asynchronous systems, where there are no upper bounds on processing and message delays, and where it is therefore provably impossible to achieve certain forms of consistent knowledge or coordinated action in the presence of even simple faults [8, 15]. Rushby [48] presents a formal verification that a system possessing the synchronization and scheduling mechanisms of TTA can be used to create the abstraction of a synchronous system. An alternative model, closer to TTA in that it does not abstract out the real-time behavior, is that of the language Giotto [17] and it would be interesting to formalize the connection between TTA and Giotto.

More broadly construed, the notion of time-triggered system encompasses a whole philosophy of real-time systems design—notably that espoused by Kopetz [22]. Kopetz' broad conception includes a distinction between *composite* and *elementary* interfaces [24] and the notion of a temporal firewall [21]. A time-triggered system does not merely schedule activity within nodes, it also manages the reliable transmission of messages between them. Messages obviously communicate data between nodes (and the processes within them) but they may also, through their presence or absence and through the data that they convey, influence the flow of control within a node or process (or, more generically, a component).

An important insight is that one component should not allow another to control its own progress. Suppose, for example, that the guarantees delivered by component X_1 are quite weak, such as, "this buffer may sometimes contain recent data concerning parameter A." Another component X_2 that uses this data must be prepared to operate when recent data about A is unavailable (at least from X_1). It might seem that predictability and simplicity would be enhanced if we were to ensure that the flow of data about A is reliable—perhaps using a protocol involving acknowledgments. But in fact, contrary to this intuition, such a mechanism would greatly increase the coupling between components and introduce more complicated failure propagations. For example, X_1 could block waiting for an acknowledgment from X_2 that may never come if X_2 has failed, thereby propagating the failure from X_2 to X_1. Kopetz [24] defines interfaces that involve such bidirectional flow of control as composite and argues convincingly that they should be eschewed in favor of elementary interfaces in which control flow is unidirectional.

The need for elementary interfaces leads to unusual protocols that are largely unknown outside the avionics field. The four-slot protocol of Simpson [67], for example, provides a completely nonblocking, asynchronous communication mechanism that nonetheless ensures timely transmission and mutual exclusion (i.e., no simultaneous reading and writing of the same buffer). A generalization of this protocol, called NBW (nonblocking write) is used in TTA [26]. A formal analysis of Simpson's protocol has recently been developed by Henderson and Paynter [16], but the larger issue of formally characterizing composite and elementary interfaces has not yet been tackled, to my knowledge.

It is debatable whether formalization of these notions is best performed as part of a broad treatment of time-triggered systems, or as part of an orthogonal topic concerned with application-independent fault tolerance. *Temporal firewalls*, another element in Kopetz' comprehensive philosophy [21], seem definitely to belong in the treatment of fault tolerance. The standard way to communicate a sensor sample is to package it with a timestamp: then the consuming process can estimate the "freshness" of the sample. But surely the useful lifetime of a sample depends on the accuracy of the original reading and on the dynamics of the real variable being measured—and these factors are better known to the process doing the sensing than to the process that consumes the sample. So, argues, Kopetz, it is better to turn the timestamp around, so that it indicates the "must use by" time, rather than the time at which the sample was taken. This is the idea of the temporal firewall, which exists in two variants. A *phase-insensitive* sensor sample is provided with a time and a guarantee that the sampled value is accurate (with respect to a specification published by the process that provides it) until the indicated time. For example, suppose that engine oil temperature may change by at most 1% of its range per second, that its sensor is completely accurate, and that the data is to be guaranteed to 0.5%. Then the sensor sample will be provided with a time 500 ms ahead of the instant when it was sampled, and the receiver will know that it is safe to use the sampled value until the indicated time. A *phase-sensitive* temporal firewall is used for rapidly changing variables where state estimation is required; in addition to sensor sample and time, it provides the parameters needed to perform state estimation. For example, along with sampled crankshaft angle, it may supply RPM, so that angle may be estimated more accurately at the time of use. The advantage of temporal firewalls is that they allow some of the downstream processing (e.g., sensor fusion) to become less application dependent.

Temporal firewalls are consistent with modern notions of *smart sensors* that co-locate computing resources with the sensor. Such resources allow a sensor to return additional information, including an estimate of the accuracy of its own reading. An attractive way to indicate (confidence in) the accuracy of a sensor reading is to return two values (both packaged in a temporal firewall) indicating the upper and lower 95% (say) confidence interval. If several such intervals are available from redundant sensors, then an interesting question is how best to combine (or *fuse*) them. Marzullo [32] introduces the sensor fusion function $\bigcap_{f,n}(S)$ for this problem; Rushby formally verifies the soundness of this construction (i.e., the fused interval always contains the correct value) [54]. A weakness of Marzullo's function is that it lacks the "Lipschitz Condition": small changes in input sensor readings can sometimes produce large changes in its output. Schmid and Schossmaier [60] have recently introduced an improved fusion function $\mathcal{F}_n^f(S)$ that does satisfy the Lipschitz condition, and is optimal among all such functions. It would be interesting to verify formally the properties of this function.

Principled fault tolerance requires not only that redundant sensor values are fused effectively, but that all redundant consumers agree on exactly the same values; this is the notion of *replica determinism* [42] that provides the foundation for *state machine replication* [62] and other methods for application-independent fault tolerance based on exact-match voting. Replica determinism in its turn depends on *interactively consistent* message passing: that is, message passing in which all nonfaulty recipients obtain the same value [39], even if the sender and some of the intermediaries in the transmission are faulty (this is also known as the problem of *Byzantine Agreement* [30]). It is well known [31] that interactive consistency cannot be achieved in the presence of a single arbitrary fault with less than two rounds of information exchange (one to disseminate the values, and one to cross-check), yet TTA sends each message in only a single broadcast. How can we reconcile this practice with theory? I suggest in [51] that the interaction of message broadcasts with the group membership algorithm (which can be seen as a continuously interleaving two-round algorithm) in TTA achieves a "Draconian consensus" in which agreement is enforced by removal of any members that disagree. It would be interesting to subject this idea to formal examination, and to construct an integrated formal treatment for application-level fault tolerance in TTA similar to those previously developed for classical state machine replication [44, 11].

The final top-level property is the most important for safety-critical applications; it is called *partitioning* and it refers to the requirement that faults in one component of TTA, or in one application supported by TTA, must not propagate to other components and applications, and must not affect the operation of nonfaulty components and applications, other than through loss of the services provided by the failed elements. It is quite easy to develop a formal statement of partitioning—but only in the absence of the qualification introduced in the final clause of the previous sentence (see [47] for an extended discussion of this topic). In the absence of communication, partitioning is equivalent to isolation and this property has a long history of formal analysis in the security community [43] and has been adapted to include the real-time attributes that are important in embedded systems [74]. In essence, formal statements of isolation state that the behavior perceived by one component is entirely unchanged by the presence or absence of other components. When communication between components is allowed, this simple statement no longer suffices, for if X_1 supplies input to X_2, then absence of X_1 certainly changes the behavior perceived by X_2. What we want to say is that the *only* change perceived by X_2 is that due to the faulty or missing data supplied by X_1 (i.e., X_1 must not be able to interfere with X_2's communication with other components, nor write directly into its memory, and so on). To my knowledge, there is no fully satisfactory formal statement of this interpretation of partitioning.

It is clear that properties of the TTA algorithms and architecture are crucial to partitioning (e.g., clock synchronization, the global schedule, existence of guardians, the single-fault assumption, and transmission window timing, are all needed to stop a faulty node violating partitioning by babbling on the bus), and there are strong informal arguments (backed by experiment) that these properties are sufficient [51], but to my knowledge there is as yet no comprehensive formal treatment of this argument.

7   Conclusion

TTA provides several challenging formal verification problems. Those who wish to develop or benchmark new techniques or tools can find good test cases among the algorithms and requirements of TTA. However, I believe that the most interesting and rewarding problems are those that concern the interactions of several algorithms, and it is here that new methods of compositional analysis and verification are most urgently needed. Examples include the interaction between the group membership and clique avoidance algorithms and their joint behavior under various fault hypotheses, the mutual interdependence of clock synchronization and group membership, and the top-level properties that emerge from the collective interaction of all the algorithms and architectural attributes of TTA. Progress on these fronts will not only advance the techniques and tools of formal methods, but will strengthen and deepen ties between the formal methods and embedded systems communities, and make a valuable contribution to assurance for the safety-critical systems that are increasingly part of our daily lives.

References

1. Anish Arora and Sandeep S. Kulkarni. Detectors and correctors: A theory of fault-tolerance components. In *18th International Conference on Distributed Computing Systems*, pages 436–443, Amsterdam, The Netherlands, 1998. IEEE Computer Society.

2. Günther Bauer and Michael Paulitsch. An investigation of membership and clique avoidance in TTP/C. In *19th Symposium on Reliable Distributed Systems*, Nuremberg, Germany, October 2000.

3. Kai Baukus, Saddek Bensalem, Yassine Lakhnech, and Karsten Stahl. Abstracting WS1S systems to verify parameterized networks. In Susanne Graf and Michael Schwartzbach, editors, *Tools and Algorithms for the Construction and Analysis of Systems (TACAS 2000)*, number 1785 in Lecture Notes in Computer Science, pages 188–203, Berlin, Germany, March 2000. Springer-Verlag.

4. Kai Baukus, Yassine Lakhnech, and Karsten Stahl. Verifying universal properties of parameterized networks. In Matthai Joseph, editor, *Formal Techniques in Real-Time and Fault-Tolerant Systems*, volume 1926 of *Lecture Notes in Computer Science*, pages 291–303, Pune, India, September 2000. Springer-Verlag.

5. Saddek Bensalem, Marius Bozga, Jean-Claude Fernandez, Lucian Ghirvu, and Yassine Lakhnech. A transformational approach for generating non-linear invariants. In Jens Palsberg, editor, *Seventh International Static Analysis Symposium (SAS'00)*, volume 1824 of *Lecture Notes in Computer Science*, pages 58–74, Santa Barbara CA, June 2000. Springer-Verlag.

6. Saddek Bensalem and Yassine Lakhnech. Automatic generation of invariants. *Formal Methods in Systems Design*, 15(1):75–92, July 1999.

7. Ahmed Bouajjani and Agathe Merceron. Parametric verification of a group membership algorithm. These proceedings.

8. Tushar D. Chandra, Vassos Hadzilacos, Sam Toueg, and Bernadette Charron-Bost. On the impossibility of group membership. In *Fifteenth ACM Symposium on Principles of Distributed Computing*, pages 322–330, Philadelphia, PA, May 1996. Association for Computing Machinery.

9. James Corbett, Matthew Dwyer, John Hatcliff, Corina Pasareanu, Robby, Shawn Laubach, and Hongjun Zheng. Bandera: Extracting finite-state models from Java source code. In *22nd International Conference on Software Engineering*, pages 439–448, Limerick, Ireland, June 2000. IEEE Computer Society.

10. S. J. Creese and A. W. Roscoe. TTP: A case study in combining induction and data independence. Technical Report PRG-TR-1-99, Oxford University Computing Laboratory, Oxford, England, 1999.

11. Ben L. Di Vito and Ricky W. Butler. Formal techniques for synchronized fault-tolerant systems. In C. E. Landwehr, B. Randell, and L. Simoncini, editors, *Dependable Computing for Critical Applications—3*, volume 8 of *Dependable Computing and Fault-Tolerant Systems*, pages 163–188. Springer-Verlag, Vienna, Austria, September 1992.

12. Jacob Elgaard, Nils Klarlund, and Anders Möller. Mona 1.x: New techniques for WS1S and WS2S. In Alan J. Hu and Moshe Y. Vardi, editors, *Computer-Aided Verification, CAV '98*, volume 1427 of *Lecture Notes in Computer Science*, pages 516–520, Vancouver, Canada, June 1998. Springer-Verlag.

13. E. A. Emerson and A. P. Sistla, editors. *Computer-Aided Verification, CAV '2000*, volume 1855 of *Lecture Notes in Computer Science*, Chicago, IL, July 2000. Springer-Verlag.

14. J.-C. Filliâtre, S. Owre, H. Rueß, and N. Shankar. ICS: Integrated Canonization and Solving. In G. Berry, H. Comon, and A. Finkel, editors, *Computer-Aided Verification, CAV '2001*, volume 2102 of *Lecture Notes in Computer Science*, pages 246–249, Paris, France, July 2001. Springer-Verlag.

15. Michael J. Fischer, Nancy A. Lynch, and Michael S. Paterson. Impossibility of distributed consensus with one faulty process. *Journal of the ACM*, 32(2):374–382, April 1985.

16. N. Henderson and S. E. Paynter. The formal classification and verification of Simpson's 4-slot asynchronous communication mechanism. In Peter Lindsay, editor, *Formal Methods Europe (FME'02)*, Lecture Notes in Computer Science, Copenhagen, Denmark, July 2002. Springer-Verlag. To appear.

17. T.A. Henzinger, B. Horowitz, and C.M. Kirsch. Giotto: a time-triggered language for embedded programming. In Henzinger and Kirsch [18], pages 166–184.

18. Tom Henzinger and Christoph Kirsch, editors. *EMSOFT 2001: Proceedings of the First Workshop on Embedded Software*, volume 2211 of *Lecture Notes in Computer Science*, Lake Tahoe, CA, October 2001. Springer-Verlag.

19. C. B. Jones. Tentative steps toward a development method for interfering programs. *ACM TOPLAS*, 5(4):596–619, 1983.

20. Shmuel Katz, Pat Lincoln, and John Rushby. Low-overhead time-triggered group membership. In Marios Mavronicolas and Philippas Tsigas, editors, *11th International Workshop on Distributed Algorithms (WDAG '97)*, volume 1320 of *Lecture Notes in Computer Science*, pages 155–169, Saarbrücken Germany, September 1997. Springer-Verlag.

21. Herman Kopetz and R. Nossal. Temporal firewalls in large distributed real-time systems. In *6th IEEE Workshop on Future Trends in Distributed Computing*, pages 310–315, Tunis, Tunisia, October 1997. IEEE Computer Society.

22. Hermann Kopetz. *Real-Time Systems: Design Princples for Distributed Embedded Applications*. The Kluwer International Series in Engineering and Computer Science. Kluwer, Dordrecht, The Netherlands, 1997.

23. Hermann Kopetz. The time-triggered model of computation. In *Real Time Systems Symposium*, Madrid, Spain, December 1998. IEEE Computer Society.

24. Hermann Kopetz. Elementary versus composite interfaces in distributed real-time systems. In *The Fourth International Symposium on Autonomous Decentralized Systems*, Tokyo, Japan, March 1999. IEEE Computer Society.

25. Hermann Kopetz and Günter Grünsteidl. TTP—a protocol for fault-tolerant real-time systems. *IEEE Computer*, 27(1):14–23, January 1994.

26. Hermann Kopetz and Johannes Reisinger. The non-blocking write protocol NBW: A solution to a real-time synchronization problem. In *Real Time Systems Symposium*, pages 131–137, Raleigh-Durham, NC, December 1993. IEEE Computer Society.

27. Sandeep Kulkarni, John Rushby, and N. Shankar. A case study in component-based mechanical verification of fault-tolerant programs. In *ICDCS Workshop on Self-Stabilizing Systems*, pages 33–40, Austin, TX, June 1999. IEEE Computer Society.

28. Sandeep S. Kulkarni. *Component-Based Design of Fault Tolerance*. PhD thesis, The Ohio State University, Columbus, OH, 1999.

29. L. Lamport and P. M. Melliar-Smith. Synchronizing clocks in the presence of faults. *Journal of the ACM*, 32(1):52–78, January 1985.

30. Leslie Lamport, Robert Shostak, and Marshall Pease. The Byzantine Generals problem. *ACM Transactions on Programming Languages and Systems*, 4(3):382–401, July 1982.

31. Nancy A. Lynch. *Distributed Algorithms*. Morgan Kaufmann Series in Data Management Systems. Morgan Kaufmann, San Francisco, CA, 1996.

32. Keith Marzullo. Tolerating failures of continuous-valued sensors. *ACM Transactions on Computer Systems*, 8(4):284–304, November 1990.

33. K. L. McMillan. Circular compositional reasoning about liveness. In Laurence Pierre and Thomas Kropf, editors, *Advances in Hardware Design and Verification: IFIP WG10.5 International Conference on Correct Hardware Design and Verification Methods (CHARME '99)*, volume 1703 of *Lecture Notes in Computer Science*, pages 342–345, Bad Herrenalb, Germany, September 1999. Springer-Verlag.

34. Paul S. Miner. Verification of fault-tolerant clock synchronization systems. NASA Technical Paper 3349, NASA Langley Research Center, Hampton, VA, November 1993.

35. Jayadev Misra and K. Mani Chandy. Proofs of networks of processes. *IEEE Transactions on Software Engineering*, 7(4):417–426, July 1981.

36. Kedar S. Namjoshi and Richard J. Trefler. On the completeness of compositional reasoning. In Emerson and Sistla [13], pages 139–153.

37. Sam Owre, John Rushby, Natarajan Shankar, and Friedrich von Henke. Formal verification for fault-tolerant architectures: Prolegomena to the design of PVS. *IEEE Transactions on Software Engineering*, 21(2):107–125, February 1995.

38. Michael Paulitsch and Wilfried Steiner. The transition from asynchronous to synchronous system operation: An approach for distributed fault-tolerant systems. In *The 22nd International Conference on Distributed Computing Systems (ICDCS 2002)*, Vienna, Austria, July 2002. IEEE Computer Society. To appear.

39. M. Pease, R. Shostak, and L. Lamport. Reaching agreement in the presence of faults. *Journal of the ACM*, 27(2):228–234, April 1980.

40. Holger Pfeifer. Formal verification of the TTA group membership algorithm. In Tommaso Bolognesi and Diego Latella, editors, *Formal Description Techniques and Protocol Specification, Testing and Verification FORTE XIII/PSTV XX 2000*, pages 3–18, Pisa, Italy, October 2000. Kluwer Academic Publishers.

41. Holger Pfeifer, Detlef Schwier, and Friedrich W. von Henke. Formal verification for time-triggered clock synchronization. In Weinstock and Rushby [72], pages 207–226.

42. Stefan Poledna. *Fault-Tolerant Systems: The Problem of Replica Determinism*. The Kluwer International Series in Engineering and Computer Science. Kluwer, Dordrecht, The Netherlands, 1996.

43. John Rushby. The design and verification of secure systems. In *Eighth ACM Symposium on Operating System Principles*, pages 12–21, Asilomar, CA, December 1981. (ACM *Operating Systems Review*, Vol. 15, No. 5).

44. John Rushby. A fault-masking and transient-recovery model for digital flight-control systems. In Jan Vytopil, editor, *Formal Techniques in Real-Time and Fault-Tolerant Systems*, Kluwer International Series in Engineering and Computer Science, chapter 5, pages 109–136. Kluwer, Boston, Dordecht, London, 1993.

45. John Rushby. A formally verified algorithm for clock synchronization under a hybrid fault model. In *Thirteenth ACM Symposium on Principles of Distributed Computing*, pages 304–313, Los Angeles, CA, August 1994. Association for Computing Machinery. Also available as NASA Contractor Report 198289.

46. John Rushby. Automated deduction and formal methods. In Rajeev Alur and Thomas A. Henzinger, editors, *Computer-Aided Verification, CAV '96*, volume 1102 of *Lecture Notes in Computer Science*, pages 169–183, New Brunswick, NJ, July/August 1996. Springer-Verlag.

47. John Rushby. Partitioning for avionics architectures: Requirements, mechanisms, and assurance. NASA Contractor Report CR-1999-209347, NASA Langley Research Center, June 1999. Available at http://www.csl.sri.com/ rushby/abstracts/partition, and http://techreports.larc.nasa.gov/ltrs/PDF/1999/cr/NASA-99-cr209347. pdf; also issued by the FAA.

48. John Rushby. Systematic formal verification for fault-tolerant time-triggered algorithms. *IEEE Transactions on Software Engineering*, 25(5):651–660, September/October 1999.

49. John Rushby. Verification diagrams revisited: Disjunctive invariants for easy verification. In Emerson and Sistla [13], pages 508–520.

50. John Rushby. Bus architectures for safety-critical embedded systems. In Henzinger and Kirsch [18], pages 306–323.

51. John Rushby. A comparison of bus architectures for safety-critical embedded systems. Technical report, Computer Science Laboratory, SRI International, Menlo Park, CA, September 2001. Available at http://www.csl.sri.com/ rushby/ abstracts/buscompare.

52. John Rushby. Formal verification of McMillan's compositional assume-guarantee rule. Technical report, Computer Science Laboratory, SRI International, Menlo Park, CA, September 2001.

53. John Rushby. Formal verification of transmission window timing for the time-triggered architecture. Technical report, Computer Science Laboratory, SRI International, Menlo Park, CA, March 2001.

54. John Rushby. Formal verificaiton of Marzullo's sensor fusion interval. Technical report, Computer Science Laboratory, SRI International, Menlo Park, CA, January 2002.

55. John Rushby and Friedrich von Henke. Formal verification of algorithms for critical systems. *IEEE Transactions on Software Engineering*, 19(1):13–23, January 1993.

56. John Rushby, Friedrich von Henke, and Sam Owre. An introduction to formal specification and verification using EHDM. Technical Report SRI-CSL-91-2, Computer Science Laboratory, SRI International, Menlo Park, CA, February 1991.

57. Hassen Saïdi and Susanne Graf. Construction of abstract state graphs with PVS. In Orna Grumberg, editor, *Computer-Aided Verification, CAV '97*, volume 1254 of *Lecture Notes in Computer Science*, pages 72–83, Haifa, Israel, June 1997. Springer-Verlag.

58. Hassen Saïdi and N. Shankar. Abstract and model check while you prove. In Nicolas Halbwachs and Doron Peled, editors, *Computer-Aided Verification, CAV '99*, volume 1633 of *Lecture Notes in Computer Science*, pages 443–454, Trento, Italy, July 1999. Springer-Verlag.

59. Ulrich Schmid. How to model link failures: A perception-based fault model. In *The International Conference on Dependable Systems and Networks*, pages 57–66, Goteborg, Sweden, July 2001. IEEE Computer Society.

60. Ulrich Schmid and Klaus Schossmaier. How to reconcile fault-tolerant interval intersection with the Lipschitz condition. *Distributed Computing*, 14(2):101–111, May 2001.

61. Fred B. Schneider. Understanding protocols for Byzantine clock synchronization. Technical Report 87-859, Department of Computer Science, Cornell University, Ithaca, NY, August 1987.

62. Fred B. Schneider. Implementing fault-tolerant services using the state machine approach: A tutorial. *ACM Computing Surveys*, 22(4):299–319, December 1990.

63. Marco Schneider. Self stabilization. *ACM Computing Surveys*, 25(1):45–67, March 1993.
64. D. Schwier and F. von Henke. Mechanical verification of clock synchronization algorithms. In *Formal Techniques in Real-Time and Fault-Tolerant Systems*, volume 1486 of *Lecture Notes in Computer Science*, pages 262–271, Lyngby, Denmark, September 1998. Springer-Verlag.
65. Natarajan Shankar. Mechanical verification of a generalized protocol for Byzantine fault-tolerant clock synchronization. In J. Vytopil, editor, *Formal Techniques in Real-Time and Fault-Tolerant Systems*, volume 571 of *Lecture Notes in Computer Science*, pages 217–236, Nijmegen, The Netherlands, January 1992. Springer-Verlag.
66. Natarajan Shankar. Combining theorem proving and model checking through symbolic analysis. In *CONCUR 2000: Concurrency Theory*, number 1877 in Lecture Notes in Computer Science, pages 1–16, State College, PA, August 2000. Springer-Verlag. Available at `ftp://ftp.csl.sri.com/pub/users/shankar/concur2000.ps.gz`.
67. H. R. Simpson. Four-slot fully asynchronous communication mechanism. *IEE Proceedings, Part E: Computers and Digital Techniques*, 137(1):17–30, January 1990.
68. T. K. Srikanth and Sam Toueg. Optimal clock synchronization. *Journal of the ACM*, 34(3):626–645, July 1987.
69. Philip Thambidurai and You-Keun Park. Interactive consistency with multiple failure modes. In *7th Symposium on Reliable Distributed Systems*, pages 93–100, Columbus, OH, October 1988. IEEE Computer Society.
70. Time-Triggered Technology TTTech Computertechnik AG, Vienna, Austria. *Specification of the TTP/C Protocol (version 0.6p0504)*, May 2001.
71. Ashish Tiwari, Harald Rueß, Hassen Saïdi, and N. Shankar. A technique for invariant generation. In T. Margaria and W. Yi, editors, *Tools and Algorithms for the Construction and Analysis of Systems: 7th International Conference, TACAS 2001*, volume 2031 of *Lecture Notes in Computer Science*, pages 113–127, Genova, Italy, April 2001. Springer-Verlag.
72. Charles B. Weinstock and John Rushby, editors. *Dependable Computing for Critical Applications—7*, volume 12 of *Dependable Computing and Fault Tolerant Systems*, San Jose, CA, January 1999. IEEE Computer Society.
73. J. Lundelius Welch and N. Lynch. A new fault-tolerant algorithm for clock synchronization. *Information and Computation*, 77(1):1–36, April 1988.
74. Matthew M. Wilding, David S. Hardin, and David A. Greve. Invariant performance: A statement of task isolation useful for embedded application integration. In Weinstock and Rushby [72], pages 287–300.

Scheduler Modeling
Based on the Controller Synthesis Paradigm

Joseph Sifakis

VERIMAG
2 Av. de Vignate
38610 Gières, France
Joseph.Sifakis@imag.fr

Abstract. The controller synthesis paradigm provides a general framework for scheduling real-time applications. Schedulers can be considered as controllers of the applications; they restrict their behavior so that given scheduling requirements are met.

We study a modeling methodology based on the controller synthesis paradigm. The methodology allows to get a correctly scheduled system from timed models of its processes, in an incremental manner, by application of composability results which simplify schedulability analysis. It consists in restricting successively the system to be scheduled by application of constraints defined from scheduling requirements. The latter are a conjunction of schedulability requirements that express timing properties of the processes and policy requirements about resource management.

The presented methodology allows a unified view of analytic approaches and model-based approaches to scheduling.

W. Damm and E.-R. Olderog (Eds.): FTRTFT 2002, LNCS 2469, p. 107, 2002.
© Springer-Verlag Berlin Heidelberg 2002

Part III

Synthesis and Scheduling

Component-Based Synthesis
of Dependable Embedded Software[*]

Arshad Jhumka, Martin Hiller, and Neeraj Suri

Department of Computer Engineering, Chalmers Univ., Sweden
{arshad,hiller,suri}@ce.chalmers.se

Abstract. Standardized and reusable software (SW) objects (or SW components – in-house or pre-fabricated) are increasingly being used to reduce the cost of software (SW) development. Given that the basic components may not have been developed with dependability as primary driver, these components need to be adapted to deal with errors from their environment. To achieve this, error containment wrappers are added to increase the reliability of the components. In this paper, we first present a modular specification approach using fault intolerant components, based on the concepts of category theory. We further introduce the concept of wrapper consistency, based upon which, we present an algorithm that systematically generates *globally consistent* fault containment wrappers for each component, to make them fault tolerant. Subsequently, we enhance the initial modular specification to deal with the wrapped components, and show that safety properties of the system are preserved under composition only if the wrappers are globally consistent.

1 Introduction and Problem Perspectives

The functionality and dependability of computer systems is increasingly being defined by software (SW). However, to reduce the high cost associated with the development of SW, *components*, for example pre-fabricated or from component repositories, are being used while having to satisfy overall system/SW dependability requirements. Given that these components may not have been developed with dependability as a primary driver, i.e., the components may be fault-intolerant, i.e., they do not tolerate faults that will violate the safety specification, the components may need to be adapted or transformed to be able to contain errors coming from their environment, i.e., made fault tolerant. This can be achieved by wrapping the different components with error containment wrappers [16,8]. Error containment wrappers can be classified into two broad categories, namely detectors and correctors [2]. Intuitively, detectors are used to detect errors, whereas correctors are detectors that correct errors whenever the system state is corrupted.

However, as pointed out in [14], the design of detectors, such as assertion checks[1], for error detection in software is a heuristic process, often with low levels

---

[*] Supported in part by Saab endowment, TFR Grants
[1] We will use the term detector, assertion or wrapper interchangeably

W. Damm and E.-R. Olderog (Eds.): FTRTFT 2002, LNCS 2469, pp. 111–128, 2002.

of efficiency to error coverage. Some conclusions mentioned were: (i) placement of detectors is crucial for them to be effective, (ii) given the randomness of the design process, some detectors detected non-existent errors in the system (so called "false positives"), leading to decreased efficiency of the system, i.e., the state of the system is such that it does not violate the safety specification [1] defined, but is however flagged as erroneous, (iii) specification-based detectors tend to have limited effectiveness, and (iv) specification-based detectors, together with code-based detectors, have a higher effectiveness in detecting errors. In other words, the state of the system is such that it does not violate the safety specification [1] defined, but is flagged as erroneous by the detector wrappers.

For problem (i) cited above, we presented an approach in [9] for locating the relevant detectors (and correctors). For problem (ii) above, in [12], we introduced the concept of *global assertion consistency* to verify global conformance across assertions. We defined global consistency as follows: Given a program P comprising a set of detectors $D = \{d_i\}$ and a safety specification S that P should satisfy, the set D is said to be *globally consistent* if $(P(D) \implies S)$. We also showed that $(P(D) \implies S)$ can be verified using the concept of *abstract interpretation* [3]. In this paper, we will show that the detection of global consistency of assertions is NP complete. Thus, for problems (ii)–(iv) above, in this paper, we develop an algorithm, based on global assertion consistency, that automatically generates consistent assertions, which can then be used to wrap the different components. Overall, the global consistency property ensures that detectors detect only those errors that will lead to safety violation of the program.

Paper Objectives. Further, once components are wrapped with detectors (and correctors), one needs to ascertain that the wrapped components, i.e., fault tolerant components, can still be composed together into a system. We show that fault tolerant wrappers used to wrap one component do not interfere with the functionality and dependability of other components. In this paper, we show that composability of fault tolerant components with globally consistent detectors is indeed preserved, showing the viability of our algorithm. Overall, our contributions in this paper are: (i) We first present a modular specification approach of a system, using concepts from category theory, (ii) We present the concept of global assertion consistency, and show that its detection is NP complete, (iii) Thus, we provide an algorithm that generates globally consistent detectors, and (iv) fault intolerant components are transformed into fault tolerant components by wrapping them with the globally consistent fault containment wrappers, and (v) We enhance our initial specification with wrapper information, and show that the fault tolerant components are composable if the wrappers are globally consistent. We place our contribution more in context towards the end of the paper when we discuss related work in Section 6. Here, we do not address temporal aspects, which is part of our ongoing work.

The paper is structured as follows: Section 2 present the system and fault models adopted in this paper. Section 3 presents an approach to specify and verify a fault intolerant specification, based on the concepts of category theory. In Section 4, we first show that detection of global consistency of detector is intractable, and then present a heuristic to tackle the problem of generating globally consistent detector wrappers. Section 5 extends our initial intolerant specification with detector wrapper constraints, and we identify properties that preserve composability of components. In order to develop a proper context for comparison, we present an overview of related work in Section 6, and we present a discussion of the approach and its applicability in Section 7. We conclude with a summary of the paper in Section 8.

2   System & Fault Models

We make the following system and fault model assumptions:

System model: We assume that software (SW) is made up of different components, communicating with each other through some form of communication, such as message-passing, shared memory etc. We will use the abstract term signal to denote these communication paradigms. We also assume gray-box knowledge of SW, i.e., the internals of the software are known, but are, non-modifiable. Thus, any transformation performed is achieved through the use of wrappers. The choice for reasoning at the gray-box level is three-fold: (i) Maintainability of the original SW is made easier since it is not modified, and "modification" is only through error containment wrappers, (ii) Reuse of fault intolerant SW is easier, and the relevant error containment wrappers can be generated, and (iii) reasoning at a gray-box level allows for modular SW construction, with usage flexibility for single processors or distributed systems.

Fault model: We assume transient data errors occurring at the communication signal level. To detect these errors in embedded systems, where the emphasis is on signal data values, assertions are often incorporated. These specify, for example, range checks, or bounds on rate of change of data values.

Next, we will present a modular specification approach for specifying a component based system, based on the concepts of category theory [6,19].

3   Modular Specification of Embedded Systems

Our modular specification framework is based on the concept of category theory [6]. Category theory allows definition of a calculus of modules, and their respective composition, i.e., module composition. It also allows module specifications and constraints to be reasoned about in the same framework. Specification languages such as Z^2 [20] are not suitable since Z does not really allow hidden interfaces etc. Its object-oriented version, Object-Z [17], could have been used but it does not offer a framework to reason about constraints in natural way, i.e., whether constraints imposed are indeed correct etc. Similarly, formal frameworks such as CSP^3 [10] are restrictive for reasoning about transforming a component into a fault tolerant one.

---

[2] We refer to Z since they represent a class of state-based specification language.

[3] We refer to CSP since they represent a class of event-based specification language

Components are algebraically specified, and they are interconnected to encapsulate their interactions. The composition operation then defines and constructs an aggregated component describing the overall system from the individual components and their interactions. We will first present the specification of basic building blocks of a component, such as *export interface*, and show how they are composed together into a component specification. Components are then composed into a system.

3.1   Specification of Basic Building Blocks

A specification consists of two parts (a) a *signature* part, and (b) an *axiom* part. The signature introduces syntactical elements that are used in the axiom part, and consists of three parts: (a1) the *Sorts* part declares the domains, (a2) the *Constants* (respectively *Variables*) part declares the time independent (respectively time dependent) functions and/or predicates, and (a3) the *Action* part declares predicates and functions representing event instances. The axiom part defines the behavior of the building block, or specification.

In practice, a component is a SW module that imports some services from its environment, and provides some services used by its environment. Formally, a component can be composed of different specifications, such as *import interface, export interface* etc. Each building block is specified algebraically, i.e., each block specification consists of a signature and axiom part. To obtain the overall component, these specifications are combined via specification morphisms.

Specification Morphism: A specification morphism $m : A \to B$ from a specification A to specification B maps any element of the signature of A to an element of the signature of B that is compatible.

3.2   Component Specification from Basic Specifications

Syntax of Component Specifications. An algebraic specification of a component C consists of four basic basic building blocks, namely (i) *parameter* (PAR), (ii) *export* (EXP), (iii) *import* (IMP), and (iv) *body* (BOD). Each building block (specification) is individually specified, and are interconnected through specification morphism, to obtain a component specification. Thus, a component specification is a tuple, *COMP = (PAR,EXP,IMP,BOD,e,s,i,v)*, consisting of 4 specifications and four specification morphisms, e, s, i and v, as shown in Fig. 1.

The BOD part of the component specification is constructed using the *pushout* operation. Specifically, the pushout of two specification morphisms $e : PAR \to EXP$ and $i : PAR \to IMP$ is an object BOD together with morphisms $v : EXP \to BOD$ and $s : IMP \to BOD$ satisfying $v \circ e = s \circ i$ and the following general property: for all objects BOD' and morphisms $s' : IMP \to BOD'$ and $v' : EXP \to BOD'$ with $v' \circ e = s' \circ i$, there is a unique morphism $b : BOD \to BOD'$ such that $v \circ b = v'$ and $s \circ b = s'$. Here, $\circ$ denotes morphism composition.

We briefly explain the role of each specification: (i) The *BODY*(BOD) part is the complete description of the component, i.e., it explains how resources provided by the import part are used to provide the services of the export interface,

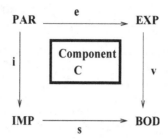

Fig. 1. Component specification with building blocks specification and specification morphisms

i.e., it transforms the services obtained from the environment into services provided to the environment. Given our gray-box approach, the BOD part cannot be modified to transform the component into a fault tolerant one.

The *IMPORT*(IMP), *EXPORT*(EXP), and the *PARAMETER*(PAR) parts are the interfaces of the component. The PAR part contains the parameters of the component, while the IMP (EXP) part defines the services needed (provided) by the component.

The four specification morphisms e, i, s, v of the components describe the links between the four specifications. Also, all items in PAR must have an image in IMP and EXP to ensure correct definition of the morphisms e and i. For example, IMP cannot introduce a type (sort) without the type being introduced in the PAR part of the specification. One important aspect of specification morphisms is that they preserve axioms. For example, one must prove that the axioms defined in the export interface can be deduced from those defined in the body specification. Thus, verification of a given component can be performed.

Semantics of Component Specification. For a given component specification $COMP = (PAR,EXP,IMP,BOD,e,s,i,v)$, the specification morphisms are interpreted as *functors* (in the reverse direction), which are functions from one category to another, i.e., they map objects onto objects and morphisms onto morphisms. More specifically, they are called *forgetful* functors since they forget those resources that are not in the image of the specification morphism, i.e., for a given specification morphism $m : SPEC \rightarrow SPEC_1$, the forgetful functor corresponding to m is given by $V_m : Cat(SPEC_1) \rightarrow Cat(SPEC)$. In pratice, this means that hidden operations and hidden data domains are forgotten, i.e., not part of the export.

On the other hand, the body (BOD) specification is interpreted according to the *functorial semantics*, since it represents the construction of the export interface from the import interface. The functorial semantics is the composition of a free functor (from import algebra to body algebra) and a forgetful functor (from body algebra to export algebra). This means that, with the functorial semantics, we allow free construction of the services to be exported with hidden data domains and hidden operations omitted from the export interface. We also have the *restriction semantics*, which is the composition of the unrestricted semantics

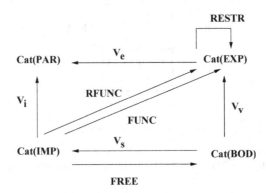

Fig. 2. Semantics of morphisms

with a restriction construction of the export with respect to the parameter part. The other specifications, i.e., PAR, IMP and EXP, have a loose interpretation, in the sense that any algebra that satisfies the specification is admissible.

Formally, from the component specification, we define a *construction semantics* of *COMP*, *FREE* as follows: $FREE : Cat(IMP) \rightarrow Cat(BOD)$ with respect to the forgetful functor $V_s : Cat(BOD) \rightarrow Cat(IMP)$. Thus, the functorial semantics of *COMP* is the functor $FUNC : Cat(IMP) \rightarrow Cat(EXP)$ which constructs for each import algebra A a corresponding export algebra B such that $B = FUNC(A)$. This construction is mainly a free construction $FREE(A)$ defined by sorts, actions and axioms in the BOD part of the component specification. The functorial semantics is a composition of the free functor and the forgetful functor with respect to the v morphism, i.e., $FUNC = V_v \circ FREE$, Fig. 2.

Thus, the meaning of a component specification is thus given as a functor which maps import algebras I to export algebras *FUNC(I)*.

Definition of component correctness:

Let $COMP = (PAR, EXP, IMP, BOD, e, s, i, v)$ be a component specification. *COMP* is said to be correct if the free functor *FREE* is strongly persistent, i.e., $ID = V_s \circ FREE$, where ID is the identity functor on *Cat(IMP)* and *FREE* preserves injectivity of homomorphisms. This just ensures that each import algebra I is protected by the free construction, i.e., $V_s \circ FREE(A) = A$.

3.3   System Specification from Components

Having specified and verified a given component, these components can now be composed together through component morphisms to obtain the complete system specification. Given two components C_i (a component importing services) and C_e (a component exporting the services required) such that all elements imported by C_i are exported (defined) by C_e, the composition operation builds a component C_{ie}. A module morphism is a pair (h, hp), see Fig. 3, of morphisms

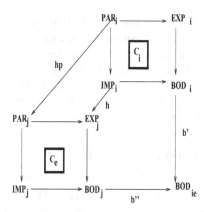

Fig. 3. Composing two components

such that h associates services imported by C_i to corresponding services exported by C_e. Morphism hp maps parameters of C_i to those of C_e. The component C_{ie} can then be computed from components C_i and C_e, i.e., it imports what component C_e imports, exports what component C_i exports, and can be computed from the pushout operation. If components C_i and C_e and morphisms h and hp are correctly defined, then component C_{ie} is correct. Also, during composition, the following should be verified: $h \circ i_i = e_e \circ hp$, where i_i is morphism i in component C_i, and e_e is morphism e in component C_e. This ensures that the associations made by hp is compatible with those defined in h.

System verification is performed as follows: any axiom in a given component C_i is translated along a given component morphism as theorem in the C_e component, i.e., one needs to ascertain that the behavior of C_i is preserved.

Also, correctness of the resulting composition C_{ie} can be derived from the correctness of C_i and C_e (using the notion of strong persistency).

Different components needed to construct the overall system are composed together, as has been shown. Given such a system specification *SPEC*, a corresponding implementation P satisfying the *SPEC* can be obtained through techniques such as refinement, which then obviates the need for verification. Given the free construction allowed, any body implementation that transforms the import services into the export services is allowed. Also, given the transitivity property of refinement and the fact that P refines *SPEC*, our framework is still valid if we reason at a lower level of abstraction, i.e., at the level of P. Thus, depending on the level of implementation detail incorporated in the specification, we can reason at different levels of abstraction within the same framework.

4   Addition of Error Containment Wrappers

The system specification provided is for a fault intolerant system, i.e., though the behavior of the system has been verified, the behavior may be violated in faulty scenarios. Hence, there is a need to add fault tolerance components to the original system, i.e., adding error containment wrappers around components.

Adding error containment wrappers around components is inherently difficult, as indicated in [14] and Section 1. We previously [12] showed that the consistency property of assertions help in designing effective detectors. For completeness, we will present a brief overview of the consistency property, as well as the proof of intractability of its detection.

4.1 Consistency Property of Assertions

An assertion EA_i in a program P defines a set of values, $S(EA_i)$, that a given variable V_i can take. Two EAs placed in a given SW system are linked to each other via code implementing a given function F_m (in subsequent discussion, we will use P to denote the relevant function F_m).

Definition 1. EA_1 and EA_2 are said to be consistent with each other *iff* $F_m(S(EA_1)) = S(EA_2)$. They are inconsistent *iff* $F_m(S(EA_1)) \cap S(EA_2) = \{\}$. They are partially consistent *iff* they are neither consistent nor inconsistent.

Thus, a predicate $cons(A_i, A_j, P)$ is true iff A_i and A_j are consistent through P(through the relevant F_m). A set of assertions $S_A = \{A_i\}$ defined in a program P is said to be globally consistent iff, $\forall i, j : cons(A_i, A_j, P)$.

Intuitively, the global consistency property states that any valid data value should not be flagged as erroneous by any of the assertions in the system. The converse is also true. Verification of consistency property can be achieved using techniques such as abstract interpretation. Given that safety specification is defined, we want to detect those states that can potentially lead to violation of the safety specification, i.e., the set of detectors, including the safety specification, should be globally consistent. The safety specification is considered as a global property defined on the system to be satisfied. However, detection of the consistency among a set of detectors is intractable. Thus, we present a heuristic, analogous to predicate transformers [4], that generates consistent detectors.

4.2 NP Completeness of Global Consistency Detection

Before presenting the heuristic, we will briefly present the proof of NP completeness of global consistency detection.

A program P consists of a set of components, $P = \{C_1 \ldots C_N\}$. Each component C_i has a set V_i of variables defined in it. A global safety property of a system is a boolean valued function B defined over the variables in $V = \bigcup_i V_i$ of the system. We define a set $L = \{L_1 \ldots L_N\}$ of detectors placed in individual components, defined over the set V of variables. We use the notation $B(L)$ to indicate the value of predicate B in a system with $L = \{L_1 \ldots L_N\}$.

Global consistency detection of wrappers (GLOB) is a decision problem. It takes the form of:

Given: Program P, global safety property B, a set of system variables V.
Determine: if there exists a set L of wrappers L_i's defined over V such that $L \cup B$ is globally consistent through P.

Claim: *GLOB is NP-complete*

Proof: First note that the problem is in NP. A verifier for the problem takes as inputs the program P, the set L of wrappers and the global property B and then verifies if the set $L \cup B$ is globally consistent. This can be done in polynomial time. Then detecting the global consistency of wrappers belongs to the set NP.

We show NP-completeness of a simplified consistency detection where all variables in V can take value "true" or "false". Assume there is only one wrapper L_i incorporated in C_i. We reduce the satisfiability problem of a boolean expression to GLOB by constructing an appropriate set of wrappers.

The set is constructed as follows: Choose an $L_i \in L$ such that $L_i =$ "false" and include a new variable $v_j \in V$ such that L_i is now "true". It is easily verified that the predicate B is true for some set L *if and only if* the global safety property is satisfiable.

4.3   Heuristic to Generate Globally Consistent Error Containment Wrappers

Given the intractability of global consistency detection, we present a heuristic that generates globally consistent wrappers. It works in a way analogous to predicate transformers. Given our access to the code (which cannot be modified), the heuristic perform a backtracking process.

We first present the main steps of the algorithm in more details, and then the implementation details:

S 1,2 The algorithm starts at the end of the sink module and backtracks to its start. Then, the process is iterated for every component.

S 3 All conditions for computing the different values of variables are calculated. Program slicing [18] techniques can be utilized for this.

S 4 Once all conditions for computing the different variables are obtained, they are substituted in the condition for computing the output signal. For example, suppose we have an output signal X and the condition for computing its value is $X := Y + 1$. Suppose that the condition for computing Y is $Y := Z + 2$, where Z is the input. Then, the new condition for X is $X := Z + 2 + 1 = X := Z + 3$.

S 5 This condition for computing the output signal is substituted in the postcondition defined on the output signal (say X), and by simplifying the constraint obtained, we can obtain a constraint defined on the input signal (say Z). This constraint will be the input detector wrapper in the given component (C_i).

S 6 This precondition is translated into the postcondition of the preceding component (C_e). Formally, we translate this precondition along morphism h to obtain the postcondition on the preceding component.

S 7+ Steps 1–6 are iterated until the source modules are reached, and constraints on system inputs obtained.

```
Derive_EA(<global_property_EA>, <module_name>,
          <module_interconnections>)
%global_property_EA is the safety specification defined
%on the system. In any round of execution, the safety spec
%is satisfied, i.e., is an invariant. Thus, the global_property_EA
%is considered as a postcondition on the output signal of the
%system, i.e., at the end of a round of execution.
1  while (NOT beginning of <module_name>)
   {
2    for (all variables V in <module_name>)
3      conditions(V) :=
       determine_from_module(<module_name>);
%Conditions for computing variable V
%determined from module
   }
4    conditions(<OutputSignal>):=
       get_all_conditions(<module_name>);
%All conditions for computing output signal

5    new_preconditions :=
output_EA[conditions(OutputSignal)/OutputSignal];
%new preconditions obtained by substituting
%output signal by the condition obtained. This is the input
%detector wrapper for the importing component.

6    postcond_preceding_module
                 := new_preconditions;
%preconditions translated as postconditions
%in preceding module. This is the output detector wrapper
%for the exporting component.
7    preceding_module :=
get_id_preceding_module(module_interconnections,
                 module_name);
%gets the id of the other module with which
%module_name is communicating

8    if (preceding_module == NIL) break;
%source module reached
9    Derive_EA(postcond_preceding_module,
             preceding_module,
             module_interconnections);
```

Overall, pre- and postconditions (input and output wrappers) are generated for each component upon backtracking. When a component C_i imports services exported by another component C_e, the precondition defined in C_i is transformed into a postcondition in C_e. Formally, the input wrapper in C_i is translated along morphism h (see before) into an output wrapper in C_e.

One potential limitation of the above algorithm is the handling of loop constructs among components, or within a component. There are techniques that can be used, such as *instrumented semantics* [7]. Techniques used for determining weakest preconditions [4] can also be used here. In the worst case, EA's which are not fully consistent may be obtained. Determining the applicability of partially consistent EA's is an avenue for future work.

4.4   Proof of Correctness of the Algorithm

Having presented the algorithm, we now present an informal proof of correctness, i.e., that the algorithm will return EAs that are consistent with each other. We make use of three lemmas for the proof.

As inputs to the algorithm, we have the global EA monitoring the output signals. We also know the input signals to the modules. States of programs can only be changed through assignment statements, however, the changes depend on the state of the program at that point, i.e., there can be multiple data paths linking the input signals and output signals, and the data path taken is determined by the state at that time. In the proof, we denote the output signal as $OutputSignal$ and F_M denotes the function implemented by a given module M.

Lemma 1 *Along any data path taken, there exists at least one assignment of the form OutputSignal := F(...) for the output signal to have updated data.*

Proof of Lemma 1: If there is no assignment where $OutputSignal$ is the target destination, then it will only contain its initialization data value or a constant value. Hence, for it to have updated data, the assignment $F(...)$ should be a function of some other variables, i.e., $F()$ should hold the conditions (variables) used to compute the $OutputSignal$.

Lemma 2 *The values held by the variables determining the value of* OutputSignal *should either be input signal data values or result from applying a function on the input signals.*

Proof of Lemma 2 If the variables which determine the data value of $Output$-$Signal$ does not hold input signal data values (or values that depend on input signal data values), it implies that $OutputSignal$ does not depend on the input signals. This is inconsistent with having input signals going into that module.

Using the two lemmas, we can deduce that $OutputSignal$ can be expressed as a function (F_M) of the input signals. Hence, in the EA monitoring $OutputSignal$, we can substitute $OutputSignal$ by the function executing on the input signals. Thus, for a global EA of the form $(a < OutputSignal < b)$ we replace $OutputSignal$ by $F_M(inputsignals)$, resulting in $(a < F_M(inputsignals) < b)$. This expression can be simplified as appropriate. Thus, preconditions monitoring the input signals are obtained. From Lemma 1 and 2, we show that the algorithm does generate preconditions from output signals specification.

Lemma 3 *The preconditions are consistent with the global EA.*

Proof of Lemma 3 From the above, the precondition is as follows:
$(a < F_M(inputsignals) < b)$. Executing F_M on the input signals will result in $OutputSignal$, hence $(a < OutputSignal < b)$, which is the global EA. Thus, the precondition and postcondition will be consistent.

Lemmas 1, 2 and 3 constitute the overall proof of correctness of the algorithm.

5   Specification of Fault Tolerant Embedded Systems

Initially, we have provided a modular specification of a fault intolerant embedded system, and explained how verification can be performed. To add fault tolerant components to the system, error containment wrappers are added to the components, given our focus on gray-box components. Since detection of globally consistent wrappers is intractable, we have proposed a heuristic that can generate globally consistent wrappers, starting from a given safety specification, i.e., the heuristic generate wrappers that are consistent with the safety specification. In subsequent sections, we show (i) how to enhance our specification with the wrapper information, i.e., constraints provided by the wrappers, and (ii) that the consistency condition on wrappers allows the fault tolerant components to be composed together. Wrappers can be added both at the input and output of a component for fault tolerance.

5.1   Addition of Detector Wrappers to Basic Specifications

Once input and output wrappers are obtained, it implies that there are constraints imposed on the components. Input wrappers constrain the values allowed by the imported functions, while output wrappers constrain the data values outputted. These constraints formulate requirements for interface data types, which may not be expressed in equational logic (as in the axiom part of the specification). Given our focus on gray-box components, we allow these constraints to be defined only at the interface level, not in the body specification. This allows for the reuse of the free construction of the equational case for corresponding specifications with constraints, except that we restrict the free constructions to those interface algebras that satisfy the given constraints.

Given (input and output) wrappers W of constraints over a component C, which is a free construction, we define $SPECW = (SPEC, W)$, as a specification with constraints. A $SPECW$-algebra is a usual $SPEC$-algebra that satisfies all constraints defined in W. Given the constraints, we include one more part to a specification, namely a *constraints* part, in addition to the *variables, axioms* and *sorts* parts already defined in the specification. We enhance each basic specifications with the constraints part that define the imposed data requirements, i.e., we wrap both import and export interfaces with relevant wrappers.

5.2   Building Fault Tolerant Components
from Fault Tolerant Building Blocks

Up to now, we have generated wrappers (constraints) on a given specification. However, given that input constraints in an importing component C_i are translated as output constraints for an exporting component C_e, and output constraints into input constraints in a given component, this translates into the ability to reason about translation of constraints along specification morphism.

Semantically, we make use of a *Constraints* functor, $Constraints : CatSpec \rightarrow Sets$, that associates a set of constraints with each specification, where $CatSpec$

is the category of specifications. This functor also maps every morphism m : $SPEC1 \to SPEC2$ onto a function $Constraints(m) : Constraints(SPEC1) \to Constraints(SPEC2)$ which assigns to every constraint $C \in Constraints$ $(SPEC1)$ on $SPEC1$ the translated constraint $Constraint(m)(C)$, denoted $m'(C)$, defined on $SPEC2$. Intuitively, this means that any constraint defined over the import interface is translated into a given constraint over the export interface of a given component. In other words, input constraints defined on a component are transformed into output constraints for the same component.

Given wrapped specifications $SPECW_1 = (SPEC_1, W_1)$, and $SPECW_2 = (SPEC_2, W_2)$, a specification morphism m from $SPECW_1$ to $SPECW_2$, denoted $m : SPECW_1 \to SPECW_2$, is called *consistent* if W_2 implies the translated constraints $m'(W_1)$, i.e., $W_2 \implies m'(W_1)$. Intuitively, it means that the predicate $cons(W_1, W_2, BOD)$ (defined in Sec. 4.1) evaluates to true under the consistency condition of morphisms, and where BOD represents the component implementation. Note that for consistency condition, we do not require $W_2 \cup A_2 \implies m'(W_1)$, where A_2 is the set of axioms for $SPEC_2$, because since we define W_2 on the specification, rather than on signatures, any algebra satisfying W_2 is already a $SPEC_2$ algebra satisfying A_2.

At this point, we need to show that the wrappers generated by our heuristic satisfy the consistent specification morphism condition.

Lemma 4: The specification morphisms of a given component are consistent.

We want to prove that the specifications, enhanced with the constraints imposed by the wrappers, yield consistent specification morphisms. To prove the above, we need to prove that $COMPW = (PARC, EXPC, IMPC, BOD, e, s, i, v)$ is correct. A given component with wrappers, $COMPW$, is *correct* if it satisfies:

1. $COMPW$ is constraints preserving, i.e., for all IMP-algebras I with $I \models CI$, we have $FUNC(I) \models CE$
2. $COMPW$ is strongly persistent with respect to the import constraints CI, i.e., $FREE_s$ is strongly persistent on all IMP-algebras I where $I \models CI$
3. $e : (PAR, CP) \to (EXP, CE)$ and $i : (PAR, CP) \to (IMP, CI)$ are consistent.

The first part amounts to proving that for every $I \models CI$, then $(I \models CI) \implies (V_f(I) \models CE)$, where $f : EXPC \to IMPC$. Given our definition of global consistency, input constraints are translated into output constraints. Thus, the component is constraint preserving.

For the second part, it is easy to see that $COMPW$ is indeed strongly persistent, i.e., the free construction, starting from an import algebra $I \models CI$, protects the algebra. Since we adopt a gray-box approach, we reuse the original free construction. So, if the original construction was strongly persistent, so is the construction with constraints.

For the third part, consistency of morphisms e and i means only that the constraints part of PAR, CP, are reflected in the constraints part of the export and import interface, CE and CI.

Theorem: If $COMPW$ is correct, then all specification morphisms e, s, i, v are consistent.

Proof: Consistency of morphisms e, i is proven by part (3) of the conditions for component correctness.

Consistency of morphism v is proven by part (1) of the correctness condition. Consistency of morphism s is based upon how induced constraints on the body part, BOD, of the component are obtained. In fact, given that we allow free construction, we do not allow any constraints in the BOD part of the component. However, given that there are constraints imposed on the import and export interface (CI, and CE), these translate into induced body constraints. Thus, $CB = s'(CI) \cup v'(CE)$. This ensures that morphism s is consistent. Note that $s' = Constraints(s)$ and $v' = Constraints(v)$, i.e., the *Constraints* functor applied to the morphisms.

It follows that the described approach of transforming a component into a fault tolerant one satisfies the consistency condition on morphisms.

Theorem: *The category of specifications with constraints and consistent specification morphisms has pushouts.*

The proof of the above theorem is direct and can be found in [6], and can be built in a similar way to that of the specification without constraints.

Thus, a component specification with constraints,
$COMPW = (PARC,EXPC,IMPC,BOD,e,s,i,v)$, consists of three specifications with constraints, namely PARC, EXPC, and IMPC where PARC = (PAR,CP), EXPC = (EXP,CE), and IMPC = (IMP,CI), a specification without constraints, namely BOD, and four specification morphisms. However, given that constraints are translated along morphisms, there is a set of constraints, CB, induced on BOD, and is given by $CB = s'(CI) \cup v'(CE)$. In [12], the induced constraints are called *annotations*. Given that we used abstract interpretation for global consistency verification, that builds an abstract context for each variable and that each abstract context is derived from constraints imposed on the import interface (by wrappers), these abstract contexts, denoted as annotations, are the induced constraints on the BOD part of the specification.

Thus, from the above theorem, the wrappers generated using the heuristic (that preserves consistency of wrappers) allow for component specification.

5.3   Fault Tolerant System Synthesis
from Fault Tolerant Components

Having discussed the construction of components with wrappers, we now look at how to construct a system from components with wrappers, i.e., components with constraints. We will keep the same approach as for the initial case of no constraints, but we will identify requirements that allow for composition of such components with wrappers.

Given two components with constraints, $COMPW_i$ and $COMPW_e$, and a a component morphism $cm : COMPW_i \to COMPW_e$, i.e., a pair $cm = (h, hp)$ of specification morphisms where $hp : (PAR_i, CP_i) \to (PAR_e, CP_e)$ and $h : (IMP_i, CI_i) \to (EXP_e, CE_e)$, the composition $COMPW_3$ of $COMPW_i$ and

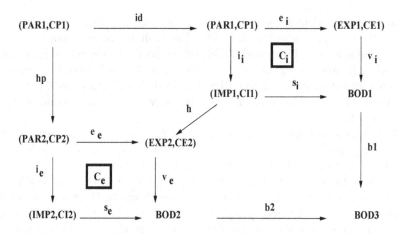

Fig. 4. Module specification from fault tolerant components

$COMPW_e$ via cm, written $COMPW_3 = COMPW_i \circ_{cm} COMPC_e$ is given as in Fig. 4.

The component morphism $cm = (h, hp)$ is called *consistent* if h and hp are consistent specification morphisms. If the morphisms h and hp are not consistent, then correctness and composability is not guaranteed.

Lemma 5: Morphism h is consistent.

Proof: Given that we translate input constraints W_i in an importing component C_i into output constraints W_e on an exporting component C_e, then $h'(W_i) = W_e$, which satisfies the condition for consistent morphism.

Lemma 6: Morphism hp is consistent

Proof: Components C_i and C_e to be composed have consistent specification morphisms. Given that during composition, $e_e \circ hp = h \circ i_i$, and from lemma 1, we get that morphism hp is consistent, where e_e, i_i means the e, i morphism of the exporting (C_e) and importing (C_i) components respectively.

Claim: The wrappers generated by the heuristic preserve the composition of the wrapped components.

Proof: The proof follows naturally from the previous two lemmas.

Given that input and output wrappers within a component are consistent (via consistent specification morphisms) and that the consistency of wrappers are preserved across different components (via consistent component morphisms), the set of wrappers in the system is called globally consistent.

6 Related Work

An approach to transform a fault intolerant system into a fault tolerant one has been presented in [13]. They represented a program as a state machine, and they proceeded to identify those transitions that may violate a given safety specification (invariant), according to the level of fault tolerance needed (i.e., fault masking, fail safe etc). Their work differs from ours in the sense that they assume white box software. In this paper, we assume gray-box software, i.e., knowledge of the component implementation is known, but is however non-modifiable. Such components may be obtained from repositories, which for maintenance reasons, are not modified.

[15] presents an transformational method for specifying and verifying fault tolerant, real time programs. The set of transitions possible in a given intolerant program is increased with faulty transitions. The authors used the concept of refinement for obtaining fault tolerant programs, and they provided different refinement conditions for fault tolerance verification. However, the authors reasoned at a white-box level, as opposed to our gray-box level approach here.

Work in [14] showed that design of detectors (assertion checks) is difficult. We have shown that detection of globally consistent detectors is NP complete, thus explaining the observation made. We further provided a heuristic that effectively tackled the problem of generation of globally consistent wrappers.

[5,19] showed usage of category theory in system specification. Our initial intolerant specification is similar to their approaches. However, work in this paper differs from theirs in many respect, namely: (i) we showed how wrappers can be automatically generated, (ii)identified consistency properties of morphisms that preserve composability.

Formal methods such as Z [20] present analogous approaches of verifying consistency of assertions, by verifying whether an output assertion is consistent with an input assertion. In Z, postconditions are always verified against preconditions. Using category theory, we have looked at a calculus of components, however we believe that a calculus of schemas, as in Z, would retain most of the properties mentioned here. However, the assertions may not be globally consistent. Invariants are defined, which need to be preserved by operations. However, their suitability is rarely assessed, giving rise to defensive programming style. CSP [10] though allows hiding during composition, but is however not suitable for our purpose here. We referred to Z and CSP here as they are representative of a class of state-based and event-based formal methods.

Finally, we mention work in [16,8] that advocates the use of wrappers for adding fault tolerance.

7   Discussion

In this section, we provide a general discussion on the heuristic and consistency of wrappers generated, and on the applicability of the approach in general.

As mentioned in the introduction, it may be the case that fault intolerant components are available, which have been formally verified. However, given the level of dependability required in embedded systems, wrappers are needed to transform these fault intolerant components into fault tolerant ones. The heuristic eases generation of wrappers that maintains composability of the components.

Thus, generation of such wrappers can be automated, such as with the use of compilers. Also, given that we reuse the same free construction by not allowing constraints being imposed on the construction of the export services, verification need not be performed over again. Given the consistency condition imposed, and that the component is correct by construction, this implies that the morphisms are consistent and that the corresponding component with wrappers is correct by construction.

We also note that the global consistency property of wrappers allow for compositional verification, which is useful in software maintenance. Initially, we mentioned that to verify such a specification, axioms in one component are translated into theorems or lemmas along component morphisms in another component. However, if a component is modified for software maintenance, the whole proof procedure needs to be re run, to ascertain correctness. This means that one free construction is chosen over another free construction. However, having consistent wrappers, hence consistent morphisms, any subsequent verification remains local, i.e., we only need to ensure that the input and output wrappers of that given component are still consistent, i.e., the change in the component preserves consistency of the specification morphisms. Given that the module morphisms are still consistent, we do not have to do a whole proof procedure again for correctness verification.

Our approach can also be automated, by incorporating the heuristic in a compiler. After the first pass of performing syntax analysis, the heuristic can be run as a second pass, whereby wrappers are generated. Also, tools such as Moka [19] can be enhanced and used to automate the consistency check.

One potential limitation, in addition to having loops, may be that the wrappers generated may be cumbersome. However, we argue that with the level of dependability and performance needed in safety-critical systems, generation and use of such wrappers is justified, especially with the fact that their generation can be automated.

8   Summary and Conclusions

In this paper, we have explained the concept of global consistency of detectors. We have shown that its detection is intractable, and we have provided a heuristic, analogous to predicate transformers, that generate globally consistent wrappers (detectors). We have first specified a fault intolerant system, and explained its subsequent verification. Then, using our heuristic, we have generated a set of fault tolerance components, i.e., detector wrappers in the form of assertions, we have shown how to systematically transform a given fault intolerant specification into a fault tolerant one. We have also shown that having globally consistent wrappers do preserve composability of components.

Earlier, we pointed out a limitation of our heuristic, which is that, due to loop structures within and among components, consistent wrappers may not be obtained. In such cases, we endeavor to take advantage of the fact that, for consistency, we require $W_2 \implies m'(W_1)$, and not the stronger $W_2 = m'(W_1)$

condition, as in this paper. Thus, as future work, we will look into generating wrappers that are consistent in the more general case, as mentioned above.

References

1. B. Alpern, F.B. Schneider, "Defining Liveness", *Information Processing Letters, 21(4):181–185, 1985*
2. A. Arora, S. Kulkarni, "Detectors and Correctors: A Theory of Fault-Tolerance Components", *Proc ICDCS*, pp 436–443, May 1998.
3. P. Cousot, R. Cousot, "Static Determination of Dynamic Properties of Programs", *Int. Symposium on Programming*, 1976
4. E.W. Dijkstra, "A Discipline of Programming", *Prentice Hall*, 1976
5. M. Doche et al, "A Modular Approach to Specify and Test an Electrical Flight Control System", *4th Intl. Workshop on Formal Methods for Industrial Critical Systems*, 1999
6. H. Ehrig, B. Mahr, "Fundamentals of Algebraic Specification 2: Modules Specifications and Constraints", *EATCS Monographs on Theoretical Computer Science*, Vol. 21, Springer Verlag, 1989
7. A. Ermedahl, J. Gustafsson, "Deriving Annotations For Tight Calculation of Execution Time", *Proc EuroPar'97, RT System Workshop*
8. T. Fraser et al, "Hardening cots software with generic software wrappers", *IEEE Symposium on Security and Privacy, pp. 2–16*, 1999
9. M. Hiller, A. Jhumka, N. Suri, "An Approach for Analysing the Propagation of Data Errors in Software", *Proc. DSN'01, pp. 161-170, 2001*
10. C. A. R. Hoare, "Communicating Sequential Processes", *Prentice Hall*, 1985
11. T. Jensen et al, "Verification of Control Flow Based Security Properties", *Proc. IEEE Symp.on Security and Privacy, pp. 89–103, 1999*
12. A. Jhumka, M. Hiller, V. Claesson, N. Suri, "On Systematic Design of Consistent Executable Assertions For Distributed Embedded Software", *to Appear ACM LCTES/SCOPES, 2002*
13. S. Kulkarni, A. Arora, "Automating the Addition of Fault Tolerance", *Proc. Formal Techniques in Real Time and Fault Tolerant Systems, pp. 82–93, 2000*
14. N.G. Leveson et al, "The use of self checks and voting in software error detection: An empirical study.", *IEEE Trans. on Soft. Eng., 16:432–443, 1990*
15. Z. Liu, M. Joseph, "Verification of Fault-Tolerance and Real-Time", *Proc. FTCS 1996, pp220-229.*
16. F. Salles et al, "Metakernels and fault containment wrappers", *Proc. FTCS*, pp. 22–29, 1998
17. G. Smith, "The Object-Z Specification Language. Advances in Formal Methods", *Kluwer Academic Publishers*, 2000
18. F. Tip, "A Survey of Program Slicing Techniques," *Journal Prog. Languages, Vol.3, No.3, pp.121–189*, Sept. 95
19. V. Wiels, "Modularite pour la conception et la validation formelles de systemes", *PhD thesis, ENSAE - ONERA/CERT/DERI*, Oct 97
20. J. Woodcock, J. Davies, "Using Z: Specification, Refinement, and Proof", *Prentice Hall*, 1996

From the Specification to the Scheduling of Time-Dependent Systems

Christophe Lohr and Jean-Pierre Courtiat

LAAS – CNRS, 7 avenue du Colonel Roche 31077 Toulouse Cedex, France
{lohr,courtiat}@laas.fr

Abstract. This paper introduces and formalizes a new variant of Timed Automata, called Time Labeled Scheduling Automata. A Time Labeled Scheduling Automaton is a single clock implementation model expressing globally the time constraints that a system has to meet. An algorithm is presented to show how a Time Labeled Scheduling Automaton can be synthesized from a minimal reachability graph derived from a high-level specification expressing the composition of different time constraints. It is shown how the reachability graph may be corrected before synthesizing the Time Labeled Scheduling Automaton to remove all its potentially inconsistent behaviors. Current applications of the model are the scheduling of interactive multimedia documents and a simple illustration is given in this area.

Keywords: Process Algebra, RT-Lotos, Timed Automata, Minimal Reachability Graph, Temporal Consistency, Time Labeled Scheduling Automata

1 Introduction

Starting from a high-level specification of a time-dependent system that explicitly expresses a composition of time constraints, our purpose is to derive an operational specification of that system based on a new temporal model, called a Time Labeled Scheduling Automaton (TLSA) for scheduling.

The TLSA model has been designed within the framework of the RT-Lotos project at LAAS-CNRS, and the associated tools have been integrated within the rtl (RT-Lotos Laboratory) tool environment. It is assumed that the system high-level specification is written in RT-Lotos [8], but results are also applicable to other formalisms that can express composition of time constraints, like timed automata [3], temporal extensions of Petri nets [17] and process algebra [11].

The main purpose of the paper is to introduce the TLSA model and to show how a TLSA can be synthesized from a (minimal) reachability graph expressing the global behavior of a specification. A TLSA is a variant of classical timed automata intended to express *globally* the time constraints that a system has to meet. It is *not* a specification model, but rather an operational implementation model using a single clock.

Performing the synthesis of a TLSA from a reachability graph presents a major advantage: it allows to take into account the results of the reachability graph

W. Damm and E.-R. Olderog (Eds.): FTRTFT 2002, LNCS 2469, pp. 129–145, 2002.

analysis at the level of the TLSA synthesis. Thus, when the verification process has detected that a reachability graph features inconsistent behaviors (a behavior is said to be *inconsistent* if it leads to a *deadlock state*, i.e. a state where no transition is enabled), it is easy to eliminate these inconsistencies from the reachability graph just by removing the paths leading to the deadlock states, and then to generate the TLSA from the corrected reachability graph. Thus, a consistent operational model of the system may be obtained without having to modify the high-level specification. This approach has been completely automated, and it has proven to be very powerful for the design and scheduling of interactive multimedia presentations [13,14,15]. It will be illustrated in the next paragraph on a simple example.

The paper is organized as follows: Section 2 provides the intuition of the TLSA model and its use, based on an example derived from the multimedia area. Section 3 formalizes the Timed Labeled Scheduling Automaton model and Section 4 proposes an algorithm to derive a TLSA from a (minimal) reachability graph. Finally, Section 5 reviews some current work in this area, and Section 6 draws some conclusions.

2   Intuition through an Example

This example deals with the specification and scheduling of interactive multimedia documents. Within this framework, a formal method is used to describe the temporal constraints characterizing both the presentation of the media composing a document and the interactions with the user, as well as the global synchronization constraints among media defined by the author of the document. The formal specification, derived from the high-level authoring model, consists essentially in a composition of simple (RT-Lotos) processes describing elementary time constraints. Reachability analysis is then performed on the formal specification to check the temporal consistency of the specification. Different variations of this temporal consistency property have been defined, depending on whether the actions leading to potential deadlock states are controllable or not (see [15,16] for details).

Consider the example depicted in Fig. 1a. The author of this multimedia scenario wishes to present three media called A, B and C respectively. The presentation durations of these media are respectively defined by the following time intervals: [3,6], [3,5] and [3,8]. This means that, for example, the presentation of media A should last at least 3 seconds and 6 seconds at the most. Thus, from the author's perspective, any value belonging to the time interval is acceptable.

Moreover, the author expresses the following synchronization constraints:

1. the presentation of media A and B should end simultaneously;
2. the presentation of media B and C should start simultaneously;
3. the start of this multimedia scenario is determined by the start of A, and its end is determined either by the end of A and B, or by the end of C.

The RT-Lotos specification is presented in Fig. 1b, and the associated (minimal) reachability graph obtained with the rtl tool is presented in Fig. 2a.

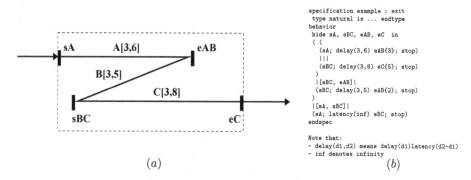

```
specification example : exit
  type natural is ... endtype
behavior
  hide sA, sBC, eAB, eC in
  ( (
      (sA; delay(3,6) eAB{3}; stop)
      |||
      (sBC; delay(3,8) eC{5}; stop)
    )
    |[sBC, eAB]|
    (sBC; delay(3,5) eAB{2}; stop)
  )
  |[sA, sBC]|
  (sA; latency(inf) sBC; stop)
endspec

Note that:
- delay(d1,d2) means delay(d1)latency(d2-d1)
- inf denotes infinity
```

(a) (b)

Fig. 1. (a) Multimedia scenario and (b) RT-Lotos specification

The minimal reachability graph allows the temporal consistency of the multimedia scenario to be analyzed. The scenario is said to be *potentially consistent*, if there exists at least one path starting with i(sA) (action i(sA) characterizes the start of medium A presentation, hence the start of the scenario presentation) and leading to the end of the scenario presentation (either the occurrence of actions i(eC) or i(eAB)). Looking at Fig. 2a, the scenario is indeed potentially consistent.

Analyzing the high-level requirements, one may note that the start of the presentation of B and C has been left completely unspecified regarding the start of A. On such a simple example, it is easy to realize that if the start of media B and C is triggered too late with respect to the start of A, some time constraints will never be met (for instance, the constraint that A and B should finish simultaneously). This characterizes potentially inconsistent behaviors in the presentation of the multimedia scenario, which are represented in the reachability graph by the paths starting from the initial state and leading to deadlock states (see, for instance, state denoted *4-(inf 3)* at the bottom of Fig. 2a).

Deadlock states are not desirable and therefore, one wants to eliminate them by removing from the reachability graph all the paths starting from the initial state and leading to these deadlock states. Deadlock states are states without outgoing edges, which are not final states. Edges leading to those deadlock states and nowhere elsewhere are called inconsistent paths and removed. By removing all the inconsistent paths from the reachability graph (see Fig. 3a) we ensure the scheduling of a consistent scenario applying the concept of controllability, that is, proposing a valid temporal interval inside which the scenario is consistent [13,14].

Fig. 2b represents the TLSA derived from the reachability graph of Fig. 2a, following the algorithm presented in Section 4. This TLSA cannot be used as a basis for scheduling the multimedia scenario, since it features the same inconsistent behaviors as its associated reachability graph. For example, let us assume the behavior where actions i(sA), i(sBC), i(eC) occur respectively at times $t_0 = 0$, $t_1 = 5$ and $t_2 = 6$, leading the scenario in state 4 of Fig. 2b. It can be note that, in this state, there is no transition enabled, since the two enabling

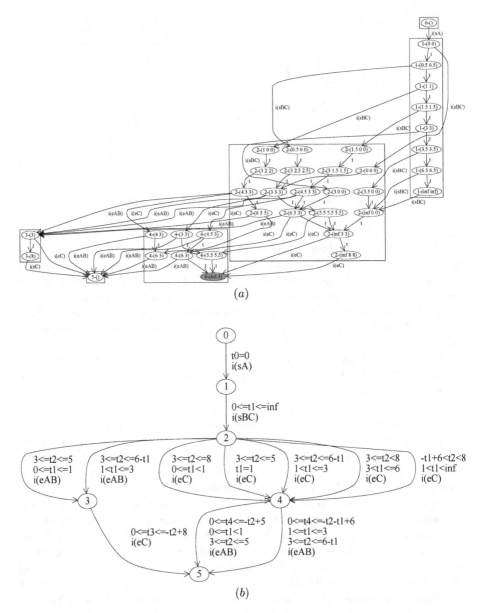

Fig. 2. (a) Minimal Reachability Graph and (b) associated TLSA

conditions (see the formal semantics of the TLSA in the next paragraph) feature either $0 \leqslant t_1 < 1$ or $1 \leqslant t_1 \leqslant 3$ whereas $t_1 = 5$.

Fig. 3b represents the TLSA derived from the reachability graph of Fig. 3a. This TLSA allows implementation of a consistent scheduling of the multimedia scenario, where the presentation of media B and C should begin no later than 3

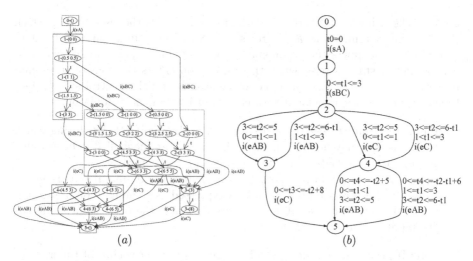

Fig. 3. (a) Consistent Minimal Reachability Graph and (b) associated TLSA

seconds after the beginning of A (see firing condition $0 \leqslant t_1 \leqslant 3$ defined for the transition between states 1 and 2). This information appears explicitly at the level of a transition of the TLSA, whereas it is hidden in the state characterization of the reachability graph.

Therefore, the proposed approach consists in the three following steps:

1. using RT-Lotos for expressing a composition of time constraints,
2. deriving the reachability graph of the RT-Lotos specification and removing all its inconsistent behaviors to obtain a *consistent* reachability graph,
3. performing the synthesis of the TLSA from the consistent reachability graph.

The TLSA may then be used for scheduling purposes, in the sense that it is an implementation model that defines when actions should occur to meet the initial composition of time constraints.

Semantics of the TLSA model will be presented in Section 3 and the algorithm for deriving a TLSA from a reachability graph will be described in Section 4.

3 Time Labeled Scheduling Automata

3.1 Introduction

Timed automata [3] have been proposed to model finite-state real-time systems. A timed automaton has a finite set of control states and a finite number of clocks. All clocks proceed at the same rate and measure the amount of time that has elapsed since they were started or reset. Each transition of the system might reset some of the clocks, and features an associated enabling condition expressed as a constraint on the values of the clocks.

A TLSA enjoys some specific features that differentiate it from classical timed automata. A TLSA has as many clocks as there are control states in the automaton these clocks being called `timers`. Each timer measures the time during which the automaton remains in a control state. No explicit function is defined to determine when timers should be started or reset. Indeed, the timer associated with a control state is reset when the automaton enters the control state, and its current value is frozen when the automaton leaves the control state[1]. Two timed conditions are associated with each transition of the automaton:

1. the *firing window* (denoted W) that defines the temporal slot during which the transition may be fired. It takes the form of an inequality to be satisfied by the timer associated with the transition input control state.
2. the *enabling condition* (denoted K) that defines the temporal constraints to be satisfied to fire the transition. It is expressed as a conjunction of inequalities to be satisfied by a subset of timers excluding the timer associated with the input control state of the transition.

Note: W, the temporal firing window, relates only to the current timer. Intuitively, W expresses the time during which the system is allowed to stay in the current control state. Note also that K, the enabling condition, relates only to past timers and expresses which transitions are enabled with respect to the past behavior of the system.

3.2 Formal Definition of a Time Labeled Scheduling Automaton

Let L be a set of action labels. Let $D = \{t \in \mathbb{Q} \mid t > 0\}$ the time domain, $D_0 = D \cup \{0\}$ and $D_0^\infty = D_0 \cup \{\infty\}$.

Let $\perp$ denote the "undefined" value, and $D_{0\perp} = D_0 \cup \{\perp\}$. By definition, we state that $\perp + \delta = \perp$, $\perp - \delta = \perp$ for any $\delta \in D_0^\infty$.

Let $T_{set} = \{t_i \mid i \in [0, n-1]\}$ be a set of *timers*, with $t_i \in D_{0\perp}$. Within this context, a timed condition is a conjunction of inequalities of the form $m \prec t_i \prec M$ where m, M are linear expressions of constants (in D_0^∞) *and timers* t_j $(t_j \in T_{set}, j \neq i)$ and $\prec \in \{<, \leqslant\}$.

Let $\mu = (\mu^0, \ldots, \mu^{n-1}) \in D_{0\perp}^n$ be the value of timers t_i with $i \in [0, n-1]$, and $\mathcal{K}$ a timed condition defined on a subset of timers t_i. Notation $\mu \vDash \mathcal{K}$ indicates that all inequalities of $\mathcal{K}$ are *true* when replacing timers t_i by their values μ^i.

Definition 1 (Time Labeled Scheduling Automaton).
A Time Labeled Scheduling Automaton is a 3-tuple (S, E, s_0) where:

- *$S = \{s_0, \ldots, s_{n-1}\}$ is a finite set of control states;*
- *E is a finite set of transitions of the form (s_i, s_j, W, K, a), where $s_i, s_j \in S$ are the source and destination control states of the transition, W and K are timed conditions, $a \in L$ is a labeling action*
- *s_0 is the initial control state.*

---

[1] For this reason, we said previously that a TLSA is a single clock model, since, in any control state, there is one and only one running timer.

The *firing window* W of a transition (s_i, s_j, W, K, a) is a timed condition defined as an inequality of the form $m \prec t_i \prec M$ where m, M are linear expressions of constants and timers t_k ($t_k \in T_{set}$, $k \neq i$). If either m or M is equal to $\perp$ when replacing timers t_k by their value μ^k, then we assume $\mu \not\models W$.

The *enabling condition* K of a transition (s_i, s_j, W, K, a) is a timed condition defined as a conjunction of inequalities of the form $\mathcal{I}_k = (m \prec t_k \prec M)$, where $k \neq i$, and m, M are linear expressions of constants and timers t_l ($t_l \in T_{set}$, $l \neq k$ and $l \neq i$). If t_k is equal to $\perp$, then we assume $\mu \models \mathcal{I}_k$; furthermore, if either m or M is equal to $\perp$ when replacing timers t_l by their value μ^l, then we assume $\mu \models \mathcal{I}_k$.

These rules are illustrated in Fig. 4.

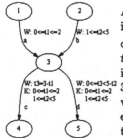

Assuming that we are in control state 1, transition $1 \xrightarrow{a} 3$ is fired inside temporal window $0 <= t_1 <= 2$. Coming from control state 1, transition $3 \xrightarrow{d} 5$ is not enabled, because $t_2 = \perp$ and then W is false (see the definition of the firing window). Looking at enabling condition K of transition $3 \xrightarrow{c} 4$, the first inequality is satisfied ($0 <= t_1 <= 2$), as well as the second one, since $t_2 = \perp$ (see the definition of the enabling condition). Transition $3 \xrightarrow{c} 4$ will then be fired at time $t_3 = 3 - t_1$.

Fig. 4. Illustrations of the firing rules

A labeled transition system $LTS(TLSA)$ is associated with each time labeled automaton $TLSA$. A state (s, μ) of $LTS(TLSA)$, also called a configuration, is fully described by specifying the control state s of $TLSA$ and the value $\mu \in D_{0\perp}^n$ of all timers of the automaton. The transitions of $LTS(TLSA)$ correspond either to explicit transitions of $TLSA$, representing the occurrence of an action, or to implicit transitions representing the passage of time. The former are described by the transition successor rule and the latter by the time successor rule.

Definition 2 (Initial state of *LTS(TLSA)*).
The initial state of $LTS(TLSA)$ is the configuration (s_0, μ_0), where $\mu_0 \in D_{0\perp}^n$ with $\mu_0 = (0, \perp, \ldots, \perp)$.

Definition 3 (Explicit transition of *LTS(TLSA)*).
Let $(s, \mu) \in LTS(TLSA)$ and $(s, s', W, K, a) \in E$ a transition of TLSA. If $\mu \models W$ and $\mu \models K$, then $(s, \mu) \xrightarrow{a} (s', F(s, s', \mu))$.
where $F : S \times S \times D_{0\perp}^n \to D_{0\perp}^n$ is the function[2] defined as:

$$F(s_i, s_j, \mu) = \mu' \quad where \quad \begin{cases} \mu'^j = 0 \\ \mu'^k = \perp \quad \forall k \neq i \mid (s_k, s_j, W, K, a) \in E \\ \mu'^l = \mu^l \quad \forall l \in [0, n-1], l \neq j, l \neq k \end{cases}$$

---

[2] In the example of Fig. 4, while firing transition $1 \xrightarrow{a} 3$, timer t_2 is re-initialized with $\perp$ by function F.

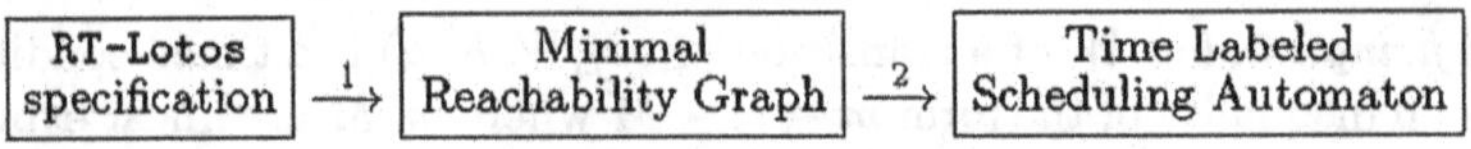

RT-Lotos specification	$\xrightarrow{\;1\;}$	Minimal Reachability Graph	$\xrightarrow{\;2\;}$	Time Labeled Scheduling Automaton

Fig. 5. Derivation of the TLSA

The role of function F is to avoid possible firing history conflicts in cyclic TLSA. In the presence of cycles and in the absence of function F, an action fired in a previous iteration around the cycle but not belonging to the current flow of execution, could influence the future conditions W and K.

Definition 4 (Implicit transition of *LTS(TLSA)*).

Let $(s, \mu) \in LTS(TLSA)$ and $\delta \in D$. If $act(s, G(s, \mu, \delta))$, then $(s, \mu) \xrightarrow{\delta} (s, G(s, \mu, \delta))$.

where $G : S \times D_{0\perp}^n \times D \to D_{0\perp}^n$ is the function defined as:

$$G(s_i, \mu, \delta) = \mu' \quad where \quad \begin{cases} \mu'^i = \mu^i + \delta \\ \mu'^k = \mu^k \quad \forall k \neq i \in [0, n-1] \end{cases}$$

and where $act : S \times D_{0\perp}^n \to \{true, false\}$ is the predicate that indicates whether there is, for configuration (s_i, μ), at least one enabled transition (s_i, s_j, W, K, a) (i.e. a transition satisfying both its firing window and its enabling condition), thus authorizing a temporal progression. This predicate is defined as:

$$act(s_i, \mu) = \bigvee_{\forall (s_i, s_j, W, K, a) \in E} (\mu \vDash W) \wedge (\mu \vDash K)$$

4   An Algorithm to Synthesize a TLSA

In this section, we develop an algorithm to synthesize a TLSA from a minimal reachability graph, itself derived from a RT-Lotos specification.

As illustrated in Fig. 5, the first sub-section summarizes the main steps of the RT-Lotos reachability analysis. The second sub-section details the algorithm which has been implemented in the rg2tlsa module integrated within the rtl tool.

4.1   RT-Lotos Reachability Analysis

RT-Lotos is one of the temporal extensions of the standard Lotos formal description technique. A detailed description of RT-Lotos is provided in [8].

RT-Lotos provides three main temporal operators, namely: the *delay* - see construct *delay(d)*, the *latency* operator - see construct *latency(l)* and the *time restrictor* operator - see construct $a\{t\}$.

As detailed in [7], the reachability analysis of RT-Lotos specifications is carried out as follows: An RT-Lotos specification is first translated into a DTA - Dynamic Timed Automaton; reachability analysis is then applied to the DTA

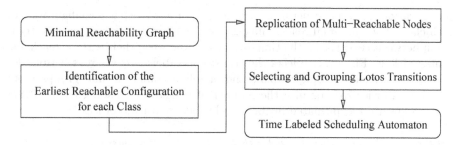

Fig. 6. Overview of the algorithm

relying on a minimization algorithm [18] that generates a minimal reachability graph, which describes the global behavior of the RT-Lotos specification.

A global state or *configuration* of a timed system includes the control state of the timed automaton (the DTA), and the clocks values. Therefore, the number of configurations is not finite. A finite analysis of such a system requires a partition of the configuration space into a finite number of regions. Algorithms to perform reachability analysis, and to minimize timed transition systems were proposed in [2,18]. The second algorithm has been adapted to DTA and implemented in the rtl tool. The resulting graph is a *minimal reachability* graph where:

- a *node* (also called a *class*) defines both a control state, and a region represented as a convex polyhedron whose dimension is equal to the number of clocks of the control state; configurations belonging to the same region have the same reachability properties since they cannot be differentiated in terms of future actions that may occur; hence, a class corresponds to a finite representation of an infinite number of configurations (s, ν).
- an *arc* corresponds either to a Lotos action occurrence or to a time progression (arc labeled by t).

Due to the minimization algorithm, all configurations of a class are not necessarily reachable from the initial configuration; it can be proven that at least one configuration per class is actually reachable [18]. The minimization algorithm allows regions larger than those required from a strict reachability point of view to be considered, minimizing thereby, the number of regions within a graph, compared to other algorithms such as [6].

The formal definition of a minimal reachability graph and the way it may be derived from a DTA are presented in [7].

4.2   TLSA Synthesis Algorithm

The input of the TLSA synthesis algorithm is a minimal reachability graph. Three main steps are defined in the algorithm in order to produce a TLSA (see Fig. 6).

The algorithm will first process each transition of the minimal reachability graph (labeled either by t or a Lotos action). It starts from the initial reachable configuration (s_0, ν_0) in order to determine the earliest reachable configuration of each class of the minimal reachability graph. Then, it determines for each transition between two classes, the time progression between their earliest reachable configurations. Finally, it selects the transitions labeled by a Lotos action, defines their associated firing window and enabling condition, and groups them together in order to minimize the number of transitions, leading to the TLSA. These steps are recapitulated in the pseudo-code algorithm of Fig. 7.

Set the clocks of the earliest reachable configuration of initial class to 0.
For each transition of the minimal reachability graph do:
> *Evaluate the earliest reachable configuration of the reached class.*
> *Set the temporal valuation of the transition with the time elapsed from the earliest reachable configuration of the starting class until the earliest reachable configuration of the reached class.*
> *Add this temporal valuation to the history of the transitions leaving the reached class.*
End loop.
For each Lotos transition do:
> *Set firing window W with the temporal valuation of the transition plus the valuations of the temporal transitions fired into the current control state.*
> *Set enabling condition K according to the history of the transition.*
End loop
Extract Lotos transitions and rename nodes with the number of their control state.
Group transitions according to W and K.

Fig. 7. Steps of the algorithm

4.2.1 Identification of the Earliest Reachable Configuration for Each Class

Let $DTA = (S, Nclock, E, s_0)$ be a dynamic timed automaton and $RG = LTS(DTA/\pi')$ its associated minimal reachability graph derived from an RT-Lotos specification (see [7] for details).

Definition 5 (Earliest reachable configuration within a class).
This is a recursive definition. Let A, B be classes of RG, S_0 the initial class of RG $((s_0, \nu_0) \in S_0)$, and transition $A \to B \in RG$.

- (s_0, ν_0) *is the earliest reachable configuration of class S_0.*
- *Let $(s, \nu) \in A$ be the earliest reachable configuration of class A, where values of ν are expressed as linear expressions of constants (defined in D_0^∞) and timers (whose values are defined in $D_{0\perp}$):*
  - *if $A \xrightarrow{t} B$, then:*
    Let δ_m be the minimal time value such that $(s, \nu + \delta_m) \in B$; δ_m is expressed as linear expressions of constants and timers. Then, $(s, \nu + \delta_m)$ is reachable and it is, furthermore, the earliest reachable configuration of class B. δ_m is called the temporal valuation of the t transition. Note that, in this case, classes A and B are associated with the same DTA state, namely control state s.

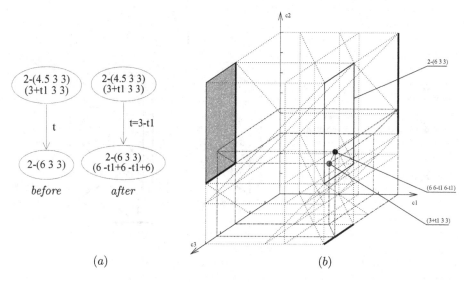

Fig. 8. Processing a t transition

- *if $A \xrightarrow{a} B$, then:*
  *Let $(s, s', K, U, a, C, \theta)$ a transition of the DTA, where s' is the control
  state of B. Let δ_M be the maximal time value such that $(s, \nu + \delta_M) \in A$;
  δ_M is expressed as linear expressions of constants and timers; note that
  if A is urgent then $\delta_M = 0$. Let δ be the time spent within all the classes
  associated with control state s before reaching the earliest configuration
  of class A. Let timer t_s be defined as: $\delta \leqslant t_s \leqslant \delta + \delta_M$. Then $(s', \nu') \in B$
  is the earliest reachable configuration of class B, where $\nu'^i = 0 \quad \forall i \in C$,
  and $\nu'^i = \nu^{\theta^{-1}(i)} + t_s - \delta \quad \forall i \in [1, Nclock(s')], i \notin C$.*

Intuitively the earliest reachable configuration of a class of RG may be defined
as the first configuration of the class that the system may reach (starting from
the initial configuration of the system) before any time progression within the
class.

The following paragraphs detail the TLSA synthesis algorithm based on examples coming from the Minimal Reachability Graph depicted in figure 3a.

- *Processing t Transitions*

Let $a = (s, (\nu_a^1, \ldots, \nu_a^N))$ be the earliest reachable configuration of class A,
with $N = Nclock(s)$; for example, as depicted in Fig. 8a, $a = (2, (3 + t1, 3, 3))$
and $A = 2 - (4.5\ 3\ 3)$.

A t transition from A to B means that there is a time progression to reach
class B. Let $b = (s, (\nu_b^1, \ldots, \nu_b^N))$ be the earliest reachable configuration of
class B. Configuration b can be defined by determining the *minimal value* δ_m,
such that $\nu_b = (\nu_a^1 + \delta_m, \ldots, \nu_a^N + \delta_m)$ belongs to the region of class B (i.e.

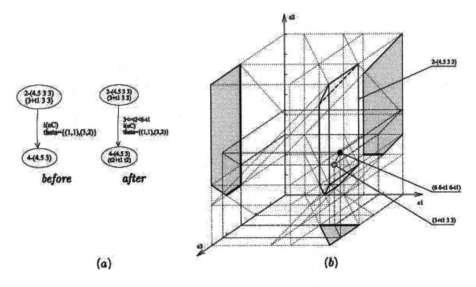

Fig. 9. Processing a Lotos transition

it satisfies the system of inequations bounding this region). For instance, the region of class $B = 2 - (6\ 3\ 3)$ is bounded by

$$\begin{cases} c_1 = 6 \\ 3 \leqslant c_2 < 8 \\ 3 \leqslant c_3 < 5 \\ -3 \leqslant c_2 - c_1 < 2 \\ -3 \leqslant c_3 - c_1 < -1 \\ -5 < c_3 - c_2 < 2 \end{cases}$$

With $\quad \begin{cases} c_1 = \nu_b{}^1 = 3 + t1 + \delta_m \\ c_2 = \nu_b{}^2 = 3 + \delta_m \\ c_3 = \nu_b{}^3 = 3 + \delta_m \end{cases} \quad$ the solution is $\quad \delta_m = 3 - t1$

Thus, the earliest reachable configuration of class B is $b = (2, (6, 6 - t1, 6 - t1),$ and the temporal valuation of transition $A \xrightarrow{t} B$ is equal to $3 - t1$.

- *Processing Lotos Transitions*

Let $a = (s, (\nu_a{}^1, \ldots, \nu_a{}^N))$ be the earliest reachable configuration of class A, with $N = Nclock(s)$; for example, in Fig. 9a, $a = (2, (3 + t1, 3, 3))$ and $A = 2 - (4.5\ 3\ 3)$. A Lotos transition from A to B means that time may progress within class A (unless A is an urgent class) before reaching class B by the occurrence of a Lotos action. Therefore, we are looking for the *maximal value* of δ_M, such that $(\nu_a{}^1 + \delta_M, \ldots, \nu_a{}^N + \delta_M)$ belongs to the region of class A. In the example, this region is bounded by

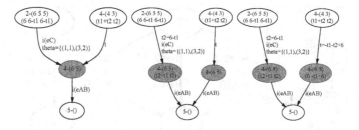

Fig. 10. Replicating a node

$$\begin{cases} 4 < c1 < 6 \\ 3 \leqslant c_2 < 8 \\ 3 \leqslant c_3 < 5 \\ -3 < c_2 - c_1 < 2 \\ -3 < c_3 - c_1 < -1 \\ -5 < c_3 - c_2 < 2 \end{cases}$$

With $\begin{cases} c_1 = 3 + t1 + \delta_M \\ c_2 = 3 + \delta_M \\ c_3 = 3 + \delta_M \end{cases}$ the solution is $\delta_M \stackrel{\leq}{=} 3 - t1$

which means that δ_M is the maximal value less than $3 - t1$.

In our example, the system has to fire two t transitions between classes associated with control state 2 before reaching class A; then $\delta = (3 - t1) + (t1) = 3$, which characterizes the time spent in all the classes associated with control state 2 before reaching class A.

Therefore, the Lotos action can be fired in class A after a progression of time t_s comprised between δ and $\delta + \delta_M$.

In the example, the system can stay $3 \leqslant t2 < 3 - t1$ units of time in the classes associated with control state 2 before firing action i(eC). This defines the *firing window* of this transition.

When the system leaves class A, the values of clocks are:

$$\begin{cases} c1 = \nu_a{}^1 + t_s - \delta \\ \vdots \\ cN = \nu_a{}^N + t_s - \delta \end{cases}$$

By applying functions C (clocks reset) and θ (copy of clocks values) (see the formal definition of the DTA in [7]) of this transition, we obtain the earliest reachable configuration of class B. In our example, the earliest reachable configuration of class $4 - (4.5\ 3)$ is: $(4, (t2 + t1, t2))$.

4.2.2 Replication of Multi-reachable Nodes

Some classes (such as $4 - (6\ 5)$ in Fig. 10) are reachable by two or more transitions. In these cases, the algorithm may determine distinct earliest reachable

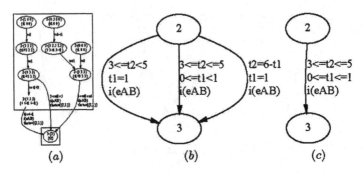

Fig. 11. Selecting and grouping Lotos transitions

configurations. As a consequence, the minimal reachability graph nodes associated with these classes must be replicated as many times as there are distinct earliest reachable configurations; outgoing transitions are replicated as well.

This case appears in particular in the presence of cycles: for each class concerned with a cycle, the algorithm finds a first earliest reachable configuration at the first iteration, then it finds a second one, corresponding to the following iterations, which may include timers affected during the cycle.

4.2.3 Selecting and Grouping Lotos Transitions

Finally, in order to produce the TLSA, the algorithm selects the Lotos transitions. It adds to these transitions their respective *firing window* and *enabling condition*. The firing window has been defined previously, and the enabling condition corresponds to the firing window's history of the Lotos transitions that lead to the class where the current transition is enabled.

The nodes of the TLSA are named according to the corresponding control state of the DTA, as it is illustrated in the transformation of Fig. 11a to Fig. 11b.

At this point, the algorithm has already produced a TLSA, although some transitions may still be redundant regarding firing windows and enabling conditions. The algorithm will then try to group together transitions having the same input and output control state and the same label. Space defined by the new *firing window* and *enabling condition* is the convex hull of polyhedra defined by the set of the *firing window* and *enabling condition* of each transition to be grouped[3]. For instance, the three transitions of Fig. 11b can be grouped together in the single transition on Fig. 11c.

5   Related Works

A certain number of work propose new types of temporal automata to express clearly the temporal relations between events.

---

[3] The vector of the current timer have only two coefficients equal to 1 and −1 in order to get a pair of inequalities - current timer superior to a constraint and current timer inferior to a constraint - which define W.

In [10], I. Kang and I.Lee employ the notion of time distance between transitions to propose a reachability algorithm. This seems to be close to how our timed conditions are expressed. However, these relations do not appear in their resulting graph, whereas the transition firing windows are explicit in the TLSA and they may themselves depend on the instants at which previous transitions were fired.

A TLSA may also be compared to event-recording-clock automata [4]. However, a TLSA does not record time of events, but instead, the time elapsed in control states. Furthermore, timed constraints compare values to linear expressions including values of other timers, and not just constants.

The problem of synthesizing scheduling automata is also the subject of several studies.

By constraining the specification of certain types of temporal constraints known as *implementable*, an algorithm to synthesize schedulers is proposed in [9]. Our approach does not make any assumption on the nature of the specified temporal constraints, the inconsistent behaviors being explicitly removed before the synthesis of the TLSA.

Another approach, proposed initially in [5] then extended in [12], aims to restrict the transition relation of temporal automata, based on a real time game, so that the resulting behaviors satisfy certain properties. Our approach is different, in the sense that the non-desirable inconsistent behaviors are removed at the level of the reachability graph. Thus, our approach is completely automatic, although it is necessary that the system knows in advance the set of all configuration classes.

Finally, in [1] the authors propose a method to build a scheduler satisfying a set of temporal constraints as well as a policy for scheduling. In the opposite, the only goal of our approach is to synthesize a temporal automata (TLSA) characterizing the set of the consistent behaviors of our high level specification expressed in RT-Lotos. However, the policy for scheduling to be applied is not described on the level of the TLSA, but on the level of the application that implement it (for example a browser for a multimedia document [15]).

6   Conclusion

We have introduced the TLSA model as an operational model intended to express globally time constraints that a system has to meet. Also an algorithm designed to synthesize a TLSA from a minimal reachability graph (derived from an RT-Lotos specification) has been described.

A TLSA expresses desirable consistent behaviors when it is synthesized from a minimal reachability graph from which all inconsistent paths (those leading to a deadlock configuration) have been removed. It describes in a simple way how to schedule events because there is one and only one running timer at a moment. Firing conditions of a transition are easy to compute: when the system enters a control state, the bounds of conditions W and K of all outgoing edges can immediately be evaluated by substitution of variables and simple arithmetic operations. So, as time progresses, the current timer has just to be compared to some constant values. Thus, the TLSA ensure the scheduling of consistent scenario applying the concept of controllability.

Works on the verification analysis and scheduling of multimedia documents based on the TLSA have been developed in [15]. In this sense, all the inconsistent behaviors of a document can be detected and removed and, further on, the scheduling of a consistent document can be accomplished by means of the concept of controllability, that is proposing a valid temporal interval inside which the scenario is always consistent. Fur this purpose, a TLSA Player was developed.

References

1. K. Altisen, G. Gossler, and J. Sifakis. A methodology for the construction of scheduled systems. In *FTRTFT 2000*, volume 1926 of *Lecture Notes in Computer Science*, pages 106–120, Pune, India, September 2000.
2. R. Alur, C. Courcoubetis, and N. Halbwachs. Minimization of timed transition systems. In *CONCUR'92*, volume 630 of *Lecture Notes in Computer Science*. Springer Verlag, 1992.
3. R. Alur and D. Dill. The theory of timed automata. In *REX Workshop "Real-Time: Theory in Practice"*, volume 600 of *Lecture Notes in Computer Science*. Springer Verlag, 1991.
4. R. Alur, L. Fix, and T.A. Heizinger. Event-clock automata : A determinizable class of timed automata. In 6th *Annual Conference on Computeraided Verification*, Lecture Notes in Computer Science 818, pages 1–13. Springer Verlag, 1994.
5. E. Asarin, O. Maler, and A. Pnueli. Symbolic controller synthesis for discrete and timed systems. In *Hybrid Systems*, pages 1–20, 1994.
6. B. Berthomieu and M. Diaz. Modeling and verification of time-dependent systems using time Petri nets. In *IEEE Transactions on Software Engineering*, volume 17. $n°3$, 1991.
7. J.P. Courtiat and R.C. R. de Oliveira. A reachability analysis of RT-Lotos specifications. In 8th *International Conference on Formal Description Techniques*, Montreal, Canada, October 1995. Chapman&Hall.
8. J.P Courtiat, C.A.S. Santos, C. Lohr, and B. Outtaj. Experience with RT-Lotos, a temporal extension of the Lotos formal description technique. *Computer Communications*, 23:1104–1123, 2000.
9. H. Dierks. Synthesising controllers from real-time specifications. In *Tenth International Symposium on System Synthesis*, pages 126–133. IEEE Computer Society, September 1997.
10. I. Kang and I. Lee. An efficient state space generation for analysis of real-time systems. In *International Symposium on Software Testing and Analysis*, pages 4–13, 1996.
11. X. Nicollin and J. Sifakis. An overview and synthesis on timed process algebras. In *REX Workshop "Real-Time: Theory in Practice"*, volume 600 of *Lecture Notes in Computer Science*. Springer Verlag, 1991.
12. A. Pnueli, E. Asarin, O. Maler, and J. Sifakis. Controller synthesis for timed automata. In *System Structure and Control*. Elsevier Science, 1998.

13. P.N.M. Sampaio and J.P. Courtiat. A formal approach for the presentation of interactive multimedia documents. In *ACM Multimedia'2000*, pages 435–438, Los Angeles, USA, October 2000.

14. P.N.M. Sampaio and J.P. Courtiat. Scheduling and presenting interactive multimedia documents. In *International Conference on Multimedia and Exposition'2001*, pages 1227–1227, Tokyo, Japan, August 2001.

15. P.N.M Sampaio, C. Lohr, and J.P. Courtiat. An integrated environment for the presentation of consistent SMIL 2.0 documents. In *ACM Symposium on Document Engineering*, Atlanta, Georgia, USA, November 2001.

16. C.A.S. Santos, P.N.M. Sampaio, and J.P. Courtiat. Revisiting the concept of hypermedia document consistency. In *ACM Multimedia'99*, Orlando, USA, November 1999.

17. P. Sénac, M. Diaz, A. Leger, and P. de Saqui-Sannes. Modelling logical and temporal synchronization in hypermedia systems. In *IEEE Journal on Selected Areas in Communications*, volume 14(1), pages 84–103, January 1996.

18. M. Yannakakis and D. Lee. An efficient algorithm for minimizing real-time transition systems. In *CAV'93*, volume 697 of *Lecture Notes in Computer Science*. Springer Verlag, 1993.

On Control
with Bounded Computational Resources[*]

Oded Maler[1], Bruce H. Krogh[2], and Moez Mahfoudh[1]

[1] VERIMAG
Centre Equation, 2, av. de Vignate
38610 Gières, France
Oded.Maler@imag.fr
[2] Dept. of Electrical and Computer Engineering
Carnegie Mellon University, 5000 Forbes Avenue
Pittsburgh, PA 15213-3890 USA
krogh@ece.cmu.edu

Abstract. We propose models that capture the influence of computation on the performance of computer-controlled systems, and make it possible to employ computational considerations in early stages of the design process of such systems. The problem of whether it is possible to meet performance requirements given resource constraints is phrased as a problem of synthesizing switching controllers for hybrid automata, for which we give algorithms that in some cases are guaranteed to terminate and in others can solve the problem in an approximate manner.

1 Background

In this work we build models that capture the influence of computational resources on the performance of computer-controlled systems. Such models allow one to employ computational considerations in early stages of the design process of control systems. We view computation as an essential resource for achieving high-quality control, a resource that in certain situations may become a bottleneck in the system. As a first step toward dealing explicitly with the interaction between control performance and the allocation of computational resources, we consider in this paper the problem of scheduling feedback computations on a single computer controlling multiple independent processes. Notwithstanding some anomalies, we may assume that the quality of control improves monotonically with the amount of computation invested (both on-line and off-line) in the control loop, as the following examples show:

[*] This work was partially supported by the EC projects IST-2001-33520 CC (Control and Computation) and IST-2001-35302 AMETIST (Advanced Methods for Timed Systems), the US Defense Advance Projects Research Agency (DARPA) contract no. F33615-00-C-1701, US Army Research Office (ARO) contract no. DAAD19-01-1-0485, and the US National Science Foundation (NSF) contract no. CCR-0121547.

W. Damm and E.-R. Olderog (Eds.): FTRTFT 2002, LNCS 2469, pp. 147–162, 2002.

1. *Sampling rates.* Usually the quality of control improves with the frequency of the basic loop (sample input, compute feedback function and output) and it approaches the ideal continuous model as the sampling rate goes to infinity. Naturally, the amount of computational effort in a digital control implementation is proportional to the sampling rate which specifies, roughly, the number of times the feedback function is evaluated in any time interval.
2. *Alternative feedback function.* In certain situations, one may choose between several feedback functions whose complexity increases with their quality. For example, in model-predictive control, where the feedback function is computed using an optimization procedure over a bounded horizon, longer decision horizons increase the dimensionality of the optimization problem and hence its complexity.
3. *Control under noise.* In order to cope with noisy measurements, sophisticated filtering and state-estimation algorithms need to be applied. These functions can be implemented using dedicated hardware or, alternatively, using the same computer that does the feedback computations. In that case they compete with these computations for the "attention" of the computer.
4. *Dynamic Identification.* When the dynamics of the controlled plant is unknown or drifting, costly identification and re-calibration algorithms should be applied occasionally in order to update the control law.

In an ideal world of unlimited computational resources[1] (which is where classical control theory evolved, at least its theoretical foundation) one could use as complex control scheme as needed to achieve a desired quality of control. However, in any digital implementation only a *bounded amount of computation* can be performed in any given time interval. When computing power is significantly larger than the complexity of the plant to be controlled (in other words, a slow plant is controlled by a fast computer) one can work with the "separation of concerns" framework which can be summarized as follows:

- The control engineer fixes the control law based on purely "functional" considerations (the quality of control). The outcome of the design is a set of feedback functions, each with its associated rate of invocation[2].
- It is the responsibility of the hardware/software engineers to meet the implied computational demands on an appropriate computer architecture (processor, I/O interface, scheduling policy). This is done without taking into account the *functional* content of the computations, i.e. their influence on the evolution of the plant. All the implementor knows about are computational tasks with *release times* and *deadlines*.

While this separation of concerns has its advantages (programmers need not know about differential equations and control engineers need not think about

---

[1] Or equivalently in a world were mathematical functions are viewed as *instantaneous* objects without computation and transmission concerns.

[2] In fact, if you inspect closely the literature on digital control, you don't find a real theory for determining the sampling rate of a control loop, but rather "bandwidth" arguments applied, sometimes, beyond their scope of validity.

computations) it is not so useful when, due to technological and economic constraints, the control of fast and complex plants should be achieved using a bounded amount of computational resources. In such situations computation may become a major bottleneck in the control system and one has to allocate computations in a smart way to meet the conflicting demands coming from different parts of the plant.

Mathematical models of plants and controllers that neglect computational issues are not suitable for computation-conscious design. On the other hand, the opposite approach, that is, the introduction of detailed models of the implementation such as operating systems and scheduling policies, may render the design and analysis of the control system intractable[3]. We present an intermediate approach whose novelty is twofold:

1. It suggests simple abstract models of computations that can be incorporated in the control design process. In these models only one essential feature of computation that is relevant for control is represented, namely *computation time.*

2. As an application we suggest a simple way to derive adaptive scheduling strategies that allocate computational resources to various parts of the plant based on the actual observed performance.

By breaking the "wall" separating control design from its digital implementation, we believe, a much larger part of the space of price/performance tradeoffs can be explored. This belief is apparently shared by other researchers from the control and real-time communities who have recently expressed interest in better mutual interaction between control and computation considerations during the design process, e.g. [SLSS96], [ABE+99], [PAB+00], [SLS+99], [ACV+01].

We present two generic models in which the controlled plant consists of several independent sub-systems which compete for the computational attention of the controller. The first model captures the computational investment in updating the control law of a system that drifts away from its current model while the second model is motivated by the problem of allocating the best feasible mix of sampling rates to sub-systems based on their current performance indices. These models can be easily adapted to other types of resource constraints.

It should be emphasized that the main contribution of this paper is conceptual. We present a new modeling methodology and demonstrate how it can be used to formulate and solve some generic problems of control under resource constraints. Despite the preliminary nature of this work, we believe it can serve as the basis for developing practical algorithms for solving real problems in the future.

2   The Setting

We assume a plant consisting of n independent sub-plants $P_1, \ldots, P_n$, controlled by n independent controllers $C_1, \ldots C_n$. The only dependency between these

---

[3] It can be argued that the type of computer science taught to control engineers is sometimes very detail-oriented and lags behind the more abstract view of computation practiced in (some) computer science quarters.

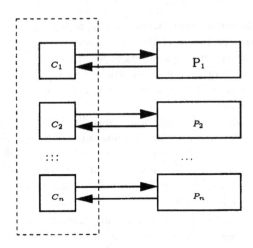

Fig. 1. Controlling n independent plants.

system components is that all controllers use the same processor to compute their feedback function (see Figure 1).

2.1   Controller Performance

The composition of a single plant P with its corresponding controller C yields a closed-loop system $S = P\|C$. We assume that we can associate with S a scalar variable x tracking the evolution of some performance index of the system along its trajectories. This measure can be either a memoryless function of the trajectory, such as the distance from a reference point in the state-space, or some average measure of the trajectory over a moving time window. It is important that an evaluation of the current value of x during the actual evolution of the plant can be made from available observations within a bounded delay so that this value can be used for adaptive scheduling.

Our mathematical assumptions concerning this measure are:

1. It lives in $[0, \infty)$ with 0 considered optimal, and our goal is to keep it always inside a bounded interval $[0, m]$.
2. Its evolution is defined by a differential inclusion of the form $\dot{x} \in F(x)$ capturing all possible behaviors under various disturbances.
3. All these behaviors are *bounded from above* by a *worst-case* dynamics which can be characterized by a differential equation $\dot{x} = f(x)$.

When several plants are controlled in parallel the overall performance of the system is represented by $\mathbf{x} = (x_1, \ldots, x_n)$ with $\dot{\mathbf{x}} = f(x)$ where $f(\mathbf{x}) = (f_1(x_1), \ldots f_n(x_n))$. Note that f is "diagonal", that is, the evolution of every x_i depends only on x_i.

In the two models defined below, we assume that the worst-case behavior for each controller for a given allocation of computational resources is *monotone*. In

Model I, the worst-case behaviors for all of the controllers is monotone increasing, representing the long-term behaviors of controllers that will always eventually require special attention to re-estimate parameters in internal models or to re-define the control function. The problem is to decide when these re-tuning computations should be made for each controller. In Model II, the performance of each controller depends on the amount of computational resources (time) allocated to compute the feedback function. For each controller it is possible to allocate sufficient resources to make the performance index decrease (improve), but there are insufficient resources to make the performance indices of *all* the controllers decrease simultaneously. In this case, the problem is to re-allocate the computational resources dynamically to assure that all of the performance indices remain within the specified bounds.

We use the notation $\mathbf{x}_0 \xrightarrow{f,t} \mathbf{x}_1$ to denote the fact that the solution of the differential equation $\dot{\mathbf{x}} = f(\mathbf{x})$, starting from $\mathbf{x}_0$, leads to $\mathbf{x}_1$ at time t. Similarly $\mathbf{x}_0 \xrightarrow{f,t} G$ indicates that the solution reaches some point $\mathbf{x}_1 \in G$. If, in addition, the trajectory stays in $H \subseteq X$ during the interval $[0,t)$ we use the notations $\mathbf{x}_0 \xrightarrow[H]{f,t} \mathbf{x}_1$ and $\mathbf{x}_0 \xrightarrow[H]{f,t} G$, respectively.

We say that a set G is f-invariant if $\mathbf{x} \xrightarrow{f,t} G$ implies $\mathbf{x} \xrightarrow{f,t'} G$ for every t', $0 \le t' \le t$ and every $\mathbf{x} \in G$. Note that convex polyhedra are f-invariant when f is constant and that hyper-rectangles are f-invariant when f is monotone.

2.2 Model I: Re-calibrating Controllers

The first model represents the long-term behavior of adaptive controllers: the performance evolves according to $\dot{\mathbf{x}} = f(\mathbf{x})$ where $f(\mathbf{x}) > \mathbf{0}$. Here the only way to avoid divergence and keep the system within a bounded subset is to invest occasionally some time in updating the various controllers. We assume that it takes d_i time[4] to update the controller for plant P_i and that this action *resets* the value of x_i to 0. For every $i \in \{1, \ldots, n\}$ the reset function $R_i : X \to X$ is defined as $R_i(x_1, \ldots, x_i, \ldots, x_n) = (x_1, \ldots, 0, \ldots, x_n)$ and its inverse is $R_i^{-1} : X \to 2^X$.

Definition 1 (Resetting Dynamical Systems). *A resetting dynamical system (RDS) is $\mathcal{A} = (X, f, \mathbf{d})$ where $X = [0, \infty)^n$, $f : X \to \mathbb{R}^n$ is a positive vector field and $\mathbf{d} = (d_1, \ldots, d_n)$ is a vector of delay constants.*

Definition 2 (Update Strategies and Runs). *An update strategy for an RDS $\mathcal{A}$ is a function $s : X \to \{1, \ldots, n, \perp\}$. A run of $\mathcal{A}$ under an update strategy s starting from $\mathbf{x}$ is*

$$\mathbf{x} \xrightarrow{t_1} \mathbf{x}' \xrightarrow{d_i} \mathbf{x}'' \xrightarrow{0} R_i(\mathbf{x}'') \xrightarrow{t_2} \ldots$$

such that $\mathbf{x} \xrightarrow[s^{-1}(\perp)]{f,t_1} \mathbf{x}'$ and $s(\mathbf{x}') = i$.

---

[4] In fact, d_i should cover both the time to perform the identification algorithm and the time for some transient behavior when the controller is changed. It is common in timed and hybrid systems models to decompose actions that take some time into time passage followed by an instantaneous transition.

In other words, a strategy is a rule that tells the system at any given point whether or not to start resetting one of the variables and which variable to reset. A run evolves without resetting as long as $s(\mathbf{x}) = \perp$ until $s(\mathbf{x}) = i$ for some i, then it continues to evolve for d_i time and resets x_i to 0. An example of a run of an RDS in $\mathbb{R}^2$ appears in Figure 2.

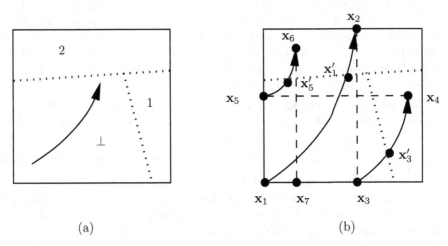

(a)   (b)

Fig. 2. (a) An update strategy in two dimensions. (b) An initial part of a run following that strategy with resets indicated by dashed lines. The run can be written as $\mathbf{x}_1 \xrightarrow{t_1} \mathbf{x}'_1 \xrightarrow{d_2} \mathbf{x}_2 \xrightarrow{0} \mathbf{x}_3 \xrightarrow{t_2} \mathbf{x}'_3 \xrightarrow{d_1} \mathbf{x}_4 \xrightarrow{0} \mathbf{x}_5 \xrightarrow{t_3} \mathbf{x}'_5 \xrightarrow{d_2} \mathbf{x}_6 \xrightarrow{0} \mathbf{x}_7$.

Definition 3 (Strategy Synthesis Problem for RDS). *Given an RDS $\mathcal{A}$ and a hyper-rectangle $G \subseteq X$ containing $\mathbf{0}$, find the maximal controlled invariant subset of G, that is, the maximal $F \subseteq G$ for which there exists an update strategy $s : F \to \{1, \ldots n, \perp\}$ such that all trajectories starting in F stay in F.*

To compute F and s we use a variant of the fixed-point computation described in [ABD+00]. This approach was first presented for timed automata [MPS95] where it is guaranteed to converge, and then adapted for hybrid automata [W97,TLS99,ABD+00].

Definition 4 (Delayed Predecessors). *Let H be a subset of X and let f be a vector field. The set*

$$\Pi_{(f,d)}(H) = \{\mathbf{x} : \exists t \geq d \; \mathbf{x} \xrightarrow{f,t} H\} \tag{1}$$

consists of all points from which the system can reach H after evolving for at least d time according to the dynamics f.

The relation between H and $\Pi(H)$ is illustrated in Figure 3. Note that we will always work inside a hyper-rectangle G and that Π is distributive over union: $\Pi(H_1 \cup H_2) = \Pi(H_1) \cup \Pi(H_2)$.

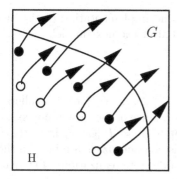
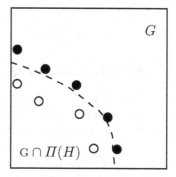

Fig. 3. A hyper-rectangle G, a set $H \subseteq G$ and the set of its delayed predecessors inside G, $G \cap \Pi_{f,d}(H)$. The dark points are outside $\Pi_{f,d}(H)$ because following f for d time leads outside H without being able to return to H.

The following algorithm computes F:

Algorithm 1 (Winning Update Strategies for RDS)

$F^0 := G$
repeat
  $F^{k+1} := G \cap \bigcup_{i \in \{1,\dots,n\}} \Pi_{(f,d_i)}(R_i^{-1}(F^k))$
until $F^{k+1} = F^k$
$F := F^k$

Claim 1 (Properties of the Algorithm) *Algorithm 1 generates a decreasing sequence of sets* $F^0, F^1, F^2, \dots$ *whose limit* F *is the maximal invariant set of Definition 3.*

Sketch of Proof: Let $d = \min\{d_i\}$. The proof is by showing that $\mathbf{x} \in F^k$ if and only if there is an update strategy such that the trajectory starting at $\mathbf{x}$ stays in G for at least kd time. This is done by induction where F^0 satisfies the property trivially and the inductive step works by showing that $\mathbf{x} \in F^{k+1}$ implies that for some i it is possible to stay in G for some t time, $t \geq d_i \geq d$ and then, after resetting, reach a point in F^k satisfying the inductive hypothesis.   ◢

The extraction of an update strategy from F can be done in two steps. First we compute a non-deterministic strategy $\hat{s} : F \to 2^{\{1,\dots,n,\perp\}}$ such that $i \in \hat{s}(\mathbf{x})$ if $\mathbf{x} \xrightarrow{f,d_i} F$ and $\perp \in \hat{s}(\mathbf{x})$ iff $\mathbf{x} \xrightarrow{f,t} F$ for some $t > d = \min\{d_i\}$. In other words $\perp \in \hat{s}(\mathbf{x})$ if updating is not urgent at $\mathbf{x}$. This non-deterministic controller is the maximal "least-restrictive" controller and any of its functional restrictions, i.e. any function s satisfying $s(\mathbf{x}) \in \hat{s}(\mathbf{x})$ is a winning strategy. Of course, practical considerations such as the description size of the strategy or the number of updates it induces will influence the actual choice of the strategy. For example, one may prefer strategies satisfying $s(\mathbf{x}) = \perp$ whenever $\perp \in \hat{s}(\mathbf{x})$.

The computational issues associated with the implementation of the algorithm and of the update strategy are discussed after the next model.

2.3 Model II: Different Quality Mixes

In this model, a plant P admits a family $\mathcal{C} = \{C^1, \ldots, C^p\}$ of controllers of increasing qualities, that is, for each j, the performance of the closed-loop system $S^j = P||C^j$ is inferior to the performance of $S^{j+1} = P||C^{j+1}$, i.e. $f^j(x) \geq f^{j+1}(x)$ for every x. One possible source of this characterization might be their sampling rates — the family $\mathcal{C}$ might consists of discrete realizations of the same continuous controller with decreasing time steps.

The set of controllers for the whole plant is $\mathcal{C} = \mathcal{C}_1 \times \ldots \times \mathcal{C}_n$ where for every i, the family $\mathcal{C}_i = \{C_i^1, \ldots, C_i^p\}$ of controllers for plant P_i contains *at least one good controller* with f_i negative. Each $C \in \mathcal{C}$ is called a control "mode" of the system, and when composed with the plant, it induces a worst-case dynamics for the performance measure $\mathbf{x}$. Our goal, as before, is to maintain $\mathbf{x}$ inside a bounded rectangle $G \subseteq \mathbb{R}_+^n$, a goal which could be trivially achieved if there were no additional constraints on control modes — we would just stay in a mode such as $(C_1^p, \ldots, C_n^p)$ where all controllers are good. We assume, however, that only a subset $\mathcal{C}' \subseteq \mathcal{C}$ of control modes is feasible due to computational resources constraints and that for every element of $\mathcal{C}'$ there is at least one plant P_i which is controlled badly (positive f_i). Hence there is no mode in which the system can stay forever while maintaining $\mathbf{x}$ bounded, and the goal should be achieved, if possible, by properly *switching* between feasible modes.

Example: A typical situation that can be modeled naturally in this framework is when each family $\{C^1, \ldots, C^k\}$ is parameterized by the frequency of sampling and computing. Assume that for every plant P_i the computation time of its feedback function is D_i, and that the frequency for each controller is φ_i^j. Hence a mode $C = (C_1^{j_1}, \ldots C_n^{j_n})$ is feasible if it satisfies the Liu and Layland schedulability condition [LL73], i.e.

$$\sum_{i=1}^{n} D_i \cdot \varphi_i^{j_i} \leq 1.$$

If, using the techniques developed in the sequel, it is shown that the plant cannot be controlled by this set of modes, moving to a faster processor will reduce D_i, increase the set of feasible modes, and might make the system controllable[5]. There could be other reasons for certain modes to be infeasible, for example a mode in which two controllers use the same actuator or where the total required power exceeds the available power.

We also assume that it takes up to d time units between the decision to switch and its actual realization. This delay constant should cover the time is takes to

---

[5] To avoid confusion with other approaches, we emphasize that we do not care about the implementation of the scheduling *inside* a mode — in this case, since everything is periodic, a static schedule is sufficient in each mode.

compute $\mathbf{x}$ from observations and for completing some cycles in the schedule corresponding to the current mode before a new schedule is started. The whole situation can now be described using a hybrid automaton whose discrete states correspond to feasible modes.

Definition 5 (Multi-mode Hybrid Automata). *A multi-mode hybrid automaton (MMHA) is $\mathcal{A} = (Q, X, f, d)$ where Q is a finite set of discrete states (modes), $X = [0, \infty)^n$, $f : Q \to (X \to \mathbb{R})$ is a family of vector fields associated with the modes and $d > 0$ is a delay constant.*

We write $f(q)$ as f^q and assume that for every q and i the sign of f_i^q is uniform all over X.

Definition 6 (Switching Strategies and Runs). *A switching strategy for a MMHA $\mathcal{A}$ is a function $s : Q \times X \to Q$ defined on a subset of $Q \times X$. The trajectory of $\mathcal{A}$ under a strategy s starting from $(q, \mathbf{x})$ is a sequence of the form*

$$(q, \mathbf{x}) \xrightarrow{t_1} (q, \mathbf{x}') \xrightarrow{d} (q, \mathbf{x}'') \xrightarrow{0} (q', \mathbf{x}'') \xrightarrow{t_2} \ldots$$

such that $\mathbf{x} \xrightarrow[s^{-1}(q)]{f^q, t} \mathbf{x}'$, $s(q, \mathbf{x}') = q'$ and $\mathbf{x}' \xrightarrow{f^q, d} \mathbf{x}''$.

In other words, $\mathbf{x}$ evolves for t_1 time following the f_q dynamics without needing to switch until $\mathbf{x}'$ where $s(q, \mathbf{x}') = q'$. After this decision point the system still evolves for d time at q and then switches to q'. An example is depicted in Figure 4 for a MMHA with two variables and two modes such that x_1 diverges in q_1 and x_2 diverges in q_2. We can now formulate the synthesis problem.

Definition 7 (Strategy Synthesis Problem for MMHA). *Given a MMHA $\mathcal{A}$ and a hyper-rectangle $G \subseteq X$ containing $\mathbf{0}$, find the maximal controlled invariant subset of $Q \times G$, that is, the maximal $\mathcal{F} \subseteq Q \times G$ for which there exists a switching strategy $s : \mathcal{F} \to Q$ such that all the trajectories starting in $\mathcal{F}$ stay in $\mathcal{F}$.*

Note that $\mathcal{F} = \bigcup_{q \in Q}(q, F_q)$ where each F_q is a subset of G. The algorithm for computing $\mathcal{F}$ is the following.

Algorithm 2 (Winning Switching Strategies for MMHA)

$$\forall q \in Q \qquad \begin{aligned} &F_q^0 := G \\ &\textbf{repeat} \\ &\qquad F_q^{k+1} := G \cap \bigcup_{q' \in Q} \Pi_{(f_q, d)}(F_{q'}^k) \\ &\textbf{until } F_q^{k+1} = F_q^k \\ &F_q := F_q^k \end{aligned}$$

Claim 2 (Properties of the Algorithm) *Algorithm 2 generates a decreasing sequence of sets $\mathcal{F}^0, \mathcal{F}^1, \mathcal{F}^2, \ldots$ whose limit $\mathcal{F}$ is the maximal invariant set of Definition 7.*

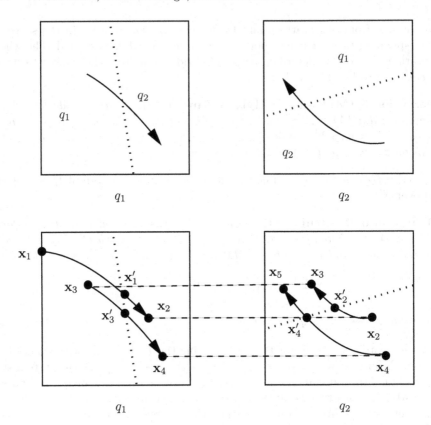

Fig. 4. A switching strategy and an initial part of a run of following this strategy. The run can be written as $(q_1, \mathbf{x}_1) \xrightarrow{t_1} (q_1, \mathbf{x}_1') \xrightarrow{d} (q_1, \mathbf{x}_2) \xrightarrow{0} (q_2, \mathbf{x}_2) \xrightarrow{t_2} (q_2, \mathbf{x}_2') \xrightarrow{d} (q_2, \mathbf{x}_3) \xrightarrow{0} (q_1, \mathbf{x}_3) \xrightarrow{t_3} (q_1, \mathbf{x}_3') \xrightarrow{d} (q_1, \mathbf{x}_4) \xrightarrow{0} (q_2, \mathbf{x}_4) \xrightarrow{t_4} (q_2, \mathbf{x}_4') \xrightarrow{d} (q_2, \mathbf{x}_5)$.

Sketch of Proof: Similarly to [AMPS98,ABD$^+$00] we show that $\mathbf{x} \in F_q^k$ if and only if it is possible, starting from $(q, \mathbf{x})$, to stay in G for at least kd time. This is true trivially for $k = 0$. The inductive step is based on the definition of Π and on the fact that for every q and k, F_q^k is included in the hyper-rectangle G which f-invariant for every monotone f. Hence, being in F_q^{k+1} implies the ability to stay for at least d time in G and then switch to some q' such that $F_{q'}^k$ satisfies the inductive hypothesis. Hence, starting from a point in the limit $\mathcal{F}$, we can stay in G indefinitely and $\mathcal{F}$ is indeed the maximal invariant set. ◢

An example of the behavior of the algorithm on a simple system appears in Figure 5.

2.4   Computational Issues

As discussed in [ABD$^+$00], abstract algorithms such as Algorithm 1 and Algorithm 2 can not be effectively implemented in a precise manner for systems where f is arbitrary because the sets of the form $\Pi_{(f,d)}(H)$ may have complex shapes. However, approximate versions of similar algorithms have already been implemented in tools such as $\mathbf{d/dt}$ [ADM01]. Such algorithms can find an under-approximation of the maximal invariant set and the corresponding switching strategy will be safe. The case when f is constant in each mode is discussed in the next section.

As in Algorithm 1, the extraction of a switching strategy from $\mathcal{F}$ can be done by first computing a least-restrictive non-deterministic strategy $\hat{s} : \mathcal{F} \to 2^Q$ defined as

$$\hat{s}(q, \mathbf{x}) = \{q' : \mathbf{x} \xrightarrow{f_q, d} F_{q'}\}.$$

This strategy allows to switch to any q' such that d time after the decision to switch the system will still be inside its safe set for q'. Any functional restriction of $\hat{s}$ is a good switching strategy. Again, due to practical considerations one may prefer strategies with less switches satisfying $s(q, \mathbf{x}) = q$ whenever $q \in \hat{s}(q, \mathbf{x})$.

Once the controller is extracted it can be implemented as a small additional module on top of the digital control system. It monitors the performance index of the systems and switches between the modes according to simple rules. Note that the controller is guaranteed to keep the system in G assuming the *worst-case* dynamics f for $\mathbf{x}$ in each mode. Due to monotonicity this implies that it will work also for any better admissible behavior of $\mathbf{x}$, probably with less switches. We believe the this approach represents a promising direction for adaptive scheduling of digital control systems.

3   Constant Slopes

In this section we study the special case where f^q is constant for each q. This case is interesting for several reasons. First, since we assume that the evolution of each variable is monotone inside a mode, systems with constant slopes exhibit the same qualitative phenomena as the more general ones. The constant derivatives can be interpreted as an upper-approximation of the real f^q or alternatively, when the system is linear, i.e. $f^q(\mathbf{x}) = A_q x$ with A_q a diagonal matrix, looking at $\log x$ we obtain a constant-slope system. From a computational point of view, such systems admit effective computation of successors and predecessors using linear algebra without numerical or symbolic integration and hence the algorithms can be easily incorporated into tools such as HyTech [HHW97], and there is even a hope that they will terminate after a finite number of steps (see below).

Constant slope systems are defined essentialy by assigining a constant vector field $\mathbf{c}^q = (c_1, \ldots, c_n)$ to every mode q. However we need an additional saturation construct to prevent variables from becoming negative[6]. Let $\lceil x \rceil = \max\{0, x\}$ and $\lceil \mathbf{x} \rceil = (\lceil x_1 \rceil, \ldots, \lceil x_n \rceil)$. For every constant c define the function

$$\bar{c}(x) = \begin{cases} c \text{ if } x > 0 \text{ or } c > 0 \\ 0 \text{ otherwise} \end{cases}$$

---

[6] This is not needed if we use the logarithmic interpretation.

and let $\bar{\mathbf{c}}(\mathbf{x})$ be its pointwise extension, that is, $\bar{\mathbf{c}}(\mathbf{x}) = (\bar{c}_1(x_1), \ldots, \bar{c}_n(x_n))$. The evolution of $\mathbf{x}$ in a mode is then defined by an equation of the form $\dot{\mathbf{x}} = \bar{\mathbf{c}}(\mathbf{x})$. We assume further that all slope vectors are integer and that so is d (rational constants can be transformed into integers by changing the time-scale).

When $f(\mathbf{x}) = \bar{\mathbf{c}}(\mathbf{x})$ the definition of the predecessor operator specializes into:

$$\Pi_{(\mathbf{c},d)}(H) = \{\mathbf{x} : \exists t \geq d \ \lceil \mathbf{x} + \mathbf{c}t \rceil \in H\}.$$

Claim 3 (Preservation of Polyhedra) *1) If H is a convex polyhedron so is $\Pi_{(\mathbf{c},d)}(H)$. 2) When $\mathbf{c}$ is positive, and H is a hyper-rectangle with integer endpoints, so are $R^{-1}(H)$ and $\Pi_{(\mathbf{c},d)}(H)$.*

Sketch of Proof: 1) Follows from the definition of Π and the elimination of t (this closure of polyhedra under constant-derivative time passage underlies the algorithmic verification of timed automata and "linear" hybrid automata [ACH+95]). 2) Let $\mathbf{c} = (c_1, \ldots, c_n)$ be a positive vector and $H = \bigwedge_i x_i \leq m_i$. To be in $\Pi_{(\mathbf{c},d)}(H)$ one must ensure for every x_i that $x_i + c_i \cdot d \leq m_i$ and hence the operator transforms H into $\bigwedge_i x_i \leq m_i - c_i d_i$. ◢
As we will see later, the second claim is not true for non-positive $\mathbf{c}$.

Corollary 1 (Effectiveness and Convergence). *1) The steps of Algorithms 1 (RDS) and 2 (MMHA) can be effectively implemented. 2) Algorithm 1 terminates after finitely many steps and the problem of finding the maximal invariant set under update strategies for constant-slope RDS is algorithmically solvable.*

Sketch of Proof: Effectiveness follows from the definition of the algorithms and the distributivity of Π over union. For convergence, Algorithm 1 performs a monotone iteration over the finite class of sets which can be written as unions of hyper-rectangles with integer endpoints and hence it reaches a fixed-point after finitely many steps. ◢

The problem of finding switching strategies for a MMHA with different slopes in every mode is much more difficult. A first observation is that a necessary condition for having such a switching policy is the existence of non-negative constants $\{\lambda_q\}_{q \in Q}$ such that $\sum_{q \in Q} \lambda_q = 1$ and

$$\sum_{q \in Q} \lambda_q \mathbf{c}^q \leq 0 \tag{2}$$

The reason is that if we look at the long term behavior of the system under *any* switching strategy and let λ_q be the average time spent at state q, then the sum in (2) represents the total "average direction" of the system which must be non-positive for the system not to diverge. The condition is not sufficient, though, because it ignores the saturation at zero and the delay. To illustrate the algorithm consider a system in $\mathbb{R}^2$ with two states and slope vectors $\mathbf{c}^1 = (a_1, -b_1)$ and $\mathbf{c}^2 = (-a_2, b_2)$ such that a_1, b_1, a_2, b_2 are positive. We assume $d = 1$ and $G = [0, m]^2$. The necessary condition for controllability is $b_2/a_2 < b_1/a_1$. After

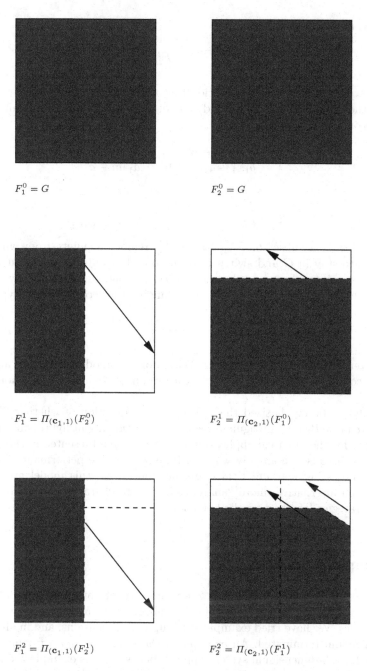

Fig. 5. Applying Algorithm 2 to a two-dimensional system with $m = 10$ and two modes $\mathbf{c}^1 = (5, -6)$ and $\mathbf{c}^2 = (-3, 2)$. We omit from the figure successive applications of the same $\Pi_{(\mathbf{c},1)}$ operator. The inequality $2x_1 + 3x_2 \leq 40$ in F_2^2 guarantees that x_1 will become smaller than 5 before x_2 becomes greater than 10.

the first iteration we obtain:

$$F_1^1 = \begin{matrix} x_1 \le m - a_1 \\ x_2 \le m \end{matrix} \qquad F_2^1 = \begin{matrix} x_1 \le m \\ x_2 \le m - b_2 \end{matrix}$$

which expresses the obvious condition that the diverging variables in each state (x_1 in the first and x_2 in the second) do not go beyond m within 1 unit of time. The second iteration gives

$$F_1^2 = \begin{matrix} x_1 \le m - a_1 \\ b_1 x_1 + a_1 x_2 \le (b_1 + a_1)m - a_1 b_2 \end{matrix}$$

and

$$F_2^2 = \begin{matrix} x_2 \le m - b_2 \\ b_2 x_1 + a_2 x_2 \le (a_2 + b_2)m - a_1 b_2 \end{matrix}$$

The set F_1^2 is a subset of F_1^1 obtained by removing points from which it is possible to stay in G and switch from q_1 to q_2 but only to points outside F_2^1. These are points where x_2 is larger than $m - b_2$ and cannot go below it before x_1 goes above m, as can be seen by re-arranging the second inequality:

$$\frac{m - x_1}{a_1} \ge \frac{x_2 - (m - b_2)}{b_1}$$

The interpretation of F_2^2 is similar. While for two modes in $\mathbb{R}^2$ the algorithm always converges, the question whether it terminates in higher dimensions is still open.

It should be emphasized that, although the question of whether $\mathcal{F}$ can be computed *exactly* is an intriguing *theoretical* question about hybrid automata, its relevance for the practical application of the approach presented in this paper is marginal, because we already work with approximative performance measures. Other interesting mathematical questions concerning this model are whether there is an alternative, more "analytical", way to characterize $\mathcal{F}$ and whether some strategies lead to periodic behaviors.

4   Implementation

We have implemented Algorithm 2 for the case of constant slopes. In order to gain insight concerning possible decidability, we have used exact rational arithmetics. We have tried examples with up to 4 dimensions, and in all of them the algorithm terminated. An example of the input file and a fragment of the output for a 3-dimensional system appears below. In this example the maximal invariant set is empty but the iteration goes through rather complex unions of convex polyhedra before converging. The software is available from the authors upon request. We are currently investigating the possibility of implementing the algorithm for more general dynamics by modifying the control synthesis algorithm of $\mathbf{d/dt}$ [ABD$^+$00].

```
Input file:

3                    % number of dimensions

10 10 10             % intial X

1                    % delay constant

3                    % no of modes

3 2 -1               % slope for state 1

2 -3 4               % slope for state 2

-2 4 3               % slope for state 3


Output file:


**** iteration #1 ******

--------- F1 --------------
    x_1  <=  7
 &  x_2  <=  8
 &  x_3  <= 10

--------- F2 --------------
    x_1  <=  8
 &  x_2  <= 10
 &  x_3  <=  6

--------- F3 --------------
    x_1  <= 10
 &  x_2  <=  6
 &  x_3  <=  7

**** iteration #2 ******

[...]
```

```
**** iteration #5 ******
--------- F1 --------------
    3 x_1 +  2 x_2  <= 20
 &  3 x_1 +  2 x_3  <= 20
 &  2 x_1 + x_2     <= 13
 &  x_1 +  3 x_3    <=  9
 &  4 x_2 +  3 x_3  <=  7
 &  x_2 +  2 x_3    <=  3
      <UNION>
    x_1 +  3 x_3    <=  2
 &  x_2 +  2 x_3    <=  7
      <UNION>
    3 x_1 +  2 x_2  <= 14
 &  3 x_1 +  2 x_3  <= 16
 &  2 x_1 + x_2     <=  9
 &  x_1 +  3 x_3    <= 10
 &  4 x_2 +  3 x_3  <= 10
 &  x_2 +  2 x_3    <=  5
      <UNION>
    - x_1  =  0
 &  x_3   <=  1
 &  x_2   <=  8
      <UNION>
    3 x_1 +  2 x_2  <= 16
 &  3 x_1 +  2 x_3  <=  8
 &  2 x_1 + x_2     <=  9
 &  x_1 +  3 x_3    <=  5
 &  4 x_2 +  3 x_3  <= 23
 &  x_2 +  2 x_3    <=  7
      <UNION>
    3 x_1 +  2 x_2  <=  9
 &  3 x_1 +  2 x_3  <= 13
 &  2 x_1 + x_2     <=  5
 &  x_1 +  3 x_3    <= 16
 &  x_1   <=  2
 &  4 x_2 +  3 x_3  <= 27
 &  x_2 +  2 x_3    <= 13
[...]
**** iteration #7 ******
--------- F1 --------------
<EMPTY>
--------- F2 --------------
<EMPTY>
--------- F3 --------------
<EMPTY>
```

5   Conclusions

The models presented in this paper capture natural, if not universal, situations of control under resource constraints: you have to handle many affairs simultaneously but your resources are insufficient for handling all of them properly. The natural solution is to invest your attention in the more burning issues, while letting the others deteriorate a bit, hoping that they will not deteriorate too much until you can pay them attention again. Our models provide methods, based on hybrid automata, for checking whether such a solution is feasible. We hope that such models and techniques will proliferate eventually into engineering practice.

Acknowledgments

This work benefited from discussions with Eugene Asarin, Amir Pnueli and Pravin Varaiya and from comments of anonymous referees.

References

ACV⁺01.   P. Albertos, A. Crespo, M. Vallés, P. Balbastre and I. Ripoll, Integrated Control Design and Real Time Scheduling, unpublished, 2001.

ABE⁺99.   K.-E. Årzén, B. Bernhardsson, J. Eker, A. Cervin, K. Nilsson, P. Persson and L. Sha, *Integrated Control and Scheduling*, Internal report TFRT-7582, Department of Automatic Control, Lund University, August 1999.

ABD⁺00.   E. Asarin, O. Bournez, T. Dang, O. Maler and A. Pnueli, Effective Synthesis of Switching Controllers for Linear Systems, *Proceedings of the IEEE*, 88, 1011-1025, 2000.

ADM01.   E. Asarin, T. Dang, and O. Maler, d/dt: a Tool for Reachability Analysis of Continuous and Hybrid systems, *5th IFAC Symposium Nonlinear Control Systems (NOLCOS)*, 2001.

ACH⁺95.   R. Alur, C. Courcoubetis, N. Halbwachs, T.A. Henzinger, P.-H. Ho, X. Nicollin, A. Olivero, J. Sifakis and S. Yovine, The Algorithmic Analysis of Hybrid Systems, *Theoretical Computer Science* 138, 3–34, 1995.

AMPS98.   E. Asarin, O. Maler, A. Pnueli and J. Sifakis, Controller Synthesis for Timed Automata, in *Proc. IFAC Symposium on System Structure and Control*, 469-474, Elsevier, 1998.

AW84.   K.J. Aström and B. Wittenmark, *Computer Controlled Systems*, Prentice-Hall, 1984.

HHW97.   T.A. Henzinger, P.-H. Ho and H. Wong-Toi, HyTech: A Model Checker for Hybrid Systems, *Software Tools for Technology Transfer* 1, 110-122, 1997.

LL73.   C.L Liu and L. Layland: Scheduling Algorithms for Multiprogramming in Hard Real-Time Environment, *Journal of the ACM* 20, 46-61, 1973.

MPS95.   O. Maler, A. Pnueli and J. Sifakis. On the Synthesis of Discrete Controllers for Timed Systems, in E.W. Mayr and C. Puech (Eds), *Proc. STACS'95*, 229-242, LNCS 900, Springer, 1995.

PAB⁺00.   L. Palopoli, L. Abeni, G. Buttazzo, F. Conticelli, and M. Di Natale, Real-Time Control System Analysis: an Integrated Approach, *Proc. RTSS'2000*, IEEE Press, 2000.

SLSS96.   D. Seto, J.P. Lehoczky, L. Sha and K.G. Shin, On Task Scheduling of Real-Time Control Systems. *Proc. RTSS'96*, 13-21, IEEE Press, 2000.

SLS⁺99.   J. Stankovic, C. Lu, S. Son, and G. Tao, The Case for Feedback Control Real-Time Scheduling, *EuroMicro Conf. on Real-Time Systems*, 1999.

TLS99.   C. Tomlin, J. Lygeros and S. Sastry, Controllers for Reachability Specifications for Hybrid Systems, *Automatica* 35, 349-370, 1999.

W97.   H. Wong-Toi, The Synthesis of Controllers for Linear Hybrid Automata, *Proc. CDC'97*, 1997.

Part IV

Timed Automata I

Decidability of Safety Properties
of Timed Multiset Rewriting

Mitsuharu Yamamoto[1], Jean-Marie Cottin[2], and Masami Hagiya[2]

[1] Faculty of Science, Chiba University
Yayoicho 1–33, Inage-ku, Chiba, Japan
mituharu@math.s.chiba-u.ac.jp
[2] Graduate School of Information Science and Technology, University of Tokyo
Hongo 7–3–1, Bunkyo-ku, Tokyo, Japan
{jcottin,hagiya}@is.s.u-tokyo.ac.jp

Abstract. We propose timed multiset rewriting as a framework that subsumes timed Petri nets and timed automata. In timed multiset rewriting, which extends multiset rewriting, each element of a multiset has a clock, and a multiset is transformed not only by usual rewriting but also by time elapse. Moreover, we can specify conditions on clocks for rewriting.

In this paper, we analyze reachability, boundedness, and coverability of timed multiset rewriting. Decidability of each property on the system depends on the presence of invariant rules and diagonal constraints. First, we show that all three properties are undecidable for systems with invariant rules. Then we show that reachability is undecidable, and both boundedness and coverability are decidable for the system without invariant rules. Finally, we show that all the three properties are undecidable if we include diagonal constraints even when excluding invariant rules.

Keywords: real-time systems, timed Petri nets, timed automata, decidability.

1   Introduction

Rewriting on multisets is a framework that can naturally model dynamic creation and destruction of objects or processes [1,2]. In order to model lifetime or timeouts of objects, a number of frameworks that can handle real-time behavior have been proposed [3,4,5,6,7]. As well as rewriting on multisets, Petri nets can model changes in the number of processes, and there are many ways to extend Petri nets so that they can provide real-time features [8].

Automata, which are used as a basis of automatic verification also have some real-time extensions [9,10]. In particular, timed automata have been studied by many researchers and automatic analysis methods using regions or zones are well-established.

In this paper, we propose timed multiset rewriting, which is a real-time extension of multiset rewriting, in a way that can naturally handle clocks as in timed automata. In timed multiset rewriting, each element has its own clock,

W. Damm and E.-R. Olderog (Eds.): FTRTFT 2002, LNCS 2469, pp. 165–183, 2002.
© Springer-Verlag Berlin Heidelberg 2002

which gives us expressive power. Moreover, it can be seen as an extension of timed Petri nets.

Among properties on timed multiset rewriting, we focus on reachability, boundedness, and coverability, all of which are naturally imported from properties on Petri nets, and discuss their decidability and analysis methods. In timed multiset rewriting, we can obtain some variations by restricting or allowing various kinds of rules or constraints. In this paper, we analyze decidability of reachability, boundedness, and coverability of timed multiset rewriting, depending on whether invariant rules and diagonal constraints are allowed or not. Decidable properties can be analyzed using regions and zones, which have been used in the analysis of timed automata, and Karp-Miller trees, which have been used in the analysis of Petri nets.

This paper is organized as follows. Section 2 provides the definition of timed multiset rewriting and shows that it is an extension of both timed automata and timed Petri nets. Sections 3 and 4 discuss reachability, boundedness, and coverability of timed multiset rewriting with and without invariant rules, respectively. The effect of diagonal constraints is discussed in Section 5. Finally, we summarize the paper in Section 6.

2   Preliminaries

In this section, we give the definition of timed multiset rewriting, and show that it is an extension of two widely studied classes of real-time systems: timed Petri nets and timed automata.

2.1   Timed Multiset Rewriting

Definition 1. *We write the set of all non-negative real numbers as* $\mathbb{R}_{\geq 0}$. *Let* S *be a finite set of elements, and* T *a set of clock variables. A* pattern *is defined as a finite multiset*

$$M = \{a_1{:}t_1,\, a_2{:}t_2, \ldots, a_n{:}t_n\}$$

(where $a_i \in S$, $t_i \in \mathbb{R}_{\geq 0} \cup T$*). Since it is a multiset, it may be the case that* $a_i = a_j$ *or* $t_i = t_j$ *for* $i \neq j$. *For a pattern* M *above, the set* $\mathrm{Var}(M)$ *of clock variables, the multiplicity* $|M|$, *and the multiplicity* $|M|_a$ *of an element* a *are defined as follows:*

$$\mathrm{Var}(M) \overset{\text{def}}{=} \{t_i \mid t_i \in T\} \qquad |M| \overset{\text{def}}{=} n$$
$$|M|_a \overset{\text{def}}{=} \textit{the number of elements } a_i \textit{ such that } a_i = a$$

When $\mathrm{Var}(M) = \emptyset$, *we call* M *a timed multiset.*

For an element $a{:}t$ *of a pattern, we simply call* a *an* element, *call* $t \in \mathbb{R}_{\geq 0} \cup T$ *a* clock, *and* $a{:}t$ *itself a* timed element.

We can consider a substitution $\sigma : \mathrm{Var}(M) \to \mathbb{R}_{\geq 0}$ *from clock variables in a pattern* M *to non-negative reals. The result of applying a substitution* σ *to* M *becomes a timed multiset, and we denote it by* $M\sigma$.

Let $\mathcal{B}(T)$ be the set of constraints whose element is a conjunction made from relations $t \bowtie c$ $(t \in T, c \in \mathbb{N}, \bowtie \in \{=, \leq, \geq, <, >\})$ between a clock variable and a natural number. When σ satisfies a constraint $\mathcal{C} \in \mathcal{B}(T)$, we write $\sigma \models \mathcal{C}$.

As its name implies, timed multiset rewriting, which is the main target of this paper, is defined as rewriting on timed multisets as defined above.

Definition 2. *A* timed multiset rewriting system *(TMSRS) is given by a tuple* $\mathcal{R} = (S, I, J)$, *where S is a set of elements, and I and J are sets of invariant rules and jump rules, respectively.*
Each invariant rule *has the following form:*

$$l \mid \mathcal{C}$$

where l is a non-empty pattern whose clocks are clock variables (no non-negative reals), and $\mathcal{C} \in \mathcal{B}(\mathrm{Var}(l))$ is a constraint on clock variables occurring in l. We say that a timed multiset M satisfies invariants I if

$$\forall \sigma.\, l\sigma \subseteq_m M \implies \sigma \models \mathcal{C} \text{ for all } l \mid \mathcal{C} \text{ in } I$$

where $\subseteq_m$ denotes multiset inclusion.
Each jump rule *has the following form:*

$$R : l \to r \text{ if } \mathcal{C}$$

where R is a label stuck to the rule and occurs only once in J, l is a non-empty pattern, r is a possibly empty pattern, and $\mathcal{C} \in \mathcal{B}(\mathrm{Var}(l) \cup \mathrm{Var}(r))$ is a constraint on clock variables occurring in either l or r. Each clock in l or r must be either a natural number or a clock variable.
When writing a pattern in I or J, we omit the surrounding "{" and "}".
Rewriting in a TMSRS $\mathcal{R}$ is classified into two kinds: jump *and* flow. *Jump corresponds to jump rules. For a jump rule $R : l \to r$ if $\mathcal{C}$ and a timed multiset M satisfying invariants I, if there exist timed multisets M' and N, and a substitution σ satisfying*

$$M = l\sigma + N, \quad M' = r\sigma + N, \quad \sigma \models \mathcal{C}, \quad M' \text{ satisfies } I$$

(where $+$ denotes multiset union), then we say that M is rewritable to M' and write $M \xrightarrow{(R,\sigma)} M'$ or simply $M \xrightarrow{R} M'$.
The other kind of rewriting, flow, corresponds to passage of time. For a timed multiset $M = \{a_1{:}t_1, \ldots, a_n{:}t_n\}$ satisfying invariants I and a positive real $d \in \mathbb{R}_{>0}$, we define $M + d$ as $M + d \stackrel{\text{def}}{=} \{a_1{:}t_1{+}d, \ldots, a_n{:}t_n{+}d\}$. If $M + d$ satisfies invariants I, then we say M is rewritable to $M' = M + d$ and write $M \xrightarrow{d} M'$.
When M is rewritable to M' using either jump or flow, we write $M \to M'$. The reflexive transitive closure and transitive closure of $\to$ are written $\to^*$ and $\to^+$, respectively.

2.2   Relation with Timed Petri Nets

A timed Petri net [8] is a Petri net augmented by the notion of age. Each token has its own age, and each arc has a time interval.

Definition 3. *A timed Petri net is given by a tuple $N = (P, T, In, Out)$ where P is a finite set of places, T is a finite set of transitions $(P \cap T = \emptyset)$, $In, Out : T \times P \to \mathcal{M}(\mathbb{N} \times (\mathbb{N} \cup \{\infty\}))$ are functions each of which takes a pair of a transition and a place and returns a finite multiset of intervals.*

Since each token has its own age, a marking M in a timed Petri net is represented by a function from a place P to a multiset $\mathcal{M}(\mathbb{R}_{\geq 0})$ of non-negative reals. In the initial marking, each token is assumed to have its age 0.

Transitions in timed Petri nets are classified into two kinds: those by firing as in the usual Petri nets, and those by passage of time. A marking M is fireable at a transition only if the age of each token (corresponding to the transition) is in the interval given by In. After firing, new tokens are created so that their ages satisfy the interval specified by Out. The transition by passage of time increases all of the ages of tokens by a positive real d.

A timed Petri net can be simulated by a TMSRS as follows.

Definition 4. *For a timed Petri net $N = (P, T, F, W, times)$, we define a TM-SRS $\mathcal{R} = (S, I, J)$ as follows:*

- $S = P$ *and* $I = \emptyset$
- *For each* $\tau \in T$, J *has the following rule:*

$$R_\tau : p_1{:}t_1^1, \ldots, p_1{:}t_1^{w_1}, \ldots, p_n{:}t_n^1, \ldots, p_n{:}t_n^{w_n} \to$$
$$q_1{:}s_1^1, \ldots, q_1{:}s_1^{v_1}, \ldots, q_m{:}s_m^1, \ldots, q_m{:}s_m^{v_m}$$
$$\textbf{if } c_1^1 \wedge \cdots \wedge c_1^{w_1} \wedge \cdots \wedge c_n^1 \wedge \cdots \wedge c_n^{w_n} \wedge$$
$$d_1^1 \wedge \cdots \wedge d_1^{v_1} \wedge \cdots \wedge d_n^1 \wedge \cdots \wedge d_m^{v_m}$$

where

$$\{p_1, \ldots, p_n\} = \{p \mid In(\tau, p) \neq \emptyset\}, \ w_i = |In(\tau, p_i)|,$$
$$\{q_1, \ldots, q_m\} = \{q \mid Out(\tau, q) \neq \emptyset\}, \ v_i = |Out(\tau, q_i)|,$$

$$\text{If } In(\tau, p_i) = \{(l_1, u_1), \ldots, (l_{w_i}, u_{w_i})\}, \begin{cases} c_i^j = l_j \leq t_i^j & \text{if } u_j = \infty \\ c_i^j = l_j \leq t_i^j \wedge t_i^j \leq u_j & \text{otherwise} \end{cases},$$

$$\text{If } Out(\tau, q_i) = \{(l_1, u_1), \ldots, (l_{v_i}, u_{v_i})\}, \begin{cases} d_i^j = l_j \leq s_i^j & \text{if } u_j = \infty \\ d_i^j = l_j \leq s_i^j \wedge s_i^j \leq u_j & \text{otherwise} \end{cases}$$

We assume t_i^j and s_i^j are clock variables in $\mathcal{R}$.
- *The initial timed multiset M_0 is a multiset of tokens in the initial marking with all their clocks 0.*

The close relation between TMSRSs and timed Petri nets naturally induces properties on TMSRSs that are originally defined on Petri nets, and they can be used for safety analysis, i.e., proving bad things never happen starting from a certain state.

Definition 5. *Assume that a TMSRS $\mathcal{R}$ and an initial timed multiset M_0 are given. A timed multiset M is* reachable *from M_0 if $M_0 \to^* M$. For a timed multiset M', M' is* coverable *from M_0 if there exists M such that $M_0 \to^* M$ and $M' \subseteq_m M$. $\mathcal{R}$ is* bounded *from M_0 if a timed multiset reachable from M_0 has a finite upper bound in its multiplicity.*

If we restrict the *Out* function's range to be $\mathcal{M}(\{(0,0)\})$, then we obtain timed-arc Petri nets. For timed-arc Petri nets, the reachability is shown to be undecidable [11], hence it is also undecidable for timed Petri nets. In [12], boundedness and coverability are shown to be decidable for discrete-time timed-arc Petri nets, i.e., the age of each token is always a natural number. The full continuous-time timed Petri nets are analyzed in [13], and their coverability is decidable.

It should be noted that there are differences between timed Petri nets and TMSRSs in their expressiveness. Besides the presence of invariant rules, timed Petri nets can not express a jump rule in which there are multiple occurrences of a single variable. This feature enables us to express preservation of clock values and a limited form of diagonal constraints, which will be discussed in Section 5.

In [7], correspondence between a timed Petri net and a system that operates on multisets is also described in the context of first-order linear logic programs, which can express more broader classes than timed Petri nets. Although [7] uses the result of the coverability of timed Petri nets for the analysis of first-order linear logic programs, it does not extend the decidable class. Thus our coverability result can also extend the decidable class for first-order linear logic programs.

2.3   Relation with Timed Automata

A timed automaton [9] is a timed extension of a usual automaton, by adding several (fixed number of) clocks to the states. It enable us to specify both discrete behavior of control and continuous behavior of time.

Definition 6. *A timed automaton is given by a tuple $A = (L, l_0, X, E, Inv)$, where L is a finite set of locations, $l_0 (\in L)$ is the initial location, $E(\subseteq L \times \mathcal{B}(X) \times 2^X \times L)$ is a set of edges, and $Inv : L \to \mathcal{B}(X)$ is an assignment of invariants to locations. In the case of $(l, g, r, l') \in E$, we write $l \xrightarrow{g,r} l'$.*

A state of a timed automaton is represented by a pair (l, u) of a location l and a clock assignment $u : X \to \mathbb{R}_{\geq 0}$. In the initial state, the location l coincides with the initial location l_0, and the clock assignment $u = u_0$ assigns 0 to each clock $x \in X$.

A timed automaton has two kinds of transitions as follows:

- *$(l, u) \to (l', u')$ where $l \xrightarrow{g,r} l'$, $u \models g$, $u' = [r \mapsto 0]u$, $u' \models Inv(l')$*
- *$(l, u) \to (l, u + d)$ if $u + d \models Inv(l)$*

The former is a transition between locations through an edge as in the usual automata, and one can reset the values of the clocks, which are specified in the edge, to 0. *The latter is a transition by time elapse without changing its location, and the value of every clock increases uniformly. For both transitions, the destination state* (l, u) *has to satisfy the invariant condition* $Inv(l)$ *that is assigned to the destination location* l.

Since the timed automaton defined above contains location invariants, it is actually a *timed safety automaton* [14], rather than the original timed automaton in [9] that has Büchi acceptance conditions instead of location invariants.

As in the case of timed Petri nets, a timed automaton can be simulated by a TMSRS. Both locations and clocks in a timed automaton are represented by clock variables in a TMSRS, permissive time progress at each location by an invariant, and a possible transition by a constraint on clock variables. A similar formulation of timed automata is also described as a special class of *real-time systems* in [15].

Definition 7. *For a given timed automaton* $A = (L, l_0, X, E, Inv)$, *we define a TMSRS* $\mathcal{R} = (S, I, J)$ *as follows.*

- $S = L \cup \{c_x \mid x \in X\}$
- *For each* $l \in L$, I *has the following invariant rule:*

$$l{:}t, c_{x_1}{:}x_1, \ldots, c_{x_n}{:}x_n \mid Inv(l)$$

  where x_i *is a clock variable occurring in* $Inv(l)$. *We assume* t *and* x_i *are clock variables in* $\mathcal{R}$.
- *For each* $e = (l, g, r, l') \in E$, J *has the following jump rule.*

$$R_e : l{:}t, c_{x_1}{:}x_1, \ldots, c_{x_n}{:}x_n \rightarrow l'{:}t, c_{x_1}{:}y_1, \ldots c_{x_n}{:}y_n \text{ **if** } g$$

  where x_i *is a clock variable occurring in either* g *or* r, *and* y_i *is* 0 *if* $x_i \in r$, *otherwise* x_i. *We assume* t *and* x_i *are clock variables in* $\mathcal{R}$.
- *The initial timed multiset* M_0 *is given by* $\{l_0{:}0\} \cup \{c_x{:}0 \mid x \in X\}$.

In timed automata, both reachability and coverability are decidable since we can enumerate all reachable states using *regions*. On the other hand, boundedness is meaningless since the multiplicity does not change through the transitions.

3   With Invariant Rules

This section is devoted to the undecidability results for reachability, boundedness, and coverability of the TMSRS given in the previous section. We consider the full version of a TMSRS including invariant rules in this section, and the next section is for a TMSRS without invariant rules.

3.1   Simulating 2-Counter Machines

The undecidability of reachability, boundedness, and coverability of a TMSRS are shown by using the fact that the halting problem of 2-counter machines is undecidable.

Definition 8. *A 2-counter machine is given by a sequence $I_1, \ldots, I_n$ of instructions, which are operations on two counters r_1 and r_2.*

The execution of a 2-counter machine starts from I_1. There is an instruction I_e that designates the end of the execution, and when the execution reaches the instruction I_e, the execution terminates. Each instruction has either of the following two types.

- *Increment: $I(i,j,k)$*

$$I_j : r_i := r_i + 1; \ \textbf{goto} \ I_k$$

- *Test&Decrement: $D(i,j,k,l)$*

$$I_j : \textbf{if} \ r_i > 0 \ \textbf{then} \ r_i := r_i - 1; \ \textbf{goto} \ I_k \ \textbf{else goto} \ I_l$$

Theorem 1. *The halting problem of 2-counter machines is undecidable.*

Next, we simulate 2-counter machines by a TMSRS. The method shown here is based on the simulation of 2-counter machines by timed-arc Petri nets given in [11], where undecidability of reachability of timed-arc Petri nets is shown using the simulation. Compared with [11], our simulation is strong enough to show undecidability of boundedness and coverability, as well as reachability, using invariant rules.

Definition 9. *We associate an element p_j for each instruction I_j in a 2-counter machine. The multiplicity of p_j is assumed to be at most 1, and it corresponds to the execution of the instruction I_j. Moreover, we associate an element r_i for each counter r_i in a 2-counter machine. The multiplicity of the timed element $r_i{:}1$ stands for the value of r_i in a 2-counter machine.*

For each type of instruction, we associate the following jump rules.

- *Increment: $I(i,j,k)$*

$$I_j : p_j{:}1 \to p_k{:}1, \ r_i{:}1$$

- *Test&Decrement: $D(i,j,k,l)$*

$$I_j^1 : p_j{:}1, r_i{:}1 \to p_k{:}1 \qquad\qquad I_j^3 : r_{3-i}{:}2, q_j{:}0 \to r_{3-i}{:}0, q_j{:}0$$
$$I_j^2 : p_j{:}2 \to q_j{:}0 \qquad\qquad\qquad\quad I_j^4 : q_j{:}0 \to p_l{:}0$$

where r_{3-i} is the counter that is not examined whether its value is 0 or not.

Moreover we add the following invariant rules:

$$r_i{:}t \mid t \le 2 \quad (i = 1, 2)$$

A state in a 2-counter machine is represented by the following timed multiset:

$$\{p_j{:}1, \overbrace{r_1{:}1, \ldots, r_1{:}1}^{n_1}, \overbrace{r_2{:}1, \ldots, r_2{:}1}^{n_2}\}$$

For brevity, the above timed multiset is denoted by (j, n_1, n_2).

The initial multiset is given by $(1, n_1, n_2)$, if the initial value of the counter r_i is n_i in a 2-counter machine.

Lemma 1. *Let CM be a 2-counter machine, and $\mathcal{R}$ a TMSRS given by Definition 9. Then for a timed multiset $M = (j, n_1, n_2)$, there exists a sequence of at least 1 rewrite starting from M and reaching the timed multiset of the form (j', n_1', n_2'). Moreover, for such a multiset (j', n_1', n_2'), if the instruction at I_j is Increment $(I(i, j, k))$, we have*

$$j' = k, \ n_i' = n_i + 1, \ n_{3-i}' = n_{3-i}$$

and if it is Test&Decrement$(D(i, j, k, l))$, we have

$$\begin{cases} j' = k, \ n_i' = n_i - 1, \ n_{3-i}' = n_{3-i} \ (\textit{if } n_i > 0) \\ j' = l, \ n_i' = 0, \ n_{3-i}' = n_{3-i} \qquad (\textit{if } n_i = 0) \end{cases}$$

Proof. 1. Case where the instruction I_j is Increment $I(i, j, k)$: We only consider the case $i = 1$, but the case $i = 2$ is similar. The only applicable jump rule is I_j and we have $(j, n_1, n_2) \xrightarrow{I_j} (k, n_1 + 1, n_2)$.

  If we apply flow, the clock assigned to p_j exceeds 1, and no more jumps are applicable. So no further rewriting reaches (j', n_1', n_2').

2. Case where the instruction I_j is Test&Decrement $D(i, j, k, l)$: As in the case of Increment, we only consider the case $i = 1$. If $n_1 = 0$, then the possible sequence of rewrites is:

$$\{p_j{:}1, r_2{:}1, \ldots, r_2{:}1\} \xrightarrow{d_1} \cdots \xrightarrow{d_n} \{p_j{:}2, r_2{:}2, \ldots, r_2{:}2\} \xrightarrow{I_j^2}$$
$$\{q_j{:}0, r_2{:}2, \ldots, r_2{:}2\} \rightarrow^* \{q_j{:}0, r_2{:}t_1, \ldots, r_2{:}t_m\} \xrightarrow{I_j^4} \{p_l{:}0, r_2{:}t_1, \ldots, r_2{:}t_m\}$$

where t_i is either 0 or 2 and $d_1 + \cdots + d_n = 1$. If t_i is 0 for $i = 1, \ldots, m$, then we can rewrite to $(l, 0, n_2)$ by flow. Otherwise, no jump rule is applicable, and neither is flow because of invariant rules.

  If $n_1 > 0$, we have two possibilities: rewrite to $(k, n_1 - 1, n_2)$ with the jump rule I_j^1, or to

$$\{p_j{:}2, r_1{:}2, \ldots, r_1{:}2, r_2{:}2, \ldots, r_2{:}2\}$$

with I_j^2 after 1 time unit. In the latter, we can further apply I_j^3 several times and then I_j^4, but at least one $r_1{:}2$ remains. Hence no further rewriting is applicable. $\qquad \square$

Theorem 2. *Let CM be a 2-counter machine, and $\mathcal{R}$ be the corresponding TMSRS. Then the following two conditions are equivalent.*

1. *If we execute CM from the state for which the initial value of r_i is n_i, then it terminates at the state for which the value of r_i is m_i.*
2. *In $\mathcal{R}$, $(1, n_1, n_2) \rightarrow^* (e, m_1, m_2)$.*

3.2   Reachability, Boundedness, and Coverability

The undecidability of reachability of a TMSRS is a direct consequence of that of timed-arc Petri nets [11]. However, we can also easily show it using the simulation given in Definition 9.

In general, the values of counters r_1 and r_2 are arbitrary when a 2-counter machine reaches I_e. However, without loss of generality, we can consider an extended machine that the final values of counters become 0 whenever it terminates, by adding appropriate instructions after I_e. We use the extended machine in the arguments on the reachability of a TMSRS.

Theorem 3. *The reachability of a TMSRS is undecidable.*

Proof. By Theorem 2, for an extended 2-counter machine CM, the initial values n_1 and n_2 and the corresponding TMSRS $\mathcal{R}$, the termination of CM and the existence of a sequence of rewrites $(1, n_1, n_2) \rightarrow^* (e, 0, 0)$ in $\mathcal{R}$ is equivalent. Since the halting problem of 2-counter machines is undecidable, the reachability of a TMSRS is also undecidable.

As in reachability, the undecidability of boundedness of a TMSRS is shown by that of the halting problem of 2-counter machines. First, we eliminate the jump rules corresponding to the instruction I_e, so that we may not apply jump rules after reaching I_e.

Since we represent the value of a counter by a multiplicity of the corresponding timed element, if a TMSRS $\mathcal{R}$ simulating a 2-counter machine CM is bounded, then the space of possible values of counters is finite. In this case, we can determine whether the machine terminates or not using some exhaustive search. Therefore, if we can show that

$$\mathcal{R} \text{ is unbounded} \Longrightarrow CM \text{ does not terminate,}$$

then the boundedness of the TMSRS determines the termination of the 2-counter machine, hence boundedness of a TMSRS is undecidable.

Lemma 2. *For a 2-counter machine CM, let $\mathcal{R}$ be a TMSRS simulating CM (with elimination of the jump rules corresponding to the instruction I_e). Then CM does not terminate whenever $\mathcal{R}$ is unbounded.*

Proof. In order to make $\mathcal{R}$ unbounded, rewriting by jump must occur infinitely often. This corresponds to the infinite execution of CM. □

Theorem 4. *The boundedness of a TMSRS is undecidable.*

Finally, the undecidability of coverability of a TMSRS is shown using the same simulation.

Lemma 3. *Let CM be a 2-counter machine, and $\mathcal{R}$ be the simulating TMSRS. Then CM terminates if and only if $\{p_e{:}1\}$ is coverable in $\mathcal{R}$.*

Proof. A sequence of rewrites reaching a timed multiset that contains $p_e{:}1$ corresponds to the execution of the 2-counter machine that reaches I_e. □

Theorem 5. *The coverability of a TMSRS is undecidable.*

4   Without Invariant Rules

As we mentioned in the previous section, reachability, boundedness, and coverability are all undecidable in general for a TMSRS. In this section, we consider restricted TMSRSs that do not contain invariant rules, and discuss reachability, boundedness, and coverability of those systems. A "TMSRS" in this section is assumed to be one without invariant rules even if we do not state it explicitly.

4.1   Reachability

In Definition 8, the simulation of timed(-arc) Petri nets by a TMSRS does not require invariant rules. Thus the undecidability result for the reachability of timed-arc Petri nets [11] is also applicable to a TMSRS without invariant rules. In fact, the essential part of the argument in [11] can also be imitated in the simulation given in Definition 9.

Theorem 6. *The reachability of a TMSRS without invariant rules is undecidable.*

4.2   Boundedness

Here we show that the boundedness of a TMSRS is decidable. In a TMSRS, there are uncountably many rewrites from a certain timed multiset, and that makes it difficult to analyze a TMSRS directly. Hence we use the notion of regions in order to make rewrites finitely many. The notion of regions was originally introduced on a fixed set of clock variables for analysis of timed automata, and it was extended to that on multisets for reachability analysis of timed processes [16].

Definition 10. *For a given TMSRS $\mathcal{R}$, we denote by C_{M} the maximum natural number occurring in $\mathcal{R}$ as a constant in a constraint.*

The region $M^\star$ corresponding to a timed multiset M is defined by the triple consisting of the following components.

1. *The multiset $\{(a{:}t) \mid a{:}t \in M, t \in \mathbb{N}, t \le C_{\mathrm{M}}\}$*
2. *The list of multisets $[B_1; B_2; \ldots; B_n]$ defined as follows. Let $0 < f_1 < f_2 < \cdots < f_n$ be all the non-zero fractional parts of clocks in M. Then B_i is defined as the multiset $\{(a{:}\lfloor t \rfloor) \mid a{:}t \in M, \mathrm{fr}(t) = f_i, t < C_{\mathrm{M}}\}$, where $\lfloor t \rfloor$ and $\mathrm{fr}(t)$ denote the integral and fractional parts of t, respectively.*
3. *The multiset of multisets $\{C_1, \ldots, C_m\}$ defined as follows. Let $I = \{c_i, \ldots, c_m\}$ be a set of natural numbers satisfying $I = \{t \mid a{:}t \in M, t > C_{\mathrm{M}}\}$. Then C_i is defined as the multiset $\{a \mid a{:}c_i \in M\}$.*

For a region U, its multiplicity $|U|$ is defined as the number of elements $((a{:}t)$ or a for all $a \in S)$ in U, and the multiplicity $|U|_a$ of an element a is defined as the number of a occurring in U.

Example 1. When $C_M = 3$ and a timed multiset M is

$$\{a{:}2.2,\ a{:}1.2,\ a{:}1.2,\ a{:}1,\ b{:}3.2,\ b{:}3,\ b{:}3,\ c{:}0.9\},$$

then $M^\star$ is

$$(\{(a{:}1),\ (b{:}3),\ (b{:}3)\},\ [\{(a{:}2),\ (a{:}1),\ (a{:}1)\};\ \{(c{:}0)\}],\ \{\{b\}\}).$$

For the above $M^\star$, $|M^\star| = 8$ and $|M^\star|_b = 3$.

Proposition 1. $|M^\star| = |M|$ and $|M^\star|_a = |M|_a$ for a multiset M and an element $a \in S$.

Proposition 2. For a region U, there exists a timed multiset M such that $M^\star = U$.

Rewriting on regions is defined as well as on timed multisets.

Definition 11. *Let $\mathcal{R}$ be a TMSRS.*

For a region U and a jump rule $R : l \to r$ if C, if there exists a timed multiset N, a region U', and an assignment σ such that

$$U = (l\sigma + N)^\star, \quad U' = (r\sigma + N)^\star, \quad \sigma \models C,$$

then we say that U is rewritable to U', and write $U \xrightarrow{R} U'$.

A rewrite by flow is defined as follows. For a region $U = (A, [B_1; \ldots; B_n], C)$ $(n \geq 0)$ satisfying either $A \neq \emptyset$ or $n > 0$, a region U' is defined as follows:

1. *Case $A \neq \emptyset$:*

$$U' \stackrel{\text{def}}{=} \begin{cases} (\emptyset, [A'; B_1; \ldots; B_n], C' + C) & \text{if } A' \neq \emptyset \\ (\emptyset, [B_1; \ldots; B_n], C' + C) & \text{if } A' = \emptyset \end{cases}$$

   where $A' \stackrel{\text{def}}{=} \{(a{:}t) \mid (a{:}t) \in A,\ t < C_M\}$, $A'' \stackrel{\text{def}}{=} \{a \mid (a{:}t) \in A,\ t = C_M\}$, and $C' = \emptyset$ if $A'' = \emptyset$ otherwise $C' = \{A''\}$.

2. *Case $A = \emptyset$ and $n > 0$:*

$$U' \stackrel{\text{def}}{=} (B'_n, [B_1; \ldots; B_{n-1}], C)$$

   where $B'_n \stackrel{\text{def}}{=} \{(a{:}t+1) \mid (a{:}t) \in B_n\}$.

Then we say that U is rewritable to U' and write as $U \xrightarrow{\tau} U'$.

When U is rewritable to U' by either jump or flow, we write $U \to U'$. The reflexive transitive closure (transitive closure, resp.) of $\xrightarrow{\tau}$ and $\to$ are denoted by $\xrightarrow{\tau}{}^*$ and $\to^*$ ($\xrightarrow{\tau}{}^+$ and $\to^+$), respectively.

Rewriting relation on timed multisets and that on regions are bisimilar to each other.

Proposition 3. *For a TMSRS $\mathcal{R}$, we have the following properties:*

- $M \xrightarrow{(R,\sigma)} N \Longrightarrow M^\star \xrightarrow{R} N^\star$
- $M \xrightarrow{d} N \Longrightarrow M^\star \xrightarrow{\tau}{}^* N^\star$
- $M^\star \xrightarrow{R} V \Longrightarrow \exists N. M \xrightarrow{R} N \wedge N^\star = V$
- $M^\star \xrightarrow{\tau} V \Longrightarrow \exists N\, d.\, d \in \mathbb{R}_{>0} \wedge M \xrightarrow{d} N \wedge N^\star = V$

Lemma 4. *For a TMSRS $\mathcal{R}$, the boundedness of rewriting on timed multisets from M and that on regions from $M^\star$ are equivalent.*

Proof. If one system is not bounded, then for any natural number n, there exists a sequence of rewrites whose result has multiplicity exceeding n. By Proposition 3, such a sequence is simulated by the other, and the multiplicity of the result also exceeds n.   □

By Lemma 4, the boundedness of a TMSRS is determined by that on regions. Therefore, we focus on the decidability of the boundedness of rewriting on regions in the rest of this subsection.

For regions introduced on TMSRSs, we can define an ordering between them that can be naturally derived from multiset inclusion, and this ordering plays a significant role in analysis using regions. This is a distinguishing characteristic of regions on multisets, compared with those defined on timed automata.

Definition 12. *Let $U = (A, B, C)$ and $U' = (A', B', C')$ be regions. We say that U' covers U and write $U \preceq U'$ if the following conditions are satisfied,*

- $A \subseteq_m A'$.
- $B \subseteq_m^* B'$ *where $\subseteq_m^*$ is a 'substring' ordering defined by $\subseteq_m$ as follows:*

$$[M_1; M_2; \ldots; M_n] \subseteq_m^* [M_1'; M_2'; \ldots; M_{n'}']$$
$$\stackrel{\text{def}}{\Longleftrightarrow} \exists \rho : \{1, \ldots, n\} \to \{1, \ldots, n'\} \text{ strictly monotone.}$$
$$\forall i \in \{1, \ldots, n\}.\, M_i \subseteq_m M_{\rho(i)}'$$

- $C \subseteq_{mm} C'$ *where $\subseteq_{mm}$ is defined as follows: $C = \{C_1, \ldots, C_n\} \subseteq_{mm} C' \stackrel{\text{def}}{\Longleftrightarrow}$ there exists $C'' = \{C_1', \ldots, C_n'\} \subseteq_m C'$ such that $C_i \subseteq_m C_i'$ for all $i = 1, \ldots, n$.*

Actually, $\preceq$ is a partial ordering. We write $U \prec U'$ if $U \preceq U'$ and $U' \not\preceq U$.

Lemma 5. *If $U \preceq U'$ and $U \to V$, then there exists V' such that $U' \to^+ V'$ and $V \preceq V'$. In particular, $U' \xrightarrow{R} V'$ when $U \xrightarrow{R} V$.*

If a TMSRS contains invariant rules I, Lemma 5 above no longer holds with respect to a rewrite by flow.

Example 2. Assume that a TMSRS has an invariant rule $a{:}t \mid t \leq 2$, and $C_M = 3$. Then a rewrite by flow

$$(\{(a{:}1)\}, [], \emptyset) \xrightarrow{\tau} (\emptyset, [\{(a{:}1)\}], \emptyset)$$

is possible. However,

$$(\{(a{:}1),\ (a{:}2)\},\ [],\ \emptyset) \xrightarrow{\ \tau\ } (\emptyset,\ [\{(a{:}1),\ (a{:}2)\}],\ \emptyset)$$

is not possible since the right hand side is a region for which the invariant rule does not hold.

Definition 13. *A quasi-ordering $\leq$ on a set X is well-quasi-ordering (wqo) if for any sequence $x_1, x_2, \ldots$ of elements in X, there exist $i < j$ such that $x_i \leq x_j$.*

Theorem 7. *The relation $\preceq$ on regions is wqo.*

Proof. There are finitely many $(a{:}t)$'s since t is a natural number bounded by C_M. Using the fact that $\leq$ on natural numbers is wqo and a finite product of wqo is also wqo, all $\subseteq_m$ in Definition 12 are wqo. Furthermore, since the 'substring' ordering derived from wqo is also wqo (Higman's lemma), $\subseteq_m^*$ is wqo. Hence $\preceq$ is wqo. □

Proposition 4. *For $\nu : S \to \mathbb{N}$, the regions U satisfying $\forall a.\,|U|_a = \nu(a)$ are finite.*

Proof. Suppose they are infinitely many. Since $|U| = |V|$ and $U \preceq V$ imply $U = V$, it contradicts the fact that $\preceq$ is wqo.

Proposition 5. *For a region U, the set $\{V \mid U \to V\}$ is finite and computable.*

Proof. For a rewrite by flow, Definition 11 directly leads to the computation of the set.

For a rewrite by jump, using Proposition 2, we can take a concrete M such that $M^* = U$. By Proposition 3, we can collect all regions V such that $U \xrightarrow{R} V$ by collecting N^* for all multisets N such that $M \xrightarrow{R} N$. For a jump rule R : $l \to r$ if C, the set $\{\sigma|_{\mathrm{Var}(l)} \mid \sigma \models C,\ l\sigma \subseteq_m M\}$ of substitutions are finite, where $\sigma|_{\mathrm{Var}(l)}$ is the restriction of the domain of σ to $\mathrm{Var}(l)$. Thus for each substitution $\sigma' : \mathrm{Var}(l) \to \mathbb{R}_{\geq 0}$, the set $G \stackrel{\text{def}}{=} \{(r\sigma)^* \mid \sigma \models C,\ \sigma|_{\mathrm{Var}(l)} = \sigma'\}$ of regions are also finite by Proposition 4 since $|(r\sigma_1)^*|_a = |(r\sigma_2)^*|_a$ for any element a and substitutions $\sigma_1, \sigma_2 \in G$. Thus the set $\{V \mid U \xrightarrow{R} V\} = \{(r\sigma + L)^* \mid \sigma \models C,\ M = l\sigma + L\}$ is finite. □

The Karp-Miller tree construction is used to determine whether a Petri net is bounded or not. Here we apply a Karp-Miller tree to a TMSRS, so that it can be used for the boundedness of a TMSRS.

Definition 14. *A Karp-Miller tree for a region U_0 is constructed as follows:*

1. *Attach the label U_0 to the root node s_0. Execute Step 2 with taking the current node as s_0.*
2. *Let s be the current node and U be its label. For each U' such that $U \to U'$ and U' does not coincide with any labels of nodes on the path from the root node to s, create a new node s' as a child of s. The label of s' is defined as follows:*

- *If U' covers the label of some node on the path from the root node to s, then attach the label ∞ to s'.*
- *Otherwise, attach the label U' to s' and execute Step 2 taking s' as the current node.*

Theorem 8. *The Karp-Miller tree for a region U_0 is finite and computable.*

Proof. First, by Proposition 5, $\{V \mid U \to V\}$ is finite and computable for a region U. Suppose the Karp-Miller tree is infinite. Any infinite tree with finite branching contains an infinite path from the root node by König's lemma. By the construction of the Karp-Miller tree, for node s and its ancestor s', if s and s' have labels U and U', respectively, then $U' \npreceq U$. Thus the existence of such an infinite path contradicts the fact that $\preceq$ is wqo.   □

Theorem 9. *For a TMSRS $\mathcal{R}$ without invariant rules, it is bounded from U_0 if and only if the Karp-Miller tree for U_0 does not include the label ∞.*

Proof. If the Karp-Miller tree for U_0 includes a node s with its label ∞, then there exist an ancestor node s' of s. By Lemma 5, we can repeatedly apply a path from s' to s and increase multiplicity as much as we want. Thus $\mathcal{R}$ is unbounded from U_0.

On the other hand, if the Karp-Miller tree for U_0 does not include the label ∞, all the possible rewrites are captured by the Karp-Miller tree. Hence $\mathcal{R}$ is bounded from U_0.   □

Therefore, we can determine whether a TMSRS $\mathcal{R}$ is bounded from a timed multiset M by examining whether the Karp-Miller tree for $M^\star$ includes ∞.

Theorem 10. *The boundedness of a TMSRS without invariant rules is decidable.*

4.3 Coverability

The a coverability of TMSRS can be shown by extending the method used in that of timed Petri nets [13], where existential zones are used as an abstract domain of configurations in timed Petri nets. However, the argument in [13] lacks the relationship between configurations and existential zones, and that buries subtle conditions required for the decidability of coverability. So, we first precisely relate multisets, which correspond to configurations in timed Petri nets, and regions as components of existential zones, and then extend the analysis method by existential zones so that it can be applied to analysis of a TMSRS.

Definition 15. *We say that a set K of timed multisets is total with respect to the closed part of a region $U = (A, B, C)$ if $\forall M \in K. M^\star = U$, and $\{M' \mid M'^\star = (A, B, \emptyset)\} \subseteq \{M_{\leq C_M} \mid M \in K\}$, where $M_{\leq C_M} \stackrel{\text{def}}{=} \{a{:}t \mid a{:}t \in M, t \leq C_M\}$.*

Lemma 6. *For regions U and V such that $U \to V$, if K is total w.r.t. the closed part of U, then $\{N \mid \exists M \in K. M \to N\}$ is also total w.r.t. the closed part of V.*

With the above lemma, two kinds of coverability are related as follows:

Lemma 7. *Assume a TMSRS $\mathcal{R}$ and timed multisets M and N are given. When all the clocks in M are natural numbers, N is coverable from M if and only if $N^\star$ is coverable from $M^\star$, with the proviso that we increase C_M enough to make clocks in both M and N smaller than or equal to C_M if needed.*

Proof. Taking the greater C_M does not affect arguments we have done so far. If we take C_M as above, $M^\star$ and $N^\star$ are written $M^\star = (A, B, \emptyset)$ and $N^\star = (A', B', \emptyset)$.

If $N^\star$ is coverable from $M^\star$, then $M^\star \to^* V$ and $N^\star \preceq V$ for some V. Since all the clocks in M are natural numbers and less than or equal to C_M, $\{M\}$ is total w.r.t. the closed part of $M^\star$. If we let $V = (A'', B'', C'')$, then we can make N' such that $N'^\star = (A'', B'', \emptyset)$ by adding some timed elements to N. By Lemma 6, there exists N'' such that $N' \subseteq_m N''$, $M \to^* N''$ and $N''^\star = V$. Thus N is coverable from M.

Conversely, if N is coverable from M, then there exists N' such that $M \to^* N'$ and $N \subseteq_m N'$. By Proposition 3, we have $M^\star \to^* N'^\star$ and $N^\star \preceq N'^\star$. That means $N^\star$ is coverable from $M^\star$.   □

A similar argument can be applied to the Karp-Miller tree on regions, and we can show that the reachability from a timed multiset whose clocks are natural numbers can be determined by the Karp-Miller tree provided it is bounded (i.e., no ∞ labels).

Although it is possible to show the decidability of the coverability of rewriting on regions using the theory of well-structured transition systems [17], we instead extend the method in [13] using existential zones since it is more concise. The argument on the relationship between two kinds of coverability is also applicable to existential zones since each existential zone can be seen as a union of some regions, and each region can be expressed by some zone. As in [13], we only consider the case that the inequalities occurring in the rewrite rules are non-strict for simplicity, but the general case can be obtained straightforwardly.

Definition 16. *An existential zone Z is a triple (m, p, D), where m is a natural number, $p : \{1, \ldots, m\} \to S$ is a mapping from indices to elements, and $D : \{0, \ldots, m\} \times \{0, \ldots, m\} \to \{-C_M, \ldots, C_M\} \cup \{\infty\}$ is a difference bound matrix.*

An existential zone $Z = (m, p, D)$ defines a set $[\![Z]\!]$ of timed multisets as follows:

$$M = \{a_1{:}t_1, \ldots, a_n{:}t_n\} \in [\![Z]\!] \overset{\text{def}}{\Longleftrightarrow}$$
$$\exists h : \{1, \ldots, m\} \to \{1, \ldots, n\} \text{ injection. } (a_{h(i)} = p(i) \text{ for } i = 1, \ldots, m) \land$$
$$(t_{h(i)} - t_{h(j)} \le D(i, j) \text{ for } i \ne j \text{ and } i, j = 1, \ldots, m) \land$$
$$(-D(0, i) \le t_{h(i)} \le D(i, 0) \text{ for } i = 1, \ldots, m)$$

We say that an existential zone Z is consistent *if $[\![Z]\!] \ne \emptyset$.*

Along [13], all we have to show is that we can compute a predecessor $Pre(Z)$ of a given existential zone Z as a finite set of existential zones $\{Z_1, \ldots, Z_n\}$ so that $M \to N$ and $N \in \llbracket Z \rrbracket$ for some N if and only if $M \in \llbracket Z_i \rrbracket$ for some i. For this purpose, we define four operations on existential regions. The first three are from [13], but among them, the addition operation is slightly different from that in [13].

Definition 17. *Suppose $[u : v]$ denotes the interval between u and v. Let $Z = (m, p, D)$ be an existential zone, $i, i_1, \ldots, i_n \in \{1, \ldots, m\}$ be natural numbers, and $a \in S$ be an element. Then the* conjunction $Z \otimes ([u : v], i)$, *the* addition $Z \oplus a$, *the* abstraction $Z \setminus i$, *and* equalization $Z \oslash \{i_1, \ldots, i_n\}$ *are defined as follows:*

conjunction $Z \otimes ([u : v], i) \stackrel{\text{def}}{=} (m, p, D')$ *where* $D'(i, 0) = \min(v, D(i, 0))$, $D'(0, i) = \min(-u, D(0, i))$, *and* $D(k, j) = D(k, j)$ *for* $k \neq j$, $(k, j) \neq (i, 0)$, *and* $(k, j) \neq (0, i)$.

addition $Z \oplus a \stackrel{\text{def}}{=} (m + 1, p', D')$ *where* $D'(m + 1, 0) = \infty$, $D'(0, m + 1) = 0$, $D'(m + 1, j) = D'(j, m + 1) = \infty$ *for* $j \in \{1, \ldots, m\}$, $D'(k, j) = D(k, j)$ *for* $j, k \in \{1, \ldots, m\}$, $p'(m + 1) = a$, *and* $p'(j) = p(j)$ *for* $j \in \{1, \ldots, m\}$.

abstraction $Z \setminus i \stackrel{\text{def}}{=} (m - 1, p', D')$ *where* $D'(j, k) = D(j, k)$ *for* $j, k \in \{0, \ldots, i - 1\}$, $D'(j, k) = D(j, k + 1)$ *and* $D'(k, j) = D(k + 1, j)$ *for* $j \in \{0, \ldots, i - 1\}$ *and* $k \in \{i, \ldots, m - 1\}$, $D'(j, k) = D(j + 1, k + 1)$ *for* $j, k \in \{i, \ldots, m - 1\}$, $p'(j) = p(j)$ *for* $j \in \{0, \ldots, i - 1\}$, *and* $p'(j) = p(j + 1)$ *for* $j \in \{i, \ldots, m - 1\}$.

equalization $Z \oslash \{i_1, \ldots, i_n\} \stackrel{\text{def}}{=} (m, p, D')$ *where* $D'(j, k) = 0$ *if* $j, k \in \{i_1, \ldots, i_n\}$, *otherwise* $D'(j, k) = D(j, k)$.

Lemma 8. *For a TMSRS $\mathcal{R}$, and a jump rule*

$$R : a_1{:}t_1, \ldots, a_k{:}t_k \to b_1{:}s_1, \ldots, b_l{:}s_l \;\textbf{if}\; C,$$

the predecessor $Pre_R(Z)$ of a given existential zone $Z = (m, p, D)$ with respect to R is given by the smallest set containing each existential zone Z' such that there is a partial injection $h : \{1, \ldots, m\} \to \{1, \ldots, l\}$ with a domain $\{i_1, \ldots, i_n\}$, and existential zones $Z_1, Z_2,$ and Z_3 satisfying the following conditions:

- $p(i_j) = b_{h(i_j)}$ *for* $j \in \{1, \ldots, n\}$.
- $Z_1 = Z \oplus a_1 \oplus \cdots \oplus a_k$.
- $Z_2 = Z_1 \otimes (\mathcal{C}(s_{h(i_1)}), i_1) \otimes \cdots \otimes (\mathcal{C}(s_{h(i_n)}), i_n) \otimes (\mathcal{C}(t_1), m+1) \otimes \cdots \otimes (\mathcal{C}(t_k), m + k)$.
- $Z_3 = Z_2 \oslash K(x_1) \oslash \cdots \oslash K(x_r)$ *is consistent.*
- $Z' = \widetilde{Z_3} \setminus i_1 \setminus \cdots \setminus i_n$

where

- $\mathcal{C}(t) \stackrel{\text{def}}{=} [t : t]$ *if $t \in \mathbb{N}$, otherwise $\mathcal{C}(t) \stackrel{\text{def}}{=} [u : v]$ satisfying $C \Leftrightarrow (t \in [u : v]) \wedge C'$ for some $C' \in \mathcal{B}(\text{Var}(C) \setminus \{t\})$, where $\text{Var}(C)$ is the set of clock variables occurring in C.*
- $\{x_1, \ldots, x_r\} = \text{Var}(C)$ *and* $K(x_i) \stackrel{\text{def}}{=} \{i_j \mid x_i = s_{h(i_j)}, j \in \{1, \ldots, n\}\} \cup \{m + j \mid x_i = t_j, j \in \{1, \ldots, k\}\}$.

- $\widetilde{Z_3} = (m_3, p_3, \widetilde{D_3})$ is a "normal form" of Z_3, i.e., $[\![\widetilde{Z_3}]\!] = [\![Z_3]\!]$ and $\widetilde{D_3}(i, j) \le \widetilde{D_3}(i, q) + \widetilde{D_3}(q, j)$ for $i, j, q \in \{0, \ldots, m + k\}$.

Together with the lemma that states the predecessor of $\xrightarrow{\tau}$ is computable in [13], we have that $Pre(Z)$ is computable for any existential zone Z.

Theorem 11. *The coverability of rewriting on existential zones is decidable. Therefore the coverability of a TMSRS from the timed multiset whose clocks are natural numbers is also decidable.*

5   With Diagonal Constraints

For timed automata, it is known that the expressiveness is not increased even if we allow diagonal constraints $(x - y \bowtie c)$ as transition conditions [9]. Moreover, if clocks are updatable by constants $(x := c)$ or by copying $(x := y)$ through transition through edges, the expressiveness remains the same. There are some classes of updatable timed automata [18] such that the emptiness problem is undecidable if the automaton has diagonal constraints whereas it is decidable if the automaton is diagonal-free.

Here we consider how diagonal constraints affect the expressiveness of TM-SRSs. Note that we already have the implicit restricted form of diagonal constraints such that $x - y = 0$ since we can use the same clock variable more than once in a single jump rule. Since the three properties on a general TMSRS are already undecidable, we consider the TMSRSs with diagonal constraints without invariant rules. Contrary to the case of timed automata, all three properties become undecidable once a TMSRS contain diagonal constraints even if clocks are updated only by constants or copying.

Definition 18. *We define a simulation of 2-counter machines by a TMSRS with diagonal constraints. The value n_i of the counter r_i is represented by a multiset $\{a_i{:}0, \ldots, a_i{:}n_i{-}1, b_i{:}n_i\}$.*

- *Increment:* $I(i, j, k)$

$$I_j^1 : p_j{:}1, a_{3-i}{:}t, b_{3-i}{:}s \rightarrow p_k{:}0, a_i{:}0, a_{3-i}{:}0, b_{3-i}{:}t \;\; \textbf{if } s - t = 1$$
$$I_j^2 : p_j{:}1, b_{3-i}{:}1 \rightarrow p_k{:}0, a_i{:}0, b_{3-i}{:}0$$

- *Test&Decrement:* $D(i, j, k, l)$

$$I_j^1 : p_j{:}0, a_i{:}t, b_i{:}s \rightarrow p_k{:}0, b_i{:}t \;\; \textbf{if } s - t = 1 \qquad I_j^2 : p_j{:}0, b_i{:}0 \rightarrow p_l{:}0, b_i{:}0$$

The simulation of Test&Decrement is straightforward, and there is no nondeterminism as in Definition 8. To increment a counter r_i, we first wait 1 time unit, then add a timed element $a_i{:}0$ and 'rewind' the clock of the other counter r_{3-i} by replacing $\{a_{3-i}{:}t, b_{3-i}{:}t{+}1\}$ with $\{a_{3-i}{:}0, b_{3-i}{:}t\}$ (or $\{b_{3-i}{:}1\}$ with $\{b_{3-i}{:}0\}$).

The above definition enables us to simulate an execution in a 2-counter machine by a TMSRS, and the undecidability of reachability, boundedness, and coverability can be shown with an argument similar to Section 3.2.

6   Conclusion

In this paper, we discussed the decidability of reachability, boundedness, and coverability of TMSRSs with or without invariant rules and diagonal constraints. All the three properties for TMSRSs with invariant rules, and the reachability of TMSRSs without invariant rules are undecidable, and they are shown by simulating 2-counter machines whose halting problem is undecidable. The boundedness and coverability of TMSRSs without invariant rules are decidable, and they are shown using regions, Karp-Miller trees, and existential zones. If we allow diagonal constraints in the rules, then all three properties are undecidable even if we disallow invariant rules.

The results of undecidability with invariant rules are too coarse to apply to the simulation of timed automata. We anticipate that if the elements in invariant rules are bounded, which is true for the simulation of timed automata, then boundedness and coverability would be decidable. Including this aspect, we should explore the system more in detail in order to make fine distinction between decidable classes.

Acknowledgement

We are grateful to Koichi Takahashi from National Institute of Advanced Industrial Science and Technology for commenting the early versions of the paper. We also thank anonymous referees for constructive and informative comments.

This work was partially supported by the Ministry of Education, Culture, Sports, Science and Technology, Grant-in-Aid for Exploratory Research, 14658088, 2002, Grant-in-Aid for Scientific Research on Priority Areas (B), 12133101, 2001, and Grant-in-Aid for Scientific Research on Priority Areas (C), 13224012, 2001.

References

1. Meseguer, J.: Conditional rewriting logic as a unified model of concurrency. Theoretical Computer Science **96** (1992) 73–155
2. Cervesato, I., Durgin, N.A., Lincoln, P., Mitchell, J.C., Scedrov, A.: A meta-notation for protocol analysis. In: IEEE CSFW. (1999) 55–69
3. Kosiuczenko, P., Wirsing, M.: Timed rewriting logic for the specification of time-sensitive systems. In Schwichtenberg, H., ed.: Proceedings of the Internat. Summer School on Proof and Computation. (1995)
4. Ölveczky, P.C., Meseguer, J.: Specifying real-time systems in rewriting logic. In: Electronic Notes in Theoretical Computer Science. Volume 4. (1996)
5. Kanovich, M., Okada, M., Scedrov, A.: Specifying real-time finite-state systems in linear logic (1998)
6. Hagiya, M., Yamamoto, M., Cottin, J.M.: Symbolic analysis of timed multiset rewriting and its application to protocol analysis (extended abstract). In: Rewriting in Proof and Computation, International Workshop, RPC'01, The Research Institute of Electrical Communication (RIEC), Tohoku University (2001) 34–41

7. Bozzano, M., Delzanno, G., Martelli, M.: An effective bottom-up semantics for first-order linear logic programs. In: FLOPS. (2001) 138–152

8. Cerone, A., Maggiolo-Schettini, A.: Time-based expressivity of time Petri nets for system specification. Theoretical Computer Science **216** (1999) 1–53

9. Alur, R., Dill, D.L.: A theory of timed automata. Theoretical Computer Science **126** (1994) 183–236

10. Henzinger, T.: The theory of hybrid automata. In: Proceedings of the 11th Annual IEEE Symposium on Logic in Computer Science (LICS '96), New Brunswick, New Jersey (1996) 278–292

11. Ruiz, V.V., Gomez, F.C., de Frutos Escrig, D.: On non-decidability of reachability for timed-arc Petri nets. In: Proc. 8th Int. Workshop on Petri Net and Performance Models (PNPM'99), 8-10 October 1999, Zaragoza, Spain. (1999) 188–196

12. de Frutos Escrig, D., Ruiz, V.V., Alonso, O.M.: Decidability of properties of timed-arc Petri nets. In Nielsen, M., Simpson, D., eds.: Lecture Notes in Computer Science: 21st International Conference on Application and Theory of Petri Nets (ICATPN 2000), Aarhus, Denmark, June 2000. Volume 1825., Springer-Verlag (2000) 187–206

13. Abdulla, P.A., Nylén, A.: Timed Petri nets and BQOs. In: Proc. ICATPN'2001, 22nd Int. Conf. on application and theory of Petri nets. Volume 2075 of LNCS. (2001) 53–70

14. T.A. Henzinger, X. Nicollin, J. Sifakis, S. Yovine: Symbolic Model Checking for Real-Time Systems. In: 7th. Symposium of Logics in Computer Science, Santa-Cruz, California, IEEE Computer Scienty Press (1992) 394–406

15. Alur, R., Henzinger, T.A.: Real-time system = discrete system + clock variables. International Journal on Software Tools for Technology Transfer **1** (1997) 86–109

16. Abdulla, P.A., Jonsson, B.: Verifying networks of timed processes. Lecture Notes in Computer Science **1384** (1998) 298–312

17. Finkel, A., Schnoebelen, P.: Well-structured transition systems everywhere ! Theoretical Computer Science **256** (2001) 64–92

18. Bouyer, P., Dufourd, C., Fleury, E., Petit, A.: Are timed automata updatable ? In: Proc. 12th Int. Conf. Computer Aided Verification (CAV'2000), Chicago, IL, USA, July 2000. Volume 1855., Springer (2000) 464–479

Extending Timed Automaton and Real-Time Logic to Many-Valued Reasoning*

Ana Fernández Vilas, José J. Pazos Arias, and Rebeca P. Díaz Redondo

Departamento de Ingeniería Telemática
Universidad de Vigo. 36200, Vigo, Spain
{avilas,jose,rebeca}@det.uvigo.es
http://www-gris.det.uvigo.es

Abstract. Past decade has witnessed a great advance in the field of dense-time formal methods for the specification, synthesis and analysis of real time systems. In this context timed automata and real-time temporal logics provide a simple, and yet general, way to model and specify the behavior of these systems. At the same time, iterative and incremental development has been massively adopted in professional practice. In order to get closer to this current trend, timed formal methods should be adapted to such lifecycle structures, getting over their traditional role of verifying that a model meets a set of fixed requirements. We advocate the suitability of many-valued reasoning in order to achieve this goal; in the scope of knowledge representation, many-valued reasoning is suitable to deal with both uncertainty and disagreement which are pervasive and desirable in an iterative and incremental design process. In this respect, this paper introduces SCTL/MUS-T methodology as an extension of timed automata and temporal logic theories to many-valued reasoning in real-time.

1   Introduction

Timed formal methods for the specification, analysis and verification of real-time systems has been around for a long time. Nowadays, there is a broad consensus [1–3] that dense-time approaches are more expressive and suitable for composition and refinement since a quantum of time is not needed to be fixed a priori. In addition to flexibility, decision procedures for dense-time are increasingly efficient every day.

The dense formal approach to real-time systems has been carried out extending a large amount of formalisms studied at length, which differ on their methods, aims, and abstraction-levels: temporal logics, first order logics, state-machines, process algebras, synchronous languages, etc. In the context of timed formal methods in general, and specifically of specification of real time systems in terms of timed process algebras and real-time logics, timed automata provide a simple, and yet general, way to model the behavior of real-time systems.

* This work was partially supported by the Xunta de Galicia Basic Research Project PGIDT01PX132203PR.

W. Damm and E.-R. Olderog (Eds.): FTRTFT 2002, LNCS 2469, pp. 185–204, 2002.
© Springer-Verlag Berlin Heidelberg 2002

While timed automata can be considered the standard timed state-machines, for what concerns properties, the situation seems not to be so clear: a variety of logics have been applied to requirements specification [4]. As far as analysis is concerned, formal techniques assuming dense time have their early origin in [5]. In this work, *Alur et al* introduced the first model checking algorithm for timed automata with real-valued clocks. The main idea behind this algorithm is the construction of an abstract finite state-space, called region graph, from the dense state-space of a timed automaton. Since obtaining an accurate finite model of the system was revealed as possible, many works have extended this solution to other kinds of analysis.

Shortly after theoretical results appeared, verification tools were developed mainly in academic area (KRONOS[1] followed by UPPAAL[2]). Both tools are based on timed automaton to a large extent, although they differ in their property specification languages. Real case studies, like the ones tackled by UPPAAL and KRONOS, have highlighted timed models and methods are ready for practitioners' usage. However, these timed theoretical foundations come up against industry reluctance about the adoption of formal methods in the software process; technology-transfer problems, which had been observed in conventional untimed systems, appear once again. In order to get closer to professional practice, formal methods are in urgent need of being incorporated into the software process. In this respect, iterative and incremental development is a major milestone.

Formalizing Incremental Design by Many-Valued Reasoning. Despite the origins of many-valued reasoning can be traced back to antiquity, its application to computer science is almost exceptional. For instance, many-valued reasoning and specifically many-valued logics are known to support the explicit modeling of uncertainty and disagreement by allowing additional truth values outside bivalence principle [6].

In spite of being a common practice in software engineering, and its proven reduction in time to market, integration of iterative and incremental development with formal methods is still immature. Research has not provided the formal bases and methodologies enabling this paradigm. As a tool for knowledge representation, we postulate that many-valued reasoning fits in appropriately with an incremental and iterative specification process. In incremental specification the system gradually takes form as more is learned about the problem, that is, both uncertainty and disagreement are pervasive and desirable in this process.

Many-valued reasoning, in its role of knowledge formalizer, has been studied in SCTL/MUS [7] methodology in order to support a formal lifecycle which is iterative and incremental in the specification process. On these bases, real-time SCTL/MUS (SCTL/MUS-T) is introduced in this paper, extending timed automaton (by defining MUS-T graphs) and real-time temporal logic (by defining SCTL-T temporal logic) to many-valued reasoning as a means of formalizing the incremental and iterative nature of the process.

---

[1] http://www-verimag.imag.fr/TEMPORISE/kronos/

[2] http://www.docs.uu.se/docs/rtmv/uppaal/

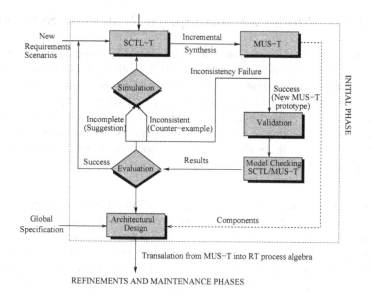

Fig. 1. *Initial* phase of the SCTL/MUS-T formalized lifecycle

The formalized lifecycle model consists, at a very abstract level, of three macro-phases: *initial, refinements* and *maintenance*. At the *initial* macro-phase (figure 1) the system is iteratively designed; a model-oriented specification (MUS-T graph, section 2) is obtained by incrementally incorporating timing scenarios identified on the target solution. At every iteration, the user identifies not only requirements, but typical scenarios of the system that is formally specified by means of a many-valued real-time logic (SCTL-T, section 3). New scenarios, which lead to a growth in the system functionality, are **synthesized** (if feasible) in the system modeled as a MUS-T graph. Also, requirements are **model checked** in the current model, the one in the current cycle, in order to decide: if the system already satisfies the requirements; if it is not able to provide, in a future design state, these requirements from the current design (inconsistency); or, if the system does not satisfy the requirements, but it is able to do it (incompleteness). Model checking and synthesis methods are introduced in section 4. Finally, in section 5, we illustrate SCTL/MUS-T methodology by means of examples extracted from the steam-boiler case study in [8].

Despite this paper focuses on the *initial* phase, the picture is completed as follows. Outcome of the *initial* phase is a set of MUS-T components which are transferred to a *refinement* phase (by translation into a real-time process algebra) where architecture decisions are incorporated and a more detailed design is successively reached, also iterative and incrementally. Finally, after delivering the system, *maintenance* turns into another development phase (*initial* + *refinements*) whose starting point is the previously developed system which is operating.

2   MUS-T: Model for Incomplete Real-Time Systems

For modeling real-time systems we define MUS-T graphs (**T**imed **M**odel of **U**nspecified **S**tates), timed extension of MUS models proposed in [7]. This extension defines a dense-time model similar to the timed automaton in [5], but event-driven. However, whereas atomic propositions on a location of a timed automaton are assertions being true or false, in order to support incompleteness and consistency-checking in an incremental process, timed events in a location of a MUS-T model can be characterized as possible (true), non-possible (false) or non-specified (unspecified).

Syntax. Before defining MUS-T graphs, some definitions concerning clocks and valuations are in order. A clock is a simple real-valued variable drawn from the finite set $\mathcal{C}$. A clock constraint $\psi \in \Psi(\mathcal{C})$ is a boolean combination of atomic formulas of the from $x \prec c$ or $x - y \prec c$, where x, y are clocks, c is an integer constant, and $\prec$ is taken from $\{\leq, \geq, <, >, =\}$. A clock valuation γ is a point in $\Re_+^{\#\mathcal{C}}$. If γ is a clock valuation, $\gamma + \tau$ for some $\tau \in \Re_+$ stands for the clock valuation obtained by adding τ to the value of every clock. Given a clock constraint ψ, $\psi(\gamma) = 1$ iff γ satisfies the clock constraint ψ, otherwise $\psi(\gamma) = 0$. Finally, let $\lambda \subseteq \mathcal{C}$ be a set of clocks, then γ_λ is the clock valuation obtained from γ by setting every clock in λ to 0. A MUS-T graph $\mathcal{M}$ is a 6-tuple $\langle s_0, S, T, I, A, \mathcal{C} \rangle$ over $\mathcal{L}_3$, where:

- $\mathcal{L}_3 = \{0, \frac{1}{2}, 1\}$ is the truth set which establishes the specification condition –possible (1), non-possible (0) or unspecified ($\frac{1}{2}$)– of the transitions in the graph.
- A is a finite set of events.
- $\mathcal{C}$ is a finite set of real-valued clocks.
- S is a finite set of locations, including two fictitious locations referred to as unspecified (s_u) and non-possible drain (s_{np}).
- s_0 is the initial location.
- $T \subseteq S \times A \times \Psi(\mathcal{C}) \times 2^{\mathcal{C}} \times S$ is the transition relation; and $CS : T \to \mathcal{L}_3$ is a total function which assigns a truth value (specification condition) to every transition.
- I_p and I_{np}: $S \to \Psi(\mathcal{C})$ are functions which assign to every location $s \in S$ a possible invariant $I_p(s)$, establishing when the progress of the time is possible in the location; and a non-possible invariant $I_{np}(s)$, establishing temporal contexts in which time cannot progress.

Every transition $t \in T$ with $CS(t) = 1$ defines a possible transition $(s, <$ $a, g_p(s,a), \lambda >, s')$ with source location s and target location s'. The timed event $< a, g_p(s,a), \lambda >$ specifies an event $a \in A$, a possible guard $g_p(s,a) \in \Psi(\mathcal{C})$ and a subset $\lambda \subseteq \mathcal{C}$ of clocks to reset in the transition. In the same way, every $t \in T$ with $CS(t) = \frac{1}{2}$ defines a partially-unspecified transition $(s, < a, g_u^P(s,a), \lambda >, s')$ with source location s, target location s' and an unspecified guarded event $< a, g_u^P(s,a), \lambda >$. Finally, transitions $t \in T$ with $CS(t) = 0$ define non-possible transitions $(s, < a, g_{np}(s, a), \{\} >, s_{np})$, with the non-possible drain s_{np} as fictitious target location.

Specification conditions partition the valuation space $\Re_+^{\#\mathcal{C}}$ in three subsets (possible, non-possible and unspecified). We enforce that partition to be complete and disjoint. For completeness, the totally-unspecified guard g_u^T is defined:

$$g_u^T(s, a) = \neg(\bigvee_i g_{p_i}(s, a)) \wedge \neg(\bigvee_j g_{u_j}^P(s, a)) \wedge \neg(g_{np}(s, a))$$

In this way, given a location s and an event a, valuation subsets defined by g_p, g_{np}, g_u^P, and g_u^T cover $\Re_+^{\#\mathcal{C}}$. $g_u^T(s, a)$ implicitly defines a totally-unspecified transition $(s, < a, g_u^T(s, a), \{\} >, s_u)$. Also, the unspecified invariant, I_u, is defined as $I_u(s) = \neg I_p(s) \wedge \neg I_{np}(s)$; given a location s, the subsets defined by I_p, I_{np} and I_u cover $\Re_+^{\#\mathcal{C}}$.

The drain-locations (s_u, s_{np}) are the fictitious target locations of non-transitions in a MUS-T graph, i.e., non-possible transitions and totally-unspecified transitions. However, their nature is definitively different, the drain-location s_{np} is zero-evolution, and the drain-location s_u is maximal-evolution. That is, $\forall\, a \in A$, $g_u^T(s_u, a) = true$ whereas $g_{np}(s_{np}, a) = true$. Similarly, $I_u(s_u) = true$ and $I_{np}(s_{np}) = true$.

Semantics. The semantics for a MUS-T graph is given in terms of a many-valued labeled transition system, which is often called dense due to the time domain. Formally, every MUS-T graph induces a dense many-valued transition system $\mathcal{S}_\mathcal{M} = \langle(s_0, \gamma^0), \mathcal{ST} = \{S \times \Re_+^{\#\mathcal{C}}\}, \mathcal{T}, A, \mathcal{C}\rangle$, over the truth set $\mathcal{L}_3$, where $\mathcal{ST}$ is the set of timed states, i.e., pairs of the form (s, γ) with $s \in S$ and $\gamma \in \Re_+^{\#\mathcal{C}}$; (s_0, γ^0) is the timed initial state with γ_0 assigning 0 to every clock; and $\mathcal{T} \subseteq \mathcal{ST} \times (A \cup \Re_+) \times \mathcal{L}_3 \times \mathcal{ST}$ is the transition relation. The transition relation $\mathcal{T}$ identifies a source and a target timed state $\in \mathcal{ST}$; a label $a \in A$ (discrete transition) or $\tau \in \Re_+$ (temporal transition); and a specification condition $\in \mathcal{L}_3$.

In general, dense time models assume orthogonality between discrete and dense changes. An execution of a timed model is a sequence of steps which alternate dense temporal transitions (incrementing the valuation an arbitrary amount of time); and discrete transitions (from one location to another). Preserving this orthogonal assumption but following the many-valued nature of a MUS-T graph, transitions $\in \mathcal{T}$ are characterized as possible (1), unspecified ($\frac{1}{2}$) or non-possible ones (0). Clock constraints on locations (invariants) and transitions (guards) implicitly define the total function $\mathcal{CS} : \mathcal{T} \to \mathcal{L}_3$, assigning a specification condition c_s to every transition $t \in \mathcal{T}$. Intuitively, the model can progress in a temporal way in a location s, with $c_s = 1$, as long as $I_p(s)$ is satisfied; with $c_s = 0$, as long as $I_{np}(s)$ is satisfied in some point; otherwise with $c_s = \frac{1}{2}$. Guards on transitions are enabling conditions, i.e. a transition $t \in \mathcal{T}$ of a MUS-T graph can only be taken, with specification condition $c_s = \mathcal{CS}(t)$, provided that clock constraints defining its guard are satisfied. Also, when a transition $\in \mathcal{T}$ occurs, all clocks in the set of clocks labeling it are reset to 0. In this way, a MUS-T graph is a many-valued timed automaton.

3   SCTL-T

We will specify requirements and scenarios of incomplete real-time systems using the temporal logic SCTL-T (**T**imed **S**imple **C**ausal **T**emporal **L**ogic), a dense real-time extension of the causal and many-valued temporal logic SCTL [7]. SCTL-T formulas match the causal pattern **Premise** Æ ⊗ **Consequence**. This generic causal formula establishes a causing condition (Premise); a temporal operator which determines the applicability of the cause (⊗); a condition which is the effect (Consequence); and a quantifier which determines the degree of satisfaction of the consequence on the applicability set (Æ). We now present the syntax and semantics of SCTL-T in three stages. The first stage introduces the quasi-boolean algebra L_6 (section 3.1), the second one defines syntax and semantics of propositional and temporal operators in SCTL-T (section 3.2); and the third one deals with recursion (section 3.3). Finally, in section 3.4 we introduce an imperative version of SCTL-T which is synthesis-oriented.

3.1   MPU: Algebra of Middle Point Uncertainty

Apart from being causal, SCTL-T is many-valued. SCTL-T semantics is given over the partially ordered set $(\mathcal{L}_6, \leq)$ of truth values, where $\mathcal{L}_6 = \{0, \frac{1}{4}, \widehat{\frac{1}{2}}, \frac{1}{2}, \frac{3}{4}, 1\}$ (Hasse diagram of figure 2). Every two elements $a, b \in \mathcal{L}_6$ have a least upper bound, $a \vee b = \sup\{a, b\}$, and a greatest lower bound $a \wedge b = \inf\{a, b\}$. Besides, the unary operation ¬ is defined by horizontal symmetry.

The 4-tuple $L_6 = (\mathcal{L}_6, \wedge, \vee, \neg)$ has the structure of a quasi-boolean algebra called algebra of **M**iddle **P**oint **U**ncertainty (MPU, see [7] for details). That is, the reduced algebra $(\mathcal{L}_6, \vee, \wedge)$ is a distributive lattice and the unary operation ¬ satisfies De Morgan, involution and antimonotonic properties. For the quasi-boolean algebra L_6, we define the causal operation, →, as follows:

$$a, b \in \mathcal{L}_6, \ \rightarrow (a, b) = \left(a \vee \widehat{\frac{1}{2}}\right) \wedge \left(\left(\neg a \wedge \widehat{\frac{1}{2}}\right) \vee b\right)$$

that is, causal connective is interpreted as usual implication when $a \geq \frac{1}{2}$, otherwise the causal formula is non-applicable ($\widehat{\frac{1}{2}}$). → is monotonic, like ∧ and ∨, and holds distributive properties and $\neg(a \rightarrow b) = a \rightarrow \neg b$.

Truth values ∈ $\mathcal{L}_6$ have its origins in the MUS-T specification condition ∈ $\mathcal{L}_3$ and the causal operation, →, defined above. A truth value expresses the capability of a MUS-T graph to satisfy a causal formula now or in future evolutions (see the table in figure 2). As being incremental, evolution means the loss of some unspecification in the model, that is, temporal or discrete transitions unspecified in the semantic graph turn into specified ones (possible or non-possible).

The partial order defined in MPU is and order relation related to the degree of satisfaction. So 0 is the least truth degree, whereas 1 is the greatest. The values $\widehat{\frac{1}{2}}$ and $\frac{1}{2}$ are middle points in this order: $\widehat{\frac{1}{2}}$ is far from the two ends (0 and 1), but it cannot get to them, whereas $\frac{1}{2}$ is near both, and it can get to either. This is the reason why it is called algebra of Middle Point Uncertainty.

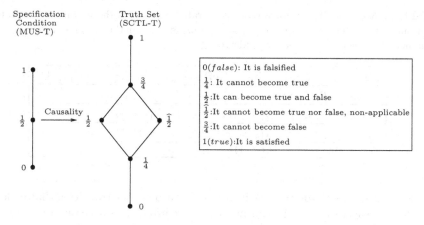

Fig. 2. SCTL-T Truth values

3.2 SCTl-T: Expressing Requirements

A SCTL-T declaration $I_i := \phi$ establishes an identifier I_i, which is taken from a set $\mathcal{I}$, and a SCTL-T formula $\phi \in \Phi_{SCTL-T}$. Φ_{SCTL-T} is given by the following grammar:

$$\langle \Phi_{SCTL-T} \rangle ::= \phi_C \forall \otimes \phi_C \mid \phi_C \exists \otimes \phi_C$$
$$\langle \phi_C \rangle ::= \psi \in \Psi \mid a \in A \mid \theta \in \Theta \mid y.\phi_C \mid \phi_C \wedge \phi_C \mid \phi_C \vee \phi_C \mid \neg \phi_C \mid \Phi_{SCTL-T}$$
$$\langle \otimes \rangle ::= \Rightarrow \mid \Rightarrow_+ \mid \Rightarrow_- \mid \Rightarrow \bigcirc \mid \Rightarrow \odot$$

where $\{\forall, \exists\}$ are the usual path quantifiers adapted to many-valued reasoning; $\otimes$, the set of temporal operators; $\theta \in \Theta ::= \{true \mid false \mid \emptyset\}$, a propositional constant of state; $a \in A$, an event in the alphabet of a MUS-T graph; $y.$, the reset quantifier which binds and resets a specification clock $y \in \mathcal{E}$; and $\mathcal{E}$, the set of specification clocks. Finally, $\psi \in \Psi$ is the set of clock constraints over model clocks $\in \mathcal{C}$ and specification clocks $\in \mathcal{E}$.

Applicability Set and Quantified Causality. Temporal operators are used to reason about transition successors and predecessors of a given timed state. A temporal operator $\in \otimes$ fixes the qualitative order between the timed state in which the premise is formulated, and the timed states in the scope of the consequence (applicability set). For every temporal operator in the syntax, an applicability set, $\perp$, is defined in table 1. Thus, $\Rightarrow \bigcirc$ and $\Rightarrow \odot$ are discrete temporal operators (successor and predecessor respectively); $\Rightarrow$, $\Rightarrow_+$ and $\Rightarrow_-$ are dense temporal operators (present, future and past respectively).

Whereas temporal operators determine the qualitative order between the premise state and the consequence states (applicability set), quantification determines the degree of satisfaction required in the consequence states. Thus, $\{\forall, \exists\}$ quantifiers provide existential and universal quantification over the applicability set. In quantified causality ($\mathbb{E} \otimes$), the truth degree of the quantified

Table 1. Applicability set for temporal operators $\in \otimes$. P is the premise of the causal formula. If the temporal operator is $\Rightarrow \bigcirc$ only events in the simplest premise in P, applicability events (AE), are considered.

$\perp ((\Rightarrow \bigcirc, P), (s, \gamma)) = \{(s', \gamma', c_s) \mid (s, \gamma) \xrightarrow{a, c_s} \circ (s', \gamma') \text{ and } a \in AE\}$
$\perp ((\Rightarrow \odot, P), (s, \gamma)) = \{(s', \gamma', c_s) \mid (s', \gamma') \xrightarrow{a, c_s} \circ (s, \gamma)\}$
$\perp ((\Rightarrow_+, P), (s, \gamma)) = \{(s, \gamma', c_s) \mid (s, \gamma) \xrightarrow{\tau, c_s} \circ (s, \gamma')\}$
$\perp ((\Rightarrow_-, P), (s, \gamma)) = \{(s, \gamma', c_s) \mid (s, \gamma') \xrightarrow{\tau, c_s} \circ (s, \gamma)\}$
$\perp ((\Rightarrow, P), (s, \gamma)) = \{(s, \gamma, 1)\}$

consequence depends on the specification condition of the transition that makes a timed state accessible in the causal formula, referred to as accessibility condition (c_s in table 1).

Informally, an existential quantification over a consequence ϕ is satisfied (truth value 1) iff it exists an applicability state $s_a = (s, \gamma, c_s)$ in which $\vdash (\phi, s_a) = 1$, and the accessibility condition c_s is 1. Thus, every future evolution of the model will satisfy the existential quantification. On the contrary, the existential quantification is not satisfied (truth value 0) iff the degree of satisfaction in every state of the applicability set is 0, whatever specification condition. On the other hand, an universal quantification over a consequence ϕ is satisfied (truth value 1) iff all timed states s_a in the applicability set with accessibility condition $\in \{\frac{1}{2}, 1\}$ satisfy the consequence ($\vdash (\phi, s_a) = 1$). It is not satisfied iff it exists an applicability timed state with $c_s = 1$ which does not satisfy the consequence ($\vdash (\phi, s_a) = 0$). See the following section for formal definition.

Semantics. Given a MUS-T graph $\mathcal{M}$, SCTL-T formulas are interpreted with respect to the many-valued dense graph $\mathcal{S}_{\mathcal{M}^\mathcal{E}}$ induced by $\mathcal{M}^\mathcal{E}$, which is $\mathcal{M}$ with $\mathcal{C}$ extended by all clocks $\mathcal{E}$ mentioned in the SCTL-T requirement. The satisfaction relation $\vdash$ is defined as:

$$\vdash : \left(\Phi_{SCTL-T} \times (S \times \Re_+^{\#\mathcal{C} \cup \mathcal{E}} \times \mathcal{L}_3) \right) \longrightarrow \mathcal{L}_6$$

where $\vdash (\phi, (s, \gamma, c_s))$ assigns a truth value $\in \mathcal{L}_6$ to the formula ϕ evaluated in a state (s, γ) with accessibility condition c_s. We start defining SCTL-T by giving the semantics of propositional constants. If (s, γ, c_s) is a timed state with accessibility condition c_s, the satisfaction relation, $\vdash$, is as follows:

i) $\psi \in \Psi$, $\vdash (\psi, (s, \gamma, c_s)) = \psi(\gamma)$.

ii) $a \in A$, $\vdash (a, (s, \gamma, c_s)) = c_s' \mid (s, \gamma) \xrightarrow{a, c_s'} \circ (s', \gamma')$.

iii) $\theta \in \Theta$, $\vdash (true, (s, \gamma, c_s)) = c_s$, i. e., $true$ is satisfied in a state (s, γ, c_s) iff this state is reached by a possible (discrete or temporal) transition ($c_s = 1$). On the contrary, $\vdash (false, (s, \gamma, c_s)) = \neg c_s$, i. e., $false$ is satisfied iff the state is reached by a non-possible transition ($c_s = 0$). Finally, $\emptyset$ is always satisfied ($\vdash (\emptyset, (s, \gamma, c_s)) = 1$).

We now proceed by defining the semantics of generic formulas by structural induction. Let ϕ, ϕ' be SCTL-T formulas, the satisfaction relation is as follows:

iv) $\vdash (y.\phi, (s, \gamma, c_s)) \equiv \vdash (\phi, (s, \gamma_{\{y\}}, c_s))$

v) $\vdash (\neg\phi, (s, \gamma, c_s)) \equiv \neg(\vdash (\phi, (s, \gamma, c_s)))$

vi) $\vdash (\phi \vee \phi', (s, \gamma, c_s)) \equiv \vdash (\phi, (s, \gamma, c_s)) \vee \vdash (\phi', (s, \gamma, c_s))$

vii) $\vdash (\phi \wedge \phi', (s, \gamma, c_s)) \equiv \vdash (\phi, (s, \gamma, c_s)) \wedge \vdash (\phi', (s, \gamma, c_s))$

viii) $\vdash (\phi \forall \otimes \phi', (s, \gamma, c_s)) \equiv \rightarrow \left(\vdash (\phi, (s, \gamma, c_s)), \bigwedge_i \neg c_{s_i}{}' \vee \vdash (\phi', (s_i{}', \gamma_i{}', c_{s_i}{}')) \right)$

where $(s_i{}', \gamma_i{}', c_{s_i}{}') \in \bot ((\otimes, \phi), (s, \gamma))$

ix) $\vdash (\phi \exists \otimes \phi', (s, \gamma, c_s)) \equiv \rightarrow \left(\vdash (\phi, (s, \gamma, c_s)), \bigvee_i c_{s_i}{}' \wedge \vdash (\phi', (s_i{}', \gamma_i{}', c_{s_i}{}')) \right)$

where $(s_i{}', \gamma_i{}', c_{s_i}{}') \in \bot ((\otimes, \phi), (s, \gamma))$

3.3   SCTL-T: Fixpoints As Recursion

As in [9], a SCTL-T requirement is a set of mutually recursive declarations of the form $\{I_0 := \phi_0, \cdots, I_n := \phi_n\}$, where SCTL-T syntax is extended with instantiation and recursive operators:

$$\langle \phi_C \rangle ::= I_i \mid \ll I_i \gg \mid [[I_i]] \ , \text{ with } I_i \in \mathcal{I}$$

An identifier I_i in the right-hand side of a declaration instantiates the formula ϕ_i in a declaration of the form $I_i = \phi_i$. Recursive operators $\ll I_i \gg$ and $[[I_i]]$ are understood respectively as the least and greatest fixed points of the predicate transformer defined by the recursion. In this way, usual operators in branching logics can be expressed in SCTL-T but with a many-valued nature. For a practical specification of scenarios and requirements without explicit fixpoint constructions we provide a set of such constructions as predefined macros[3]. Additionally, we enforce requirements to be alternation free in order to simplify and make fully local model checking and synthesis algorithms.

Preliminary Definitions. Before defining semantics of fixpoints, some definitions concerning many-valued fixpoints are in order. One way to provide semantics of a state-based temporal logic (SCTL-T, for instance) is to map formulas to set of states, but in many-valued reasoning a mapping from formulas to partitions of states is needed. Let $\mathcal{M}$ be a MUS-T graph. We define the set $\mathcal{P}^6$ of all 6-cardinality partitions of its state-space, $\mathcal{ST}$, where every $P \in \mathcal{P}^6$ is:

$$P = \{\langle P \rangle_0, \langle P \rangle_{\frac{1}{4}}, \langle P \rangle_{\frac{1}{2}}, \langle P \rangle_{\frac{1}{2}}, \langle P \rangle_{\frac{3}{4}}, \langle P \rangle_1\}$$

---

[3] In the examples in this paper (section 5) macro-symbols stand for the usual meanings, that is, $\mathcal{G}$, it is always *Going* to be the case; $\mathcal{F}$, at least once in the *Future*; $\mathcal{H}$, it *Has* always been the case; $\mathcal{P}$, at least once in the *Past*; $\mathcal{U}$, *Until*; $\mathcal{S}$, *Since*; $\mathcal{U}_w$, *Weak Until*; and $\mathcal{S}_w$, *Weak Since*

For every P, $P' \in \mathcal{P}^6$, union ($\cup_\mathcal{P}$), intersection ($\cap_\mathcal{P}$), complement ($-^\mathcal{P}$) and inclusion ($\subseteq_\mathcal{P}$) are defined as:

$$s \in \langle P \cup_\mathcal{P} P' \rangle_j \text{ iff } j = \sup\{i, i' \mid s \in \langle P \rangle_i \text{ and } s \in \langle P' \rangle_{i'}\}$$

$$s \in \langle P \cap_\mathcal{P} P' \rangle_j \text{ iff } j = \inf\{i, i' \mid s \in \langle P \rangle_i \text{ and } s \in \langle P' \rangle_{i'}\}$$

$$s \in \langle \overline{P}^\mathcal{P} \rangle_j \text{ iff } s \in \langle P \rangle_{\neg j}$$

$$P \subseteq_\mathcal{P} P' \text{ iff } \langle P \rangle_i \subseteq \bigcup_{i \leq j \leq 1} \langle P' \rangle_j \ \forall \, i$$

where $\subseteq$ and $\cup$ stand for the set inclusion and union in $\mathcal{ST}$; $\leq$ is the partial order relation in $\mathcal{L}_6$; inf and sup are, respectively, the greatest lower bound and least upper bound in this partial order; and $\neg$ is the complement in $\mathcal{L}_6$.

The set of all 6-cardinality partitions $\mathcal{P}^6$ forms a lattice under the inclusion $\subseteq_\mathcal{P}$ defined above, where for every $P, P' \in \mathcal{P}^6$, the least upper bound is $P \cup_\mathcal{P} P'$; and the greatest lower bound is $P \cap_\mathcal{P} P'$. Besides, $P_\perp = \{\mathcal{ST}, \{\} \cdots \{\}\}$, is the least element in the lattice; and $P_\top = \{\{\} \cdots \{\}, \mathcal{ST}\}$, is the greatest element in the lattice. Each element P of the lattice can also be thought as a predicate on $\mathcal{ST}$, where the predicate is viewed as being i for exactly the states $\in \langle P \rangle_i$.

Semantics. A SCTL-T declaration $I_j := \phi_j$ which includes a recursive operator $\ll I_i \gg$ (or $[\![I_i]\!]$) with $i \leq j$, defines the predicate transformer $I_i = f(I_i)$. Let $f : \mathcal{P}^6 \to \mathcal{P}^6$ be such a predicate transformer; then f is monotonic provided that $P \subseteq_\mathcal{P} P'$ implies $f(P) \subseteq_\mathcal{P} f(P')$. Since every logical connective, except negation, is monotonic, and all the negations can be pushed down to the atomic propositions using De Morgan's laws and dualities, every predicate transformer defined by a SCTL-T recursion is monotonic, guaranteeing the existence of the fixpoints [10]. As identifiers do not appear free in SCTL-T formulas, but bound by recursive operators, enforcing an even number of negations in the scope of recursive operators is not needed. So, SCTL-T semantics is extended as follows:

x) $\vdash (I_i, (s, \gamma, c_s)) \equiv \vdash (\phi_i, (s, \gamma, c_s))$, where ϕ_i is such that $I_i := \phi_i$.

xi) $\vdash (\ll I_i \gg, (s, \gamma, c_s)) \equiv j \in \mathcal{L}_6 \mid (s, \gamma) \in \; < \bigcap_\mathcal{P} \{P \mid f(P) \subseteq P\} >_j$

xii) $\vdash ([\![I_i]\!], (s, \gamma, c_s)) \equiv j \in \mathcal{L}_6 \mid (s, \gamma) \in \; < \bigcup_\mathcal{P} \{P \mid f(P) \supseteq P\} >_j$

3.4   SCTL-T: Expressing Scenarios

Using scenarios a designer proposes a situation and decides what behavior would be appropriate to that context. We formalize scenarios defining a synthesis-oriented version of SCTL-T (SCTL-T^s). To be precise, we formalize scenarios with the simple "declarative past causes imperative future" idea in [11]. The general idea behind imperative future is to rewrite each formula to be synthesized into a set of SCTL-T^s formulas of the form:

declarative past $\{\forall\}\{\Rightarrow, \Rightarrow_+, \Rightarrow \bigcirc\}^4$ *imperative future*

---

[4] Temporal operators overloaded for synthesis

and then treat such formulas as scenarios showing how the future can be constructed given the past constructed so far. Formally, a synthesis rule $SR \in \mathcal{SR}$ is a causal formula where the premise specifies the synthesis context and the consequence specifies the new non-strict future behavior:

$$\langle \mathcal{SR} \rangle ::= ini \otimes_s \phi_{fs} | \phi_p \otimes_s \phi_{fs}$$
$$\langle \otimes_s \rangle ::= \Rightarrow | \forall \Rightarrow \bigcirc | \forall \Rightarrow_+$$
$$\langle \phi_{fs} \rangle ::= \psi | a | \neg a | \theta | y.\phi_{fs} | a\{y\} | \phi_{fs} \wedge \phi_{fs} | \phi_{fs} \forall \otimes_f \phi_{fs}$$

where ϕ_p is a non-strict past formula $\in \Phi_{SCTL-T}$, $\otimes_f$ is the set of non-strict future temporal operators[5]; and $\otimes_s$ are the overloaded versions of non-strict future temporal operators for imperative specification. Finally in order to allow the explicit management of model clocks from the logic, we introduce an imperative form of bind, $a\{x\}$, which adds a clock x to $\mathcal{C}$ (if it does not exists) and resets the clock in a discrete transition labeled by a.

Incremental synthesis is based on the following principle: changes in the model refer to specifying transitions which are unspecified in the semantic graph (from $\frac{1}{2}$ up to 1, or from $\frac{1}{2}$ down to 0). Any other change in the specification condition reflects an inconsistency failure which should identify a set of scenarios in conflict.

Regarding the synthesis algorithm, unfortunately, tableau construction for dense real-time logics allowing punctuality is undecidable [4]. Incremental synthesis applies a bounded model construction algorithm similar to the one in [12]. In the bounded synthesis approach, given a SCTL-T requirement and a source MUS-T model, a satisfying target model is synthesized (if feasible) within given bounds on the number of clocks in $\mathcal{C}$ and constants in clock constraints. The synthesis algorithm proceeds as an imperative model checking algorithm, that is, selecting synthesis contexts (states in the model satisfying the declarative part) and then adding, in these contexts, the new future behavior specified by the imperative part (enforcing a truth value 1). That is, given a synthesis rule $SR := \phi_p \otimes_s \phi_{fs}$, if $\phi_p = ini$, (s_0, γ^0) is the single synthesis context, otherwise (s, γ) is a synthesis contexts iff $\vdash (\phi_p, (s, \gamma)) = 1$ (applicable rule in this context).

Synthesis rules are global-scope (invariants), so it is necessary to reuse locations in order to avoid MUS-T graphs indefinitely growing. In brief, reuse criteria are defined as preserving simulations and bisimulations, at different demanding levels, between the non-reusing model and the reusing one.

The incremental synthesis of a SCTL-T scenario in a MUS-T graph can be viewed as a form of the more traditional controller synthesis problem where all specified transitions (possible and non-possible) in a MUS-T graph are considered to be uncontrollable, meanwhile all unspecified transitions are considered to be controllable. In this sense, the timed version of the controller synthesis problem in [13] could be applied to the synthesis of SCTL-T scenarios by handling the unspecified transitions, that is, turning unspecified transitions into possible or non-possible ones. However, a MUS-T graph is really a multi-valued graph

---

[5] For readability we provide $\forall \Rightarrow \overset{\forall \rightarrow}{\bigcirc} \equiv \forall \Rightarrow \bigcirc \forall \Rightarrow_+$, and its overloaded $\forall \Rightarrow \overset{\forall \rightarrow}{\bigcirc}$.

with a potential arbitrary number of clocks in which only the clocks in the set $\mathcal{C}$ are specified, so the controller synthesis solution cannot be applied.

4   Many-Valued Reasoning

SCTL/MUS-T is a dense-time methodology, so automation of model checking and synthesis involves obtaining an exact abstraction of the infinite and dense state-space. In this respect, two many-valued strong time abstracting bisimulations (FSTaB and BSTaB) are defined which preserve truth values in SCTL-T. To be precise, FSTaB preserves non-strict future SCTL-T formulas without clock constraints and BSTaB preserves strict past SCTL-T formulas without clock constraints. Complete SCTL-T preservation can be obtained using a technique similar to the one used in [5], that is, extending the MUS-T graph with the set of specification clocks and considering an equivalence relation that also distinguishes the clock constraints in the formula.

Many-Valued Strong Time Abstracting Bisimulations.   Consider a MUS-T graph $\mathcal{M}$, and a subset $A^S \subseteq A$ of preserving events. A **F**orward **S**trong **T**ime-abstracting **B**isimulation (FSTaB) with preserving events A^S abstracts away the exact amount of time elapsed in a time transition and discrete events not in the subset A^S. This is done by replacing all labels $\tau \in \Re_+$ by the label $\epsilon \notin (A \cup \Re_+)$, and all labels $a \in A - A^S$ by the label $d \notin (A \cup \Re_+)$

A binary relation $\cong_S$ on the states $\mathcal{ST}$ ($\cong_S \subseteq \mathcal{ST} \times \mathcal{ST}$) is a FSTaB with preserving events A^S, iff for all states $st_1 \cong_S st_2$, where $st_1 = (s_1, \gamma_1)$ and $s_2^t = (s_2, \gamma_2)$, the following conditions hold:

$$\forall\, st_1' \mid st_1 \xrightarrow{a,l} st_1' \in \mathcal{T}, \exists\, st_2' \mid st_2 \xrightarrow{a,l} st_2' \text{ and } st_1' ; \cong_S st_2';$$

$$\forall\, st_1' \mid st_1 \xrightarrow{\epsilon,l} st_1' \in \mathcal{T}, \exists\, st_2' \mid st_2 \xrightarrow{\epsilon,l} st_2' \text{ and } st_1' \cong_S st_2';$$

$$\forall\, st_1' \mid st_1 \xrightarrow{d,l} st_1' \in \mathcal{T}, \exists\, st_2' \mid st_2 \xrightarrow{d,l} st_2' \text{ and } st_1' \cong_S st_2';$$

the above conditions also hold if the roles s_1 and s_2 are reversed.

In the same way, a binary relation $\cong_S$ on the states $\mathcal{ST}$ is a **B**ackward **T**ime-abstracting **B**isimulation, BSTaB, with preserving events A^S, iff for all states $st_1 \cong_S st_2$ the same conditions hold backward. Finally, let ψ a clock constraint or a reset predicate $x = 0$ for some clock x, a binary relation $\cong$ preserves ψ iff for all states $st_1 \cong_S st_2$, $\psi(st_1) = \psi(st_2)$.

Lemma 1. *Let $\mathcal{M}$ be a MUS-T graph and $\cong_S$ be a FSTaB with preserving events A^S on $\mathcal{M}$. For any non-strict future formula $\phi \in \Phi_{SCTL-T}$ with events $\in A^S$ and any pair of states $st \cong_S st'$, $\vdash (\phi, (st, c_s)) = \vdash (\phi, (st', c_s))$.*

Lemma 2. *Let $\mathcal{M}$ be a MUS-T graph and $\phi \in \Phi_{SCTL-T}$ with events A_ϕ, a set of specification clocks $\mathcal{E}_\phi$, and a set of clock constraints Ψ_ϕ. Let $\mathcal{M}^{\mathcal{E}}$ be the*

MUS-T graph $\mathcal{M}$ extended with the clocks in $\mathcal{E}_\phi$ and $\cong_S$ a F-BSTaB on $\mathcal{M}^\mathcal{E}$ with preserving events $A^S = A_\phi$. If $\cong_S$ preserves reset predicates $y_i = 0 \; \forall \; y_i \in \mathcal{E}_\phi$; and clock constraints in the formula $\psi_i \in \Psi_\phi$, then $\cong_S$ preserves the truth value of ϕ. That is, for any pair of states $st_1 \cong_S st_2$, $\vdash (\phi, (st_1, c_s)) = \vdash (\phi, (st_2, c_s))$.

For shortness, the reader is referred to [8] for proofs of the above lemmas. Finally, the region equivalence in [5] is a F-BSTaB with the above characteristics. Since this equivalence induces a finite partition of the state-space, the quotient of a MUS-T graph with respect to this F-BSTaB bisimulation is finite.

SCTL-T Model Checking and Synthesis. Model checking and synthesis of SCTL-T formulas use the STaBs defined above to compute a finite quotient of a given MUS-T graph. In this respect, minimization algorithms, computing the minimal quotient, have been adapted to timing reasoning [14] in order to overcome the state-explosion problem. Minimization algorithms are based on the facts that a forward bisimulation induces a pre-stable partition and vice-versa, and, in the same way, a backward bisimulation induces a post-stable partition and vice-versa. Minimization is done by partition refinement, that is, the coarser pre(post)-stable partition of the state-space $\mathcal{ST}$ is computed starting from an initial partition and successively refining it until it becomes pre(post)-stable.

5   Case Study: A Fragment

In [8] it is showed a complete example which applies the SCTL/MUS-T methodology to the steam-boiler case study [15]. In brief, the steam-boiler has a water boiler tank, a pump, and a number of sensor one of which measures water level. The entire physical system operates under guidance of a controller. The controller must keep the water level between extreme values M_1 and M_2 at all times. It should also try to keep the water level between normal operating levels N_1 and N_2 as much as possible. The controller operates in five modes (initialization, normal, rescue, degraded and emergency stop) following a cycle and a priori does not terminate; this cycle takes place every 5 seconds. The reader is referred to the complete case study in [8] for details of modes which are not included in this paper; also, only design for non-failure environment (accurate measure and non-failure pump) is included. In normal model, the controller makes its decision to turn on or turn off the pump based on the current water level; no action is taken if this level lies in the range $[N_1, N_2]$. The controller works periodically with each cycle consisting of three tasks: sensor regulation, report computation (optional behavior) and actuating the pump.

Controller Requirements. Events in the controller of the steam-boiler are identified as synchronization events (in a non-failure environment) and internal events (controller tasks). The set of synchronization events is $\{p_{on}, p_{off}, na,$ $n1_\downarrow, n2_\uparrow, n_\leftrightarrow, m1_\downarrow, m2_\uparrow\}$ where p_{on}, p_{off} and na stand for opening, closing and non-actuating the pump; $n_\leftrightarrow$ ($> N1$ and $< N2$), $m1_\downarrow$ ($< M1$), $m2_\uparrow$ ($> M2$),

Table 2. Controller requirements

R_1	$x.BS \; \forall\Rightarrow\bigcirc \; (\emptyset \Rightarrow \mathcal{AF}[ES \wedge x \leq 3 \wedge x \geq 1])$
R_2	$x.BR \; \forall\Rightarrow\bigcirc \; (\emptyset \Rightarrow \mathcal{AF}[ER \wedge x = 3])$
R_3	$x.act \Rightarrow \mathcal{AF}[x = 5 \Rightarrow act]$
R_4	$x.act \Rightarrow \mathcal{EF}[act \wedge x = 5]$
R_5	$x.act \; \forall\Rightarrow\bigcirc \; \mathcal{AG}[(x < 5 \Rightarrow \neg act) \vee (x \geq 5)]$
R_6	$(n1_\downarrow \vee n2_\uparrow \vee n_\leftrightarrow) \; \forall\Rightarrow\bigcirc \; (\emptyset \Rightarrow \mathcal{AF}[ES \Rightarrow \mathcal{AF}[act]])$
R_7	$(n1_\downarrow \vee n2_\uparrow \vee n_\leftrightarrow) \; \forall\Rightarrow\bigcirc \; (\emptyset \Rightarrow \mathcal{EF}[ES \; \forall\Rightarrow\bigcirc \; (BR \Rightarrow \mathcal{AF}[act])])$

$n1_\downarrow$ ($< N1$) and $n2_\uparrow$ ($> N2$) stand for the measures of the water sensor. Internal events are identified as BS, ES (start and completion of sensor regulation); BR, ER (start and completion of report computation) and act (entering actuation task). Identified controller requirements (in table 2) matches the following informal specification:

- **Task Completion** (R_1, R_2): Once regulation starts it is always completed within no less than 1 and no more than 3 seconds. Besides, once report computation starts it takes 3 seconds.
- **Actuation Cycle** (R_3, R_4, R_5): Actuation only occurs once every 5 seconds. Actuation is not possible if such delay from the last one has not elapsed.
- **Cycle Sequence** (R_6, R_7): Once water level has been read, provided that the boiler does not reach any extreme limit ($M1$ or $M2$), a new cycle starts which always includes regulation and, possibly, report computation.

Controller Scenarios. The design process is based on identifying timing scenarios of the system and specifying them as SCTL-T^s synthesis rules (table 3):

- **Init** (S_{INI}): At the beginning the controller enters the regulation task. This is the only task at this moment.
- **Regulation** (S_{REG}): Sensor regulation takes no less than 1 and no more than 3 seconds.
- **Entering Actuation** (S_{EA}): Actuation phase starts (act) 5 seconds after the last actuation or the beginning of regulation.
- **Actuation** (S_{ACT}, S_{AM}): In the actuation phase controller checks the water sensor ($n1_\downarrow$, $n2_\uparrow$, $m1_\downarrow$, $m2_\uparrow$, $n_\leftrightarrow$), this checking is assumed to be instantaneous. On the basis of the water level, controller decides to open (p_{on}), close (p_{off}) or not to actuate (na) the pump (Actuation Mode); also actuation is assumed to be instantaneous.
- **Actuation Completion and New Cycle** (S_{NC}): Once controller has actuated, provided that extreme values are not reached, a new cycle starts.
- **Report Computation** –optional behavior– (S_{RC}): Report computation, if it occurs, comes after completion of regulation and takes 3 seconds.

Applying SCTL/MUS-T. The methodology is articulated as subsequent iterations consisting of formalizing the specification which captures the controller

Table 3. Controller scenarios

S_{INI}^0	$ini\ \forall{\Rightarrow}{\bigcirc}\ \ BS \wedge \neg(ER \vee BR \vee ES)$
S_{INI}^1	$ini \Rightarrow (\emptyset\ \forall{\Rightarrow}_+\ false)$
S_{REG}^0	$BS\{x_s\}\ \forall{\Rightarrow}{\bigcirc}\ \ ((x_s \leq 3 \Rightarrow true)\ \wedge\ (x_s > 3 \Rightarrow false))$
S_{REG}^1	$BS\{x_s\}\ \forall{\Rightarrow}{\bigcirc}\ \ ((x_s \geq 1 \wedge x_s \leq 3) \Rightarrow ES)$
S_{EA}^0	$x.\emptyset \Rightarrow \mathcal{EP}[BS \wedge x = 5] \Rightarrow act$
S_{EA}^1	$x.\emptyset \Rightarrow \mathcal{EP}[BS \wedge x < 5] \Rightarrow \neg act$
S_{EA}^2	$(x.\emptyset\ \exists{\Rightarrow}{\odot}\ (\emptyset \Rightarrow \mathcal{EP}[act \wedge x < 5])) \Rightarrow \neg act$
S_{EA}^3	$x.\emptyset \Rightarrow \mathcal{AP}[act \wedge x = 5] \Rightarrow act$
S_{ACT}^0	$act\ \forall{\Rightarrow}{\bigcirc}\ (\emptyset\ \forall{\Rightarrow}_+\ false)$
S_{ACT}^1	$act\ \forall{\Rightarrow}{\bigcirc}\ n1_\downarrow \wedge n2_\uparrow \wedge m1_\downarrow \wedge m2_\uparrow \wedge n_\leftrightarrow$
S_{ACT}^2	$(\emptyset\ \forall{\Rightarrow}{\odot}\ \neg act) \Rightarrow \neg(n1_\downarrow \vee n2_\uparrow \vee m1_\downarrow \vee m2_\uparrow \vee n_\leftrightarrow)$
S_{AM}^0	$(n1_\downarrow \wedge n2_\uparrow \wedge m1_\downarrow \wedge m2_\uparrow \wedge n_\leftrightarrow) \Rightarrow \neg p_{on} \wedge \neg p_{off}$
S_{AM}^1	$n1_\downarrow\ \forall{\Rightarrow}{\bigcirc}\ (na \wedge p_{on} \wedge \neg p_{off})$
S_{AM}^2	$n2_\uparrow\ \forall{\Rightarrow}{\bigcirc}\ (na \wedge p_{off} \wedge \neg p_{on})$
S_{AM}^3	$n_\leftrightarrow\ \forall{\Rightarrow}{\bigcirc}\ na \wedge \neg p_{on} \wedge \neg p_{off}$
S_{AM}^4	$\neg(n1_\downarrow \wedge n2_\uparrow)\ \forall{\Rightarrow}{\bigcirc}\ \neg p_{on} \wedge \neg p_{off}$
S_{AM}^5	$(\emptyset\ \exists{\Rightarrow}{\odot}\ act)\ \forall{\Rightarrow}{\bigcirc}\ (\neg act \wedge (\emptyset\ \forall{\Rightarrow}_+\ false))$
S_{NC}	$p_{on} \vee p_{off} \vee na\ \forall{\Rightarrow}{\bigcirc}\ BS$
S_{RC}^0	$(\emptyset\ \exists{\Rightarrow}{\odot}\ ES) \vee BR\{x_r\}\ \forall{\Rightarrow}{\bigcirc}\ (x_r = 3 \Rightarrow ER)$
S_{RC}^1	$(\emptyset\ \exists{\Rightarrow}{\odot}\ ES) \vee BR\}\ \forall{\Rightarrow}{\bigcirc}\ (x_r \leq 3 \Rightarrow true) \wedge (x_r > 3 \Rightarrow false)$

requirements; incremental design of the controller by means of formalizing typical behaviors as scenarios; and verification and validation of design decisions conforming to the requirements specification. The advantages which many-valued reasoning provides comes from the many-valued results obtained from model checking and incremental synthesis:

– Incremental synthesis results: A SCTL-T scenario is successfully synthesized provided that its imperative part is $\geq \frac{1}{2}$. Otherwise the imperative part is $\widehat{\frac{1}{2}}$, non-applicable, or $< \widehat{\frac{1}{2}}$, so the synthesis is not feasible. In the last case the scenarios in conflict are supplied allowing the designer to inspect what scenarios are error-prone, a misunderstanding of the system is uncovered.
– Model checking results: If a SCTL-T requirement is not satisfied (< 1) the designer is guided as follows. In case of inconsistency failure, $< \widehat{\frac{1}{2}}$, counterexamples are computed. By animating the counterexamples the designer inspects which scenarios, or maybe the requirement, are error-prone. In case of incompleteness failure ($\geq \frac{1}{2}$) completion suggestions are computed, then the model, extended with supplied suggestions, is animated in order to explore what alternative conforms to wishes and new scenarios are discovered.

On the basis of the specified requirements and scenarios, appendix A outlines a part of the SCTL/MUS-T process following the lifecycle in figure 1.

6　Conclusions

With respect to other formal approaches proposed in the literature, our lifecycle model is based on an iterative and incremental structure in which real-time characteristics are considered from the beginning of the process. One advantage of this approach is early detection of timing failures; considering timing requirements comparatively late in the process, as performance requirements, would cause ad hoc changes to the system. Also, as the system gradually takes form as more is learned about the problem, alternative solutions can be explored. Regarding the specification process, scenarios of using the system are often easier to identify at the beginning than generic requirements that can be made clear only after a deeper knowledge about the system has been gained. Despite this paper only includes some parts of the steam-boiler case study, the complete process in [8] reveals that specially at early phases: requirements often change guided by verification results, new scenarios are discovered throughout the process; and misunderstanding of the system is uncovered by conflicts in requirements or scenarios. So, reaching a good design entails a lot of interaction with designers.

Loose or partial specifications has previously been pursued in [16] by using the real-time process calculi TMS (**T**imed **M**odal **S**pecifications). TMS allow partial specifications by introducing two modalities in transitions, *may* and *must*. Intuitively, the more *must* transitions and the fewer *may* transitions a TM specification has, the finer or more specified it is. Despite this characterization supports refinements in and incremental process, consistency checking is not implicit since *not-must* transitions are not considered. Besides, the far or the close a TM specification is from satisfying a property-oriented specification is not measured by means of many-valued reasoning.

Finally, we are working on distributing methodology for collaborative specification [17] since development of complex systems usually involves many stakeholders, each with their own perspectives on the system. In this context, a MUS-T model turns into a MUS-T view provided by every single stakeholder. Inconsistencies will relate not just MUS-T models in successive cycles of a single lifecycle, but MUS-T views from parallel lifecycles in the distributed process.

References

1. Alur, R.: Techniques for Automatic Verification of Real-Time Systems. PhD thesis, Department of Computer Science, Stanford University (1991)
2. Gollu, A., Puri, A., Varaiya, P.: Discretization of Timed Automata. In: Decision and Control, 33rd IEEE Conference. (1994) 957–958
3. Asarin, E., Maler, O., Pnueli, A.: On Discretization of Delays in Timed Automata and Digital Circuits. In: Concurrency Theory, 9th International Conference (CONCUR'98). Volume 1466 of LNCS. Springer Verlag (1998) 470–484
4. Alur, R., Henzinger, T.A.: Logics and Models of Real Time: A Survey. In: Real Time: Theory and Practice, REX Workshop. Volume 600 of LNCS. Springer Verlag (1992) 74–106
5. Alur, R., Courcoubetis, C., Dill, D.: Model Checking in Dense Real-time. Information and Computation **104** (1993) 2–34

6. Chechik, M., Devereux, B., Easterbrook, S.M., Lai, A., Petrovykh, V.: Efficient Multiple-Valued Model-Checking Using Lattice Representations. In: Concurrency Theory, 12th International Conference (CONCUR'01). (2001) 21–24

7. Pazos Arias, J.J., García Duque, J.: SCTL-MUS: A Formal Methodology for Software Development of Distributed Systems. A Case Study. Formal Aspects of Computing **13** (2001) 50–91

8. Fernández Vilas, A.: Tratamiento Formal de Sistemas con Requisitos de Tiempo Real Críticos. PhD thesis, Dept. Ingeniería Telemática, Universidad de Vigo (2002)

9. Sokolsky, O.V., Smolka, S.A.: Local Model Checking for Real-Time Systems. In: Computer Aided Verification, 7th International Conference (CAV'95). Volume 939 of LNCS., Springer Verlag (1995) 211–224

10. Tarski, A.: A Lattice-Theoretical Fixpoint Theorem and its Applications. Pacific Journal of Mathematics **5** (1955) 285–309

11. Barringer, H., Fisher, M., Gabbay, D., Gough, G., Owens, R.: METATEM: An Introduction. Formal Aspects of Computing **7** (1995) 533–549

12. Laroussinie, F., Larsen, K.G., Weise, C.: From Timed Automata to Logic - And Back. In: Mathematical Foundations of Computer Science, 20th International Symposium (MFCS'95). Volume 969 of LNCS., Springer Verlag (1995) 529–539

13. Wong Toi, H., Hoffmann, G.: The Control of Dense Real Time Discrete Event Systems. In: Decision and Control, 30th IEEE Conference. (1991) 1527–1528

14. Alur, R., Courcoubetis, C., Halbwachs, N., Dill, D.L., Wong Toi, H.: Minimization of Timed Transition Systems. In: Concurrency Theory, 3rd International Conference (CONCUR'92). Volume 630 of LNCS., Spinger Verlag (1992) 340–354

15. Abrial, J.R., Borger, E., Langmaack, H.: Formal Methods for Industrial Applications: Specifying and Programming the Steam Boiler Control. Volume 1165 of LNCS. Springer Verlag (1996)

16. Cerans, K., Godskesen, J.C., Larsen, K.G.: Timed Modal Specifications – Theory and Tools. In: Computer Aided Verification, 5th International Conference (CAV'93). Volume 697 of LNCS., Springer Verlag (1993) 253–267

17. García Duque, J., Pazos Arias, J.J.: Reasoning over Inconsistent Viewpoints: How levels of agreement can evolve? In: Living With Inconsistency, 2nd International Workshop (ICSE'01). (2001)

A   Controller Synthesis

In this appendix we outline part of the SCTL/MUS-T design process in [8]. At the beginning, init (S_{INI}) and regulation rules (S_{REG}) are applied, synthesized MUS-T prototype is showed in figure 3(a)[6]. Then, context of entering actuation is identified. However, rule S_{EA}^{0}, which establishes the context of the first actuation, is never applicable; to be precise S_{EA}^{0} is such that its declarative part is 0 in every instance of locations INI and REG, i.e., rule will not be applicable now nor future evolutions; and $\in \{0, \frac{1}{2}\}$ in instances of location WAIT.

By animating the actual prototype, we can check that a time delay 5 can only be reached by unspecified parts of the model: both by unspecified discrete

---

[6] In the figures representing MUS-T models only partially unspecified events (dashed lines) are showed. Transitions which are not showed are totally unspecified transition with target location s_u.

transitions in locations {INI, REG}; or by unspecified temporal transitions in location REG. As enabling discrete transitions entails falsifying regulation completion (R_1), the designer expectations meet enabling temporal transitions in the location WAIT. A new scenario $S_{REG}^2 := ES \ \forall \Rightarrow \bigcirc \ (\emptyset \ \forall \Rightarrow_+ \ true)$ is incorporated. In this way, S_{EA}^0 turns into applicable in the location WAIT.

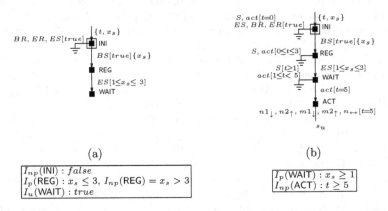

(a)   (b)

| I_{np}(INI) : $false$ |
| I_p(REG) : $x_s \leq 3$, I_{np}(REG) = $x_s > 3$ |
| I_u(WAIT) : $true$ |

| I_p(WAIT) : $x_s \geq 1$ |
| I_{np}(ACT) : $t \geq 5$ |

Fig. 3. 3(a): Rules $\{S_{INI}, S_{REG}\}$. 3(b): Rules $\{S_{EA}^0, S_{EA}^1\}$, S_{EA}^2 is a conflicting rule. S stands for the set $\{n1_\downarrow, n2_\uparrow, m1_\downarrow, m2_\uparrow, n_\leftrightarrow\}$.

Then, entering actuation (S_{EA}) scenarios are synthesized (figure 3(b)). Synthesizing event act as possible makes S_{EA}^2 applicable and $\neg act$ is synthesized in every discrete successor of location ACT. However, in these successors S_{EA}^0 is also applicable and a conflict between S_{EA}^0 and S_{EA}^2 is discovered. Conflict arises from the fact that S_{EA}^0 enables consecutive events act within 0 delay if a 5 time delay exists from event BS. So, S_{EA}^0 is refined as:

$$S_{EA}^0 := (x.\emptyset \Rightarrow \mathcal{EP}[BS \wedge x = 5]) \wedge \mathcal{A}[\neg act \ \mathcal{S} \ BS] \Rightarrow act$$

By applying rules $\{S_{ACT}, S_{AM}\}$ the model in figure 4(a) is obtained. In the synthesis an WLUM [7] criterion has been selected for the rule S_{AM}^4; the remainder rules does not match up any criterion. Once rules have been synthesized, controller requirements are verified over the current prototype. Relevant results are the following ones:

– **Task Completion:** $\vdash R_1 \in \{\widehat{\frac{1}{2}}, \frac{1}{2}\}$, so it is not falsified in the current prototype. That is, once regulation starts there are not executions in which regulation does not finish $(\neg ES)$ within the specified interval. However a totally-unspecified model would provide the same $(\frac{1}{2})$. The minimal model

---

[7] Examples only use WLUM (**W**ithout **L**oss of **U**nspecification in the **M**odel) criterion. Intuitively, WLUM criterion selects existing locations in the model in which specified behavior in a scenario can be reached without making changes.

obtained by turning unspecified behaviors into non-possible ones results in truth values $\in \{\widehat{\frac{1}{2}}, 1\}$, that is, the model satisfies the requirement or the requirement is non-applicable. Finally, R_2 requirement is always $\frac{1}{2}$ both in the actual model and in the minimal one, since it is an optional behavior.

- **Actuation cycle:** As the weakest requirement, $\vdash R_4 \in \{\widehat{\frac{1}{2}}, \frac{1}{2}\}$, that is, although R_4 is not falsified, an actuation cycle within 5 seconds is not ensured.

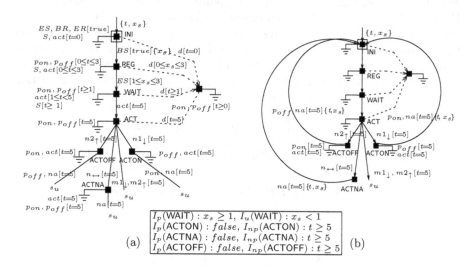

$$
\begin{array}{l}
I_p(\text{WAIT}) : x_s \geq 1,\; I_u(\text{WAIT}) : x_s < 1 \\
I_p(\text{ACTON}) : false,\; I_{np}(\text{ACTON}) : t \geq 5 \\
I_p(\text{ACTNA}) : false,\; I_{np}(\text{ACTNA}) : t \geq 5 \\
I_p(\text{ACTOFF}) : false,\; I_{np}(\text{ACTOFF}) : t \geq 5
\end{array}
$$

Fig. 4. 4(a): Rules $\{S_{ACT}, S_{AM}\}$. d stands for a generic discrete transition. 4(b): Rule S_{NC} with WLUM criterion + implicit reset.

On the basis of the last result, cyclic behavior should be synthesized by means of S_{NC} rule. New prototype is showed in figure 4(b) where an WLUM criterion with implicit reset has been selected. By validating this model, we discover instances of location WAIT being potential deadlock. Avoiding this potential deadlock can be reached by restricting stop invariant or enabling discrete evolution for $t > 5$. Once again, controller requirements are verified:

- **Task Completion:** Same results.
- **Actuation cycle:** Although $\vdash R_4 \in \{\widehat{\frac{1}{2}}, \frac{1}{2}, 1\}$, it is the weakest requirement in this set. By verifying R_3 requirement in the minimal model, we obtain truth values $\in \{0, \widehat{\frac{1}{2}}\}$. Animating the counterexample, we can discover executions, staying in WAIT infinitely, that contain a temporal delay greater than 5 without an *act* possible-event. As we saw above, WAIT is a potential deadlock. Restricting the time model can stay in this location is needed: $S_{ACT}^3 := act \;\forall{\Rightarrow}_+\; false$; and, consequently, $I_p(\text{WAIT}) = x_s \geq 1 \land t \leq 5$. In this way, $\vdash R_3 \in \{\widehat{\frac{1}{2}}, 1\}$ in the minimal model, i.e., requirement is satisfied or is non-applicable $(\widehat{\frac{1}{2}})$.

– **Cycle Sequence:** Both requirements result in truth values $\in \{\widehat{\frac{1}{2}}, \frac{1}{2}\}$. However, in the minimal model, R_7 requirement is falsified in instances in which it is applicable ($\neq \widehat{\frac{1}{2}}$), that is, there is not any execution in which report computation is carried out.

Applying S_{RC} rule, the controller fragment in figure 5(a) is obtained where report computation is still optional (unspecified transition). S_{RC} synthesis makes S_{EA}^3 rule applicable and $\{S_{ACT}, S_{AM}\}$ as well (figure 5(a), WLUM criterion selected). However, in this model, R_2 requirement (report completion) is impossible to satisfy (truth value $\frac{1}{4}$) in some instances. Misscompletion arises from the fact that actuation urgency (every 5 seconds) disables ER. So, it is necessary to refine report computation, that is, BR only must be enabled when the system has enough time both to complete this task (3 seconds), and to enter actuation task (5 seconds from the last actuation):

$$S_{RC}^2 := (x.\emptyset \Rightarrow \mathcal{AP}[act \wedge x > 2]) \Rightarrow \neg BR$$

Besides all events are forbidden until report computation is completed:

$$S_{RC}^3 := (\emptyset \; \forall{\Rightarrow}\odot \; BR) \; \forall{\Rightarrow}\overset{\forall\rightarrow}{\bigcirc} \; (x_r < 3 \; \forall{\Rightarrow}\bigcirc \; false)$$

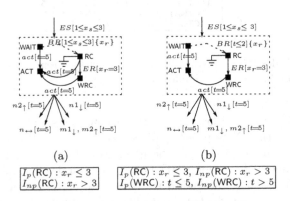

(a)   (b)

$I_p(\text{RC}) : x_r \leq 3$	$I_p(\text{RC}) : x_r \leq 3, I_{np}(\text{RC}) : x_r > 3$
$I_{np}(\text{RC}) : x_r > 3$	$I_p(\text{WRC}) : t \leq 5, I_{np}(\text{WRC}) : t > 5$

Fig. 5. MUS-T fragment obtained by rules S_{RC}.

In this way the controller fragment in figure 5(b) is obtained in which degree of satisfaction of R_2 is $\frac{3}{4}$. That is, although report computation is still optional, it is impossible to falsify in future evolutions. Besides R_2 will be satisfied (1) turning BR transition into a possible one.

Fault Diagnosis for Timed Automata

Stavros Tripakis

VERIMAG
Centre Equation, 2, avenue de Vignate, 38610 Gières, France
`tripakis@imag.fr`

Abstract. We study the problem of fault-diagnosis in the context of dense-time automata. The problem is, given the model of a plant as a timed automaton with a set of observable events and a set of unobservable events, including a special event modeling faults, to construct a deterministic machine, the diagnoser, which reacts to observable events and time delays, and announces a fault within a delay of at most Δ time units after the fault occurred. We define what it means for a timed automaton to be diagnosable, and provide algorithms to check diagnosability. The algorithms are based on standard reachability analyses in search of accepting states or non-zeno runs. We also show how to construct a diagnoser for a diagnosable timed automaton, and how the diagnoser can be implemented using data structures and algorithms similar to those used in most timed-automata verification tools.

Keywords: Fault diagnosis, Partial observability, Timed Automata.

1 Introduction

In this paper we study the problem of *fault diagnosis* in the context of *dense-time automata*. Our work is inspired from [21,22], who have studied the problem in the context of *discrete event systems* (DES) [19].

In the DES framework, the fault diagnosis problem is as follows. We are given the description of the behavior of a plant, in the form of a finite-state automaton. A behavior of the plant corresponds to a run of the automaton, that is, a sequence of events. An event is either *observable* or *unobservable*. One or more special unobservable events model *faults* that may occur during the operation of the plant. The objective is to design a *diagnoser*. The diagnoser is a deterministic machine which reacts to observable events by changing state instantaneously. The requirements are as follows. If the plant performs a fault event, the diagnoser should detect it after at most n steps (i.e., moves of the plant), where n has a known upper bound. Detection means, for instance, that the diagnoser enters a special state which announces that the fault has occurred. Another obvious requirement is that the diagnoser does not create any false alarms, that is, whenever it announces a fault, the fault has indeed occurred. Finally, once a fault is announced, the diagnoser cannot stop announcing it (i.e., on-line fault repairs are not modeled).

W. Damm and E.-R. Olderog (Eds.): FTRTFT 2002, LNCS 2469, pp. 205–221, 2002.

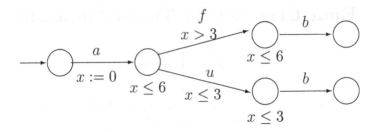

Fig. 1. A diagnosable timed automaton.

Not every plant is *diagnosable*. For example, a plant with two behaviors, a, f, b and a, u, b, is not diagnosable if f, u are unobservable and f is the fault. Indeed, the diagnoser, observing only a, b, has no way to know whether a fault actually occurred or not. On the other hand, a plant with behaviors a, f, b, c and a, u, b, d is diagnosable: after seeing c or d, the diagnoser can distinguish what happened.

Our motivation has been to extend the above framework to dense-time automata [3]. Such an extension is useful, since it permits us to model plants with timed behaviors, for example, "a followed by b within a delay of 7 time units". It also allows for diagnosers to base their decisions not only on the sequences of events observed, but also on the time delays between these events. That is, the diagnoser not only observes events, but can also measure the time elapsed between two successive events and, consequently, between any two events.

For example, consider the plant modeled by the timed automaton of Figure 1. The plant has two sets of behaviors: *faulty* behaviors (where f occurs) and non-faulty behaviors. If events a and b are observable, then the plant is diagnosable. Indeed, in all behaviors, a and b occur, in that order. In every faulty behavior, the delay between a and b is greater than 3 time units, while in every non-faulty behavior, the delay is at most 3. Thus, a diagnoser observing a and b, and measuring their interarrival delay can tell whether a fault occurred or not.

The contributions of this paper are as follows. First, we propose a notion of diagnosability for timed automata. This notion, called Δ-diagnosability, ensures that a fault can always be detected at most Δ time units after the time it occurs. Second, we provide an algorithm to check whether a given automaton A is diagnosable. The algorithm is based on a reachability analysis in search of *non-zeno runs* in a special product automaton of A with itself. Third, we provide an algorithm to find the minimum Δ such that A is Δ-diagnosable (assuming that it is already known that A is diagnosable). The algorithm conducts a *binary search* on the constant Δ, each time performing a reachability analysis of the above product, composed with an observer automaton with one clock.

Finally, we show how to build a diagnoser for A. The diagnoser works as a *state estimator* for A, that is, a state of the diagnoser is a set of all possible states that A could be in, according to what has been observed so far. The diagnoser changes state each time it observes an event a or a delay δ, and it is guaranteed not to produce any false alarms and to announce a fault at most Δ time units after the fault occurs. We also show how a diagnoser can be implemented effectively using finitary data structures to represent its current state, and how the transition function of the diagnoser can be effectively computed on these structures.

The rest of the paper is organized as follows. In Section 2, we present our model. In Section 3, we introduce the notion of diagnosability and show how it can be algorithmically checked. In Section 4, we define diagnosers and show how they can be implemented. Related work is discussed in Section 5.

2   Timed Automata with Faults and Unobservable Events

Let $\mathcal{X}$ be a finite set of variables taking values in the set of non-negative reals, denoted R. We call these variables *clocks*. A *valuation* on $\mathcal{X}$ is a function $v : \mathcal{X} \to$ R which assigns a value to each clock in $\mathcal{X}$. Given a valuation v and a *delay* $\delta \in$ R, $v + \delta$ denotes the valuation v' such that for all $x \in \mathcal{X}$, $v'(x) = v(x) + \delta$. Given a valuation v and a subset of clocks $X \subseteq \mathcal{X}$, $v[X := 0]$ denotes the valuation v' such that for all $x \in X$, $v'(x) = 0$ and for all $y \in \mathcal{X} - X$, $v'(y) = v(y)$.

A *polyhedron* on $\mathcal{X}$ is a set of valuations which can be represented as a boolean expression with atomic constraints of the form $x \leq k$ or $x - y \leq k$, where $x, y \in \mathcal{X}$ and k is an integer constant. For example, $x = 0 \land y > 3$ is a polyhedron. By definition, polyhedra are closed by boolean operations $\land, \lor, \neg$, which correspond to set intersection, union and complementation. Polyhedra are also closed by existential quantification: for $x \in \mathcal{X}$, $\exists x . \zeta$ denotes the polyhedron $\{v \mid \exists v' \in \zeta, \forall y \in \mathcal{X}, y \neq x \Rightarrow v(y) = v'(y)\}$. For example, $\exists x . (x \leq 3 \land y \leq x)$ is the polyhedron $y \leq 3$. We use true to denote the polyhedron $\bigwedge_{x \in \mathcal{X}} x \geq 0$ and false to denote the empty polyhedron. We also use $\mathbf{0}$ to denote the singleton $\bigwedge_{x \in \mathcal{X}} x = 0$.

A *timed automaton* [3,15] is a tuple $A = (Q, \mathcal{X}, \Sigma, E, I)$, where:

- Q is a finite set of *discrete states*; $q^0 \in Q$ is the *initial* discrete state.
- $\mathcal{X}$ is a finite set of clocks.
- Σ is a finite set of *events*. Σ is the union of two disjoint sets $\Sigma = \Sigma_o \cup \Sigma_u$, and $f \in \Sigma_u$ is a distinguished event, called the *fault* event[1]. An event in Σ_o is called *observable*, otherwise, it is called *unobservable*.
- E is a finite set of *transitions*. Each transition is a tuple $e = (q, q', a, \zeta, X)$, where $q, q' \in Q$, $a \in \Sigma$, ζ is a polyhedron on $\mathcal{X}$ and $X \subseteq \mathcal{X}$. We use source(e) to denote q, dest(e) for q', event(e) for a, guard(e) for ζ, and reset(e) for X. Given an event $a \in \Sigma$, $E(a)$ denotes the set of all transitions $e \in E$ such that event(e) = a.
- I is the *invariant function* which associates with each discrete state $q \in Q$ a polyhedron on $\mathcal{X}$, $I(q)$. We require that $\mathbf{0} \in I(q^0)$.

---

[1] For simplicity, we assume a single type of fault. The definitions and results generalize directly to more than one fault types. In Section 3 we discuss how this can be done.

A *state* of A is a pair $s = (q, v)$, where $q \in Q$ and v is a valuation on $\mathcal{X}$, such that $v \in I(q)$. We denote q by discrete(s). The *initial state* of A is $s^0 = (q^0, \mathbf{0})$. Each delay $\delta \in \mathsf{R}$ defines a partial function on the states of A: if $s = (q, v)$ is a state of A, and $\forall \delta' \leq \delta$, $v + \delta' \in I(q)$, then $\delta(s) = (q, v + \delta)$, otherwise, $\delta(s)$ is undefined. Each transition $e = (q, q', a, \zeta, X) \in E$ defines a partial function on the states of A: if $s = (q, v)$ is a state of A such that $v \in \zeta$ and $v[X := 0] \in I(q')$, then $e(s) = (q', v[X := 0])$, otherwise, $e(s)$ is undefined.

A *timed sequence* over a set of events Σ is a finite or infinite sequence $\gamma_1, \gamma_2, \cdots$, where each γ_i is either an event in Σ or a delay in R. We require that between any two events in ρ there is exactly one delay (possibly 0). For example, if a and b are events, $a, 0, b, 3, c$ and $a, 1, 1, 1, \ldots$ are valid timed sequences, while a, b and $a, 1, 2, b$ are not. Let $\mathcal{TS}_\Sigma$ denote the set of all timed sequences over Σ.

If ρ is a finite timed sequence, time(ρ) denotes the sum of all delays in ρ. If ρ is infinite, then time(ρ) denotes the limit of the sum (possibly ∞). We say that ρ is *non-zeno* if time(ρ) = ∞. Note that a non-zeno timed sequence is necessarily infinite, although it might contain only a finite number of events.

We define a *projection* operator P as follows. Given a (finite or infinite) timed sequence ρ and a set of events $\Sigma' \subseteq \Sigma$, $P(\rho, \Sigma')$ is the timed sequence obtained by erasing from ρ all events in Σ' and summing the delays between successive events in the resulting sequence. For example, if $\rho = 1, a, 4, b, 1, c, 0, d, 3, e$, then $P(\rho, \{b, d\}) = 1, a, 5, c, 3, e$. Note that, in the definition of $P(\rho, \Sigma')$, Σ' is the set of events to be erased. Also notice that, time(ρ) = time($P(\rho, \Sigma')$), for any ρ and Σ'.

Given a state s of A, a *run of A starting at s* (or simply *a run of A*, if $s = s^0$) is a (finite or infinite) timed sequence $\rho = \gamma_1, \gamma_2, \cdots$, for which there exists a sequence of states $s_0, s_1, s_2, \cdots$, such that $s_0 = s$ and for each $i = 1, 2, \ldots$, if γ_i is a delay $\delta \in \mathsf{R}$ then $s_i = \delta(s_{i-1})$, whereas if γ_i is an event $a \in \Sigma$, then $s_i = e(s_{i-1})$, for some $e \in E(a)$. If ρ is a finite run $\gamma_1, \gamma_2, \cdots, \gamma_n$ starting from s, we say that s_n is *reachable from s via ρ*. A finite run ρ defines a function on the states of A as follows. If s is a state of A, $\rho(s)$ is the set of all states reachable from s via ρ (note that $\rho(s)$ might be empty). The set of all states of A reachable from s^0 via some run is denoted R_A.

A is *well-timed* if for all $s \in R_A$, there is a non-zeno run of A starting at s.

A run $\rho = \gamma_1, \gamma_2, \cdots$ is called *faulty* if for some $i = 1, 2, \ldots, \gamma_i = f$. Let j be the smallest i such that $\gamma_i = f$, and let $\rho' = \gamma_j, \gamma_{j+1}, \cdots$. Given $\delta \in \mathsf{R}$, if time(ρ') $\geq \delta$, then we say that *at least δ time units pass after the first occurrence of f in ρ*, or, in short, that *ρ is δ-faulty*.

The following lemma states an important property of the model, which will be used in the sequel.

Lemma 1. *If for all $\Delta \in \mathsf{N}$, A has a Δ-faulty run, then A has a non-zeno faulty run.*

Proof   Our proof relies on the *region graph* [3] of A, call it G. G is a finite quotient graph with respect to a *time-abstracting bisimulation* [28]. Each node of G (called a region) contains a set of bisimilar states of A. The edges of G

correspond either to transitions of A or to symbolic passage of time. We refer the reader to timed-automata papers for more details on the region graph. What is important for our proof is that every run of A is inscribed in a path of G and, vice-versa, every path of G contains a set of runs of A.

Let R_f be the set of regions of G which are reachable by a faulty path. Note that for every $r \in R_f$, all successors of r are also in R_f. Let G_f be the restriction of G to R_f. We claim that G_f has a strongly-connected component (SCC) Λ, such that for every clock x, x is either reset and can grow strictly greater than zero in Λ, or remains unbounded in Λ: this implies the existence of a faulty non-zero run [4]. Suppose our claim is false, that is, for every SCC Λ in G_f, there is a clock x which remains upper bounded in Λ and is never reset or never grows above zero. In both cases, x never grows in Λ above some constant Γ_Λ (in the last case, $\Gamma_\Lambda = 0$). Then, for every run ρ inscribed in Λ, time$(\rho) \leq \Gamma_\Lambda$. Since there is a finite number of SCCs in a finite graph, the time spent in any faulty run is bounded by some Γ (obtained as the maximum of Γ_Λ^x, plus the times spent in the finite paths linking the SCCs). But this contradicts the hypothesis.

$\square$

3 Diagnosability

We assume that the behavior of the plant to be diagnosed can be modeled as a timed automaton A. We also assume that A is well-timed. This is a reasonable assumption, since, in real plants, time elapses without upper bound. Therefore, if A can reach a state from which time cannot progress, this is due to a modeling error. Well-timedness can be algorithmically checked using, for instance, the techniques proposed in [27].

3.1 The Notion of Diagnosability for Timed Automata

In discrete-event systems, diagnosability has been defined with respect to a parameter n (a natural constant), representing the maximum delay required for the diagnoser to detect a fault [21,22]. Since time is not an inherent part of the DES model, delays are captured by counting events: the diagnoser must detect a fault after at most n steps of the plant, where a step corresponds to an event (observable or not).

For timed automata, we propose a more natural definition: a timed automaton A is diagnosable with respect to a delay Δ, if a fault can be detected in A at most Δ time units after it occurs. Note that, since A is well-timed, Δ time units will eventually elapse.

Definition 2 (Diagnosability for Timed Automata). *Consider a timed automaton A. We say that A is Δ-diagnosable, for a natural number $\Delta \in \mathsf{N}$, if for any two finite runs ρ_1, ρ_2 of A, if ρ_1 is Δ-faulty, then either ρ_2 is faulty or $P(\rho_1, \Sigma_u) \neq P(\rho_2, \Sigma_u)$. We say that A is diagnosable if there exists some $\Delta \in \mathsf{N}$, such that A is Δ-diagnosable.*

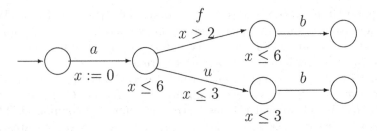

Fig. 2. A non-diagnosable timed automaton.

Example 3. Assuming that events a and b are observable, f and u are unobservable and f is the fault, the timed automaton of Figure 1 is 3-diagnosable. On the other hand, the slightly modified automaton shown in Figure 2 is not diagnosable. Indeed, the two runs $a, 2.5, f, 0.1, b$ and $a, 2.5, u, 0.1, b$ have the same projection $a, 2.6, b$, but only the first one is faulty. Moreover, an arbitrary amount of time can elapse after b in both runs, and their projections will remain identical.

We make some remarks about Definition 2.

For the sake of simplicity, we consider only one type of fault. This is not an essential assumption. The framework can be extended in a straightforward manner so that a number of different faults are considered, modeled by a set of events $\Sigma_f \subseteq \Sigma_u$. Then, the diagnosability definition would state that for each $f \in \Sigma_f$, there should not be two runs ρ_1 and ρ_2, such that f occurs in ρ_1 and at least Δ time passes afterwards[2], the projections of ρ_1 and ρ_2 to observable events are the same, but f does not occur in ρ_2. Checking diagnosability with multiple faults can be done by checking diagnosability separately for each fault. Building diagnosers which detect multiple faults can also be done by a simple extension of the single-fault construction.

We do not model on-line "repairs" of faults, that is, we assume that faults cannot be "undone". This means that, once a fault has occurred, we consider the behavior erroneous and we would like to detect the fault, no matter what the plant does afterwards.

We define diagnosability with respect to a natural constant Δ, rather than, say, a real number. This allows us to speak of Δ_{min} in the lemma that follows. If Δ is taken to be real, we can find plants which are diagnosable for all $\Delta > 3$, say, but not for $\Delta = 3$. Assuming Δ natural also gives a simple enumerative procedure to find Δ_{min}, as we show in Section 3.3.

Lemma 4. *Let A be Δ-diagnosable. Then, for any $\Delta' > \Delta$, A is Δ'-diagnosable. Also, there exists Δ_{min} such that A is Δ_{min}-diagnosable and for all $\Delta' < \Delta_{min}$, A is not Δ'-diagnosable.*

---

[2]   We could also consider a definition with a different delay Δ_f for each fault $f \in \Sigma_f$.

Lemma 5. *A is Δ-diagnosable iff there exists a function $\phi : \mathcal{TS}_{\Sigma_o} \to \{0,1\}$, such that for every finite run ρ of A, if ρ is not faulty, then $\phi(P(\rho, \Sigma_u)) = 0$, whereas if ρ is Δ-faulty, then $\phi(P(\rho, \Sigma_u)) = 1$.*

Proof   Assume A is Δ-diagnosable. Define ϕ as follows. Given $\pi \in \mathcal{TS}_{\Sigma_o}$, if there exists a finite run τ of A, such that $P(\tau, \Sigma_u) = \pi$ and τ is Δ-faulty, then $\phi(\pi) = 1$, otherwise, $\phi(\pi) = 0$. Now, consider some finite run ρ of A and let $\pi = P(\rho, \Sigma_u)$. If ρ is Δ-faulty, then $\phi(\pi) = 1$, by definition of ϕ. If ρ is not faulty, then we claim that $\phi(\pi) = 0$. Suppose not. Then, there exists a finite run τ of A, such that τ is Δ-faulty and $P(\tau, \Sigma_u) = \pi$. But this means that $P(\tau, \Sigma_u) = P(\rho, \Sigma_u)$, which contradicts the hypothesis that A is Δ-diagnosable.

Conversely, assume A is not Δ-diagnosable, that is, there exist two finite runs ρ_1 and ρ_2 of A, such that ρ_1 is Δ-faulty, ρ_2 is not faulty, and $P(\rho_1, \Sigma_u) = P(\rho_2, \Sigma_u) = \pi$. Now, $\phi(\pi)$ cannot be 0, because $\phi(P(\rho_1, \Sigma_u))$ must be 1, and $\phi(\pi)$ cannot be 1 either, because $\phi(P(\rho_1, \Sigma_u))$ must be 0. So, ϕ cannot exist. $\Box$

3.2   Checking Diagnosability

Checking diagnosability and building diagnosers are well-known problems for finite-state models. Diagnosability can be decided in polynomial time, whereas building a diagnoser relies on a *subset construction* and is exponential in the worst case [29].

In the dense-time case, in order to check whether a given timed automaton A is diagnosable or not, we first form a special parallel product of A with itself. This product, denoted $(A\|_{\Sigma_o} A)^{-f_2}$, has as set of states the cartesian product of the states of A and contains twice as many clocks as A. Checking diagnosability of A will be reduced to finding non-zeno faulty paths in $(A\|_{\Sigma_o} A)^{-f_2}$.

$(A\|_{\Sigma_o} A)^{-f_2}$ is obtained in two phases. First, we build a product $A\|_{\Sigma_o} A$ as follows:

1. We make two "copies" of A, A_1 and A_2, by renaming unobservable events, discrete states and clocks of A:
   - Each discrete state q of A is renamed q_1 in A_1 and q_2 in A_2. The initial state q^0 is copied into q_1^0 and q_2^0.
   - Each clock x of A is renamed x_1 in A_1 and x_2 in A_2.
   - Each unobservable event u of A is renamed u_1 in A_1 and u_2 in A_2. Let Σ_u^1 and Σ_u^2 denote the corresponding sets of renamed unobservable events. Observable events are not renamed.
   - The transitions are copied and renamed accordingly. For example, $e = (q, q', u, x \leq 3, \{y\})$ becomes $e_1 = (q_1, q_1', u_1, x_1 \leq 3, \{y_1\})$ in A_1 (assuming the event u is unobservable, otherwise it would not be renamed).
2. $A\|_{\Sigma_o} A$ is obtained as the usual parallel composition of A_1 and A_2, where transitions of A_1 and A_2 labeled with the same (observable) event are forced to *synchronize*. For example, if $e_i = (q_i, q_i', a, \zeta_i, X_i)$ are transitions of A_i, for $i = 1, 2$, and a is an observable event, then $e = ((q_1, q_2), (q_1', q_2'), a, \zeta_1 \wedge \zeta_2, X_1 \cup X_2)$ is the synchronized transition of $A\|_{\Sigma_o} A$. All other transitions *interleave*. The invariant of a product state (q_1, q_2) is $I(q_1) \wedge I(q_2)$.

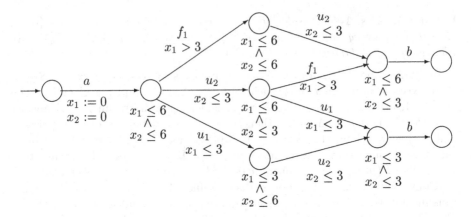

Fig. 3. The product $(A\|_{\Sigma_o} A)^{-f_2}$ for the timed automaton of Figure 1.

Now, let $(A\|_{\Sigma_o} A)^{-f_2}$ be the timed automaton obtained from $A\|_{\Sigma_o} A$ by removing all transitions labeled f_2 from the latter. An example is shown in Figure 3.

The intuition is that every run of $(A\|_{\Sigma_o} A)^{-f_2}$ corresponds to two runs of A which yield the same observation, that is, the same projection to observable events. We obtain this property by synchronizing the two copies in all observable events. (Note that time advances synchronously in both copies.)

To prove this, we need some notation. Let ρ be a run of $(A\|_{\Sigma_o} A)^{-f_2}$. ρ is called faulty if f_1 appears in it. We denote by ρ^1 (resp., ρ^2) the timed sequence obtained by taking the projection $P(\rho, \Sigma_u^2)$ (resp., $P(\rho, \Sigma_u^1)$) and then renaming each event $u_1 \in \Sigma_u^1$ (resp., $u_2 \in \Sigma_u^2$) back into u. That is, ρ^1 and ρ^2 are timed sequences over Σ. For example, if $\rho = a, 1, u_2, 3, u_1$, then $\rho^1 = a, 4, u$ and $\rho^2 = a, 1, u, 3$.

Lemma 6. ρ *is a run of* $(A\|_{\Sigma_o} A)^{-f_2}$ *iff* ρ^1 *and* ρ^2 *are runs of A, ρ^2 is not faulty and* $P(\rho^1, \Sigma_u) = P(\rho^2, \Sigma_u)$. *For such* ρ, ρ^1, ρ^2, *the following also hold:*

1. ρ *is faulty iff* ρ^1 *is faulty.*
2. $\mathsf{time}(\rho) = \mathsf{time}(\rho^1) = \mathsf{time}(\rho^2)$.

Proposition 7 (Diagnosability Check). *A is diagnosable iff every faulty run of* $(A\|_{\Sigma_o} A)^{-f_2}$ *is zeno.*

Proof   Let ρ be a non-zeno faulty run of $(A\|_{\Sigma_o} A)^{-f_2}$. Pick some $\Delta \in \mathbb{N}$. Let ρ_Δ be the finite prefix of ρ up to exactly Δ time units after the first occurrence of f_1 in ρ. Since ρ is non-zeno, ρ_Δ is well-defined and it is clearly a run of $(A\|_{\Sigma_o} A)^{-f_2}$. Thus, by Lemma 6, ρ_Δ^1 and ρ_Δ^2 are both runs of A, ρ_Δ^2 is not faulty, and $P(\rho_\Delta^1, \Sigma_u) = P(\rho_\Delta^2, \Sigma_u)$. Moreover, ρ_Δ^1 is Δ-faulty: this is because the time elapsing after f_1 in ρ_Δ is equal to the time elapsing after f in ρ_Δ^1. Because of $\rho_\Delta^1, \rho_\Delta^2$, A is not Δ-diagnosable. Since such runs can be found for any Δ, A is not diagnosable.

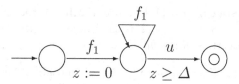

Fig. 4. Observer automaton $\mathsf{Obs}(\Delta)$.

In the other direction, assume A is not diagnosable. This means that for any $\Delta \in \mathsf{N}$, there exist two finite runs ρ_Δ^1 and ρ_Δ^2 of A, such that ρ_Δ^1 contains f, ρ_Δ^2 does not, $P(\rho_\Delta^1, \Sigma_u) = P(\rho_\Delta^2, \Sigma_u)$, and at least Δ time units elapse after the first occurrence of f in ρ_Δ^1. Therefore, by Lemma 6, for any $\Delta \in \mathsf{N}$, there exists a run ρ_Δ of $(A\|_{\Sigma_o} A)^{-f_2}$ such that ρ_Δ is Δ-faulty. By Lemma 1, A has a non-zeno faulty run. $\qquad\square$

From Proposition 7, it follows that checking diagnosability for timed automata is decidable. Indeed, $(A\|_{\Sigma_o} A)^{-f_2}$ can be automatically generated from A using simple copying and renaming operations, and the standard syntactic parallel composition of timed automata. Finding non-zeno runs of a timed automaton was first shown to be decidable in [4] using the region graph construction, with a worst-case complexity of PSPACE. Since the size of $(A\|_{\Sigma_o} A)^{-f_2}$ is polynomial in the size of A, it follows that the worst case complexity of checking diagnosability is also PSPACE.

In practice, non-zeno runs can be found more efficiently, using the algorithms proposed in [8]. These algorithms work on the *simulation graph*, which is a much coarser graph than the region graph, and can be constructed on-the-fly using, for instance, a *depth-first search*. The above algorithms have been implemented in the model-checking tool Kronos [26,9].

3.3   Finding the Maximum Delay for Fault Detection

In the previous section we showed how to check whether a given timed automaton A is diagnosable. Now, we show how to find the required delay for fault detection, Δ_{min}, introduced in Lemma 4.

Consider the *observer* automaton shown in Figure 4. The automaton is parameterized by the constant $\Delta \in \mathsf{N}$, that is, for each given Δ, there is a different automaton, which will be denoted $\mathsf{Obs}(\Delta)$. The clock z of $\mathsf{Obs}(\Delta)$ is a new clock, different from all clocks in A or $(A\|_{\Sigma_o} A)^{-f_2}$. The event u is a new unobservable event, different from all events in A or $(A\|_{\Sigma_o} A)^{-f_2}$. The rightmost discrete state of $\mathsf{Obs}(\Delta)$ (drawn with two concentric circles) is its *accepting* state. Let $(A\|_{\Sigma_o} A)^{-f_2}\|_{f_1} \mathsf{Obs}(\Delta)$ be the parallel product of $(A\|_{\Sigma_o} A)^{-f_2}$ and $\mathsf{Obs}(\Delta)$, where the two automata synchronize only on the transitions labeled f_1. Then, we have the following result.

Proposition 8 (Maximum Delay for Fault Detection). *For any timed automaton A and any $\Delta \in N$, A is Δ-diagnosable iff the accepting state of $(A\|_{\Sigma_o} A)^{-f_2}\|_{f_1} \mathsf{Obs}(\Delta)$ is unreachable.*

If we know that a given automaton A is diagnosable, then we can use Proposition 8 in the following way. We check repeatedly, for $\Delta = 0, 1, 2, ...$, whether the accepting state of $(A\|_{\Sigma_o} A)^{-f_2}\|_{f_1} \mathsf{Obs}(\Delta)$ is reachable. Since A is diagnosable, reachability will eventually fail. This will happen for the first time when $\Delta = \Delta_{min}$.

The above method is simple, but not very efficient (especially when Δ_{min} is large), since it requires $\Delta_{min} + 1$ reachability tests. An alternative way is to use the well-known *binary search* technique, which involves $O(\log \Delta_{min})$ reachability tests. The binary search starts by performing the reachability test repeatedly for $\Delta = 0, 1, 2, 4, 8, ...$, until the first time the test fails. Assume this happens for $\Delta = 2^k$. Then, we know that A is 2^k-diagnosable but not 2^{k-1}-diagnosable, so, Δ_{min} must lie in the interval $[2^{k-1} + 1, 2^k]$. We search this interval by "splitting" it in two, $[2^{k-1} + 1, M]$ and $[M, 2^k]$, checking reachability for the middle value M, and repeating the procedure recursively, for $[2^{k-1} + 1, M]$, if the test fails, and for $[M, 2^k]$, if it succeeds.

4   Diagnosers

For this section, we fix a timed automaton A, which is well-timed and Δ-diagnosable.

Our objective is to construct a *diagnoser* for A, as illustrated in Figure 5. The diagnoser is a deterministic machine which instantaneously observes each observable event generated by the plant and measures delays between successive events. It is also realistic to assume that the diagnoser sets a *time-out*, so that, even if no event happens for some time, the diagnoser will still react to the passage of time.

Each time an event or a delay is observed, the diagnoser changes its state. A state of the diagnoser is marked yes (a fault has been detected) or not-yet (no fault has been detected so far). A valid diagnoser should announce a fault only if a fault indeed occurred. Moreover, when a fault occurs, the diagnoser should announce it at most Δ time units later. Finally, a diagnoser should never stop announcing a fault once it has announced it.

Definition 9 (Diagnoser). *A diagnoser for a timed automaton A is a tuple $(\mathcal{W}, W^0, f_e, f_t, f_d)$, where $\mathcal{W}$ is a set of states, $W^0 \in \mathcal{W}$ is the initial state, $f_e : \mathcal{W} \times \Sigma_o \to \mathcal{W}$ is the event transition function, $f_t : \mathcal{W} \times \mathsf{R} \to \mathcal{W}$ is the time transition function, and $f_d : \mathcal{W} \to \{\text{not-yet}, \text{yes}\}$ is the decision function. The time transition function must satisfy the usual semi-group property, that is, for all $W \in \mathcal{W}$, for all $\delta, \delta', \delta'' \in \mathsf{R}$, if $\delta = \delta' + \delta''$, then $f_t(W, \delta) = f_t(f_t(W, \delta'), \delta'')$.*

A finite timed sequence $\rho = \gamma_1, \gamma_2, \cdots, \gamma_n$ over Σ_o defines a function on the states $\mathcal{W}$ of the diagnoser. If $W \in \mathcal{W}$, $\rho(W)$ is defined to be the last state W_n in

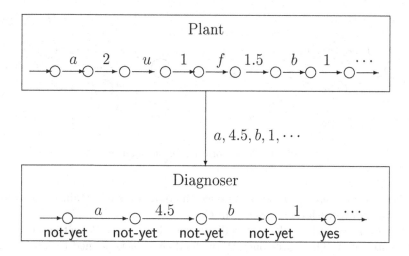

Fig. 5. Illustration of a diagnoser.

a sequence of states $W_0, W_1, \cdots, W_n$, where $W_0 = W$, and for each $i = 1, 2, ...,$ if γ_i is a delay $\delta \in \mathsf{R}$, then $W_i = f_t(W_{i-1}, \delta)$, whereas if γ_i is an event $a \in \Sigma_o$, then $W_i = f_t(W_{i-1}, a)$.

A diagnoser is called *valid* if it satisfies the following conditions:

1. If ρ is a non-faulty finite run of A, then $f_d(\ \pi(W^0)\ ) =$ not-yet, where $\pi = P(\rho, \Sigma_u)$.
2. If ρ is a finite Δ-faulty run of A, then $f_d(\ \pi(W^0)\ ) =$ yes, where $\pi = P(\rho, \Sigma_u)$.
3. If ρ_1, ρ_2 are finite runs of A, ρ_1 is a prefix of ρ_2, and $\pi_i = P(\rho_i, \Sigma_u)$, for $i = 1, 2$, then, if $f_d(\ \pi_1(W^0)\ ) =$ yes, then $f_d(\ \pi_2(W^0)\ ) =$ yes. That is, once the diagnoser has output yes, it can no longer output not-yet.

4.1   Constructing a Diagnoser

We now show how to construct a diagnoser for A. The diagnoser will work as a *state estimator* for A, that is, each state of the diagnoser will correspond to a set of possible states of the timed automaton.

For simplicity of the presentation, we will assume that the set of discrete states Q of A is partitioned in two disjoint sets: $Q = Q_f \cup (Q - Q_f)$, such that, for every run ρ of A, discrete$(\rho(s^0)) \in Q_f$ iff ρ is faulty. In other words, once a fault occurs, A moves to Q_f and never exits this set of discrete states, and while no fault occurs, A moves inside $Q - Q_f$. It is easy to transform any automaton to an automaton satisfying the above condition, possibly by having to duplicate some discrete states and transitions (the transformed automaton will have at most twice as many discrete states as the original automaton). An example of such a transformation is shown in Figure 6. The motivation for the transformation is to reduce the fault detection problem into a state estimation

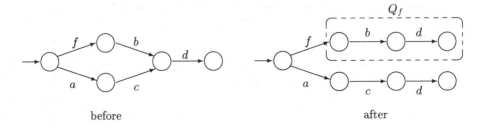

Fig. 6. Transforming an automaton.

problem: a fault has been detected once the diagnoser is certain that the plant is in some state with discrete part in Q_f.

We are now ready to define the diagnoser. Recall that R_A is the set of reachable states of A. The state-space W of the diagnoser is defined to be $W = 2^{R_A}$.

The decision function f_d of the diagnoser is defined as follows:

$$f_d(W) = \begin{cases} \text{yes, if } \forall s \in W, \text{discrete}(s) \in Q_f \\ \text{not-yet, otherwise.} \end{cases} \quad (1)$$

Recall that, for a given event $a \in \Sigma$, $E(a)$ denotes the set of transitions of A labeled by a. Given a set of events $\Sigma' \subseteq \Sigma$, let $\text{Runs}(A, \Sigma')$ be the set of finite runs of A containing only events in Σ'. Then, the transition functions of the diagnoser are defined as follows:

$$f_e(W, a) = \{e(s) \mid s \in W, e \in E(a)\} \quad (2)$$
$$f_t(W, \delta) = \{\rho(s) \mid s \in W, \rho \in \text{Runs}(A, \Sigma_u), \text{time}(\rho) = \delta\}. \quad (3)$$

It can be seen that f_t defined as above satisfies the semi-group property.

The initial state of the diagnoser is defined to be

$$W^0 = \{\rho(s^0) \mid \rho \in \text{Runs}(A, \Sigma_u), \text{time}(\rho) = 0\}, \quad (4)$$

that is, W^0 contains all states reached in zero delay from the initial state of the automaton, by performing only unobservable actions.

The following lemma states that a diagnoser acts as a state estimator for A.

Lemma 10. *For every finite run ρ of A, if $s = \rho(s^0)$ and $\pi = P(\rho, \Sigma_u)$, then $s \in \pi(W^0)$. Conversely, for every finite run π of the diagnoser, for all $s \in \pi(W^0)$, there exists a finite run ρ of A, such that $s = \rho(s^0)$ and $P(\rho, \Sigma_u) = \pi$.*

Proposition 11. *If A is a Δ-diagnosable timed automaton, then the tuple (W, W^0, f_e, f_t, f_d) defined above is a valid diagnoser for A.*

Proof   Let ρ be a finite run of A and let $\pi = P(\rho, \Sigma_u)$.

Assume first that ρ is non-faulty. From the assumption about the structure of A, it must be that for all $s \in \rho(s^0)$, we have discrete$(s) \notin Q_f$. Also, $\rho(s^0) \neq \emptyset$, since ρ is a run of A. Let $s \in \rho(s^0)$. By Lemma 10, $s \in \pi(W^0)$. Thus, by the definition of f_d, $f_d(\pi(W^0)) = $ not-yet. This proves the first condition for validity.

Now, assume that ρ is Δ-faulty. By Lemma 10, $s = \rho(s^0) \in \pi(W^0)$ and, since ρ is faulty, discrete$(s) \in Q_f$. Now, pick some $s' \in \pi(W^0)$. By Lemma 10, there exists a finite run ρ' of A, such that $s' = \rho'(s^0)$ and $P(\rho', \Sigma_u) = \pi$. Since A is Δ-diagnosable, ρ' has to be faulty. Therefore, discrete$(s') \in Q_f$. That is, for all $s' \in \pi(W^0)$, we have discrete$(s') \in Q_f$. Thus, by the definition of f_d, $f_d(\pi(W^0)) = $ yes, which proves the second condition for validity.

As for the third condition, recall that, once A enters the set Q_f, it never exits. Thus, if W is a state of the diagnoser such that for all $s \in W$, discrete$(s) \in Q_f$, then, at any future state W', the same will hold, thus, the decision of the diagnoser will not change. □

4.2   Diagnoser Implementation and Run-Time Considerations

In this section, we show how diagnoser states can be represented using finitary data structures and how the decision and transition functions can be effectively computed on these structures. In fact, we will use technology not much different from that used in timed-automata model-checkers such as Kronos [9] or Uppaal [1].

A state of the diagnoser will be a list $[(q_1, \zeta_1), ..., (q_k, \zeta_k)]$, where $q_i \in Q$ and ζ_i is a polyhedron on X, the set of clocks of A. Such a polyhedron can be effectively represented using well-known data structures called *difference bound matrices* (DBMs) [13]. Set-theoretic operations on such polyhedra, such as union, intersection, test for emptiness, and so on, can be conducted on the corresponding DBMs. The initial state s^0 of A can be represented by the list $[(q_0, \bigwedge_{x \in X} x = 0)]$.

The decision function of the diagnoser can be easily computed by scanning the list: if the list contains some pair (q_i, ζ_i) such that $q_i \notin Q_f$, then the function returns not-yet, otherwise it returns yes.

The event transition function $f_e(W, a)$ can be computed as follows. If $W = [(q_1, \zeta_1), ..., (q_k, \zeta_k)]$ is the current list, start with a new empty list W', and for each $(q_i, \zeta_i) \in W$, for each $e \in E(a)$ such that source$(e) = q_i$, if $\zeta_i \cap$ guard$(e) \neq \emptyset$, then (dest$(e), \zeta'$) is added to r', where ζ' is the polyhedron

$$\left((\exists x \in \text{reset}(e) . \zeta_i) \cap \left(\bigwedge_{x \in \text{reset}(e)} x = 0 \right) \right) \cap I(\text{dest}(e)),$$

which contains all $v[\text{reset}(e) := 0] \in I(\text{dest}(e))$, such that $v \in \zeta_i \cap$ guard(e). Since the number of pairs in W is finite, and there is a finite number of transitions e, the number of pairs in W' is also finite.

The time transition function $f_t(W, \delta)$ can be computed for any delay δ which is a rational number[3], using a *reachability* procedure. There are two differences

---

[3] In practice, the granularity of δ will be restricted by the numerical accuracy of the machine.

between the standard reachability procedure for timed automata, and the one for computing $f_t(W, \delta)$. For $f_t(W, \delta)$, reachability is restricted only to unobservable transitions of A. Standard reachability can be easily modified to meet this condition: simply select only transitions labeled with unobservable events. Also, standard reachability computes the set of states reachable at any time, whereas reachability for $f_t(W, \delta)$ computes the set of states reachable in *exactly* δ time units. This condition can be satisfied as follows.

First, we compute the set of states reachable from W in *at most δ time units*. Call this set $W_{\leq \delta}$. $W_{\leq \delta}$ can be represented as a finite list of DBMs, and can be computed by extending W with a new clock z initially set to 0 and exploring only the states satisfying $z \leq \delta$. Once $W_{\leq \delta}$ is computed, we take the intersection $W_{\leq \delta} \cap (z = \delta)$: this set contains all states reachable from W in exactly δ time units. Finally, the clock z is eliminated by existential quantification, and the final result is obtained:

$$f_t(W, \delta) = \exists z \cdot \left(W_{\leq \delta} \cap (z = \delta) \right). \tag{5}$$

```
set W to W^0 ;                          /* initialize diagnoser state */
set timer x to 0 ;                      /* set an incrementing timer */
loop
   if (f_d(W) = yes) then
      announce fault ;
   end if ;
   await (event interrupt) or (x = TO) ; /* await event or timer interrupt */
   if (event a interrupt) then
      set W to f_e(f_t(W, x), a) ;       /* update state by time and discrete step */
   else
      set W to f_t(W, TO) ;             /* update state by time step */
   end if ;
   set timer x to 0 ;                    /* reset timer for new time interrupt */
end loop.
```

Fig. 7. Diagnoser implementation loop.

Figure 7 shows how the implementation of a diagnoser would look like, in pseudo-code. After initializing its state and setting a timer to 0, the diagnoser enters an infinite loop. Inside the loop, the diagnoser checks whether a fault has occurred and if so it announces it. Then, it waits until an (observable) event is received, or the timer times-out (this happens after TO time units, where TO is a parameter), updates its state accordingly, and repeats the loop. Such an implementation requires an execution platform which provides some kind of event interrupts, time-outs and clock readings[4].

---

[4] The memory required for such an implementation is generally unbounded, since the set of reachable states of the diagnoser is generally unbounded. This is not surprising,

A diagnoser implemented like the one shown in Figure 7 will function correctly, provided the loop can be executed sufficiently fast. In practice, this means that the maximum time to compute the transition function should not be greater than the minimum delay between two observable events. This requirement is similar to the *synchrony hypothesis*, which implies the correct execution of programs written in *synchronous languages* such as Esterel [2] or Lustre [14].

5 Related Work and Discussion

Fault diagnosis has been studied by different communities and in different contexts, e.g., see [20,21,24,7,6], and citations therein. We restrict our discussion to work closely related to timed systems.

[11,32] study fault-diagnosis on a discrete-time model, called *timed discrete-event systems* (TDES). In TDES, time passing is modeled by a special (observable) event "tick" and the problem of diagnosis can be easily reduced to the untimed case and solved using untimed techniques. Discretization of time is also used in [23], to reduce the problem into a finite-state diagnosis problem.

[16] use a timed automaton model without clocks, but where time intervals are associated with discrete states. They propose *template monitoring* as a technique for distributed fault diagnosis, where templates are sets of constraints on the occurrence times of events.

Fault diagnosis is closely related to observation and state estimation problems. Such problems are considered in the context of hybrid automata in [6,17]. These methods rely on an observable part of (or function of) the plant's continuous variables. Based on the observable continuous variables (and possibly discrete observations as well), the dynamics of the unobservable variables must be determined. This approach cannot be used to solve our problem, because we assume that *no* clock of the timed automaton is directly observable. Instead, the diagnoser must infer the values of clocks based only on the events it observes. This is a reasonable assumption, since the plant model is often an abstraction of a physical process, which has no clocks anyway.

Fault-diagnosis is also related to the *controller-synthesis* problem, introduced for discrete-event systems in [19]. The problem has been studied for timed and hybrid models as well (e.g., see [31,10,12,5,18,30,25]). Some of these works are restricted to a discrete-time framework, for example [10,18]. The rest make a major assumption, namely, that the state of the plant (including the values of all clocks) is *fully observable*. This is unrealistic, except for the case where the plant is deterministic and all its events are observable[5].

[30] discusses how partial observability of plant states can be taken into account, by assuming the existence of a function $vis(\cdot)$ from the state space of

---

since the set of states of a timed automaton is also generally infinite. Thus, even if the diagnoser was represented as a timed automaton, an unbounded memory would be generally needed to implement clocks.

[5] In this case, the controller can replicate the clocks of the plant and reset them whenever it sees the corresponding observable event.

the plant to a domain of possible observations: when the plant is at state s, the controller observes $vis(s)$. Then, [30] shows how to synthesize *memoryless* controllers in the above framework. The controllers are memoryless in the sense that their decision depends only on the current observation and not past ones. This is why the algorithm is incomplete: it might fail to synthesize a controller, even though one exists. Another drawback is that the function $vis(\cdot)$ is not always easy to come up with, for example, when starting with an observation framework based on events, as we do here.

Acknowledgements

I would like to thank Eugene Asarin, Oded Maler and Peter Niebert.

References

1. Uppaal web-site: `www.docs.uu.se/docs/rtmv/uppaal/`.
2. Esterel web-site: `www.esterel.org`.
3. R. Alur and D.L. Dill. A theory of timed automata. *Theoretical Computer Science*, 126:183–235, 1994.
4. Rajeev Alur. *Techniques for Automatic Verification of Real-Time Systems*. PhD thesis, Department of Computer Science, Stanford University, 1991.
5. E. Asarin, O. Maler, A. Pnueli, and J. Sifakis. Controller synthesis for timed automata. In *Proc. IFAC Symposium on System Structure and Control*. Elsevier, 1998.
6. A. Balluchi, L. Benvenuti, M. Di Benedetto, and A. Sangiovanni-Vincentelli. Design of observers for hybrid systems. In *Hybrid Systems: Computation and Control*, 2002. To appear.
7. P. Baroni, G. Lamperti, P. Pogliano, and M. Zanella. Diagnosis of large active systems. *Artificial Intelligence*, 110, 1999.
8. A. Bouajjani, S. Tripakis, and S. Yovine. On-the-fly symbolic model checking for real-time systems. In *Proc. of the 18th IEEE Real-Time Systems Symposium, San Francisco, CA*, pages 232–243. IEEE, December 1997.
9. M. Bozga, C. Daws, O. Maler, A. Olivero, S. Tripakis, and S. Yovine. Kronos: a model-checking tool for real-time systems. In *Proc. of the 10th Conference on Computer-Aided Verification, CAV'98*. LNCS 1427, Springer-Verlag, 1998.
10. B.A. Brandin and W.M. Wonham. Supervisory control of timed discrete-event systems. *IEEE Transactions on Automatic Control*, 39(2), 1994.
11. Yi-Liang Chen and Gregory Provan. Modeling and diagnosis of timed discrete event systems – a factory automation example. In *ACC*, 1997.
12. D.D. Cofer and V.K. Garg. On controlling timed discrete event systems. In *Hybrid Systems III: Verification and Control*. LNCS 1066, Springer-Verlag, 1996.
13. D.L. Dill. Timing assumptions and verification of finite-state concurrent systems. In J. Sifakis, editor, *Automatic Verification Methods for Finite State Systems*, Lecture Notes in Computer Science 407, pages 197–212. Springer–Verlag, 1989.
14. N. Halbwachs, P. Caspi, P. Raymond, and D. Pilaud. The synchronous dataflow programming language Lustre. *Proceedings of the IEEE*, 79(9), September 1991.
15. T.A. Henzinger, X. Nicollin, J. Sifakis, and S. Yovine. Symbolic model checking for real-time systems. *Information and Computation*, 111(2):193–244, 1994.

16. L.E. Holloway and S. Chand. Time templates for discrete event fault monitoring in manufacturing systems. In *Proc. of the 1994 American Control Conference*, 1994.
17. S. Narasimhan and G. Biswas. An approach to model-based diagnosis of hybrid systems. In *Hybrid Systems: Computation and Control*, 2002. To appear.
18. J. Raisch and S. O'Young. A DES approach to control of hybrid dynamical systems. In *Hybrid Systems III: Verification and Control*. LNCS 1066, Springer-Verlag, 1996.
19. P. Ramadge and W. Wonham. Supervisory control of a class of discrete event processes. *SIAM J. Control Optim.*, 25(1), January 1987.
20. Amit Kumar Ray and R. B. Misra. Real-time fault diagnosis - using occupancy grids and neural network techniques. In *Industrial and Engineering Applications of Artificial Intelligence and Expert Systems, IEA/AIE*. LNCS 604, Springer-Verlag, 1992.
21. M. Sampath, R. Sengupta, S. Lafortune, K. Sinnamohideen, and D. Teneketzis. Diagnosability of discrete event systems. *IEEE Transactions on Automatic Control*, 40(9), September 1995.
22. M. Sampath, R. Sengupta, S. Lafortune, K. Sinnamohideen, and D. Teneketzis. Failure diagnosis using discrete event models. *IEEE Transactions on Control Systems Technology*, 4(2), March 1996.
23. J. Sztipanovits, R. Carnes, and A. Misra. Finite state temporal automata modeling for fault diagnosis. In *9th AIAA Conference on Computing in Aerospace*, 1993.
24. J. Sztipanovits and A. Misra. Diagnosis of discrete event systems using ordered binary decision diagrams. In *7th Intl. Workshop on Principles of Diagnosis*, 1996.
25. C. Tomlin, J. Lygeros, and S. Sastry. Synthesizing controllers for nonlinear hybrid systems. In *Hybrid Systems: Computation and Control*. LNCS 1386, Springer-Verlag, 1998.
26. S. Tripakis. *The formal analysis of timed systems in practice*. PhD thesis, Université Joseph Fourrier de Grenoble, 1998.
27. S. Tripakis. Verifying progress in timed systems. In *ARTS'99*, LNCS 1601, 1999.
28. S. Tripakis and S. Yovine. Analysis of timed systems using time-abstracting bisimulations. *Formal Methods in System Design*, 18(1):25–68, January 2001.
29. J.N. Tsitsiklis. On the control of discrete event dynamical systems. *Mathematics of Control, Signals and Systems*, 2(2), 1989.
30. H. Wong-Toi. The synthesis of controllers for linear hybrid automata. In *Proc. of IEEE Conference on Decision and Control*, 1997.
31. H. Wong-Toi and G. Hoffmann. The control of dense real-time discrete event systems. In *Proc. of the 30th IEEE Conference on Decision and Control*, 1991.
32. S. Hashtrudi Zad, R.H. Kwong, and W.M. Wonham. Fault diagnosis in finite-state automata and timed discrete-event systems. In *38th IEEE Conference on Decision and Control*, 1999.

Part V

Bounded Model Checking

Verification of Timed Automata
via Satisfiability Checking*

Peter Niebert[2], Moez Mahfoudh[1], Eugene Asarin[1], Marius Bozga[1],
Oded Maler[1], and Navendu Jain[3]

[1] VERIMAG, 2 Av. de Vignate, 38610 Gières, France
{Moez.Mahfoudh,Eugene.Asarin,Marius.Bozga,Oded.Maler}@imag.fr
[2] Laboratoire d'Informatique Fondamentale, CMI, 39 rue Joliot-Curie
13453 Marseille Cedex 13, France
niebert@cmi.univ-mrs.fr
[3] Computer Science and Eng. Dept., Indian Inst. of Technology
Hauz Khas, New Delhi, India
navendu@cse.iitd.ac.in

Abstract. In this paper we show how to translate bounded-length verification problems for timed automata into formulae in *difference logic*, a propositional logic enriched with timing constraints. We describe the principles of a satisfiability checker specialized for this logic that we have implemented and report some preliminary experimental results.

1   Introduction

The generic problem of verification can be phrased as follows: given a description of a transition system, check whether its set of possible behaviors contains a behavior violating some desired property. It is known for quite a while that the problem is decidable for finite-state systems and various specification formalisms [QS81,EC82,LP84,VW86] via graph search algorithms. However, most systems of interest are given as a composition of many interacting sub-systems and their global state-space is prohibitively-large for enumerative graph algorithms. To treat such systems one needs symbolic techniques that perform the reachability computation on an implicit syntactic representation of the system. This is the basis of what is called *symbolic model-checking* [McM93,BCM+93].

To be more concrete, consider a system over a set $\mathcal{B}$ of state variables and its transition relation $R(\mathcal{B}, \mathcal{B}')$, written using an auxiliary set of "next-state" variables $\mathcal{B}'$. The global transition relation is expressed as a conjunction of the local transition formulae for the system components:

$$R(\mathcal{B}, \mathcal{B}') = R_1(\mathcal{B}, \mathcal{B}') \wedge R_2(\mathcal{B}, \mathcal{B}') \wedge \ldots \wedge R_n(\mathcal{B}, \mathcal{B}').$$

The standard algorithm for checking whether from a set of initial states F one can reach a set G works as follows:

* This work was partially supported by the EC project IST-2001-35302 AMETIST (Advanced Methods for Timed Systems).

W. Damm and E.-R. Olderog (Eds.): FTRTFT 2002, LNCS 2469, pp. 225–243, 2002.
© Springer-Verlag Berlin Heidelberg 2002

repeat
$$F(\mathcal{B}) := \exists \mathcal{B}'[\ F(\mathcal{B}') \wedge R(\mathcal{B}', \mathcal{B})]$$
until $\ F(\mathcal{B}) \wedge G(\mathcal{B}) \neq \emptyset$

At every iteration k of the algorithm, the formula F characterizes the states reachable from the initial set within exactly k steps. The Boolean operations and the $\exists$-operation are implemented usually using BDDs, a canonical representation for propositional formulae [Bry86]. A variant of the algorithm which keeps a representation of all states reachable within at most k steps is guaranteed to terminate after finitely many steps.

In recent years it has been realized that this way of solving the reachability problem is not always the most efficient, and that the representation of intermediate sets of states by BDDs can explode in size. Instead of an alternating sequence of next-state computation and elimination of intermediate states, one can construct a formula expressing the existence of a path of length k, and then apply generic SAT solvers to the formula [SS90,BCRZ99,BCCZ99]. The formula looks like this:

$$\exists \mathcal{B}^0, \ldots, \exists \mathcal{B}^k \ F(\mathcal{B}^0) \wedge R(\mathcal{B}^0, \mathcal{B}^1) \wedge R(\mathcal{B}^1, \mathcal{B}^2) \wedge \ldots \wedge R(\mathcal{B}^{k-1}, \mathcal{B}^k) \wedge G(\mathcal{B}^k).$$

The advantage in using a SAT solver for such a formula lies in the fact that we are not restricted anymore to a fixed order of variable elimination and can use any of the numerous techniques for solving the satisfiability problem (which is, perhaps, the most celebrated discrete computational problem). Of course, this idea is most useful for systems that do exhibit undesired behavior, and is less so for correct systems of large diameter, but bug hunting is a respectable activity especially for systems too large for complete verification.

In this work we take this idea further and apply it to *timed systems* where the computational difficulty is much bigger. To this end we define *difference logic*, a propositional logic augmented with numerical variables and difference constraints between pairs of such variables. We then define a procedure for expressing bounded reachability problems for timed automata as formulae in this logic. These formulae are then checked for satisfiability by a new SAT solver for difference logic that we have designed and implemented. Preliminary experimental results are reported.

The rest of the paper is structured as follows. In section 2 we define difference logic and the conjunctive normal form for its formulae. The derivation of formulae for bounded reachability problems for "flat" timed automata is described in Section 3 followed by a compositional version of this transalation in Section 4. Section 5 is dedicated to the description of the solver, while some preliminary experimental results are described in Section 6. We conclude with some related work.

2   Difference Logic

In this section we define the class of formulae that we consider. This class has already been used elsewhere (see e.g. [MLAH99,LPWY99,ABK$^+$97,BM00,ACG99]) and is probably part of folklore, but to give it a name let us call it *difference logic* (DL). We use two slightly different variants, DLZ and DLR depending on the domain of the numerical variables.

Definition 1 (Difference Logic). *Let $\mathcal{B} = \{B_1, B_2, \ldots\}$ be a set of Boolean variables and $\mathcal{X} = \{X_1, X_2, \ldots\}$ be a set of numerical variables. The set of atomic formulae of $DL(\mathcal{B}, \mathcal{X})$ consists of the Boolean variables in $\mathcal{B}$ and numerical constraints of the following forms:*

$$X_i - X_j \geq c$$

(with $c \in \mathbb{Z}$ for DLZ and $c \in \mathbb{Q}$ for DLR) and

$$X_i - X_j > c$$

with $c \in \mathbb{Q}$ for DLR only[1].

The set $\mathcal{F}$ of all DL formulae is the smallest set containing the atomic formulae which is closed under negation ($\varphi \in \mathcal{F}$ implies $\neg\varphi \in \mathcal{F}$) and a collection of binary Boolean connectives ($\varphi_1, \varphi_2 \in \mathcal{F}$ implies $\varphi_1 \vee \varphi_2, \varphi_1 \wedge \varphi_2, \varphi_1 \rightarrow \varphi_2, \ldots \in \mathcal{F}$).

An $(\mathcal{X}, \mathcal{B})$-*valuation* consists of two functions (overloaded with the name v) $v : \mathcal{B} \rightarrow \{T, F\}$ and $v : \mathcal{X} \rightarrow \mathbb{Z}$ for DLZ or $v : \mathcal{X} \rightarrow \mathbb{R}$ for DLR. The valuation v is extended to all $DL(\mathcal{B}, \mathcal{X})$ formulae by letting

$$v(X_i - X_j \geq c) = T \text{ iff } v(X_i) - v(X_j) \geq c$$

and applying the obvious rules for the Boolean connectives.

A formula φ is satisfied by a valuation v iff $v(\varphi) = T$ (we denote it also by $v \models \varphi$). A formula φ is satisfiable if it has a satisfying valuation.

Proposition 1. *The satisfiability problem for $DL(\mathcal{B}, \mathcal{X})$ is NP-complete.*

Proof. NP-hardness is an immediate consequence of the Boolean case, Cook's theorem [GJ79]. For NP-easiness, a non-deterministic algorithm works by guessing which atomic formulae (Boolean variables and inequalities) appearing in the formula are true and which are false. A polynomial time test then has to check that this assignment renders the entire formula true (linear time in the size of the formula) and that the corresponding set of constraints on the reals is in fact satisfiable. The satisfiability of a *conjunction* of difference constraints (a special case of linear programming) can be solved in polynomial (cubic) time using a variant of the Floyd-Warshall algorithm [CLRS01].   □

We work with formulae in conjunctive normal with at most 3 literals in a clause.

Definition 2 (3CNF). *A Boolean literal is a formula of the form B or $\neg B$ with $B \in \mathcal{B}$. A numerical literal is a formula of the form $X - Y \geq c$ (also $X - Y > c$ for DLR). A 3-clause is a disjunction $C = L_1 \vee L_2 \vee L_3$ of at most 3 literals at most one of which is a numerical literal. A formula of difference logic is in 3CNF if it is a conjunction $\bigwedge_{k \in K} C_k$ of a set of 3-clauses C_k.*

---

[1] Over integers, the constraint $X - Y > c$ is of course equivalent to $X - Y \geq c + 1$, hence $>$-constraints are obsolete in the integer case and life is easier without them.

The restriction to at most one numerical literal per clause plays an important role in the implementation of our procedure. The restriction to 3-clauses is less pertinent — it simplifies the description of proof methods based on the Davis-Putnam approach. We have developed another version with unbounded clause size.

As in propositional logic (see [T70]), translations from arbitrary formulae to 3CNF need not be costly if auxiliary Boolean variables are introduced:

Proposition 2. *From an arbitrary $DL(\mathcal{B}, \mathcal{X})$ formula φ one can derive a $DL(\mathcal{B}', \mathcal{X})$ formula φ' over an extended set of Boolean variables $\mathcal{B}' \supseteq \mathcal{B}$, such that*

- *φ' is in 3CNF;*
- *any $(\mathcal{B}, \mathcal{X})$-valuation v satisfying φ can be extended to a $(\mathcal{B}', \mathcal{X})$-valuation v' satisfying φ'.*
- *(the projection of) any valuation v' satisfying φ' satisfies equally φ.*
- *$|\varphi'| = O(|\varphi|)$.*

Proof. (Sketch) A simple construction to achieve this is to introduce for each composed sub-formula ψ of φ a fresh variable B_ψ to express whether for a given valuation ψ holds. Then the structure of φ can be broken up into local semantic constraints by coding, using 3CNF clauses, the semantic relation of ψ with its immediate sub-formulae. For instance, if $\psi = \psi_1 \vee \psi_2$ then we will add the three clauses $\{\neg B_\psi \vee B_{\psi_1} \vee B_{\psi_2}, B_\psi \vee \neg B_{\psi_1}, B_\psi \vee \neg B_{\psi_2}\}$ to our set of clauses. In addition to these structural clauses, a clause B_φ is used to express that φ should be true. It is easy to extend a satisfying valuation of φ to a satisfying valuation for the set of clauses constructed this way and, conversely, projecting the additional variables of a satisfying valuation of φ' yields a satisfying valuation of φ.   □

As a tiny example, consider the formula φ consisting of a clause

$$(Y - Z \geq -2 \vee Z - X \geq 1)$$

with two numerical literals. To transform it to 3CNF we use an additional Boolean variable B to represent $Y - Z \geq -2$. Using the fact that $B \leftrightarrow Y - Z \geq -2$ can be written as

$$(B \leftarrow Y - Z \geq -2) \wedge (B \rightarrow Y - Z \geq -2)$$

we get

$$(B \vee Z - X \geq 1) \wedge (\neg B \vee Y - Z \geq -2) \wedge (B \vee Z - Y > 2).$$

In practice, optimized translations introducing less variables and with certain additional structural properties are possible (see [GW99] for a more detailed discussion).

3   From Flat Timed Automata to Difference Logic

Timed automata [AD94] are automata augmented with clock variables. Their behavior consists of an alternation of discrete transitions and passage of time where the automtaton stays in a state and the clock values grow with a uniform rate. Clock values can enable transitions, disable staying in a state and be reset by transitions. We will start with "flat" timed automata and define their translation to DL, and later will proceed to a product of interacting automata. A similar translation, proposed in [HNSY94], is the basis for the algorithmic verification of timed automata. An integer bounded inequality over a set C of variables is either $C \leq d$, $C < d$, $C \geq d$ or $C > d$ for $C \in C$ and an integer constant d.

Definition 3 (Timed Automaton). *A timed automaton is a tuple $A = (Q, C, S, \Delta)$ where Q is a finite set of states, C is a finite set of clock variables, S is a function which associates with every state q a conjunction S_q of integer bounded inequalities over C (staying conditions), and Δ is a transition relation consisting of tuples of the form (q, g, ρ, q') where q and q' are states, $\rho \subseteq C$ and g (the transition guard) is a conjunction of integer bounded inequalities over C.*

A *clock valuation* is a function $\mathbf{v} : C \to \mathbb{R}_+$, or equivalently a $|C|$-dimensional vector over $\mathbb{R}_+$. We denote the set of all clock valuations by $\mathcal{H}$. A configuration of the automaton is hence a pair $(q, \mathbf{v}) \in Q \times \mathcal{H}$ consisting of a discrete state (sometimes called "location") and a clock valuation. Every subset $\rho \subseteq C$ induces a reset function $\text{Reset}_\rho : \mathcal{H} \to \mathcal{H}$ defined for every clock valuation $\mathbf{v}$ and every clock variable $C \in C$ as

$$\text{Reset}_\rho \, \mathbf{v}(C) = \begin{cases} 0 & \text{if } C \in \rho \\ \mathbf{v}(C) & \text{if } C \notin \rho \end{cases}$$

That is, Reset_ρ resets to zero all the clocks in ρ and leaves the other clocks unchanged. We use $\mathbf{1}$ to denote the unit vector $(1, \ldots, 1)$ and $\mathbf{0}$ for the zero vector.

Definition 4 (Steps and Runs). *A step of the automaton is one of the following:*

- *A discrete step:*

$$(q, \mathbf{v}) \xrightarrow{\delta} (q', \mathbf{v}'),$$

  where $\delta = (q, g, \rho, q') \in \Delta$, such that $\mathbf{v}$ satisfies g and $\mathbf{v}' = \text{Reset}_\rho(\mathbf{v})$.
- *A time step:*

$$(q, \mathbf{v}) \xrightarrow{t} (q, \mathbf{v} + t\mathbf{1}),$$

  where $t \geq 0$, and $\mathbf{v} + t\mathbf{1}$ satisfies S_q.

A finite run of a timed automaton is a finite sequence of steps

$$(q_0, \mathbf{v}_0) \xrightarrow{z_1} (q_1, \mathbf{v}_1) \xrightarrow{z_2} \cdots \xrightarrow{z_n} (q_n, \mathbf{v}_n).$$

Steps and runs can be extended to include *time stamps* that indicate the absolute time since the beginning of the run. This can be viewed as having an additional clock which is never reset to zero. An extended discrete step is thus

$$(q, \mathbf{v}, T) \xrightarrow{\delta} (q', \mathbf{v}', T),$$

and an extended time step is

$$(q, \mathbf{v}, T) \xrightarrow{t} (q, \mathbf{v} + t\mathbf{1}, T + t).$$

Note that a single behavior of the automaton can be represented by infinitely many runs due to splitting of time steps. For example, the step above can be split into

$$(q, \mathbf{v}, T) \xrightarrow{t'} (q, \mathbf{v} + t'\mathbf{1}, T + t') \xrightarrow{t-t'} (q, \mathbf{v} + t\mathbf{1}, T + t).$$

In particular the definition of a time step allows $t = 0$ which means that idle transitions that do nothing and take no time can be inserted anywhere inside a run. This will be used in the sequel. We will refer to a run in which there are no two consecutive time steps as a *minimal run*.

To build a DL formula that characterizes valid runs of the automaton we assume first that Q can be encoded by a set $\mathcal{B}$ of Boolean variables so that $\Phi_q(\mathcal{B})$ is the formula over those variables denoting a state q. Such state formulae can be extended using disjunction into formulae of the form Φ_P for every $P \subseteq Q$. In order to express step formula we will use auxiliary sets of variables $\mathcal{B}'$ and $\mathcal{C}'$ to denote the values of state and clock variables after the step.

The formula $\Phi_\rho(\mathcal{C}, \mathcal{C}')$ expressing the effect of applying Reset_ρ is

$$\Phi_\rho(\mathcal{C}, \mathcal{C}') \equiv \bigwedge_{C_m \in \rho} C_m' = 0 \wedge \bigwedge_{C_m \notin \rho} C_m' = C_m.$$

The formula $\Phi_\tau(\mathcal{C}, \mathcal{C}')$ for the passage of time is

$$\Phi_\tau(\mathcal{C}, \mathcal{C}') \equiv \exists t \ t \geq 0 \wedge \bigwedge_m C_m' - C_m = t.$$

The formula $\Psi_\delta(\mathcal{B}, \mathcal{C}, \mathcal{B}', \mathcal{C}')$ for a step associated with a transition $\delta = (q, g, \rho, q')$ is

$$\Psi_\delta(\mathcal{B}, \mathcal{C}, \mathcal{B}', \mathcal{C}') \equiv \Phi_q(\mathcal{B}) \wedge \Phi_g(\mathcal{C}) \wedge \Phi_\rho(\mathcal{C}, \mathcal{C}') \wedge \Phi_{q'}(\mathcal{B}')$$

where $\Phi_g(\mathcal{C})$ is just the substitution of $\mathcal{C}$ in the guard g. The formula $\Psi_q(\mathcal{B}, \mathcal{C}, \mathcal{B}', \mathcal{C}')$ for a time step at state q is

$$\Psi_q(\mathcal{B}, \mathcal{C}, \mathcal{B}', \mathcal{C}') \equiv \Phi_q(\mathcal{B}) \wedge \Phi_\tau(\mathcal{C}, \mathcal{C}') \wedge \Phi_{s,q}(\mathcal{C}') \wedge \Phi_q(\mathcal{B}')$$

where $\Phi_{s,q}(\mathcal{C}')$ is just the substitution of $\mathcal{C}'$ in S_q. The formula for a valid step is

$$\Psi(\mathcal{B}, \mathcal{C}, \mathcal{B}', \mathcal{C}') \equiv \bigvee_{q \in Q} \Psi_q \vee \bigvee_{\delta \in \Delta} \Psi_\delta.$$

The formula $\Psi_k(\mathcal{B}^0, \mathcal{C}^0, \ldots, \mathcal{B}^k, \mathcal{C}^k)$ characterizing a run of length k is written as

$$\Psi_k \equiv \Psi(\mathcal{B}^0, \mathcal{C}^0, \mathcal{B}^1, \mathcal{C}^1) \wedge \Psi(\mathcal{B}^1, \mathcal{C}^1, \mathcal{B}^2, \mathcal{C}^2) \wedge \ldots \wedge \Psi(\mathcal{B}^{k-1}, \mathcal{C}^{k-1}, \mathcal{B}^k, \mathcal{C}^k).$$

Due to idling this formula is satisfied also by runs whose minimal run is of length smaller than k. Finally a run of length k starting from a set G and ending in a set H is written as

$$\Phi_G(\mathcal{B}^0, \mathcal{C}^0) \wedge \Psi_k(\mathcal{B}^0, \mathcal{C}^0, \ldots, \mathcal{B}^k, \mathcal{C}^k) \wedge \Phi_H(\mathcal{B}^k, \mathcal{C}^k).$$

As the alert reader might have noticed, the inequalities in Φ_τ are outside the scope of DL. After eliminating t we obtain

$$\Phi_\tau(\mathcal{C}, \mathcal{C}') \equiv \bigwedge_i \bigwedge_{j \neq i} (C_i' - C_i) = (C_j' - C_j) \geq 0$$

with numerical constraints that relate 4 numerical variables. This can be, however, circumvented by a change of variables which has an intuitive meaning (see also [BJLY98]). Consider a state extended with a time-stamp T. For every clock C_i, the variable $X_i = T - C_i$ represents the last time when C_i was reset (we use the notation $\mathcal{X} = T - \mathcal{C}$ for the whole transformation). It is not hard to see that an $(\mathcal{X}, T)$-valuation gives a state representation "isomorphic" to a $\mathcal{C}$-valuation: the guard and staying conditions should be evaluated on $T - \mathcal{X}$ instead of on $\mathcal{C}$, passage of time affects only T while a reset of C_i at time T corresponds to the assignment $X_i := T$. All the above formulae can be transformed into formulae in $\mathcal{X}$ and T as follows. The reset formula becomes

$$\Phi_\rho(\mathcal{X}, \mathcal{X}', T) \equiv \bigwedge_{C_m \in \rho} X_m' = T \wedge \bigwedge_{C_m \notin \rho} X_m' = X_m.$$

Time passage is written as

$$\Phi_\tau(\mathcal{X}, T, \mathcal{X}', T') \equiv \bigwedge_m X_m' = X_m \wedge \exists t\, t \geq 0 \wedge T' - T = t$$

and after elimination of t as

$$\Phi_\tau(\mathcal{X}, T, \mathcal{X}', T') \equiv \bigwedge_m X_m' = X_m \wedge T' - T \geq 0.$$

The transition formula becomes

$$\Psi_\delta(\mathcal{B}, \mathcal{X}, T, \mathcal{B}', \mathcal{X}', T') \equiv \Phi_q(\mathcal{B}) \wedge \Phi_g(\mathcal{X}, T) \wedge \Phi_\rho(\mathcal{X}, \mathcal{X}', T) \wedge \Phi_{q'}(\mathcal{B}') \wedge T = T'$$

where $\Phi_g(\mathcal{X}, T)$ is the substitution of $T - \mathcal{X}$ in the guard g instead of $\mathcal{C}$. A time step at state q is expressed as

$$\Psi_q(\mathcal{B}, \mathcal{X}, T, \mathcal{B}', \mathcal{X}', T') \equiv \Phi_q(\mathcal{B}) \wedge \Phi_\tau(\mathcal{X}, T, \mathcal{X}', T') \wedge \Phi_{s,q}(\mathcal{X}', T') \wedge \Phi_q(\mathcal{B}')$$

where $\Phi_{s,q}(\mathcal{X}',T')$ is the substitution of $T' - \mathcal{X}'$ in S_q. The formula for a step is

$$\Psi(\mathcal{B},\mathcal{X},T,\mathcal{B}',\mathcal{X}',T') \equiv \bigvee_{q \in Q} \Psi_q \vee \bigvee_{\delta \in \Delta} \Psi_\delta.$$

The formula $\Psi_k(\mathcal{B}^0,\mathcal{X}^0,T^0,\ldots,\mathcal{B}^k,\mathcal{X}^k,T^k)$ for a run of length k is

$$\Psi_k \equiv \Psi(\mathcal{B}^0,\mathcal{X}^0,T^0,\mathcal{B}^1,\mathcal{X}^1,T^1) \wedge \ldots \wedge \Psi(\mathcal{B}^{k-1},\mathcal{X}^{k-1},T^{k-1},\mathcal{B}^k,\mathcal{X}^k,T^k).$$

All these formulae are in DL and the price is the addition of k numerical variables that represent the dates at which the corresponding transitions were taken.

Proposition 3 (Translation). *Let $\mathcal{A}$ be a timed automaton with n states, m clocks and l transitions. The problem of reachability within at most k transitions can be expressed by a DL formula with $(k+1)\log n$ Boolean variables and $(k+1)(m+1)$ numerical variables. The size of the formula is $O(k(n+l)m^2 \log n)$.*

4   Compositional Translation

In this section we describe the construction of DL formulae for reachability problems for a product of interacting timed automata. There are many variants of composition operators and we will concentrate in the presentation on communication by variables, that is, any automaton may observe the state of the other automata and refer to their values in its transition guards and staying conditions. Consider several timed automata $\{\mathcal{A}_i\}_{i \in I}$ of the form $\mathcal{A}_i = (Q_i, C_i, S_i, \Delta_i)$ running in parallel. We assume the states of each automaton $\mathcal{A}_i$ are encoded using a distinct set $\mathcal{B}_i$ of Boolean variables and let $\mathcal{B} = \bigcup \mathcal{B}_i$ and $\mathcal{C} = \bigcup \mathcal{C}_i$.

To express the mutual interaction between automata we use some notations. The set of automata whose state should be observed while taking the transition $\delta_i \in \Delta_i$ with a guard g_i is

$$J_{\delta_i} = \{j : Q_j \text{ appears in } g_i\}.$$

Likewise, the set of automata to be observed during time passage in a state $q_i \in Q_i$ is

$$J_{q_i} = \{j : Q_j \text{ appears in } S_{q_i}\}.$$

Finally the set of automata whose passage of time might be influenced by transitions in automaton $\mathcal{A}_i$ is

$$J_i' = \{j : \exists q_j \in Q_j \text{ s.t. } Q_i \text{ appears in } S_{q_j}\}.$$

A local discrete step of an automaton $\mathcal{A}_i$ is

$$(q_i, \mathbf{v}_i, T) \xrightarrow{\delta_i} (q_i', \mathbf{v}_i', T),$$

such that the transition guard g_i of $\delta_i \in \Delta_i$ is satisfied by the clocks of $\mathcal{A}_i$ *and* by the states of all other automata in J_{δ_i} at time T. A time step of $\mathcal{A}_i$ is

$$(q_i, \mathbf{v}_i, T) \xrightarrow{t} (q_i, \mathbf{v}_i + t\mathbf{1}, T + t).$$

such that S_{q_i} is satisfied by the clocks of $\mathcal{A}_i$ and by states of the automata in J_{q_i} during the interval $[T, T + t)$.

The first approach for constructing global runs and their corresponding formulae is rather straightforward. A global discrete step is of the form

$$((q_1, \ldots, q_i, \ldots, q_n), (\mathbf{v}_1, \ldots, \mathbf{v}_i, \ldots, \mathbf{v}_n), T) \xrightarrow{\delta_i}$$
$$((q_1, \ldots, q_i', \ldots, q_n), (\mathbf{v}_1, \ldots, \mathbf{v}_i', \ldots, \mathbf{v}_n), T)$$

such that $(q_i, \mathbf{v}_i, T) \xrightarrow{\delta_i} (q_i', \mathbf{v}_i', T)$ is a discrete step of some[2] automaton $\mathcal{A}_i$. A global time step is

$$((q_1, \ldots, q_n), (\mathbf{v}_1, \ldots, \mathbf{v}_n), T) \xrightarrow{t} ((q_1, \ldots, q_n), (\mathbf{v}_1 + t\mathbf{1}, \ldots, \mathbf{v}_n + t\mathbf{1}), T + t)$$

such that for every q_i, S_{q_i} is satisfied by $\mathbf{v}_i + t\mathbf{1}$ and by $(q_1, \ldots, q_n)$. This means that whenever one automaton makes a discrete transition at time T, any other automaton that makes a time step in an interval $[T', T'']$ containing T, must "split" that step (see Figure 1).

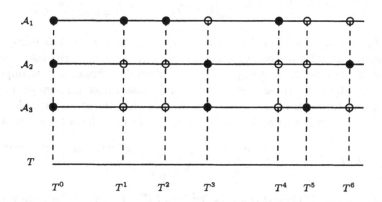

Fig. 1. A fragments of a run of 3 automata where the black dots represent discrete transitions. The local minimal runs need to be refined by splitting time steps in order to to conform with the minimal run of the global automaton. For example, $\mathcal{A}_1$ splits its time step at $[T^2, T^4)$ into two steps at $[T^2, T^3)$ and $[T^3, T^4)$.

To build the formulae we replace, as before, clock variables by date variables $\mathcal{X}_i$ for each automaton ($\mathcal{X} = \bigcup \mathcal{X}_i$) and use one global time stamp variable T common to all automata. We construct for each $\mathcal{A}_i$ its step formulae $\Phi_i(\mathcal{B}, \mathcal{X}_i, T, \mathcal{B}_i', \mathcal{X}_i', T')$ and the conjunction of those characterizes a global step. The use of the same variable T by all automata guarantees synchronization, i.e. that whenever $\mathcal{A}_i$ refers to the state variables of $\mathcal{A}_j$, their values correspond to the same time instant.

---

[2] This definition corresponds to full interleaving of transitions but in the implementation we allow several simultaneous transitions in the same step.

When the automata are loosely-coupled it might be more economical to express the steps of each automaton using its *private time-scale* and impose synchronization between those time scales only when the automata interact (this approach was introduced in [BJLY98] as an attempt to apply partial-order methods to timed automata). For each automaton $\mathcal{A}_i$ we use a different time-stamp variable T_i ($\mathcal{T} = \bigcup T_i$) such that the values of its date variables are $\mathcal{X}_i = T_i - \mathcal{C}_i$. Then we have, for every $\mathcal{A}_i$ and a reset ρ_i

$$\Phi_{\rho_i}(\mathcal{X}_i, \mathcal{X}'_i, T_i) \equiv \bigwedge_{C_m \in \rho_i} X'_m = T_i \wedge \bigwedge_{C_m \notin \rho_i} X'_m = X_m.$$

Time passage for $\mathcal{A}_i$ is written as

$$\Phi_{\tau_i}(\mathcal{X}_i, T_i, \mathcal{X}'_i, T'_i) \equiv \bigwedge_m X'_m = X_m \wedge T'_i - T_i \geq 0.$$

The transition formula for $\delta_i \in \Delta_i$ is

$$\Psi_{\delta_i}(\mathcal{B}, \mathcal{X}, \mathcal{T}, \mathcal{B}'_i, \mathcal{X}', \mathcal{T}') \equiv \frac{\Phi_{q_i}(\mathcal{B}_i) \wedge \Phi_{g_i}(\mathcal{B}, \mathcal{X}_i, T_i) \wedge \Phi_{\rho_i}(\mathcal{X}_i, \mathcal{X}'_i, T_i) \wedge}{\Phi_{q'_i}(\mathcal{B}'_i) \wedge T_i = T'_i \wedge \bigwedge_{j \in J_{\delta_i} \cup J'_i} T_i = T_j}$$

where $\Phi_{g_i}(\mathcal{B}, \mathcal{X}_i, T_i)$ is the substitution of $T_i - \mathcal{X}_i$ and the corresponding values of the state-variables of the other automata in g_i. Note that the last condition enforces identity on time stamps only for automata whose state is important for the transition, i.e. those that guard it and those whose time steps might be disabled due to the transition. Needless to say, only the state variables of the automata in J_{δ_i} will appear in the formula. The formula for a time step at q_i is

$$\Psi_{q_i}(\mathcal{B}, \mathcal{X}, \mathcal{T}, \mathcal{B}', \mathcal{X}', \mathcal{T}') \equiv \frac{\Phi_{q_i}(\mathcal{B}_i) \wedge \Phi_{\tau_i}(\mathcal{X}_i, T_i, \mathcal{X}'_i, T'_i) \wedge \Phi_{s,q_i}(\mathcal{B}, \mathcal{X}', T'_i) \wedge}{\Phi_{q_i}(\mathcal{B}'_i) \wedge \bigwedge_{j \in J_{q_i}} (T_i = T_j)}$$

where $\Phi_{s,q_i}(\mathcal{B}, \mathcal{X}'_i, T'_i)$ is just the substitution of $T'_i - \mathcal{X}'_i$ and all the state variables in S_{q_i}. The formula for a step of $\mathcal{A}_i$ is

$$\Psi_i(\mathcal{B}, \mathcal{X}_i, \mathcal{T}, \mathcal{B}'_i, \mathcal{X}'_i, \mathcal{T}') \equiv \bigvee_{q \in Q_i} \Psi_q \vee \bigvee_{\delta \in \Delta_i} \Psi_\delta.$$

The formula for a global step is

$$\Psi(\mathcal{B}, \mathcal{X}, \mathcal{T}, \mathcal{B}', \mathcal{X}', \mathcal{T}') \equiv \bigwedge_{i \in I} \Psi_i(\mathcal{B}, \mathcal{X}_i, \mathcal{T}, \mathcal{B}_i, \mathcal{X}'_i, \mathcal{T}')$$

and the formula for a run with at most k transitions is

$$\Psi_k \equiv \Psi(\mathcal{B}^0, \mathcal{X}^0, \mathcal{T}^0, \mathcal{B}^1, \mathcal{X}^1, \mathcal{T}^1) \wedge \ldots \wedge \Psi(\mathcal{B}^{k-1}, \mathcal{X}^{k-1}, \mathcal{T}^{k-1}, \mathcal{B}^k, \mathcal{X}^k, \mathcal{T}^k).$$

In this construction we pay the price of introducing more time-stamp variables in order to obtain less steps for the same run.

5   The Solver

5.1   Handling Mixed Constraints

The challenge for a satisfiability checker for DL lies, of course, in the interaction between Boolean and numerical constraints. We sketch some of the popular approaches to this problem. Given the scope of the topic and its inter-disciplinary nature, this is not intended to be an exhaustive nor an objective survey.

Numerical constraints were traditionally treated in the context of continuous optimization where efficient algorithms exist, for example, for conjunction of linear constraints (linear programming). Attempting to extend this approach to mixed constraints leads to the so-called mixed integer-linear programming where Booleans are viewed as integers. When there are only few such "integer" variables one may convert them into reals ranging in $[0, 1]$, use efficient linear programming algorithms to find a satisfying assignment for the relaxed problem and then try to push the assignments for the converted Booleans back to $\{0, 1\}$. Although certain classes of problems admit successful relaxation schemes, we do not believe that this approach will work when the combinatorial part of the problem is significant and the discrete variables have no metric meaning.

An opposite approach, which tries to keep everything inside the propositional world, is to replace every numerical constraint by a new Boolean variable (similarly to what we partially do while transforming to CNF) until a purely propositional problem remains. After a satisfying assignment for this problem is found, linear programming can be used to see whether the numerical constraints implied by the extended assignment are satisfiable. If they are not satisfiable, a new propositional instance should be found, and so on. The advantage of this approach is in the ability to use of-the-shelf efficient SAT solvers. However, the interaction between the numerical and logical constraints is restricted only to the final phase and this might lead to a lot of backtracking.

The approach, often described under the title of *constraint propagation* or *constraint logic programming* [JM94], treats both types of constraints rather equally. Here the key idea is an incremental search in the space of solution, where every decision concerning one variable can be propagated to reduce the domains of other variables. Such methods have been applied rather successfully to problems with increasingly complex numerical constraints, both linear and non-linear. Some recent "hybrid" techniques that combine constraint propagation with linear programming proved to be very powerful. More on the relation between these approaches can be found in [H00].

Given that DL, with its restricted class of linear constraints, is perhaps the most conservative numerical extension of propositional logic, we have chosen to construct our solver as an extended propositional solver. Our algorithm gives priority to propositional reasoning but derives information from numerical constraints as soon as they become isolated and easy to manipulate. The key idea of our approach is that a conjunction of difference constraints can be represented using a *difference bounds matrix*, a data-structure used extensively in the verification of timed automata [Dil89]. The Floyd-Warshall algorithm is used to normalize the constraints, to find contradictions in the set of numerical clauses and also to extract a solution from a consistent set of inequalities in polynomial time.

Typical SAT solvers perform both syntactic transformations of formulae that may simplify clauses and remove variables, and a search in the space of valuations for the remaining variables. Our solver, inspired by the Davis-Putnam procedure, gives priority to the former and resorts to search ("branching") only when simplifications are impossible. In other popular solvers such as GRASP [MS99] and Chaff [MMZ+], search is the primary mechanism and syntactic transformations are incorporated as "learning", that is adding new clauses implied by failures in the search.

5.2   Boolean Proof Methods

In this section we sketch the way we treat the Boolean part, some of which is common to other approaches for realizing the Davis-Putnam proof procedure (see, e.g. [Zha95]). This will serve as an introduction to the treatment of numerical constraints (there are some interesting analogies between the Boolean and numerical proof methods). Our presentation largely follows that of [GW99].

The proof method relies on applying satisfiability-preserving transformations to 3CNF DL formulae, some of which might reduce the number of satisfying valuations. Successive applications of these rules can lead to a satisfying valuation or to a (resolution) proof of unsatisfiability.

Simplifications: Elimination of redundant clauses which are weaker than others, independently of the rest of the formula. On the level of literals, a literal L_2 is weaker than another literal L_1 if for any valuation v, $v \models L_1$ implies $v \models L_2$. For Boolean literals this is the case for identical literals. For numerical constraints, $X - Y \geq c$ is weaker than $X - Y \geq d$ if $d \geq c$. This weaker-than relation generalizes to clauses in the obvious way.
Elimination of redundant literals by resolution: If there are two clauses $C_1 = L_1 \vee C'$ and $C_2 = \neg L_1 \vee C'$, replace C_1 and C_2 by C'.

Boolean unit resolution: If there is a clause L_1 and a clause $C = L_2 \vee C'$ such that L_1 and L_2 are contradictory, replace C by C'. Boolean literals are contradictory if one is the negation of the other.

Boolean pure variables detection: If there is a boolean literal L such that the formula can be writtem as $\bigwedge_i C_i \wedge \bigwedge_j (L \vee C'_j)$ where L does not occur in any of the clauses C_i and C'_j. Then we can set $L := T$ and the formula is reduced $\bigwedge_i C_i$.

Detection of logical cycles: If there is a chain of two literal clauses $\neg L_1 \vee L_2, \neg L_2 \vee L_3, \ldots \neg L_n \vee L_1$, apply a renaming of $L_2, \ldots, L_n$ to L_1 (this renaming has to be remembered in order to reconstruct complete valuations of the original formula). A cycle including the same literal negatively and positively exposes a contradiction and the formula is unsatisfiable. In practice, the detection of cycles is implemented using Tarjan's linear-time algorithm for computing strongly connected components [Tar72]. For performance considerations, this rule is only applied if the number of two literal clauses is below a certain value (800 in the current implementation).

Detection of Boolean contradictions: An empty clause is not satisfiable, hence the entire formula containing an empty clause is not satisfiable. Note that numerical contradictions will show up as Boolean contradictions via resolution.

The empty conjunction: If we arrive at a formula containing no more clauses, it is trivially satisfiable by any valuation.

All of the above transformations can reduce the size of a formula without affecting its semantics. Sometimes, however, checking the conditions for applying these rules might be costly (quadratic in the size of the formula).

The Davis-Putnam rules go beyond these transformations by replacing a formula by a stronger one while preserving (non)satisfiability. Instead of describing the general Davis-Putnam framework, we only mention an interesting rule which preserves the 3CNF structure without introducing new variables.

Boolean Davis-Putnam rule: Supposing that there is a Boolean literal L such that the formula can be represented as $\bigwedge_i C_i \wedge \bigwedge_j (L \vee C'_j) \wedge \bigwedge_k (\neg L \vee L_k)$ where L does not occur in any of the clauses C_i, C'_j. That is, all negative occurrences of L are in 2-clauses. Then we can set $L := \bigwedge_k L_k$ (and memorize this assignment) and substitute $\bigwedge_k L_k$ for L throughout the formula.

Note that this transformation, while preserving satisfiability, can decrease the number of solutions. Secondly, while going back to 3CNF, some clauses may have to be copied in case of more than a single negative occurrence of L. It is a question of heuristics, when the application of this rule is sensible. Obviously, in the case of a single negative occurrence of L this will result in a simplification.

Branching. When the above transformations yield neither a solution nor a contradiction we resort to branching over valuations of Boolean variables: A Boolean variable is chosen and either assumed to be false or true, thus eliminating it. By recursion, eventually all variables will be eliminated. However, the scheme as stated requires backtracking, possibly leading to an exponential-time linear-space complexity.

5.3   Numerical Proof Methods

The main novelty of our approach is in the treatment of numerical difference constraints. We sketch here the major ideas as applicable to the integer interpretation.

Numerical unit resolution: When a formula contains a numerical 1-literal clause $X - Y \geq c$, we can replace numerical literals $X - Y \geq d$ with $d \leq c$ by T and numerical literals $Y - X \geq d$ with $c > -d$ by F.

Computing numerical implications: Consider a chain of clauses $X_1 - X_2 \geq c_1, \ldots, X_{n-1} - X_n \geq c_n$. For every j, k such that $1 \leq j < k \leq n$ we can conclude that $X_j - X_k \geq \sum_{j \leq i \leq k} c_i$. These implied inequalities can be used to remove weaker numerical literals from the formula. In particular, when the chain involves a cycle (X_j and X_k are identical) then it can be replaced by F if it is positive. Moreover, if this sum is zero, one can eliminate the variables $X_{j+1}, \ldots, X_{k-1}$ and express them using X_j.

Similarly to the treatment of Boolean chains and cycles, the above numerical implications are computed using a graph algorithm, in this case the Floyd-Warshall *all vertex shortest path algorithm with negative weights* [CLRS01]. The data-structure for representing conjunctions of difference constraints is the *difference bounds matrix* used extensively in the verification of timed automata. In this matrix an inequality of the form $X_i - X_j \geq c$ is represented by putting $-c$ in the (i, j)-entry of the matrix (when two variables are not related by a constraint c is set to $-\infty$).

In the following, we develop an analogue of the Davis-Putnam rule for numerical constraints. We say that in a numerical literal $X - Y \geq c$ the variable X occurs positively and Y occurs negatively. Let v and v' be two valuation which are identical except for one variable X. One can see that if $v'(X) \geq v(X)$ then $v \models L$ implies $v' \models L$ for every literal L where X occurs positively and $v' \models L$ implies $v \models L$ when X occurs negatively in L.

Davis-Putnam for literal $\geq$-constraints: Assume, we have only a few (ideally, one) positive occurrences of X in literal clauses $X - Y_i \geq c_i$ with $i \in I$ and all other occurrences – in particular those in mixed clauses – are negative. Then we can set $X := max\{Y_i + c_i \mid i \in I\}$ (or $X := Y_i + c_i$ in the ideal case) and eliminate X from all clauses: Each literal $Z - X \geq d$ will be replaced by a conjunction $\bigwedge_{i \in I} Z - Y_i \geq d + c_i$. Analogously, if we have only a few negative occurrence of X in the one-literal clauses $Y_i - X \geq c$ with $i \in I$, we can safely set $X := min\{Y - c_i \mid i \in I\}$.

This rule is correct in not affecting the satisfiability of the formula because any valuation v satisfying it must satisfy $v(X) \geq v(Y_i) + c_i$. The valuation $v' = v[X := max\{v(Y_i) + c_i\}]$ where only the value of X is changed such that $v'(X) \leq v(X)$ also satisfies the formula, because it satisfies $X - Y_i \geq c_i$ for all $i \in I$ and all other clauses containing negative occurrences of X will also remain true.

5.4   The Overall Algorithm

The algorithm consists of two major parts: The branching procedure and the non-branching rules. Since the cost of Davis-Putnam rules is potentially higher than that of the other rules, Boolean and numerical rules are performed in the following order:

1. Boolean simplifications;
2. Unit resolution;
3. Strongly connected component algorithm on the two literal Boolean clauses with subsequent detection of contradictions or elimination of equivalent literals;

4. Shortest path algorithm for the normalization of numerical constrains with subsequent detection of contradictions or elimination of tightly coupled variables and numerical unit resolution;
5. Application of the Boolean Davis-Putnam rule;
6. Application of the numerical Davis-Putnam rule;
7. Pass to branching.

Whenever a change in the clause set occurs at one of the stages (1)-(6), the algorithm restarts at (1).

6   Implementation and Experimental Results

The solver has been written from scratch in order to keep its size small. In its current status it still needs a lot of tuning and application-specific heuristics, in particular, for selecting variables for branching. Consequently, its current performance is inferior to that of more mature tools for timed verification. We hope that this situation will change in the near future. We will report the result of preliminary experiments after a brief description of the implementation architecure.

6.1   Implementation

The central data-structure of the solver is the clause table in which we keep Boolean and mixed clauses, while while purely numerical clauses are stored in a difference bounds matrix. The interaction between the two happens when, following a simplification, a mixed clause is transformed into a numerical literal and passes from the clause table to the matrix. Numerical implications are computed on the matrix and may affect Boolean clauses, for example by numerical unit resolution.

Due to branching we need to organize these data structures in a stack. Heuristic improvements can be used to render stack operations less expensive, e.g. a special technique for storing stacks of sparse matrices.

We have tried to keep the translation from DL to 3CNF separated as much as possible from the rest of the solver. And indeed, a new version of the solver, not restricted to 3CNF has been written recently in a very short time. This version consumes less memory but still needs more tuning to compete in time performance with the 3CNF version.

We have started implementing translators from various formats of timed automata as used in the tools Kronos, OpenKronos and IF [Y97, BDM+98, BFG+00]. Since these tools admit a variety of syntax, synchronization mechanisms and semantic definitions, this process is not yet complete. The translations that are currently working are a direct translation from job-shop scheduling problems[3], a translation from flat timed automata in the Kronos format, and a

---

[3] This translation does not go through timed automata but encodes the obvious constraints on the start times of steps in jobs.

Table 1. Size of reachability formulae (in 3CNF) and solution time as a function of path length for a simple automaton. In all cases the formula is satisfiable.

path length	# bool vars	# real vars	# bool clauses	# mixed clauses	time (secs)
1	51	7	87	52	0.01
10	492	34	888	520	0.24
20	982	64	1778	1040	1.46
50	2452	154	4448	2600	10.34
100	4902	304	8898	5200	43.20

global-time compositional translation for the sub-class of timed automata corresponding to digital circuits with bi-bounded inertial delays [BS94] following their modeling as timed automata [MP95,BJMY].

6.2 Experimental Results

Long Runs of Simple Automata. As a first example we took a simple timed automaton with 4 states and one clock and created, via our translator, DL formulae for paths of varying length. Table 1 show how the size and properties of the formulae change with the length of the path, as well as the time it takes to check satisfiability. The good results here are misleading, because most of the complexity in this example is along the temporal dimension and hence the solver does not need to perform a lot of branching.

Job-Shop Scheduling. The classical job-shop scheduling problem translates very naturally into DL. The problem can be stated as an optimization problem ("find an optimal schedule") or as a decision problem ("is there a schedule of length smaller than L?"). We have experimented with a well-known benchmark example taken from [ABZ88] with 10 machines and 10 jobs, each having 10 steps. The known optimal schedule is of length 1179. The 3CNF DL formula for a feasible schedule has 1452 Boolean variables, 102 real variables, 1901 Boolean clauses and 2453 mixed clauses. While posing the verification problem we observe a phenomenon which, we think, is very typical in such situations: when L is much larger than the length of the optimal schedule, a satisfying assignment is easily found. Likewise, when L is much smaller than the optimum, we detect quickly a contradiction. As we approach the optimum from both sides, the computational cost grows. The results appear in Table 2.

All experiments were performed on a standard PC powered by a 600MHz Pentium III. The maximum memory usage reached was about 90MB (for the hard job-shop examples and the formula for a path of length 100 for the simple automaton). Other experiments required less than 10MB.

7 Related Work and Conclusions

The idea to extend the applicability of SAT-based verification from finite-state systems to systems augmented with unbounded variables or clocks is a very nat-

Table 2. The results for the job-shop benchmark. The second column indicates the (a-priori known) answer to the question whether there exists a schedule of length $\leq L$. The symbol ∞ indicates that the solver did not terminate within 25 minutes.

L	answer	time(secs)
100	No	4.72
500	No	4.47
750	No	4.57
1000	No	31.03
1100	No	∞
1179	Yes	∞
1200	Yes	∞
1300	Yes	∞
1400	Yes	18.88
1500	Yes	13.36
2000	Yes	12.59
3000	Yes	12.79
5000	Yes	13.59
10000	Yes	14.53

ural one and has been pursued independently by several groups. In [ACG99] a solver for a similar logic was applied to AI temporal planning problems. The closest work to ours is that of [ABC+02,ACKS02] where the authors develop an extended SAT solver to verify timed automata against temporal logic specifications. The major differences with respect to the present paper is in their use of a more general linear constraint solver, and in the limited interaction between the Boolean and numerical parts. The work of [MRS02] considers more general numerical constraints and gives priority to propositional reasoning by encoding numerical constraints as Booleans and then using decision procedures to eliminate "spurious solutions". Other investigations in this methodology appear in [SSB02] where DL formulae are called separation formulae.

We have proposed an alternative approach for solving timing related verification and optimization problems. It is worth mentioning other works, such as [BFH+01,AM01], that go in the opposite direction by applying timed automata verification techniques to scheduling problems that were traditionally solved using constraint resolution. We hope that all this effort will eventually lead to performance improvements and to a better understanding of the computational difficulty of temporal reasoning.

References

[AM01]   Y. Abdeddam and O. Maler, Job-Shop Scheduling using Timed Automata *Proc. CAV'01*, 478-492, LNCS 2102, Springer 2001.

[ABZ88]   J. Adams, E. Balas and D. Zawack, The Shifting Bottleneck Procedure for Job Shop Scheduling, *Management Science* 34, 391-401, 1988.

[AD94]   R. Alur and D.L. Dill, A Theory of Timed Automata, *Theoretical Computer Science* 126, 183-235, 1994.

[ACG99]   A. Armando, C. Castellini and E. Giunchiglia, SAT-based Procedures for Temporal Reasoning, *Proc. ECP'99*, LNCS, Springer, 1999.

[ABK⁺97]   E. Asarin, M. Bozga, A. Kerbrat, O. Maler, A. Pnueli, and A. Rasse, Data Structures for the Verification of Timed Automata, *Proc. Hybrid and Real-Time Systems*, 346-360, LNCS 1201, Springer, 1997.

[ABC⁺02]   G. Audemard, P. Bertoli, A. Cimatti, A. Kornilowics and R. Sebastiani, A SAT-Based Approach for Solving Formulas over Boolean and Linear Mathematical Propositions, in *Proc. CADE'02*, 193-208, LNCS 2392, Springer, 2002.

[ACKS02]   G. Audemard, A. Cimatti, A. Kornilowics and R. Sebastiani, Bounded Model Checking for Timed Systems, Technical report ITC-0201-05, IRST, Trento, 2002.

[BFH⁺01]   G. Behrmann, A. Fehnker T.S. Hune, K.G. Larsen, P. Pettersson and J. Romijn, Efficient Guiding Towards Cost-Optimality in UPPAAL, *Proc. TACAS 2001*, 174-188, LNCS 2031, Springer, 2001.

[BJLY98]   J. Bengtsson, B. Jonsson, J. Lilius and W. Yi, Partial Order Reductions for Timed Systems, *Proc. Concur'98*, 485-500, LNCS 1466, Springer, 1998.

[BCRZ99]   A. Biere, E.M. Clarke, R. Raimi, and Y. Zhu, Verifying Safety Properties of a PowerPC Microprocessor using Symbolic Model Checking without BDDs, *Proc. CAV'99*, 60-71, LNCS 1633, Springer, 1999.

[BCCZ99]   A. Biere, A. Cimatti, E.M. Clarke and Y. Zhu, Symbolic Model Checking without BDDs, *Proc. TACAS'99*, 193-207, LNCS 1579, Springer, 1999.

[BM00]   O. Bournez and O. Maler, On the Representation of Timed Polyhedra, *Proc. ICALP 2000*, 793-807, LNCS 1853, Springer, 2000.

[BDM⁺98] M. Bozga, C. Daws, O. Maler, A. Olivero, S. Tripakis, and S. Yovine, Kronos: a Model-Checking Tool for Real-Time Systems, *Proc. CAV'98*, LNCS 1427, Springer, 1998.

[BFG⁺00]   M. Bozga, J.-C. Fernandez, L. Ghirvu, S. Graf, J.-.P. Krimm and L. Mounier, IF: A Validation Environment for Timed Asynchronous Systems, *Proc. CAV'00*, LNCS, Springer, 2000.

[BJMY]   M. Bozga, H. Jianmin, O. Maler and S. Yovine, Verification of Asynchronous Circuits using Timed Automata, *Proc. TPTS'02*, 2002.

[Bry86]   R.E. Bryant, Graph-based Algorithms for Boolean Function Manipulation, *IEEE Transactions on Computers* 35, 677-691, 1986.

[BS94]   J.A. Brzozowski and C-J.H. Seger, *Asynchronous Circuits*, Springer, 1994.

[BCM⁺93] J.R. Burch, E.M. Clarke, K.L. McMillan, D.L. Dill, and L.J. Hwang, Symbolic Model-Checking: 10^{20} States and Beyond, *Proc. LICS'90*, IEEE, 1990.

[CLRS01]   T. Cormen, C. Leiserson, R. Rivest, and C. Stein. *Introduction to Algorithms*. MIT Press, McGraw-Hill, 2001.

[Dil89]   D.L. Dill, Timing Assumptions and Verification of Finite-State Concurrent Systems, *Proc. CAV'89*, 197-212, LNCS 407, Springer, 1989.

[EC82]   E.A. Emerson and E.M. Clarke, Using Branching Time Temporal Logic to Synthesize Synchronization Skeletons, *Science of Computer Programming* 2, 241-266, 1982.

[GJ79]   M. Garey and D. Johnson. *Computers and Intractability*. W. H. Freeman, 1979.

[GW99]   J.F. Groote and J.P. Warners. The Propositional Formula Checker Heer-Hugo. Technical Report 691, Centrum voor Wiskunde en Informatica (CWI) Amsterdam, 1999.

[HNSY94] T. Henzinger, X. Nicollin, J. Sifakis, and S. Yovine, Symbolic Model-checking for Real-time Systems, *Information and Computation* 111, 193-244, 1994.

[H00]   J. Hooker, *Logic-Based Methods for Optimization: Combining Optimization and Constraint Satisfaction*, Wiley, 2000

[JM94]   J. Jaffar and M. J. Maher. Constraint Logic Programming: A Survey, *Journal of Logic Programming*, 19/20, 503-581, 1994.

[LPWY99] K. Larsen, J. Pearson, C. Weise, and W. Yi, Clock difference diagrams. *Nordic Journal of Computing* 6, 271-298, 1999.

[LP84]   O. Lichtenstein, A. Pnueli, Checking that Finite-state Concurrent Programs Satisfy their Linear Specification, *Proc. POPL'84*, 97-107, ACM, 1984.

[MP95]   O. Maler and A. Pnueli, Timing Analysis of Asynchronous Circuits using Timed Automata, *Proc. CHARME'95*, 189-205, LNCS 987, Springer, 1995.

[MS99]   J.P. Marques-Silva and K.A. Sakallah, GRASP: A Search Algorithm for Propositional Satisfiability, *IEEE Transactions on Computers* 48, 506-21, 1999.

[McM93]   K.L. McMillan, *Symbolic Model-Checking: an Approach to the State-Explosion problem*, Kluwer, 1993.

[MLAH99] J. Møller, J. Lichtenberg, H. Andersen, and H. Hulgaard, Difference Decision Diagrams, *Proc. CSL'99*, 1999.

[MMZ+]   M. Moskewicz, C. Madigan, Y. Zhao, L. Zhang and S. Malik, Chaff: Engineering an Efficient SAT Solver, *Proc. DAC 2001*, 2001.

[MRS02]   L. de Moura, H. Rueß and M. Sorea, Lazy Theorem Proving for Bounded Model Checking over Infinite Domains, *Proc. CADE'02*, 437-453, LNCS 2392, Springer, 2002.

[QS81]   J.P. Queille and J. Sifakis, Specification and Verification of Concurrent Systems in Cesar, *Proc. 5th Int. Symp. on Programming*, 337-351, LNCS 137, Springer, 1981.

[SS90]   G. Stålmarck and M. Saflund, Modeling and Verifying Systems and Software in Propositional Logic, *Safety of Computer Control Systems (SAFECOMP'90)*, 31-36, Pergamon Press, 1990.

[SSB02]   O. Strichman, S.A. Seshia, and R.E. Bryant, Deciding Separation Formulas with SAT, in *Proc. CAV'2002*, Springer, 2002.

[Tar72]   R. Tarjan. Depth-first Search and Linear Graph Algorithms. *SIAM J. Comput.* 1, 146-160, 1972.

[T70]   G. Tseitin, On the Complexity of Derivation in Propositional Calculus, in *Studies in Constructive Mathematics and Mathematical Logic* 2, 115-125, Consultants Bureau, New York, 1970.

[VW86]   M.Y. Vardi and P. Wolper, An Automata-theoretic Approach to Automatic Program Verification, *Proc. LICS'86*, 322-331, IEEE, 1986.

[Y97]   S. Yovine, Kronos: A Verification Tool for Real-time Systems, *International Journal of Software Tools for Technology Transfer* 1, 123-133, 1997.

[Zha95]   G. Zhang. The Davis-Putnam Resolution Procedure, In *Advances in Logic Programming and Automated Reasoning*, volume 2. Ablex Publishing Corporation, 1995.

Take It NP-Easy:
Bounded Model Construction
for Duration Calculus

Martin Fränzle

Department of Computer Science
Carl-von-Ossietzky Universität Oldenburg
P.O. Box 2503, D-26111 Oldenburg, Germany
Martin.Fraenzle@Informatik.Uni-Oldenburg.De
Phone/Fax: +49-441-798-3046/2145

Abstract. Following the recent successes of bounded model-checking, we reconsider the problem of constructing models of discrete-time Duration Calculus formulae. While this problem is known to be non-elementary when arbitrary length models are considered [Han94], it turns out to be only NP-complete when constrained to bounded length.

As a corollary we obtain that model construction is in NP for the formulae actually encountered in case studies using Duration Calculus, as these have a certain small-model property.

First experiments with a prototype implementation of the procedures demonstrate a competitive performance.

Keywords: Discrete-time Duration Calculus; Model construction; Bounded model construction; Complexity

1 Introduction

Duration Calculus, as introduced in [ZHR91] and thoroughly analyzed in [HZ97] and [Frä97], is a logic for reasoning about embedded real-time systems at a high level of abstraction from operational detail. While the abstractness of the vocabulary of Duration Calculus is desirable for system specification and analysis, it proved to be a burden for automatic verification support. Checking dense-time models against Duration Calculus requires certain behavioral properties of the model, like number of state changes being finitely bounded over any finite time interval [Frä97,Frä02], unless the use of temporal operators or of negation is seriously restricted, as in [ZZYL94,BLR95,Lak96]. Otherwise, the model property turns out to be undecidable [HZ97,Frä97,Frä02].

Discrete-time Duration Calculus, i.e. Duration Calculus interpreted over the natural numbers as a time domain instead of $\mathbb{R}_{\geq 0}$, has more favorable decidability properties, as first pointed out in [ZHS93] and more deeply analyzed by Hansen in [Han94]. Following this discovery, there have been various experiments towards building automatic verification support for discrete-time Duration Calculus, e.g. [SS94a,SS94b,Pan00]. However, none of these systems has come to be

W. Damm and E.-R. Olderog (Eds.): FTRTFT 2002, LNCS 2469, pp. 245–264, 2002.

routinely used for checking non-trivial formulae. We believe that the primary reason is that the computational complexity of those systems, be it either Sestoft's and Skakkebæk's method [SS94a,SS94b] or Pandya's MONA-based procedure for a very rich Duration Calculus [Pan00], is extremely high.

While extreme, namely non-elementary, complexity is in general unavoidable as deciding or model-checking Duration Calculus is worst-case non-elementary [HZ97,Frä02], this need not be the typical case, as the MONA experience shows [BKR96]. In fact, the author's findings, when doing a prototype implementation of a Duration Calculus checker in 1996, were that considerably more efficient ad-hoc constructions for typical specification formulae were easy to find:

> "However, the non-elementary complexity of the decision procedure need not be an obstacle to practical applications, as deep nesting of chop and negation which leads to the blow-up in complexity is hardly ever encountered in practice, except within iterated application of some derived standard operators. In most cases, more efficient decision procedures than obtained through unfolding their definitions can be easily devised for these derived operators. [...] While such a special treatment of derived operators does not influence the worst-case complexity, it does reduce complexity of checking formulae where deep nesting of negation and chop only occurs through iterated application of derived operators. In a prototypic implementation of the decision procedure performed by the author, enhanced treatment of timed leads-to and some other frequently encountered derived operators resulted in a dramatic increase of performance when applied to the gas-burner example [RRH93]."
>
> [Frä97, p. 51]

In the current paper, we set out to give a formal justification for that observation. Following the recent successes of bounded model checking [BCZ99], we investigate the complexity of bounded model construction for Duration Calculus, which turns out to be NP-complete. We then identify a class of formulae having a small-model property and show that typical Duration Calculus specification formulae belong to this class, which proves that checking such formulae is NP-easy.

The structure of this paper is as follows: we start by introducing Duration Calculus in Section 2. Section 3 reviews effective construction of arbitrary-length models of Duration Calculus formulae and its computational complexity. Section 4 defines the bounded model construction problem, provides effective constructions for it, and shows it to be NP-complete. In Section 5, we turn to showing that typical Duration Calculus formulae encountered in case studies have a small-model property that renders them NP-easily checkable by bounded model construction. Section 6, finally, provides some first performance figures obtained from comparing a prototype implementation of the BMC procedure to Pandya's MONA-based DCValid tool [Pan00].

2   Duration Calculus

Duration Calculus (abbreviated DC in the remainder) is a real-time logic that is specially tailored towards reasoning about durational constraints on time-dependent Boolean-valued states. Since its introduction in [ZHR91], many variants of Duration Calculus have been defined [Zho93], some aiming at even increased expressiveness [Ska94,ZL94,ZH96,Pan96,Pan00], others at investigation of mechanizability aspects of durational calculi and therefore restricting the vocabulary [ZHS93,SS94a,Han94,ZZYL94]. Aiming at a mechanizable design calculus, we follow the second line and present a slight subset of the Duration Calculus defined in [ZHR91]. The particular restrictions of our logic follow those taken in [Han94,Frä97]. Our subset allows full treatment of the gas burner case study [RRH93], the primary case study of the ProCoS project. This indicates that our subset offers an interesting vocabulary for specifying embedded real-time controllers.

Syntax. The syntax of DC used in this paper is as follows.

$$\langle formula \rangle ::= \int \langle state\,assertion \rangle \geq 1 \mid \neg \langle formula \rangle \mid$$
$$(\langle formula \rangle \wedge \langle formula \rangle) \mid$$
$$(\langle formula \rangle \frown \langle formula \rangle)$$
$$\langle state\,assertion \rangle ::= \langle state\,variable \rangle \mid \neg \langle state\,assertion \rangle \mid$$
$$(\langle state\,assertion \rangle \wedge \langle state\,assertion \rangle)$$
$$\langle state\,variable \rangle ::\in Varname \ ,$$

where *Varname* is a countable set of state variable names.

While the meaning of the Boolean connectives used in DC formulae should be obvious, the temporal connective $\frown$ (pronounced "chop"), which is inherited from Interval Temporal Logic [Mos85], may need some explanation. Formulae are interpreted over, first, trajectories providing valuation of state variables that varies over time and, second, over finite intervals of time, called "observation intervals". A formula $\phi \frown \psi$ is true of an observation interval iff the observation interval can be split into a left and a right subinterval s.t. ϕ holds of the left part and ψ of the right part. A duration formula $\int P \geq 1$ is true of an observation interval iff the state assertion P, interpreted over the trajectory, is true for at least one time instant in the observation interval. Fig. 1 provides an illustration of the meaning of these formulae.

Despite its simple syntax, DC is very expressive, as can be seen from the following abbreviations frequently used in formulae:

- $\int P \geq k \stackrel{\text{def}}{=} \underbrace{\int P \geq 1 \frown \ldots \frown \int P \geq 1}_{k\ times}$ asserts that state assertion P holds for

  at least k time units within the current observation interval,
- $\int P < k \stackrel{\text{def}}{=} \neg \int P \geq k$ means that P holds for strictly less than k time units in the current observation interval,
- $\ell \geq k \stackrel{\text{def}}{=} \int \textbf{true} \geq k$, where **true** is an arbitrary tautologous state assertion, denotes the fact that the observation interval has length k or more[1],

---

[1] Note that ℓ in $\ell \sim k$ is not a state variable, but a piece of concrete syntax that denotes the length of the current observation interval.

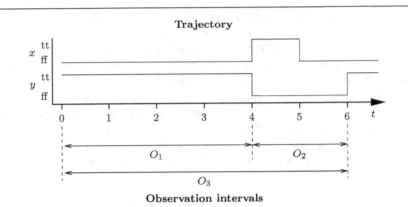

Observation intervals

The formula $\int y \geq 1$ holds on observation interval $O_1 = [0, 4]$, as the accumulated duration of y being true over this interval exceeds 1. Analogously, $\int(x \wedge \neg y) \geq 1$ holds on observation interval $O_2 = [4, 6]$. Therefore, the formula $(\int y \geq 1) \frown (\int(x \wedge \neg y) \geq 1)$ holds on the catenation $O_3 = [0, 6]$ of the other two observation intervals.

Fig. 1. The meaning of $\int P \geq 1$ and of the chop modality

---

- $\ell < k \stackrel{\text{def}}{=} \neg \ell \geq k$ confines the length of the observation interval to be strictly less than k,
- as usual, the Boolean connectives can be expressed through

$$(\phi \vee \psi) \stackrel{\text{def}}{=} \neg(\neg\phi \wedge \neg\psi) \ ,$$

$$(\phi \Rightarrow \psi) \stackrel{\text{def}}{=} (\neg\phi \vee \psi) \ ,$$

$$(\phi \Longleftrightarrow \psi) \stackrel{\text{def}}{=} ((\phi \Rightarrow \psi) \wedge (\psi \Rightarrow \phi)) \ ,$$

$$\mathbf{true} \stackrel{\text{def}}{=} (\phi \vee \neg\phi) \ ,$$

$$\mathbf{false} \stackrel{\text{def}}{=} \neg\mathbf{true} \ .$$

- Furthermore, the temporal operators $\Diamond$ and $\Box$, meaning 'in some subinterval of the observation interval' and 'in each subinterval of the observation interval', can be defined as

$$\Diamond\phi \stackrel{\text{def}}{=} (\mathbf{true} \frown \phi \frown \mathbf{true}) \ ,$$

$$\Box\phi \stackrel{\text{def}}{=} \neg\Diamond\neg\phi \ .$$

In the definition of $\Diamond\phi$ we omitted the inner parentheses as chop is associative. As the formula $(\mathbf{true} \frown \phi \frown \mathbf{true})$ is satisfied on an observation interval iff the observation interval can be split into three adjacent subintervals, the leftmost and the rightmost satisfying $\mathbf{true}$, the middle one satisfying ϕ, $\Diamond\phi$ indeed means 'in some subinterval of the observation interval ϕ holds'. $\Box\phi$ is simply its dual, meaning 'in no subinterval of the observation interval $\neg\phi$', or equivalently 'in each subinterval of the observation interval ϕ'.

Semantics. Duration Calculus is interpreted over trajectories

$$traj \in Traj \stackrel{\text{def}}{=} \{traj : Time \to Varname \to \mathbb{B}\}$$

that provide a time-dependent, Boolean-valued interpretation of state variables. Unlike most expositions of DC, we will deal here with a discrete-time interpretation of DC, i.e. use $Time \stackrel{\text{def}}{=} \mathbb{N}$. Satisfaction of a formula ϕ by a trajectory $traj$ is defined as a limit property over a chain of finite chunks from $traj$ called *observations*, where an observation is a pair $(traj, [a, b]) \in Obs \stackrel{\text{def}}{=} Traj \times TimeInterval$ with *TimeInterval* being the set of finite closed intervals in *Time*.

Before we expand on that limit property, we will define when an *observation* $(traj, [a, b])$ *satisfies a formula* ϕ, denoted $traj, [a, b] \models \phi$. For an atomic duration formula $\int P \geq 1$, this is defined by

$$traj, [a, b] \models \int P \geq 1 \quad \text{iff} \quad \sum_{t=a}^{b-1} \chi \circ [\![P]\!] \circ traj(t) \geq 1 \; ,$$

where $[\![P]\!](\sigma)$ canonically lifts a Boolean-valued interpretation $\sigma : Varname \to \mathbb{B}$ of state variables to an interpretation of the state assertion P, e.g. $[\![a \wedge \neg c]\!](\sigma) = \sigma(a) \wedge \neg\sigma(c)$, and χ maps truth values to $\{0, 1\}$ according to the convention $\chi(\text{false}) = 0$ and $\chi(\text{true}) = 1$. I.e., $\int P \geq 1$ holds on $(traj, [a, b])$ iff P holds in at least one time instant in $\{a, \ldots, b-1\}$.

The interpretation of Boolean connectives is classical:

$$\begin{array}{llll} traj, [a, b] \models \neg\phi & \text{iff} & traj, [a, b] \not\models \phi \; , \\ traj, [a, b] \models (\phi \wedge \psi) & \text{iff} & traj, [a, b] \models \phi & \text{and} & traj, [a, b] \models \psi \; . \end{array}$$

Satisfaction of a chop formula $\phi \frown \psi$, finally, requires that the observation interval can be split into two subintervals $[a, m]$ and $[m, b]$ s.t. ϕ resp. ψ hold on the two subintervals:

$$traj, [a, b] \models (\phi \frown \psi) \quad \text{iff} \quad \exists m \in Time \cap [a, b] . \begin{pmatrix} traj, [a, m] \models \phi & \text{and} \\ traj, [m, b] \models \psi \end{pmatrix} .$$

A trajectory $traj$ *satisfies a formula* ϕ, denoted $traj \models \phi$, iff any prefix-observation of $traj$ satisfies ϕ — formally, $traj \models \phi$ iff $traj, [0, t] \models \phi$ for each $t \in Time$. Note that this is the original definition of satisfaction as used in [ZHR91] and that a different notion, namely $traj \models \phi$ iff $traj, [b, e] \models \phi$ for each $b \leq e \in Time$, has been introduced in more recent expositions, e.g. [HZ97]. We stick to the original definition as it yields a strictly more expressive logics, being able to simulate the new definition through encoding ϕ by $\neg(\text{true} \frown \neg\phi)$ and, furthermore, being able to express initialization properties not expressible with the new semantics.

For notational convenience, we denote the set of models of ϕ, i.e. the set of trajectories satisfying ϕ, by $\mathcal{M}[\![\phi]\!]$. As usual, we say that ϕ *is valid* iff $\mathcal{M}[\![\phi]\!] = Traj$.

Besides the infinite-trajectory semantics given above, it is also possible to provide a finite-trace interpretation of DC: we say that a *finite* trace $tr \in (Varname \rightarrow \mathbb{B})^*$ satisfies ϕ, denoted $tr \models \phi$, iff there is some trajectory $traj \in Traj$ and some observation interval $[a, b] \in TimeInterval$ such that

$$\forall t \in \{0, \ldots, \text{len}(tr) - 1\} \cdot traj(a + t) = tr(t),$$
$$a + \text{len}(tr) - 1 = b,$$
$$traj, [a, b] \models \phi \ ,$$

where $\text{len}(tr)$ denotes the length of the sequence tr. We then say that tr is a *finite model of* ϕ. The set of finite models of ϕ is denoted $\mathcal{M}_{\text{fin}}[\![\phi]\!]$. Due to the definition, it is easy to see that the existence of *finite* models is closely coupled to validity, which was previously defined via *infinite* models:

Lemma 1. *A DC formula ϕ is valid (i.e., $\mathcal{M}[\![\phi]\!] = Traj$) iff $\neg\phi$ has no finite model (i.e., $\mathcal{M}_{\text{fin}}[\![\neg\phi]\!] = \emptyset$).*

Proof. By definition of validity, a DC formula ϕ is invalid iff there is some trajectory $traj \in Traj$ and some $t \in \mathbb{N}$ such that $traj, [0, t] \models \neg\phi$. As satisfaction of DC formulae is invariant to translation of the observation interval (cf. any of [ZHR91,Rav95,Frä97,HZ97]), this is the case iff there is $traj' \in Traj$ and $b \leq e \in Time$ with $traj', [b, e,] \models \neg\phi$. By definition of satisfaction by finite traces, this is equivalent to $\neg\phi$ having a finite model.   □

It follows from the previous lemma that when aiming at decision procedures for DC, the tool support may w.l.o.g. concentrate on constructing the finite models.

3   Unbounded Model Construction

We will now turn to the problem of effectively constructing for some arbitrary formula ϕ some finite model of ϕ, if such exists, or deciding that none exists, otherwise. This problem, in the remainder called the *unbounded model construction problem* as no bound on the length of the models is imposed, has been extensively studied before. While unbounded model construction poses severe decidability problems in a dense-time setting (i.e., $Time = \mathbb{R}$), as shown in [ZHS93] and more deeply analyzed in [Frä97], it can be done through a straightforward mapping to star-free regular expressions in the discrete-time setting, as first recognized by Hansen in 1994 [Han94]:

Lemma 2. *Given a DC formula ϕ, a star-free regular expression accepting a language that corresponds directly to the finite models of ϕ can be constructed effectively (in linear time).*

   Hence, an automaton generating (a representation of) the finite models of ϕ can be constructed effectively.

Proof. It is straightforward to map DC formulae to star-free regular expressions describing their finite models [Han94]. An appropriate mapping R of formulae ϕ with $\mathit{free}(\phi) \subseteq V$, where $V \subseteq \mathit{Varname}$ is arbitrarily chosen, to a star-free regular expression over $\alpha \overset{\text{def}}{=} V \to \mathbb{B}$ is

$$R[\![\textstyle\int P \geq 1]\!] \overset{\text{def}}{=} \alpha^* \left(\bigcup_{p \in \widetilde{P}} p \right) \alpha^* \; ,$$

$$R[\![\neg\phi]\!] \overset{\text{def}}{=} \overline{R[\![\phi]\!]} \; ,$$

$$R[\![\phi \wedge \psi]\!] \overset{\text{def}}{=} R[\![\phi]\!] \cap R[\![\psi]\!] \; ,$$

$$R[\![\phi \frown \psi]\!] \overset{\text{def}}{=} R[\![\phi]\!] \cdot R[\![\psi]\!] \; ,$$

where $\widetilde{P}$ denotes the set of valuations in the alphabet α that satisfy P. It is straightforward to prove by induction on the structure of the formula that $tr \models \phi$ iff $w \in \mathcal{L}_{R[\![\phi]\!]}$ for $w \overset{\text{def}}{=} \langle tr(0)|_V, tr(1)|_V, tr(2)|_V, \ldots, tr(\mathrm{len}(tr) - 1)|_V \rangle$. $\qquad\square$

Given a DC formula ϕ, the translation $R[\![\phi]\!]$ yields a star-free regular expression of size at most $2^{|\mathit{free}(\phi)|} \cdot |\phi|$. As checking emptiness of extended regular expressions is non-elementary [MS73], this provides a non-elementary algorithm for model construction of discrete-time DC. Furthermore, it is easy to see that in general one cannot do better, as was also observed in [Han94]:

Theorem 1 (Non-elementariness of propositional DC). *The problem of deciding existence of a finite model to a DC formula is non-elementary.*

Proof. The emptiness problem of extended regular expressions, which is non-elementary according to [MS73], has a linear encoding in DC: let re be an extended regular expression over an alphabet of the form $\alpha = V \to \mathbb{B}$, with $V \subset \mathit{Varname}$ being finite. For any $a \in \alpha$ let P_a be the state assertion

$$P_a \overset{\text{def}}{=} \bigwedge_{\substack{u \in V, \\ a(u)=\texttt{true}}} u \quad \wedge \quad \bigwedge_{\substack{v \in V, \\ a(v)=\texttt{false}}} \neg v \quad .$$

We will encode words $w = \langle w_1, \ldots, w_n \rangle \in \alpha^*$ by finite traces first satisfying P_{w_1}, then P_{w_2}, and so on. To achieve this, we use the mapping F of star-free regular expressions to DC formula defined by

$$F[\![a]\!] \overset{\text{def}}{=} \textstyle\int P_a \geq 1 \wedge \ell < 2 \; ,$$

$$F[\![re_1 \cap re_2]\!] \overset{\text{def}}{=} F[\![re_1]\!] \wedge F[\![re_2]\!] \; ,$$

$$F[\![re_1 \cdot re_2]\!] \overset{\text{def}}{=} F[\![re_1]\!] \frown F[\![re_2]\!] \; ,$$

$$F[\![\overline{re_1}]\!] \overset{\text{def}}{=} \neg F[\![re_1]\!] \; .$$

It is easy to show by structural induction that for any extended regular expression re the formula $F[\![re]\!]$ is satisfied by a finite model tr iff $w \in \mathcal{L}_{re}$ for $w \overset{\text{def}}{=} \langle tr(0)|_V, tr(1)|_V, tr(2)|_V, \ldots, tr(\mathrm{len}(tr) - 1)|_V \rangle$.

As the mapping $tr \mapsto \langle tr(0)|_V, tr(1)|_V, tr(2)|_V, \ldots, tr(\mathrm{len}(tr) - 1)|_V \rangle$ from finite traces to α^* is surjective, this implies that $F[\![re]\!]$ has a finite model iff $\mathcal{L}_{re} \neq \emptyset$. Thus F provides a linear encoding of the emptiness problem of extended regular expressions into the $\{\lceil P \rceil\}$-fragment of DC, which proves that deciding existence of a finite model of a DC formula is non-elementary due to the non-elementary complexity of language emptiness for extended regular expressions [MS73]. □

4 Bounded Model Construction

Given a natural number k and a DC formula ϕ, the *bounded model construction problem for k and ϕ* (BMC(ϕ, k) for short) is to assign to ϕ a model of length k iff such a model of ϕ exists.

It is obvious that this problem is computationally much simpler than the unbounded model construction problem: one could, for example, generate all strings $w \in \alpha^k$ and test for membership $w \in \mathcal{L}_\phi$, which would yield an algorithm that is exponential in k (as there are $|\alpha|^k$ words to generate) and polynomial in $|\alpha| \cdot |\phi|$ (as checking membership is in P for star-free regular languages) — which however means that it is worst-case exponential in $|\phi|$ also, as $|\alpha| = 2^{|free(\phi)|}$ may grow exponentially in $|\phi|$. However, we will show in the sequel that the problem is in fact much simpler, namely NP-complete in both k and $|\phi|$.

We start by showing that bounded model construction for DC is NP-hard:

Lemma 3. *For each $k \geq 1$, BMC(ϕ, k) is NP-hard in $|\phi|$.*

Proof. The duration formula $\int P \geq 1$ is satisfiable by a model of length $k \geq 1$ iff the propositional formula P is satisfiable. As satisfiability of propositional formulae is NP-complete, NP-hardness of BMC($\cdot, k$) follows. □

For showing NP-easiness, we will provide a polynomial reduction to propositional logic.

4.1 Straightforward Encoding into Propositional Logic

We start with a straightforward reduction, which is fine for most practical purposes, though not optimal if not augmented with further analysis, as we will show.

As usual in propositional satisfiability-based bounded model checking, we represent the values of the different state variables in the different time instants by propositional variables. Therefore, we assume that we have a renaming scheme on variables, which yields for any state variable x and any index $k \in \mathbb{N}$ a unique propositional variable name x_k. We will use overloading to denote the straightforward lifting of this mapping to state expressions. Hence, P_k denotes the propositional formula obtained from mapping all state variables $x, y, \ldots$ in the state assertion P to $x_k, y_k, \ldots$. The reduction of BMC(ϕ, k) to propositional logic is then obtained by the mapping

$$\mathrm{BMC}_{\mathrm{straight}}[\![\phi, k]\!] = T_0^k[\![\phi]\!],$$

$$T_i^j[\![\textstyle\int P \geq 1]\!] = \bigvee_{l=i}^{j-1} P_l$$

$$T_i^j[\![\phi \wedge \psi]\!] = T_i^j[\![\phi]\!] \wedge T_i^j[\![\psi]\!]$$

$$T_i^j[\![\neg\phi]\!] = \neg T_i^j[\![\phi]\!]$$

$$T_i^j[\![\phi \frown \psi]\!] = \bigvee_{m=i}^{j} T_i^m[\![\phi]\!] \wedge T_m^j[\![\psi]\!]$$

where, as usual, the empty disjunction $\bigvee_{k=i}^{i-1} P_k$ equals `false`.

It is straightforward to show by induction on the structure of ϕ that the models of $\mathrm{BMC}_{\mathrm{straight}}[\![\phi, k]\!]$ are in one-to-one correspondence to ϕ's models of length k:

Lemma 4. *For each valuation σ of propositional variables, the equivalence $\sigma \models \mathrm{BMC}_{\mathrm{straight}}[\![\phi, k]\!]$ iff $tr_\sigma^k \models \phi$ holds, where*

$$tr_\sigma^k(t)(x) \stackrel{\mathrm{def}}{=} \begin{cases} \sigma(x_t) & \text{iff } 0 \leq t < k \\ \text{undefined} & \text{otherwise} \end{cases}$$

for each $t \in \mathbb{N}$ and $x \in free(\phi)$.

As the mapping $\sigma \mapsto tr_\sigma^k$ is a surjective mapping onto the traces of length k, it follows that the reduction to propositional logic performed by $\mathrm{BMC}_{\mathrm{straight}}$, together with satisfiability checking for propositional logic, solves the bounded model construction problem:

Lemma 5. *A DC formula ϕ has a model of length $k \in \mathbb{N}$ iff $\mathrm{BMC}_{\mathrm{straight}}[\![\phi, k]\!]$ is satisfiable.*

Unfortunately, $\mathrm{BMC}_{\mathrm{straight}}[\![\phi, k]\!]$ yields a propositional formula of worst-case size $k^{(\mathrm{chopdepth}(\phi)+1)}|\phi|$, where $\mathrm{chopdepth}(\phi)$ denotes the maximum nesting-depth of chop operators in ϕ. Consequently, $\mathrm{BMC}_{\mathrm{straight}}[\![\phi, k]\!]$ can be of exponential size in $\mathrm{chopdepth}(\phi)$ and thus also in $|\phi|$. Hence, Lemma 5 shows soundness and completeness of the construction, yet does not suffice to show that bounded model construction for DC is NP-easy. Instead, it just proves that bounded model construction for DC is at most singly exponential.

4.2 Improved Encoding into Propositional Logic

A closer inspection of the formulae generated by $\mathrm{BMC}_{\mathrm{straight}}[\![\phi, k]\!]$ reveals that nested chops will in fact generate the same propositional (sub-)formulae multiple times. E.g., $\mathrm{BMC}_{\mathrm{straight}}[\![\int P \geq 1 \frown (\int Q \geq 1 \frown (\int R \geq 1 \frown \int S \geq 1)), k]\!]$ yields a propositional formula which $\frac{(k+1)k}{2}$ times contains the particular subformula $T_k^k[\![\int S \geq 1]\!]$. This can be avoided by introducing auxiliary propositional variables for "caching" the truth values of common subformulae.

The simplest such scheme generates exactly $\frac{(k+1)k}{2}$ auxiliary variables per subformula of ϕ. Each such variable encodes the truth value of the corresponding subformula in one of the $\frac{(k+1)k}{2}$ possible subintervals of $\{0, \ldots, k\}$. This scheme resembles the linear-time translation of arbitrary propositional satisfiability problems to CNF due to Tseitin [Tse68], where subformulae are replaced by fresh propositional variables alongside with suitable definitions of these auxiliary variables.

To make this scheme operational, we assume that we have a mapping from DC formulae and time intervals to propositional variables which assigns to any DC formula ϕ and any index pair $i, j \in \mathbb{N}$ of indices with $i \leq j$ a unique propositional variable name $[\phi]_{i,j}$. We furthermore assume that these variable names $[\phi]_{i,j}$ are different from all propositional variable names x_k assigned by the mapping of state variables and indices to propositional variables. The propositional variable $[\phi]_{i,j}$ will be used to represent the truth value of (sub-)formula ϕ on observation interval $[i, j]$. This can be achieved by associating to $[\phi]_{i,j}$ an appropriate defining term in propositional logic, as in

$$\mathrm{BMC}_{\mathrm{poly}}[\![\phi, k]\!] = t^k[\![\phi]\!] \wedge [\phi]_{0,k}$$

$$t^k[\![\smallint P \geq 1]\!] = \bigwedge_{\substack{i \in \{0,\ldots,k-1\} \\ j \in \{i+1,\ldots,k\}}} ([\smallint P \geq 1]_{i,j} \iff (P_i \vee [\smallint P \geq 1]_{i+1,j}))$$

$$\wedge \bigwedge_{i \in \{0,\ldots,k\}} \neg[\smallint P \geq 1]_{i,i}$$

$$t^k[\![\phi \wedge \psi]\!] = t^k[\![\phi]\!] \wedge t^k[\![\psi]\!] \wedge \bigwedge_{\substack{i \in \{0,\ldots,k\} \\ j \in \{i,\ldots,k\}}} ([\phi \wedge \psi]_{i,j} \iff [\phi]_{i,j} \wedge [\psi]_{i,j})$$

$$t^k[\![\neg \phi]\!] = t^k[\![\phi]\!] \wedge \bigwedge_{\substack{i \in \{0,\ldots,k\} \\ j \in \{i,\ldots,k\}}} ([\neg \phi]_{i,j} \iff \neg[\phi]_{i,j})$$

$$t^k[\![\phi \frown \psi]\!] = t^k[\![\phi]\!] \wedge t^k[\![\psi]\!] \wedge \bigwedge_{\substack{i \in \{0,\ldots,k\} \\ j \in \{i,\ldots,k\}}} \left(\begin{array}{c} [\phi \frown \psi]_{i,j} \iff \\ \bigvee_{m=i}^{j}([\phi]_{i,m} \wedge [\psi]_{m,j}) \end{array} \right) .$$

This yields an encoding of $\mathrm{BMC}(\phi, k)$ into propositional logic of size at most $O\left(k^3 \cdot |\phi|\right)$.

Because of the auxiliary variables, the correspondence between models of the propositional formula $\mathrm{BMC}_{\mathrm{poly}}[\![\phi, k]\!]$ and models of ϕ of length k is slightly weaker than for $\mathrm{BMC}_{\mathrm{straight}}$:

Lemma 6. *For any valuation σ of propositional variables, $\sigma \models \mathrm{BMC}_{\mathrm{poly}}[\![\phi, k]\!]$ implies $tr^k_\sigma \models \phi$.*

Vice versa, $tr \models \phi$ for some finite trace tr implies that there is some valuation σ with $tr = tr^{\mathrm{len}(tr)}_\sigma$ and $\sigma \models \mathrm{BMC}_{\mathrm{poly}}[\![\phi, \mathrm{len}(tr)]\!]$.

Again, it follows that the reduction to propositional logic performed by BMC_{poly}, together with satisfiability checking for propositional logic, solves the bounded model construction problem:

Lemma 7. *A DC formula ϕ has a model of length $k \in \mathbb{N}$ iff $\text{BMC}_{\text{poly}}[\![\phi, k]\!]$ is satisfiable.*

However, as BMC_{poly} provides a polynomial encoding, this shows that bounded model construction for DC is NP-easy:

Lemma 8. $\text{BMC}(\phi, k)$ *is NP-easy in $|\phi| + k$, i.e. there is a non-deterministic algorithm of complexity polynomial in $|\phi| + k$ which solves the bounded model construction problem $\text{BMC}(\phi, k)$.*

Proof. For arbitrary DC formulae ϕ and $k \in \mathbb{N}$, the mapping $\text{BMC}_{\text{poly}}[\![\phi, k]\!]$ provides a propositional encoding of $\text{BMC}(\phi, k)$ of size $O\left(k^3 \cdot |\phi|\right)$, i.e. polynomial in $|\phi|$ and k. NP-easiness of $\text{BMC}(\phi, k)$ thus follows from NP-easiness of satisfiability of propositional formulae. □

Together with Lemma 3 this yields

Theorem 2 (NP-completeness). $\text{BMC}(\phi, k)$ *is NP-complete if unary notation is used for k, i.e. if the size of the problem $\text{BMC}(\phi, k)$ is considered to be $|\phi| + k$.*

Note that this shows that bounded model construction is considerably cheaper than unbounded model construction. However, given the non-elementariness result of Theorem 1, this also shows that the shortest countermodels to DC formulae may in general be of non-elementary size.

4.3 Further Optimizations

It is easy to see that the translation by BMC_{poly} is still not optimal. For practical purposes, some enhancements are in order which, while not further reducing the complexity class, lead to more compact and more rapidly checkable propositional formulae. The most important such optimization is to take into account whether a subformula occurs in positive or in negative context and to replace the bi-implications occurring in the definitions of the auxiliary variables in BMC_{poly} by sufficient forms of one-sided implications. Therefore, instead of translating, e.g., $t^k[\![\phi \frown \psi]\!]$ to

$$t^k[\![\phi]\!] \wedge t^k[\![\psi]\!] \wedge \bigwedge_{\substack{i \in \{0,\ldots,k\} \\ j \in \{i,\ldots,k\}}} \left([\phi \frown \psi]_{i,j} \iff \bigvee_{m=i}^{j} ([\phi]_{i,m} \wedge [\psi]_{m,j}) \right)$$

we may translate positive occurrences (i.e., occurrences that appear under an even number of negations in the overall formula) to

$$t^k[\![\phi]\!] \wedge t^k[\![\psi]\!] \wedge \bigwedge_{\substack{i \in \{0,\ldots,k\} \\ j \in \{i,\ldots,k\}}} \left([\phi \frown \psi]_{i,j} \Rightarrow \bigvee_{m=i}^{j} ([\phi]_{i,m} \wedge [\psi]_{m,j}) \right)$$

and negative occurrences (i.e., occurrences appearing under an odd number of negations) to

$$t^k[\![\phi]\!] \wedge t^k[\![\psi]\!] \wedge \bigwedge_{\substack{i \in \{0,\ldots,k\} \\ j \in \{i,\ldots,k\}}} \left(\begin{matrix} [\phi \frown \psi]_{i,j} \Leftarrow \\ \bigvee_{m=i}^{j}([\phi]_{i,m} \wedge [\psi]_{m,j}) \end{matrix} \right) .$$

Further optimizations can be used for reducing the number of auxiliary variables, in particular by common subexpression elimination and by, e.g., avoiding introduction of a further auxiliary variable $[\neg\phi]_{i,k}$ in negations, instead using $\neg[\phi]_{i,k}$ whenever the truth value of subformula $\neg\phi$ in the time interval $\{i,\ldots,j\}$ is needed. In fact, all optimizations proposed for the generation of small CNFs from propositional formulae (cf. [NW99,PG86]) can be adapted to bounded model construction for DC formulae. However, all these optimizations, while being inevitable for a reasonably efficient implementation, will not lead to a further reduction of the worst-case complexity, as the NP-hardness result of Lemma 3 shows.

5   A Class of NP-Easy Formulae

The NP-easiness result of the previous section gives hope that bounded model construction for DC is actually affordable. However, as the non-elementariness result of Theorem 1 shows, the shortest models of DC formulae may have non-elementary length s.t. the usefulness of debugging DC specifications by bounded model construction may be doubtful. Fortunately, as we will show in this section, it turns out that most DC formulae actually used in specifications have models of length linear in the formula size, thus rendering BMC a very powerful technique.

We start by defining a certain kind of linear-size patterns that suffice for describing the trace sets of these formulae:

Definition 1. *Given $n \in \mathbb{N}$, we call a sequence $\langle u_0, u_1, \ldots, u_k \rangle$ with $u_i \in (Varname \to \mathbb{B})^*$ for each $i \leq k$ an n-pattern iff*

$$\sum_{i=0}^{k} \mathrm{len}(u_i) \leq n .$$

The trace set $\mathcal{L}_{pat}$ defined by an n-pattern $pat = \langle u_0, u_1, \ldots, u_k \rangle$ is the set defined by the regular expression $u_0(\alpha^*)u_1(\alpha^*)u_2(\alpha^*)\ldots(\alpha^*)u_k$ over the (infinite) alphabet $\alpha \stackrel{\mathrm{def}}{=} (V \to \mathbb{B})$, i.e.

$$\mathcal{L}_{pat} \stackrel{\mathrm{def}}{=} \mathcal{L}_{u_0(\alpha^*)u_1(\alpha^*)u_2(\alpha^*)\ldots(\alpha^*)u_k} .$$

Given a constant $c \in \mathbb{N}$, a DC formula ϕ is said to give rise to c-linear patterns iff there is a set Pat of $c|\phi|$-patterns that defines the finite models of ϕ in that

$$\mathcal{M}_{\mathrm{fin}}[\![\phi]\!] = \bigcup_{pat \in Pat} \mathcal{L}_{pat} .$$

Note that in the definition of the trace set $\mathcal{L}_{u_0(\alpha^*)u_1(\alpha^*)u_2(\alpha^*)...(\alpha^*)u_k}$ associated to a pattern $pat = \langle u_0, u_1, \ldots, u_k \rangle$, unconstrained segments α^* are interspersed only inside the pattern, but not before u_0 or after u_k. Therefore, it is possible to represent a single trace tr by a pattern, using the pattern $pat = \langle tr \rangle$ of length 1. Similarly, one can represent trace sets beginning or ending in a certain trace by patterns of the forms $pat = \langle tr, \varepsilon \rangle$ or $pat = \langle \varepsilon, tr \rangle$, respectively.

The crucial point about formulae having c-linear patterns is that such formulae have models of small size:

Lemma 9. *If ϕ gives rise to c-linear patterns then ϕ has some model of length at most $c|\phi|$, or no model at all.*

Proof. If ϕ gives rise to c-linear patterns then its finite models can be described by a set Pat of $c|\phi|$-patterns such that $\mathcal{M}_{\mathrm{fin}}[\![\phi]\!] = \bigcup_{pat \in Pat} \mathcal{L}_{pat}$. If $\mathcal{M}_{\mathrm{fin}}[\![\phi]\!] \neq \emptyset$ then $Pat \neq \emptyset$. As the conjecture is trivially satisfied if $\mathcal{M}_{\mathrm{fin}}[\![\phi]\!] = \emptyset$, we assume in the remainder that $\mathcal{M}_{\mathrm{fin}}[\![\phi]\!] \neq \emptyset$. Then let $pat = \langle u_0, u_1, \ldots, u_k \rangle \in Pat$. As $\mathcal{L}_{pat} = \mathcal{L}_{u_0(\alpha^*)u_1(\alpha^*)u_2(\alpha^*)...(\alpha^*)u_k}$, it follows that $u_0 \cdot u_1 \cdot \ldots \cdot u_k \in \mathcal{M}_{\mathrm{fin}}[\![\phi]\!]$. The conjecture follows as $\mathrm{len}(u_0 \cdot u_1 \cdot \ldots \cdot u_k) = \sum_{i=0}^{k} \mathrm{len}(u_i) \leq c|\phi|$ holds due to pat being a $c|\phi|$-pattern. □

Combining above small-model property with the NP-easiness of bounded model construction, we obtain an NP-easiness result for constructing models of formulae which have c-linear patterns.

Theorem 3 (NP-easiness of model construction). *If ϕ gives rise to c-linear patterns then checking for existence of a finite model of ϕ and — if possible — constructing a finite model of ϕ is NP-easy. I.e., for formulae giving rise to c-linear patterns, there is a non-deterministic algorithm of complexity polynomial in the size of the formula that decides existence of a finite model and, if such exists, constructs such a model.*

Proof. If ϕ gives rise to c-linear patterns then, according to Lemma 9, it has a model of length at most $c|\phi|$, if any. Hence, performing $\mathrm{BMC}(\phi, k)$ for each $k \leq c|\phi|$ suffices for checking existence of a finite model and for constructing a finite model of ϕ. Due to Theorem 2, this is NP-easy. □

Corollary 1. *Deciding validity of negations of c-linear formulae is in NP.*

Proof. Follows immediately from Lemma 1 and Theorem 3. □

Given this result, it is interesting to see that the so-called DC implementables, a subset of DC proposed by Ravn for describing system designs [Rav95], are actually negations of formulae giving rise to 1-linear patterns. In order to show this we first prove suitable closure properties of formulae giving rise to n-linear patterns:

Lemma 10. *Given $c \in \mathbb{N}$, let ϕ and ψ be DC formulae giving rise to c-linear patterns; let π be an arbitrary DC formula and P an arbitrary state assertion. Then*

1. $\phi \wedge \psi$ *gives rise to c-linear patterns;*
2. $\phi \vee \psi$ *gives rise to c-linear patterns;*
3. $\phi \frown \psi$ *gives rise to c-linear patterns;*
4. $\int P \geq 1$ *gives rise to 1-linear patterns;*
5. **true** *gives rise to 1-linear patterns;*
6. $l < k \wedge \pi$ *gives rise to 1-linear patterns.*

Proof. 1. Given an n-pattern pat_1 and an m-pattern pat_2, the intersection of the trace sets defined by those two patterns can obviously be defined by a set of $(n+m)$-patterns. It follows that $\mathcal{M}_{\mathrm{fin}}[\![\phi \wedge \psi]\!]$ can be defined by a set of $c(|\phi| + |\psi|)$-patterns, as, by the premise of the lemma, $\mathcal{M}_{\mathrm{fin}}[\![\phi]\!]$ can be defined by $c|\phi|$-patterns and $\mathcal{M}_{\mathrm{fin}}[\![\psi]\!]$ can be defined by $c|\psi|$-patterns. Hence, as any $(c|\phi \wedge \psi| - 1)$-pattern is also a $c|\phi \wedge \psi|$-pattern, $\mathcal{M}_{\mathrm{fin}}[\![\phi \wedge \psi]\!]$ can be defined by a set of $c|\phi \wedge \psi|$-patterns. I.e., $\phi \wedge \psi$ gives rise to c-linear patterns.

2. Straightforward, as the trace sets definable by sets of n-patterns are closed under union.

3. Analogous to the proof of statement 1.

4. As was already observed in the proof of Lemma 2, the patterns $(\alpha^*)p(\alpha^*)$, where p ranges over the valuations that satisfy P, describe the finite models of $\int P \geq 1$. This is a set of 1-patterns.

5. $\mathcal{M}_{\mathrm{fin}}[\![\mathbf{true}]\!]$ can be described by the 0-pattern $\langle \varepsilon \rangle$.

6. If W is the set of traces of length at most k that satisfy π then the set $Pat = \{\langle w \rangle \mid w \in W\}$ of patterns defines $\mathcal{M}_{\mathrm{fin}}[\![l < k \wedge \pi]\!]$. All patterns in Pat are by definition k-patterns and thus $|l < k \wedge \pi|$-patterns, as $k < |l < k \wedge \pi|$ [2].

$\square$

Given these closure properties, it is easy to see that the DC formulae encountered in major case studies, including the "prototype" of all duration formulae, namely the safety requirement $\square(l < 30 \Rightarrow \int gas \wedge \neg flame < 6)$ of the ProCoS gas burner [RRH93], are typically negations of formulae giving rise to 1-linear patterns.

Corollary 2 (NP-easiness of typical specification patterns). *The following formulae are negations of DC formulae giving rise to 1-linear patterns:*

1. *the DC implementables, as defined in [Rav95],*
2. *the safety requirement $\square(l < 30 \Rightarrow \int gas \wedge \neg flame < 6)$ of the ProCoS gas burner [RRH93]*

The validity problem of these formulae (and their positive Boolean combinations) thus is in NP.

Proof. 1. DC implementables are built from formulae of the three forms **true**, $\int P \geq 1$, and $l < k \wedge \pi$ using chop and Boolean junctors, with use of negation

---

[2] Note that we measure the length of formulae after expanding abbreviations such that $|l < k| = |\neg(\underbrace{\int \mathbf{true} \geq 1 \frown \ldots \frown \int \mathbf{true} \geq 1)}_{k \text{ times}}| > k$.

being limited to a single, outermost, negation. Hence, the fact that DC implementables give rise to 1-linear patterns follows from Lemma 10 by induction on the structure of DC implementables.

2. According to Lemma 10, part 6, the formula $\neg(l < 30 \Rightarrow \int gas \wedge \neg flame < 6)$ gives rise to 1-linear patterns, as the abbreviations expand to $l < 30 \wedge \neg(\int gas \wedge \neg flame < 6)$. The conjecture follows, as $\Box\phi$ is equivalent to $\neg(\text{true} \frown (\neg\phi) \frown \text{true}$, the formula true gives rise to 1-linear patterns (Lemma 10, part 5), and the formulae giving rise to 1-linear patterns are closed under chop (Lemma 10, part 3).

It follows from Corollary 1 that the validity problem of these formulae is in NP.

$\square$

This shows that validity checking is in fact cheap for typical DC-based specification formulae, thus giving a formal argument supporting the observation made in [Frä97, p. 51] and cited in the introduction. Note that above result also sheds some light on the relative expressiveness of DC implementables compared to timed automata, as the latter have a PSPACE-complete emptiness problem [AD94][3], while checking a set of DC implementables for validity is in NP according to Corollary 2. This shows that DC implementables, while often considered to be merely a different syntax for timed automata, are in fact subtly different.

6   Experimental Results

In order to evaluate the proposed method, we have developed a prototype implementation in SWI-Prolog. It employs the compilation scheme BMC_{poly} with the optimizations explained in Section 4.3 and generates propositional formulae in conjunctive clause form (CNFs)[4]. As a backend for checking the resulting satisfiability problems we used ZChaff in version zchaff.2001.2.17[5]. As a reference we took Pandya's DC-Valid tool [Pan00] in version 1.4β, which translates DC into the monadic second order logic over strings M2L-Str and uses MONA [BKR96] in version 1.4 as a verification backend. All experiments were performed on a 500 MHz Pentium III M with 384 MByte RAM and 300 MByte swap space, running under Linux. In the sequel, we do just report the runtimes of the verification backends (i.e. ZChaff and MONA), as a comparison of the translation times needed by the front ends does not make much sense due to the vastly different implementation basis (SWI-Prolog vs. C). However, it should be clear that even an efficient implementation of BMC would presumably spend considerably more time in the frontend than DCValid does, as the translation task is substantially more involved.

---

[3] While timed automata are usually interpreted over dense time, Alur's and Dill's prove of PSPACE completeness of the emptiness problem does also cover the discrete-time interpretation and applies even if the time constants are given in unary notation, like we do in our syntax of DC.

[4] In fact, the implementation generalizes BMC_{poly} by compiling formula $t^k[\![\phi]\!] \wedge \bigvee_{e=0}^{k}[\![\phi]\!]_{0,e}$ instead of BMC_{poly}, thus recognizing all models of length *at most* k.

[5] http://www.ee.princeton.edu/ chaff/zchaff.php

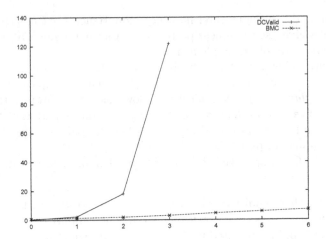

Fig. 2. Verification time for $\Box(\ell \leq 30 \Rightarrow \int gas \wedge \neg flame \leq n)$. Horizontal axis: n; vertical axis: time spent in verification backend (in seconds).

The first group of experiments dealt with checking validity of formulae of the shape $\Box(\ell \leq m \Rightarrow \int P \leq n)$, where $n < m$. It is easy to see that an automaton recognizing the models of such a formula needs $mn - \frac{n(n-1)}{2}$ states. Therefore, one might expect state explosion when checking this very typical DC formula for large m and n. We tried with moderate $m = 30$ and various small n by checking

$$\phi_n \stackrel{\text{def}}{=} \Box(\ell \leq 30 \Rightarrow \int gas \wedge \neg flame \leq n)$$

for different n. The formula is invalid for all $n < 30$. The results are shown in Fig. 2. DCValid failed for all $n > 3$ due to MONA running out of memory. $BMC(\phi_n, k)$ has been performed with $k = 31$, which is the size for which a model can be guaranteed, if there is one. The largest CNF generated by BMC for this problem had 101616 clauses with 53774 Atoms; ZChaff's memory usage remained below 10 MByte.

Another group of experiments dealt with Boolean combinations of individually tractable specifications. We concentrated on the apparently easy case of variable-disjoint conjuncts or disjuncts. Therefore, we simply replicated the formula $\Box(\ell \leq 10 \Rightarrow \int s \leq 3)$ under bound renaming. The DCValid/MONA-system suffered from state explosion in *both* cases, running out of memory already with 3 conjuncts or disjuncts, while BMC remained stable (Fig. 3).

However, even though some of the CNFs stemming from above problems are extremely large (multiple 100k clauses and clause lengths > 30 for some clauses), they may be considered to be friendly instances for Boolean satisfiability checkers as all of them are stemming from invalid formulae, thus yielding a satisfiable SAT problem[6]. Hence we tried a problem that has both valid and

---

[6] Note that the SAT checker is actually used for searching finite models of the *negation* of the formula

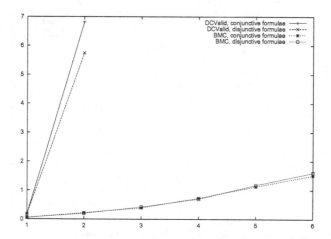

Fig. 3. Verification time for $\bigwedge_{i=1}^{n} \Box(\ell \leq 10 \Rightarrow \int s_i \leq 3)$ and $\bigvee_{i=1}^{n} \Box(\ell \leq 10 \Rightarrow \int s_i \leq 3)$. Horizontal axis: n; vertical axis: time spent in verification backend (in seconds). MONA ran out of memory for $n > 2$. BMC was performed for 15 steps.

invalid instances. It is a scheduling problem for three processes. The processes are modeled through state variables r_i indicating when process i is running. Mutual exclusion is enforced through a conjunction of DC formulae $\Box \int r_i \wedge r_j = 0$ for all $i \neq j$. Furthermore, the demand that all processes run *exactly* 2 time units[7] within any n time unit window — $n \in \mathbb{N}$ being the parameter of the problem — has been formalized through a conjunction of formulae $\Box(\ell = n \Rightarrow \int r_i = 2)$ for all i. This formula set is invalid for $n \geq 6$, then yielding a prefix of a valid schedule as counterexample, and valid, i.e. not schedulable, for $n < 6$. The findings were that BMC outperformed DCValid on the invalid instances, yet was inferior to DCValid on the valid instances (Fig. 4).

Similar findings have been obtained on other cases. Thus, it seems that BMC and DCValid can in fact complement each other, BMC being fast on invalid instances and thus being a powerful debugging aid, DCValid being faster on valid instances and thus being suitable for certifying the final product.

7 Discussion

Within this paper, we have shown that ideas taken from bounded model checking [BCZ99] may indeed prove useful for validity checking of Duration Calculus formulae. While previous approaches to DC decision procedures suffered from extreme — in the worst case non-elementary — computational complexity, bounded model construction is 'only' NP-complete (Theorem 2), yet sufficient for practical DC specifications (Corollary 2).

---

[7] A version using 3 time units runtime per process turned out to be intractable by DCValid.

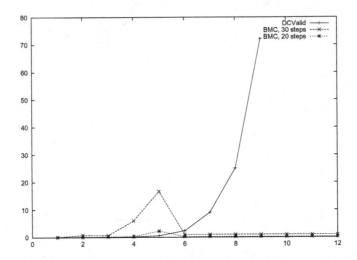

Fig. 4. Verification time for the three-process schedulability problem. Horizontal axis: n; vertical axis: time spent in verification backend (in seconds). BMC time drops sharply when moving from the region where the formula is valid ($n \leq 5$) to the invalid region ($n \geq 6$).

Related findings have been reported by Ayari and Basin in [AB00], where the complexity of bounded model construction for monadic second order logic has been investigated. While the complexity does not drop to NP in that case, it does go down from non-elementary to PSPACE-complete for M2L-Str when bounded model construction is performed instead of unbounded one. For WS1S, the complexity remains non-elementary even in the bounded case [AB00]. However, as M2L-Str is sufficient for encoding DC with quantifiers, as performed in [Pan00][8], it is planned to combine Ayari's and Basin's PSPACE-complete bounded model construction for M2L-Str with our bounded model construction for DC for being able to efficiently check quantified DC.

Acknowledgments

The line of research reported herein owes much to David Basin and Ahmed Ayari, with whom we discussed bounded model construction of monadic second order logics, as described in [AB00]. This motivated us to consider bounded model construction for Duration Calculus. Furthermore, I would like to thank my colleagues Christian Herde and Olaf Bär for many fruitful discussions on variants of the Tseitin transformation [Bär01].

---

[8] In fact, Pandya's tool labels its output as being WS1S. Yet, the formulae generated have all quantifiers bounded s.t. the WS1S and the M2l-Str interpretation coincide.

References

AB00.   A. AYARI AND D. BASIN. Bounded model construction for monadic second-order logics. In E. A. Emerson and A. P. Sistla, eds., *Computer Aided Verification (CAV 2000)*, volume 1855 of *Lecture Notes in Computer Science*, pages 99–113. Springer-Verlag, 2000.

AD94.   R. ALUR AND D. L. DILL. A theory of timed automata. *Theoretical Computer Science*, 126(2):183–235, 1994.

Bär01.   O. BÄR. Übersetzung von SMI in um lineare Arithmetik erweiterte CNF. Diplomarbeit, Fachbereich Informatik der Carl v. Ossietzky Universität Oldenburg, Germany, December 2001.

BCZ99.   A. BIERE, A. CIMATTI, AND Y. ZHU. Symbolic model checking without BDDs. In *TACAS'99*, volume 1579 of *Lecture Notes in Computer Science*. Springer-Verlag, 1999.

BKR96.   M. BIEHL, N. KLARLUND, AND T. RAUHE. Mona: Decidable arithmetic in practice. In Jonsson and Parrow [JP96], pages 459–462.

BLR95.   A. BOUAJJANI, Y. LAKHNECH, AND R. ROBBANA. From duration calculus to linear hybrid automata. In P. Wolper, ed., *Computer Aided Verification (CAV '95)*, volume 939 of *Lecture Notes in Computer Science*. Springer-Verlag, 1995.

Frä97.   M. FRÄNZLE. *Controller Design from Temporal Logic: Undecidability need not matter.* Dissertation, Technische Fakultät der Christian-Albrechts-Universität Kiel, Germany, 1997. Available as Bericht Nr. 9710, Institut für Informatik und Prakt. Mathematik der Christian-Albrechts-Universität Kiel, Germany, and via WWW under URL
           http://ca.informatik.uni-oldenburg.de/~fraenzle/diss.html.

Frä02.   M. FRÄNZLE. Model-checking dense-time duration calculus. Accepted for *Formal Aspects of Computing*, to appear 2002.

Han94.   M. R. HANSEN. Model-checking discrete duration calculus. *Formal Aspects of Computing*, 6(6A):826–845, 1994.

HZ97.   M. R. HANSEN AND ZHOU CHAOCHEN. Duration calculus: Logical foundations. *Formal Aspects of Computing*, 9(3):283–330, 1997.

JP96.   B. JONSSON AND J. PARROW, eds. *Formal Techniques in Real-Time and Fault-Tolerant Systems (FTRTFT '96)*, volume 1135 of *Lecture Notes in Computer Science*. Springer-Verlag, 1996.

Lak96.   Y. LAKNECH. *Specification and Verification of Hybrid and Real-Time Systems.* Dissertation, Technische Fakultät der Christian-Albrechts-Universität Kiel, Germany, 1996.

LdRV94.   H. LANGMAACK, W.-P. DE ROEVER, AND J. VYTOPIL, eds. *Formal Techniques in Real-Time and Fault-Tolerant Systems (FTRTFT '94)*, volume 863 of *Lecture Notes in Computer Science*. Springer-Verlag, 1994.

Mos85.   B. MOSZKOWSKI. A temporal logic for multi-level reasoning about hardware. *IEEE Computer*, 18(2):10–19, 1985.

MS73.   A. R. MEYER AND L. STOCKMEYER. Nonelementary word problems in automata and logic. In *Proc. AMS Symposium on Complexity of Computation*, April 1973.

NW99.   A. NONNENGART AND C. WEIDENBACH. Computing small clause normal forms. In A. Robinson and A. Voronkov, eds., *Handbook of Automated Reasoning*. Elsevier Science B.V., 1999.

Pan96.   P. K. PANDYA. Weak chop inverses and liveness in mean-value calculus. In Jonsson and Parrow [JP96], pages 148–167.

Pan00.   P. PANDYA. Specifying and deciding quantified discrete-time duration calculus formulae using DCVALID. Technical report TCS00-PKP-1, Tata Institute of Fundamental Research, India, 2000.

PG86.   D. A. PLAISTED AND S. GREENBAUM. A structure-preserving clause form translation. *Journal of Symbolic Computation*, 2:293–304, 1986.

Rav95.   A. P. RAVN. *Design of Embedded Real-Time Computing Systems*. Doctoral dissertation, Department of Computer Science, Danish Technical University, Lyngby, DK, October 1995. Available as technical report ID-TR: 1995-170.

RRH93.   A. P. RAVN, H. RISCHEL, AND K. M. HANSEN. Specifying and verifying requirements of real-time systems. *IEEE Transactions on Software Engineering*, 19(1):41–55, January 1993.

Ska94.   J. U. SKAKKEBÆK. Liveness and fairness in duration calculus. In B. Jonsson and J. Parrow, eds., *CONCUR'94*, volume 836 of *Lecture Notes in Computer Science*, pages 283–298. Springer-Verlag, 1994.

SS94a.   J. U. SKAKKEBÆK AND P. SESTOFT. Checking validity of duration calculus formulas. ProCoS Technical Report ID/DTH JUS 3/1, Technical University of Denmark, March 1994.

SS94b.   J. U. SKAKKEBÆK AND N. SHANKAR. Towards a duration calculus proof assistant in PVS. In Langmaack et al. [LdRV94], pages 660–679.

Tse68.   G. TSEITIN. On the complexity of derivations in propositional calculus. In A. Slisenko, ed., *Studies in Constructive Mathematics and Mathematical Logics*, 1968.

ZH96.   ZHOU CHAOCHEN AND M. R. HANSEN. Chopping a point. Handout at the 4th ProCoS Working Group Meeting, March 1996.

Zho93.   ZHOU CHAOCHEN. Duration calculi: An overview. In D. Bjørner, M. Broy, and I. V. Pottosin, eds., *Formal Methods in Programming and Their Applications*, volume 735 of *Lecture Notes in Computer Science*, pages 256–266. Springer-Verlag, 1993.

ZHR91.   ZHOU CHAOCHEN, C. A. R. HOARE, AND A. P. RAVN. A calculus of durations. *Information Processing Letters*, 40(5):269–276, 1991.

ZHS93.   ZHOU CHAOCHEN, M. R. HANSEN, AND P. SESTOFT. Decidability and undecidability results for duration calculus. In P. Enjalbert, A. Finkel, and K. W. Wagner, eds., *Symposium on Theoretical Aspects of Computer Science (STACS 93)*, volume 665 of *Lecture Notes in Computer Science*, pages 58–68. Springer-Verlag, 1993.

ZL94.   ZHOU CHAOCHEN AND LI XIAOSHAN. A mean value calculus of durations. In A. W. Roscoe, ed., *A Classical Mind — Essays in Honour of C.A.R. Hoare*, chapter 25, pages 431–451. Prentice-Hall Intl., 1994.

ZZYL94.   ZHOU CHAOCHEN, ZHANG JINGZHONG, YANG LU, AND LI XIAOSHAN. Linear duration invariants. In Langmaack et al. [LdRV94], pages 86–109.

Towards Bounded Model Checking*
for the Universal Fragment of TCTL

Wojciech Penczek[1], Bożena Woźna[2], and Andrzej Zbrzezny[2]

[1] Institute of Computer Science, PAS
Ordona 21, 01-237 Warsaw, Poland
and
Podlasie Academy
Institute of Informatics, Siedlce, Poland
penczek@ipipan.waw.pl
[2] Institute of Mathematics and Computer Science, PU
Armii Krajowej 13/15, 42-200 Częstochowa, Poland
{b.wozna,a.zbrzezny}@wsp.czest.pl

Abstract. Bounded Model Checking (BMC) based on SAT methods consists in searching for a counterexample of a particular length and to generate a propositional formula that is satisfiable iff such a counterexample exists. Our paper shows how the concept of bounded model checking can be extended to deal with TACTL (the universal fragment of TCTL) properties of Timed Automata.

1 Introduction

Model checking [13] consists in verifying that a finite state concurrent program P satisfies a property φ (denoted $P \models \varphi$). When P is represented by its model M_P and the property φ is given by a temporal logic formula, one checks that $M_P \models \varphi$. Generating M_P for P and checking that $M_P \models \varphi$ is automated. The complexity of model checking methods strongly depends on the translation from P to M_P and on the temporal logic to which the formula φ belongs to.

Recently, the interest in automated verification is moving towards concurrent real-time systems. The properties to be verified are usually expressed in either a standard temporal logic like LTL [13] and CTL [18,19], or in its timed version like MITL [5] and TCTL [1]. The practical applicability of model checking is strongly restricted by the state explosion problem. Therefore, many different reduction techniques have been introduced in order to alleviate the state explosion. The major methods include application of partial order reductions [7,14,26,29,30,31,37,38], symmetry reductions [20], abstraction techniques [15,16], BDD-based symbolic storage methods [11,27], and SAT-related algorithms [8,12,22,33,35].

Bounded model checking (BMC) based on SAT methods has been recently introduced as a complementary technique to BDD-based symbolic model checking

* Partly supported by the State Committee for Scientific Research under the grant No. 8T11C 01419.

W. Damm and E.-R. Olderog (Eds.): FTRTFT 2002, LNCS 2469, pp. 265–288, 2002.
© Springer-Verlag Berlin Heidelberg 2002

for LTL [8,9]. An extension of the BMC method to verification of the properties expressed in ACTL has been shown for the first time in [34]. The main modification of the original algorithm for LTL consists in the translation of a model M to several symbolic paths (instead of one), which can start at arbitrary states of the model. Moreover, the translation for an ACTL formula is simpler than for LTL as there are no nested path modalities. The basic idea of BMC is to search for a counterexample of a particular length and to generate a propositional formula that is satisfiable iff such a counterexample exists. The efficiency of this method is based on an observation that if a system is faulty, then only a fragment of its state space is sufficient for finding an error [8,9,34].

In the standard approach to verification of real time systems, Timed Automata are used as model generators, whereas the properties are expressed as formulas of TCTL [1]. There are two alternative methods of building an abstract model for a Timed Automaton. The first one is based on the notion of a clock region graph [1], which is built by BFS-algorithm. The second method exploits the partitioning algorithm [2,3,36], which iteratively builds the minimal model w.r.t. the initial covering of the concrete state space.

The aim of our paper is to generalize the method of bounded model checking to verification of Timed Automata. Since the application of BMC to the whole language of CTL (so TCTL) seems to be very difficult, if not impossible, as one might need to search all the state space of the model, we consider the universal fragment of TCTL, called TACTL. Using a discretization method of [6], we translate the validity of a TACTL formula φ in the clock region model of a Timed Automaton $\mathcal{A}$ ($M_{\mathcal{A}} \models \varphi$) to a propositional formula. This formula is then tested for satisfiability using ZChaff [28,40] to verify whether $M_{\mathcal{A}} \models \varphi$. Since the length of the propositional formula is polynomial in the size of $\mathcal{A}$ and φ, the state explosion problem inherent in model checking is taken care by the efficient satisfiability solver.

The rest of the paper is organized as follows. The next section contains the discussion of the related work. Then, in section 3 Timed Automata are introduced. Logics TCTL and TACTL are defined in section 4. Section 5 defines region graphs. Bounded model checking for ACTL and TACTL is presented in the next two sections. Generalizations and further optimizations are discussed in Section 8. Section 9 contains experimental results, whereas final remarks are given in Section 10.

2   Related Work

Our paper is an extended and improved version of [33], where a general approach to applying BMC for a subset of TACTL was described.

The idea of BMC for a temporal logic is taken from the papers by Clarke et al. [8,9]. Timed Automata have been defined and investigated in many papers [1,4,36]. We adopt the definition given in [36]. Model checking for TCTL was considered by several authors using different approaches: over clock region models [1], on-the-fly [10], space-efficient [25], and over minimal models [36].

Our approach is closely related to [4] and [36], from which we draw the idea of the translation of model checking problem for TACTL to the model checking problem for *fair*-ACTL (ACTL^F). Motivation for considering only the universal fragment of CTL can be found in [21,32]. Similar arguments apply to TCTL.

3   Timed Automata

We start with introducing Timed Automata and their runs. Hereafter, $\mathbb{N} = \{0, 1, 2, \ldots\}$ denotes the set of natural numbers and $\mathbb{R}_+$ denotes the set of non-negative real numbers. Let $X = \{x_1, \ldots, x_n\}$ be a finite set of variables, called *clocks*. A *clock valuation* is a function $v : X \to \mathbb{R}_+$, assigning to each clock x a non-negative value $v(x)$. The set of all the valuations is denoted by $\mathbb{R}_+^n$. For a subset Y of X by $v[Y := 0]$ we mean the valuation v' such that $\forall x \in Y, v'(x) = 0$ and $\forall x \in X \setminus Y, v'(x) = v(x)$. For $\delta \in \mathbb{R}_+$, $v + \delta$ denotes the valuation v'' such that $\forall x \in X, v''(x) = v(x) + \delta$. The set Ψ_X of *clock constraints* over the set of clocks X is defined inductively as follows:

$$\psi := x_i \sim c \mid x_i - x_j \sim c \mid \psi \wedge \psi$$

where $x_i, x_j \in X$, $i, j \in \{1, \ldots, n\}$, $\sim \in \{\leq, <, =, >, \geq\}$, and $c \in \mathbb{N}$.

A clock valuation v *satisfies* the clock constraint $\psi \in \Psi_X$, if

$$\begin{aligned} v &\models x_i \sim c && \text{iff } v(x_i) \sim c \\ v &\models x_i - x_j \sim c && \text{iff } v(x_i) - v(x_j) \sim c \\ v &\models \psi \wedge \psi' && \text{iff } v \models \psi \text{ and } v \models \psi' \end{aligned}$$

For each $\psi \in \Psi_X$ by $\mathbb{p}(\psi)$ we denote the set of all the clock valuations satisfying ψ, i.e., $\mathbb{p}(\psi) = \{v \in \mathbb{R}_+^n \mid v \models \psi\}$. Similarly, $\mathbb{P}(\Psi_X) = \{\mathbb{p}(\psi) \subseteq \mathbb{R}_+^n \mid \psi \in \Psi_X\}$. Now, we are ready to define Timed Automata.

Definition 1. *A* timed automaton $\mathcal{A}$ *is a 6-tuple* $(\Sigma, S, s^0, E, X, \mathbb{I})$*, where* Σ *is a finite set of actions,* S *is a finite set of locations,* $s^0 \in S$ *is an initial location,* $E \subseteq S \times \Sigma \times \Psi_X \times 2^X \times S$ *is a transition relation,* X *is a finite set of clocks,* $\mathbb{I} : S \longrightarrow \Psi_X$ *is a state invariant.*

Each element e *of* E *is denoted by* $e := s \xrightarrow{l,\psi,Y} s'$*. This represents a transition from the location* s *to the location* s' *on the input action* l*. The set* $Y \subseteq X$ *gives the clocks to be reset with this transition, whereas* $\psi \in \Psi_X$ *is the enabling condition for* e*.*

Given a transition $e := s \xrightarrow{l,\psi,Y} s'$, we write $source(e)$, $target(e)$, $guard(e)$ for s, s' and ψ, respectively. The clocks of a Timed Automaton allow to express the timing properties. An enabling condition constrains the execution of a transition without forcing it to be taken. An invariant condition allows an automaton to stay at a some state only as long as the constraint is satisfied.

A (concrete) state of $\mathcal{A}$ is a pair $q = (s, v)$, where $s \in S$ and $v \in \mathbb{R}_+^n$. The set of all the concrete states is denoted by Q, i.e., $Q = S \times \mathbb{R}_+^n$. The initial state of $\mathcal{A}$ is defined as $q^0 = (s^0, v^0)$ with $v^0(x_i) = 0$ for all $x_i \in X$.

Let $l \in \Sigma$ and $\delta \in \mathbb{R}_+$. A timed consecution relation in $\mathcal{A}$ is defined by action- and time-successors as follows:

- $(s, v) \xrightarrow{l} (s', v')$ iff there is a transition $s \xrightarrow{l, \psi, Y} s' \in E$ such that $v \models \psi$ and $v' = v[Y := 0]$ and $v' \models \mathbb{I}(s')$,
- $(s, v) \xrightarrow{\delta} (s', v')$ iff $s = s'$ and $v' = v + \delta$ and $v' \models \mathbb{I}(s')$; $((s', v')$ is denoted by $(s, v) + \delta)$.

Let $q \in Q$. A q-run ρ of $\mathcal{A}$ is a maximal sequence of concrete states:
$q_0 \xrightarrow{\delta_0} q_0 + \delta_0 \xrightarrow{l_0} q_1 \xrightarrow{\delta_1} q_1 + \delta_1 \xrightarrow{l_1} q_2 \xrightarrow{\delta_2} \cdots$, where $q_0 = q$, $l_i \in \Sigma$ and $\delta_i \in \mathbb{R}_+$ for each $i \geq 0$.

A state q of $\mathcal{A}$ is a *deadlock* if there is no delay $\delta \in \mathbb{R}_+$ and an action $l \in \Sigma$ such that $q \xrightarrow{\delta} q' \xrightarrow{l} q'$, for some $q', q'' \in Q$. A run ρ has a deadlock iff there is a deadlock state in ρ. A run ρ is said to be *progressive* iff $\Sigma_{i \in \mathbb{N}} \delta_i$ is unbounded. A run ρ is said to be *maximal* iff ρ is infinite and progressive or ρ has a deadlock. A Timed Automaton is *progressive* iff all its infinite runs are progressive. For simplicity of presentation, we consider only progressive Timed Automata. Progressiveness can be checked using the sufficient conditions of [36]. In Section 8 we discuss unrestricted Timed Automata.

4   Logics TCTL and TACTL

This section defines the logic TCTL [1] and two its sublogics: TACTL and TECTL interpreted over concrete models of Timed Automata. As usual let $\mathcal{PV} = \{p_1, p_2, \ldots\}$ be a set of propositional variables.

Definition 2. *A (concrete) model for a Timed Automaton $\mathcal{A}$ is a pair $M_{\mathcal{A}} = ((Q, f, q^0), \mathcal{V})$, where $Q = S \times \mathbb{R}_+^n$ is a set of the concrete states of $\mathcal{A}$, f is a function returning a set of all the maximal q-runs for each concrete state $q \in Q$, q^0 is the initial state, $\mathcal{V} : S \longrightarrow 2^{\mathcal{PV}}$ is a valuation function.*

The formulas of TCTL are defined inductively as follows:

$$\alpha, \beta := p \mid \neg \alpha \mid \alpha \vee \beta \mid \alpha \wedge \beta \mid \mathrm{E}(\alpha \mathrm{U}_I \beta) \mid \mathrm{EG}_I \alpha,$$

where $p \in \mathcal{PV}$ and I is an interval in $\mathbb{R}_+$ with integer bounds of the form $[n, m]$, $[n, m)$, $(n, m]$, (n, m), (n, ∞), and $[n, \infty)$, for $n, m \in \mathbb{N}$.

Intuitively, E means there exists a run, $\alpha \mathrm{U}_I \beta$ is true in a run if β is true for some state within interval I and always earlier α holds.

The logic TECTL is the restriction of TCTL such that the negation can be applied only to propositions, i.e., $\neg \alpha$ is replaced by $\neg p$ above. The set of all the TECTL formulas is denoted by $\mathcal{TF}$. TACTL is the language, which can be defined by replacing each occurrence of the path quantifier E by A in the set $\mathcal{TF}$.

Let $\rho = q_0 \xrightarrow{\delta_0} q_0 + \delta_0 \xrightarrow{l_0} q_1 \xrightarrow{\delta_1} q_1 + \delta_1 \xrightarrow{l_1} q_2 \xrightarrow{\delta_2} \cdots$ be a q_0-run, $q_0 = (s_0, v_0)$, and $|\rho|$ be the length of ρ, i.e., the number of δ_i's if finite and ∞, otherwise.

$q_0 \models p$ iff $p \in \mathcal{V}(s_0)$, $q_0 \models \neg\alpha$ iff $q_0 \not\models \alpha$,

$q_0 \models \alpha \vee \beta$ iff $q_0 \models \alpha$ or $q_0 \models \beta$, $q_0 \models \alpha \wedge \beta$ iff $q_0 \models \alpha$ and $q_0 \models \beta$,

$q_0 \models \mathrm{E}(\alpha \mathrm{U}_I \beta)$ iff $\exists\, \rho \in f(q_0) \exists_{i < |\rho|+1} \; [\Sigma_{j \leq i} \delta_j \in I$ and $(q_i + \delta_i) \models \beta$ and

$$(\forall j \leq i)(\forall \delta \leq \delta_j)\, q_j + \delta \models \alpha \vee \beta],$$

$q_0 \models \mathrm{EG}_I \alpha$ iff $\exists\, \rho \in f(q_0)\, (\forall_{i < |\rho|+1})\, (\forall \delta \leq \delta_i)$with $\Sigma_{j \leq i} \delta_j \in I$, $(q_i + \delta) \models \alpha$.

Note that without a loss of generality we can define the length of a run ρ taking into account the number of time delays (δ_i) only. The action step (l_i) can be seen as a time step with $\delta_i = 0$, for $i \in \mathbb{N}$.

For model $M_{\mathcal{A}}$ and a TCTL formula φ, we say that $M_{\mathcal{A}} \models \varphi$ iff $M_{\mathcal{A}}, q^0 \models \varphi$. The *model checking* problem for TCTL is defined as follows: given a TCTL formula φ and a Timed Automaton $\mathcal{A}$ together and a valuation function $\mathcal{V}$, determine whether $M_{\mathcal{A}} \models \varphi$.

Since $M_{\mathcal{A}}$ is usually infinite, we need to define its finite abstraction, which preserves TCTL or TACTL. Such an abstraction is a region graph, which is defined in the next section.

5   Region Graphs

Given a Timed Automaton $\mathcal{A}$. Let $\Psi \subseteq \Psi_X$ be a non-empty set containing all the clock constrains occurring in any enabling condition used in the transition relation E or in a state invariant of $\mathcal{A}$. Moreover, let c_{max} be the largest constant appearing in Ψ. For $\sigma \in \mathbb{R}_+$, $frac(\sigma)$ denotes the fractional part of σ, and $\lfloor \sigma \rfloor$ denotes its integral part.

Definition 3 (Equivalence of clock valuations). *For two clock valuations v and v' in $\mathbb{R}_+^n$, $v \simeq_\Psi v'$ iff for all $x, y \in X$ the following conditions are met:*

1. *$v(x) > c_{max}$ implies $v'(x) > c_{max}$*
2. *if $v(x) \leq c_{max}$ then*
   - *a.) $\lfloor v(x) \rfloor = \lfloor v'(x) \rfloor$, and*
   - *b.) $frac(v(x)) = 0$ implies $frac(v'(x)) = 0$,*
3. *for all clock constraints of the form $x - y \sim c$ with $c \in \mathbb{N}$ and $c \leq c_{max}$, $v \models x - y \sim c$ implies $v' \models x - y \sim c$.*

We use $[v]$ to denote the equivalence class of the relation $\simeq_\Psi$ to which v belongs. Such a class is called a *zone*. The set of all the zones is denoted by $Z(n)$. A zone $[v']$ is *final* iff $v(x) > c_{max}$ for all $v \in [v']$ and $x \in X$. A zone $[v']$ is *open* if there is a clock $x \in X$ such that $v(x) > c_{max}$ for all $v \in [v']$. A zone $[v]$ *satisfies* the clock constraint $\psi \in \Psi_X$, if $[v] \models \psi$ iff $\forall v' \in [v]$, $v' \models \psi$. A *region* is a pair $(s, [v])$, where $s \in S$ and $[v] \in Z(n)$. Note that the set of all the regions is finite.

Definition 4 (Time successor). *Let $[v]$ and $[w]$ be two distinct zones. The zone $[w]$ is said to be the* time successor *of $[v]$, denoted $\tau([v])$, iff for each $v' \in [v]$ there exists $\delta \in \mathbb{R}_+$ such that $v' + \delta \in [w]$ and $v' + \delta' \in [v] \cup [w]$ for all $\delta' \leq \delta$.*

The time successor exists for every zone except for the *final* one.

Definition 5 (Action successor). *The zone* $[w]$ *is said to be the* action successor *of* $[v]$ *by a transition* $e : s \xrightarrow{l,\psi,Y} s' \in E$, *denoted* $e([v])$, *iff* $[v] \models \psi$ *and* $[w] = [v[Y := 0]]$.

Definition 6. *The* region graph *of a Timed Automaton* $\mathcal{A}$ *is a finite structure* $\mathcal{RG}(\mathcal{A}) = (\mathcal{W}, \rightarrow, w^0)$, *where* $\mathcal{W} = S \times Z(n)$, $w^0 = (s^0, [v^0])$ *and* $\rightarrow \subseteq \mathcal{W} \times (E \cup \{\tau\}) \times \mathcal{W}$ *is defined as follows:*

1. $(s, [v]) \xrightarrow{e} (s', [v'])$ *iff* $[v'] = e([v])$, $s = source(e)$, $s' = target(e)$, *and* $[v'] \models \mathbb{I}(s')$, *for* $e \in E$,
2. $(s, [v]) \xrightarrow{\tau} (s, [v'])$ *iff* $[v'] \models \mathbb{I}(s)$ *and* $([v'] = \tau([v])$ *or* $[v'] = [v]$ *if* $[v]$ *is final).*

The model based on the region graph of $\mathcal{A}$ *and a valuation function* $\mathcal{V}$ *is defined as* $(\mathcal{RG}(\mathcal{A}), \mathcal{V}')$, *where* $\mathcal{V}' : \mathcal{W} \longrightarrow 2^{\mathcal{PV}}$ *such that* $\mathcal{V}'((s, [v])) = \mathcal{V}(s)$.

6   Bounded Model Checking for TACTL

In this section we describe a method of BMC for TACTL, and show its correctness. The main idea of our method consists in translating the TACTL model checking problem to the ACTL model checking problem [1,36] and applying the bounded model checking for ACTL [34].

In general, the model checking problem for TACTL can be translated to the model checking problem for ACTL$^\mathrm{F}$ [1]. However, since we have assumed that we deal with progressive Timed Automata only, this translation can be made to the ACTL model checking [36]. The idea is as follows. Given a Timed Automaton $\mathcal{A}$, a valuation function $\mathcal{V}$, and a TACTL formula ψ. First we extend $\mathcal{A}$ with a set of new clocks, to obtain a new automaton $\mathcal{A}'$. Then we construct the region graph for $\mathcal{A}'$ and ψ, and augment the valuation function $\mathcal{V}$. Finally we transform ψ to the ACTL formula ψ'.

More precisely, let X be the set of clocks of $\mathcal{A}$, and $\{I_1, \ldots, I_m\}$ be a set of the non-trivial intervals appearing in ψ. The automaton $\mathcal{A}'$ is like $\mathcal{A}$ except for the set of clocks X', which is defined as follows. $X' = X \cup \{x_{n+1}, \ldots, x_{n+m}\}$, i.e., $X' = \{x_1, \ldots, x_{n+m}\}$. Let $\mathcal{RG}(\mathcal{A}', \psi) = (\mathcal{W}, \rightarrow, w^0)$ be a region graph for $\mathcal{A}'$ and ψ. The set of propositional variables $\mathcal{PV}'$ and the valuation function $\mathcal{V}'$ augments $\mathcal{PV}$ and $\mathcal{V}$ as follows. By $p_{x_{n+i}=0}$ and $p_{x_{n+i} \in I_i}$ we denote the new propositions for every interval I_i appearing in ψ and by $\mathcal{PV}_X$ the set of these propositions. The proposition $p_{x_{n+i}=0}$ is true at a state $(s, [v])$ of $\mathcal{RG}(\mathcal{A}', \psi)$ if $(\exists v' \in [v])v'(x_{n+i}) = 0$. The proposition $p_{x_{n+i} \in I_i}$ is true at a state $(s, [v])$ of $\mathcal{RG}(\mathcal{A}', \psi)$ if $(\exists v' \in [v])$ $v'(x_{n+i}) \in I_i$. Let $\mathcal{V}_X$ be the function labeling each state of the graph $\mathcal{RG}(\mathcal{A}', \psi)$ with the set of propositions from $\mathcal{PV}_X$ true at that state. Let $\mathcal{PV}' = \mathcal{PV} \cup \mathcal{PV}_X$. We define the valuation function $\mathcal{V}' : \mathcal{W} \rightarrow 2^{\mathcal{PV}'}$ as follows: $\mathcal{V}'((s, [v])) = \mathcal{V}(s) \cup \mathcal{V}_X((s, [v]))$.

Since the bounded model checking method consists in searching for counterexamples, in practice we check the validity of the negation of a tested formula. Therefore, here we give a translation of a TECTL formula φ to an ECTL formula (instead of the TACTL formula $\psi = \neg\varphi$). Then, we show the semantics of the formula φ defined over a model based on the region graph $\mathcal{RG}(\mathcal{A}', \varphi)$.

A TECTL formula φ is translated inductively to the ECTL formula φ' as follows:

- $p \in \mathcal{PV}$ is translated to p,
- $\alpha \vee \beta$ is translated to $\alpha' \vee \beta'$,
- $\alpha \wedge \beta$ is translated to $\alpha' \wedge \beta'$,
- $\mathrm{EG}_{I_r}\alpha$ is translated to $\mathrm{EG}(\alpha' \vee \neg p_{x_{n+r} \in I_r})$,
- $\mathrm{E}(\alpha\mathrm{U}_{I_r}\beta)$ is translated to $\mathrm{E}((\alpha' \vee (\beta' \wedge p_{x_{n+r} \in I_r}))\mathrm{U}(\beta' \wedge p_{x_{n+r} \in I_r}))$.

Definition 7 (Semantics). *Let $M = ((\mathcal{W}, \rightarrow, w^0), \mathcal{V}')$ be a model based on the region graph $\mathcal{RG}(\mathcal{A}', \varphi)$ and φ be TECTL formulas. A path in M is a maximal sequence $\pi = (w_0, w_1, \cdots)$ of states such that $w_i \rightarrow w_{i+1}$ for each $i < |\pi|$, where $|\pi|$ is the length of π, i.e., the number of its states when finite and ∞ when infinite. For a path $\pi = (w_0, w_1, \cdots)$, let $\pi(i) = w_i$, for each $i \in |\pi|$. $M, (s, [v]) \models \varphi$ denotes that φ is true at the state $(s, [v])$ of M. M is omitted if it is implicitly understood. Let $[v_r]$ denote $[v[x_{n+r} := 0]]$, for $r \in \{1, \ldots, m\}$. The relation $\models$ is defined inductively as follows:*

$(s, [v]) \models p$ *iff* $p \in \mathcal{V}'((s, [v]))$, $(s, [v]) \models \alpha \vee \beta$ *iff* $(s, [v]) \models \alpha$ *or* $(s, [v]) \models \beta$,

$(s, [v]) \models \neg p$ *iff* $p \notin \mathcal{V}'((s, [v]))$, $(s, [v]) \models \alpha \wedge \beta$ *iff* $(s, [v]) \models \alpha$ *and* $(s, [v]) \models \beta$,

$(s, [v]) \models \mathrm{EG}_{I_r}\alpha$ *iff* $\exists\pi[\pi(0) = (s, [v_r])$ *and* $\forall_{j<|\pi|}\pi(j) \models (\alpha \vee \neg p_{x_{n+r} \in I_r})]$,

$(s, [v]) \models \mathrm{E}(\alpha\mathrm{U}_{I_r}\beta)$ *iff* $\begin{cases} \exists\pi[\pi(0) = (s, [v_r]) \text{ and } \exists_{j<|\pi|}(\pi(j) \models (\beta \wedge p_{x_{n+r} \in I_r}) \\ \text{and } \forall_{0 \le i < j}\pi(i) \models (\alpha \vee (\beta \wedge p_{x_{n+r} \in I_r})))]. \end{cases}$

Definition 8 (Validity). *A TECTL formula φ is valid in $M = ((\mathcal{W}, \rightarrow, w^0), \mathcal{V}')$ (denoted $M \models \varphi$) iff $M, w^0 \models \varphi$.*

It is easy to show that the validity over the model based on the region graph is equivalent to the validity over the concrete model, i.e., $M \models \varphi$ iff $M_{\mathcal{A}} \models \varphi$, for each $\varphi \in$ TECTL (see [36]).

In order to deal with the bounded model checking method, we have to define the bounded semantics, which allows us to interpret the formulas over a fragment of the considered model only. For that purpose we need the definitions of a k–path, a loop, and a k–model.

Definition 9 (k–path). *Let $M = ((\mathcal{W}, \rightarrow, w^0), \mathcal{V}')$ be a model based on the region graph $\mathcal{RG}(\mathcal{A}', \varphi)$ and $k \in \mathbb{N}$. A k-path is a finite sequence $\pi = (w_0, \cdots, w_k)$ of states of $\mathcal{W}$ such that $w_i \rightarrow w_{i+1}$ for each $0 \le i < k$.*

Though a k–path is finite, it still can represent an infinite path if there is a *back loop* from the last state of the k–path to any of the previous states.

Definition 10 (loop). *We call a k–path π a loop if $\pi(k) \rightarrow \pi(l)$ for some $0 \le l \le k$.*

Definition 11 (k–model). *Let $M = ((\mathcal{W}, \rightarrow, w^0), \mathcal{V}')$ be a model and $k \in \mathbb{N}$. The k–model for M is a structure $M_k = ((\mathcal{W}, Path_k, w^0), \mathcal{V}')$, where $Path_k$ is the set of all the k–paths of M.*

For a subset $Path' \subseteq Path_k$ we define

$$States(Path') = \{w \in W \mid (\exists \pi \in Path')(\exists i \leq k) \, \pi(i) = w\}.$$

Definition 12. *Let* $M_k = ((W, Path_k, w^0), V')$ *be a* k-*model of* M. *A structure* $M'_k = ((W', Path'_k, w^0), V'|_{W'})$ *is a submodel of* M_k *if* $Path'_k \subseteq Path_k$, $W' = States(Path'_k)$.

Similarly to the ACTL case, described in [35], we define the bounded semantics for TECTL formulas φ over k-models M_k of M (submodels M'_k of M_k).

Definition 13 (Bounded semantics). *Let* M_k *be a* $k-$*model and* α, β *be* TECTL *formulas.* $M_k, (s, [v]) \models \alpha$ *denotes that* α *is true at the state* $(s, [v])$ *of* M_k. M_k *is omitted if it is implicitly understood. Let* $[v_r]$ *denote* $[v[x_{n+r} := 0]]$, $\alpha_r = (\alpha \vee \neg p_{x_{n+r} \in I_r})$, *and* $\beta_r = (\beta \wedge p_{x_{n+r} \in I_r})$, *for* $r \in \{1, \ldots, m\}$. *The relation* $\models$ *is defined inductively as follows:*

$(s, [v]) \models p$ *iff* $p \in V'((s, [v]))$, $(s, [v]) \models \alpha \vee \beta$ *iff* $(s, [v]) \models \alpha$ *or* $(s, [v]) \models \beta$,

$(s, [v]) \models \neg p$ *iff* $p \notin V'((s, [v]))$, $(s, [v]) \models \alpha \wedge \beta$ *iff* $(s, [v]) \models \alpha$ *and* $(s, [v]) \models \beta$,

$(s, [v]) \models \text{EG}_{I_r}\alpha$ *iff* $\begin{cases} \exists \pi \in Path_k [\pi(0) = (s, [v_r]) \text{ and } \forall_{0 \leq j \leq k}\pi(j) \models \alpha_r], \\ \text{if } \pi \text{ is a loop or } \pi(k) \text{ is a deadlock,} \\ false, \quad otherwise, \end{cases}$

$(s, [v]) \models \text{E}(\alpha \text{U}_{I_r}\beta)$ *iff* $\begin{cases} \exists \pi \in Path_k [\pi(0) = (s, [v_r]) \text{ and } \exists_{0 \leq j \leq k}(\pi(j) \models \beta_r \text{ and} \\ \forall_{0 \leq i < j}\pi(i) \models (\alpha \vee \beta_r)]. \end{cases}$

Definition 14 (Validity for Bounded Semantics). *A* TECTL *formula* φ *is valid in a* k-*model* M_k *(denoted* $M \models_k \varphi$*) iff* $M_k, w^0 \models \varphi$.

Hereafter, let $|M|$ denote the number of states of the model M.
The main theorem of this section states that we can always find a bound k of M such that $M \models_k \varphi$ is equivalent to $M \models \varphi$.

Theorem 1. *Let* M *be a model and* φ *be a* TECTL *formula.* $M \models \varphi$ *iff there is* $k \in \{0, \ldots, |M|\}$ *such that* $M \models_k \varphi$.

Proof (Sketch). Follows from the following facts:

- The model checking problem of TECTL can be translated to the model checking problem for ECTL^F [1,36].
- Since we have assumed that we deal with progressive Timed Automata only, the above translation can be made to the ECTL model checking.
- By Theorem 1 of [35] we can always find a bound $k \leq |M|$ such that the bounded and unbounded validity for ECTL are equivalent.

Now, we define a function f_k, which determines the number of the k-paths of a submodel M'_k, which is sufficient for checking a TECTL formula.

Definition 15. *Define a function* $f_k : \mathcal{TF} \to \mathbb{N}$ *as follows:*

- $f_k(p) = f_k(\neg p) = 0$, *where* $p \in \mathcal{PV}'$

$$- f_k(\alpha \vee \beta) = max\{f_k(\alpha), f_k(\beta)\}$$
$$- f_k(\alpha \wedge \beta) = f_k(\alpha) + f_k(\beta)$$
$$- f_k(EG_I\alpha) = (k+1) \cdot f_k(\alpha) + 1$$
$$- f_k(E(\alpha U_I\beta)) = k \cdot f_k(\alpha) + f_k(\beta) + 1$$

Now, we can present a BMC method for TACTL.
Let $M = ((\mathcal{W}, \rightarrow, w^0), \mathcal{V}')$ be the model based on $\mathcal{RG}(\mathcal{A}', \psi)$ for a TACTL formula ψ. To answer the question whether $M \not\models \psi$, we use the following algorithm:

1. Let $\varphi = \neg\psi$ be a TECTL formula,
2. Iterate for $k := 1$ to $|M|$.
3. Select the $k-$model M_k of M.
4. Select the submodels M'_k of M_k with $|Path'_k| \leq f_k(\varphi)$, where f_k is a function of k and φ (see Definition 15).
5. Translate the transition relation of the $k-$paths of all of the submodels M'_k to a propositional formula $[M^{\varphi,w^0}]_k$.
6. Translate φ over all M'_k to a propositional formula $[\varphi]_{M_k}$.
7. Check the satisfiability of $[M, \varphi]_k := [M^{\varphi,w^0}]_k \wedge [\varphi]_{M_k}$.

Hence, checking φ over M_k is translated to checking the satisfiability of the propositional formula $[M^{\varphi,w^0}]_k \wedge [\varphi]_{M_k}$. So that one can use the most efficient algorithms for solving the SAT-problem.

We assume that $\mathcal{W} \subseteq \{0,1\}^n$ and $n = \lceil log_2(|\mathcal{W}|) \rceil$. So, each state can be represented by a vector of state variables $\boldsymbol{w} = (\boldsymbol{w}[1], \ldots, \boldsymbol{w}[n])$, where $\boldsymbol{w}[i]$ is a propositional variable for $i = 1, \ldots, n$. Moreover, a finite sequence $\boldsymbol{w}_0, \ldots, \boldsymbol{w}_k$ of vectors of state variables we call a *symbolic $k-$path*.

Hereafter, let $\mathcal{SV}$ be a set of the state variables containing the symbols *true* and *false*, and let $\mathcal{SF}$ be a set of propositional formulas built over $\mathcal{SV}$. Moreover, let $LL^\varphi \subset \mathbb{N}_+$ be a finite set of natural numbers. The elements of LL^φ are used as the indices of the symbolic $k-$paths used for translating the transition relation of the submodels M'_k.

To construct $[M, \varphi]_k$, we first define a propositional formula $[M^{\varphi,w^0}]_k$ that constrains $|LL^\varphi|$ symbolic k-paths to represent k-paths of M_k. For $j \in LL^\varphi$, the j-th symbolic $k-$path is denoted by $\boldsymbol{w}_{0,j}, \ldots, \boldsymbol{w}_{k,j}$, where $\boldsymbol{w}_{i,j}$, for $i = 1, \ldots, k$, are vectors of state variables. Then, we translate the TECTL formula φ to a propositional formula that constrains the sets of $|LL^\varphi|$ symbolic k-paths that satisfy φ.

Let $lit : \mathcal{SV} \times \{0,1\} \rightarrow \mathcal{SF}$ be a function defined as follows: $lit(r, 0) = \neg r$ and $lit(r, 1) = r$. Furthermore, let $\boldsymbol{w}, \boldsymbol{w}'$ be vectors of state variables. We define the following propositional formulas:

$-$ $dead(\boldsymbol{w})$ iff $\boldsymbol{w}$ is a deadlock,
$-$ $I_w(\boldsymbol{w})$ iff $\bigwedge_{i=1}^n lit(\boldsymbol{w}[i], w[i])$; encodes a state w of the model M,
$-$ $T(\boldsymbol{w}, \boldsymbol{w}')$ iff $\boldsymbol{w} \rightarrow \boldsymbol{w}'$ or $(dead(\boldsymbol{w}) \wedge \boldsymbol{w} = \boldsymbol{w}')$,
$-$ $p(\boldsymbol{w})$ iff $p \in \mathcal{V}'(\boldsymbol{w})$, for $p \in \mathcal{PV}'$,
$-$ $H(\boldsymbol{w}, \boldsymbol{w}')$ iff $\boldsymbol{w} = \boldsymbol{w}'$,

- $L_{k,j}(l)$ iff $T(\boldsymbol{w}_{k,j}, \boldsymbol{w}_{l,j})$; encodes a backward loop from the k-th state to the l-th state in the symbolic k-path j, for $0 \le l \le k$.

Definition 16. *Let M be a model, w be a state of M and φ be a TECTL formula. The propositional formula $[M^{\varphi,w}]_k$, for $|LL^\varphi| = f_k(\varphi)$, is defined as follows:*

$$[M^{\varphi,w}]_k := I_w(\boldsymbol{w}_{0,0}) \wedge \bigwedge_{j \in LL^\varphi} \Big(\bigwedge_{i=0}^{k-1} T(\boldsymbol{w}_{i,j}, \boldsymbol{w}_{i+1,j}) \Big)$$

where $\boldsymbol{w}_{0,0}$ and $\boldsymbol{w}_{i,j}$ for $i = 0, \dots, k$ and $j \in LL^\varphi$ are vectors of state variables.

The above formula encodes all the k-paths generated by the transition relation T, as well as the initial vector $\boldsymbol{w}_{0,0}$ to be equal to w.

By $\boldsymbol{w}_{m_r,n_r}$ we denote the vector of state variables representing the states that are like the ones represented by $\boldsymbol{w}_{m,n}$ except for the value of the clock x_{n+r}, which is reset to 0. The translation of a TECTL formula is similar to the untimed case, since all the temporal subformulas of φ are interpreted at the initial states of the considered new k-paths starting at states $\boldsymbol{w}_{m_r,n_r}$. This means that no loop can return to a state preceding the present state.

We use $[\varphi]_k^{[m,n]}$ to denote the translation of a TECTL formula φ at $\boldsymbol{w}_{m,n}$ to a propositional formula.

(1) Translation of a TECTL formula

$[p]_k^{[m,n]} := p(\boldsymbol{w}_{m,n})$, $[\alpha \wedge \beta]_k^{[m,n]} := [\alpha]_k^{[m,n]} \wedge [\beta]_k^{[m,n]}$,

$[\neg p]_k^{[m,n]} := \neg p(\boldsymbol{w}_{m,n})$, $[\alpha \vee \beta]_k^{[m,n]} := [\alpha]_k^{[m,n]} \vee [\beta]_k^{[m,n]}$,

$[\mathrm{E}(\alpha \mathrm{U}_{I_r} \beta)]_k^{[m,n]} := (let \ \beta' := \beta \wedge p_{x_{n+r} \in I_r})$
$$\bigvee_{i \in LL^\varphi} \Big(H(\boldsymbol{w}_{m_r,n_r}, \boldsymbol{w}_{0,i}) \wedge \bigvee_{j=0}^{k} ([\beta']_k^{[j,i]} \wedge \bigwedge_{t=0}^{j-1} [\alpha \vee \beta']_k^{[t,i]}) \Big),$$

$[\mathrm{EG}_{I_r} \alpha]_k^{[m,n]} := (let \ \alpha' := \alpha \vee \neg p_{x_{n+r} \in I_r}) \ \bigvee_{i \in LL^\varphi} \Big(H(\boldsymbol{w}_{m_r,n_r}, \boldsymbol{w}_{0,i}) \wedge$
$$\Big(\bigvee_{l=0}^{k} L_{k,i}(l) \vee dead(w_{k,i}) \Big) \wedge \bigwedge_{j=0}^{k} [\alpha']_k^{[j,i]} \Big).$$

Let $[\varphi]_{M_k}$ denote $[\varphi]_k^{[0,0]}$.

The following theorem shows the correctness of our translation.

Theorem 2. *Let $M = ((\mathcal{W}, \rightarrow, w^0), \mathcal{V}')$ be a model, M_k be a k-model of M, and φ be a TECTL formula. Then, $M \models_k \varphi$ iff $[\varphi]_{M_k} \wedge [M^{\varphi,w^0}]_k$ is satisfiable.*

Proof (Sketch). Follows from the following facts:

- The model checking problem of TECTL can be translated to the model checking problem for ECTL^F [1,36].
- Since we deal with progressive Timed Automata only, the above translation can be made to ECTL model checking. Our definition of the Translation (1) is based on this translation.
- Theorem 2 of [35] shows that the translation of the model checking problem for ECTL to the SAT problem is correct.

Corollary 1. $M \models_k \neg\varphi$ iff $[\varphi]_{M_k} \wedge [M^{\varphi,w^0}]_k$ is unsatisfiable for $k = |M|$.

7 Implementation of BMC for Timed Automata

In this section we show how BMC can be applied to verification of *Timed Automata*. Following [6], we consider Timed Automata satisfying the following two conditions (**): the space of clocks valuations is bounded by some $c \in \mathbb{N}$, (i.e., range over $C^n = [0, c)^n$) and there is at most one transition associated with every pair of states. The readers can convince themselves that it costs few states to convert any Timed Automaton into one satisfying these properties [6].

Two clock valuations $v = (\lfloor v_1 \rfloor + frac(v_1), \ldots, \lfloor v_n \rfloor + frac(v_n))$ and $v' = (\lfloor v'_1 \rfloor + frac(v'_1), \ldots, \lfloor v'_n \rfloor + frac(v'_n))$ are *zone-equivalent*, written $v \simeq v'$, if

$$\bigwedge_{i=1}^{n} \left((\lfloor v'_i \rfloor = \lfloor v_i \rfloor) \wedge ((frac(v'_i) = 0) \Leftrightarrow (frac(v_i) = 0)) \right) \wedge$$
$$\bigwedge_{i,j \in \{1,\ldots,n\}} \left((frac(v_i) \le frac(v_j)) \Leftrightarrow (frac(v'_i) \le frac(v'_j)) \right)$$

Since the clock valuations are bounded by c, it is obvious that the above definition is equivalent to the Definition 3.

To implement BMC for Timed Automata we have to encode both the transition relation of the region graph of a Timed Automaton and the TECTL formula by propositional formulas. The encoding of the formula was discussed in the previous section. This section shows the encoding of the transition relation.

The method is based on the *discretization* scheme of [6], which preserves the qualitative behaviour of the automaton. Below, we present the above scheme consisting in representing each region of the region graph by one or more appropriately chosen representative states. The set of the representatives of a region is obtained by discretizing the space of clock valuations as follows.

Let $\Delta = 1/(2n)$ be a discretization step and $\widetilde{C} = \{m\Delta \mid 0 \le m < 2nc\}$. In other words, we cut every unit interval into $2n$ equal segments and pick the endpoints. The discretized clock space (the domain over which discretized clocks range is $\widetilde{\mathbb{B}^n} = \widetilde{C^n} \cap \{(v_1, \ldots, v_n) \mid \forall_{i,j \in \{1,\ldots,n\}} |v_i - v_j| = 2m\Delta, \ m \ge 0\}$.

Note that we take from $\widetilde{C^n}$ only points such that the difference between any pair of clock valuations is an even multiple of Δ (see Figure 1).

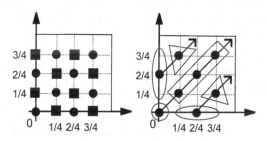

Fig. 1. Left: discretizing $[0, 1)^2$: the circle points are the elements of $\widetilde{\mathbb{B}^n}$ while the squared points belong to $\widetilde{C^n} \setminus \widetilde{\mathbb{B}^n}$. Right: illustration of the Definition 17 and Lemma 2.

For any zone Z, its discretization is defined as $\widetilde{Z} = Z \cap \widetilde{\mathbb{B}^n}$. A discretized zone is called a $d-zone$. It is not hard to see that, for every zone Z, we have $Z \neq \emptyset$ iff $\widetilde{Z} \neq \emptyset$. Another important property of this scheme is the following:

Lemma 1 ([6]). *Let $v = \widetilde{v} + \epsilon$, for some $\widetilde{v} \in \widetilde{\mathbb{B}^n}$ and $|\epsilon| < \Delta$. Then, $v \in Z \Rightarrow$ $(\widetilde{v} \in Z \vee \widetilde{v} + \Delta \in Z)$. (Hence at least one of them belongs also to $\widetilde{Z}$).*

Note that this fails to be true for points outside $\widetilde{\mathbb{B}^n}$. Consider $v = (0, \frac{3}{4})$ and zone $Z = (0 < x < 1) \wedge (0 < y < 1) \wedge (y > x)$. Here $v + \epsilon \in Z$ but neither v nor $v + \Delta = (\frac{1}{4}, 1)$ belong to Z.

The *Discrete Time Successor* of $\widetilde{Z}$, denoted by $\tau(\widetilde{Z})$, is the restriction of $\tau(Z)$ to points in $\widetilde{\mathbb{B}^n}$ and times values in $\widetilde{C}$.

Definition 17 (Discrete Time Successor). *Let $\widetilde{Z}$, $\widetilde{Z}'$ be two distinct d-zones. The d-zone $\widetilde{Z}'$ is the discrete time successor of $\widetilde{Z}$ iff for each $v \in \widetilde{Z}$ there exists $\delta \in \widetilde{C}$ such that $v + \delta \in \widetilde{Z}'$ and $v + \delta' \in \widetilde{Z} \cup \widetilde{Z}'$ for all $\delta' \in \widetilde{C}$ with $\delta' \leq \delta$.*

Lemma 2 ([6]. Discretization Preserves Time Successor). *For every zone Z and Z' if $Z' = \tau(Z)$, then $\widetilde{Z}' = \tau(\widetilde{Z})$.*

Obviously, the reverse of Lemma 2 also holds.
Below we show that it is sufficient to represent each zone by one representative.

Lemma 3. *Let $\widetilde{Z}$, $\widetilde{Z}'$ be two distinct d-zones and $v \in \widetilde{Z}$ be any representative of $\widetilde{Z}$. $\widetilde{Z}' = \tau(\widetilde{Z})$ iff there exists $\delta \in \widetilde{C}$ such that $v + \delta \in \widetilde{Z}'$ and $v + \delta' \in \widetilde{Z} \cup \widetilde{Z}'$ for all $\delta' \in \widetilde{C}$ with $\delta' \leq \delta$.*

Proof. (=>) The proof is obvious.
(<=) Let $v = (v_1, \ldots, v_n) \in \widetilde{Z}$ and there exists $\delta \in \widetilde{C}$ such that $v + \delta \in \widetilde{Z}'$ and $v + \delta' \in \widetilde{Z} \cup \widetilde{Z}'$ for all $\delta' \in \widetilde{C}$ with $\delta' \leq \delta$. We show, that $\widetilde{Z}' = \tau(\widetilde{Z})$.

Let $u = (u_1, \ldots, u_n) \in \widetilde{Z}$ and $u \neq v$. Since u and v belong to the same d-zone $\widetilde{Z}$, then their integral parts are equal and also the ordering of the fractional parts is the same. Moreover, for all $i \in \{1, \ldots, n\}$ we have $0 \leq |v_i - u_i| < 1$ (i.e., $0 \leq |frac(v_i) - frac(u_i)| < 1$) and $frac(v_i) - frac(u_i) = m\Delta$ for $m \in \{-2n + 1, \ldots, 2n - 1\}$. Hence, $frac(v_i) = frac(u_i) + m\Delta$ for all $i \in \{1, \ldots, n\}$. Therefore, $v + \delta = (v_1 + \delta, \ldots, v_n + \delta) = (u_1 + m\Delta + \delta, \ldots, u_n + m\Delta + \delta) = u + (m\Delta + \delta)$. Since $v + \delta \in \widetilde{Z}'$, then $u + (m\Delta + \delta) \in \widetilde{Z}'$. Let $\delta_1 = (m\Delta + \delta)$. It is obvious, that $u + \delta'_1 \in \widetilde{Z} \cup \widetilde{Z}'$ for all $\delta'_1 \in \widetilde{C}$ with $\delta'_1 \leq \delta_1$. Since u has been an arbitrary valuation different from v, we conclude that $\widetilde{Z}' = \tau(\widetilde{Z})$.

This discretization is not closed under the reset of the values of the clocks - for example, resetting the first coordinate of $(\Delta, \Delta) \in \widetilde{\mathbb{B}^2}$ we obtain $(0, \Delta) \in \widetilde{C^2} \backslash \widetilde{\mathbb{B}^2}$. This is important, because Lemma 2 does not hold on $\widetilde{C^n}$, but only on $\widetilde{\mathbb{B}^n}$. In order to calculate the *Discrete Action Successors* of a d-zone $\widetilde{Z}$ we delete points of $\widetilde{Z}$ that went out of $\widetilde{\mathbb{B}^n}$ and add one or more zone-equivalent points from $\widetilde{\mathbb{B}^n}$.

Before we give the definition of the discrete action successors, we define the following operations on zones and its discretization:
$$Z[Y := 0] = \{v[Y := 0] \mid v \in Z\}, \quad \widetilde{Z}[Y := 0] = \{v[Y := 0] \mid v \in \widetilde{Z}\}.$$

Note that $\widetilde{Z}[Y := 0]$ is a subset of $\widetilde{C^n}$, but not necessarily a subset of $\widetilde{\mathbb{B}^n}$.

Definition 18 (Discrete Action Successor). *Let* $\widetilde{Z}$, $\widetilde{Z'}$ *be two d-zones. The d-zone* $\widetilde{Z'}$ *is said to be the discrete action successor of d-zone* $\widetilde{Z}$ *by transition* $e : s \xrightarrow{l, \psi, Y} s' \in E$ *(denoted* $e(\widetilde{Z})$*) iff* $\widetilde{Z} \subseteq \mathbb{p}(\psi)$ *and* $e(\widetilde{Z}) = \{v' \in \widetilde{\mathbb{B}^n} \mid v' \simeq v$ *and* $v \in \widetilde{Z}[Y := 0]\}$.

Note that $e(\widetilde{Z}) = e(Z) \cap \widetilde{\mathbb{B}^n}$.

Lemma 4 (Discretization for Action Successor). *For every zone* Z *and* Z' *if* $Z' = e(Z)$, *then* $\widetilde{Z'} = e(\widetilde{Z})$.

Proof. Let $Z' = e(Z)$. By the definition of the Action Successor, Z' is the action successor of Z by the transition $e : s \xrightarrow{l, \psi, Y} s' \in E$, iff $Z \subseteq \mathbb{p}(\psi)$ and $Z' = Z[Y := 0]$. Since, $\widetilde{Z} \subseteq Z$ and $\widetilde{\mathbb{p}(\psi)} \subseteq \mathbb{p}(\psi)$, it is obvious that $\widetilde{Z} \subseteq \mathbb{p}(\psi)$. Now, we show that $\widetilde{Z'} = e(\widetilde{Z})$.

$(e(\widetilde{Z}) \subseteq \widetilde{Z'})$ Let $v' \in e(\widetilde{Z})$. By Definition 18 there is $v \in \widetilde{Z}[Y := 0]$ such that $v \simeq v'$. Hence, by discretization $v \in \widetilde{Z'}$.

$(\widetilde{Z'} \subseteq e(\widetilde{Z}))$ Let $v' \in \widetilde{Z'}$. By discretization and by assumption $Z' = e(Z)$, we have that $v' \in e(Z) \cap \widetilde{\mathbb{B}^n}$. Thus, $v' \in e(Z)$ and $v' \in \widetilde{\mathbb{B}^n}$. Since $v' \in e(Z)$, $v' = v[Y := 0]$ for some $v \in Z$. So, it is clear that $v' \in Z[Y := 0]$. Therefore, from $v' \in \widetilde{\mathbb{B}^n}$ and $v' \in Z[Y := 0]$, it follows that $v' \in Z[Y := 0] \cap \widetilde{\mathbb{B}^n}$. So, $v' \in e(\widetilde{Z})$.

Obviously, the reverse of Lemma 4 also holds.

We are given a Timed Automaton $\mathcal{A} = (\Sigma, S, s^0, E, X, \mathbb{I})$, a valuation function $\mathcal{V}$, and a TECTL formula φ. We assume that $\mathcal{A}$ is progressive and satisfies the conditions (**). Let $\mathcal{A}''$ be the Timed Automaton like $\mathcal{A}'$ defined in Section 6, but converted to satisfy the conditions (**) [1].

Hereafter, we assume that $\mathcal{A}''$ has altogether n clocks and $\widetilde{\mathcal{A}''}$ denotes the automaton $\mathcal{A}''$ with the discretized clock space. Let M be the model based on the region graph of $\mathcal{A}''$ and φ.

Definition 19. *The region graph for the Timed Automaton* $\widetilde{\mathcal{A}''}$ *and* φ *is a finite structure* $\widetilde{\mathcal{RG}}(\widetilde{\mathcal{A}''}, \varphi) = (\widetilde{W}, \rightarrow, \widetilde{w^0})$, *where* $\widetilde{W} = \{(s, \widetilde{Z}) \mid (s, Z) \in S \times Z(n)\}$, $\widetilde{w^0} = (s^0, \widetilde{Z^0})$, *where* $Z^0 = [v^0]$ *and* $\rightarrow \subseteq \widetilde{W} \times (E \cup \{\tau\}) \times \widetilde{W}$ *is defined as follows:*

- $(s, \widetilde{Z}) \xrightarrow{e} (s', \widetilde{Z'})$ *iff* $\widetilde{Z'} = e(\widetilde{Z})$, $s = source(e)$, $s' = target(e)$, *and* $\widetilde{Z'} \subseteq \mathbb{p}(\mathbb{I}(s')) \cap \widetilde{\mathbb{B}^n}$, *for* $e \in E$,
- $(s, \widetilde{Z}) \xrightarrow{\tau} (s, \widetilde{Z'})$ *iff* $\widetilde{Z'} \subseteq \mathbb{p}(\mathbb{I}(s)) \cap \widetilde{\mathbb{B}^n}$ *and* $\widetilde{Z'} = \tau(\widetilde{Z})$.

---

[1] This conversion is usually not necessary as we state in Section 8

The discretized model based on the region graph of $\widetilde{\mathcal{A}''}$ and a TECTL formula φ is defined as $\widetilde{M} = (\widetilde{\mathcal{RG}}(\widetilde{\mathcal{A}''}, \varphi), \widetilde{\mathcal{V}''})$, where $\widetilde{\mathcal{V}''} : \widetilde{\mathcal{W}} \longrightarrow 2^{\mathcal{PV'}}$ with $\widetilde{\mathcal{V}''}((s, \widetilde{Z})) = \mathcal{V}''((s, Z))$, where $\mathcal{V}''$ is the valuation function for $\mathcal{A}''$, defined like $\mathcal{V}'$ for $\mathcal{A}'$ in Section 6.

Since the discretized model $\widetilde{M}$ is isomorphic with the model M for $\mathcal{A}''$ and φ, we have $\widetilde{M} \models_k \varphi$ iff $M \models_k \varphi$, for TECTL formula φ.

Now, we can construct a propositional formula $[\widetilde{M}, \varphi]_k$ that is satisfiable iff $\widetilde{M} \models_k \varphi$. An implementation of $[\widetilde{M}, \varphi]_k$ is shown in the appendix.

8   Generalizations and Further Optimizations

As to unrestricted Timed Automata we can reduce the verification of TECTL formulas to progressive runs only, by defining the translation from TECTL to ECTL^{F}, i.e., the fair version of ECTL, and adapting the translation from ECTL to SAT to deal with the fair paths.

While we construct the automaton $\mathcal{A}'$ we add the new m clocks, which correspond to the non-trivial intervals appearing in φ. Since these clocks are never reset the valuations of them are unbounded. It is however not necessary to convert $\mathcal{A}'$ to an automaton with the bounded clock space. Note that in our bounded semantics the valuations of the clocks are always bounded. However, dealing directly with the unconverted $\mathcal{A}'$ has a problem of not closing loops by time successors. This can be compensated by using one of the following two methods.

The first method relies on freezing the value of each new clock x_i when x_i exceeds the maximal integer bound of the interval I_i. An alternative solution can be applied when checking formulas indexed with intervals of the form $(a, b), (a, b], [a, b)$ or $[a, b]$. To each location of $\mathcal{A}'$ we add the self-loop with the enabling conditions ψ defined as follows. Let b_i be the right bound of the interval I_i, and $N_{X' \setminus X}$ be a set of indices of the clocks from $X' \setminus X$. Then, $\psi := \bigwedge_{i \in N_{X' \setminus X}} x_i \geq b_i$. For our example, we have used the latter solution.

In the final version of the implementation we are going to use the former method, which allows to encode and discretize open zones. Then, we would not need to convert Timed Automata to satisfy the conditions (**), avoiding an increase in the number of state variables.

It is known that some aggregation of time successors can be made in the region graph model [25] without influencing the validity of a tested formula. This allows to find counterexamples on shorter paths.

9   Experimental Results

We have implemented a model checker BBMC based on bounded model checking for TACTL. For input consisting of a description of a Timed Automaton $\mathcal{A}$ and a TACTL formula ψ expressing some desired specification, BBMC first negates the formula ψ obtaining the TECTL formula φ. Then, it builds the propositional formula $\mu = [\varphi]_{M_k} \wedge [M^{\varphi,w^0}]_k$, which is satisfiable iff the formula φ is valid in the model of $\mathcal{A}'$. Given the formula μ, the model checker outputs the set of clauses C. Each clause is a set of literals, where each literal is either a positive or a negative propositional variable. Notice, that the size of the set C can be exponential with respect to the size of μ. In order to avoid the exponential explosion we use a structure preserving transformation, such that the resulting set C is satisfiable iff the formula μ is satisfiable, although C is not logically equivalent to the original formula μ.

The output format for the set of clauses C generated by our model checker is in the DIMACS format [23] for satisfiability problems. We have made use of the satisfiability solver ZChaff [28,39,40], which uses the DIMACS format. It is an implementation of the Chaff solver, maintained by Lintao Zhang. ZChaff is known to solve problems with more than one million variables and 10 million clauses.

We have performed our experiments on the IBM PC compatible computer equipped with the processor AMD Duron 800 MHz, 256 MB main memory and the operating system Windows 98. We have tested the Timed Automaton describing the standard *railroad crossing system* (RCS, for short).

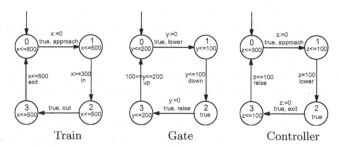

Fig. 2. Timed Automaton for Train, Gate, and Controller

This is a well-known example in the literature of real-time verification (see [24]). The system consists of three components, Train, Gate and Controllers, as shown in Figure 2, which execute in parallel and synchronize through the events: *approach, exit, lower* and *down*. When a train approaches the crossing, Train sends an *approach* signal to Controller and enters the crossing at least 300 seconds later. When a train leaves the crossing, Train sends an *exit* signal to Controller. The *exit* signal is sent within 500 seconds after the *approach* signal. Controller sends a signal *lower* to Gate exactly 100 seconds after the *approach* signal and sends a *raise* signal within 100 seconds after *exit*. Gate responds to *lower* by moving *down* within 100 seconds and responds to *raise* by moving *up* between 100 and 200 seconds. The product Timed Automaton composed of Train, Gate and Controllers is shown in Figure 3. A node (i, j, k) represents that Train, Gate, and Controllers are at nodes i, j and k, respectively. The invariant of a node is the conjunction of the invariants of the three components. For input, our model checker takes the encoded transition relation of the product Timed Automaton of Figure 3.

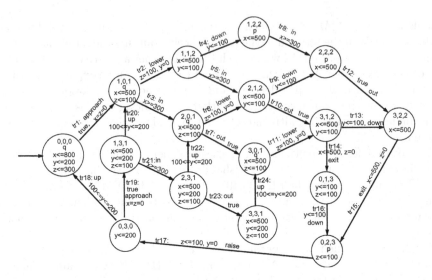

Fig. 3. Timed Automaton for Railroad Crossing System (RCS)

Let M_{RCS} be the model of the Timed Automaton for RCS. For the railroad crossing system, we want to verify the following utility property: whenever the gate is down, it is moved back up within K seconds for some K. This property is given by the TACTL formula: $\psi = \mathrm{AG}(p \Rightarrow \mathrm{AF}_{<K}q)$ with the proposition p true at the states of M_{RCS} when the gate is down, and the proposition q true at the states of M_{RCS} when the gate is moved back up.

Without loss of generality we can assume that the time unit is equal to 100 seconds. So, this means that we test $\psi = \mathrm{AG}(p \Rightarrow \mathrm{AF}_{<\frac{K}{100}}q)$ instead of $\psi = \mathrm{AG}(p \Rightarrow \mathrm{AF}_{<K}q)$, and each value c, which appears in the guards and the invariants, is divided by 100.

Note that, for each $k > 0$ the value of the function f_k for the formula $\varphi = \neg\psi$ (i.e., $\mathrm{EF}(p \wedge \mathrm{EG}_{<K}\neg q)$) is equal to 2. This means that a counterexample, if exists, can be found on two symbolic k−paths. Moreover, it is easy to see, that the length of a counterexample, i.e., the value of k, depends on K. In Table 1 we show the experimental results for two symbolic k−paths. The first column of Table 1 shows the right bound of the interval appearing in the subscript of our formula, (i.e., the interval $[0, K)$); the second shows the length of the symbolic k−paths, (i.e. the value k); the third and fourth show the numbers of propositional variables and clauses generated by BBMC respectively; the fifth and sixth show the time and memory consumed by BBMC to generate the set of clauses; the next two columns show the time and the memory consumed by ZChaff, and the last shows the solution of our problem, i.e., satisfiable iff $M_{RCS} \not\models_k \psi$ (i.e., satisfiable if $M_{RCS} \not\models \psi$).

Since our method is devoted for finding an error, for the subscript $K >= 7$ we do not present the results, because the property: *whenever the gate is down, it is moved back up within 700 seconds, i.e., 7 time unit*, is true [24].

Table 1. Experimental results for RCS system on two symbolic k−paths

		BBMC				ZChaff		
K	k	variables	clauses	sec	MB	sec	MB	Solution
1	1	9697	28828	4.8	3.88	0.6	2.75	unsatisfiable
1	4	26275	79060	40.6	33.06	6.8	9.06	unsatisfiable
1	5	31801	95804	64.5	57.06	24.3	11.06	satisfiable
2	1	9701	28840	4.8	5.31	0.3	2.63	unsatisfiable
2	4	26285	79090	40.6	26.50	23.7	9.81	unsatisfiable
2	5	31813	95840	64.7	49.38	7.5	9.75	satisfiable
3	1	9685	28792	4.8	5.25	0.3	2.63	unsatisfiable
3	5	31765	95696	64.8	53.50	54.0	14.62	unsatisfiable
3	6	37285	112422	97.0	69.31	63.0	15.69	satisfiable
4	1	9703	28846	4.8	4.94	0.3	2.63	unsatisfiable
4	6	37353	112626	97.3	61.38	312.6	39.75	unsatisfiable
4	8	48413	146138	191.0	106.90	178.0	42.62	satisfiable
5	1	9689	28804	4.8	6.38	0.4	2.69	unsatisfiable
5	6	37299	112464	97.1	62.88	234.7	39.88	unsatisfiable
5	12	70431	212856	622.3	175.70	3593.0	144.00	satisfiable
6	1	9693	28816	4.8	5.38	0.4	2.69	unsatisfiable
6	8	48361	145982	203.3	108.60	502.7	74.69	unsatisfiable
6	16	92553	279886	1527.0	154.80	5054.0	147.80	satisfiable

10   Final Remarks

We have shown that the BMC method for the logic TACTL is feasible. Our method has been implemented and checked on several examples. In Section 9 we gave experimental results for the system RCS finding counterexamples on paths of length up to 16. This experiment is maybe not sufficiently convincing to the reader about the efficiency of our method since the model of RCS is only of degree 3, i.e., the maximal branching of its states is equal to 3. However, we believe that using our method will allow us to search for errors in timed systems, for which complete minimal bisimulation state spaces cannot be generated (e.g. *the mutual exclusion protocol* for 7 processes [36]). This is motivated by the fact that we do not need to generate the whole model and can encode the transition relation in a very efficient way.

So far the transition relation of the product automaton has been an input for our implementation. This solution is obviously not efficient for Timed Automata composed of many components, like the above mentioned MUTEX, since the explosion in states and transitions is already present in the product automaton itself. Therefore, we are planning to change the input so that the translation of the transition relation of the product automaton is obtained from the local transition relations of the components.

Obviously exploiting region graph models for model checking of TCTL is not the best possible option, even if only parts of models are used, as we do it. Therefore, we are working on replacing region graphs with minimized bisimulation graphs. This is, however, far non-trivial due to the fact that minimal bisimulation models cannot be built by the DFS or BFS algorithm on which the translation of the transition relation is based. Moreover, it seems likely that our method can be efficiently used for detecting deadlocks and checking reachability in Timed Automata using surjective (simulating) models.

References

1. R. Alur, C. Courcoubetis, and D. Dill. Model checking in dense real-time. *Information and Computation*, 104(1):2–34, 1993.
2. R. Alur, C. Courcoubetis, D. Dill, N. Halbwachs, and H. Wong-Toi. An implementation of three algorithms for timing verification based on automata emptiness. In *Proc. of RTSS'92*, p. 157–166. IEEE Comp. Soc. Press, 1992.
3. R. Alur, C. Courcoubetis, D. Dill, N. Halbwachs, and H. Wong-Toi. Minimization of timed transition systems. In *Proc. of CONCUR'92*, volume 630 of *LNCS*, p. 340–354. Springer-Verlag, 1992.
4. R. Alur and D. Dill. A theory of Timed Automata. *Theoretical Computer Science*, 126(2):183 – 235, 1994.
5. R. Alur, T. Feder, and T. Henzinger. The benefits of relaxing punctuality. *Journal of the ACM*, 43(1):116–146, 1996.
6. E. Asarin, M. Bozga, A. Kerbrat, O. Maler, A. Pnueli, and A. Rasse. Data-structures for the verification of Timed Automata. In *Proc. of HART'97*, volume 1201 of *LNCS*, p. 346–360. Springer-Verlag, 1997.
7. J. Bengtsson, B. Jonsson, J. Lilius, and W. Yi. Partial order reductions for timed systems. In *Proc. of CONCUR'98*, volume 1466 of *LNCS*, p. 485–500. Springer-Verlag, 1998.
8. A. Biere, A. Cimatti, E. Clarke, M.Fujita, and Y. Zhu. Symbolic model checking using SAT procedures instead of BDDs. In *Proc. of DAC'99*, p. 317–320, 1999.
9. A. Biere, A. Cimatti, E. Clarke, and Y. Zhu. Symbolic model checking without BDDs. In *Proc. of TACAS'99*, volume 1579 of *LNCS*, p. 193–207. Springer-Verlag, 1999.
10. A. Bouajjani, S. Tripakis, and S. Yovine. On-the-fly symbolic model checking for real-time systems. In *Proc. of RTSS'97*, p. 232 – 243. IEEE Comp. Soc. Press, 1997.
11. R. Bryant. Graph-based algorithms for boolean function manipulation. *IEEE Transaction on Computers*, 35(8):677–691, 1986.
12. E. Clarke, A. Biere, R. Raimi, and Y. Zhu. Bounded model checking using satisfiability solving. In *Formal Methods in System Designe*, volume 19(1), p. 7–34, 2001.
13. E. M. Clarke, O. Grumberg, and D. Peled. *Model Checking*. MIT Press, 1999.
14. D. Dams, R. Gerth, B. Knaack, and R. Kuiper. Partial-order reduction techniques for real-time model checking. In *Proc. of the 3rd Int. Workshop on Formal Methods for Industrial Critical Systems*, p. 157 – 169, 1998.
15. D. Dams, O. Grumberg, and R. Gerth. Abstract interpretation of reactive systems: Abstractions preserving ACTL*, ECTL* and CTL*. In *Proc. of PROCOMET'94*. Elsevier Science Publishers, 1994.
16. C. Daws and S. Tripakis. Model checking of real-time reachability properties using abstractions. In *Proc. of TACAS'98*, volume 1384 of *LNCS*, p. 313–329. Springer-Verlag, 1998.

17. Richard H. Eckhouse. *Minicomputer systems. Organization and programming*. Prentice-Hall, 1975.

18. E. A. Emerson. *Handbook of Theoretical Computer Science*, volume B: Formal Methods and Semantics, chapter Temporal and Modal Logic, p. 995–1067. Elsevier Science Publishers, 1990.

19. E. A. Emerson and E. M. Clarke. Using branching-time temporal logic to synthesize synchronization skeletons. *Science of Computer Programming*, 2(3):241–266, 1982.

20. E. A. Emerson and A. P. Sistla. Symmetry and model checking. *Formal Methods in System Design*, 9:105–131, 1995.

21. O. Grumberg and D. E. Long. Model checking and modular verification. In *Proc. of CONCUR'91*, volume 527 of *LNCS*, p. 250–265. Springer-Verlag, 1991.

22. K. Heljanko and I. Niemelä. Bounded LTL model checking with stable models. In *Proc. of LPNMR'2001*, volume 2173 of *LNCS*, p. 200–212. Springer-Verlag, 2001.

23. D. S. Johnson and M. A. Trick, editors. *Cliques, Coloring and Satisfiability: The Second DIMACS Implementation Challenge*, volume 26 of *ACM/AMS DIMACS Series*. Amer. Math. Soc., 1996.

24. I. Kang and I. Lee. An Efficient State Space Generation for the Analysis of Real-time Systems. In *Proc. of Int. Symposium on Software Testing and Analysis*, 1996.

25. O. Kupferman, T. A. Henzinger, and M. Y. Vardi. A space-efficient on-the-fly algorithm for real-time model checking. In *Proc. of CONCUR'96*, volume 1119 of *LNCS*, p. 514–529. Springer-Verlag, 1996.

26. J. Lilius. Efficient state space search for Time Petri Nets. In *Proc. of MFCS*, volume 18 of *ENTCS*. Elsevier Science Publishers, 1999.

27. K. L. McMillan. *Symbolic Model Checking: An Approach to the State Explosion Problem*. Kluwer Academic Publishers, 1993.

28. M. Moskewicz, C. Madigan, Y. Zhao, L. Zhang, and S. Malik. Chaff: Engineering an efficient sat solver. In *Proc. of DAC'01*, June 2001.

29. F. Pagani. Partial orders and verification of real-time systems. In *Proc. of FTRTFT'96*, volume 1135 of *LNCS*, p. 327–346. Springer-Verlag, 1996.

30. D. Peled. Partial order reduction: Linear and branching temporal logics and process algebras. In *Proc. of POMIV'96*, volume 29 of *ACM/AMS DIMACS Series*, p. 79–88. Amer. Math. Soc., 1996.

31. W. Penczek and A. Półrola. Abstractions and partial order reductions for checking branching properties of Time Petri Nets. In *Proc. of ICATPN'01*, volume 2075 of *LNCS*, p. 323–342. Springer-Verlag, 2001.

32. W. Penczek, M. Szreter, R. Gerth, and R. Kuiper. Improving partial order reductions for universal branching time properties. *Fundamenta Informaticae*, 43:245–267, 2000.

33. W. Penczek and B. Woźna. Towards bounded model checking for Timed Automata. In *Proc. of CS&P'01*, p. 195–209, 2001.

34. W. Penczek, B. Woźna, and A. Zbrzezny. Bounded Model Checking for the Universal Fragment of CTL. *Fundamenta Informaticae*, 2002. to appear.

35. W. Penczek, B. Woźna, and A. Zbrzezny. Branching Time Bounded Model Checking for Elementary Net Systems. *Report ICS PAS*, 940, January 2002.

36. S. Tripakis and S. Yovine. Analysis of timed systems using time-abstracting bisimulations. *Formal Methods in System Design*, 18(1):25–68, 2001.

37. P. Wolper and P. Godefroid. Partial-order methods for temporal verification. In *Proc. of CONCUR'93*, volume 715 of *LNCS*, p. 233–246. Springer-Verlag, 1993.

38. T. Yoneda and B.H. Schlingloff. Efficient verification of parallel real-time systems. *Formal Methods in System Design*, 11(2):197–215, 1997.

39. L. Zhang, C. Madigan, M. Moskewicz, and S. Malik. Efficient conflict driven learning in a boolean satisfiability solver. In *Proc. of ICCAD'01*, Nov. 2001.
40. Lintao Zhang. Zchaff. http://www.ee.princeton.edu/~chaff/zchaff.php, 2001.

11   Appendix

Here, we give a detailed description of the implementation of the propositional formula $[M, \varphi]_k$. Let's start with introducing the following auxiliary functions.

- $\Theta_t : [0, \ldots, 2^t{-}1] \to \{0, 1\}^t$ is a function, which converts each natural number smaller than 2^t to the bit-vector of the length t.
- $BP : \{0, 1\} \to \mathcal{SV}$ is an injective function, which converts a bit to the (const) state proposition such that $BP(0) = false$ and $BP(1) = true$.
- $sum_t : \mathcal{SV}^t \times \{0, 1\}^t \to \mathcal{SF}^t$ is a function that adds a bit-vector to a vector of state variables in the binary way, defined as follows.
  Let $u = (u[1], \ldots, u[t])$ be a vector of state variables, $b = (b[1], \ldots, b[t])$ be a bit-vector and $a = (a[1], \ldots, a[t])$ be an auxiliary vector of propositional formulas, which encodes the move-bits for the vectors u and b, defined as:
  - $a[1] := false$,
  - $a[i] := (u[i{-}1] \wedge BP(b[i{-}1])) \vee (u[i{-}1] \wedge a[i{-}1]) \vee (BP(b[i{-}1]) \wedge a[i{-}1])$, for $i = 2, \ldots, t$.
  Let $p, q \in \mathcal{SF}$. Define the operator $\oplus$ as $p \oplus q := \neg(p \leftrightarrow q)$. Then,

$$sum_t(u, b) = (u[1] \oplus BP(b[1]) \oplus a[1], \ldots, u[t] \oplus BP(b[t]) \oplus a[t])$$

- $neg_t : \{0, 1\}^t \to \{0, 1\}^t$ is an one-to-one function encoding the negation of a bit-vector, defined as follows: $neg_t((b[1], \ldots, b[t])) = (\neg b[1], \ldots, \neg b[t])$, where $\neg 1 = 0$ and $\neg 0 = 1$.
- $minus_t : \mathcal{SF}^t \times \{0, 1\}^t \to \mathcal{SF}^t$ is a function encoding the binary subtraction, defined as follows. Let u be a vector of propositional formulas, b be a bit-vector, and let the value encoded by u be greater than the value encoded by b.

$$minus_t(u, b) = sum'_t(u, sum'_t(neg_t(b), \Theta_t(1)))$$

where sum'_t is like sum_t except for the t'th move-bit, which is removed. The definition of the function $minus_t$ is written on the basis of the standard algorithm of the subtraction of the binary numbers, which is used by digital circuits (see [17]).

- Let $\Phi \subseteq \Psi_{X'}$ be a set of clock constraints only of the form $x \sim c$ and $x{-}y \sim c$, where $x, y \in X'$ and $\sim \in \{\leq, <, =, >, \geq\}$, and $c \in \mathbb{N}$. Define the function $scc : \Psi_{X'} \to 2^\Phi$ (a straight condition calculating) as follows:
  - $scc(\text{"}x \sim c\text{"}) = \{\text{"}x \sim c\text{"}\}$
  - $scc(\text{"}x - y \sim c\text{"}) = \{\text{"}x - y \sim c\text{"}\}$
  - $scc(\phi_1 \wedge \phi_2) = scc(\phi_1) \cup scc(\phi_2)$
  The function scc returns the set of clock constraints of the form $x \sim c$ and $x - y \sim c$, (i.e., from the set Φ) for all the clock' constraints.

- Let $\varXi \subseteq \varPsi_{X'}$ be a set of clock constraints of the form $x \sim c$ only, where $x \in X'$, $\sim \in \{\leq, <, =, >, \geq\}$, and $c \in \mathbb{N}$. Moreover, let INT be the set of the intervals of the form $[a, b]$, $[a, b)$, $(a, b]$, (a, b), (a, ∞), and $[a, \infty)$, for $a, b \in \mathbb{N}$. We define the function $inter : INT \times X' \to 2^{\varXi}$ as follows:

  - $inter((a, \infty), x) = \{"x > a"\}$,
  - $inter([a, \infty), x) = \{"x \geq a"\}$,
  - $inter([a, b], x) = \{"x \geq a", "x \leq b"\}$,
  - $inter([a, b), x) = \{"x \geq a", "x < b"\}$,
  - $inter((a, b], x) = \{"x > a", "x \leq b"\}$,
  - $inter((a, b), x) = \{"x > a", "x < b"\}$.

The function $inter$ returns the set of clock constraints of the form $x \sim c$, (i.e., from the set $\varXi$) for each interval and clock $x \in X'$.

Let a, b be vectors of propositional formulas over $\mathcal{SF}$. Define the following auxiliary operator:

- $a = b := \forall_{1 \leq i \leq t}\, a[i] = b[i]$,

and the following auxiliary propositional formulas:

- $zero(a) := \bigwedge_{i=1}^{t} \neg a[i]$
- $gez(a) := \bigvee_{i=1}^{t} a[i]$
- $eq(a, b) := \bigwedge_{i=1}^{t} a[i] \Leftrightarrow b[i]$
- $ge(a, b) := \bigvee_{i=1}^{t} \left(a[i] \wedge \neg b[i] \wedge \bigwedge_{j=i+1}^{t} a[j] \Leftrightarrow b[j] \right)$
- $geq(a, b) := eq(a, b) \vee ge(a, b)$
- $le(a, b) := \neg geq(a, b)$
- $leq(a, b) := \neg ge(a, b)$

Note that above definitions are also correct when a or b are bit-vectors.

To construct the formula $[\widetilde{M}, \varphi]_k$ we have to implement the following propositional formulas:

- I encoding the initial state of M,
- T encoding the transition relation of M, and
- $[\varphi]_{M_k}$ encoding the translation of the formula φ to a propositional formula, which has been already defined in Section 6.

Let $\widetilde{M}$ be a model based on the region graph of $\widetilde{\mathcal{A}}''$ and the TECTL formula φ. By $m = log_2(|S|)$ we denote the number of state variables sufficient to encode the locations of $\widetilde{\mathcal{A}}''$, where $|S|$ is the number of locations of $\widetilde{\mathcal{A}}''$. We encode the elements of $\widetilde{W}$ by subsets of $\{0, 1\}^m \times \{0, 1\}^{n \cdot (\lceil log_2(c) \rceil + \lceil log_2(4n) \rceil)}$. This means that a state of $\widetilde{W}$ can be represented by a pair of vectors of state variables $(s, v) = ((s[1], \ldots, s[m]), (v[1], \ldots, v[r]))$, where $r = n \cdot (\lceil log_2(c) \rceil + \lceil log_2(4n) \rceil)$ and $s[i], v[j]$ are propositional variables, for $i \in \{1, \ldots, m\}$ and $j \in \{1, \ldots, r\}$. Moreover, we require that the values of clocks are given in the binary system as the sum of the integral and the fractional part, but we encode only the integral part and the numerator of the fractional part.

Hereafter, by s, $s1$, and $s2$ we mean vectors of state variables representing locations of $\mathcal{A}''$, and by vj (i.e., v, $v1,v2$) we mean a vector of state variables representing clock valuations.

Each vector vj consists of n "subvectors" $\mathcal{I}_i^{vj}$ with $\lceil log_2(c) \rceil$ state variables representing the integral part of the value of the clock x_i, and n "subvectors" $\mathcal{F}_i^{vj}$ with $\lceil log_2(4n) \rceil$ state variables representing the fractional part of the value of the clock x_i, for $i \in \{1, \ldots, n\}$.

By u we mean a vector of propositional formulas over $\mathcal{SF}$. The vector u like v consists of n "subvectors" $\mathcal{I}_i^u$ with $\lceil log_2(c) \rceil$ propositional formulas representing the integral part of the value of the clock x_i, and n "subvectors" $\mathcal{F}_i^u$ with $\lceil log_2(4n) \rceil$ propositional formulas representing the fractional part of the value of the clock x_i, for $i \in \{1, \ldots, n\}$.

Moreover, let $idx : S \times \{0,1\} \to 2^{\{1,\ldots,m\}}$ be a function defined as follows. $idx(s, i)$ returns the set of indices of the bits of the bit-vector representing s, which are set to i, for $i \in \{0,1\}$.

Now, we define the following propositional formulas:

- It follows from Lemma 3 that we can assume each d-zone to be represented by its arbitrary point. So, let $z \in \widetilde{Z}$ be any representative of $\widetilde{Z}$. The formula I is implemented as follows:

$$I_{(s,\widetilde{Z})}((s,v)) := \bigwedge_{i \in idx(s,1)} s[i] \wedge \bigwedge_{i \in idx(s,0)} \neg s[i] \wedge eq(v, vec(z)), \text{ where}$$

  $vec : \widetilde{\mathbb{B}^n} \to \{0,1\}^r$ is an injective function converting each clock valuation $(v_1, \ldots, v_n)$ to the bit-vector $b = (b_{I_1}, b_{F_1}, \ldots, b_{I_n}, b_{F_n})$ of the length r, where b consists of $2n$ bit-vectors: b_{I_i}, b_{F_i} for $i \in \{1, \ldots, n\}$. Each b_{I_i} is the binary representation of the integral part of v_i and b_{F_i} is the binary representation of the numerator of the fractional part of v_i.

To implement the formula T, we first implement the formula AS encoding the discrete action successor relation, and then implement the formula TS encoding the discrete time successor relation. To implement the formula AS we have to define the function $reset$ and the formulas $Guard$, Inv, and $adjust$. To simplify the notation of the above formulas we start with defining the formulas $Bool$ and $even$.

- Let $\phi \in \Phi$, $t = \lceil log_2(c) \rceil$ and a denote the bit-vector of the length t, which is the binary representation of $a \in \{0, \ldots, c\}$. $Bool(\phi, u) :=$

$$\begin{cases} le(\mathcal{I}_i^u, a), & \text{if } \phi = x_i < a \\ le(\mathcal{I}_i^u, a) \vee \big(eq(\mathcal{I}_i^u, a) \wedge zero(\mathcal{F}_i^u)\big), & \text{if } \phi = x_i \leq a \\ ge(\mathcal{I}_i^u, a) \vee \big(eq(\mathcal{I}_i^u, a) \wedge gez(\mathcal{F}_i^u)\big), & \text{if } \phi = x_i > a \\ geq(\mathcal{I}_i^u, a), & \text{if } \phi = x_i \geq a \\ eq(\mathcal{I}_i^u, a) \wedge zero(\mathcal{F}_i^u), & \text{if } \phi = (x_i = a) \\ le(\mathcal{I}_i^u, sum_t(\mathcal{I}_j^u, a)) \vee \big(eq(\mathcal{I}_i^u, sum_t(\mathcal{I}_j^u, a)) \wedge le(\mathcal{F}_i^u, \mathcal{F}_j^u)\big), & \text{if } \phi = x_i - x_j < a \\ le(\mathcal{I}_i^u, sum_t(\mathcal{I}_j^u, a)) \vee \big(eq(\mathcal{I}_i^u, sum_t(\mathcal{I}_j^u, a)) \wedge leq(\mathcal{F}_i^u, \mathcal{F}_j^u)\big), & \text{if } \phi = x_i - x_j \leq a \\ ge(\mathcal{I}_i^u, sum_t(\mathcal{I}_j^u, a)) \vee \big(eq(\mathcal{I}_i^u, sum_t(\mathcal{I}_j^u, a)) \wedge ge(\mathcal{F}_i^u, \mathcal{F}_j^u)\big), & \text{if } \phi = x_i - x_j > a \\ ge(\mathcal{I}_i^u, sum_t(\mathcal{I}_j^u, a)) \vee \big(eq(\mathcal{I}_i^u, sum_t(\mathcal{I}_j^u, a)) \wedge geq(\mathcal{F}_i^u, \mathcal{F}_j^u)\big), & \text{if } \phi = x_i - x_j \geq a \\ eq(\mathcal{I}_i^u, sum_t(\mathcal{I}_j^u, a)) \wedge eq(\mathcal{F}_i^u, \mathcal{F}_j^u), & \text{if } \phi = x_i - x_j = a \end{cases}$$

- $even(\boldsymbol{u}):= \bigwedge_{i,j\in\{1,\dots,n\}}(\mathcal{F}_i^u[1] \Leftrightarrow \mathcal{F}_j^u[1])$.

  The formula $even$ encodes all the clocks valuations satisfying the conditions $\forall_{i,j\in\{1,\dots,n\}}|v_i - v_j| = 2m$ for some $m \geq 0$.

- $Guard(e,\boldsymbol{u}):= \bigwedge_{\phi\in scc(guard(e))} Bool(\phi,\boldsymbol{u}) \wedge even(\boldsymbol{u})$.

  $Guard$ is a propositional formula, which encodes the enabling conditions for a transition e of $\widetilde{\mathcal{A}''}$.

- $Inv(s,\boldsymbol{u}):= \bigwedge_{\phi\in scc(\mathbb{I}(s))} Bool(\phi,\boldsymbol{u}) \wedge even(\boldsymbol{u})$.

  The above formula encodes the invariant of a location s of $\widetilde{\mathcal{A}''}$.

  Let $Y_e \subseteq \{1,\dots,n\}$ be a finite set of the indices of the clocks to be reset with the transition e. For $e \in E$, let $reset_e : \mathcal{SV}^r \to \mathcal{SV}^r$ be a function defined as follows: $reset_e(\boldsymbol{v}) = \boldsymbol{v1}$, where: $\forall_{i\in Y_e}\left(\bigvee_{j=1}^{\lceil log_2(c)\rceil}\mathcal{I}_i^{v1}[j] = false$ and $\bigvee_{j=1}^{\lceil log_2(4n)\rceil}\mathcal{F}_i^{v1}[j] = false\right)$ and $\forall_{i\in\{1,\dots,n\}\backslash Y_e}\left(\mathcal{I}_i^{v1} = \mathcal{I}_i^v$ and $\mathcal{F}_i^{v1} = \mathcal{F}_i^v\right)$.

  The function $reset_e$ returns the vector of the state variables that constrains all the clock valuations reset with the transition $e \in E$, to be valid valuations in $\widetilde{C^n}$, for each vector of state variables.

  In order to calculate the action successors we need to define a propositional formula, called $adjust$, based on the "adjustment" function α from [6]. After applying the reset function, $adjust$ replaces each vector of state variables $\boldsymbol{v1}$, representing values of clocks went out of $\widetilde{\mathbb{B}^n}$, by the vector of state variables $\boldsymbol{v2}$, representing values of clocks from $\widetilde{\mathbb{B}^n}$, equivalent to $\boldsymbol{v1}$.

- $adjust(\boldsymbol{v1},\boldsymbol{v2}) := \begin{cases} (eq(\boldsymbol{v1},\boldsymbol{v2}) \wedge even(\boldsymbol{v1}))\vee \\ ((\bigvee_{m=0}^{n-1} adjust_m(\boldsymbol{v1},\boldsymbol{v2})) \wedge \neg even(\boldsymbol{v1})), \end{cases}$

  where $adjust_m$ is defined as follows. Let $\boldsymbol{l} = \Theta_{\lceil log_2(4n)\rceil}(l)$, for $l \in \{0,\dots,2n\}$.

$$adjust_m(\boldsymbol{v1},\boldsymbol{v2}) := \begin{cases} \bigwedge_{i=1}^n eq(\mathcal{I}_i^{v1},\mathcal{I}_i^{v2}) \wedge \left(zero(\mathcal{F}_i^{v1}) \wedge zero(\mathcal{F}_i^{v2})\vee \right. \\ \bigvee_{l=0}^{m-1}(eq(\mathcal{F}_i^{v1},2l+1) \wedge eq(\mathcal{F}_i^{v2},2l+2))\vee \\ \left. \bigvee_{l=m+1}^{n-1}(eq(\mathcal{F}_i^{v1},2l+1) \wedge eq(\mathcal{F}_i^{v2},2l))\right) \end{cases}$$

- $AS((\boldsymbol{s1},\boldsymbol{v1}),(\boldsymbol{s2},\boldsymbol{v2})):= \begin{cases} \bigvee_{e\in E}\left(\bigwedge_{i\in idx(source(e),1)} s1[i] \wedge \right. \\ \bigwedge_{i\in idx(source(e),0)} \neg s1[i] \wedge \\ \bigwedge_{i\in idx(target(e),1)} s2[i] \wedge \\ \bigwedge_{i\in idx(target(e),0)} \neg s2[i] \wedge Guard(e,\boldsymbol{v1}) \wedge \\ \left. Inv(target(e),\boldsymbol{v2}) \wedge adjust(reset_e(\boldsymbol{v1}),\boldsymbol{v2})\right). \end{cases}$

To implement the formula TS, encoding the discrete time successor relation, we have to first define the formulas $equiv$ and $cleverSum$.

- $equiv(\boldsymbol{u},\boldsymbol{v}) := \begin{cases} \bigwedge_{i=1}^n\left(eq(\mathcal{I}_i^v,\mathcal{I}_i^u) \wedge (zero(\mathcal{F}_i^v) \Leftrightarrow zero(\mathcal{F}_i^u))\right)\wedge \\ \bigwedge_{i,j\in\{1,\dots,n\}}(leq(\mathcal{F}_i^u,\mathcal{F}_j^u) \Leftrightarrow leq(\mathcal{F}_i^v,\mathcal{F}_j^v)). \end{cases}$

  The formula $equiv$ encodes the equivalence relation of the clock valuations, i.e., the relation $\simeq$.

Let $t_1 = \lceil log_2(c)\rceil$, $t_2 = \lceil log_2(4n)\rceil$, $\boldsymbol{d} = \Theta_{\lceil log_2(4n)\rceil}(d)$ for $d \in \{0,\dots,2n-1\}$, $\boldsymbol{0} = \Theta_{\lceil log_2(4n)\rceil}(0)$, $\boldsymbol{2n} = \Theta_{\lceil log_2(4n)\rceil}(2n)$, $\boldsymbol{1} = \Theta_{\lceil log_2(c)\rceil}(1)$.

$$- \ cleverSum(\boldsymbol{v1}, \boldsymbol{d}, \boldsymbol{v2}) := \begin{cases} \bigwedge_{i=1}^{n} \Big((eq(sum_{t_2}(\mathcal{F}_i^{v1}, \boldsymbol{d}), \boldsymbol{2n}) \wedge eq(\mathcal{F}_i^{v2}, \boldsymbol{0}) \wedge \\ eq(sum_{t_1}(\mathcal{I}_i^{v1}, \boldsymbol{1}), \mathcal{I}_i^{v2})) \vee (le(sum_{t_2}(\mathcal{F}_i^{v1}, \boldsymbol{d}), \boldsymbol{2n}) \wedge \\ eq(\mathcal{I}_i^{v1}, \mathcal{I}_i^{v2}) \wedge eq(sum_{t_2}(\mathcal{F}_i^{v1}, \boldsymbol{d}), \mathcal{F}_i^{v2})) \Big) \end{cases}$$

The formula *cleverSum* encodes the addition of the bit-vector $\boldsymbol{d}$ to all vectors $\mathcal{F}_i^{v1}$ and $\mathcal{I}_i^{v1}$ representing the value of the clock $x_i \in X'$, for $i = 1, \ldots, n$. The result of the addition is put in the vector $\boldsymbol{v2}$, i.e., $\boldsymbol{v2}$ contains either the value zone-equivalent to the value $\boldsymbol{v1}$ or its time successor.

$$- \ TS((\boldsymbol{s1}, \boldsymbol{v1}), (\boldsymbol{s2}, \boldsymbol{v2})) := \begin{cases} eq(\boldsymbol{s1}, \boldsymbol{s2}) \wedge \Big(\bigvee_{d=0}^{2n-1} cleversum(\boldsymbol{v1}, \boldsymbol{d}, \boldsymbol{v2}) \Big) \wedge \\ \neg equiv(\boldsymbol{v1}, \boldsymbol{v2}) \wedge \Big(\bigvee_{s \in S} (eq(\boldsymbol{s2}, s) \wedge Inv(s, \boldsymbol{v2})) \Big). \end{cases}$$

Now, we are ready to implement the formula T.

$- \ T((\boldsymbol{s1}, \boldsymbol{v1}), (\boldsymbol{s2}, \boldsymbol{v2})) := AS((\boldsymbol{s1}, \boldsymbol{v1}), (\boldsymbol{s2}, \boldsymbol{v2})) \vee TS((\boldsymbol{s1}, \boldsymbol{v1}), (\boldsymbol{s2}, \boldsymbol{v2})).$

Next, we implement the formulas to be used in the definition of $[\varphi]_{M_k}$.

$- \ H((\boldsymbol{s1}, \boldsymbol{v1}), (\boldsymbol{s2}, \boldsymbol{v2})) := eq(\boldsymbol{s1}, \boldsymbol{s2}) \wedge eq(\boldsymbol{v1}, \boldsymbol{v2}).$

- Let $\mathcal{V}_S : \mathcal{PV} \to 2^S$ be a function returning the set of locations of which a proposition p is true, for each $p \in \mathcal{PV}$, defined as $\mathcal{V}_S(p) = \{s \in S \mid p \in \mathcal{V}(s)\}$. The formula encoding all the states labeled by the proposition $p_i \in \mathcal{PV}$ is defined as $p_i((\boldsymbol{s}, \boldsymbol{v})) := \bigvee_{s \in \mathcal{V}_S(p_i)} eq(\boldsymbol{s}, s)$.

- The formula encoding all the states labeled by the proposition $p_{x_i \in I} \in \mathcal{PV}_X$ is defined as $p_{x_i \in I}((\boldsymbol{s}, \boldsymbol{v})) := \bigwedge_{\xi_i \in inter(I, x_i)} Bool(\xi_i, \boldsymbol{v})$, where ξ_i denotes an inequality over $x_i \in X'$.

$- \ p((\boldsymbol{s}, \boldsymbol{v}))$ iff $\begin{cases} p_i((\boldsymbol{s}, \boldsymbol{v})), & \text{if } p_i \in \mathcal{PV} \\ p_{x_i \in I}((\boldsymbol{s}, \boldsymbol{v})), & otherwise. \end{cases}$

Below, we implement the formula *dead* encoding the deadlock.

- Let $add : \mathcal{SV}^r \times \{0, 1\}^{\lceil log_2(4n) \rceil} \to \mathcal{SF}^r$ be a function, which returns a vector of propositional formulas such that each vector $\boldsymbol{u}_i$ (i.e., the vector consisting of $\mathcal{I}_i^u$ and $\mathcal{F}_i^u$) encodes the sum of the values represented by $\boldsymbol{d}$ and $\boldsymbol{v}_i$ (i.e., the vector consisting of $\mathcal{I}_i^v$ and $\mathcal{F}_i^v$) as the proper fractions, defined as follows. Let $d \in \{0, \ldots, 2n - 1\}$. Then, $add(\boldsymbol{v}, \boldsymbol{d}) = \boldsymbol{u}$, where for all $i = 1, \ldots, n$.

$$\mathcal{I}_i^u[j] := \begin{cases} \big(le(sum_{t_2}(\mathcal{F}_i^v, \boldsymbol{d}), \boldsymbol{2n}) \wedge \mathcal{I}_i^v[j] \big) \vee \big(eq(sum_{t_2}(\mathcal{F}_i^v, \boldsymbol{d}), \boldsymbol{2n}) \wedge \\ (sum_{t_1}(\mathcal{I}_i^v, \boldsymbol{1}))[j] \big) \vee \big(ge(sum_{t_2}(\mathcal{F}_i^v, \boldsymbol{d}), \boldsymbol{2n}) \wedge (sum_{t_1}(\mathcal{I}_i^v, \boldsymbol{1}))[j] \big) \end{cases}$$

for all $j = 1, \ldots, \lceil log_2(c) \rceil$,

$$\mathcal{F}_i^u[j] := \begin{cases} (le(sum_{t_2}(\mathcal{F}_i^v, \boldsymbol{d}), \boldsymbol{2n}) \wedge (sum_{t_2}(\mathcal{F}_i^v, \boldsymbol{d}))[j]) \vee \\ (eq(sum_{t_2}(\mathcal{F}_i^v, \boldsymbol{d}), \boldsymbol{2n}) \wedge (zero(\mathcal{F}_i^v))[j]) \vee \\ (ge(sum_{t_2}(\mathcal{F}_i^v, \boldsymbol{d}), \boldsymbol{2n}) \wedge (minus_{t_2}(sum_{t_2}(\mathcal{F}_i^v, \boldsymbol{d}), \boldsymbol{2n}))[j]) \end{cases}$$

for all $j = 1, \ldots, \lceil log_2(4n) \rceil$.

$$dead((\boldsymbol{s}, \boldsymbol{v})) := \begin{cases} \neg \Big[\bigvee_{s \in S} \big(eq(\boldsymbol{s}, s) \wedge \bigvee_{d=1}^{2n-1} (Inv(s, add(\boldsymbol{v}, \boldsymbol{d})) \wedge \\ cleversum(\boldsymbol{v}, \boldsymbol{d}, add(\boldsymbol{v}, \boldsymbol{d})) \wedge \neg equiv(add(\boldsymbol{v}, \boldsymbol{d}), \boldsymbol{v})) \big) \Big] \vee \\ \bigvee_{e \in E} \big(eq(\boldsymbol{s}, source(e)) \wedge Guard(e, \boldsymbol{v}) \wedge Inv(source(e), \boldsymbol{v}) \big) \Big] \end{cases}$$

Part VI

Verification and Conformance Testing

A Typed Interrupt Calculus

Jens Palsberg and Di Ma

Department of Computer Science
Purdue University, W. Lafayette, IN 47907
{palsberg,madi}@cs.purdue.edu

Abstract. Most real-time systems require responsive interrupt handling. Programming of interrupt handlers is challenging: in order to ensure responsiveness, it is often necessary to have interrupt processing enabled in the body of lower priority handlers. It would be a programming error to allow the interrupt handlers to interrupt each other in a cyclic fashion; it could lead to an unbounded stack. Until now, static checking for such errors could only be done using model checking. However, the needed form of model checking requires a whole-program analysis that cannot check program fragments. In this paper, we present a calculus that contains essential constructs for programming interrupt-driven systems. The calculus has a static type system that guarantees stack boundedness and enables modular type checking. A number of common programming idioms have been type checked using our prototype implementation.

1 Introduction

Interrupt-driven systems. Interrupts and interrupt handlers are often used in systems where fast response to an event is essential. Embedded interrupt-driven systems generally have a fixed number of interrupt sources with a handler defined for each source. When an interrupt occurs, control is transferred automatically to the handler for that interrupt source, unless interrupt processing is disabled. If disabled, the interrupt will wait for interrupt processing to be enabled. To get fast response times, it is necessary to keep interrupt processing enabled most of the time, including in *the body* of lower priority interrupt handlers. This opens the door for interrupt handlers to be themselves interrupted, making it difficult to understand whether real-time deadlines can be met. Conversely, to write reliable code with a given real-time property, it is simplest to disable interrupts in the body of interrupt handlers. This may delay the handling of other interrupts and therefore make it difficult for the system to have other desired real-time properties. The resultant tension between fast response times and easy-to-understand, reliable code drives developers to write code that is often difficult to test and debug.

A nasty programming error. A particularly nasty programming error is to allow the interrupt handlers to interrupt each other indefinitely, leading to an unbounded stack. For example, consider the following two interrupt handlers.

W. Damm and E.-R. Olderog (Eds.): FTRTFT 2002, LNCS 2469, pp. 291–310, 2002.

```
handler 1 {                          handler 2 {
  // do something                      // do something
  enable-handling-of-interrupt-2       enable-handling-of-interrupt-1
  // do something else                 // do something else
  iret                                 iret
}                                    }
```

Suppose an interrupt from source 1 arrives first, and so handler 1 is called. Before returning, handler 1 enables handling of interrupts from source 2, and unfortunately an interrupt from source 2 arrives before handler 1 has returned. Thus handler 2 is called, and it, in turn, enables handling of interrupts from source 1 before returning, allowing a highly undesirable cycle and an unbounded stack.

A traditional type system does not check for this kind of error. The error is not about misusing data; it is about needing unbounded resources. Until now, static checking for such errors could only be done using model checking. However, the needed form of model checking is a whole-program analysis that cannot check program fragments [13,3]. The goal of this paper is to present a type system that guarantees stack boundedness and enables modular type checking. To do that, we need a minimal setting in which to study interrupt-driven systems.

The need for a new calculus. For many programming paradigms, there is a small calculus which allows the study of properties in a language-independent way and which makes it tractable to prove key properties. For example, for functional programming there is the λ-calculus [2], for concurrent programming there is Milner's calculus of communicating systems [7], for object-oriented programming there is the Abadi-Cardelli object calculus [1], and for mobile computation there is the π-calculus [8] and the ambient calculus [4]. These calculi do not offer any notion of interrupts and interrupt handling. While such concepts might be introduced on top of one of those calculi, we believe that it is better to design a new calculus with interrupts at the core. A new calculus should focus on the essential concepts and leave out everything else.

What are the essential concepts? While some modern, general-purpose CPUs have sophisticated ways of handling internal and external interrupts, the notion of an interrupt mask register (imr) is widely used. This is especially true for CPUs that are used in embedded systems with small memory size, a need for low power consumption, and other constraints. The following table lists some characteristics of four CPUs that are often used in embedded systems:

Well-known product	Processor	# of interrupt sources	master bit
Microcontroller	Zilog Z86	6	yes
iPAQ Pocket PC	Intel strongARM, XScale	21	no
Palm	Motorola Dragonball (68000 Family)	22	yes
Microcontroller	Intel MCS-51 Family (8051 etc)	6	yes

Each of these processors have similar-looking imr's. For example, consider the imr for the MCS-51 (which calls it the interrupt enable (IE) register):

| EA | – | ET2 | ES | ET1 | EX1 | ET0 | EX0 |

The bits have the following meanings:

- EA: enable/disable all interrupt handling,
- –: reserved (not used), and
- each of the remaining six bits corresponds to a specific interrupt source.

We will refer to the EA bit (and similar bits on other processors) as the *master bit*. The idea is that for a particular interrupt handler to be enabled, *both* the master bit and the bit for that interrupt handler have to be enabled. This semantics is supported by the Z86, Dragonball, MCS-51, and many other processors. When an interrupt handler is called, a return address is stored on the stack, and the processor automatically turns *off* the master bit. At the time of return, the processor turns the master bit back *on*. Not all processors use this scheme: the strongARM does not have a master bit. In this paper we focus on modeling processors that do have a master bit.

In the rest of the paper, we will use a representation of the imr which is independent of particular architectures. We represent the imr as a bit sequence $b_0 b_1 \ldots b_n$, where $b_i \in \{0, 1\}$, b_0 is the master bit, and, for $i > 0$, b_i is the bit for interrupts from source i which is handled by handler i. Notice that the master bit is the most significant bit, and that the bit for handler 1 is the second-most significant bit, and so on. This layout is different from some processors, and it simplifies the notation used later.

Our results. We present a calculus that contains essential constructs for programming interrupt-driven systems. A program in the calculus consists of a main part and some interrupt handlers. A program execution has access to:

- an interrupt mask register that can be updated during computation,
- a stack for storing return addresses, and
- a memory of integer variables; output is done via memory-mapped I/O.

The calculus is intended for modeling embedded systems that should run "forever," and for which termination would be considered a disastrous error. To model that, the calculus is designed such that no program can terminate; non-termination is guaranteed.

Each element on the stack is a return address. When we measure the size of the stack, we simply count the number of elements on the stack.

For our calculus, we present a type system that guarantees stack boundedness and enables modular type checking. A number of common programming idioms have been type checked using our prototype implementation.

A type for a handler contains information about the imr on entry and the imr at the point of return. Given that a handler can be called at different points in the program where the imr may have different values, the type of a handler is an intersection type [5,6] of the form:

$$\bigwedge_{j=1}^{n} ((\widehat{imr})^j \xrightarrow{\delta^j} (\widehat{imr}')^j).$$

where the jth component of the intersection means:

if the handler is called in a situation where the imr can be conservatively approximated by $(\widehat{imr})^j$, then at the point of return, the imr can conservatively be approximated by $(\widehat{imr}')^j$, and during that call, the stack will grow by at most δ^j elements, excluding the return address for the call itself.

The annotations δ^j help with checking that the stack is bounded. Our type system with annotated types is an example of a type-based analysis [10].

Rest of the paper. In Section 2 we introduce our interrupt calculus and type system via six examples. In Section 3 we present the syntax and semantics of the interrupt calculus, and we prove that no program can terminate. In Section 4 we present our type system and prove stack boundedness, and in Section 5 we conclude. In the appendix we prove the theorem of type preservation which is a key lemma in the proof of stack boundedness.

2   Examples

We will introduce our interrupt calculus and type system via six examples of increasing sophistication. The first five programs have been type checked using our prototype implementation, while the sixth program illustrates the limitations of our type system. We will use the concrete syntax that is supported by our type checker; later, in Sections 3–4, we will use an abstract syntax. Note that an imr value, say, 11 will in the concrete syntax be written as 11b, to remind the reader that it is a binary value. Also, the type of a handler

$$\bigwedge_{j=1}^{n} ((\widehat{imr})^j \xrightarrow{\delta^j} (\widehat{imr}')^j).$$

will be written $((\widehat{imr})^1 \to (\widehat{imr}')^1 : \delta^1) \ldots ((\widehat{imr})^n \to (\widehat{imr}')^n : \delta^n)$.

The program in Figure 1 is a version of Example 3-5 from Wayne Wolf's textbook [14, p.113]. The program copies data from one device to another device. The program uses memory-mapped I/O; two variables map to the device registers:

- indata: the input device writes data in this register and
- outdata: the output device reads data from this register.

```
Maximum stack size: 1

imr = imr or 11b
loop {                              handler 1 [ ( 11b -> 11b : 0 ) ] {
    if ( gotchar == 0 ) {              achar    = indata
        outdata    = achar             gotchar  = 0
        gotchar    = 1                 iret
    } else {                        }
        skip
    }
}
```

Fig. 1. A program for copying data from one device to another device.

```
maximum stack size: 1           handler 1 [ ( 111b -> 111b : 0 ) ] {
                                    skip
imr = imr or 111b                   iret
loop {                           }
    skip                         handler 2 [ ( 111b -> 111b : 0 ) ] {
    imr = imr or 111b               skip
}                                   iret
                                 }
```

Fig. 2. Two selfish handlers

The line `maximum stack size: 1` is a part of the program text. It tells the type checker to check that the stack can never be of a size greater than one. The number 1 is a count of return addresses on the stack; nothing else than return addresses can be put on the stack in our calculus. The header of the handler contains the annotation `11b -> 11b : 0`. It is a type that says that if the handler is called in a situation where the imr can be conservatively approximated by 11, then it will return in a situation where the imr can be conservatively approximated by 11, and the stack will not grow during the call. The value 11 should be read as follows. The leftmost bit is the master bit, and the next bit is the bit for handler 1. The value 11 means that handler 1 is enabled.

The program in Figure 2 is much like the program in Figure 1, except that there are now two handlers. The handlers cannot be interrupted so the maximum stack size is 1. Notice that since there are two handlers, the imr has three bits. They are organized as follows. The leftmost bit is, as always, the master bit. The next bit is the bit for handler 1, and the rightmost bit is the bit for handler 2.

The program in Figure 3 illustrates how to program a notion of prioritized handlers where handler 1 is of higher priority than handler 2. While handler 1 cannot be interrupted by handler 2, it is possible for handler 2 to be interrupted by handler 1. Handler 2 achieves that by disabling its own bit in the imr with the statement `imr = imr and 110b`, and then enabling the master bit with the statement `imr = imr or 100b`. Thus, handler 2 can be interrupted before it returns. Accordingly, the maximum stack size is 2. The type for handler 1 is an intersection type that reflects that handler 1 can be called both from the main

```
                                    handler 1 [ ( 111b -> 111b : 0 )
                                                ( 110b -> 110b : 0 ) ] {
maximum stack size: 2                   skip
                                        iret
imr = imr or 111b                   }
loop {                              handler 2 [ ( 111b -> 111b : 1 ) ] {
   skip                                 skip
   imr = imr or 111b                    imr = imr and 110b
}                                       imr = imr or  100b
                                        iret
                                    }
```

Fig. 3. Two prioritized handlers

```
                                    handler 1 [ ( 111b -> 101b : 1 )
                                                ( 110b -> 100b : 0 ) ] {
                                        imr = imr and 101b
maximum stack size: 2                   imr = imr or  100b
                                        iret
imr = imr or 111b                   }
loop {                              handler 2 [ ( 111b -> 110b : 1 )
   imr = imr or 111b                            ( 101b -> 100b : 0 ) ] {
}                                       imr = imr and 110b
                                        imr = imr or  100b
                                        iret
                                    }
```

Fig. 4. Two cooperative handlers

part and from handler 2. If it is called from the main part, then the imr is 111, and if it is called from handler 2, then the imr is 110. The type for handler 2 has annotation 1 because handler 2 can be interrupted by handler 1, which, in turn, cannot be interrupted.

The program in Figure 4 illustrates how both handlers can allow the other handler to interrupt. Each handler uses the discipline of disabling its own bit in the imr before setting the master bit to 1. This ensures that the maximum stack size is two.

The program in Figure 5 illustrates that n handlers can lead to a bounded stack where the bound is greater than n. In this case we have two handlers and a maximum stack size of three. A stack size of three is achieved by first calling handler 1, then calling handler 2, and finally calling handler 1 again.

While our type system can type check many common programming idioms, as illustrated above, there are useful programs that it cannot type check. For example, the program in Figure 6, written by Dennis Brylow, is a 60 second timer. The OUT variable will be 0 for 60 seconds after a request for interrupt 2. There are two interrupt handlers:

```
                              handler 1 [ ( 111b -> 111b : 2 )
                                          ( 110b -> 100b : 0 ) ] {
                                imr = imr and 101b
                                imr = imr or   100b
maximum stack size: 3             iret
                              }
imr = imr or 111b             handler 2 [ ( 111b -> 100b : 1 )
loop {                                    ( 101b -> 100b : 1 ) ] {
   imr = imr or 111b            imr = imr and 110b
}                               imr = imr or   010b
                                imr = imr or   100b
                                imr = imr and 101b
                                iret
                              }
```

Fig. 5. Two fancy handlers

```
maximum stack size: 1
                              handler 1 [ ( 111b -> 111b : 0 )
SEC = SEC + 60                            ( 110b -> 110b : 0 ) ] {
imr = imr or 110b               SEC = SEC + (-1)
loop {                          iret
   if( SEC == 0 ) {           }
   OUT = 1                    handler 2 [ ( 111b -> 110b : 0 )
   imr = imr and 101b                     ( 101b -> 110b : 0 ) ] {
   imr = imr or   001b          SEC = 60
   } else {                     imr = imr and 110b
   OUT = 0                      imr = imr or   010b
   }                            iret
}                             }
```

Fig. 6. A timer

- The first handler is for an external timer that is expected to request an interrupt once each second.
- The second handler is a trigger. When it arrives, the OUT variable will become 0 for 60 seconds. Then OUT will become 1, and remain so until the next trigger event.

Our type system cannot handle this pattern where handler 2 disables itself and then enables handler 1, and where the main program disables handler 1 and enables handler 2. Thus, while the program in Figure 6 has a maximum stack size of 2, it does not type check in our type system.

3   The Interrupt Calculus

3.1   Syntax

We will use an abstract syntax that is slightly more compact than the concrete syntax used in Section 2.

We use x to range over a set of program variables, we use imr to range over bit strings, and we use c to range over integer constants.

$$
\begin{array}{lll}
\text{(program)} & p & ::= (m, \overline{h}) \\
\text{(main)} & m & ::= \text{loop } s \mid s \, ; \, m \\
\text{(handler)} & h & ::= \text{iret} \mid s \, ; \, h \\
\text{(statements)} & s & ::= x = e \mid imr = imr \wedge imr \mid imr = imr \vee imr \mid \\
& & \quad \text{if0 } (x) \, s_1 \text{ else } s_2 \mid s_1 \, ; \, s_2 \mid \text{skip} \\
\text{(expression)} & e & ::= c \mid x \mid x + c \mid x_1 + x_2
\end{array}
$$

The over bar notation $\overline{h}$ denotes a sequence $h_1 \ldots h_n$; we will use the notation $\overline{h}(i) = h_i$.

We use a to range over m and h. We identify programs that are equivalent under the smallest congruence generated by the rules:

$$
\begin{array}{c}
(s_1 \, ; \, s_2) \, ; \, m = s_1 \, ; \, (s_2 \, ; \, m) \\
(s_1 \, ; \, s_2) \, ; \, h = s_1 \, ; \, (s_2 \, ; \, h) \\
(s_1 \, ; \, s_2) \, ; \, s = s_1 \, ; \, (s_2 \, ; \, s).
\end{array}
$$

With these rules, we can rearrange any m or h into one of the seven forms:

> loop s iret $x = e; a$ $imr = imr \wedge imr; a$ $imr = imr \vee imr; a$
>
> (if0 (x) s_1 else s_2); a skip; a.

3.2   Semantics

We use R to denote a *store*, that is, a partial function mapping program variables to integers.

We use σ to denote a *stack* generated by the grammar: $\sigma ::= \text{nil} \mid a :: \sigma$. We define the size of a stack as follows: $|\text{nil}| = 0$ and $|a :: \sigma| = 1 + |\sigma|$.

If $imr = b_0 b_1 \ldots b_n$, where $b_i \in \{0, 1\}$, then we will use the notation $imr(i) = b_i$. The predicate *enabled* is defined as follows:

$$
enabled(imr, i) = (imr(0) = 1) \wedge (imr(i) = 1), \qquad i \in 1..n.
$$

We use 0 to denote the imr value where all bits are 0. We use t_i to denote the imr value where all bits are 0's except that the ith bit is set to 1. We will use $\wedge$ to denote bitwise logical conjunction, $\vee$ to denote bitwise logical disjunction, $\leq$ to denote bitwise logical implication, and $(\cdot)^\bullet$ to denote bitwise logical negation. Notice that $enabled(t_0 \vee t_i, j)$ is true for $i = j$ and false otherwise. The imr values, ordered by $\leq$, form a lattice with bottom element 0.

A *program state* is a tuple $\langle \overline{h}, R, imr, \sigma, a \rangle$. We will refer to a as *the current statement*; it models the instruction pointer of a CPU. We use P to range over program states. If $P = \langle \overline{h}, R, imr, \sigma, a \rangle$, then we use the notation $P.stk = \sigma$. For $p = (m, \overline{h})$, the initial program state for executing p is $P_p = \langle \overline{h}, \lambda x.0, 0, \text{nil}, m \rangle$, where the function $\lambda x.0$ is defined on the variables that are used in the program p.

A small-step operational semantics for the language is given by the reflexive, transitive closure of the relation $\rightarrow$ on program states:

$$\langle \overline{h}, R, imr, \sigma, a \rangle \rightarrow \langle \overline{h}, R, imr \wedge \mathsf{t}_0^{\bullet}, a :: \sigma, \overline{h}(i) \rangle \qquad (1)$$
$$\text{if } enabled(imr, i)$$

$$\langle \overline{h}, R, imr, \sigma, \mathsf{iret} \rangle \rightarrow \langle \overline{h}, R, imr \vee \mathsf{t}_0, \sigma', a \rangle \quad \text{if } \sigma = a :: \sigma' \quad (2)$$

$$\langle \overline{h}, R, imr, \sigma, \mathsf{loop}\ s \rangle \rightarrow \langle \overline{h}, R, imr, \sigma, s; \mathsf{loop}\ s \rangle \qquad (3)$$

$$\langle \overline{h}, R, imr, \sigma, x = e; a \rangle \rightarrow \langle \overline{h}, R\{x \mapsto eval_R(e)\}, imr, \sigma, a \rangle \qquad (4)$$

$$\langle \overline{h}, R, imr, \sigma, \mathsf{imr} = \mathsf{imr} \wedge imr'; a \rangle \rightarrow \langle \overline{h}, R, imr \wedge imr', \sigma, a \rangle \qquad (5)$$

$$\langle \overline{h}, R, imr, \sigma, \mathsf{imr} = \mathsf{imr} \vee imr'; a \rangle \rightarrow \langle \overline{h}, R, imr \vee imr', \sigma, a \rangle \qquad (6)$$

$$\langle \overline{h}, R, imr, \sigma, (\mathsf{if0}\ (x)\ s_1\ \mathsf{else}\ s_2); a \rangle \rightarrow \langle \overline{h}, R, imr, \sigma, s_1; a \rangle \quad \text{if } R(x) = 0 \quad (7)$$

$$\langle \overline{h}, R, imr, \sigma, (\mathsf{if0}\ (x)\ s_1\ \mathsf{else}\ s_2); a \rangle \rightarrow \langle \overline{h}, R, imr, \sigma, s_2; a \rangle \quad \text{if } R(x) \neq 0 \quad (8)$$

$$\langle \overline{h}, R, imr, \sigma, \mathsf{skip}; a \rangle \rightarrow \langle \overline{h}, R, imr, \sigma, a \rangle \qquad (9)$$

We define the function $eval_R(e)$ as follows:

$$eval_R(c) = c$$
$$eval_R(x) = R(x)$$
$$eval_R(x + c) = R(x) + c$$
$$eval_R(x_1 + x_2) = R(x_1) + R(x_2).$$

Rule (1) models that if an interrupt is enabled, then it may occur. The rule says that if $enabled(imr, i)$, then it is a possible transition to push the current statement on the stack, make $\overline{h}(i)$ the current statement, and turn off the master bit in the imr. Notice that we make no assumptions about the interrupts arrivals; any enabled interrupt can occur at any time, and, conversely, no interrupt has to occur.

Rule (2) models interrupt return. The rule says that to return from an interrupt, remove the top element of the stack, make the removed top element the current statement, and turn on the master bit.

Rule (3) is an unfolding rule for loops, and Rules (4)–(9) are standard rules for statements.

3.3 Nontermination

We say that a program p *can terminate* if $P_p \rightarrow^* P'$ and there is no P'' such that $P' \rightarrow P''$.

We say that a program state $\langle \overline{h}, R, imr, \sigma, a \rangle$ is *consistent* if and only if (1) $\sigma = \mathsf{nil}$ and $a = m$; or (2) $\sigma = h^k :: \ldots :: h^1 :: m :: \mathsf{nil}$ and $a = h$, for $k \geq 0$, where $k = 0$ means $\sigma = m :: \mathsf{nil}$.

Lemma 1. (Consistency Preservation) *If P is consistent and $P \rightarrow P'$, then P' is consistent.*

Proof. A straightforward cases analysis of $P \rightarrow P'$.

Lemma 2. (Progress) *If P is consistent, then there exists P' such that $P \to P'$.*

Proof. There are two cases of P:

- $P = \langle \overline{h}, R, imr, \text{nil}, m \rangle$. There are two cases of m:
  - if $m = \text{loop } s$, then Rule (3) gives $P' = \langle \overline{h}, R, imr, \text{nil}, s; \text{loop } s \rangle$, and
  - if $m = s; m'$, then Rules (4)–(9) ensure that there exists a state P' such that $P \to P'$.
- $P = \langle \overline{h}, R, imr, h^k :: \ldots :: h^1 :: m :: \text{nil}, h \rangle$, $k \geq 0$. There are two cases of h:
  - if $h = \text{iret}$, then either $k = 0$ and $s = m :: \text{nil}$, and Rule (2) gives $P' = \langle \overline{h}, R, imr \lor t_0, \text{nil}, m \rangle$, or $k > 0$ and hence $P' = \langle \overline{h}, R, imr \lor t_0, h^{k-1} :: \ldots :: h^1 :: m :: \text{nil}, h^k \rangle$, and
  - if $h = s; h'$, then Rules (4)–(9) ensure that there exists a state P' such that $P \to P'$.

Theorem 1. (Nontermination) *No program can terminate.*

Proof. Suppose a program p can terminate, that is, suppose $P_p \to^* P'$ and there is no P'' such that $P' \to P''$. Notice first that P_p is consistent by consistency criterion (1). From Lemma 1 and induction on the number of execution steps in $P_p \to^* P'$, we have that P' is consistent. From Lemma 2 we have that there exists P'' such that $P' \to P''$, a contradiction.

4   Type System

4.1   Types

We will use imr values as types. When we intend an imr value to be used as a type, we will use the mnemonic device of writing it with a hat, for example, $\widehat{imr}$.

We will use the bitwise logical implication $\leq$ as the subtype relation. For example, $101 \leq 111$. We will also use $\leq$ to specify the relationship between an imr value and its type. When we want to express that an imr value imr has type $\widehat{imr}$, we will write $imr \leq \widehat{imr}$. The meaning is that $\widehat{imr}$ is a conservative approximation of imr, that is, if a bit in imr is 1, then the corresponding bit in $\widehat{imr}$ is also 1.

We use K to range over the integers, and we use δ to range over the nonnegative integers.

We use τ to range over intersection types of the form:

$$\bigwedge_{j=1}^{n} ((\widehat{imr})^j \xrightarrow{\delta^j} (\widehat{imr}')^j).$$

We use $\overline{\tau}$ to range over a sequence $\tau_1 \ldots \tau_n$; we will use the notation $\overline{\tau}(i) = \tau_i$.

4.2   Type Rules

We will use the following forms of type judgments:

Type Judgment	Meaning
$\vdash h : \tau$	Interrupt handler h has type τ
$\overline{\tau}, \widehat{imr} \vdash_K \sigma$	Stack σ type checks
$\overline{\tau}, \widehat{imr} \vdash_K m$	Main part m type checks
$\overline{\tau}, \widehat{imr} \vdash_K h : \widehat{imr}'$	Handler h type checks
$\overline{\tau}, \widehat{imr} \vdash_K s : \widehat{imr}'$	Statement s type checks
$\overline{\tau} \vdash_K P$	Program state P type checks

The judgment $\overline{\tau}, \widehat{imr} \vdash_K m$ means that if the handlers are of type $\overline{\tau}$, and the imr has type $\widehat{imr}$, then m type checks. The integer K bounds the stack size to be at most K. We can view K as a "stack budget" in the sense that any time an element is placed on the stack, the budget goes down by one, and when an element is removed from the stack, the budget goes up by one. The type system ensures that the budget does not go below zero.

The judgment $\overline{\tau}, \widehat{imr} \vdash_K h : \widehat{imr}'$ means that if the handlers are of type $\overline{\tau}$, and the imr has type $\widehat{imr}$, then h type checks, and at the point of returning from the handler, the imr has type $\widehat{imr}'$. The integer K means that during the call, the stack will grow by at most K elements. Notice that "during the call" may include calls to other interrupt handlers.

The judgment $\overline{\tau}, \widehat{imr} \vdash_K s : \widehat{imr}'$ has a meaning similar to that of $\overline{\tau}, \widehat{imr} \vdash_K h : \widehat{imr}'$.

A judgment for a program state is related to the concrete syntax used in Section 2 in the following way. We can dissect the concrete syntax into four parts: (1) a maximum stack size K, (2) the types $\overline{\tau}$ for the handlers, (3) a main part m, and (4) a collection $\overline{h}$ of handlers. When we talk about a program $(m, \overline{h})$ in the abstract syntax, the two other parts K and $\overline{\tau}$ seem left out. However, they reappear in the judgment: $\overline{\tau} \vdash_K P_{(m,\overline{h})}$. Thus, that judgment can be read simply as: "the program type checks."

For two sequences $\overline{h}, \overline{\tau}$ of the same length, we will use the abbreviation:

$$\vdash \overline{h} : \overline{\tau}$$

to denote the family of judgments

$$\vdash \overline{h}(i) : \overline{\tau}(i)$$

for all i in the common domain of $\overline{h}$ and $\overline{\tau}$.

We will use the abbreviation:

$$safe(\overline{\tau}, \widehat{imr}, K) = \begin{bmatrix} \forall i \in 1 \ldots n \\ \text{if } enabled(\widehat{imr}, i) \\ \text{then, whenever } \overline{\tau}(i) = \ldots \wedge (\widehat{imr} \xrightarrow{\delta} \widehat{imr}') \wedge \ldots, \\ \text{we have } \widehat{imr}' \leq \widehat{imr} \wedge \delta + 1 \leq K \end{bmatrix} .$$

The idea of $safe(\overline{\tau}, \widehat{imr}, K)$ is to guarantee that it is safe for an interrupt to occur. If an interrupt occurs at a time when the imr has type $\widehat{imr}$ and the "stack budget" is K, then the handler for that interrupt should return with an imr that has a type which is a *subtype* of $\widehat{imr}$. This ensures that $\widehat{imr}$ is still a type for the imr after the interrupt. Moreover, the stack should grow at most δ elements during the call, plus a return address for the call itself.

As a mnemonic, we will sometimes use imr_r for the return imr value of an interrupt handler, and we will sometimes use imr_b for the imr value when an interrupt handler is called.

$$\frac{\vdash \overline{h} : \overline{\tau} \qquad imr \le \widehat{imr} \qquad \overline{\tau}, \widehat{imr} \vdash_K m}{\overline{\tau} \vdash_K \langle \overline{h}, R, imr, \mathsf{nil}, m \rangle} \tag{10}$$

$$\frac{\vdash \overline{h} : \overline{\tau} \qquad imr \le \widehat{imr}}{\overline{\tau}, \widehat{imr} \vdash_K h : \widehat{imr_r} \qquad \widehat{imr_r} \le \widehat{imr_b} \qquad \overline{\tau}, \widehat{imr_b} \vdash_K \sigma}{\overline{\tau} \vdash_K \langle \overline{h}, R, imr, \sigma, h \rangle} \tag{11}$$

$$\frac{\overline{\tau}, \widehat{imr} \vdash_{K+1} m}{\overline{\tau}, \widehat{imr} \vdash_K m :: \mathsf{nil}} \tag{12}$$

$$\frac{\overline{\tau}, \widehat{imr} \vdash_{K+1} h : \widehat{imr_r} \qquad \widehat{imr_r} \le \widehat{imr_b} \qquad \overline{\tau}, \widehat{imr_b} \vdash_{K+1} \sigma}{\overline{\tau}, \widehat{imr} \vdash_K h :: \sigma} \tag{13}$$

$$\frac{\overline{\tau}, (\widehat{imr})^j \wedge \mathsf{t}_0^{\bullet} \vdash_{\delta^j} h : (\widehat{imr}')^j \qquad j \in 1..n}{\vdash h : \bigwedge_{j=1}^n ((\widehat{imr})^j \xrightarrow{\delta^j} (\widehat{imr}')^j)} \tag{14}$$

$$\frac{\overline{\tau}, \widehat{imr} \vdash_K s : \widehat{imr}}{\overline{\tau}, \widehat{imr} \vdash_K \mathsf{loop}\ s} \quad \left[safe(\overline{\tau}, \widehat{imr}, K) \right] \tag{15}$$

$$\frac{\overline{\tau}, \widehat{imr} \vdash_K s : \widehat{imr}' \qquad \overline{\tau}, \widehat{imr}' \vdash_K m}{\overline{\tau}, \widehat{imr} \vdash_K s; m} \tag{16}$$

$$\overline{\tau}, \widehat{imr} \vdash_K \mathsf{iret} : \widehat{imr} \vee \mathsf{t}_0 \quad \left[safe(\overline{\tau}, \widehat{imr}, K) \right] \tag{17}$$

$$\frac{\overline{\tau}, \widehat{imr} \vdash_K s : \widehat{imr}' \qquad \overline{\tau}, \widehat{imr}' \vdash_K h : \widehat{imr}''}{\overline{\tau}, \widehat{imr} \vdash_K s; h : \widehat{imr}''} \tag{18}$$

$$\overline{\tau}, \widehat{imr} \vdash_K x = e : \widehat{imr} \quad \left[safe(\overline{\tau}, \widehat{imr}, K) \right] \tag{19}$$

$$\overline{\tau}, \widehat{imr} \vdash_K \mathsf{imr} = \mathsf{imr} \wedge imr' : \widehat{imr} \wedge imr' \quad \left[safe(\overline{\tau}, \widehat{imr}, K) \right] \tag{20}$$

$$\overline{\tau}, \widehat{imr} \vdash_K \mathsf{imr} = \mathsf{imr} \vee imr' : \widehat{imr} \vee imr' \quad \left[safe(\overline{\tau}, \widehat{imr}, K) \right] \tag{21}$$

$$\frac{\overline{\tau}, \widehat{imr} \vdash_K s_1 : \widehat{imr}' \qquad \overline{\tau}, \widehat{imr} \vdash_K s_2 : \widehat{imr}'}{\overline{\tau}, \widehat{imr} \vdash_K \mathsf{if0}\ (x)\ s_1\ \mathsf{else}\ s_2 : \widehat{imr}'} \quad \left[safe(\overline{\tau}, \widehat{imr}, K) \right] \tag{22}$$

$$\frac{\overline{\tau}, \widehat{imr} \vdash_K s_1 : \widehat{imr}_1 \qquad \overline{\tau}, \widehat{imr}_1 \vdash_K s_2 : \widehat{imr}_2}{\overline{\tau}, \widehat{imr} \vdash_K s_1; s_2 : \widehat{imr}_2} \tag{23}$$

$$\overline{\tau}, \widehat{imr} \vdash_K \text{skip} : \widehat{imr} \quad \left[safe(\overline{\tau}, \widehat{imr}, K) \right] \tag{24}$$

Rules (10)–(11) are for type checking program states. The actual imr value imr is abstracted to a type $\widehat{imr}$ which is used to type check the current statement. In Rule (11), the last two hypotheses ensure that interrupts can return to their callers in a type-safe way. This involves type checking the stack, which is done by Rules (12)–(13).

Rule (14) says that the type of a handler is an intersection type so the handler must have all of the component types of the intersection. For each component type, the annotation δ^j is used as the bound on how much the stack can grow during a call to the handler. Notice that an intersection of different components cannot be reduced into a single component. The rule type checks the handler with the master bit initially turned off.

Rules (15)–(24) are type rules for statements. They are flow-sensitive to the imr, and most of them have the side condition $safe(\overline{\tau}, \widehat{imr}, K)$. The side condition ensures that if an enabled interrupt occurs, then the handler can both be called and return in a type-safe way.

4.3   Type Preservation and Stack Boundedness

Theorem 2. (Type Preservation) *Suppose P is a consistent program state. If $\overline{\tau} \vdash_K P$, $K \geq 0$, and $P \to P'$, then $\overline{\tau} \vdash_{K'} P'$ and $K' \geq 0$, where $K' = K + |P.stk| - |P'.stk|$.*

Proof. See Appendix A.

Theorem 3. (Multi-Step Type Preservation) *Suppose P is a consistent program state. If $\overline{\tau} \vdash_K P$, $K \geq 0$, and $P \to^* P'$, then $\overline{\tau} \vdash_{K'} P'$ and $K' \geq 0$, where $K' = K + |P.stk| - |P'.stk|$.*

Proof. We need to prove that

$\forall n \geq 0$, if $\overline{\tau} \vdash_K P$, $K \geq 0$, and $P \to^n P'$, then $\overline{\tau} \vdash_{K'} P'$ and $K' \geq 0$, where $K' = K + |P.stk| - |P'.stk|$.

We proceed by induction on n. In the base case of $n = 0$, we have $P = P'$, so $K' = K + |P.stk| - |P.stk| = K$. From $P' = P$ and $K' = K$, we have $\overline{\tau} \vdash_{K'} P'$ and $K' \geq 0$.

In the induction step, assume that the property is true for n. Suppose $\overline{\tau} \vdash_K P$, $K \geq 0$, and $P \to^n P' \to P''$. From the induction hypothesis, we have $\overline{\tau} \vdash_{K'} P'$ and $K' \geq 0$, where

$$K' = K + |P.stk| - |P'.stk| \tag{25}$$

From Lemma 1 we have that P' is consistent. From Theorem 2, we have $\overline{\tau} \vdash_{K''} P''$ and $K'' \geq 0$, where

$$K'' = K' + |P'.stk| - |P''.stk| \qquad (26)$$

From Equations (25) and (26), we have

$$
\begin{aligned}
K'' &= K' + |P'.stk| - |P''.stk| \\
&= K + |P.stk| - |P'.stk| + |P'.stk| - |P''.stk| \\
&= K + |P.stk| - |P''.stk|
\end{aligned}
$$

as desired.

Corollary 1. (Stack Boundedness) *If* $\overline{\tau} \vdash_K P_p$, $K \geq 0$, *and* $P_p \rightarrow^* P'$, *then* $|P'.stk| \leq K$.

Proof. Notice first that P_p is consistent. From $\overline{\tau} \vdash_K P_p$, $K \geq 0$, $P_p \rightarrow^* P'$, and Theorem 3, we have $\overline{\tau} \vdash_{K'} P'$ and $K' \geq 0$, where $K' = K + |P_p.stk| - |P'.stk|$. From $K' = K + |P_p.stk| - |P'.stk|$ and $|P_p.stk| = 0$, we have $K' = K - |P'.stk|$, so, since $K' \geq 0$, we have $|P'.stk| \leq K$, as desired.

5   Conclusion

Our calculus is a good foundation for studying interrupt-driven systems. In tune with the need of embedded systems, no program can terminate. Our type system guarantees stack boundedness, and a number of idioms have been type checked using our prototype implementation.

Our calculus can be viewed as the core of our ZIL language [9,12]. ZIL is an intermediate language that strongly resembles Z86 assembly language except that it uses variables instead of registers. We use ZIL as an intermediate language in compilers.

Future work includes implementing the type checker for a full-scale language, such as ZIL, and experimenting with type checking production code. Another challenge is to design a more powerful type system which can type check the timer program in Figure 6. It may be possible to integrate the interrupt calculus with a calculus such as the π-calculus. This could give the advantage that existing methods, techniques, and tools can be used.

To enable our type system to be used easily for legacy systems, we need a way to infer the types of all interrupt handlers. Such type inference may be related to model checking. An idea might be to first execute a variant of a model checking algorithm for pushdown automata [13,3], and then use the computed information to construct types (for a possibly related result, see [11]). At present, it is open whether type inference for our type system is decidable.

Acknowledgment

Our work is supported by the National Science Foundation ITR award 0112628. We thank Dennis Brylow, Mayur Naik, James Rose, Vidyut Samanta, and Matthew Wallace for many helpful discussions.

A   Proof of Theorem 2

Lemma 3. (Safe-Guarantee, Statements) *If* $\overline{\tau}, \widehat{imr} \vdash_K s : \widehat{imr}'$, *then* $safe(\overline{\tau}, \widehat{imr}, K)$.

Proof. By induction on the derivation of $\overline{\tau}, \widehat{imr} \vdash_K s : \widehat{imr}'$; we omit the details.

Lemma 4. (Safe-Guarantee, Handlers) *If* $\overline{\tau}, \widehat{imr} \vdash_K h : \widehat{imr}'$, *then* $safe(\overline{\tau}, \widehat{imr}, K)$.

Proof. By induction on the derivation of $\overline{\tau}, \widehat{imr} \vdash_K h : \widehat{imr}'$, using Lemma 3; we omit the details.

Lemma 5. (Safe-Guarantee, Main) *If* $\overline{\tau}, \widehat{imr} \vdash_K m$, *then* $safe(\overline{\tau}, \widehat{imr}, K)$.

Proof. By induction on the derivation of $\overline{\tau}, \widehat{imr} \vdash_K m$, using Lemma 3; we omit the details.

Lemma 6. (Safe-Weakening) *If* $K_1 \leq K_2$ *and* $safe(\overline{\tau}, \widehat{imr}, K_1)$, *then* $safe(\overline{\tau}, \widehat{imr}, K_2)$.

Proof. From $K_1 \leq K_2$ and

$$
safe(\overline{\tau}, \widehat{imr}, K_1) = \begin{bmatrix} \forall i \in 1 \ldots n \\ \text{if } enabled(\widehat{imr}, i) \\ \text{then, whenever } \overline{\tau}(i) = \ldots \wedge (\widehat{imr} \xrightarrow{\delta} \widehat{imr}') \wedge \ldots, \\ \text{we have } \widehat{imr}' \leq \widehat{imr} \wedge \delta + 1 \leq K_1 \end{bmatrix}
$$

we have

$$
\begin{bmatrix} \forall i \in 1 \ldots n \\ \text{if } enabled(\widehat{imr}, i) \\ \text{then, whenever } \overline{\tau}(i) = \ldots \wedge (\widehat{imr} \xrightarrow{\delta} \widehat{imr}') \wedge \ldots, \\ \text{we have } \widehat{imr}' \leq \widehat{imr} \wedge \delta + 1 \leq K_2 \end{bmatrix}
$$

that is, $safe(\overline{\tau}, \widehat{imr}, K_2)$.

Lemma 7. (K-Weakening, Statements) *If $K_1 \leq K_2$ and $\overline{\tau}, \widehat{imr} \vdash_{K_1} s : \widehat{imr}'$, then $\overline{\tau}, \widehat{imr} \vdash_{K_2} s : \widehat{imr}'$.*

Proof. We proceed by induction on the derivation of $\overline{\tau}, \widehat{imr} \vdash_{K_1} s : \widehat{imr}'$. There are six subcases depending on which one of Rules (19)–(24) was the last one used in the derivation of $\overline{\tau}, \widehat{imr} \vdash_{K_1} s : \widehat{imr}'$.

– Rule (19). We have

$$\overline{\tau}, \widehat{imr} \vdash_{K_1} x = e : \widehat{imr} \qquad \left[safe(\overline{\tau}, \widehat{imr}, K_1) \right].$$

From $K_1 \leq K_2$, $safe(\overline{\tau}, \widehat{imr}, K_1)$, and Lemma 6, we have $safe(\overline{\tau}, \widehat{imr}, K_2)$. Hence, $\overline{\tau}, \widehat{imr} \vdash_{K_2} x = e : \widehat{imr}$.
– Rule (20). The proof is similar to that for Rule (19).
– Rule (21). The proof is similar to that for Rule (19).
– Rule (22). We have

$$\frac{\overline{\tau}, \widehat{imr} \vdash_{K_1} s_1 : \widehat{imr}' \quad \overline{\tau}, \widehat{imr} \vdash_{K_1} s_2 : \widehat{imr}'}{\overline{\tau}, \widehat{imr} \vdash_{K_1} \text{if0 } (x) \ s_1 \text{ else } s_2 : \widehat{imr}'} \qquad \left[safe(\overline{\tau}, \widehat{imr}, K_1) \right].$$

From the induction hypothesis, we have $\overline{\tau}, \widehat{imr} \vdash_{K_2} s_1 : \widehat{imr}'$ and $\overline{\tau}, \widehat{imr} \vdash_{K_2} s_2 : \widehat{imr}'$. From $K_1 \leq K_2$, $safe(\overline{\tau}, \widehat{imr}, K_1)$, and Lemma 6, we have $safe(\overline{\tau}, \widehat{imr}, K_2)$. Hence, $\overline{\tau}, \widehat{imr} \vdash_{K_2} \text{if0 } (x) \ s_1 \text{ else } s_2 : \widehat{imr}'$.
– Rule (23). We have

$$\frac{\overline{\tau}, \widehat{imr} \vdash_{K_1} s_1 : \widehat{imr}_1 \quad \overline{\tau}, \widehat{imr}_1 \vdash_{K_1} s_2 : \widehat{imr}_2}{\overline{\tau}, \widehat{imr} \vdash_{K_1} s_1; s_2 : \widehat{imr}_2}.$$

From the induction hypothesis, we have $\overline{\tau}, \widehat{imr} \vdash_{K_2} s_1 : \widehat{imr}_1$ and $\overline{\tau}, \widehat{imr}_1 \vdash_{K_2} s_2 : \widehat{imr}_2$. Hence, $\overline{\tau}, \widehat{imr} \vdash_{K_2} s_1; s_2 : \widehat{imr}_2$.
– Rule (24). The proof is similar to that for Rule (19).

Lemma 8. (K-Weakening, Handlers) *If $K_1 \leq K_2$ and $\overline{\tau}, \widehat{imr} \vdash_{K_1} h : \widehat{imr}'$, then $\overline{\tau}, \widehat{imr} \vdash_{K_2} h : \widehat{imr}'$.*

Proof. We proceed by induction on the derivation of $\overline{\tau}, \widehat{imr} \vdash_{K_1} h : \widehat{imr}'$. There are two subcases depending on which one of Rules (17)–(18) was the last one used in the derivation of $\overline{\tau}, \widehat{imr} \vdash_{K_1} h : \widehat{imr}'$.

– Rule (17). We have

$$\overline{\tau}, \widehat{imr} \vdash_{K_1} \text{iret} : \widehat{imr} \vee \mathsf{t}_0 \qquad \left[safe(\overline{\tau}, \widehat{imr}, K_1) \right].$$

From $K_1 \leq K_2$, $safe(\overline{\tau}, \widehat{imr}, K_1)$, and Lemma 6, we have $safe(\overline{\tau}, \widehat{imr}, K_2)$. Therefore, we have

$$\overline{\tau}, \widehat{imr} \vdash_{K_2} \text{iret} : \widehat{imr} \vee \mathsf{t}_0.$$

– Rule (18). We have

$$\frac{\overline{\tau}, \widehat{imr} \vdash_{K_1} s : \widehat{imr}' \qquad \overline{\tau}, \widehat{imr}' \vdash_{K_1} h : \widehat{imr}''}{\overline{\tau}, \widehat{imr} \vdash_{K_1} s; h : \widehat{imr}''}.$$

From Lemma 7, we have

$$\overline{\tau}, \widehat{imr} \vdash_{K_2} s : \widehat{imr}'.$$

From the induction hypothesis, we have

$$\overline{\tau}, \widehat{imr}' \vdash_{K_2} h : \widehat{imr}''.$$

From $\overline{\tau}, \widehat{imr} \vdash_{K_2} s : \widehat{imr}'$ and $\overline{\tau}, \widehat{imr}' \vdash_{K_2} h : \widehat{imr}''$, we can use Rule (18) to derive $\overline{\tau}, \widehat{imr} \vdash_{K_2} s; h : \widehat{imr}''$.

We can now prove Theorem 2, which we restate here:

Suppose P is a consistent program state. If $\overline{\tau} \vdash_K P$, $K \geq 0$, and $P \rightarrow P'$, then $\overline{\tau} \vdash_{K'} P'$ and $K' \geq 0$, where $K' = K + |P.stk| - |P'.stk|$.

Proof. There are nine cases depending on which one of Rules (1)–(9) was used to derive $P \rightarrow P'$.

– Rule (1). We have $\langle \overline{\tau}, R, imr, \sigma, a \rangle \rightarrow \langle \overline{h}, R, imr \wedge \mathsf{t}_0^\bullet, a :: \sigma, \overline{h}(i) \rangle$ and $enabled(imr, i)$. Since P is consistent, there are two subcases.
Subcase 1: We have $P = \langle \overline{h}, R, imr, \mathsf{nil}, m \rangle$ and
$P' = \langle \overline{h}, R, imr \wedge \mathsf{t}_0^\bullet, m :: \mathsf{nil}, \overline{h}(i) \rangle$. From $\overline{\tau} \vdash_K P$ and Rule (10), we have the derivation:

$$\frac{\vdash \overline{h} : \overline{\tau} \qquad imr \leq \widehat{imr} \qquad \overline{\tau}, \widehat{imr} \vdash_K m}{\overline{\tau} \vdash_K \langle \overline{h}, R, imr, \mathsf{nil}, m \rangle}.$$

From $\overline{\tau}, \widehat{imr} \vdash_K m$, and Lemma 5, we have that:

$$safe(\overline{\tau}, \widehat{imr}, K) = \begin{bmatrix} \forall i \in 1 \dots n \\ \text{if } enabled(\widehat{imr}, i) \\ \text{then, whenever } \overline{\tau}(i) = \dots \wedge (\widehat{imr} \xrightarrow{\delta} \widehat{imr}') \wedge \dots, \\ \text{we have } \widehat{imr}' \leq \widehat{imr} \wedge \delta + 1 \leq K \end{bmatrix}$$

is true. From $safe(\overline{\tau}, \widehat{imr}, K)$ and $enabled(\widehat{imr}, i)$, it follows that:

$$\overline{\tau}(i) = \dots \wedge (\widehat{imr} \xrightarrow{\delta} \widehat{imr}') \wedge \dots \qquad \widehat{imr}' \leq \widehat{imr} \qquad \delta + 1 \leq K.$$

From $\vdash \overline{h} : \overline{\tau}$ and Rule (14), we have $\overline{\tau}, \widehat{imr} \wedge \mathsf{t}_0^\bullet \vdash_\delta h_i : \widehat{imr}'$. From $\delta \leq K - 1, \overline{\tau}, \widehat{imr} \wedge \mathsf{t}_0^\bullet \vdash_\delta h_i : \widehat{imr}'$, and Lemma 8, we have

$$\overline{\tau}, \widehat{imr} \wedge \mathsf{t}_0^\bullet \vdash_{K-1} h_i : \widehat{imr}'.$$

From $\overline{\tau}, \widehat{imr} \vdash_K m$ and Rule (12), we have $\overline{\tau}, \widehat{imr} \vdash_{K-1} m :: \text{nil}$. From $\vdash \overline{h} : \overline{\tau}, imr \wedge \mathsf{t}_0^\bullet \leq \widehat{imr} \wedge \mathsf{t}_0^\bullet, \overline{\tau}, \widehat{imr} \wedge \mathsf{t}_0^\bullet \vdash_{K-1} h_i : \widehat{imr}', \widehat{imr}' \leq \widehat{imr}$, $\overline{\tau}, \widehat{imr} \vdash_{K-1} m :: \text{nil}$, and $K' = K + |P.stk| - |P'.stk| = K - 1 \geq \delta \geq 0$, we can use Rule (11) to derive $\overline{\tau} \vdash_{K'} P'$.

Subcase 2: We have $P = \langle \overline{h}, R, imr, \sigma, h \rangle$, $P' = \langle \overline{h}, R, imr \wedge \mathsf{t}_0^\bullet, h :: \sigma, \overline{h}(i) \rangle$. From $\overline{\tau} \vdash_K P$ and Rule (11), we have the derivation:

$$\dfrac{\dfrac{\vdash \overline{h} : \overline{\tau} \quad imr \leq \widehat{imr}}{} \quad \overline{\tau}, \widehat{imr} \vdash_K h : \widehat{imr}_r \quad \widehat{imr}_r \leq \widehat{imr}_b \quad \overline{\tau}, \widehat{imr}_b \vdash_K \sigma}{\overline{\tau} \vdash_K \langle \overline{h}, R, imr, \sigma, h \rangle}.$$

From $\overline{\tau}, \widehat{imr} \vdash_K h : \widehat{imr}_r$, and Lemma 4, we have that

$$safe(\overline{\tau}, \widehat{imr}, K) = \begin{bmatrix} \forall i \in 1 \ldots n \\ \text{if } enabled(\widehat{imr}, i) \\ \text{then, whenever } \overline{\tau}(i) = \ldots \wedge (\widehat{imr} \xrightarrow{\delta} \widehat{imr}') \wedge \ldots, \\ \text{we have } \widehat{imr}' \leq \widehat{imr} \wedge \delta + 1 \leq K \end{bmatrix}$$

is true. From $safe(\overline{\tau}, \widehat{imr}, K)$ and $enabled(\widehat{imr}, i)$, it follows that

$$\overline{\tau}(i) = \ldots \wedge (\widehat{imr} \xrightarrow{\delta} \widehat{imr}') \wedge \ldots \qquad \widehat{imr}' \leq \widehat{imr} \qquad \delta + 1 \leq K.$$

From $\vdash \overline{h} : \overline{\tau}$ and Rule (14), we have $\overline{\tau}, \widehat{imr} \wedge \mathsf{t}_0^\bullet \vdash_\delta h_i : \widehat{imr}'$. From $\delta \leq K - 1, \overline{\tau}, \widehat{imr} \wedge \mathsf{t}_0^\bullet \vdash_\delta h_i : \widehat{imr}'$, and Lemma 8, we have

$$\overline{\tau}, \widehat{imr} \wedge \mathsf{t}_0^\bullet \vdash_{K-1} h_i : \widehat{imr}'.$$

From $\overline{\tau}, \widehat{imr} \vdash_K h : \widehat{imr}_r, \widehat{imr}_r \leq \widehat{imr}_b, \overline{\tau}, \widehat{imr}_b \vdash_K \sigma$, and Rule (13), we have

$$\overline{\tau}, \widehat{imr} \vdash_{K-1} h :: \sigma.$$

From $\vdash \overline{h} : \overline{\tau}, imr \wedge \mathsf{t}_0^\bullet \leq \widehat{imr} \wedge \mathsf{t}_0^\bullet, \overline{\tau}, \widehat{imr} \wedge \mathsf{t}_0^\bullet \vdash_{K-1} h_i : \widehat{imr}', \widehat{imr}' \leq \widehat{imr}$, $\overline{\tau}, \widehat{imr} \vdash_{K-1} h :: \sigma$, and $K' = K + |P.stk| - |P'.stk| = K - 1 \geq \delta \geq 0$, we can use Rule (11) to derive $\overline{\tau} \vdash_{K'} P'$.

– Rule (2). We have $\langle \overline{h}, R, imr, \sigma, \mathsf{iret} \rangle \to \langle \overline{h}, R, imr \vee \mathsf{t}_0, \sigma', a \rangle$, and $\sigma = a :: \sigma'$. Since P is consistent, there are two subcases.

Subcase 1: We have $P = \langle \overline{h}, R, imr, m :: \text{nil}, \mathsf{iret} \rangle$ and $P' = \langle \overline{h}, R, imr \vee \mathsf{t}_0, \text{nil}, m \rangle$. From $\overline{\tau} \vdash_K P$, Rule (11), and Rule (12), we have the derivation:

$$\dfrac{\dfrac{\vdash \overline{h} : \overline{\tau} \quad imr \leq \widehat{imr}}{} \quad \overline{\tau}, \widehat{imr} \vdash_K \mathsf{iret} : \widehat{imr} \vee \mathsf{t}_0 \quad \widehat{imr} \vee \mathsf{t}_0 \leq \widehat{imr}_b \quad \dfrac{\overline{\tau}, \widehat{imr}_b \vdash_{K+1} m}{\overline{\tau}, \widehat{imr}_b \vdash_K m :: \text{nil}}}{\overline{\tau} \vdash_K \langle \overline{h}, R, imr, m :: \text{nil}, \mathsf{iret} \rangle}.$$

From $\vdash \overline{h} : \overline{\tau},\, imr \vee t_0 \leq \widehat{imr} \vee t_0 \leq \widehat{imr_b},\, \overline{\tau}, \widehat{imr_b}\ \vdash_{K+1}\ m$, and $K' = K + |P.stk| - |P'.stk| = K+1$, we can use Rule (10) to derive $\overline{\tau} \vdash_{K'} P'$.

Subcase 2: We have $P = \langle \overline{h}, R, imr, h^k :: \sigma', \mathsf{iret} \rangle$ and $P' = \langle \overline{h}, R, imr \vee t_0, \sigma', h^k \rangle$. From $\overline{\tau} \vdash_K P$, Rule (11), and Rule (13), we have the derivation:

$$\frac{\vdash \overline{h} : \overline{\tau} \quad imr \leq \widehat{imr}}{\overline{\tau}, \widehat{imr}\ \vdash_K\ \mathsf{iret} : \widehat{imr} \vee t_0 \quad \widehat{imr} \vee t_0 \leq \widehat{imr_b} \quad \overline{\tau}, \widehat{imr_b}\ \vdash_K\ h^k :: \sigma'}{\overline{\tau}\ \vdash_K\ \langle \overline{h}, R, imr, h^k :: \sigma', \mathsf{iret} \rangle}.$$

where $\overline{\tau}, \widehat{imr_b}\ \vdash_K\ h^k :: \sigma'$ is derived as follows:

$$\frac{\overline{\tau}, \widehat{imr_b}\ \vdash_{K+1}\ h^k : \widehat{imr}_r^k \quad \widehat{imr}_r^k \leq \widehat{imr_b}^k \quad \overline{\tau}, \widehat{imr_b}^k\ \vdash_{K+1}\ \sigma}{\overline{\tau}, \widehat{imr_b}\ \vdash_K\ h^k :: \sigma}.$$

From $\vdash \overline{h} : \overline{\tau},\, imr \vee t_0 \leq \widehat{imr} \vee t_0 \leq \widehat{imr_b},\, \overline{\tau}, \widehat{imr_b}\ \vdash_{K+1}\ h^k : \widehat{imr}_r^k,\, \widehat{imr}_r^k \leq \widehat{imr_b}^k,\, \overline{\tau}, \widehat{imr_b}^k\ \vdash_{K+1}\ \sigma$, and $K' = K + |P.stk| - |P'.stk| = K+1$ we can use Rule (11) to derive $\overline{\tau} \vdash_{K'} P'$.

- Rule (3). We have $\langle \overline{h}, R, imr, \mathsf{nil}, \mathsf{loop}\ s \rangle \rightarrow \langle \overline{h}, R, imr, \mathsf{nil}, s; \mathsf{loop}\ s \rangle$. From $\overline{\tau} \vdash_K P$, Rule (10), and Rule (15), we have the derivation:

$$\frac{\vdash \overline{h} : \overline{\tau} \quad imr \leq \widehat{imr} \quad \dfrac{\overline{\tau}, \widehat{imr}\ \vdash_K\ s : \widehat{imr}}{\overline{\tau}, \widehat{imr}\ \vdash_K\ \mathsf{loop}\ s}}{\overline{\tau}\ \vdash_K\ \langle \overline{h}, R, imr, \mathsf{nil}, \mathsf{loop}\ s \rangle}.$$

From $\overline{\tau}, \widehat{imr}\ \vdash_K\ s : \widehat{imr},\, \overline{\tau}, \widehat{imr}\ \vdash_K\ \mathsf{loop}\ s$, and Rule (16) we have $\overline{\tau}, \widehat{imr}\ \vdash_K\ s; \mathsf{loop}\ s$. From $\vdash \overline{h} : \overline{\tau},\, imr \leq \widehat{imr},\, \overline{\tau}, \widehat{imr}\ \vdash_K\ s; \mathsf{loop}\ s$, and $K' = K + |P.stk| - |P'.stk| = K$, we can use Rule (10) to derive $\overline{\tau} \vdash_{K'} P'$.

- Rule (4). We have $\langle \overline{h}, R, imr, \sigma, x = e; a \rangle \rightarrow \langle \overline{h}, R\{x \mapsto eval_R(e)\}, imr, \sigma, a \rangle$. Since P is consistent, there are two subcases.

Subcase 1: $P = \langle \overline{h}, R, imr, \mathsf{nil}, x = e; m \rangle$ and $P' = \langle \overline{h}, R\{x \mapsto eval_R(e)\}, imr, \mathsf{nil}, m \rangle$.

From $\overline{\tau} \vdash_K P$, Rule (10), and Rule (16), we have the derivation:

$$\frac{\vdash \overline{h} : \overline{\tau} \quad imr \leq \widehat{imr} \quad \dfrac{\overline{\tau}, \widehat{imr}\ \vdash_K\ x = e : \widehat{imr} \quad \overline{\tau}, \widehat{imr}\ \vdash_K\ m}{\overline{\tau}, \widehat{imr}\ \vdash_K\ x = e; m}}{\overline{\tau}\ \vdash_K\ \langle \overline{h}, R, imr, \mathsf{nil}, x = e; m \rangle}.$$

From $\vdash \overline{h} : \overline{\tau},\, imr \leq \widehat{imr}, \overline{\tau}, \widehat{imr}\ \vdash_K\ m$, and $K' = K + |P.stk| - |P'.stk| = K$, we can use Rule (10) to derive $\overline{\tau} \vdash_{K'} P'$.

Subcase 2: $P = \langle \overline{h}, R, imr, \sigma, x = e; h \rangle$ and $P' = \langle \overline{h}, R\{x \mapsto eval_R(e)\}, imr, \sigma, h \rangle$. From $\overline{\tau} \vdash_K P$, Rule (11), and

Rule (18), we have the derivation:

$$
\cfrac{
  \vdash \overline{h} : \overline{\tau} \quad imr \leq \widehat{imr} \quad
  \cfrac{
    \overline{\tau}, \widehat{imr} \vdash_K x = e : \widehat{imr} \quad
    \overline{\tau}, \widehat{imr} \vdash_K h : \widehat{imr}_r
  }{
    \overline{\tau}, \widehat{imr} \vdash_K x = e; h : \widehat{imr}_r
  }
  \qquad
  \cfrac{
    \widehat{imr}_r \leq \widehat{imr}_b \quad \overline{\tau}, \widehat{imr}_b \vdash_K \sigma
  }{}
}{
  \overline{\tau} \vdash_K \langle \overline{h}, R, imr, \sigma, x = e; h \rangle
}.
$$

From $\vdash \overline{h} : \overline{\tau}, imr \leq \widehat{imr}, \overline{\tau}, \widehat{imr} \vdash_K h : \widehat{imr}_r, \widehat{imr}_r \leq \widehat{imr}_b,$
$\overline{\tau}, \widehat{imr}_b \vdash_K \sigma$, and $K' = K + |P.stk| - |P'.stk| = K$, we can use Rule (11)
to derive $\overline{\tau} \vdash_{K'} P'$.

- Rules (5)–(9). The proofs are similar to that for Rule (4); we omit the details.

References

1. Martín Abadi and Luca Cardelli. *A Theory of Objects*. Springer-Verlag, 1996.
2. Henk P. Barendregt. *The Lambda Calculus: Its Syntax and Semantics*. North-Holland, Amsterdam, 1981.
3. Dennis Brylow, Niels Damgaard, and Jens Palsberg. Static checking of interrupt-driven software. In *Proceedings of ICSE'01, 23rd International Conference on Software Engineering*, pages 47–56, Toronto, May 2001.
4. Luca Cardelli and Andrew D. Gordon. Mobile ambients. In M. Nivat, editor, *Proceedings of Foundations of Software Science and Computation Structures*, pages 140–155. Springer-Verlag (*LNCS* 1378), 1998.
5. M. Coppo, M. Dezani-Ciancaglini, and B. Venneri. Principal type schemes and lambda-calculus semantics. In J. Seldin and J. Hindley, editors, *To H. B. Curry: Essays on Combinatory Logic, Lambda Calculus and Formalism*, pages 535–560. Academic Press, 1980.
6. J. Roger Hindley. Types with intersection: An introduction. *Formal Aspects of Computing*, 4:470–486, 1991.
7. R. Milner. *A Calculus of Communicating Systems*. Springer-Verlag (*LNCS* 92), 1980.
8. Robin Milner, Joachim Parrow, and David Walker. A calculus of mobile processes, part I/II. *Information and Compuation*, 100(1):1–77, September 1992.
9. Mayur Naik and Jens Palsberg. Compiling with code-size constraints. In *LCTES'02, Languages, Compilers, and Tools for Embedded Systems joint with SCOPES'02, Software and Compilers for Embedded Systems*, June 2002.
10. Jens Palsberg. Type-based analysis and applications. In *Proceedings of PASTE'01, ACM Workshop on Program Analysis for Software Tools*, pages 20–27, June 2001.
11. Jens Palsberg and Christina Pavlopoulou. From polyvariant flow information to intersection and union types. *Journal of Functional Programming*, 11(3):263–317, May 2001.
12. Jens Palsberg and Matthew Wallace. Reverse engineering of real-time assembly code. Manuscript, 2002.
13. Andreas Podelski. Model checking as constraint solving. In *Proceedings of SAS'00, International Static Analysis Symposium*, pages 22–37. Springer-Verlag (*LNCS* 1824), 2000.
14. Wayne Wolf. *Computers as Components, Principles of Embedded Computing System Design*. Morgan Kaufman Publishers, 2000.

Parametric Verification
of a Group Membership Algorithm*

Ahmed Bouajjani and Agathe Merceron

LIAFA, Univ. of Paris 7, Case 7014, 2 place Jussieu, F-75251 Paris 5, France
{Ahmed.Bouajjani,Agathe.Merceron}@liafa.jussieu.fr

Abstract. We address the problem of verifying clique avoidance in the TTP protocol. TTP allows several stations embedded in a car to communicate. It has many mechanisms to ensure robustness to faults. In particular, it has an algorithm that allows a station to recognize itself as faulty and leave the communication. This algorithm must satisfy the crucial 'non-clique' property: it is impossible to have two or more disjoint groups of stations communicating exclusively with stations in their own group. In this paper, we propose an automatic verification method for an arbitrary number of stations N and a given number of faults k. We give a faithful abstraction that allows to model the algorithm by means of unbounded (parametric) counter automata. We have checked the non-clique property on this model in the case of one fault, using the ALV tool as well as the LASH tool.

Keywords: Formal verification, fault-tolerant protocols, parametric counter automata, abstraction.

1   Introduction

The verification of complex systems, especially of software systems, requires the adoption of powerful methodologies based on combining, and sometimes iterating, several analysis techniques. A widely adopted approach consists in combining abstraction techniques with verification algorithms (e.g., model-checking, symbolic reachability analysis, see, e.g., [16,1,23]). In this approach, non-trivial abstraction steps are necessary to construct faithful abstract models (typically finite-state models) on which the required properties can be automatically verified. The abstraction steps can be extremely hard to carry out depending on how restricted the targeted class of abstract models is. Indeed, many aspects in the behavior of complex software systems cannot (or can hardly) be captured using finite-state models. Among these aspects, we can mention, e.g., (1) the manipulation of variables and data-structures (counters, queues, arrays, etc.) ranging over infinite domains, (2) parameterization (e.g., sizes of the data structures, the number of components in the system, the rates of

* This work was supported in part by the European Commission (FET project ADVANCE, contract No IST-1999-29082).

W. Damm and E.-R. Olderog (Eds.): FTRTFT 2002, LNCS 2469, pp. 311–330, 2002.

errors/faults/losses, etc.). For this reason, it is often needed to consider abstraction steps which yield infinite-state models corresponding to extended automata, i.e., a finite-control automata supplied with unbounded data-structures (e.g., timed automata, pushdown automata, counter automata, FIFO-channel automata, finite-state transducers, etc.) [1]. Then, symbolic reachability analysis algorithms (see, e.g., [14,7,8,9,18,12,24,10,4,2,3]) can be applied on these (abstract) extended automata-based models in order to verify the desired properties of the original (concrete) system. Of course, abstraction steps remain non-trivial in general for complex systems, even if infinite-state extended automata are used as abstract models.

In this paper, we consider verification problems concerning a protocol used in the automotive industry. The protocol, called TTP/C, was designed at the Technical University of Vienna in order to allow the communication between several devices (micro-processors) embedded in a car, whose function is to control the safe execution of different driving actions [20,19].

The protocol involves many mechanisms to ensure robustness to faults. In particular, the protocol involves a mechanism which allows to discard devices (called stations) which are (supposed to be) faulty. This mechanism must ensure the crucial property: *all active stations form one single group of communicating stations, i.e., it is impossible to have two (or more) disjoint groups of active stations communicating exclusively with stations in their own group.*

Actually, the algorithm is very subtle and its verification is a real challenge for formal and automatic verification methods. Roughly, it is a parameterized algorithm for N stations arranged in a ring topology. Each of the stations broadcasts a message to all stations when it is its turn to emit. The turn of each station is determined by a fixed time schedule. Stations maintain informations corresponding to their view of the global state of the system: a membership vector, consisting of an array with a parametric size N, telling which stations are active. Stations exchange their views of the system and this allows them to recognize faulty stations. Each time a station sends a message, it sends also the result of a calculation which encodes its membership vector. Stations compare their membership vectors to those received from sending stations. If a receiver disagrees with the membership vector of the sender, it counts the received message as incorrect. If a station disagree with a majority of stations (in the round since the last time the station has emitted), it considers itself as faulty and leaves the active mode (it refrains from emitting and skips its turn). Stations which are inactive can return later to the active mode (details are given in the paper). Besides the membership vector, each station s maintains two integer counters in order to count in the last round (since the previous emission of the station s) (1) the number of stations which have emitted and from which s has received a correct message with membership vector equal to its own vector at that moment (the stations may disagree later concerning some other emitting station), and (2) the number of stations from which s received an incorrect message (the incorrect message may be due to a transmission fault or to a different membership vector). The information maintained by each station s depends tightly on its position in the ring relatively to the positions of the faulty stations and relatively to the stations which agree/disagree with s w.r.t. each fault.

The proof of correction of the algorithm and its automatic verification are far from being straightforward, especially in the parametric case, i.e., for any number of stations, and any number of faults.

The first contribution of this paper is to prove that the algorithm stabilizes to a state where all membership vectors are equal after precisely two rounds from the occurrence of the last fault in any sequence of faults.

Then, we address the problem of verifying automatically the algorithm. We prove that, for every fixed number of faults k, it is possible to construct an exact abstraction of the algorithm (parameterized by the number of stations N) by means of a parametric counter automaton. This result is surprising since (1) it is not easy to abstract the information related to the topology of the system (ordering between the stations in the ring), and (2) each station (in the concrete algorithm) has local variables ranging over infinite domains (two counters and an array with parametric bounds). The difficulty is to prove that it is possible to encode the information needed by all stations by means of a finite number of counters. Basically, this is done as follows: (1) We observe that a sequence of faults induces a partition of the set of active stations (classes correspond to stations having the same membership vector) which is built by successive refinements: Initially, all stations are in the same set, and the occurrence of each fault has the effect of splitting the class containing the faulty station into two subclasses (stations which recognizes the fault, and the other ones). (2) We show that there is a partition of the ring into a finite number of regions (depending on the positions of the faulty stations) such that, to determine at any time whether a station of any class can emit, it is enough to know how many stations in the different classes/zones have emitted in the last two rounds. This counting is delicate due to the splitting of the classes after each fault.

Finally, we show that, given a counter automaton modeling the algorithm, the stabilization property (after 2 rounds following the last fault) can be expressed as a constrained reachability property (in CTL with Presburger predicates) which can be checked using symbolic reachability analysis tools for counter automata (e.g., ALV [13] or LASH [21]). We have experimented this approach in the case of one fault. We have built a model for the algorithm in the language of ALV, and we have been able to verify automatically that it converges to a single clique after precisely two rounds from the occurrence of the fault. Actually, we have provided a refinement of the abstraction given in the general case which allows to build a simpler automaton. This refinement is based on properties specific to the 1 fault case that have been checked automatically using ALV.

The paper is organized as follows. Section 2 presents the protocol. In Section 3, we prove the crucial non-clique property for n stations: the stations that are still active do have the same membership vector at the end of the second round following fault k. Considering the 1 fault case, section 4 presents how to abstract faithfully the protocol parameterized by the number of stations n as an automaton with counters that can be symbolically model checked. Section 5

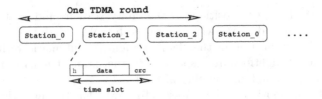

Fig. 1. A TDMA round for 3 stations.

generalizes the approach for a given number of faults k. Section 6 concludes the paper. By lack of space, all proofs are omitted. They can be found in [11].

2   Informal Description of the Protocol

TTP is a time-triggered protocol. It has a finite set S of N stations and allows them to communicate via a shared bus. Messages are broadcast to all stations via the bus. Each station that participates in the communication sends a message when it is the *right* time to do so. Therefore, access to the bus is determined by a time division multiple access (TDMA) schema controlled by the global time generated by the protocol. A TDMA round is divided into *time slots*. The stations are statically ordered in a ring and time slots are allocated to the stations according to their order. During its time slot, a station has exclusive message sending rights. A TDMA round for three stations is shown in Figure 1. When one round is completed, a next one takes place following the same pattern.

TTP is a fault-tolerant protocol. Stations may fail while other stations continue communicating with each other. TTP provides different services to ensure robustness to faults, such as replication of stations, replication of communication channels, bus guardian, fault-tolerant clock synchronization algorithm, implicit acknowledgment, clique avoidance mechanism, [20,19,5]. Several classes of faults are distinguished. A symmetric fault occurs when a station is *send faulty*, i.e., no other station can receive it properly, or *receive faulty*, i.e., it cannot receive properly any message. Asymmetric faults occur when an emitting station is received properly by more than 1 station, but less then all stations. In this paper, we allow asymmetric faults to occur and consider symmetric faults as a special case of asymmetric faults. TTP provides special mechanisms to deal with other failures like processor faults, transient faults, but we do not consider them here. For the protocol to work well, it is essential that (asymmetric) faults do not give rise to cliques. In [20,19] *cliques* are understood as disjoint sets of stations communicating exclusively with each other. In this paper, we focus on implicit acknowledgment and clique avoidance mechanism, to be introduced shortly, and show that they prevent the formation of different cliques, clique is cast in its graph theoretical meaning. When it is working or in the `active` state, a station sends messages in its time slot, listens to messages broadcast by other stations and carries local calculations.

2.1 Local Information

Each station s stores locally some information, in particular a *membership vector* m_s and two counters, $CAcc_s$ and $CFail_s$. A *membership vector* is an array of booleans indexed by S. It indicates the stations that s receives correctly (in a sense that will be made precise below). If s received correctly the last message, also called *frame*, sent by s', then $m_s[s'] = 1$, otherwise $m_s[s'] = 0$. A sending station is supposed to receive herself properly, thus $m_s[s] = 1$ for a working station s. The counters $CAcc_s$ and $CFail_s$ are used as follows. When it is ready to send, s resets $CAcc_s$ and $CFail_s$ to 0. During the subsequent round, s increases $CAcc_s$ by 1 each time it receives a correct frame (this includes the frame it is sending itself) and it increases $CFail_s$ by 1 each time it receives an incorrect frame. When no frame is sent (because the station that should send is not working), neither $CFail_s$ nor $CAcc_s$ are increased.

2.2 Implicit Acknowledgment

Frames are broadcast over the bus to all stations but they are not explicitly acknowledged. TTP has *implicit acknowledgment*. A frame is composed of a header, denoted by h in Figure 1, a data field, denoted by data and a CRC field denoted by crc. The data field contains the data, like sensor-recorded data, that a station wants to broadcast. The CRC field contains the calculation of the Cyclic Redundancy Check done by the sending station. CRC is calculated over the header, the data field and the individual membership vector. When station s is sending, it puts in the CRC field the calculation it has done with its own membership vector m_s. Station s' receiving a frame from station s recognizes the frame as *valid* if all the fields have the expected lengths. If the frame is valid, station s' performs a CRC calculation over the header and the data field it has just received, and its own membership vector $m_{s'}$. It recognizes the frame as *correct* if it has recognized it as valid and its CRC calculation agrees with the one put by s in the CRC field. Therefore, a correct CRC implies that sender s and receiver s' have the same membership vector. *We also assume a converse:* if s and s' do not have the same membership vector, the CRC is not correct. The CRC check justifies *implicit acknowledgment*. Receiver s' has $m_{s'}[s'] = 1$. A correct CRC implies $m_{s'} = m_s$, thus $m_s[s'] = 1$. Hence s has correctly received the last frame sent by s', i.e., s' is implicitly acknowledged by s. Implicit acknowledgment in TTP contains an additional feature involving first and second successors [19]. Our result on cliques is established for a version where these complications are not present.

2.3 Clique Avoidance Mechanism

The *clique avoidance mechanism* reads as follows: Once per round, at the beginning of its time slot, a station s checks whether $CAcc_s > CFail_s$. If it is the case, it resets both counters as already said above and sends a message. If it is not the case, the stations fails. It puts its own membership vector bit to 0, i.e.,

$m_s[s] = 0$, and leaves the `active` state, thus will not send in the subsequent rounds. The intuition behind this mechanism is that a station that fails to recognize a majority of frames as correct, is most probably not working properly. Other working stations, not receiving anything during the time slot of s, put the bit of s to 0 in their own membership vector.

2.4   Re-integration

Faulty stations that have left the active state can re-integrate the active state [19,5]. The integration algorithm works as follows. An integrating station s copies the membership vector from some active station. As soon as the integrating station has a copy, it updates its membership vector listening to the traffic following the same algorithm as other working stations. During its first sending slot, it resets both counters, $CAcc_s$ and $CFail_s$ to 0, without sending any frame. During the following round, it increases its counters and keeps updating its membership vector as working stations do. At the beginning of its next sending slot, s checks whether $CAcc_s > CFail_s$. If it is the case, it puts $m_s[s]$ to 1 and sends a frame, otherwise it leaves the `active` state again. Receiving stations, if they detect a valid frame, put the membership of s to 1 and then perform the CRC check as described above.

2.5   Example

Consider a set S composed of 4 stations and suppose that all stations received correct frames from each other for a while. This means that they all have identical membership vectors and $CFail = 0$. After station s_3 has sent, the membership vectors as well as counters $CAcc$ and $CFail$ look as follows. Remember that there is no global resetting of $CAcc$ and $CFail$. Resetting is relative to the position of the sending station.

stations	$m[s_0]$	$m[s_1]$	$m[s_2]$	$m[s_3]$	$CAcc$	$CFail$
s_0	1	1	1	1	4	0
s_1	1	1	1	1	3	0
s_2	1	1	1	1	2	0
s_3	1	1	1	1	1	0

We suppose that a fault occurs while s_0 is sending and that no subsequent fault occurs for at least two rounds, calculated from the time slot of s_0. We assume also that the frame sent by s_0 is recognized as correct by s_2 only. So the set S is split in two subsets, $S_1 = \{s_0, s_2\}$ and $S_0 = \{s_1, s_3\}$.

1. Membership vectors and counters after s_0 has sent:

stations	$m[s_0]$	$m[s_1]$	$m[s_2]$	$m[s_3]$	$CAcc$	$CFail$
s_0	1	1	1	1	1	0
s_1	0	1	1	1	3	1
s_2	1	1	1	1	3	0
s_3	0	1	1	1	1	1

2. Membership vectors and counters after s_1 has sent. Notice that, because s_0 and s_2 do not have the same membership vector as s_1, the CRC check does not pass, so they don't recognize the frame sent by s_1 as correct.

stations	$m[s_0]$	$m[s_1]$	$m[s_2]$	$m[s_3]$	CAcc	CFail
s_0	1	0	1	1	1	1
s_1	0	1	1	1	1	0
s_2	1	0	1	1	3	1
s_3	0	1	1	1	2	1

3. Membership vectors and counters after s_2 has sent:

stations	$m[s_0]$	$m[s_1]$	$m[s_2]$	$m[s_3]$	CAcc	CFail
s_0	1	0	1	1	2	1
s_1	0	1	0	1	1	1
s_2	1	0	1	1	1	0
s_3	0	1	0	1	2	2

4. Memberships and counters after the time slot of s_3, which cannot send by the clique avoidance mechanism and leaves the active state:

stations	$m[s_0]$	$m[s_1]$	$m[s_2]$	$m[s_3]$	CAcc	CFail
s_0	1	0	1	0	2	1
s_1	0	1	0	0	1	1
s_2	1	0	1	0	1	0
s_3	0	0	0	0	0	0

5. Memberships and counters after s_0 has sent again:

stations	$m[s_0]$	$m[s_1]$	$m[s_2]$	$m[s_3]$	CAcc	CFail
s_0	1	0	1	0	1	0
s_1	0	1	0	0	1	2
s_2	1	0	1	0	2	0
s_3	0	0	0	0	0	0

6. Memberships and counters after the time slot of s_1, which cannot send by the clique avoidance mechanism and leaves the active state:

stations	$m[s_0]$	$m[s_1]$	$m[s_2]$	$m[s_3]$	CAcc	CFail
s_0	1	0	1	0	1	0
s_1	0	0	0	0	0	0
s_2	1	0	1	0	2	0
s_3	0	0	0	0	0	0

Membership vectors are coherent again at this point of time.

3   Proving Clique Avoidance

In this section, we prove that if k faults occur at a rate of more than 1 fault per two TDMA rounds and if no fault occur during two rounds following fault k, then at the end of that second round, all active stations have the same membership vector, so they form a single *clique* in the graph theoretical sense.

Let us denote by W the subset of S that contains all working stations. We may write $m_s = S'$ for a station s with $S' \subseteq S$ as a short hand for $m_s[s'] = 1$ iff $s' \in S'$. To prove coherence of membership vectors we start with the following situation. We suppose that stations of W have identical membership vectors and all have $CFail_s = 0$. Because $m_s[s] = 1$ for any working station, this implies that $m_s = W$ for any $s \in W$. Faults occur from this initial state.

Let us define a graph as follows: the nodes are the stations, and there is an arc between s and s' iff $m_s[s'] = 1$. We recall that, in graph theory, a *clique* is a complete subgraph, i.e., each pair of nodes is related by an arc. Thus initially, W forms a single clique in the graph theoretical sense.

3.1   Introductory Example

Let us illustrate how things might work in the case of two faults. The first fault occurs when s_0 sends. We suppose that only s_1 fails to receive correctly the frame sent by s_0. S is split as $S_1 = \{s_0, s_2, s_3\}$ and $S_0 = \{s_1\}$. Membership vectors and counters after s_0 has sent:

stations	$m[s_0]$	$m[s_1]$	$m[s_2]$	$m[s_3]$	$CAcc$	$CFail$
s_0	1	1	1	1	1	0
s_1	0	1	1	1	3	1
s_2	1	1	1	1	3	0
s_3	1	1	1	1	2	0

Membership vectors and counters after s_1 has sent:

stations	$m[s_0]$	$m[s_1]$	$m[s_2]$	$m[s_3]$	$CAcc$	$CFail$
s_0	1	0	1	1	1	1
s_1	0	1	1	1	1	0
s_2	1	0	1	1	3	1
s_3	1	0	1	1	2	1

Membership vectors and counters after s_2 has sent. At this point, we suppose that a second fault occurs. Neither s_3 nor s_0 recognize the frame sent by s_2 as correct. S_1 is split in $S_{11} = \{s_2\}$ and $S_{10} = \{s_0, s_3\}$:

stations	$m[s_0]$	$m[s_1]$	$m[s_2]$	$m[s_3]$	$CAcc$	$CFail$
s_0	1	0	0	1	1	2
s_1	0	1	0	1	1	1
s_2	1	0	1	1	1	0
s_3	1	0	0	1	2	2

Membership vectors and counters after the time slot of s_3, which is prevented from sending by the clique avoidance mechanism:

stations	$m[s_0]$	$m[s_1]$	$m[s_2]$	$m[s_3]$	$CAcc$	$CFail$
s_0	1	0	0	0	1	2
s_1	0	1	0	0	1	1
s_2	1	0	1	0	1	0
s_3	0	0	0	0	0	0

One notices that s_0, then s_1 are prevented from sending by the clique avoidance mechanism. Membership vectors and counters after the time slot of s_1:

stations	$m[s_0]$	$m[s_1]$	$m[s_2]$	$m[s_3]$	CAcc	CFail
s_0	0	0	0	0	0	0
s_1	0	0	0	0	0	0
s_2	0	0	1	0	1	0
s_3	0	0	0	0	0	0

Coherence is achieved again after the time slot of s_1, where s_2 remains the only active station. Though S_{11} is smaller that S_{10}, the position of s_2 in the ring as the first station of the round with the second fault allows it to capitalize on frames accepted in the round before and to win over the set S_{10}.

3.2   Proving a Single Clique after k Faults

The proof proceeds as follows. First we show a preliminary result. If W is divided into subsets S_i is such a way that all stations in a subset have the same membership vector, then stations inside a subset behave similarly: if there is no fault, they recognize the same frames as correct or as incorrect. Then we show that the occurrence of faults does produce such a partitioning, i.e., after fault k, W is divided into subsets S_w, where $w \in \{0,1\}^k$. Indeed, as illustrated by the example at the end of section 2, after 1 fault, W is split in S_1, the stations that recognize the frame as correct, and S_0, the stations that do not recognize the frame as correct. Because any station recognizes itself as correct, S_1 is not empty. Now, suppose that a second fault occurs. Assume that the second fault occurs when a station from set S_1 sends. As before, set S_1 splits into S_{11}, the stations that recognize the frame as correct, and S_{10}, the stations that do not recognize the frame as correct, as illustrated in the example in Subsection 3.1. Again S_{11} is not empty. And the process generalizes. If a station s from a set S_w sends when fault k occurs, S_w splits into S_{w1} and S_{w0} with $S_{w1} \neq \emptyset$. Then, we show that two stations s and s' have the same membership vector if and only if they belong to the same set S_w. Using the preliminary lemma, we have a result about the incrementation of the counters CAcc and CFail, namely, all stations from a set S_w increment CAcc if a station from S_w sends, and increment CFail if a station from $S_{w'}$ sends, where $w \neq w'$. From this, we can deduce our main result: in the second round after fault k, only stations from a single set S_w can send. It follows that, at the end of the second round, there is only one clique and it is not empty.

The preliminary result reads as follows.

Lemma 1 *Suppose that W is divided into m subsets $S_1, \ldots, S_m$ such that s and s' have the same membership vector iff s and s' belong to the same subset S_i, $1 \leq i \leq m$. Let $s \in S_i$, $1 \leq i \leq m$. Suppose no fault occurs. Then, each time some other station s' from S_i is sending, s increases $CAcc_s$ by 1 and keeps the membership bit of s' to 1. Each time some station $s' \in S_j$, $j \neq i$ is sending, s increases $CFail_s$ by 1 and puts the membership bit of s' to 0.*

Now we show how faults partition the set W.

Proposition 2 *At the end of the time slot of s^k, the station where fault k occurs, $k \geq 1$, W is divided into subsets S_w, with $w \in \{0,1\}^k$, such that:*

1. *there exists at least one w with $S_w \neq \emptyset$,*
2. *any two stations $s \in S_w$ and $s' \in S_{w'}$ have the same membership vector iff $w = w'$,*
3. *for any $w \in \{0 \mid 1\}^k$ with $S_w \neq \emptyset$, for any $s, s' \in S_w$, $m_s[s'] = 1$.*

Now, observe that in the second round following fault k, the last fault, at least one station can send.

Lemma 3 *In the second round following fault k, at least one station is sending.*

Finally, we show that only stations from a unique set S_w are able to send in the second round following fault k.

Theorem 1. *Let $s \in S_w$ be the first station to send in the second round following fault k. Then, only stations from set S_w can send in the second round following fault k.*

From Theorem 1, one deduces that, at the end of the second round following fault k, for any station $s \in S_w$: $m_s = S_w$. This gives our safety property about cliques.

Corollary 4 *At the end of the second round following fault k, all working stations form a single clique in the graph theoretical sense.*

By Lemma 3, we know that the clique formed at the end of the second round is not empty. This implies that faults never prevent all stations from sending.

Corollary 5 *At the end of the second round following fault k, the set of working stations is not empty.*

3.3   Integrating Stations

Proposition 2 and Theorem 1 can be generalized to the case where integrating stations are allowed. Indeed, an integrating station s copies the membership vector from some active station s' which belongs to some S_w and updates it as active stations do. So it keeps having the same membership vector as stations of some set $S_{w'}$, with w being a prefix of w', as faults occur. This is shown in Proposition 6, which is a sharper version of Proposition 2.

Proposition 6 *At the end of the time slot of s^k, the station where fault k occurs, $k \geq 1$, W is divided into subsets S_w, with $w \in \{0,1\}^k$, such that:*

1. *there exists at least one w with $S_w \neq \emptyset$,*
2. *any two stations $s \in S_w$ and $s' \in S_{w'}$ have the same membership vector iff $w = w'$,*
3. *for any $w \in \{0 \mid 1\}^k$ with $S_w \neq \emptyset$, for any $s, s' \in S_w$, $m_s[s'] = 1$.*

4. This partition stays stable till the occurrence of fault $k + 1$.

5. The station s^{k+1} ready to send when fault $k + 1$ occurs belongs to some set S_w, $w \in \{0,1\}^k$, or has its membership vector identical to a station of some set S_w, $w \in \{0,1\}^k$.

At its first time slot, an integrating station s resets its counters but does not send. During the subsequent round, it increments $CAcc_s$ and $CFail_s$ as working stations do. When its time slot comes again, s, having the same membership vector as stations of S_w, performs the clique avoidance mechanism. $CAcc_s > CFail_s$ means that stations from S_w, without s, have emitted more than stations from any other set. Thus s can emit and, that way, contributes to reinforce S_w. If $CAcc_s \leq CFail_s$, then s cannot emit and nothing will be changed concerning the size of S_w. This argument is used to prove Theorem 1 in the case of integrating stations. Corollaries 4 and 5 hold as well.

4   Automatic Verification: The 1 Fault Case

In the case of a single fault, the set W of active stations is divided into two subsets, S_1 and S_0. The set S_1 is not empty as it contains s^1, the station that was sending when the fault occurs. We assume that no other fault occurs for the next two rounds, a round is taken with the beginning of the time slot of s^1. We want to prove automatically for an arbitrary number N of stations that, at the end of the second round following the fault, all working stations form a single non-empty clique. To achieve this goal, we need a formalism to model the protocol and a formalism to specify the properties that the protocol must satisfy. To model the protocol, we take an automaton with parameters and counters. To specify the properties, we take the temporal logic CTL.

We have seen that each station maintains two counters, $CAcc$ and $CFail$ and a membership vector m. To be able to model the protocol with an arbitrary number N of stations by an automaton, we need an abstraction that allows us to forget all individual membership vectors and counters, and, at the same time, allows us to represent correctly the emission of frames.

We divide the presentation in two main parts: first round, and second and later rounds following the fault.

4.1   First Round Following the Fault: Abstraction

In the case of 1 fault, Propositions and Lemmata of section 3 take a simpler form given by the Corollaries below. Essentially, stations from S_1 increment $CAcc$ when stations from S_1 send, and they increment $CFail$ and do $m[s] = 0$ when some station s from S_0 sends. Stations from S_0 behave similarly.

Corollary 7 *At the end of the time slot of s^1, all stations in S_1 have the same membership vector, namely W and all stations in S_0 have the same membership vector, namely $W \setminus \{s^1\}$.*

Corollary 8 *In the round following the time slot of s^1, after a station s of S_0 has sent, any station s' of S_1 which is still in the* active *state, puts the membership bit of s to* false, *i.e. $m_{s'}[s] = 0$, and increases $CFail_{s'}$ by 1.*

Corollary 9 *In the round following the time slot of s^1, after a station s of S_1 has sent, any station s' of S_1, which is still in the* active *state, keeps the membership bit of s to* true *and increases $CAcc_{s'}$ by 1.*

With these corollaries, it is equivalent to know which set, S_1 or S_0, a station belongs to, or to know its membership vector. Hence, we may abstract away individual membership vectors and keep only the two sets.

Let us see now that we can abstract away all individual counters $CAcc$ and $CFail$. Let $d1$ be a counter to count how many stations of S_1 have sent so far in the round since the fault occurred. Let $d0$ be a similar counter for S_0. These two global counters are enough to calculate $CAcc_s$ and $CFail_s$ for each station s ready to send. Indeed, let s be a station ready to send. Assume $s \in S_1$. How much is $CFail_s$? It is exactly given by $d0$. How much is $CAcc_s$? Generally, it is more than $d1$. One has to add all stations that have emitted before the fault since the last time slot of s, because s has recognized them all as correct, see Figure 2. However, this number can be calculated exactly with the help of $d1$ and $d0$ only as Proposition 2 shows.

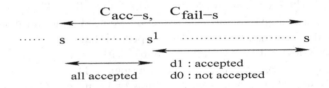

Fig. 2. Illustrating proof of Theorem 2.

Theorem 2. *Let s a station ready to send in the round following fault 1.*

1. *If $s \in S_1$, then $CAcc_s = |W| - d0$ and $CFail_s = d0$.*
2. *If $s \in S_0$, then $CAcc_s = |W| - d1$ and $CFail_s = d1$.*

Corollaries 7 to 9 and Theorem 2 give us a powerful abstraction: we abstract away the N individual membership vectors, we abstract away the statical order and the individual $CAcc$ and $CFail$. Instead we fix two sets, S_1 and S_2, and two counters $d1$ and $d0$, and we can model correctly stations sending and failing.

4.2   First Round Following the Fault: The Model

The protocol with N stations including the first round following 1 fault is modeled by the automaton with parameters and counters shown in the TOP part of Figure 3. Let us read it from left to right.

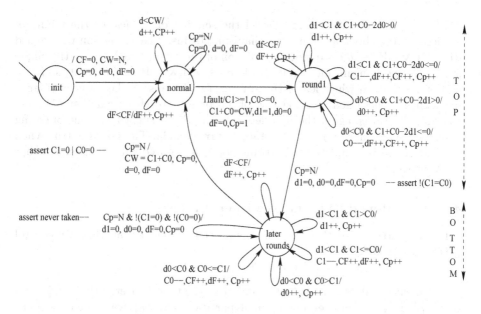

Fig. 3. The automaton with parameters and counters modeling N stations.

Transition from initial state `init` to state `normal` initializes counters. The counter of working stations, CW, takes as initial value the parameter N which is the total number of stations. The counter of stations that are not working anymore, or have failed, CF is set to 0 as well as three other counters, Cp, d and dF. Cp counts how many time slots in total have elapsed in the round. d counts how many working stations have sent in the round. dF counts how many slots of non-working stations have elapsed in the round.

State `normal` models the protocol when there are no faults. Transition with guard $d < CW$ models the sending of a frame by a working station while transition with guard $dF < CF$ corresponds to the time slot of a non-working station, where no frame is sent. Notice the non-determinism as we abstract the statical order among stations. Transition with guard $Cp = N$ is the starting of a new round.

Transition with guard *1fault* from `normal` to `round1` is taken when a fault occurs. The input *1fault* can be seen as a signal that can have the value *true* at random. This transition sets the items defined in the abstraction: $C1$ is the number of stations belonging to S_1, i.e., the number of stations that recognize the frame of the faulty station as correct and $C0$ is similar for S_0. These parameters must fulfill 3 constraints as given in the abstraction: $C1 \geq 1$, as the faulty station recognizes itself as correct, $C0 \geq 0$ and $C1 + C0 = CW$. The counter $d1$, to count how many stations of the set S_1 have sent in the round, is set to 1 and its counterpart $d0$, for S_0, is set to 0. Finally, Cp is reset to 1 as the round is now taken from the slot of the faulty station.

Transitions of state round1 model the sending of frames, or the failing of stations by the clique avoidance mechanism. For instance, transition with guard $d1 < C1 \& CW - 2d0 > 0$ models a station of the set S_1 which passes the clique avoidance mechanism and sends, while $d1 < C1 \& CW - 2d0 \leq 0$ models a station from set S_1 which leaves the active state because of the clique avoidance mechanism. These guards make use of Theorem 2 to check whether $CAcc_s - CFail_s > 0$. Notice again the non-determinism. State round1 has one outgoing transition with guard $Cp = N$ to state later rounds. The guard is true when the first round is completed. This transition is annotated with an assertion that we want to prove.

4.3   First Round Following the Fault: Properties

A first property, called $P1$, that has been proved as true, is that whenever control leaves state round1:

$$!(C1 = C0) \qquad (P1).$$

P1 means that, when the first round after the fault is over, either $|S_1| > |S_0|$ or $|S_0| > |S_1|$, whatever the original partition $\{S_1, S_0\}$ was when the fault occurred.

We have analyzed what leads to $C1 > C0$, or $C0 > C1$ upon leaving round1. First, we have shown that, if $|S_1| > |S_0|$ when the fault occurs, then $C1 > C0$ when control leaves round1, and vice-versa. Let us denote by InS_1, InS_0, the initial number of stations in the set S_1, respectively in the set S_0, when a fault occurs. Adding the constraint $InS_1 > InS_0$, we have proved that whenever control leaves state round1:

$$(InS_1 = C1) \qquad (P2).$$

Since counters $C1$ and $C0$ may not increase, this implies $C1 > C0$ when control enters state later rounds. It also implies that all stations from S_1 did send in the first round.

Then we have investigated the case $|S_1| = |S_0|$ when the fault occurs. If set S_1 comes first in the statical order, then $C_1 > C_0$, and vice versa if S_0 comes first. Adding the constraint $InS_1 = InS_0$ we have proved:

$$AG \ (d1 = InS_1 \text{ and } d0 < InS_1) \ \Rightarrow \ AG(C1 = InS_1)) \qquad (P3),$$

$$AG \ ((d1 = InS_1 \text{ and } d0 < InS_1) \ \Rightarrow \ (C1 + C0 - 2 * d1 <= 0)) \qquad (P4).$$

Again, this implies $C1 > C0$ when control leaves state round1. It also implies that all stations from S_1 did send in the first round.

4.4   Second and Later Rounds Following the Fault: Abstraction

From Theorem 2, we deduce $CAcc_{s^1}$ and $CFail_{s^1}$ for the faulty station s^1 at the end of the first round.

Corollary 10 *At the end of the first round $CAcc_{s^1} = |S_1|$ and $CFail_{s^1} = |S_0|$.*

From Corollaries 8 and 9, we deduce that at the end of the first round, all stations in S_1 have the same membership vector, namely S_1. A similar result holds for stations in S_0.

Corollary 11 *Let s be any station and consider m_s at the end of the first round following the fault.*

1. *If $s \in S_1$ then $m_s[s'] = 1$ iff $s' \in S_1$.*
2. *If $s \in S_0$ then $m_s[s'] = 1$ iff $s' \in S_0$.*

Let us notice that S_1 and S_0 form two cliques in the graph theoretical sense. If none of this set is empty, at the end of the first round, stations are split in two cliques. This is illustrated at the end of section 2, after the time slot of s_3.

Using Properties $P1$ as well as Corollaries 10 and 11, one can deduce that $|S_1|$ and $|S_0|$ give good approximations of $CAcc$ and $CFail$ in subsequent rounds. Indeed, suppose first that $|S_1| > |S_0|$ at the end of the first round. Stations in S_1 continue sending, while stations in S_0 are not able to send. $CAcc_s$ stays stable for any station $s \in S_1$ during the second round, while $CFail_s$ decreases. For a station $s' \in S_0$, the contrary happens. A dual result holds when $|S_1| < |S_0|$.

Lemma 12 *Consider the sets A and F with $A = S_1$ and $F = S_0$ at the end of the first round and let s be any station about to send in the second round.*

1. *Suppose $|A| > |F|$.*
   (a) *If $s \in S_1$ then $CAcc_s \geq |A|$ and $CFail_s \leq |F|$.*
   (b) *Let $s \in S_0$ then $CAcc_s \leq |F|$ and $CFail_s \geq |A|$.*
2. *Suppose $|F| > |A|$.*
   (a) *If $s \in S_0$ then $CAcc_s \geq |F|$ and $CFail_s \leq |A|$.*
   (b) *If $s \in S_1$ then $CAcc_s \leq |A|$ and $CFail_s \geq |F|$.*

4.5   Second and Later Rounds: The Model and Properties

We use lemma 12 to model the full protocol in later rounds as shown in the BOTTOM part of Figure 3. Transition with guard $d1 < C1$ & $C1 > C0$ models stations from S_1 that are sending, while $d1 < C1$ & $C1 \leq C0$ corresponds to stations from S_1 which leave the active state because of the clique avoidance mechanism. Similar transitions correspond to stations from S_0.

If membership vectors are coherent again at the end of the second round, transition with guard $Cp = N$ & $!(C1 = 0)$ & $!(C0 = 0)$, that models the start of a new round with both sets non empty, should never be taken. Indeed, the invariant below at state **later rounds** is true:

$$AG \ !(!(C1 = 0) \ \textbf{and} \ !(C0 = 0) \ \textbf{and} \ (Cp = N)) \qquad (P6).$$

$P6$ is annotated as an assertion in Figure 3. $P6$ proves that the corresponding transition is never enabled, thus control leaves state **later rounds** as soon as $Cp = N$, i.e., after 1 round.

Further the following property is also verified as true when control moves from state `later rounds` to state `normal`:

$$AG \ (C1 = 0 \text{ or } C0 = 0) \qquad (P7).$$

$P7$ means that either S_1 or S_0 is empty at the end of the second round. Hence, all active stations have the same membership vectors at the end of the second round and form again a single clique in the graph theoretical sense.

4.6   Implementation

The automaton in Figure 3 has been translated in the formalism of Action Language and If, and automatically verified using the corresponding verifier [13], [21] respectively. Verification has been conducted modularly. First, the TOP part with properties $P1$ to $P4$ have been verified, then the BOTTOM part with properties $P6$ and $P7$. The transition system construction took 0.84 sec. and the verification of $P1$ took 0.41 sec. using 16572416 bytes of memory with ALV, and LASH needed 27643969 byte(s) for the same property.

5   Automatic Verification: The k Faults Case

To model the protocol for an arbitrary number N of stations and a given number k of faults, as for the case of 1 fault, we use a fixed (but proportional to k) number of counters to abstract the individual membership vectors and the individual $CAcc$ and $CFail$. However, we will see that the case of k faults is not a mere generalization, it is more complex than the case of 1 fault.

5.1   First Round

Let $1 \leq i \leq k$. By Proposition 2, after the occurrence of fault i, W is divided into sets S_w with $w \in \{0,1\}^i$. We find it handy for the following to indicate the length of the string w with the superscript i. We associate two counters Cw^i and dw^i to each set S_{w^i} that is formed after the occurrence of any fault i. The counters Cw^i counts how many stations belong to set S_{w^i} when fault i occurs. The counters dw^i count how many stations from the set S_{w^i} have sent between fault i and fault $i + 1$ in case $i < k$, and counts how many stations from the set S_{w^i} have sent so far in the first round following fault k in case $i = k$. Again because of Proposition 2, we assume that, for any $w \in \{0,1\}^{i-1}$, $Cw^i 1 + Cw^i 0 = Cw^i$, $Cw^i 1 \geq 1$ and $dw^i 1 \geq 1$. For each fault i, we associate a counter $Cp(i)$ that counts how many time slots have elapsed since fault i.

These counters are almost enough to know $CAcc_s$ and $CFail_s$ for any station s in the first round following fault k. Indeed, let s be a station ready to send. s belongs to some set S_{w^k}. In the rounds preceding fault k and during the round following fault k, s recognizes as correct frames sent by stations from $S_{w'}$, where w' is a prefix of w^k, and recognizes as incorrect all other frames. This information is recorded with the counters dw^i, $w \in \{0,1\}^i$ and $1 \leq i \leq k$.

There is one more subtlety. The clique avoidance mechanism needs that $CAcc_s$ and $CFail_s$ count one round only, the round being relative to the position of the sending station s. To do so properly, we distinguish two cases.

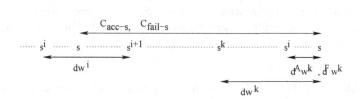

Fig. 4. Evaluating $CAcc_s$ and $CFail_s$ after fault k.

The first case is when fault k occurs in the first round following fault 1 and the time slot of s still belongs to that round. One must take into account that s has recognized as correct all stations that have sent before fault 1, which is a generalization of Theorem 2.

The second case is when the time slot of the sending station s lies between station s^i and s^{i+1} and fault k occurs in the first round following fault i, $i \geq 1$. After fault i, s belongs to some set S_{w^i} and the number of frames accepted as correct by s is given by dw^i. However, to count correctly $CAcc_s$, dw^i is too much. One has to withdraw all stations accepted by s whose time slots are between s^i and s. This is illustrated in Figure 4. We introduce auxiliary counters $d^A w^k$ and $d^F w^k$. These counters are set to 0 when fault k occurs. Counter $d^A w^k$ counts how many stations from set S_{w^k} have sent so far, as counters dw^k do, and counter $d^F w^k$ counts how many stations from set S_{w^k} were preventing from sending so far by the clique avoidance mechanism and moved to the set of non-working stations. The difference with dw^k is that these counters are reset to 0 each time a counter $Cp(i)$ reaches N after fault k. Thus $dw^i - \Sigma_{w'^k} d^A w'^k - \Sigma_{w'^k} d^F w'^k$, with w^i a prefix of w'^k, gives exactly how many frames between s and s^{i+1} the station s has recognized as correct in the round, and $dw^i - \Sigma_{w'^k} d^A w'^k - \Sigma_{w'^k} d^F w'^k + dw^{i+1} + \cdots + dw^k$ gives exactly how many frames in total s has recognized as correct in the round, i.e., $CAcc_s$. A similar idea works for $CFail_s$.

Proposition 13 *Let $s \in S_{w^k}$ a station ready to send in the round following fault k.*

1. *If $Cp(1) \leq N$ at the time slot of s, then:*
   $CAcc_s = |W| - \Sigma_{w'} dw'$, *and* $CFail_s = \Sigma_{w'} dw'$,
   where w' must not be prefix of w^k.
2. *Let $i < k$ such that $Cp(i) \geq N$ and $Cp(i+1) < N$ at the time slot of s. Then:*
   $CAcc_s = (\Sigma_{j=i}^{j=k} dw^j) - \Sigma_{w'^k} d^A w'^k - \Sigma_{w'^k} d^F w'^k$, w^j *are prefixes of w^k and of w'^k, and*
   $CFail_s = (\Sigma_{j=i}^{j=k} \Sigma_{w'^j} dw'^j) - \Sigma_{w''^k} d^A w''^k - \Sigma_{w''^k} d^F w''^k$, w'^j, w''^k *must not be prefixes of w^k.*

5.2   Later Rounds and the Model

At the end of the first round, counters dw^k are kept as they are while counters $d^F w^k$ are reset to 0 and incremented during the second round as before, i.e., $d^F w^k$ counts how many stations from set S_{w^k} were preventing from sending so far by the clique avoidance mechanism and moved to the set of non-working stations. For the second round following fault k, $CAcc_s$ and $CFail_s$ are calculated with these counters only.

Proposition 14 *Let $s \in S_w^k$ a station ready to send in the second round following fault k. Then:*
$CAcc_s = dw^k - d^F w^k$, *and*
$CFail_s = \Sigma_{w'^k} dw'^k - \Sigma_{w'^k} d^F w'^k$ *with* $w'^k \neq w^k$.

The proof of this lemma uses the fact that if a station sends in the second round following fault k, then it has sent also in the first round following fault k.

Using all these counters, an automaton similar to the one given in Figure 3 can be designed and, in theory[1], automatically verified. Properties analogous to $P6$ and $P7$ have to be checked to prove that after the second round following fault k, there is only 1 clique.

6   Conclusion

We have proposed an approach for verifying automatically a complex algorithm which is industrially relevant. The complexity of this algorithm is due to its very subtle dynamic which is hard to model. We have shown that this dynamic can be captured faithfully by means of unbounded (parametric) counter automata. Even if the verification problem for these infinite-state models is undecidable in general, there exists many symbolic reachability analysis techniques and tools which allow to handle such models.

Our approach allows to build a model (counter automaton) for the algorithm with an arbitrary number n of stations, but for a given number k of faults. We have experimented our approach by verifying in a fully automatic way the model in the case of one fault, using the ALV tool and the LASH tool.

Related Work: [5] provides a manual proof of the algorithm in the 1 fault case. Theorem 1 generalizes this result to the case of any number of faults. On the other hand, [5] considers the first and second successor feature in the implicit acknowledgment algorithm, which is omitted in our work.

As far as we know, all the existing works on automated proofs or verifications of the membership algorithm of TTP concern the case of one fault, and only symmetric fault occurrences are assumed. In our work, we consider the more general framework where several faults can occur, and moreover, these faults can be asymmetric. In [22], a mechanised proof using PVS is provided. [17,6,15] adopt an approach based on combining abstraction and finite-state model-checking.

---

[1] In the case of 2 faults, we got memory problems, both with ALV and LASH.

[17] has checked the algorithm for 6 stations. [6,15] consider the parametric verification of n stations; [15] provides an abstraction proved manually whereas [6] uses an automatic abstraction generation technique, both abstractions leading to a finite-state abstraction of the parameterized network. The abstractions used in those works seem to be non-extensible to the case of asymmetric faults and to the k faults case. To tackle this more general framework, we provide an abstraction which yields a counter automaton and reduce the verification of the algorithm to the symbolic reachability analysis of the obtained infinite-state abstract model. Moreover, our abstraction is exact in the sense that it models faithfully the emission of frames by stations.

Future Work: One future work is to consider the feature involving first and second successor in the implicit acknowledgment algorithm. Our work indicates that this feature could be left out, as far as clique avoidance and coherence of membership vectors is concerned, since without it, stabilization occurs after two rounds following the last fault in the general case of k asymmetric faults. However, this feature allows a quicker detection of send-faulty stations. We conjecture that all results of Section 3 go through. However the abstraction issue seems more tricky. Another interesting direction is to automatize, for instance using a theorem prover, the abstraction proof which allows to build the counter automaton modeling the algorithm. More generally, an important issue is to design automatic abstraction techniques allowing to produce infinite-state models given by extended automata. Finally, a challenging problem is to design an algorithmic technique allowing to verify automatically the algorithm by taking into account simultaneously both of its parameters, i.e., for any number of stations *and for any number of faults.*

References

1. Abdulla P.A, Annichini A., Bensalem S., Bouajjani A., Habermehl P., Lakhnech Y: Verification of Infinite-State Systems by Combining Abstraction and Reachability Analysis. CAV'99, Lecture Notes in Computer Science, Vol 1633. Springer-Verlag, (1999)
2. Abdulla P.A, Jonsson B.: Channel Representations in Protocol Verification. CONCUR'01, Lecture Notes in Computer Science, Vol 2154. Springer-Verlag, (2001) 1–15
3. Abdulla P.A, Jonsson B.: Ensuring Completeness of Symbolic Verification Methods for Infinite-State Systems. Theoretical Computer Science, Vol 256. (2001) 145–167
4. Annichini A., Asarin E., Bouajjani A.: Symbolic Techniques for Parametric Reasoning about Counter and Clock Systems. CAV'00, Lecture Notes in Computer Science, Vol 1855. (2000)
5. Bauer G., Paulitsch M.: An investigation of membership and clique avoidance in TTP/C. Proceedings 19th IEEE Symposium on Reliable Distributed Systems (SRDS'00), IEEE Computer Society, (2000), 118–124
6. Baukus K., Lakhnech Y., Stahl K.: Verifying Universal Properties of Parameterized Networks. Proceedings of the 5th International Symposium on Formal Techniques in Real-Time and Fault Tolerant Systems, FTRTFT 2000, Pune, India

7. Boigelot B., Wolper P.: Symbolic Verification with Periodic Sets. CAV'94, Lecture Notes in Computer Science, Vol 818. Springer-Verlag, (1994)
8. Bouajjani A., Esparza J., Maler O.: Reachability Analysis of Pushdown Automata: Application to Model Checking. CONCUR'97, Lecture Notes in Computer Science, Vol 1243. Springer-Verlag, (1997)
9. Bouajjani A., Habermehl P.: Symbolic Reachability Analysis of FIFO-Channel Systems with Nonregular Sets of Configurations. ICALP'97, Lecture Notes in Computer Science, Vol 1256. Springer-Verlag, (1997) Full version in TCS, Vol 221 (1/2) (1999) 221–250
10. Bouajjani A., Jonsson B., Nilsson M., Touili T.: Regular Model Checking. CAV'00, Lecture Notes in Computer Science, Vol 1855. Springer-Verlag, (2000)
11. Bouajjani A., Merceron A.: Parametric Verification of a Group Membership Algorithm. Technical Report, Liafa, University of Paris 7, (2002)
12. Bultan T., Gerber R., League C.: Verifying Systems With Integer Constraints and Boolean Predicates: A Composite Approach. Proc. of the Intern. Symp. on Software Testing and Analysis, ACM Press (1998)
13. Bultan T., Yavuz-Kahveci T.: Action Language Verifier. Proceedings of the 16th IEEE International Conference on Automated Software Engineering (ASE 2001), IEEE Computer Society, Coronado Island, California, (2001)
14. Cousot P., Halbwachs H.: Automatic Discovery of Linear Restraints Among Variables of a Program. POPL'78, ACM Press (1978)
15. Creese S., Roscoe A.W.: TTP: a case study in combining induction and data independence. Oxford University Programming Research Group, Technical Report TR-1-99, (1999)
16. Graf S., Saidi H.: Construction of abstract state graphs with pvs. CAV'97, Lecture Notes in Computer Science, Vol 1254. Springer-Verlag, (1997)
17. Katz S., Lincoln P., Rushby J.: Low-overhead Time-Triggered Group Membership. WDAG'97, Lecture Notes in Computer Science, Vol 1320. Springer-Verlag, (1997)
18. Kesten Y., Maler O., Marcus M., Pnueli A., Shahar E.: Symbolic Model Checking with Rich Assertional Languages. CAV'97, Lecture Notes in Computer Science, Vol 1254. Springer-Verlag, (1997)
19. Kopetz H.: TTP/C Protocol - Specification of the TTP/C Protocol. www.tttech.com (1999)
20. Kopetz H., Grünsteidl G.: A time triggered protocol for fault-tolerant Real-Time Systems. IEEE Computer, (1999) 14–23
21. LASH: The Liège Automata-based Symbolic Handler (LASH). www.montefiore.ulg.ac.be/~boigelot/research/lash/
22. Pfeifer H.: Formal verification of the TTP Group Membership Algorithm. IFIP TC6/WG6.1 International Conference on Formal Description Techniques for Distributed Systems and Communication protocols and Protocol Specification, Testing and Verification, FORTE/PSTV 2000, Pisa, Italy (2000)
23. Saidi H., Shankar N.: Abstract and Model Check while you Prove. CAV'99, Lecture Notes in Computer Science, Vol 1633. Springer-Verlag, (1999)
24. Wolper W., Boigelot B.: Verifying systems with infinite but regular state spaces. CAV'98, Lecture Notes in Computer Science, Vol 1427. Springer-Verlag, (1998)

A Method for Testing the Conformance
of Real Time Systems

Ahmed Khoumsi

University of Sherbrooke, Dep. GEGI, Sherbrooke J1K2R1, Canada
khoumsi@gel.usherb.ca

Abstract. The aim of *conformance testing* is to check whether an implementation conforms to a specification. We consider the case where the specification contains timing constraints and is described by a model called Timed Automata (TA). The state space of a TA can be infinite due to the infinite number of time values. In a recent work, we proposed a method to finitely represent the state space. The proposed method transforms a TA into an equivalent finite state automaton using two special types of events, *Set* and *Exp*, and denoted se-FSA.

In the present article, we propose a conformance testing method which is applicable when the specification is described by a TA. First, we use the above-mentioned transformation procedure for representing the specification by a se-FSA. Second, we propose a procedure for generating test sequences from the se-FSA describing the specification. And third, we propose a simple architecture for executing the generated test sequences.

Keywords: Real-time systems, Conformance testing, Generalized Wp-Method, Timed Automata (TA), se-FSA, *Set*, *Exp*, Test cases generation, Test architecture.

1 Introduction

1.1 Modelling Timed Systems

Real-time systems are systems for which, in addition to the correct order of events, constraints on delays separating certain events must be satisfied. Among the models that have been developed for studying rigorously timed systems, we will consider the model of Timed Automata (TA) introduced in [1,2]. In such a model, time measures are modeled by real variables and represent exact values of time. The state of such TA is defined by a *location* and (real) values of clocks. Its state space can be infinite, due to the infinite number of clock values. The region graph approach [3] proposes a finite representation of the state space obtained by merging states, which are in some sense equivalent, into a region. However, the region graph approach can still suffer from state explosion [3]. In the worst case, the number of states is exponential in the number of clocks and polynomial in the magnitudes of the constants used in timing constraints.

W. Damm and E.-R. Olderog (Eds.): FTRTFT 2002, LNCS 2469, pp. 331–351, 2002.

1.2   Testing Timed Systems

Conformance testing (or more simply *testing*) aims to check whether an implementation, which is referred to as an *implementation under test* ($\mathcal{IUT}$), conforms to a specification. In the case of timed systems, the specification contains timing constraints and is generally described by a real-time enrichment of well known models. As an example, a TA [1] is obtained from a finite state automaton (FSA) by annotating every transition of the FSA by a timing constraint and by clock(s) to reset. Few work has been done for *testing* timed systems, for example [4,5,6,7,8,9,10,11,11,12,13,14]. For lack of space, let us introduce only the methods in [8,9,10,11] because they use the same approach as us, that is, they are inspired by test methods for untimed systems.

- The authors of [8] propose a theoretical framework for testing timed systems which are described by a variant of the TA of [1]. The TA describing the specification is transformed into a region automaton, which in turn is transformed into another FSA, referred to as a Grid Automaton. Test sequences are then generated from the Grid Automaton. The idea behind the construction of the Grid automaton is to represent each clock region with a finite set of clock valuations, referred to as the representatives of the clock region. The main limitations of this approach are:
  - the Grid Automaton has more states than the corresponding region graph,
  - the authors assume that outputs can occur only on integer values of clocks.
- The authors of [9] improve [8] by providing a more complete method for generating test sequences. They do not reduce the state explosion problem but, contrary to [8], the exact instants of outputs remain unknown, only the respect or the violation of time constraints is important.
- The authors of [10] propose a method which reduces the state explosion problem induced by the methods of [8,9]. An important limitation of this method is that it is applicable only when a *single* clock is used to describe all the timing constraints of the specification.
- The authors of [11] remove the single-clock limitation of [10], but they create another limitation by assuming that in the TA which describes the specification, the set of possible values of clocks in a location *does not depend* on the path which has been executed to reach this location.

1.3   Our Contribution and Structure of the Article

The purpose of this paper is to propose a method for testing dense real-time systems. The proposed method is based on a procedure which transforms a timed automaton (TA) into an equivalent finite state automaton (FSA) using two special types of events: *Set* and *Exp*. Such FSA is denoted se-FSA. The transformation method is presented in detail in [15]. Let us note that [15] and the present article are complementary in the sense that [15] shows how the transformation is realized, while the present article uses the transformation as a black box and shows its application for testing purpose.

Let us present our contribution in comparison to [8,9,10,11].

Comparison to [8,9]: With our method, the TA describing the specification is transformed into a se-FSA, while in [8,9] the same TA is transformed into a region automaton (RA) and then into a grid automaton (GA). The advantage of our method is that the se-FSA can contain much less states than the corresponding RA and GA. In fact, state explosion in RA and GA increases with 1) the number of clocks and 2) the magnitudes of the constants used in the transitions' timing constraints, while using se-FSA allows to avoid the state explosion due to (2). After the transformation of the TA describing the specification into a se-FSA, we develop a procedure for the automatic generation of test sequences and propose an architecture for executing the generated test sequences.

Comparison to [10,11]: Similarly to our method, the methods in [10,11] reduce the state explosion problem of the methods in [8,9]. But contrary to [10], our method is applicable when *several* clocks are used. And contrary to [11], our method is applicable even if the set of possible values of clocks in a location *depends* on the path which has been executed to reach this location. We also propose a test architecture which is simpler than the one of [10,11]. Besides, unlike [10,11], nondeterminism and complete specification aspects are studied more rigorously.

Let us discuss about the fact that our method avoids the state explosion due to the magnitudes of the constants used in the transitions' timing constraints. In reachability analysis, several minimization methods allow to reduce significantly the state space, sometimes even more than our method [16,17,18,19,20]. There is also a method that transforms region automata (RA) into zone automata (ZA). In the worst theoretical case, this method does not reduce the state space, but in practice (i.e., in most cases), the state space is significantly reduced [21]. But all those methods keep only the minimal necessary information that allows to determine the reachable transitions. In our case, we need to keep *all* the (order and timing) information that is contained in the original TA.

The rest of the paper is organized as follows. Sect. 2 describes Timed automata (TA) and presents the fault model considered. Sect. 3 presents the transformation procedure of [15]. Sect. 4 presents the conformance relation and proposes a simple test architecture. In Sect. 5, we show how to generate test sequences from a se-FSA. And in Sect. 6, we conclude and discuss some future research issues.

2   TA Model and Fault Model

2.1   Timed Automata (TA)

We will use the following definitions and notations: "derivative" means "derivative w.r.t. (physical) time", "reset" means "set to zero", "$\sup(a, b)$" means "the greatest of a and b", $[a, b]$ and $[a, b[$ are the intervals defined by $\{x | a \le x \le b\}$ and $\{x | a \le x < b\}$, and $C = \{c_1, \cdots, c_{N_c}\}$ is a set of clocks.

Definition 1 *(Continuous time, clock)* Continuous time is a real variable that evolves indefinitely and the derivative of which is equal to 1. A clock is a continuous time which can be reset with the occurrence of an event.

Definition 2 *(Canonical enabling condition, CEC, Enabling condition, EC, $\mathcal{EC}_C$)* A Canonical Enabling Condition (CEC) is any formula of the form "$c_i \sim k$", where $\sim \in \{<, >, \le, \ge, =\}$ and k is a nonnegative integer constant. An Enabling Condition (EC) is any CEC or conjunction of CECs. Let then $\mathcal{EC}_C$ denote the set of ECs depending of clocks of C (we consider that *True* $\in \mathcal{EC}_C$).

Definition 3 *(Reset, $\mathcal{P}_C$)* A Reset is any subset of C. Let then $\mathcal{P}_C$ denote the set of resets.

Definition 4 *(Timed Automaton, TA)* A Timed Automaton (TA) [1,11] is defined by $(\mathcal{L}, \mathcal{E}, \mathcal{C}, Tr, l_0)$ where: $\mathcal{L}$ is a finite set of locations, l_0 is the initial location, $\mathcal{E}$ is a finite set of events, $\mathcal{C}$ is a finite set of clocks, and $Tr \subseteq \mathcal{L} \times \mathcal{E} \times \mathcal{L} \times \mathcal{EC}_C \times \mathcal{P}_C$ is a transition relation. There are two types of events: the reception of an input u (written $?u$) and the sending of an output u (written $!u$).

A transition is therefore defined by Tr $= \langle q; \sigma; r; EC; Z \rangle$ where: q and r are origin and destination locations, σ is the event of the transition, Tr can occur only if $EC = true$, and after the occurrence of Tr, the clocks in Z are reset. Z is called *reset* of Tr.

The clocks used in a TA that describes a given system are just a way to express timing constraints of the system, they do not correspond necessarily to real clocks that are used by the system. For example, to specify that the delay d between two transitions Tr1 and Tr2 is such that $d \in [1,3]$, we may use a clock c_1 as follows: the Z of Tr1 is $\{c_1\}$, and the EC of Tr2 is $(c_1 \ge 1) \wedge (c_1 \le 3)$.

Example 1 *(Timed Automaton, TA)* We consider a system modeled by the TA of Fig. 1, where locations are represented by nodes, and a transition Tr $= \langle q; \sigma; r; EC; \{c_i, c_j, \cdots\} \rangle$ is represented by an arrow linking q to r and labelled by $(\sigma; EC; c_i := 0, c_j := 0, \cdots)$. The absence of EC or of clocks to reset is indicated by "-". As described in Fig. 1:

- the system is initially in l_0 and reaches l_1 at the reception of σ;
- from l_1, the system reaches l_2 by sending μ;
- from l_2, the system reaches l_0 either by receiving ϕ or by sending ρ.

The timing constraints are as follows, where $\delta_{e_1 e_2}$ denotes the delay separating e_1 and e_2: $\delta_{?\sigma!\mu} \le 3$, $\delta_{?\sigma?\phi} < 2$, $\delta_{?\sigma!\rho} \ge 2$, $\delta_{!\mu?\phi} \ge 1$, and $\delta_{!\mu!\rho} \ge 1$.

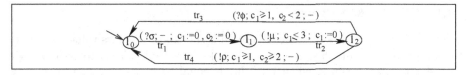

Fig. 1. Example of TA

2.2 Fault Model

Faults that may arise in an implementation of a timed system can be categorized by: 1) faults independent of timing constraints and 2) timing faults [22]. For the first category, we consider the following two types of faults determined in [23]: (i) an implementation has an *output fault* if it does not respond with the expected output in one of its states, and (ii) an implementation has a *transfer fault* if, after the reception of an input or the sending of an ouput, it enters a different state than the expected one. A fault of the second category occurs when $\mathcal{IUT}$ does not respect timing constraints described in its specification. We will consider all the types of timing constraints that can be modelled in a TA. More precisely, in a given sequence of executed events $e_1 e_2 \cdots e_n$, between every pair (e_i, e_j) where $i < j$, we may have a timing constraint in the form $\delta_{e_i e_j} \sim k$, where $\delta_{e_i e_j}$ is the delay between e_i and e_j, $\sim \in \{<, >, \leq, \geq, =\}$, and k is a nonnegative integer constant. During the execution of a sequence, the tester respects timing constraints of inputs and checks whether timing constraints of outputs are satisfied. The aim of our test method is to detect faults of category 1 and category 2. Note that after the transformation procedure mentioned in Sect. 1.3 and presented in Sect. 3, timing faults will be represented in the form of faults of category 1.

3 Transformation Procedure of Timed Automata

Let us recall that the aim of this article is not the development of the transformation (which is done in [15]), but the *use* of the transformation for the development of a method for testing real-time systems. The transformation method transforms a TA into an *equivalent* and *minimal* FSA. The latter is denoted se-FSA and uses two special types of events: *Set* and *Exp*, in addition to the events of the TA. The TA and the corresponding se-FSA are *equivalent* in the sense that they specify the same order and timing constraints (of events other than *Set* and *Exp*). More clarifications and details about this equivalence are given in Section 3.5. The se-FSA is *minimal* in the sense that it contains much less states than any other known FSA that is equivalent to the corresponding TA. Let us, for example, compare the state spaces of the grid automaton (GA) [8,9] and the se-FSA obtained from the same TA. The state space of the GA increases with the number of clocks and the magnitudes of the constants used in the transitions' timing constraints. The state space of the se-FSA is smaller because it increases only with the number of clocks.

3.1 *Set* and *Exp* Events

$Set(c_i, k)$ means: clock c_i is set to zero and will expire when its value is equal to
   k. More generally, $Set(c_i, k_1, k_2, \cdots, k_p)$ means that c_i is set to zero and will
   expire several times, when its value is equal to $k_1, k_2, \cdots, k_p$, respectively.
   We consider without loss of generality that $k_1 < k_2 < \cdots < k_p$.
$Exp(c_i, k)$ means: clock c_i expires and its current value is k. During the period
   which separates a $Set(c_i, k)$ and the corresponding $Exp(c_i, k)$, the latter is
   said is *foreseen*.

Therefore, $Set(c_i, k)$ is followed (after a delay k) by $Exp(c_i, k)$, and
$Set(c_i, k_1, k_2, \cdots, k_p)$ is followed (after delays $k_1, \cdots, k_p$) by $Exp(c_i, k_1)$,
$Exp(c_i, k_2), \cdots, Exp(c_i, k_p)$. When a $Set(c_i, m)$ occurs, every $Exp(c_i, *)$ which
was foreseen before this $Set(c_i, m)$ is cancelled.
    As we will see in Sect. 4, *Set* and *Exp* events are concrete events. In fact, *Set*s
are sent by Test-Controller and received by Clock-Handler, and *Exp*s are sent by
Clock-Handler and received by Test-Controller. If we conceptually include Clock-
Handler in the system under test, then *Set*s (resp. *Exp*s) can be considered as
inputs (resp. outputs) and, thus, will be prefixed by "?" (resp. "!").

3.2 Principle of Transformation Explained in a Simple Example

The procedure that transforms a TA into a se-FSA is quite complex although its
basic principle is simple [15]. Let us first explain this principle in the following
example that uses a single clock. We consider the following timing constraint:
the delay between two events a and b falls within the interval $[1, 3[$. In a TA,
such a constraint is expressed by: 1) using two transitions tr_i and tr_j which
represent the occurrences of a and b, 2) resetting a clock c at the occurrence of
tr_i, and 3) associating to tr_j the EC $((c \geq 1) \wedge (c < 3))$. This timing constraint
can also be expressed as follows: we replace the reset of c by a $Set(c, 1, 3)$ (the
latter will be followed by $Exp(c, 1)$ and $Exp(c, 3)$) and we specify that tr_j occurs
after or simultaneously to $Exp(c, 1)$ and before $Exp(c, 3)$. Therefore, the above
timing constraint will be represented in a se-FSA by the following two sequences:
"$\langle a, Set(c, 1, 3) \rangle \cdot Exp(c, 1) \cdot b \cdot Exp(c, 3)$" and
"$\langle a, Set(c, 1, 3) \rangle \cdot \langle Exp(c, 1), b \rangle \cdot Exp(c, 3)$". (Consecutive events are separated by
".", and simultaneous events are grouped in "$\langle \rangle$".)

3.3 A Few Details About the Construction of *Set* and *Exp*

The example used in Sect. 3.2 gives the impression that the transformation
procedure is trivial. Actually, such a procedure is quite complex because it is
applicable to the general case where *several* clocks are used [15]. A simpler
version, which is applicable when a single clock is used, is presented in [10]. Let
us consider the example of Fig. 1 in order to show a particular aspect which can
occur only when several clocks are used. The four transitions are identified by
tr_i, $i = 1, 2, 3, 4$. If we apply the principle of Sect. 3.2:

- the reset "$c_1 := 0$" in tr_1 is replaced by $Set(c_1, 3)$ because it is used to express the timing constraint "$c_1 \leq 3$" in tr_2;
- the reset "$c_2 := 0$" in tr_1 is replaced by $Set(c_2, 2)$ because it is used to express the timing constraints "$c_2 < 2$" and "$c_2 \geq 2$", in tr_3 and tr_4 respectively;
- the reset "$c_1 := 0$" in tr_2 is replaced by $Set(c_1, 1)$ because it is used to express the timing constraint "$c_1 \geq 1$" in tr_3 and tr_4.

Let us consider the $Exps$ that can occur from location l_2 and correspond to the ECs of outgoing transitions of l_2, i.e., tr_3 and tr_4. These $Exps$ are $Exp(c_1, 1)$ and $Exp(c_2, 2)$, whose corresponding $Sets$ are in tr_2 and tr_1 respectively. In order to determine the possible orders of $Exp(c_1, 1)$ and $Exp(c_2, 2)$ in l_2, let t_1 and t_2 be the instants of transitions tr_1 and tr_2, respectively.

"$!Exp(c_1, 1)$ before $!Exp(c_2, 2)$" implies $t_2 + 1 < t_1 + 2$, i.e., $t_2 - t_1 < 1$,

"$!Exp(c_1, 1)$ simultaneous to $!Exp(c_2, 2)$" implies $t_2 + 1 = t_1 + 2$, i.e., $t_2 - t_1 = 1$,

"$!Exp(c_1, 1)$ after $!Exp(c_2, 2)$" implies $t_2 + 1 > t_1 + 2$, i.e., $t_2 - t_1 > 1$.

Therefore, in l_2 we can determine the order of the two Exp events if we know whether the delay between tr_1 and tr_2 (i.e., $t_2 - t_1$) is smaller than, equal to or greater than 1. For this purpose, we add $?Set(c_i, 1)$ to tr_1 (transition occurring at instant t_1). Clock c_i can be c_1 or c_2 because: (i) c_1 and c_2 are set in tr_1, (ii) c_1 and c_2 are not set between tr_1 and tr_2, and (iii) c_i is used to estimate the delay between tr_1 and tr_2. If, for example, we select c_2, tr_1 will contain $?Set(c_2, 1)$ and $?Set(c_2, 2)$ which can be combined into $?Set(c_2, 1, 2)$.

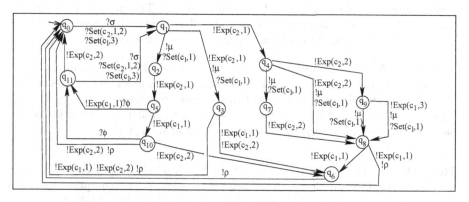

Fig. 2. Transformation of the TA of Fig. 1 into a se-FSA

3.4   An Example

If we apply the transformation to the TA of Fig. 1, we obtain the se-FSA of Fig. 2 which represents all the possible occurrences of: 1) the events of the TA, to which certain Set events are associated; and 2) the Exp events. Timing constraints specified in the TA have been transformed in the form of order constraints relatively to Exp events. Note that an Exp event occurs:

- alone in transitions $q_1 \rightarrow q_4$, $q_2 \rightarrow q_5$, $q_5 \rightarrow q_{10}$, $q_{10} \rightarrow q_6$, $q_7 \rightarrow q_8$, $q_8 \rightarrow q_6$, $q_4 \rightarrow q_9$ and $q_{11} \rightarrow q_0$;
- simultaneously to another *Exp* event in transitions $q_3 \rightarrow q_6$ and $q_3 \rightarrow q_0$;
- simultaneously to an event of the TA in transitions $q_1 \rightarrow q_3$, $q_5 \rightarrow q_{11}$, $q_{10} \rightarrow q_0$, $q_3 \rightarrow q_0$, $q_8 \rightarrow q_0$, $q_4 \rightarrow q_8$ and $q_9 \rightarrow q_8$.

More generally, each transition of a se-FSA may consist of: (a) an input or an output, (b) *Exp* events, and (c) *Set* events. Events in (a,b) are theoretically simultaneous and are immediately followed by events in (c), if any.

3.5   Equivalence between a TA and the Corresponding se-FSA

The transformation procedure guarantees that every TA and the corresponding se-FSA are equivalent [15]. Intuitively, the TA and se-FSA are equivalent in the sense that their order and timing constraints are equivalent. To clarify the notion of equivalence, let us first define the timed language of TA and the timed language of se-FSA.

Timed Language of TA. In a sequence of transitions $Tr_1 \, Tr_2 \cdots$ of a TA A, there exists a timing constraint $\delta_{i,j} \sim k$ on the delay $\delta_{i,j}$ between Tr_i and Tr_j, for $i < j$, iff Tr_i resets a clock c, Tr_j has a timing constraint $c \sim k$, and every Tr_m such that $i < m < j$ (if any) does not reset c. In this study, we assume that from every location, the TA has not several outgoing transitions labelled by the same event and whose ECs can be satisfied simultaneously. This assumption allows to simplify the transformation procedure and will be replaced in Section 5.2 by a more restrictive assumption which is useful for the test generation process.

Definition 5 *(Timed event, timed execution)* A *timed event* is formally represented by a pair (e, τ) where e is an event and τ is the instant of occurrence of e. A *timed execution* is any sequence of timed events "$(e_1, \tau_1)(e_2, \tau_2) \cdots (e_i, \tau_i) \cdots$", where $\tau_1 < \tau_2 < \cdots < \tau_i < \cdots$. Such a sequence represents an execution of the sequence $e_1 e_2 \cdots e_i \cdots$ such that every e_i occurs at instant τ_i.

Remark 1 In Def. 5, we have used symbol $<$ instead of $\leq$. This means that we do not consider simultaneous transitions in a TA. This assumption has been used in order to simplify the transformation procedure. We think that this is not a restrictive assumption because simultaneousness is very unlikely.

Definition 6 *(Acceptance of timed execution by TA, timed language of TA)* Let A be a TA and $Seq = (e_1, \tau_1)(e_2, \tau_2) \cdots$ be a timed execution where $e_1, e_2, \cdots$ are members of the alphabet of A. Seq is accepted by A iff there exists a sequence of transitions $Tr_1 \, Tr_2 \cdots$ of A such that, for $i, j = 1, 2, \cdots$ and $i \neq j$: the event of Tr_i is e_i, and for every timing constraint $\delta_{i,j} \sim k$ on the delay between Tr_i and Tr_j, we have $\tau_j - \tau_i \sim k$. The timed language of A, denoted TL_A, is the set of timed executions accepted by A.

Timed Language of se-FSA

Definition 7 *(Timed event of se-FSA, timed execution of se-FSA)* A timed event is formally represented by a pair (E, τ), where E consists of one or several (simultaneous) events and τ is the instant of occurrence of E. A *timed execution* is any sequence of timed events "$(E_1, \tau_1)(E_2, \tau_2) \cdots (E_i, \tau_i) \cdots$", where $\tau_1 < \tau_2 < \cdots < \tau_i < \cdots$. Such a sequence represents an execution of the event sequence $E_1 E_2 \cdots E_i \cdots$ such that every E_i occurs at instant τ_i.

Definition 8 *(Consistant timed execution)* A timed execution $SEQ = (E_1, \tau_1)(E_2, \tau_2) \cdots$ is consistent iff, for every $E_i, E_j, i < j$:
If E_i contains a $Set(c, k)$, E_j contains a $Exp(c, k)$, and no E_m (where $i < m < j$) contains a $Set(c, *)$, Then $\tau_j = \tau_i + k$.

Definition 9 *(Acceptance of timed execution by se-FSA, timed language of se-FSA)* Let B be a se-FSA and $SEQ = (E_1, \tau_1)(E_2, \tau_2) \cdots$ be a timed execution where $E_1, E_2, \cdots$ are members of the alphabet of B, i.e., each E_i labels a transition of B. SEQ is accepted by B iff : SEQ is consistent and there exists a sequence of transitions $tr_1 tr_2 \cdots$ of B such that, for $i = 1, 2, \cdots$, tr_i is labelled by E_i. The timed language of A, denoted TL_B, is the set of timed executions accepted by B.

Definition 10 *(Equivalence between TA and se-FSA)* A TA A is equivalent to a se-FSA B iff TL_A is obtained from TL_B by removing all the Set and Exp events.

4 Conformance Relation and Test Architecture

4.1 Conformance Relation

A conformance relation defines the meaning of "an implementation conforms to a specification". We make the following usual hypothesis.

Hypothesis 1 The environment (e.g., the test system $\mathcal{TS}$) sends the inputs by respecting the specification. This assumption can be more precisely defined as follows, where S is a TA describing the specification and TL_S is the timed language of S (see Sect. 3.5): after the execution by $\mathcal{IUT}$ of any (empty or non-empty) timed execution Seq of TL_S, $\mathcal{TS}$ can send an input i to $\mathcal{IUT}$ at an instant τ iff $Seq \cdot (i, \tau) \in TL_S$.

Definition 11 *(Conformance)* Assuming Hypothesis 1, $\mathcal{IUT}$ conforms to S iff: after the execution by $\mathcal{IUT}$ of any (empty or non-empty) timed sequence Seq of TL_S, $\mathcal{IUT}$ can generate an output o at an instant τ iff $Seq \cdot (o, \tau) \in TL_S$.

In Hyp. 1 and Def. 11, the empty timed execution is considered as a member of TL_S, and Symbol "." represents the concatenation operator.

4.2   Test System ($\mathcal{TS}$) and System under Test ($\mathcal{SUT}$)

We propose a test system ($\mathcal{TS}$) which consists of two modules called Test-Controller and Clock-Handler, respectively. The advantage of such a $\mathcal{TS}$ is that it guarantees the following equivalence.

> **TESTING EQUIVALENCE:** Let S1 be a TA and S2 be the se-FSA obtained from S1 using the transformation procedure of Sect. 3. The following two points are equivalent:
> 1. $\mathcal{IUT}$ conforms to S1.
> 2. $\mathcal{SUT}$ consisting of $\mathcal{IUT}$ and Clock-Handler conforms to S2.

The test system ($\mathcal{TS}$) consists of Clock-Handler and Test-Controller (see Fig. 3).

Clock-Handler receives *Set* events and sends *Exp* events. Clock-Handler creates a process $PC_i(k)$ with the reception of $Set(c_i, k)$. After a delay k since its creation, $PC_i(k)$ sends $Exp(c_i, k)$ and then terminates. Clock-Handler creates a process $PC_i(k_1, k_2, \cdots, k_p)$ with the reception of $Set(c_i, k_1, k_2, \cdots, k_p)$. After each delay k_i since its creation, $PC_i(k_1, k_2, \cdots, k_p)$ sends $Exp(c_i, k_i)$. $PC_i(k_1, k_2, \cdots, k_p)$ terminates after the sending of $Exp(c_i, k_p)$. If a $Set(c_i, m)$ is received before the termination of $PC_i(*)$, then the latter is killed and a new process $PC_i(m)$ is created.

Test-Controller controls the execution of any test sequence generated from S2. More concretely, it sends inputs to $\mathcal{IUT}$, receives outputs from $\mathcal{IUT}$, sends *Set* events to Clock-Handler, and receives *Exp* events from Clock-Handler.

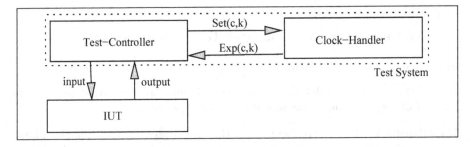

Fig. 3. Structure of the test system

Our test system ($\mathcal{TS}$) has the structure represented in Fig. 3. Let **S1** be a TA describing the specification of $\mathcal{IUT}$, **S2** be the se-FSA derived from **S1** using the transformation procedure of Sect. 3, and **Seq** be the set of test sequences generated from **S2** using a method which will be presented in Sect. 5. We consider therefore that a system conforms to **S2** if it conforms to every sequence of **Seq**.

The proposed architecture allows to check whether $\mathcal{SUT}$ (consisting of $\mathcal{IUT}$ and Clock-Handler) conforms to each sequence of **Seq** and therefore to **S2**. From the testing equivalence, we deduce that this architecture allows to check whether $\mathcal{IUT}$ conforms to **S1**. Recall that every *Set* event follows *immediately* (i.e., is practically simultaneous to) the sending of an input or the reception of an output of $\mathcal{IUT}$.

Here is a very simple example that illustrates the test equivalence. S1 specifies that a task T must be realized in less than two units of time. S2, obtained from S1 by the transformation procedure, specifies that: (i) at the beginning of the task an alarm is programmed for occurring after two units of time, and (ii) the task must be terminated before the alarm. The programming of the alarm corresponds to a *Set* event and the occurrence of the alarm corresponds to an *Exp* event. Test-Controller orders $\mathcal{IUT}$ to start the task T and, simultaneously, programs the alarm by sending a $Set(c, 2)$ to Clock-Handler. Test-Controller deduces that $\mathcal{IUT}$ conforms to S1 iff it receives $Exp(c, 2)$ from Clock-Handler *after* it receives from $\mathcal{IUT}$ the indication that the task is terminated.

5 Test Cases Generation

5.1 Transforming se-FSA into io-FSA

Our aim is to use a test generation method applicable to FSAs whose transitions are labelled in the form input/output. Such FSAs are commonly called Mealy-automata, and we will denote them io-FSA. For that purpose, the se-FSA obtained by the transformation procedure of Sect. 3 needs to be relabelled in the form of a io-FSA. In a "classical" io-FSA, the transitions are generally labelled in the form (X/Y), where X is an input and Y is the corresponding output, and an empty X or Y is indicated by $-$. In our case, as we will see in the following, each transition of the obtained io-FSA is labelled in one of the forms: $(-/Y)$, $(X/-)$ or $(-/Y):(X/-)$. In the latter form, the symbol ":" means that the output Y is *immediately* followed by the input X. Note that in our case, X (resp. Y) may consist of one or *several* inputs (resp. outputs). Let us explain how the relabelling is realized and the semantics of the obtained io-FSA. For that purpose, let us consider the different types of transitions in a se-FSA, where $\mathcal{E}$ (resp. $\mathcal{S}$) denotes any set of *Exp* (resp. *Set*) events:

1. A transition labelled by an input i of $\mathcal{IUT}$, and possibly by $\mathcal{E}$ and $\mathcal{S}$, is relabelled $(-/\mathcal{E}):(i,\mathcal{S}/-)$. If $\mathcal{E}$ is empty, the transition is labelled $(i,\mathcal{S}/-)$. If $\mathcal{S}$ is empty, the transition is labelled $(-/\mathcal{E}):(i/-)$. If $\mathcal{E}$ and $\mathcal{S}$ are empty, the transition is labelled $(i/-)$. Intuitively, Test-Controller receives $\mathcal{E}$ from Clock-Handler and then sends i to $\mathcal{IUT}$ and $\mathcal{S}$ to Clock-Handler. $\mathcal{E}$ and i are theoretically simultaneous and are immediately followed by $\mathcal{S}$.
2. A transition labelled by an output o of $\mathcal{IUT}$, and possibly by $\mathcal{E}$ and $\mathcal{S}$, is relabelled $(-/(o,\mathcal{E})):(\mathcal{S}/-)$. If $\mathcal{E}$ is empty, the transition is labelled $(-/o):(\mathcal{S}/-)$. If $\mathcal{S}$ is empty, the transition is labelled $(-/(o,\mathcal{E})$. If $\mathcal{E}$ and $\mathcal{S}$ are empty, the transition is labelled $(-/o)$. Intuitively, Test-Controller receives o from $\mathcal{IUT}$ and $\mathcal{E}$ from Clock-Handler, and then sends $\mathcal{S}$ to Clock-Handler. o and $\mathcal{E}$ are theoretically simultaneous and are immediately followed by $\mathcal{S}$.
3. A transition labelled by $\mathcal{E}$ is relabelled $(-/\mathcal{E})$. Intuitively, Test-Controller receives $\mathcal{E}$ from Clock-Handler. When $\mathcal{E}$ consists of several *Exps*, the latter are theoretically simultaneous.

This relabelling does not change the semantics of transitions and is just a rewriting of labels with another syntax. Therefore, the se-FSA and the corresponding io-FSA model exactly the same thing. This relabelling is not absolutely necessary. Its advantage is that we obtain an automaton with labels in the form a/b. For example, the se-FSA of Fig. 2 is relabelled into the io-FSA of Fig. 4 where:

Transitions related to the input σ: $Tr_1 = Tr_{22} = (\sigma, Set(c_1, 3), Set(c_2, 1, 2)/-)$.

Transitions related to the input ϕ: $Tr_6 = (-/Exp(c_1, 1)):(\phi/-)$, $Tr_{13} = (\phi/-)$.

Transitions related to the output μ: $Tr_2 = Tr_{10} = Tr_{19} = (-/\mu):(Set(c_1, 1)/-)$,

$\quad Tr_3 = (-/\mu, Exp(c_2, 1)):(Set(c_1, 1)/-)$,

$\quad Tr_{11} = (-/\mu, Exp(c_2, 2)):(Set(c_1, 1)/-)$,

$\quad Tr_{20} = (-/\mu, Exp(c_1, 3)):(Set(c_1, 1)/-)$.

Transitions related to the output ρ: $Tr_8 = (-/Exp(c_1, 1), Exp(c_2, 2), \rho)$,

$\quad Tr_{14} = (-/\rho, Exp(c_2, 2))$, $Tr_{18} = (-/\rho, Exp(c_1, 1))$, $Tr_{21} = (-/\rho)$.

Transitions related no neither input nor output of $\mathcal{IUT}$:

$\quad Tr_4 = Tr_5 = (-/Exp(c_2, 1))$,

$\quad Tr_7 = Tr_{17} = (-/Exp(c_1, 1))$, $Tr_9 = (-/Exp(c_1, 1), Exp(c_2, 2))$,

$\quad Tr_{12} = Tr_{15} = Tr_{16} = Tr_{23} = (-/Exp(c_2, 2))$.

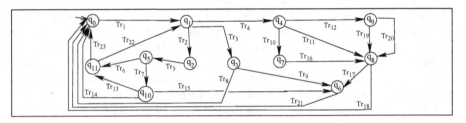

Fig. 4. io-FSA obtained after the relabeling of the se-FSA of Fig. 2. $Tr_0, Tr_1, \cdots, Tr_{23}$ are defined above.

5.2   Discussions and Hypotheses Related to Nondeterminism

In a TA, a transition labelled by an input (resp. output) of $\mathcal{IUT}$ is called input (resp. output) transition. We assume that the TA describing the specification is deterministic, i.e., from any location of the TA, we cannot have:

- several outgoing input transitions labelled by the same input and whose ECs can be satisfied simultaneously;
- an outgoing output transition and another outgoing (input or output) transition whose ECs can be satisfied simultaneously.

Note that the above assumption is stronger than the one just above Def. 5. The latter assumption is used to simplify the transformation procedure while the above assumption is used to simplify the test generation process.

Even with the assumption that the TA describing the specification is deterministic, the corresponding io-FSA (and se-FSA) may be nondeterministic, because of the use of *Exp* events. More precisely, there are two types of nondeterministic states in a io-FSA. In the following: $\mathcal{E}$ and $\mathcal{E}'$ denote two any distinct sets of *Exp* events (each of them may consist of one or several *Exp* events), i and o denote an input and an output of $\mathcal{IUT}$ respectively, and "*" means "anything" (which may be empty, i.e., *nothing*).

Type 1: We consider states corresponding to a situation where an output o of $\mathcal{IUT}$ and a set $\mathcal{E}$ of *Exp* event(s) are both possible ($\mathcal{E}$ can be a singleton). When a state of this type is reached, we cannot foresee the order between o and $\mathcal{E}$, because we cannot foresee the instant of o. We deduce that a state of type 1 is *nondeterministic*.

For example, in State q_1 of the io-FSA of Fig. 4, the three outgoing transitions Tr_2, Tr_3, Tr_4 correspond to the three cases where the output μ is *before*, *simultaneous to*, and *after* $Exp(c_2, 1)$, respectively. We cannot foresee which of the three transitions will occur. $q_3, q_4, q_8, q_9, q_{10}$ are other states of type 1.

Type 2: We consider states corresponding to a situation where two different sets of *Exp* events, $\mathcal{E}$ and $\mathcal{E}'$, are possible ($\mathcal{E}$ and $\mathcal{E}'$ can be a singleton). Actually, such a situation does not correspond necessarily to a nondeterminism. When a state of this type is reached, we can foresee which of $\mathcal{E}$ or $\mathcal{E}'$ will occur, because we know the instants when the corresponding *Set* events have occurred.

Let us consider the case where we cannot control the instants of the *Set* events corresponding to $\mathcal{E}$ and $\mathcal{E}'$. This case may occur, for example, when these *Set* events are associated to (i.e., immediately follow) outputs of $\mathcal{IUT}$, whose instants cannot be controlled. In such a case, before the occurrence of the *Set* events, we can neither select nor foresee which of $\mathcal{E}$ or $\mathcal{E}'$ will occur. In such a case, a state of type 2 is *nondeterministic*.

To summarize about a state s of type 2, which one of $\mathcal{E}$ and $\mathcal{E}'$ will occur: (i) can always be foreseen *after* the occurrences of the corresponding *Set* events, and (ii) in certain cases, can be neither selected nor foreseen *before* the occurrences of the corresponding *Set* events. When there exist cases corresponding to (ii), state s is nondeterministic.

As an example, State 3 of Figure 5 is a state of type 2. We have Case (i) because, when state 3 is reached (i.e., after the occurrences of $Set(c_1, 2)$ and $Set(c_2, 1)$), we determine that State 4 (resp. State 6, resp. State 5) is reached if the delay between $Set(c_1, 2)$ and $Set(c_2, 1)$ is smaller than (resp. greater than, resp. equal to) 1. And we have Case (ii) because, before state 3 is reached, we do not know the delay which will separate $Set(c_1, 2)$ and $Set(c_2, 1)$ and, thus, we cannot determine which of the three states 4, 5, or 6 will be reached. ($?\sigma$ and $!\mu$ are an input and an output of $\mathcal{IUT}$, respectively.)

Since we intend to generate test sequences from a io-FSA and since the latter can be nondeterministic, we must use a test cases generation method that is applicable to nondeterministic FSAs. In this study, we have opted for the Generalized Wp-Method (GWp-Method) [24]. In order to test nondeterministic

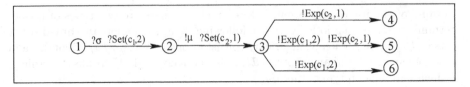

Fig. 5. Nondeterministic state of type 2.

implementations, we need to make a so-called *complete-testing assumption* which can be expressed as follows: it is possible, by applying a given input sequence t to a given $\mathcal{IUT}$ a finite number of times, to exercise all possible execution paths of the $\mathcal{IUT}$ that are traversed by t [24,25]. In our context, this assumption can also be expressed as follows: for every nondeterministic state s of type 1 or 2, it is possible, after a finite number of executions that lead to s, to execute all the outgoing transitions of s. Without such a complete-testing assumption, no test suites can guarantee full fault coverage for nondeterministic implementations.

A io-FSA (obtained from a deterministic TA), although nondeterministic, is *observable* in the sense that a state and a transition label uniquely determine the next state. In other terms, in a io-FSA, we cannot have two outgoing transitions of the same state that have the same label. *Observability* is interesting because GWp-Method is applicable for testing *observable* nondeterministic systems. In [24], an algorithm is proposed for transforming an arbitrary nondeterministic FSA into an observable nondeterministic FSA. Since our io-FSA is observable, we avoid the step of such a transformation.

5.3   Discussions and Hypotheses Related to Complete Specification

The GWp-Method we intend to use is applicable only if the io-FSA describing the specification is completely specified over its set of inputs, otherwise we must complete it. For clarity, let us first consider a specification described by a "classical" io-FSA, whose transitions are labelled in the form "i/o", where i and o denote an input and an output respectively. GWp-Method can be applied for generating test sequences from this kind of io-FSA, only if the latter is *completely specified* over the set of inputs. When such a io-FSA is not completely specified, here are two methods for completing it. For every state s and for every input i which is not specified in s:

First completion method: we add a selfloop labelled "$i/-$". Here, we assume that non-specified inputs are accepted and ignored by $\mathcal{IUT}$.

Second completion method: we add a transition labelled "$i/error$" which leads to an *Error* state, from which all inputs are ignored. Here, we assume that when $\mathcal{IUT}$ receives a non-specified input, then it sends an *error* message and enters an *Error* state from which all inputs are ignored.

Let us now consider a specification described by the type of io-FSA of Sect. 5.1; henceforth "io-FSA" denotes this type of io-FSA. With our test architecture, where *Set* events are *inputs* (see Sect. 4), the set of inputs of the io-FSA is the set of all the elements i, $(i, \mathcal{S})$ and $\mathcal{S}$, where i is an input of $\mathcal{IUT}$, $\mathcal{S}$ consists of one of several *Set* events, and:

- each element i is an input of the $\mathcal{IUT}$ and corresponds to a transition of the io-FSA which is labelled in one of the two forms "$(-/\mathcal{E}) : (i/-)$" or "$(i/-)$",
- each element $(i, \mathcal{S})$ corresponds to a transition of the io-FSA which is labelled in one of the two forms "$(-/\mathcal{E}) : (i, \mathcal{S}/-)$" or "$(i, \mathcal{S}/-)$",
- each element $\mathcal{S}$ corresponds to a transition of the io-FSA which is labelled in one of the two forms "$(-/(o, \mathcal{E})) : (\mathcal{S}/-)$" or "$(-/o) : (\mathcal{S}/-)$".

Completing such a io-FSA cannot be done as simply as for a traditional io-FSA. For example:

- If we apply the first completion method, the addition of a selfloop labelled "$(i, \mathcal{S})/-$" or "$\mathcal{S}/-$" in a state s means that *Set* events have no influence on $\mathcal{SUT}$. This assumption is unrealistic because setting a clock has an influence on Clock-Handler.
- If we apply the second completion method, the addition of a transition labelled "$(i, \mathcal{S})/error$" from a state s to state *Error*, means that $\mathcal{SUT}$ (consisting of $\mathcal{IUT}$ and Clock-Handler) does not accept $(i, \mathcal{S})$. Since Clock-Handler never refuses a *Set* event, this implies that the $\mathcal{IUT}$ refuses i. Therefore, this addition is unrealistic if i is specified in s, i.e., if s has an outgoing transition using i.

More generally, the problem for completing a io-FSA is that the states reached by the added transitions cannot always be determined. In fact, since clocks are set in order to specify timing constraints, adding transitions which sets clocks that are currently in use, distorts the specification. (A clock c is said *in use* when: c has been previously reset in order to check the timing constraint of a transition which has not still occurred.) In order to circumvent such a problem, we can make the following assumption:

Hypothesis 2 In the TA describing the specification, the transitions associated to the same event (input or ouput) of $\mathcal{IUT}$ reset the *same* set of clocks.

When Hypothesis 2 is not satisfied, let $Tr_1, Tr_2, \cdots, Tr_k$ be any set of transitions associated to the same event e of $\mathcal{IUT}$ and which reset the clocks sets $Z_1, Z_2, \cdots, Z_k$ respectively, and let $Z = Z_1 \cup Z_2 \cup \cdots \cup Z_k$. Let $l_1, l_2, \cdots l_k$ be the original locations of $Tr_1, Tr_2, \cdots, Tr_k$, respectively. In order to respect Hypothesis 2, we need to replace each Z_i by Z. But this replacement is correct (i.e., does not distort the specification) if and only if no clock in $Z \setminus Z_i$ is in use in l_i, for $i = 1, \cdots, k$. ($Z \setminus Z_i = \{x | x \in Z, x \notin Z_i\}$.) Henceforth, we assume Hypothesis 2. The latter seems to be a strong assumption and we intend to investigate the development of a test method where Hypothesis 2 is not necessary.

Assuming Hypothesis 2, the transformation procedure of [15] (see Sect. 3) needs to be modified such that the transitions associated to the same event (input or ouput) of $\mathcal{IUT}$ contain the same Set events. Let us, for example, consider two transitions Tr1 and Tr2 associated to the same event e of $\mathcal{IUT}$, which reset the same set of clocks $\{c_1, c_2\}$. The Set events generated by the transformation procedure of [15] can for example be: $(Set(c_1, u_1), Set(c_2, u_2))$ for Tr1, and $(Set(c_1, v_1), Set(c_2, v_2))$ for Tr2. The transformation procedure of [15] needs to be modified such that the two transitions Tr1 and Tr2 are associated to the same Set events $(Set(c_1, u_1, v_1), Set(c_1, u_2, v_2))$. With Hypothesis 2, such a modification can be easily integrated in the transformation algorithm of [15].

With hypothesis 2 and the above-mentioned modification of the transformation procedure of [15], we obtain a completely specified io-FSA if before applying the transformation procedure, the original TA is transformed as follows. For every location l and for every input i, let Z be the set of clocks that are reset by every transition associated to i, and EC (a boolean function depending on clock values) define the domain where i is *not* specified from l. In the general case, such a EC can be defined in the form EC_1 OR EC_2 OR $\cdots$ OR EC_n, where each EC_i is a CEC or a conjunction of CECs. In this case, we add to l several outgoing transitions $\langle ?i; -; EC_1; Z \rangle, \langle ?i; -; EC_2; Z \rangle, \cdots, \langle ?i; -; EC_n; Z \rangle$ that lead to a same location from which an outgoing transition $\langle !error; E; - \rangle$ leads to an $Error$ state, from which all inputs are ignored. E is an enabling condition that bounds the delay after which $\mathcal{IUT}$ sends the $error$ message. Here, we assume that when $\mathcal{IUT}$ receives a non-specified input, then it sends an $error$ message and enters an $Error$ state from which all inputs are ignored. Let us note that $EC = true$ in the particular case where l has no outgoing transition with i.

For example, in the TA of Fig. 1, we add: $\langle ?\sigma; -; c_1 := 0, c_2 := 0 \rangle$ to locations l_1 and l_2, $\langle ?\phi; -; - \rangle$ to locations l_0 and l_1, $\langle ?\phi; c_1 < 1; - \rangle$ and $\langle ?\phi; c_2 \geq 2; - \rangle$ to location l_2. These added transitions are followed by $\langle !error; E; - \rangle$ that leads to an $Error$ state. If we apply the transformation procedure of [15] to this new TA, we obtain a se-FSA which completes the se-FSA of Fig. 2 by adding ($\mathcal{E}$ denotes one or several Exp events):

- a transition labelled $(\sigma, ?Set(c_1, 3), ?Set(c_2, 1, 2))$ to all states, except for q_0 and q_{11};
- a transition labelled $(\mathcal{E}, ?\sigma, ?Set(c_1, 3), ?Set(c_2, 1, 2))$ to every state with an outgoing transition labelled $\mathcal{E}$;
- a transition labelled $?\phi$ to all states, except for q_{10};
- a transition labelled $(\mathcal{E}, ?\phi)$ to every state with an outgoing transition labelled $\mathcal{E}$, except for q_5.

These added transitions are followed by $!error$ which leads to an $Error$ state. If we transform this new se-FSA into a io-FSA, we obtain a io-FSA which completes the io-FSA of Fig. 4 by adding:

- a transition labelled $(\sigma, Set(c_1, 3), Set(c_2, 1, 2)/-)$ to all states, except for q_0 and q_{11};
- a transition labelled $(-/\mathcal{E}) : (\sigma, Set(c_1, 3), Set(c_2, 1, 2)/-)$ to every state with an outgoing transition labelled $(-/\mathcal{E})$;
- a transition labelled $(\phi/-)$ to all states, except for q_{10};

– a transition labelled $(-/\mathcal{E}):(\phi/-)$ to every state with an outgoing transition labelled $(-/\mathcal{E})$, except for q_5.

These added transitions are followed by $(-/error)$ which leads to an *Error* state.

Hypothesis 2 and the modification of the transformation procedure of [15] can be justified by the fact that they allow us to avoid the following situation: having to add, in a io-FSA, a transition Tr1 to a state s which has an outgoing transition Tr2, such that Tr1 and Tr2 have the same event e (input or output) of $\mathcal{IUT}$ and different *Set* events. Such a situation is problematic because the added Tr1 can: neither lead to *Error* state because Tr2 implies that e is accepted by $\mathcal{IUT}$, nor be a selfloop because *Set* events of Tr1 have an effect on Clock-Handler.

5.4 Other Usual Necessary Hypotheses for Using GWp-Method

Hypothesis 3 There exists a *reset* action which brings $\mathcal{IUT}$ to its initial state.

Hypothesis 4 The specification (in the form of io-FSA) from which test sequences are generated is minimal, in the sense that it does not contain equivalent states. This hypothesis is guaranteed by the transformation procedure of [15].

Hypothesis 5 We assume that the behaviour of $\mathcal{SUT}$ (see Section 4.2) can be described by a io-FSA. This implies that $\mathcal{IUT}$ can be described by a FSA. Note that this hypothesis is equivalent to the test hypothesis in [26].

Hypothesis 6 Let n be the number of states of the io-FSA (or se-FSA) that describes the specification, and m be an upper bound of the number of states of the io-FSA that describes $\mathcal{SUT}$. We assume that $m \geq n$.

5.5 Formulation of GWp-Method

Let us first reformulate the *Test Equivalence* of Sect. 4 when "se-FSA" is replaced by "io-FSA". Let S1 be a TA and S2 be the corresponding io-FSA; S2 is obtained from S1 by using the transformations of Sect. 3 and 5.1, consecutively. The following two points are equivalent:

1. $\mathcal{IUT}$ conforms to S1.
2. $\mathcal{SUT}$ (consisting of $\mathcal{IUT}$ and Clock-Handler) conforms to S2.

Recall that our original objective was to check whether a $\mathcal{IUT}$ conforms to a TA. Using the above equivalence, we can transform our objective into: checking whether a $\mathcal{SUT}$ conforms to a io-FSA. And rightly, GWp-Method [24] is a method for generating test sequences which allow to determine whether a system (in our case, $\mathcal{SUT}$) conforms to a given io-FSA.

Note that there is no need to prove the above test equivalence, because it is equivalent to the test equivalence of Sect. 4.2. In fact, the transformation of a se-FSA into a io-FSA is just a syntactic transformation that consists of relabelling the transitions of the se-FSA. The semantics of each transition is not modified.

In the following: $q_0, q_1, q_2, \cdots, q_s$ are the states of the io-FSA (q_0 being the initial state), $Tr_0, Tr_1, \cdots, Tr_t$ are the transitions of the io-FSA, "." represents the concatenation operation, n and m are defined in Hypothesis 6, I is the set of inputs of the considered io-FSA, $I*$ is the corresponding (infinite) set of input sequences, I^k consists of all the input sequences of $I*$ whose length is k, and $I[k] = \{\epsilon\} \cup I \cup I^2 \cup \cdots \cup I^k$. GWp-Method defines and constructs *State Cover Set*, *Transition Cover Set*, *State Identification Set*, and *Test Suite* as follows:

A State Cover Set: $Q = \{Q_{q_0}, Q_{q_1}, \cdots, Q_{q_s}\}$, where Q_{q_i} is an input sequence which brings SUT from q_0 to q_i.

A Transition Cover Set: $P = P_{Tr_0} \cup P_{Tr_1} \cup \cdots \cup P_{Tr_t}$, where
$P_{Tr_k} = \{Q_{q_i}, Q_{q_i} \cdot Inp(k)\}$, $Inp(k)$ denotes the input(s) of Tr_k, and q_i and q_j are origin and destination states of Tr_k. Note that $Q \subseteq P$.

The Set: $R = P \setminus Q$. Let then $r_0, r_1, \cdots, r_p$ be the input sequences of R.

A State Identification Set $\mathcal{W} = \{W_{q_0}, W_{q_1}, \cdots, W_{q_s}\}$, where W_{q_i} is a set of input sequences which can be used to identify state q_i. We also consider the set $W_{q_0} \cup W_{q_1} \cup \cdots \cup W_{q_s}$ from which we remove every input sequence which is the prefix of another input sequence of the same set. The result is denoted W and called *Charaterization Set*.

A Test Suite $T = T_1 \cup T_2$, where:
$T_1 = reset \cdot Q \cdot I[m-n] \cdot W$ and $T_2 = reset \cdot (R \cdot I^{m-n}) \oplus \mathcal{W}$.
Operator $\oplus$ can be defined as follows: $A \oplus \{W_{q_0}, W_{q_1}, \cdots, W_{q_s}\} = ((a_0 \cdot \mathcal{W}_0) \cup (a_1 \cdot \mathcal{W}_1) \cdots \cup (a_k \cdot \mathcal{W}_k))$, where $A = \{a_0, a_1, \cdots a_k\} \subset I*$, $\mathcal{W}_i = W_{p_{i,1}} \cup W_{p_{i,2}} \cup \cdots \cup W_{p_{i,k_i}}$, and $p_{i,j}$ (for $j = 1, \cdots k_i$) being all the states that can be reached after the execution of the input sequence a_i. The input sequences of T allow to test all the states and transitions of the io-FSA [24].

5.6   Procedure for Generating Test Sequences

The proposed test generation procedure, which receives a io-FSA A as input, consists of the following three steps:

Step 1: In each state of A without any outgoing output transition (i.e., transition labelled $-/*$), add the self-loop ($-/-$) which models "waiting without receiving any output". For example, in the io-FSA of Fig. 4, we add the selfloop $Tr_0 = -/-$ in state q_0.
Step 1 is useful because there are cases where we can obtain information about the current state just by waiting and observing what happens.

Step 2: Test sequences (which are input sequences) are generated by using GWp-Method.

Step 3: The set of test sequences is minimized by removing redundant test sequences. This is done by removing every test sequence which is the prefix of another test sequence.

5.7   Example

Let us compute $Q, P, R, \mathcal{W}$ and W for the example in Fig. 4. In the following: "$- : i$" represents the input of a transition labelled "$(-/o) : (i/-)$" and means "the input i *immediately* follows the output o"; and the (possibly empty) inputs of consecutive transitions are separated by ".".

Let ϵ denote the empty input sequence, $-$ denote the empty input which means "waiting for an output", $A = (\sigma, Set(c_1, 3), Set(c_1, 1, 2))$ denote the inputs of Tr_1 and Tr_{22}, $B = (\phi)$ denote the input of Tr_{13}, $C = (-:\phi)$ denote the input of Tr_6, and $D = (-:Set(c_1, 1))$ denote the input of $Tr_2, Tr_3, Tr_{10}, Tr_{11}, Tr_{19}, Tr_{20}$. We obtain the following $Q, P, R, \mathcal{W}$ and W:

$Q = \{\epsilon, A, A{\cdot}D, A{\cdot}{-}, A{\cdot}D{\cdot}{-}, A{-}{\cdot}D{-}{-}, A{-}{\cdot}D, A{-}{\cdot}D{-}, A{-}{-}, A{\cdot}D{-}{-}, A{\cdot}D{\cdot}{-}C\}$,
$R = \{-, A{\cdot}D{\cdot}{-}{-}{\cdot}B, A{\cdot}D{\cdot}{-}{-}{\cdot}{-}, A{\cdot}D{\cdot}{-}C{\cdot}A, A{\cdot}D{\cdot}{-}C{\cdot}{-}, A{\cdot}{-}{-}{\cdot}D, A{-}{\cdot}D{\cdot}{-}{-}\}$,
$P = Q \cup R$, $\mathcal{W} = \{W_0, W_1, W_2, W_3, W_4, W_5, W_6, W_7, W_8, W_9, W_{10}, W_{11}\}$, where
$W_0 = W_3 = \{-\}$, $W_2 = W_6 = W_8 = W_{10} = W_{11} = \{-{\cdot}-\}$, $W_7 = \{-{\cdot}-{\cdot}-\}$,
$W_1 = \{-{-}{-}, D{\cdot}{-}, -{\cdot}D\}$, $W_4 = \{-{\cdot}D{\cdot}{-}, D{-}{\cdot}{-}{\cdot}{-}\}$, $W_5 = \{-{\cdot}B{\cdot}{-}\}$, $W_9 = \{D{\cdot}{-}\}$.
$W = \{-{\cdot}-{\cdot}-, D{\cdot}{-}{\cdot}{-}{\cdot}{-}, -{\cdot}D{\cdot}{-}, -{\cdot}B{\cdot}{-}\}$.

In order to compute T_1 and T_2, we must also know m which is an upper bound of the number of states of $\mathcal{IUT}$. In other to reduce the number and length of test sequences, m must be as small as possible. Since $m \geq n$ (see Hyp. 6), the ideal situation is $m = n$. For lack of space, we do not present a computation of T_1 and T_2 (for example when $m = n$), but note that parameters they depend on (i.e., $Q, P, R, \mathcal{W}, W$) have been computed.

6   Conclusion and Future Work

6.1   Contributions

This article presents a study for testing timed systems. Our main contributions in comparison to [8,9,10,11] are the following:

1. In [8,9], the elapsing of each fraction of unit of time is represented by a transition ν. Therefore, a state explosion problem arises. Our method reduces state explosion by representing only "relevant" time elapsing.
2. The test method in [10] is applicable iff a *single* clock is used. Our method generalizes the method of [10] by being applicable when one or *several* clocks are used.
3. The test method of [11] is applicable iff the set of possible values of clocks in a location of a TA *does not depend* on the path which has been executed to reach this location. This assumption is not used in our method.
4. Unlike [10,11], *nondeterminism* due to the use of *Exp* events and *complete specification* are studied in a rigorous manner.
5. The proposed test architecture is much *simpler* than the one in [10,11].

6.2   Future Work

In the near future, we intend to investigate the improvement of the transformation method and of the test method, such that certain or all of the following assumptions become unnecessary:

- We assumed Hypothesis 2 which states that in the TA describing the specification, the transitions associated to the same event of IUT reset the *same* set of clocks.
- We assumed that the TA is deterministic.
- We assumed that consecutive transitions of the TA cannot be simultaneous.

We also intend to study the following issues:

- We considered state and transition coverage. It would be interesting to adapt our test approach for data-based coverage.
- We considered a *centralized* IUT. When the latter is *distributed* in several sites: 1) a distributed test architecture consisting of several local testers must be designed and 2) every generated test sequence must be distributed into local test sequences which are executed by the different testers, respectively.

References

1. R. Alur and D. Dill. A theory of timed automata. *Theoretical Computer Science*, 126:183–235, 1994.
2. A. Khoumsi, G.v. Bochmann, and R. Dssouli. Protocol synthesis for real-time applications. In *Proc. PSTV/FORTE*, Beijing, China, October 1999. Also available in http://www.gel.usherb.ca/khoumsi/Research/Public/PSTVFORTE99.ps.
3. R. Alur, C. Courcoubetis, and D. Dill. Model checking for real-time systems. In *Proc. IEEE Symposium on Logic in Computer Science*, 1990.
4. F. Liu. Test generation based on an FSM model with timers and counters. Master's thesis, University of Montreal, Department IRO, 1993.
5. D. Mandrioli, S. Morasca, and A. Morzenti. Generating test cases for real-time systems from logic specifications. *ACM Transactions on Computer Systems*, 13(4):365–398, November 1995.
6. D. Clarke and I. Lee. Automatic generation of tests for timing constraints from requirements. In *Proc. 3rd International Workshop on Object-Oriented Real-Time Dependable Systems*, Newport Beach, California, February 1997.
7. A. En-Nouaary, R. Dssouli, and A. Elqortobi. Génération de tests temporisés. In *Proc. 6th Colloque Francophone de l'Ingénierie des Protocoles*. HERMES, 1997.
8. J. Springintveld, F. Vaadranger, and P. Dargenio. Testing timed automata. Technical Report CTIT97-17, University of Twente, Amsterdam, The Netherlands, 1997.
9. A. En-Nouaary, R. Dssouli, F. Khendek, and A. Elqortobi. Timed test generation based on state characterization technique. In *Proc. 19th IEEE Real-Time Systems Symposium (RTSS)*, Madrid, Spain, December 1998.
10. A. Khoumsi, M. Akalay, R. Dssouli, A. En-Nouaary, and L. Granger. An approach for testing real time protocol entities. In *Proc. 13th Intern. Workshop. on Testing of Communicating Systems (TestCom)*, Ottawa, Canada, Aug.-Sept. 2000. Kluwer Academic Publishers. Also available in http://www.gel.usherb.ca/khoumsi/Research/Public/TESTCOM00.ps.

11. A. Khoumsi, A. En-Nouaary, R. Dssouli, and M. Akalay. A new method for testing real time systems. In *Proc. 7th Intern. Conf. on Real-Time Computing Systems (RTCSA)*, Cheju Island, South Korea, December 2000. Also available in http://www.gel.usherb.ca/khoumsi/Research/Public/RTCSA00.ps.

12. B. Nielsen and A. Skou. Automated test generation timed automata. In *Work in Progress-Session of the 21st IEEE Real-Time Systems Symposium (RTSS)*, Walt Disney World, Orlando, Florida, USA, November 2000.

13. B. Nielsen and A. Skou. Automated test generation timed automata. In *Tools and Algorithms for the Construction and Analysis of Systems (TACAS)*, pages 343–357, Genova, Italy, April 2001.

14. B. Nielsen and A. Skou. Test generation for time critical systems: Tool and case study. In *Proc. 13th Euromicro Conf. on Real-Time Systems*, pages 155–162, Delft, The Netherlands, June 2001.

15. A. Khoumsi. A new transformation of timed automata into finite state automata. In *Submitted to the 23rd IEEE Real-Time Systems Symposium (RTSS)*, 2002.

16. R. Alur, C. Courcoubetis, N. Halbwachs, D. Dill, and H. Wong-Toi. Minimization of timed transitions systems. In *CONCUR*, pages 340–354. Springer-Verlag LNCS 630, 1992.

17. M. Yannakakis and D. Lee. An efficient algorithm for minimizing real-time transition systems. In *Proc. 5th Conf. on Computer Aided Verification*, pages 210–224. Springer-Verlag LNCS 697, 1993.

18. I. Kang and I. Lee. State minimization for concurrent system analysis based on state space exploration. In *Proc. Conf. On Computer Assurance*, pages 123–134, 1994.

19. I. Kang and I. Lee. An efficient state space generation for analysis of real-time systems. In *Proc. Intern. Symposium on Software Testing and Analysis (ISSTA'96)*, 1996.

20. S. Tripakis and S. Yovine. Analysis of timed systems based on time-abstracting bisimulations. In *Proc. 8th Intern. Conf. on Computer Aided Verification*, pages 229–242. Springer-Verlag LNCS 1102, 1995.

21. R. Alur. Timed automata. In *Proc. 11th Intern. Conf. on Computer Aided Verification*, pages 8–22. Springer-Verlag LNCS 1633, 1999.

22. A. En-Nouaary, F. Khendek, and R. Dssouli. Fault coverage in testing real-time systems. In *Proc. 6th Intern. Conf. on Real-Time Computing Systems and Applications (RTCSA)*, Hong-Kong, December 1999.

23. G. Luo, R. Dssouli, G.v. Bochmann, P. Venkataram, and A. Ghedamsi. Test generation with respect to distributed interfaces. *Computer Standards and Interfaces*, 16:119–132, 1994.

24. G. Luo, G. v. Bochmann, and A. Petrenko. Test selection based on communicating nondeterministic finite-state machines using a generalized wp-method. *IEEE Transactions on Software Engineering*, 20(2):149–162, 1994.

25. S. Fujiwara and G. v. Bochmann. Testing nondeterministic finite-state machine with fault-coverage. In *Proc. 4th Intern. Workshop on Protocol Test Systems (WPTS)*, pages 267–280. North-Holland, 1992.

26. J. Tretmans. *A Formal Approach to Conformance Testing*. PhD thesis, University of Twente, The Netherlands, December 1992.

Part VII

UML Models
and Model Checking

A Probabilistic Extension of UML Statecharts

Specification and Verification

David N. Jansen[1], Holger Hermanns[2], and Joost-Pieter Katoen[2]

[1] Universiteit Twente, Information Systems Group
Postbus 217, 7500 AE Enschede, The Netherlands
dnjansen@cs.utwente.nl
[2] Universiteit Twente, Formal Methods and Tools Group
Postbus 217, 7500 AE Enschede, The Netherlands
{hermanns,katoen}@cs.utwente.nl

Abstract. This paper introduces means to specify system randomness within UML statecharts, and to verify probabilistic temporal properties over such enhanced statecharts which we call probabilistic UML statecharts. To achieve this, we develop a general recipe to extend a statechart semantics with discrete probability distributions, resulting in Markov decision processes as semantic models. We apply this recipe to the requirements-level UML semantics of [8]. Properties of interest for probabilistic statecharts are expressed in PCTL, a probabilistic variant of CTL for processes that exhibit both non-determinism and probabilities. Verification is performed using the model checker PRISM. A model checking example shows the feasibility of the suggested approach.

Keywords: Markov decision processes, model checking, probabilities, semantics, UML statecharts.

1 Introduction

The Unified Modelling Language (UML) is more and more pervading system design and engineering. Accordingly, it is not far fetched to predict that the coming years shall see substantial efforts to extend the UML and the accompanying design methodology towards soft real-time, fault-tolerance, quality of service and the like. First work in this direction has been undertaken, e. g., in [5,9,14,16].

One of the principal modelling paradigms needed to express such aspects is the concept of *probability,* allowing one to quantitatively describe the randomness the system is exposed to, the randomness the system itself exhibits, or both. For instance, probability is a useful means to describe varying workload, to quantify uncertainty in the system timing, as well as to properly model randomised distributed algorithms. Furthermore, probability is also an abstraction means, e. g., it allows one to hide data dependencies by just representing the likelihood of particular branches to be taken.

There are two facets of the probability concept that are worth to be distinguished. On the one hand, each reactive system is exposed to external stimuli that exhibit some kind of randomness. We call this *environmental randomness.*

W. Damm and E.-R. Olderog (Eds.): FTRTFT 2002, LNCS 2469, pp. 355–374, 2002.

On the other hand, the system behaviour itself may ask for a probabilistic description, either because the system embodies a randomised algorithm, or because probability is used for abstraction. We call this *system randomness.*

This paper addresses system randomness. It introduces probabilistic UML-statecharts as a means to support the design of probabilistic systems. More concretely, the paper extends statecharts by probabilistic elements: a transition is allowed to lead to one of several states depending on a probability distribution; each probability distribution is guarded by a trigger, inspired by [20]. The interference of probabilities, priorities and nondeterminism raises some subtle semantic issues. We attack these issues in a way that allows one still to employ an arbitrary priority scheme to resolve or reduce nondeterminism. The semantics is formally defined as a mapping on (strictly) alternating probabilistic transition systems [10], a subset of Markov decision processes (MDP) [19]. To allow verification of probabilistic temporal properties over probabilistic UML-statecharts, properties are expressed in the probabilistic branching-time temporal logic PCTL [1], the prime logic for property specification and verification of models that exhibit both probabilities and nondeterminism. These properties can be checked using the model checker PRISM [15].

Care is taken to achieve a conservative extension of standard UML statecharts. Among the various published semantics for statecharts, we take as a representative the requirements-level semantics of Eshuis and Wieringa [8], which is based on the semantics by Damm et al. [6] which in turn formalises the Statemate semantics of statecharts [13]. A requirements-level model focuses on the design; an implementation-level model describes the implementation of a design. Requirements-level semantics mostly use the perfect technology assumption, which abstracts from limitations (in speed and memory) imposed by an implementation [18]. The chosen semantics combines the Statemate semantics with communication and classification. We have chosen it because it is simple and close to the most used semantics for UML. A detailed justification of this semantics and comparisons to Statemate semantics as well as implementation-level semantics can be found in [8]. The setup of our probabilistic extension, however, is independent of the UML basis we take. This means that other formal statechart semantics can equally well be enhanced with a similar probabilistic extension, as long as certain principal conditions are respected. We give an account of these conditions in Sect. 7.

We omit some minor features of the semantics, that could be added easily but would clutter up the exposition. These features include actions on initial transitions and entry and exit actions. We also leave out real-time aspects. To facilitate model-checking of the underlying model, we confine ourselves to bounded integer variables and employ a closed world assumption.

In summary, this paper makes the following contributions. (i) It introduces a generic recipe to conservatively extend a statechart dialect with probabilistic features. (ii) It details this recipe for the requirement-level semantics of [8], and identifies subtle interferences between the imposed priority scheme, and the order of resolving nondeterminism and probabilistic choice. (iii) It proposes to use the probabilistic logic PCTL to specify properties over statecharts and shows how model checking of probabilistic statecharts can be performed effectively.

Organisation of the paper. Sect. 2 and 3 introduce syntax and semantics of probabilistic statecharts. In Sect. 4, we show that this semantics conservatively extends the non-probabilistic statechart semantics. Sect. 5 presents a logic for P-statecharts and Sect. 6 demonstrates model checking with a larger example. Sect. 7 discusses our approach in the broader context of statechart semantics and of probabilistic models.

2   Probabilistic UML Statecharts

This section introduces probabilistic UML-statecharts (P-statecharts, for short), together with some drawing conventions. We first fix some notations. We assume familiarity with basic measure and probability theory [21].

Notation. The powerset of a set A is denoted by $\mathbb{P}(A)$. A probability space is denoted $(\Omega, \mathcal{A}, P)$ where Ω is the set of possible outcomes of the probabilistic experiments, $\mathcal{A} \subseteq \mathbb{P}(\Omega)$ is a σ-algebra of measurable sets and $P : \mathcal{A} \to [0, 1]$ is a probability measure. For discrete probability spaces, we sometimes write (Ω, P) instead of $(\Omega, \mathbb{P}(\Omega), P)$.

Collection of statecharts. A system consists of a finite collection of communicating statecharts. In the following, we assume a given finite collection of P-statecharts, denoted by $\{PSC_1, \ldots, PSC_n\}$.

Syntax. A single P-statechart PSC_i consists of the following elements:

- A finite set $Nodes_i$ of nodes with a tree structure, described by a function $children_i : Nodes_i \to \mathbb{P}(Nodes_i)$. (If $x' \in children_i(x)$, then x is the parent of x'. Of course, $children_i$ has to fulfil several constraints to make it describe a tree structure. For simplicity, these are omitted here.) Descendants are children or children of children, etc. The root is denoted $root_i$.
  The function $type_i : Nodes_i \to \{\text{BASIC}, \text{AND}, \text{OR}\}$ assigns to every node its type. Nodes that are leaves of the tree have type BASIC; children of AND nodes have type OR; $type_i(root_i) = \text{OR}$; other nodes have type OR or AND. The partial function $default_i : Nodes_i \multimap Nodes_i$ identifies for each OR node one of its children as the default (or initial) node.
- A finite set $Events$ of events. (Note that the set of events is identical for all P-statecharts in the collection.) We will use the symbol $\bot$ to denote "no event required"; $\bot \notin Events$.
- A finite set $Vars_i$ of variables together with an initial valuation $V_{0,i} : Vars_i \to \mathbb{Z}$, which assigns initial values to the variables. (We only allow bounded integer variables.)
- A set $Guards_i$ of guard expressions. Guard expressions are boolean combinations of the atoms $j.isin(x)$, for $j \in \{1, \ldots, n\}$ and $x \in Nodes_j$ (with the intuitive meaning "the P-statechart PSC_j is in node x"), and comparisons like $expr \leqslant expr$ and $expr > expr$, for arithmetic expressions made up from the variables and integer constants.

- A set $Actions_i$ of actions. Actions are $\mathsf{v} := expr$, which denotes an assignment to $\mathsf{v} \in Vars_i$, and **send** $j.\mathsf{e}$ (for $j \in \{1, \ldots, n\}$ and $\mathsf{e} \in Events$) with the intuitive meaning "send event e to the P-statechart PSC_j".
- A finite set $PEdges_i$ of P-edges. A P-edge is a tuple (X, e, g, P) where $X \subseteq Nodes_i$ is a non-empty set of source state nodes, $e \in Events \cup \{\bot\}$, $g \in Guards_i$ is a guard, and P is a probability measure in the discrete probability space $(\mathbb{P}(Actions_i) \times (\mathbb{P}(Nodes_i) \setminus \{\varnothing\}), P)$. We assume that there is a bijective index function $\iota : \{1, \ldots, |PEdges_i|\} \to PEdges_i$ to simplify the identification of P-edges.

Note that $Guards_i$ and $Actions_i$ are defined in terms of the other components. We will therefore denote a P-statechart simply by $(Nodes_i, Events, Vars_i, PEdges_i)$.

The above definition differs from the usual statecharts syntaxes (e. g., [8]) in the way edges are refined into P-edges. A P-edge (X, e, g, P) can be considered as a hyperedge with source node set X, and possibly multiple targets (A, Y), each target having a certain probability $P(A, Y)$. Note that a target is an action set A together with a non-empty set Y of successor nodes. Once the P-edge is triggered by event e and guard g holds in node X, a target (A, Y) is selected with probability $P(A, Y)$.

Drawing a P-Statechart. We adopt the following drawing conventions. The root node is not drawn. Nodes that are not children of an AND-node are drawn as rectangles with rounded corners. A parent node encloses its children. Children of an AND-node partition the node by dashed lines. Each OR-node encloses a black dot and indicates its default node by an arrow directed from the dot to the default node. A trivial P-edge (where probability 1 is assigned to a unique action set/node set) with event e, guard g and action set A is denoted as an arrow $\xrightarrow{\mathsf{e[g]}/A}$. A P-edge possessing a non-trivial probability space consists of two parts: first an arrow with event and guard $\xrightarrow{\mathsf{e[g]}}$ that points to a symbol ℗ (a so-called P-pseudonode), then several arrows emanating from the P-pseudonode, each with a probability and an action set $\xrightarrow{p/A}$. This notation is inspired by C-pseudonodes Ⓒ, used for case selection purposes e. g., in [12]. If the event on a P-edge is $\bot$, we may omit it. Further, if the guard is *true*, we may omit it. Similarly an empty set of actions may be omitted.

Example 1. Figure 1 depicts a P-statechart which shows the behaviour when playing with an *unreliable, but fair coin*: the event "flip" may or may not be ignored. If the system reacts, it outputs "heads" or "tails", each with 50 % chance. If the output is heads, the system stops playing. It is unspecified how (un)reliable the system is.

3   P-Statechart Semantics

This section discusses the semantics of P-Statechart, which is an adaptation of the nonprobabilistic semantics in [8]. The semantics is defined in two phases.

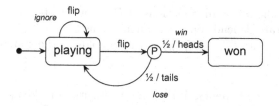

Fig. 1. Example P-statechart. The labels printed in italics (*ignore* etc.) are not part of the diagram, but are included to facilitate referencing the edges near the labels.

First, it is defined what will be a step. This encompasses the resolution of nondeterminism, probabilistic choice and priorities within a single P-statechart. Subsequently, these steps are used as the buiding blocks in a mapping of a collection of P-statecharts onto a Markov decision process.

Closed-world assumption. Opposed to [8] we assume a closed system model in the sense that we do *not* consider the system to be subject to inputs from the environment. This "closed-world assumption" simplifies model checking. The "open-world" semantics of [8] provides for input from the environment of the statecharts, and therefore, their state transitions consist of several phases, cluttering up the semantics. However, if one wants to consider specific environmental inputs, one can easily add another component that generates the desired events.

Intuitive semantics for a single P-statechart. The intuitive behaviour of a P-statechart can be described as follows. The statechart is always in some state (which consists of one or several nodes). A P-edge is taken if the P-statechart is in the source node(s), the event of the edge happens and its guard holds. Then, the system chooses one of the possible results (probabilistically and nondeterministically); it leaves the source nodes, executes the chosen action and enters the chosen target nodes of the P-edge. More than one edge may be taken simultaneously, even within a single statechart.

3.1 Step Construction

This section describes how a step is constructed for a single P-statechart PSC_i.

Configurations and states. A *configuration* C_i of P-statechart PSC_i is a set of nodes that fulfils the conditions:

- $root_i \in C_i$.
- If an OR-node is in C_i, then exactly one of its children is in C_i.
- If an AND-node is in C_i, then all its children are in C_i.

The set of all configurations of PSC_i is denoted $Conf_i$. A *state* of PSC_i is a triple (C_i, I_i, V_i) where C_i is a configuration, $I_i \subseteq Events$ is a set of events (to which the statechart still has to react), and $V_i : Vars_i \rightarrow \mathbb{Z}$ is a valuation of the variables. The set of all valuations of PSC_i is denoted Val_i. The validity of guard g in a state depends on the configurations $C_1, \ldots, C_n$ and the valuations $V_1, \ldots, V_n$. We write $(C_{1\ldots n}, V_{1\ldots n}) \vDash g$ iff g holds in the state of the collection of P-statecharts.

Edges. An edge is a triple (j, A, Y), where j identifies a P-edge, $A \subseteq Actions_i$ is a set of actions and $Y \subseteq Nodes_i$ is a set of target nodes. The set $Edges_i$ is defined as: $\{(j, A, Y) \mid \exists X, e, g, P : \iota(j) = (X, e, g, P) \in PEdges_i \wedge P(\{(A, Y)\}) > 0\}$.

Scope. The *scope* of an edge (j, A, Y) is the smallest (in the parent–child-hierarchy) OR-node that contains both the source nodes $\iota(j).X$ and the target nodes Y. Since this node only depends on source and target nodes, we refer to it as $scope(\iota(j).X, Y)$. (The scope is the smallest node that is not affected when the edge is executed.)

Steps. A step is a set of edges that are taken together as a reaction to events. The edges in a step for P-statechart PSC_i depend on its current state (C_i, I_i, V_i). A step has to obey several constraints, which are in close correspondance to [8]:

  Enabledness. All edges in the step must be enabled. A P-edge (X, e, g, P) is enabled if the current configuration C_i contains its source state nodes X, the event e is in the current input set I_i and the guard g holds: $(C_{1\ldots n}, V_{1\ldots n}) \vDash g$. An edge is enabled if its corresponding P-edge is enabled[1].
  Consistency. All edges in the step must be pairwise consistent. This means that they are either identical or that their scopes are different children of some AND-node or their descendants (in the latter case, the scopes are called orthogonal in [8]). If two edges are not consistent, they are called inconsistent.
  Priority. We assume a given priority scheme (a partial order on the edges) that resolves some of the inconsistencies: If an enabled edge e is not in the step, then there must be an edge in the step that is inconsistent with e and does not have lower priority than e.
  Maximality. A step must be maximal. This means that adding any edge leads to a violation of the above conditions[2].

We now give an algorithm to construct a step of a single statechart which – by construction – satisfies the conditions above. The algorithm employs a specific order with respect to the resolution of nondeterminism and probabilities. Assume that the current state is (C_i, I_i, V_i).

1. Calculate the set of enabled P-edges: for $j \in \{1, \ldots, |PEdges_i|\}$,

$$j \in EnP(C_i, I_i, V_i) \text{ iff } \iota(j).X \subseteq C_i \wedge (\iota(j).e \in I_i \cup \{\bot\}) \wedge (C_{1\ldots n}, V_{1\ldots n}) \vDash \iota(j).g$$

---

[1] It may happen that no P-edge, and consequently no edge, is enabled. Because of the closed world assumption, this is a deadlock.

[2] If there is no unique maximum, the system is nondeterministic.

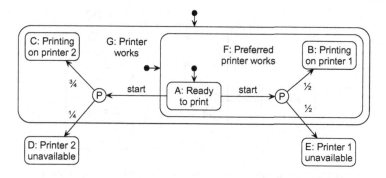

Fig. 2. Example of priority depending on target state

2. Draw samples from the probability spaces of the enabled P-edges, reducing the set $EnP(C_i, I_i, V_i)$ to a set $En(C_i, I_i, V_i)$ of enabled edges.
3. Calculate $Steps(En(C_i, I_i, V_i))$, where $Steps(E)$ (for $E \subseteq Edges_i$) contains all maximal, prioritized, consistent sets of edges $\subseteq E$.
4. Choose nondeterministically an element of $Steps(En(C_i, I_i, V_i))$.

Task 2 can be formalised as follows: For every state (C_i, I_i, V_i), we define a discrete probability space $\mathcal{PR}_{(C_i, I_i, V_i)}$ over $\mathbb{P}(Edges_i)$. Its probability measure is the lift of the following probability weight to sets of sets: for any selection of A_j and Y_j (for $j \in EnP(C_i, I_i, V_i)$),

$$P(\{(j, A_j, Y_j) \mid j \in EnP(C_i, I_i, V_i)\}) = \prod_{j \in EnP(C_i, I_i, V_i)} (\iota(j).P)(A_j, Y_j)$$

and $P(E) = 0$ otherwise. Note that if $EnP(C_i, I_i, V_i) = \varnothing$, then P is the trivial probability weight such that $P(\varnothing) = 1$.

Tasks 3 and 4 can be achieved by applying the original algorithm for *nextstep* (see [8]) to the calculated set $En(C_i, I_i, V_i)$. It is a nondeterministic algorithm that calculates a maximal, prioritized, consistent step, given a set of enabled edges. As a consequence, the above algorithm (consisting of Tasks 1–4) leads to a step that is enabled, consistent, prioritized and maximal.

It is worth to highlight that (after calculating the enabled possibilities in Task 1), we first choose probabilistically (in Task 2) according to the probabilities given by the P-edges. Only after that, in Tasks 3 and 4, we resolve the nondeterminism between the remaining possibilities. This order – first resolve probabilism, then nondeterminism – is essential, as shown by the following two examples, and can only be reversed by sacrificing the expressivity of P-statecharts, e. g., by disallowing arrows to cross node boundaries from a P-pseudonode to a target node.

Priority depends on probabilistic choices. In the mostly used priority schemes, priority depends on the scope. For example, in the UML priority scheme, smaller (in the parent–child-hierarchy) scopes have higher priority, according to [12]. The P-statechart in Fig. 2 describes a fragment of a system with two printers, of which

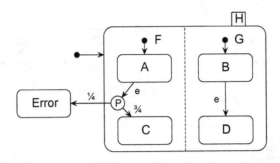

Fig. 3. Example of consistency depending on target state

the preferred printer (printer 1) is available only with probability $\frac{1}{2}$, and the other (printer 2) is available in $\frac{3}{4}$ of the cases. The probabilities are independent. If a print request is started, the system directs it to the best available printer. The edge leading from A: Ready to print to C: Printing on printer 2 (denoted A → C) with scope G: Printer works has higher priority than A → D and A → E (with scopes *root*), but A → C has lower priority than the edge A → B (with scope F: Preferred printer works), because F: Preferred printer works is a descendant of G: Printer works. So, if in configuration $\{A, F, G, root\}$ event start happens, the step produced by the above algorithm is:

- $\{A \rightarrow B\}$ with probability $P(\{A \rightarrow B, A \rightarrow C\}) + P(\{A \rightarrow B, A \rightarrow D\}) = \frac{1}{2}$, as edge A → B has priority over all other edges.
- $\{A \rightarrow C\}$ with probability $P(\{A \rightarrow E, A \rightarrow C\}) = \frac{1}{2} \cdot \frac{3}{4} = \frac{3}{8}$, as A → C has priority over A → E.
- Either $\{A \rightarrow D\}$ or $\{A \rightarrow E\}$ with probability $P(\{A \rightarrow E, A \rightarrow D\}) = \frac{1}{2} \cdot \frac{1}{4} = \frac{1}{8}$. The choice between these two steps is purely nondeterministic.

As the edges that belong to one P-edge have different scopes, it is impossible to resolve the priorities prior to resolving the probabilistic choice. Although this is exemplified using the priority scheme of [12], a similar P-statechart can be drawn for the Statemate priority scheme (which also depends on the scope).

The priority scheme of [22] does not depend on the scope, but only on the source nodes. For such a priority scheme, the above phenomenon is not a problem; but the next example is independent from priorities.

Consistency depends on probabilistic choices. The P-statechart in Fig. 3 shows a system which reacts to an event e in two independent components, of which one causes an error with probability $\frac{1}{4}$. The edge A → Error is inconsistent with B → D, as the scopes *root* and G are not (descendants of) different children of an AND-node (orthogonal). So, if in configuration $\{A, B, F, G, H, root\}$ event e happens, the step produced by the above algorithm is:

- $\{C, D, F, G, H, root\}$ with probability $P(A \rightarrow C) = \frac{3}{4}$.
- Either $\{A, D, F, G, H, root\}$ or $\{Error, root\}$ with probability $P(A \rightarrow Error) = \frac{1}{4}$; most priority schemes only allow one of the two cases.

Thus, the probability of taking edge B → D as a reaction to event e depends on the resolution of the probabilistic choice in the parallel node F. It is impossible to resolve the nondeterminism first, as there may or may not be inconsistent edges.

In summary, the influence of the target state in the construction of a step, as present in both the consistency definition and the priority scheme, forces us to resolve probabilism *prior* to establishing consistency and priority.

3.2   Step Execution

After having settled how steps are selected within a single P-statechart, we now consider their joint execution in the collection $\{PSC_1, \ldots, PSC_n\}$. The execution of a step is the same as in [8], as probabilistic aspects are not involved anymore. On the level of a single statechart, executing a step consists of two parts: updating the variables and events occurring in the actions and determining the new state. As the actions of one P-statechart may influence the sets of events of other P-statecharts, we describe the step execution of the complete collection of P-statecharts.

Default completion. The *default completion* C' of some set of nodes C is the smallest superset of C such that C' is a configuration. If C' contains an OR-node x but C contains none of its descendants, C' contains its default node $default_i(x)$.

Executing a step. Given configurations $(C_1, \ldots, C_n)$, steps $(T_1, \ldots, T_n)$, and valuations $(V_1, \ldots, V_n)$, we define for P-statechart PSC_i the new state (C_i', I_i', V_i') by:

- C_i' is the default completion of the union of $\bigcup\limits_{(j,A,Y) \in T_i} Y$ and

$$\{x \in C_i \mid \forall(j, A, Y) \in T_i : x \text{ is not a descendant of } scope(\iota(j).X, Y)\}.$$

- $I_i' = \bigcup\limits_{k=1}^{n} \{e \mid \exists(j, A, Y) \in T_k : \text{send } i.e \in A\}$
- $V_i' = V_i[\{v := expr \mid v := expr \in A, (j, A, Y) \in T_i\}]$, the same valuation as before except for the assignments in any action of the step. If these assignments are inconsistent, V_i' is undefined.

We denote this as: $Execute(C_{1\ldots n}, T_{1\ldots n}, V_{1\ldots n}) = ((C_1', I_1', V_1'), \ldots, (C_n', I_n', V_n'))$.

3.3   Markov Decision Process Semantics

Recall that in the step construction algorithm we resolve probabilistic choices prior to resolving non-determinism. A semantic model – that contains both non-determinism and discrete probabilities – preferably obeys the same order. Bundle probabilistic transition systems (BPTS) [7] is one of the rare models for which this is indeed the case. Although this model would be appropriate as semantical model, we prefer to use the (more standard) model of Markov decision processes (MDP) [19]. This slightly complicates the semantics, but has the nice property that it facilitates model checking of probabilistic properties.

We now embed the step semantics described above in a global semantics, mapping a collection of P-statecharts onto a finite Markov decision process. To allow the interpretation of temporal logic formulas later on, we equip an MDP with a state-labelling that assigns a set of atomic propositions to states. We assume a given fixed set AP of atomic propositions.

Markov decision processes. An *MDP* is a quadruple $(S, Distr, L, s_0)$ where:

- S is a finite, non-empty set of states.
- $Distr$ assigns to each state a finite, non-empty set of distributions on S.
- $L : S \rightarrow \mathbb{P}(AP)$ assigns to each state a set of atomic propositions.
- $s_0 \in S$ is the initial state.

In state s, the atomic propositions in $L(s)$ hold. Informally speaking, an MDP exhibits the following behaviour. Whenever the system is in state s, a probability distribution $\mu \in Distr(s)$ is chosen nondeterministically. Then, the system chooses probabilistically the next state according to the selected distribution μ.

Paths in an MDP. A *path* is an infinite sequence of states $(s_0, s_1, \ldots)$ such that s_0 is the initial state and the probability that s_{i+1} is reached from s_i is > 0, for each i. A path represents a possible behaviour of an MDP.

MDP semantics of a collection of P-statecharts. In an MDP, first a non-deterministic choice is made (among the available distributions) after which a next state is selected probabilistically. This order is reversed for the construction of a step of a P-statechart. To overcome this difference, we add auxiliary states to the MDP. Recall that (original) states consist of, per P-statechart, a configuration, a set of events, and a valuation, written (C, I, V). Auxiliary states will correspond to the outcome of Task 2 of the step construction algorithm and consist of, per P-statechart, a configuration, a set of enabled edges and a valuation, written (C, E, V). Each auxiliary state will be labelled with the distinguished atomic proposition $\triangle$. It offers a non-deterministic choice of trivial distributions (assigning probability 1 to a single state) only, such that each successor state is an original state (not labelled $\triangle$). Original states, in turn, do only possess singleton sets of probability distributions (hence there is no non-determinism), and all states with positive probability will be states labelled $\triangle$. This type of MDPs is also known as (strictly) alternating probabilistic transition systems [10].

Let the set $AP = \{\triangle\} \cup \bigcup_{i=1}^{n} \{i.isin(x) \mid x \in Nodes_i\}$. For a finite collection of P-statecharts (indexed from 1 to n), the MDP $(S, Distr, L, s_0)$ is defined by:

- $S = O \cup A$ where

$$O = \mathop{\times}_{i=1}^{n} (Conf_i \times \mathbb{P}(Events) \times Val_i) \quad \text{and} \quad A = \mathop{\times}_{i=1}^{n} (Conf_i \times \mathbb{P}(Edges_i) \times Val_i).$$

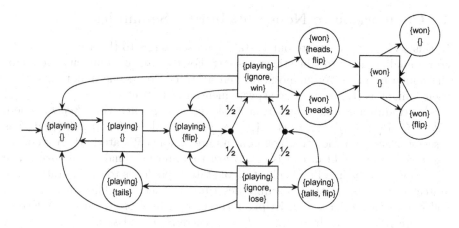

Fig. 4. MDP semantics of the P-statechart of Fig. 1

- $Distr((s_1, \ldots, s_n)) =$
  - $\{(s_1', \ldots, s_n') \mapsto \prod_{i=1}^{n} \mu_i(s_i')\}$, if $(s_1, \ldots, s_n) \in O$, where μ_i is the distribution corresponding to $\mathcal{PR}_{s_i} = (\mathbb{P}(Edges_i), P)$, defined by $\mu_i(C_i, E', V_i) = P(\{E'\})$ for $E' \subseteq Edges_i$ and $\mu_i(s) = 0$ for other states[3].
  - $\{\mu_s^1 \mid \exists T_i \in Steps(E_i) : s = Execute(C_{1\ldots n}, T_{1\ldots n}, V_{1\ldots n})\}$ otherwise. μ_s^1 denotes the trivial distribution that assigns probability 1 to state s.

- $L((s_1, \ldots, s_n)) = \begin{cases} \bigcup_{i=1}^{n} \{i.isin(x) \mid x \in C_i\} & \text{if } (s_1, \ldots, s_n) \in O \\ \{\triangle\} & \text{otherwise} \end{cases}$

- $s_0 = ((C_{0,1}', \varnothing, V_{0,1}), \ldots, (C_{0,n}', \varnothing, V_{0,n})) \in O$, where $C_{0,i}'$ is the default completion of $\{root_i\}$ and $V_{0,i}$ is the initial valuation in the ith P-statechart.

where $s_i = (C_i, I_i, V_i)$ if $(s_1, \ldots, s_n) \in O$ and $s_i = (C_i, E_i, V_i)$ otherwise.

Example 2. To illustrate how P-statecharts are mapped onto MDPs, we consider the "unreliable, but fair coin" P-statechart from Fig. 1. We compose this P-statechart with an event generator, which generates "flip" events at random. (If we don't add a component which generates "flip" events, the only reachable state of the system would be the initial state, due to the closed world assumption.) The MDP semantics of this collection of two P-statecharts is illustrated in Fig. 4. Here, original states of the form $(C, I, \varnothing)$ (where I is a set of events) are shown by circles with the sets C and I inscribed. Auxiliary states of the form $(C, E, \varnothing)$ (where E is a set of edges) are shown by boxes with the sets C and E inscribed. The names used for edges are shown in italics in Fig. 1; the nodes and edges of the event generator are omitted.

---

[3] If no edges are enabled in P-statechart i, this will lead to $\mu_i(C_i, \varnothing, V_i) = 1$.

4   Comparison to Non-probabilistic Semantics

In this section, we compare our P-statechart semantics to the semantics of the corresponding non-probabilistic statechart. For the sake of simplicity, we adapt the semantics of [8] to our notation and abstract from some minor aspects of their semantics (the very same aspects mentioned in Sect. 1).

A (traditional) statechart is a tuple $(Nodes, Events, Vars, Edges)$ where $Edges \subseteq \mathbb{P}(Nodes) \times (Events \cup \{\bot\}) \times Guards \times \mathbb{P}(Actions) \times \mathbb{P}(Nodes)$ is a set of edges, and the other components are as for a P-statechart. A step is – like before – an enabled, consistent, prioritized and maximal set of edges. The execution of steps in a finite collection of statecharts leads to a new state of the statecharts similar to the procedure described in Sect. 3.2. The semantics of a collection of statecharts is a Kripke structure (instead of an MDP). A Kripke structure KS is a quadruple (S, T, L, s_0), where S, L and s_0 are defined as for MDPs and $T \subseteq S \times S$ is the (non-probabilistic) transition relation.

Projections. To facilitate the comparison, we define three projections: one that abstracts from the probabilistic choices in a P-statechart (called α_1), and one that abstracts from the probabilistic choices in an MDP (called α_2). The projections replace probabilities by nondeterminism. Let $\alpha_1(PSC_i) = SC_i$ where SC_i is obtained from PSC_i by replacing the set of P-edges $PEdges_i$ by the set of edges $Edges'_i$ and by adding some variables to handle the interplay between probabilities and priorities correctly: For every nontrivial P-edge where edges have different priorities, we add one variable to make a nondeterministic choice between the possible continuations of the P-edge. So, $Edges'_i$ has the form
$$\{(X, e, g \wedge \ldots, A \cup \{\ldots\}, Y) \mid \exists d : \exists P : \iota(d) = (X, e, g, P) \wedge (d, A, Y) \in Edges_i\},$$
where the ... stand for checks of and assignments to new variables, where necessary. We also add an extra state *Init* to initialize the variables. Later on, we will use a third projection π to remove the additional variables and *Init* again. Further, $\alpha_1(\{PSC_1, \ldots, PSC_n\}) = \{\alpha_1(PSC_1), \ldots, \alpha_1(PSC_n)\}$.

Example 3. Figure 5 illustrates α_1: it contains a possible translation of Fig. 2 to a statechart. As both P-edges in the P-statechart have edges of different priority, α_1 adds two variables.

The projection α_2 is defined by: $\alpha_2(S, Distr, L, s_0) = (S', T, L \restriction_{S'}, s_0)$, where:

- $S' = \{((C_1, I_1, V_1), \ldots, (C_n, I_n, V_n)) \in S \mid I_i \subseteq Events\}$
- $T = \{(s, s') \mid \exists \mu \in Distr(s) : (\exists \tilde{s} \in S : \mu(\tilde{s}) > 0 \wedge \exists \mu' \in Distr(\tilde{s}) : \mu'(s') > 0)\}$

State set S' contains all non-auxiliary states, and $(s, s') \in T$ whenever s can move to s' via some auxiliary state $\tilde{s}$ in the original MDP with positive probability.

Theorem 1. *The following diagram commutes:*

$$
\begin{array}{ccc}
\{PSC_1, \ldots, PSC_n\} & \xrightarrow{\ \alpha_1\ } & \{SC_1, \ldots, SC_n\} \\
\downarrow{\scriptstyle sem_1} & & \downarrow{\scriptstyle \pi \circ sem_2} \\
MDP & \xrightarrow{\ \alpha_2\ } & KS
\end{array}
$$

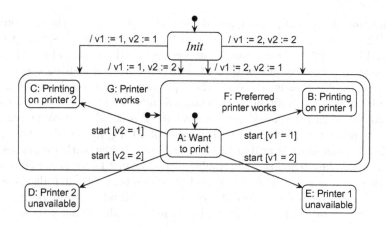

Fig. 5. A translation of Fig. 2 to a statechart

where sem_1 denotes our MDP-semantics and sem_2 denotes the KS-semantics of [8].

Proof. The proof is straightforward (but tedious) by checking the components of the resulting Kripke structures. The central idea is sketched below: The sets of steps in both semantics correspond to each other.

Assume given a state $s_i = (C_i, I_i, V_i)$ of one P-statechart (according to sem_1) and a step T_i with positive probability. We have to prove that there is a corresponding step T_i' in a corresponding state s_i' of $sem_2(\alpha_1(S))$.

The state s_i' is (C_i, I_i, V_i') [4], where V_i' extends V_i with suitable values for the new variables, such that the guards added to the edges in T_i by α_1 become true. The edges in T_i' are extensions of the edges in T_i by assignments to the new variables. We have some freedom of choice in these assignments, as T_i does not prescribe anything. (This is the point where nondeterminism replaces probabilism.) If one considers a path, one can choose the target that enables the next step in the path. The set T_i' is a step: it contains only edges enabled in s_i' and it is consistent, prioritized and maximal because T_i is a step.

The other parts of the proof are easy.

Corollary 1. *The P-statechart semantics is a conservative extension of the statechart semantics of [8].*

5   Property Specification for P-Statecharts

As a property specification language for P-statecharts we propose to use the probabilistic branching time logic PCTL, which extends CTL with probabilistic features. PCTL was originally interpreted over fully probabilistic systems, i. e.,

---

[4] States are not subjected to probabilities, that's why s_i and s_i' are so similar.

systems that do not exhibit any non-determinism [11]. We use the interpretation of PCTL over MDPs defined by Baier and Kwiatkowska [1,15][5], similar to pCTL and pCTL* [3]. PCTL allows one to express properties such as (Ψ) "the probability that a system crashes within 13 steps without ever visiting certain states is at most 10^{-5}". In order to decide these properties, the non-determinism is resolved by means of schedulers (also known as adversaries or policies). Temporal formulas are then interpreted with respect to all schedulers or some schedulers. Here, we restrict ourselves to the fragment of PCTL for which actual model-checking tool-support is available; i.e., we only consider path properties interpreted for all fair schedulers. Formulas of the form "There is a fair scheduler such that ..." can be checked via duality. The model-checking algorithm thus returns "true" for property (Ψ), iff (Ψ) holds for all fair schedulers that resolve the non-determinism. For simplicity, we do not consider next-formulas.

Syntax and informal semantics. The syntax of PCTL is given by the following grammar, where a denotes an atomic proposition, $p \in [0,1]$ denotes a probability and $\sqsupseteq$ is a placeholder for a comparison operator $<, \leqslant, =, \geqslant, >$:

$$\varphi, \psi ::= \textbf{true} \mid \textbf{false} \mid a \mid v \leqslant k \mid v \geqslant k \mid \varphi \wedge \psi \mid \neg\varphi \mid \mathcal{P}_{\sqsupseteq p}[\varphi \, \mathcal{U}^{\leqslant k} \, \psi] \mid \mathcal{P}_{\sqsupseteq p}[\varphi \, \mathcal{U} \, \psi]$$

The meaning of **true**, comparisons, conjunction and negation is standard. Recall from Sect. 3.3 that atomic propositions are $\triangle$ and $i.isin(x)$, which holds in states where P-statechart i is in node x. Formula $\mathcal{P}_{\sqsupseteq p}[\varphi \, \mathcal{U}^{\leqslant k} \, \psi]$ holds in a state if the probability of the set of paths that reach a ψ-state in at most k steps while passing only through φ-states is $\sqsupseteq p$. Property Ψ, e.g., is expressed as $\mathcal{P}_{\leqslant 10^{-5}}[\neg\varphi \, \mathcal{U}^{\leqslant 13} \, crash]$ where φ describes the states that should be avoided. $\mathcal{P}_{\sqsupseteq p}[\varphi \, \mathcal{U} \, \psi]$ has the same meaning, but does not put a bound on the number of steps needed to reach the ψ-state. The temporal operator $\Diamond$ can be defined e.g., as $\mathcal{P}_{\sqsupseteq p}[\Diamond^{\leqslant k}\varphi] = \mathcal{P}_{\sqsupseteq p}[\textbf{true} \, \mathcal{U}^{\leqslant k} \, \varphi]$. (A formal interpretation on MDPs is omitted here, and can be found in [1]).

Schedulers and fair schedulers. The above explanation is ambiguous if non-determinism is present, because the probability will (in general) depend on the resolution of non-determinism. Non-determinism is resolved by schedulers. A *scheduler* selects, for each initial fragment of a path through the MDP, one of the possible (non-deterministic) continuations. It does not resolve probabilistic choices. Several types of schedulers do exist, see [1]. Here, we consider *fair* schedulers. A fair scheduler only selects fair paths. A path π is *fair* if, for each state s that appears infinitely often in π, each of the possible non-deterministic continuations in s also appears infinitely often. Thus, for instance, $\mathcal{P}_{\leqslant 10^{-5}}[\neg\varphi \, \mathcal{U}^{\leqslant 13} \, crash]$ is valid if for all fair schedulers the probability to reach a crash-state within 13 steps (without visiting a φ-state) is at most 10^{-5}. From now on, we assume all PCTL-formulas to be interpreted over all fair schedulers.

Example 4. For the P-statechart in Fig. 1, we express the following properties:

---

[5] Baier and Kwiatkowska sometimes call the logic PBTL.

- "The probability that eventually the game will be over is 1":

$$\mathcal{P}_{=1}[\lozenge \ \neg 1.isin(playing)]$$

- "In less than 50 % of the cases, the game will be won within at most 20 steps":

$$\mathcal{P}_{<0.5}[\lozenge^{\leqslant 20} \ 1.isin(won)]$$

PCTL interpreted over P-statecharts. In our setting, a formula is interpreted over a finite collection of P-statecharts $\{PSC_1, \ldots, PSC_n\}$ and one of its states $(s_1, \ldots, s_n)$ where $s_i = (C_i, I_i, V_i)$. Formally, the semantics is defined via the MDP semantics, i.e., $\{PSC_1, \ldots, PSC_n\} \vDash \varphi$ iff the corresponding MDP satisfies $\overline{\varphi}$. Here $\overline{}$ denotes a syntactic translation needed to "hop along" the auxiliary ($\triangle$-labelled) MDP states. It is defined by induction over the structure of formulas. For elementary PCTL-formulas, such as atomic propositions and variable constraints, this translation is simply the identity, e.g., $\overline{\mathbf{true}} = \mathbf{true}$. For the remaining operators we have:

$$\overline{\varphi \wedge \psi} = \overline{\varphi} \wedge \overline{\psi}$$
$$\overline{\neg \varphi} = \neg \overline{\varphi}$$
$$\overline{\mathcal{P}_{\sqsupseteq p}[\varphi \, \mathcal{U}^{\leqslant k} \, \psi]} = \mathcal{P}_{\sqsupseteq p}[(\overline{\varphi} \vee \triangle) \, \mathcal{U}^{\leqslant 2k} \, \overline{\psi}]$$
$$\overline{\mathcal{P}_{\sqsupseteq p}[\varphi \, \mathcal{U} \, \psi]} = \mathcal{P}_{\sqsupseteq p}[(\overline{\varphi} \vee \triangle) \, \mathcal{U} \, \overline{\psi}]$$

6   Example: Hawks and Doves

This section applies P-statecharts and PCTL to the specification and verification of the behaviour of a small example taken from theoretical biology. Conflicts between animals are often analysed using simulation techniques. We consider the following variant of the hawk–dove-game [4,17]. In a population of animals, individuals combat for some advantage (such as food, dominance, or mates), their success being measured in points. Individuals may fight using several strategies. In particular, we consider

Hawk strategy: Hawk-like individuals will fight with great effort, until they win the contest (+5 points) or are severely injured (−3 points).

Dove strategy: Dove-like individuals will fight with limited effort, until they win the contest (+5 points) or give up after some fight (−1 point). When facing a hawk, they immediately give up (±0 points).

We consider a small scenario with three individuals and an arbiter. In every round, the arbiter chooses nondeterministically a pair of individuals; they will be opponents in the next contest. The two individuals select probabilistically the hawk or dove strategy. The arbiter decides who wins. Figures 6 and 7 show the P-statechart for one individual and the arbiter, respectively. The players all start off with 17 points and the individual scores may float in the interval $[0, 55]$ (otherwise they stop). Applying the MDP semantics of Sect. 3 together with

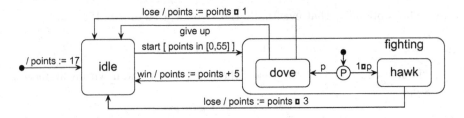

Fig. 6. Statechart of a contestant in the hawk–dove-game

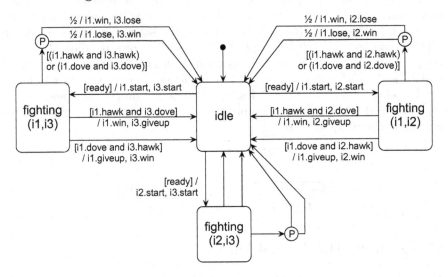

Fig. 7. Statechart of the arbiter in the hawk–dove-game. We have omitted some P-edge labels from and to node fighting(i2,i3), which are analogous the other fighting nodes.

some further optimisations (leaving out trivial intermediary states, encoding the configuration efficiently) leads to a system of 3,147,947 reachable states. The size of the state space is mainly dominated by the integer variables storing the scores. Different scenarios were checked with the model checker PRISM [15] where each scenario consisted of different types of animals. These types were generated by taking different values for p, the probability to behave like a dove. Formulas are checked for the initial state. The three considered scenarios are the following.

One daring and two careful players. This is a scenario with two individuals (c_1 and c_2) for which $p = 0.75$ and one individual (d) with $p = 0.5$. The probability that any individual dies (its points drop below 0) turns out to be very small, with the daring individual running a higher risk of being killed, since

$$\mathcal{P}_{\leqslant 10^{-7}}[(\neg dead(c_1) \wedge \neg dead(d))\, \mathcal{U}\, dead(c_2)] \quad \text{is refuted}$$

(and likewise with c_1 and c_2 reversed), but

$$\mathcal{P}_{\leqslant 10^{-7}}[(\neg dead(c_1) \wedge \neg dead(c_2))\, \mathcal{U}\, dead(d)] \quad \text{holds.}$$

The actual probability of d dying first is at most (depending on the scheduler) $7.206 \cdot 10^{-7}$, while the probability of the careful one dying first is at most $5.923 \cdot 10^{-8}$ (each). On the other hand, the daring individual is likely to outperform the others on accumulating a certain number of points, say 37. This follows from verifying:

$$\mathcal{P}_{<0.5}[(points_{c_1} < 37 \wedge points_d < 37) \, \mathcal{U} \, points_{c_2} \geqslant 37] \quad \text{which is valid, and}$$

$$\mathcal{P}_{\leqslant 0.75}[(points_{c_1} < 37 \wedge points_{c_2} < 37) \, \mathcal{U} \, points_d \geqslant 37] \quad \text{which is refuted.}$$

Three aggressive players. In this scenario each animal (d_1, d_2, d_3) plays hawk with probability 0.9 (i. e., $p = 0.1$). The probability that some of the individuals dies is relatively high, e. g.,

$$\mathcal{P}_{\leqslant 0.01}[(\neg dead(d_1) \wedge \neg dead(d_2)) \, \mathcal{U} \, dead(d_3)] \quad \text{is refuted}$$

(and likewise for the permutations of the d_i). So, there are schedulers which will lead to d_3 dying first with more than 1 % chance. The probability that one of the individuals gets more than 37 points within 100 steps is always less than 0.75, as

$$\mathcal{P}_{<0.75}[\diamondsuit^{\leqslant 100} \, (points_{d_1} \geqslant 37)] \quad \text{holds.}$$

Three careful players. In the opposite situation (the three individuals play dove with probability 0.9), the individuals (c_1, c_2, c_3) are less likely to die and more likely to get a reward fast. The probability that any of the individuals dies is rather low as, e. g.,

$$\mathcal{P}_{\leqslant 10^{-10}}[(\neg dead(c_1) \wedge \neg dead(c_2)) \, \mathcal{U} \, dead(c_3)] \quad \text{holds.}$$

So, for any scheduler, the probability of c_3 dying first never exceeds 10^{-10}. The probability that one of the individuals gets more than 37 points within 100 steps turns out to be greater than 0.8, since

$$\mathcal{P}_{\leqslant 0.8}[\diamondsuit^{\leqslant 100} \, (points_{c_1} \geqslant 37)] \quad \text{is refuted.}$$

Conclusion. As a general conclusion of the experiments we may state that it is good for a population as a whole if the animals are careful; but an individual may be at an advantage if it is more daring than the others.

7   Discussion and Conclusion

This section discusses our approach in the broader context of statechart semantics and of probabilistic models.

Contribution. This paper has developed a recipe to conservatively extend a statechart dialect with probabilistic features. We have applied this recipe to the requirement-level UML semantics of [8], mapping the probabilistic extension onto Markov decision processes as semantic models. Further, we have shown how to use the probabilistic logic PCTL to specify properties over probabilistic statecharts and how model checking of probabilistic statecharts can be performed effectively.

Adaptation to other statechart semantics. Various semantics have been published for statecharts, [2] lays out the spectrum of the many possibilities in defining a semantics. The extension to P-statecharts described in this paper can be applied to a wide range of other semantic definitions. The main idea of our extension is:

1. Syntactically, probabilities are trigger-guarded, i. e., reactions to triggers may depend on the result of a probabilistic experiment, whereas the triggers themselves are not subjected to probabilities. This restricts our approach to describing system randomness, opposed to environmental randomness.
2. Semantically, we reduce the P-statechart probabilistically to a (traditional) statechart, and this is done just before a step. The step is constructed and executed in the traditional statechart setting, and the step's result is interpreted in the P-statechart again. Such a reduction is possible as long as the effects of probabilistic experiments are encapsulated in the steps.

In principle it is possible to define a (traditional) statechart semantics which – if interpreted in the probabilistic extension – would break the encapsulation of probabilities within a step. For instance, one could imagine a semantics where a state variable depends on the enabledness of specific outgoing edges (which could only be decided after resolving the probabilism). However, such a feature appears to be rarely used, the overview given in [2] does not mention any feature like this.

Possible simplifications. Sect. 3.3 has mentioned BPTS as the most natural model for a P-statechart semantics. Thus, we could have simplified the semantics if there were a BPTS model checker available.

On the other hand, observe that the examples in Sect. 3.1 depend on the fact that some P-edge allows a probabilistic choice between target nodes with different parents. For most priority schemes, and for consistency, not the actually entered nodes are relevant, but their parents. If we disallow probabilistic choices between target nodes with different parents, we could resolve nondeterminism and probabilism in a different order and simplify several points: Theorem 1 can be formulated and proved simpler. It becomes feasible to give a direct semantics in terms of MDPs (i. e., without intermediary states), which is closer to the intuition behind P-statecharts. However, it is no more possible to express behaviours like the examples in Sect. 3.1.

Lessons learnt. It is easy to formulate an intuitive extension of statecharts with probabilities. However, when we started formalising and detailing it, a delicate balance had to be found with the other features of statecharts. Our first version of Theorem 1, for example, didn't work properly in the case that some edge has a higher priority than another edge which belongs to the same P-edge.

We have tried to formulate the extension as powerful as possible. This also revealed the problems of extending statecharts more clearly. For some applications, a simpler extension, or a simpler variant of basic statecharts is enough. In that case, one should ask whether the result is worth the effort.

Future work. Apart from exploring the specification and verification approach to system randomness on larger case studies, we are intending to investigate the very same approach in the context of environmental randomness. This asks for modelling and verification support for probabilistic and timing aspects of external stimuli a reactive system is exposed to.

Acknowledgements

The authors thank Rik Eshuis for pointing out a flaw in an earlier version of Theorem 1. Roel Wieringa is thanked for his comments on a draft version of the paper.

References

1. Christel Baier and Marta Kwiatkowska. Model checking for a probabilistic branching time logic with fairness. *Distributed Computing*, 11(3):125–155, 1998.
2. Michael von der Beeck. A comparison of statecharts variants. In H. Langmaack, W.-P. de Roever, and J. Vytopil, editors, *Formal Techniques in Real-Time and Fault-Tolerant Systems : ... proceedings*, pages 128–148, Berlin, 1994. Springer.
3. Andrea Bianco and Luca de Alfaro. Model checking of probabilistic and nondeterministic systems. In P. S. Thiagarajan, editor, *Foundations of Software Technology and Theoretical Computer Science : ... proceedings*, volume 1026 of *LNCS*, pages 499–513, Berlin, 1995. Springer.
4. Philip H. Crowley. Hawks, doves, and mixed-symmetry games. *Journal of Theoretical Biology*, 204(4):543–563, June 2000.
5. M. Dal Cin, G. Huszerl, and K. Kosmidis. Evaluation of dependability critical systems based on guarded statechart models. In *4th Int. Symp. on High Assurance Systems Engineering (HASE)*, pages 37–45. IEEE, 1999.
6. Werner Damm, Bernhard Josko, Hardi Hungar, and Amir Pnueli. A compositional real-time semantics of statemate designs. In Willem-Paul de Roever, Hans Langmaack, and Amir Pnueli, editors, *Compositionality : the significant difference. COMPOS '97*, volume 1536 of *LNCS*, pages 186–238, Berlin, 1998. Springer.
7. Pedro R. D'Argenio, Holger Hermanns, and Joost-Pieter Katoen. On generative parallel composition. In Christel Baier, Michael Huth, Marta Kwiatkowska, and Mark Ryan, editors, *PROBMIV'98 First International Workshop on Probabilistic Methods in Verification : Indianapolis, Ind. ... 1998*, volume 22 of *Electronic Notes in Theoretical Computer Science*. Elsevier, 2000. URL: http://www.elsevier.nl/locate/entcs/volume22.html.
8. Rik Eshuis and Roel Wieringa. Requirements-level semantics for UML statecharts. In Scott F. Smith and Carolyn L. Talcott, editors, *Formal Methods for Open Object-Based Distributed Systems IV : ... FMOODS*, pages 121–140, Boston, 2000. Kluwer Academic Publishers.
9. Stefania Gnesi, Diego Latella, and Mieke Massink. A stochastic extension of a behavioural subset of UML statechart diagrams. In L. Palagi and R. Bilof, editors, *Fifth International Symposium on High-Assurance Systems Engineering (HASE)*, pages 55–64. IEEE Computer Society Press, 2000.
10. H. A. Hansson. *Time and Probability in Formal Design of Distributed Systems*. PhD thesis, University of Uppsala, 1991.

11. Hans Hansson and Bengt Jonsson. A logic for reasoning about time and reliability. *Formal Aspects of Computing*, 6:512–535, 1994.
12. David Harel and Eran Gery. Executable object modeling with statecharts. *Computer*, 30(7):31–42, July 1997. IEEE.
13. David Harel and Amnon Naamad. The STATEMATE semantics of statecharts. *ACM Transactions on Software Engineering and Methodology*, 5(4):293–333, 1996.
14. Peter King and Rob Pooley. Derivation of Petri net performance models from UML specifications of communications software. In Boudewijn R. Haverkort, Henrik C. Bohnenkamp, and Connie U. Smith, editors, *Computer Performance Evaluation : Modelling Techniques and Tools ; ... TOOLS 2000*, volume 1786 of *LNCS*, pages 262–276, Berlin, 2000. Springer.
15. Marta Kwiatkowska, Gethin Norman, and David Parker. Probabilistic symbolic model checking with prism: A hybrid approach. In Joost-Pieter Katoen and Perdita Stevens, editors, *Tools and Algorithms for the Construction and Analysis of Algorithms : ... TACAS*, volume 2280 of *LNCS*, pages 52–66, Berlin, 2002. Springer.
16. C. Lindemann, A. Thümmler, A. Klemm, M. Lohmann, and O. P. Waldhorst. Quantitative system evaluation with DSPNexpress 2000. In *Workshop on Software and Performance (WOSP)*, pages 12–17. ACM, 2000.
17. J. Maynard Smith and G. R. Price. The logic of animal conflict. *Nature*, 246, November 1973.
18. S. McMenamin and J. Palmer. *Essential Systems Analysis*. Yourdon Press, New York, 1984.
19. Martin L. Puterman. *Markov Decision Processes : Discrete Stochastic Dynamic Programming*. Wiley, New York, 1994.
20. R. Segala and N. Lynch. Probabilistic simulations for probabilistic processes. *Nordic Journal of Computing*, 2:250–273, 1995.
21. A. N. Shiryaev. *Probability*, volume 95 of *Graduate texts in mathematics*. Springer, New York, 1996.
22. UML Revision Task Force. *OMG UML Specification 1.3*. Object Management Group, 1999. http://www.omg.org/cgi-bin/doc?ad/99-06-08.

Eliminating Queues
from RT UML Model Representations*

Werner Damm[1] and Bengt Jonsson

Uppsala University, Dept. of Computer Systems
S-751 05 Uppsala,
damm@offis.de, bengt@docs.uu.se

Abstract. This paper concerns analyzing UML based models of distributed real time systems involving multiple active agents. In order to avoid the time-penalties incurred by distributed execution of synchronous operation calls, it is typically recommended to restrict inter-task communication to event-based communication through unbounded FIFO buffers. This means that such systems potentially have an infinite number of states, making them out of reach for analysis techniques intended for finite-state systems. We present a symbolic analysis technique of such systems, which can be tuned to give a finite, possibly inexact representation of the state-space. The central idea is to eliminate FIFO buffers completely, and represent their contents implicitly, by their effect on the receiving agent. We propose a natural class of protocols which we call mode separated, for which this representation is both finite and exact. This result has impact on both responsiveness and predictability of end-to-end latencies, as well for the protocol verification, enabling automatic verification methods to be applied.

Keywords: Real-time distributed systems, RT UML, protocol verification, verification of infinite state systems

1 Introduction

We are interested in analysing UML based models of distributed real time systems involving multiple active agents. A central part of this modelling relates to the specification of protocols regulating the co-operation of such agents. Such protocols define the interface between the (possibly complex) processing internal to the agent and those aspects which must be visible to other agents to achieve the global co-operation. A concrete instance of this modelling paradigm is the European Standard on Wireless Train Control currently under development [1], where "agents" correspond to trains, railroad-crossings, switches, or other control points, and the protocol specifies dialogues between such agents, ensuring e.g. that a train only passes a railroad crossing once it has been secured. A simplified model of such a protocol can be found in e.g. [2]. [3] gives a representative example using an executable object model based on UML state-charts for such classes of applications.

---

* This research was partially supported by DFG USE and the STINT foundation.
[1] On sabbatical leave from Dept. of Computer Science, University of Oldenburg. Oldenburg, FRG

W. Damm and E.-R. Olderog (Eds.): FTRTFT 2002, LNCS 2469, pp. 375–393, 2002.

Protocols in transportation applications often relate to safety critical functions of distributed systems. Missing a signalling message in the train system application could potentially cause accidents, hence system components related to such protocol aspects typically would have high safety integrity levels. This paper provides a contribution in assessing the use of UML for modelling such applications. It focuses on those concepts of UML involved in the specification of inter-agent protocols, and assesses the potential to use automatic model-checking based algorithms in their verification. The key result of this paper is, that indeed such verification methods can be applied, given further support for the use of UML and analysing such application classes.

A salient feature imposed from UML is, that state-machines representing the agents communicate by exchanging events, which end up in unbounded FIFO buffers at the receiver side. The verification problem for such models thus entails verification of infinite state systems. In fact, two dimensions of infinity have to be addressed, since in addition to unbounded communication channels such UML models would typically also involve an unbounded number of state-machines. In this paper we focus on providing exact finite abstractions of the communication protocols for a given bounded number of so called *mode-separated* state machines. Intuitively, such state machines use a particular protocol to enter what we call *modes*, i.e. machine states representing global knowledge about the system state.

The analysis of protocols with unbounded FIFO queues has been considered rather extensively in protocol verification (e.g. [4,5,6,7]), and a number of symbolic representations, most of them being variants of regular expressions, have been proposed [8,9,10,11,12,13]. In the current work, we take a different approach, by avoiding to represent explicitly the buffers.

Central to our approach is the observation that in order to capture the behavior of an agent, it is not necessary to represent the concrete contents of the queue of unconsumed incoming events - all that really matters is its future impact on the receiving protocol machine. Thus, instead of giving a symbolic representation of the queue content, we partially evaluate the effect of consuming the events in the queue on the state of the receiver machine. We represent this effect by designating as *pending* the set of possible transitions that could be triggered by consuming events currently in the input buffer. By making a transition pending, we indicate that the part of its guard which requires event consumption can be neglected, when the computation of the state machines eventually analyses enabledness of this transition.

The advantages of using the receiver state machine for representing queue contents is that redundant and irrelevant messages will not be represented at all. A further advantage is that when the symbolic representation grows in complexity, we can use the structure of the receiving state machine as a guide for suitable overapproximations. In fact, our technique allows to tune the degree of approximation. An exact representation cannot in general be finite (this follows from undecidability of the analysis problem [14]) hence we also turn our attention to characterizing classes of protocols for which an exact and finite symbolic representation exists.

A key attribute of the application classes we consider is that the slackness between agents, roughly meaning how closely the local state of one machine is determined by the local state of the other machines, is bounded. Typically, the cooperation protocols are *mode separated*, meaning that they are split into distinct modes, each of which is intuitively associated with a global state of the system. Alluding to the train system application, modes of a train could follow a pattern of moves originating from a purely local processing state on a track segment well separated from other trains or control points, to an approach mode requiring the initiation of a protocol ensuring a safe passage, to a pass-mode characterising the actual passage of the control point, to a clean-up mode following the passage of the control point. Each such mode typically is supported by distinct phases of the protocol, often requiring a dialogue involving multiple events to be exchanged. Safety concerns stipulate a separation of such modes: there must be no disagreement between agents concerning the sequence of modes visited during an execution, in particular a mode should be re-entered only after all transitions related to the previous activation of this mode have been completed, and modes should not share transitions. In our context, we will give a formal definition of the concept of mode separation, and show that this property implies that our symbolic representation yields a *finite exact* abstraction of the system of state machines.

We conjecture that the technique we are proposing has independent value in ensuring responsiveness of UML based implementations for real-time applications. It can be realised as a pre-compilation phase, compiling away the FIFO buffer, and yielding a model with instantaneous processing of emitted events. This should substantially ease analysis of end-to-end response time, and eliminate the need of determining appropriate FIFO buffer sizes. Moreover, by considering pending transitions as purely local transitions, run-to-completion steps in the precompiled model effectively process multiple events in one sweep, significantly speeding up response time. This is in particular relevant for applications, where events signal hazardous situations requiring immediate attention.

The paper is structured as follows. In the following section, we introduce as a formal model of multi-agent systems an (infinite state) transition system with explicit representations of channel contents, reducing the verification problem of the application domain to a formal reachability analysis of its state space. The subsequent section formalises the idea of introducing pending transitions into the model of a protocol machine, and shows that this yields a finite abstraction for mode-separated protocols. Section 5 gives a simple syntactic condition called mode separation, guaranteeing the abstraction to be exact.

2   Formal Model of UML State Machines

In this section we give a formal model capturing the mathematical essence of UML based specifications of co-operation protocols. We focus here on the co-operation of two active objects, whose behaviour for simplicity we assume to be defined by UML statecharts. The model we propose is scalable to an arbitrary number of active objects, since it explicitly takes into account the effect of an unrestricted environment, which at any point in time can insert events into the event queue of either active object. This section is based on [15] giving a full semantics of the behavioural model of UML. In this paper, we restrict ourselves to pure event-based asynchronous communication between state-machines. Emitting an event does not block the sender machine, and causes the event to be inserted into the event queue of the receiving machine.

We assume as given a set E of events, with typical elements $e, e1, e2, ...$. We denote the emitting of event e to the partner state-machine by $e!$, to the sending machine by $self!e$, and to the environment by $env!e$. An emitted event will then be in-

serted into the receiver's event queue; events emitted to the environment cause no
state change in the observed system. The consumption of an event e is denoted by
$e?$; note that UML does not allow to qualify such a reception to some selected sender.

A further simplification taken in this paper is to ignore all aspects dealing with local data and operation calls. Thus the action language is reduced to emitting events or
performing some un-interpreted local action, denoted α_j – with j ranging over the
natural numbers - , for which we assume as given their semantics $[[\alpha_j]]$. We similarly
abstract from conditions on data values, by incorporating a countable set γ_j of symbols for local conditions, with semantics $[[\gamma_j]]$. Such conditions can appear as guards
of transitions, as may the consumption of an event, or a conjunction of both. Thus, we
assume a set A of *actions* with $A = \{ \alpha_j, e!, self!e, env!e \mid e \in E, j \in \omega \}$ and a set G
of *guards* with $G = \{ \gamma_j, e?, e?[\gamma_j] \mid e \in E, j \in \omega \}$.

A UML *state-machine* M is a tuple

$$M = (Q, T, q0)$$

where
- Q is some finite set of states
- $T \subseteq Q \times (G \times A) \times Q$ is the set of labelled transitions
- $q0 \in Q$ is the initial state

We analyse a system $S = M1 \parallel M2$ built from two asynchronously communicating UML state machines $M1$ and $M2$, working in the context of some unspecified
environment.

The dynamic behaviour of S is captured as a transition relation over its configurations. A *configuration* c of S is a tuple

$$c = \, << q1, \sigma1, \gamma1, v1>, < q2, \sigma2, \gamma2, v2 >>$$

where

- $q1, q2$ denote the current state of $M1$ and $M2$, respectively
- $\sigma1, \sigma2$ denote the current valuation of local data of $M1$, $M2$, resp.
- $\gamma1, \gamma2 \in E^*$ denote the current content of event queues associated
                 with $M1$, $M2$, resp.
- $v1, v2 \subseteq E$ denote the set of events emitted in the current step by M1,
                 M2, to the environment

We denote the set of all configurations of S by C_s, or simply C if the denoted
system is clear from the context.

A central concept in the execution semantics of UML statecharts is the notion of
run-to-completion steps (*RTC steps* for short). We call a state q of a UML state machine *stable*, if consuming an event is the only way the computation can proceed,
Formally, we define stability of a given state q and data-valuation σ of state-
machine Mj as follows:

$$stable(q, \sigma) \leftrightarrow (\forall t=(q, <\tau, \alpha>, q') \in Tj \; [[\tau]](\sigma) = false)$$

In other words: any transition originating from q with a pure local guard is disabled
given the current valuation of data-variables σ. Under the RTC semantics, performing
local computations has priority over consuming events. Thus, a new event is only
dispatched, once the state machine has become stable.

In summary, the transition relation on configurations will thus cover all of the following:

- *local-j*: Mj is taking a local computation step (j=1,2)
- *dispatch-j*: Mj is stable and an event is dispatched and accepted (j=1,2)
- *discard-j:* Mj is stable and the dispatched is not accepted (j=1,2)
- *env-j:*   The environment generates an event for machine Mj (j=1,2)

Since UML assumes an interleaving semantics, the transition relation capturing the dynamic semantics of S is thus defined as the *disjunction* of these sub-relations. We now proceed to define each of the sub-relations.

Local-1

$$c = <<q1, \sigma1, \gamma1, v1>, <q2, \sigma2, \gamma2, v2>> !_{local-1}$$
$$c' = <<q1', \sigma1', \gamma1', v1'>, <q2', \sigma2', \gamma2', v2'>>$$

iff

- $<q2, \sigma2> = <q2', \sigma2'>$
- $v2' = \{\}$
- $\exists (q1, <\tau, a>, q1') \in T1 \ \wedge \ [[\tau]](\sigma) = true \ \wedge$
  $(\exists \in \omega \ a \equiv \alpha j \ \wedge \ \sigma1' = [[\alpha j]](\sigma1) \ \wedge \ \gamma1' = \gamma1 \ \wedge v1' = \{\} \wedge \gamma2' = \gamma2)$
  $\vee (\exists e \in E \ a \equiv e! \ \wedge \ \gamma2' = \gamma2 \bullet e \sigma1' = \sigma1 \ \wedge \ \gamma1' = \gamma1 \wedge v1' = \{\})$
  $\vee (\exists e \in E \ a \equiv self!e \ \wedge \ \gamma1' = \gamma1 \bullet e \wedge \ \sigma1' = \sigma1 \ \wedge \ \gamma2' = \gamma2 \wedge v1' = \{\})$
  $\vee (\exists e \in E \ a \equiv env!e \ \wedge \ \gamma1' = \gamma1 \wedge \ \gamma2' = \gamma2 \wedge \ \sigma1' = \sigma1 \ \wedge \ v1' = \{e\})$

There are four cases to consider for actions a. For a local action αj, we evaluate its semantics $[[\alpha j]]$ on the current valuation of data variables $\sigma1$, leading to an updated valuation $\sigma1'$, while leaving both queues unchanged. The other cases deal with emitting events, which are either placed in the queue of $M2$, or in the queue of $M1$, depending on the appearance of the qualifier *self*, or simply emitted without side-effect on the current configuration if addressed to the environment.

Dispatch-1

$$c = <<q1, \sigma1, \gamma1, v1>, <q2, \sigma2, \gamma2, v2>> !_{dispatch-1}$$
$$c' = <<q1', \sigma1', \gamma1', v1'>, <q2', \sigma2', \gamma2', v2'>>$$

iff

- $<q2, \sigma2> = <q2', \sigma2'>$
- $v2' = \{\}$
- $stable(q1, \sigma1) \ \gamma1' = tail(\gamma1)$
- $\exists (q1, <e?[\tau], a>, q1') \in T1 \ e = head(\gamma1) \ \wedge \ [[\tau]](\sigma) = true \ \wedge$
  $((\exists \in \omega \ a \equiv \alpha j \ \wedge \ \sigma1' = [[\alpha j]](\sigma1) \ \wedge \ \gamma1' = tail(\gamma1) \ \wedge \ \gamma2' = \gamma2 \wedge v1' = \{\})$
  $\vee (\exists e \in E \ a \equiv e \ \wedge \ \gamma2' = \gamma2 \bullet e \wedge \ \sigma1' = \sigma1 \ \wedge \ \gamma1' = tail(\gamma1) \ \wedge v1' = \{\})$
  $\vee (\exists e \in E \ a \equiv self!e \ \wedge \ \gamma1' = tail(\gamma1) \bullet e \wedge \ \sigma1' = \sigma1 \ \wedge \ \gamma2' = \gamma2 \wedge v1' = \{\})$
  $\vee (\exists e \in E \ a \equiv env!e \ \wedge \ \gamma2' = \gamma2 \wedge \ \sigma1' = \sigma1 \ \wedge \ \gamma1' = tail(\gamma1) \ \wedge v1' = \{e\}))$

In a stable configuration, the first event of the queue is dispatched. If there is a transition originating from the current state whose trigger matches the dispatched event, and whose associated local condition evaluates to *true*, then one of these is picked, and its action part is evaluated as above. The case of a trigger without local condition is understood to be subsumed by this clause, by assuming the local condition *true*.

Discard-1

$$c = <<q1, \sigma1, \gamma1, v1>, <q2, \sigma2, \gamma2, v2>>\,!_{\;discard-1}$$
$$c' = <<q1', \sigma1', \gamma1', v1'>, <q2', \sigma2', \gamma2', v2'>>$$

iff

- $<q2, \sigma2, \gamma2> = <q2', \sigma2', \gamma2'>$
- $stable(q1, \sigma1) \wedge \gamma1' = tail(\gamma1)$
- $v1' = v2' = \{\}$
- $<q1, \sigma1> = <q1', \sigma1'>$
- $\forall(q1, <e?[\tau], a>, q1') \in T1 \ \ e = head(\gamma1) \rightarrow [[\tau]](\sigma) = false$

If no transition from the current state matches the dispatched event, then the event is *discarded*: it is deleted from the event-queue, and has no other effect on the current state configuration. UML actually allows the specification of so-called *deferred events* for each state; if in the above situation, *e* would have been in the defer-set of *q1*, then *e* would remain in the queue, and the dispatcher would consider the subsequent event. We do not consider handling of deferred events.

Env-1

$$c = <<q1, \sigma1, \gamma1, v1>, <q2, \sigma2, \gamma2, v2>>\,!_{\;env-1}$$
$$c' = <<q1', \sigma1', \gamma1', v1'>, <q2', \sigma2', \gamma2', v2'>>$$

iff

- $<q2, \sigma2, \gamma2> = <q2', \sigma2', \gamma2'>$
- $v1' = v2' = \{\}$
- $<q1, \sigma1> = <q1', \sigma1'>$
- $\exists e \in E \ \gamma1' = \gamma1 \bullet e$

At any point in time, the environment may choose to insert some arbitrary event into the event queue associated with machine *M1*.

We finally define the transition relation $!_s$ associated with system *S*, or $!$ for short, as the union of the above transition relations:

$$!_s = !_{local-1} \cup !_{local-2} \cup !_{dispatch-1} \cup !_{dispatch-2} \cup !_{discard-1} \cup !_{discard-2} \cup !_{env-1} \cup !_{env-2}$$

Figure 1 shows an artificial example system to illustrate our approach, together with a possible computation sequence of this system. The example shows on the top the architecture of the system, consisting of components *M1* and *M2*, which communicate using the associations shown. The behaviour of the components is defined by the two state-machines depicted below *M1* and *M2*, respectively. If triggered to take a *move*, controller *M2* chooses arbitrarily the direction *d* of the move of the robot, and signals controller *M1* in charge of engine control the selected direction. It then checks its sensors for detecting possible obstacles; if the chosen direction is clear of obstacles, the interlock for moves is removed, by emitting the corresponding *clear* event to *M1*. *M2* initiates the step motor depending on the chosen direction, and awaits clearance of the interlock before emitting a *go*, causing the actual move. The *check* event generated by the environment models a cyclic scheduler, while the *move* command is intended to be issued by some operator, and is thus not synchronized to steps of the system.

Note. that states *1,2,3* of *M2* are *instable*, while all its other states are *stable*. Thus, an example of a *run-to-completion* step of *M2* from state *6* is the one which is triggered by consuming a *move* command, followed by the local processing steps passing through states *1,2,3,* possibly iterating in state *3* waiting for an obstacle to move, and finally passing to state *4*. The only *instable* state of *M1* is state *4*. The sample configuration sequence shows purely local computation steps (such as reading sensors in *c3! c4*), environment steps (such as emitting the spurious *move* command in *c7! c8*), discarding events (such as the older *move* command in *c10! c11*), and dispatching events (such as *ack* in *c11! c12*).

Configurations provide a fine grained view of a systems execution semantics. In the context of system design, we are typically only interested in a *grey box* view of the systems behaviour, where observability is restricted to message exchange between system components themselves, as well as between system components and the environment, such as typically captured by scenarios or message sequence charts. We define this view as follows. For a configuration sequence from an initial configuration

$$\pi = c0 \; !_{\;s} \; c1 \; !_{\;s} \; ... \; !_{\;s} \; cn \; ,$$

label the *j*th transition $c(j-1) \; !_{\;s} \; cj$ by *<source, e, dest>* if it involves emission of event e from *source* to *dest*, where *source* and *dest* are either *M1, M2,* or *env*. Let *obs(π)* be the sequence of such labels in *π*. We then define the observational semantics *[[S]]* of *S* as the set of seuqences of labels associated with such configuration sequences:

$$[[S]] = \{ \; obs(\pi) \; | \; \pi \text{ is a finite configuration sequences of } S \; \}$$

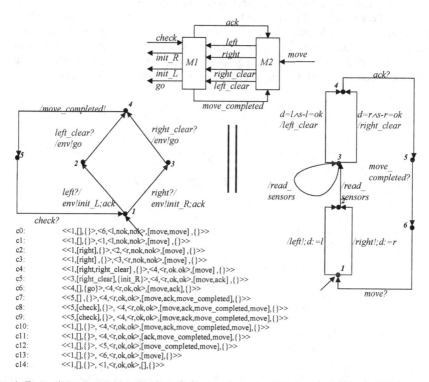

Fig. 1. Example system with robot *M1* and controller *M2* with possible computation sequence at bottom left.

3   Symbolic Evaluation of Events

The aim of this section is to define a finite state representation of a given system S which induces the same observational semantics as the standard representation of S as defined in the previous section. The central idea has already been elaborated in the introduction: rather than storing an event in the receivers queue, we directly evaluate the effect of emitting the event on the receivers state machine. Concretely, this effect is that transitions which previously required consumption of an event now become only locally guarded or unguarded, and can be performed without event dispatching. We refer to such transitions as *pending*.

We will introduce a simple colouring scheme to classify transitions in a state machine. Let us paint the current state *red*. Transitions that are reachable from the current state by taking only locally guarded or unguarded transitions are also *red*. A pending transition is painted *green* if it can be reached from the initial state, or from another green transition, by taking only locally guarded or unguarded transitions. All other transitions remain uncoloured. We must define rules for recolouring of transitions during computation steps. Intuitively, such rules will either extend the green region to represent reception of events into the event queue, or turn green regions red to represent dispatching of events from the event queue, while red regions turn uncoloured. Our construction thus eliminates unbounded FIFO buffers by the green-set – just another representation of the effect of emitting events.

There are a number of caveats to this intuitive idea, and we take the simple example of Figure 2 to illustrate these. The left box below the state-machine shows the sequence of events received by this state-machine in a possible computation sequence. The right box shows a suggestion for the set of transitions that should be coloured green, a transition being represented by its source and destination state.

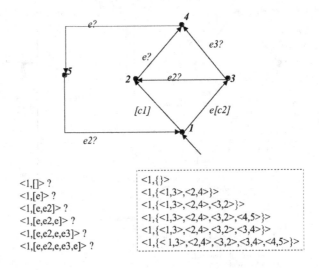

<1,[]> ?
<1,[e]> ?
<1,[e,e2]> ?
<1,[e,e2,e]> ?
<1,[e,e2,e,e3]> ?
<1,[e,e2,e,e3,e]> ?

<1,{}>
<1,{<1,3>,<2,4>}>
<1,{<1,3>,<2,4>,<3,2>}>
<1,{<1,3>,<2,4>,<3,2>,<4,5>}>
<1,{<1,3>,<2,4>,<3,2>,<3,4>}>
<1,{< 1,3>,<2,4>,<3,2>,<3,4>,<4,5>}>

Fig. 2. Example system with sequence of received events at left, and possible green-set at right.

Initially, we start with an empty queue, represented symbolically by an empty green set. Now consider the effect of emitting event e, with state 1 painted red. Recall, that this colouring also extends to transition $<1,2>$. Hence, adjacent to the red region, we have two transitions willing to consume the emitted event, $<1,3>$ and $<2,4>$, and we colour them green. Next, event $e2$ becomes emitted – and we find the transition $<3,2>$ adjacent to the green region, waiting to consume $e2$, and include it in the green set. The next occurrence of e makees $<4,5>$ green. Next, consider the arrival of yet another event $e3$. With state 3 being green, we find a transition matching the emitted event, and include it in the green set.

There are two flaws with this construction, when striving for exactness. First, notice that by introducing transition $<3,2>$ in the green set, the pragmatics of having transition $<2,4>$ in the green set becomes ambiguous: is it because we have received messages corresponding to the "slow" path $<1,3>$ $<3,2>$ to state 2, and that actually $<2,4>$ represents the second occurrences of e being emitted, or is it because we have performed the local step $<1,2>$ and are about to swallow the first occurrence of e ? This highlights the need to cater for non-determinism by keeping the green sets for the different alternatives *separated*. This separation can come for free if the choices are processed in state disjoint regions of the state-machineö otherwise it can be enforced artificially, by adding primed copies of a state in confusion situations such as above.

The second flaw can be observed when processing event $e3$. By now colouring transition $<3,4>$ green, the symbolic representation can actually *choose,* whether to pick this transition, once state 3 becomes the current state, or whether to follow the already green $<3,2>$-transition. Thus our representation has lost ordering information – and consuming the wrong event could easily spoil the capability of imitating a real-computation sequence. We cater for this by never extending the green set with transitions, which are in conflict to an already taken global choice.

We now turn to defining our symbolic representation, in which some main ideas are to use copies of states to maintain separation of alternative computations, and to delete sets of "dead" transitions. Let Q^{ω} denote the set Q together with an unbounded supply of numbered copies of Q. The k-th copy of state q is denoted $q(k)$; we identify q with $q(0)$. For a given state q of machine M its *local post-set* q^* is defined to be the set of states reachable from q by taking only locally guarded or unguarded transitions. We extend this function to *copies* of state q. *Symbolic configurations* SC_S of our system S take the form

$$sc = <<q1, \; \sigma1, \; \Gamma1, \; v1>, \; <q2, \; \sigma2, \; \Gamma2, \; v2>>$$

where $\Gamma j \subseteq Qj^{\omega} \times G \times A \times Qj^{\omega}$ denotes the current set of red and green transitions or copies thereof in machine Mj. The set Γj satisfies the property that its locally guarded and unguarded transitions generate a graph, whose connected components form the nodes a tree, where the green transitions are arcs. The current state qj is in the root component of this tree. In other words, for all reachable states q, all paths from qj to q contain the same sequence of event-consuming transitions. Moreoever, the set Γj has no unreachable states.

We now define a transition relation on symbolic configurations. The transition relation relies on two key operations $extend(e, \Gamma j, qj)$, and $reduce(\Gamma j, qj)$ on the sets Γj of red and green transitions. Intuitively, *extend* spreads the green colour from the current potential leaves of Γj by evaluating symbolically the effect of consuming e in each of these leaves. The function *reduce* acts like a garbage collector: it removes from Π all transitions which are no longer reachable once the actual state has progressed to qj. In an actual implementation, *reduce* should incorporate a reclaiming scheme of indices for state-copies.

Define a *potential leaf* of Π as a state-copy $q(k)$ such that the disjunction of local guards of (local and non-local) transitions from $q(k)$ is not *true*. The function *extend(e, Π,qj)*, takes as parameters the emitted event, the current set Π of red and green transitions, and the current state of Mj. It extends Π as follows.

- For each potential leaf $q(k)$ in Π we add, for each transition $<q,<e[\tau],a>,q'>$ from q triggered by e, a transition of form $<q(k),<e[\tau],a>,q'(l)>$ from $q(k)$ to a copy of q' which is not previously in Π.
- If there are transitions from q labeled by other events than e, we add one transition of form $<q(k),<e[\neg\rho],>,q(l)>$ from $q(k)$ to a fresh copy of itself, guarded by the negation $\neg\rho$ of the disjunction ρ of local guards of all e-consuming transitions that emanate at q. This is an explicit representation of a discard step, which must be added to avoid the order confusion observed in the previous example.

Thereafter Π is extended by adding appropriate copies of locally guarded and unguarded transitions that are reachable from the destinations of added green transitions.

The function *reduce(Π,qj')* takes as parameters the current set Π of red and green transitions, and a new current state of Mj. It deletes from Π all transitions, which are not reachable from qj'.

The initial symbolic configuration starts with Π being the set of unguarded and locally guarded transitions that are reachable from the initial state of Mj.

Slocal-1

$$sc = <<q1,\sigma1,\Gamma1,v1>, <q2,\sigma2,\Gamma2,v2>>!\ s_{local-1}$$
$$sc' = <<q1',\sigma1',\Gamma1',v1'>,<q2',\sigma2',\Gamma2',v2'>>$$

iff

- $<q2,\sigma2>=<q2',\sigma2'>$
- $v2'=\{\}$
- $\exists(q1,<\tau,a>,q1')\in T1 \land [[\tau]](\sigma) = true$

$(\exists j\in\omega\ a\equiv\alpha j \land \sigma1'=[[\alpha j]](\sigma1) \land \Gamma1'=\Gamma\land v1'=\{\}\land \Gamma2'=\Gamma2)$
$\lor (\exists e\in E\ a\equiv e! \land \Gamma2'=extend(e,\Gamma2,q2)\land \sigma1'=\sigma1 \land \Gamma1'=\Gamma\land v1'=\{\})$
$\lor (\exists e\in E\ a\equiv selfe \land \Gamma1'=extend(e,\Gamma,q1)\land \sigma1'=\sigma1 \land \Gamma2'=\Gamma2\land v1'=\{\})$
$\lor (\exists e\in E\ a\equiv env!e \land \Gamma2'=\Gamma2 \land \Gamma1'=\Gamma\land \sigma1'=\sigma1 \land v1'=\{e\})$

where

$$\Gamma = reduce(\Gamma1,q1')$$

There are four sub-cases to consider, corresponding to the four disjuncts in the definition of local computation steps. The first disjunct does not involve event-processing and hence leaves both queues unchanged. However, the green-set $\Gamma1$ of $M1$ may contain alternatve sub+trees that are no longer reachable after the transition to $q1'$, hence the function $reduce(\Gamma1,q1')$ should be applied first. In the third case, we note that emitting the event to itself is handled by setting

Γl to *extend(e, Γ, q1)*, and that in the final case of emitting an event to the environment the green set remains unchanged.

Green-1

$$sc = <<q1, \sigma l, \Gamma l, v l>, <q2, \sigma 2, \Gamma 2, v 2>>!_{green-1}$$
$$sc' = <<q1', \sigma l', \Gamma l', v l'>, <q2', \sigma 2', \Gamma 2', v 2'>>$$

iff

- $<q2, \sigma 2> = <q2', \sigma 2'>$
- $v2' = \{\}$
- *stable(q1, σl)*
- $\exists (q1, <e?[\tau], a>, q1'(r)) \in \Gamma l \ [[\tau]](\sigma) = true \ \wedge$
  $(\exists j \in \omega \ a \equiv \alpha j \ \wedge \ \sigma l' = [[\alpha j]](\sigma l) \ \wedge \ \Gamma l' = \Gamma \wedge v l' = \{\} \wedge \ \Gamma 2' = \Gamma 2)$
  $\vee (\exists e \in E \ a \equiv e! \ \wedge \ \Gamma 2' = extend(e, \Gamma 2, q2) \wedge \ \sigma l' = \sigma l \ \wedge \ \Gamma l' = \Gamma \wedge v l' = \{\})$
  $\vee (\exists e \in E \ a \equiv self! e \ \wedge \ \Gamma l' = extend(e, \Gamma, q1) \wedge \ \sigma l' = \sigma l \ \wedge \ \Gamma 2' = \Gamma 2 \wedge v l' = \{\})$
  $\vee (\exists e \in E \ a \equiv env! e \ \wedge \ \Gamma 2' = \Gamma 2 \ \wedge \ \Gamma l' = \Gamma \wedge \ \sigma l' = \sigma l \ \wedge \ v l' = \{e\})$

where

$$\Gamma = reduce(\Gamma l, q1')$$

Green-steps intuitively correspond to dispatch or discard steps and thus may only be taken if there is no locally enabled transition leaving the current state *q1*. They move the current state forward along one of the adjacent green transitions, thus possibly also resolving choices. All other concepts have been elaborated before.

Senv-1

$$sc = <<q1, \sigma l, \Gamma l, v l>, <q2, \sigma 2, \Gamma 2, v 2>>!_{senv-1}$$
$$sc' = <<q1', \sigma l', \Gamma l', v l'>, <q2', \sigma 2', \Gamma 2', v 2'>>$$

iff

- $<q2, \sigma 2, \Gamma 2> = <q2', \sigma 2', \Gamma 2'>$
- $v l' = v 2' = \{\}$
- $<q1, \sigma l> = <q1', \sigma l'>$
- $\exists e \in E \ \Gamma l' = extend(e, \Gamma l, q1)$

As before, the environment can choose at any time to emit some event *e*, which in the symbolic computation model is then evaluated by updating the green-set.

We finally define the symbolic transition relation $!_{sS}$ associated with system *S*, as the union of the above transition relations:

$$!_{sS} = !_{slocal-1} \cup !_{slocal-2} \cup !_{green-1} \cup !_{green-2} \cup !_{senv-1} \cup !_{senv-2}$$

Figure 3 shows how the symbolic transition relation operates, and in particular how the problems highlighted for the system in Figure 2 are handled. As before, we represent emitting *e* by including $<1,3>$ and $<2,4>$ in the green set. The subsequent emission of *e2* would - as noted before – cause a duplication of state *2* in the green set, hence we use a primed copy of this state when painting transition $<3,2>$. This allows us to nicely separate the two alternatives when processing the subsequent emittance of event *e*: the left hand choice leads to the inclusion of $<4,5>$, which has no bearing on the computation path following the other alternative to the copy *2′* of state *2*, which in its turn can now move forward to a fresh copy of state *4*, by including $<2',4'>$ in the green set. The subsequent emittance of *e3* is ignored: the global choice between the two transitions originating from state *3* has already been decided in favour of *<3,2>*. The subsequent emittance of event *e* causes a copy *<4',5'>* of transition *<4,5>* to be included in the green set.

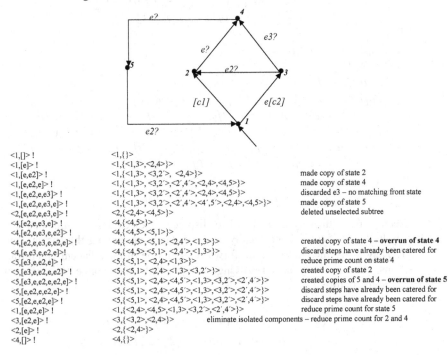

<1,[]> !	<1,{}>	
<1,[e]> !	<1,{<1,3>,<2,4>}>	
<1,[e,e2]> !	<1,{<1,3>, <3,2'>, <2,4>}>	made copy of state 2
<1,[e,e2,e]> !	<1,{<1,3>, <3,2'>,<2',4'>,<2,4>,<4,5>}>	made copy of state 4
<1,[e,e2,e3]> !	<1,{<1,3>, <3,2'>,<2',4'>,<2,4>,<4,5>}>	discarded e3 – no matching front state
<1,[e,e2,e3,e]> !	<1,{<1,3>, <3,2'>,<2',4'>,<4',5'>,<2,4>,<4,5>}>	made copy of state 5
<2,[e,e2,e3,e]> !	<2,{<2,4>,<4,5>}>	deleted unselected subtree
<4,[e2,e,e3,e]> !	<4,{<4,5>}>	
<4,[e2,e,e3,e,e2]> !	<4,{<4,5>,<5,1>}>	
<4,[e2,e,e3,e,e2,e]> !	<4,{<4,5>,<5,1>, <2,4'>,<1,3>}>	created copy of state 4 – **overrun of state 4**
<4,[e,e3,e,e2,e]> !	<4,{<4,5>,<5,1>, <2,4'>,<1,3>}>	discard steps have already been catered for
<5,[e3,e,e2,e]> !	<5,{<5,1>, <2,4>,<1,3>}>	reduce prime count on state 4
<5,[e3,e,e2,e,e2]> !	<5,{<5,1>, <2,4>,<1,3>,<3,2'>}>	created copy of state 2
<5,[e3,e,e2,e,e2,e]> !	<5,{<5,1>, <2,4>,<4,5'>,<1,3>,<3,2'>,<2',4'>}>	created copies of 5 and 4 – **overrun of state 5**
<5,[e,e2,e,e2,e]> !	<5,{<5,1>, <2,4>,<4,5'>,<1,3>,<3,2'>,<2',4'>}>	discard steps have already been catered for
<5,[e2,e,e2,e]> !	<5,{<5,1>, <2,4>,<4,5'>,<1,3>,<3,2'>,<2',4'>}>	discard steps have already been catered for
<1,[e,e2,e]> !	<1,{<2,4>,<4,5>,<1,3>,<3,2'>,<2',4'>}>	reduce prime count for state 5
<3,[e2,e]> !	<3,{<3,2'>,<2,4>}>	eliminate isolated components – reduce prime count for 2 and 4
<2,[e]> !	<2,{<2,4>}>	
<4,[]> !	<4,{}>	

Fig. 3. Symbolic transition sequence of the example system of Figure 2.

We now mimic a state configuration resolving the initial choice of transitions originating from state *1* in favour of transition *<1,2>*. In general, configuration steps advancing the current state are modelled by deleting those components from the green set no longer reachable from the current state, thus the complete sub-tree *{<1,3>,<3,2'>,<2',4'>,<4',5'>}* induced by the alternate choice is deleted. By the same policy, just advancing the current state will cause the taken transition to be deleted from the green set, as shown in the subsequent computation step reaching state *4*. This artificial example is too loosely synchronised to avoid *state-overrun* – the partner machine being able to now emit events *e2* and *e* causes a state overrun for state *4*: if including *<2,4,>* in the green-set, we could no longer separate behaviour induced by the current and the subsequent visit of this state. By using a fresh copy of state *4*, we avoid this problem – at the price of loosing boundedness of the green-set.

For a sequence of symbolic configurations

$$s\pi \;=\; sc0 \;!\;_{s}\; sc1 \;!\;_{s}\; ... \;!\;_{s}\; scn$$

where $sc0$ is an initial symbolic configuration, label the jth transition $cj\text{-}1 \;!\;_{s}\; cj$ by *<source,* *e , dest>* if it involves emission of event e from *source* to *dest*, Let *obs(sπ)* be the sequence of such labels in $s\pi$. The key property of our construction is the preservation of the observational semantics.

Theorem 1

[[S]] = {obs(sπ) | sπ is a finite sequence of symbolic configurations of S }

Proof:

$\subseteq$ In this direction, the theorem states that *the symbolic semantics is a safe approximation of the possible computation sequences of each protocol machine.* The theorem follows by composition if for each protocol machine we prove that each computation sequence in the concrete semantics corresponds to a computation sequence in the symbolic semantics, with the same external behaviour. Let us specialize the notation to machine *M1*. We establish a simulation relation between configurations $<q1, \sigma1, \gamma1, v1>$ in the concrete semantics, and symbolic configurations $<q1, \sigma1, \Gamma1, v1>$ in the symbolic semantics. The simulation relation identifies the state *q1*, valuation $\sigma1$, and set of emitted events *v1*. A (concrete) configuration $<q1, \sigma1, \gamma1, v1>$ is simulated by a symbolic configuration $<q1, \sigma1, \Gamma1, v1>$ under the following condition:

> **if** *M1* can perform a sequence π of transitions from *q1* to a state *qf* while consuming the events $\gamma1$ in dispatch and discard transitions, **then** the sequence π (possibly with states replaced by their appropriate copies) can be performed in $\Gamma1$ from *q1* to a potential leaf which is (possibly a copy of) *qf*.

In order to prove that this simulation relation is preserved by the transitions, we note that the definition of the concrete and symbolic semantics differ only on the following points:

1. Each extension of the input queue ($\gamma1' = \gamma1 \bullet e$) correspond to an application of the function *extend(e, $\Gamma1$, q1)*.
2. Each change of control state, from *q1* to *q1'* say, corresponds to deleting the corresponding root of $\Gamma1$ and resizing it with respect to *q1'* using *reduce($\Gamma1$, q1'(r))*. If the transition consumes an element of the input queue in a dispatch or discard transition, then that element is removed from the input queue ($\gamma1' = tail(\gamma1)$) .

We should thus check that

1. the function *extend(e, $\Gamma1$, q1)* extends $\Gamma1$ by adding paths that correspond to the paths that consume *e* starting from a potential leaf of $\Gamma1$;
2. shrinking of $\Gamma1$ by moving to a child of the previous root corresponds exactly to following the first step of paths that start with this transition.

Both properties should be clear by construction.

$\supseteq$ We prove this direction by establishing, that the "inverse" of the preceding simulation relation,

> Each path in $\Gamma1$ from *q1* to a potential leaf *qf(k)* corresponds to a sequence of transitions in *M1* from *q1* to *qf*, possibly with discard transitions added, that consume the events $\gamma1$ in dispatch and discard transitions

is also a simulation relation in the other direction. This follows form the fact that each state in Π can be reached from the root by a *unique* sequence of consumed events from the input buffer, and that Π contains no "spurious" potential leaves.

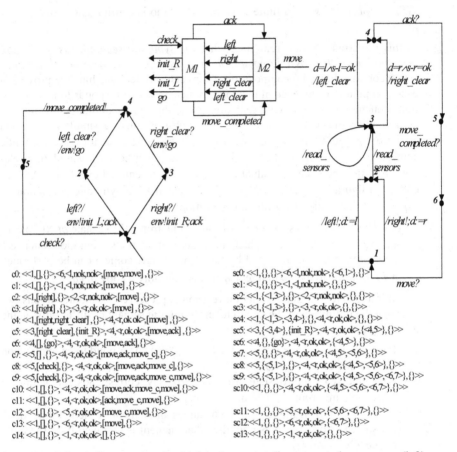

c0: <<1,[],{}>,<6,<1,nok,nok>,[move,move] ,{}>>
c1: <<1,[],{}>,<1,<1,nok,nok>,[move] ,{}>>
c2: <<1,[right],{}>,<2,<τ,nok,nok>,[move] ,{}>>
c3: <<1,[right] ,{}>,<3,<τ,ok,ok>,[move] ,{}>>
c4: <<1,[right,right_clear] ,{}>,<4,<τ,ok,ok>,[move] ,{}>>
c5: <<3,[right_clear],{init_R}>,<4,<τ,ok,ok>,[move,ack] ,{}>>
c6: <<4,[],{go}>,<4,<τ,ok,ok>,[move,ack],{}>>
c7: <<5,[] ,{}>,<4,<τ,ok,ok>,[move,ack,move_c],{}>>
c8: <<5,[check],{}>, <4,<τ,ok,ok>,[move,ack,move_c],{}>>
c9: <<5,[check],{}>, <4,<τ,ok,ok>,[move,ack,move_c,move],{}>>
c10: <<1,[],{}>, <4,<τ,ok,ok>,[move,ack,move_c,move],{}>>
c11: <<1,[],{}>, <4,<τ,ok,ok>,[ack,move_c,move],{}>>
c12: <<1,[],{}>, <5,<τ,ok,ok>,[move_c,move],{}>>
c13: <<1,[],{}>, <6,<τ,ok,ok>,[move],{}>>
c14: <<1,[],{}>, <1,<τ,ok,ok>,[],{}>>

sc0: <<1,{},{}>,<6,<1,nok,nok>,{<6,1>},{}>>
sc1: <<1,{},{}>,<1,<1,nok,nok>,{},{}>>
sc2: <<1,{<1,3>},{}>,<2,<τ,nok,nok>,{},{}>>
sc3: <<1,{<1,3>},{}>,<3,<τ,ok,ok>,{},{}>>
sc4: <<1,{<1,3>,<3,4>},{},<4,<τ,ok,ok>,{},{}>>
sc5: <<3,{<3,4>},{init_R}>,<4,<τ,ok,ok>,{<4,5>},{}>>
sc6: <<4,{},{go}>,<4,<τ,ok,ok>,{<4,5>},{}>>
sc7: <<5,{},{}>,<4,<τ,ok,ok>,{<4,5>,<5,6>},{}>>
sc8: <<5,{<5,1>},{}>,<4,<τ,ok,ok>,{<4,5>,<5,6>},{}>>
sc9: <<5,{<5,1>},{}>,<4,<τ,ok,ok>,{<4,5>,<5,6>,<6,7>},{}>>
sc10:<<1,{},{}>,<4,<τ,ok,ok>,{<4,5>,<5,6>,<6,7>},{}>>
sc11:<<1,{},{}>,<5,<τ,ok,ok>,{<5,6>,<6,7>},{}>>
sc12:<<1,{},{}>,<6,<τ,ok,ok>,{<6,7>},{}>>
sc13:<<1,{},{}>,<1,<τ,ok,ok>,{},{}>>

Fig. 4. Symbolic representation (right) of corresponding computation sequence (left).

In Figure 4, we illustrate the practical value of the construction using the example of the previous section. The symbolic configuration sequence is paired up with the original computation sequence. The example exhibits a number of properties typical for well structured protocols: separation of alternatives comes for free, and the protocol is free from state overrun. As a consequence, the symbolic representation is finite state.

We conclude this section by proposing an approach to selectively over-approximate the set of observations. The idea is that in the case that our symbolic construction grows unboundedly, by potentially creating an unbounded number of copies of a given state q, we will allow the symbolic representation to blur the distinction between different copies of state q. We may then over-approximate the set of possible behaviours, including behaviours which are not feasible in S, but we can guarantee finiteness of the resulting symbolic transition system. As an example, this

technique can be used to deal with "inessential loops", in which a state machine receives copies of events without being dependent on the number of copies received. In
general, by allowing the user to over-approximate the behaviour for a selected set of
states, the user can *tune* the trade-off between succinctness and exactness of the symbolic representation.

We now describe how to modify the symbolic representation when states in the
subset Rj are not copied in the symbolic transition rules. A first effect is that the set
of *potential leaves* can no longer be uniquely deduced from the green-set Γj. In order
to increase precision, we therefore extend our symbolic representation by explicitly
including a set of *potential leaves*. Formally, *relaxed symbolic configurations* of our
system S take the form

$$rsc = << q1 , \sigma1, \Gamma1, F1, v1>, < q2 , \sigma2 , \Gamma2, F2, v2 >>$$

where $Fj \subseteq Qj$ denotes the current set of *potential leaves* of machine Mj. The effect
of an event emission is, as before, computed using the function $extend(e, \Gamma j, Fj, qj)$,
which now takes the set of potential leaves as an explicit argument, but otherwise is
defined as previously. After following a transition $<q, <e[\tau], a>, q'>$, the set Fj is
updated. As before, it will contain state or state-copies, for which the disjunction of
local guards of outgoing transitions is not *true*, but additionally it will contain states
(or state copies) which are reachable from q' by local transitions and from which the
disjunction of guards of local transitions is not *true*. The rationale for including these
extra states is that they may correspond to revisits of relaxed states, and therefore
outgoing transitions that consume events should be ignored when determining
whether they can now be potential leaves. To illustrate the modified construction, in
Figure 4 we revisit the artificial example of Figure 2, assuming states *2,4* and *5* to be
relaxed. The set of potential leaves is listed as third component of the symbolic state.

We conclude this section by stating that the relaxed symbolic representation yields
a safe approximation of the queue-based semantics.

Theorem 2

Let R1, R2 be sets of relaxed sates of machines *M1, M2*, respectively. Then

$[[S]] \subseteq \{obs(rs\pi) \mid rs\pi$ is a finite sequence of symbolic configurations of $S \}$

Proof
The construction in the first half of the proof of Theorem 1 can still be carried out
without modification

4   About Exact Finite Symbolic Representations

In the symbolic analysis method outlined in the previous section, we may need to
designate certain states as relaxed in order to keep the symbolic state space finite. At
the same time, relaxed states induce an over-approximation of the state-space. In this
section, we will give conditions under certain combinations of exact and relaxed
states yield a finite and exact analysis of (properties of) a protocol. A central idea is to
identify a core *skeleton* of the protocol in each machine, such that the synchronization
between the machines is "sufficiently tight" so that the symbolic analysis is faithful, at
least with respect to this skeleton.

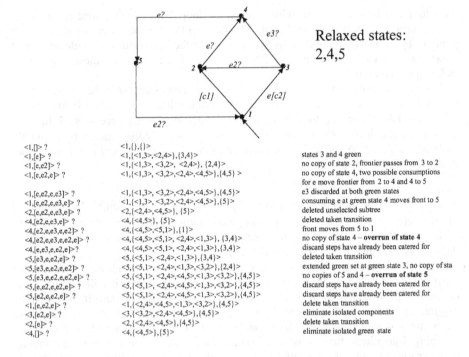

Relaxed states:
2,4,5

<1,[]> ?	<1,{},{}>	
<1,[e]> ?	<1,{<1,3>,<2,4>},{3,4}>	states 3 and 4 green
<1,[e,e2]> ?	<1,{<1,3>, <3,2>, <2,4>}, {2,4}>	no copy of state 2, frontier passes from 3 to 2
<1,[e,e2,e]> ?	<1,{<1,3>, <3,2>,<2,4>,<4,5>},{4,5} >	no copy of state 4, two possible consumptions for e move frontier from 2 to 4 and 4 to 5
<1,[e,e2,e,e3]> ?	<1,{<1,3>, <3,2>,<2,4>,<4,5>},{4,5}>	e3 discarded at both green states
<1,[e,e2,e,e3,e]> ?	<1,{<1,3>, <3,2>,<2,4>,<4,5>},{5}>	consuming e at green state 4 moves front to 5
<2,[e,e2,e,e3,e]> ?	<2,{<2,4>,<4,5>}, {5}>	deleted unselected subtree
<4,[e2,e,e3,e]> ?	<4,{<4,5>}, {5}>	deleted taken transition
<4,[e2,e,e3,e,e2]> ?	<4,{<4,5>,<5,1>},{1}>	front moves from 5 to 1
<4,[e2,e,e3,e,e2,e]> ?	<4,{<4,5>,<5,1>, <2,4>,<1,3>}, {3,4}>	no copy of state 4 – overrun of state 4
<4,[e,e3,e,e2,e]> ?	<4,{<4,5>,<5,1>, <2,4>,<1,3>},{3,4}>	discard steps have already been catered for
<5,[e3,e,e2,e]> ?	<5,{<5,1>, <2,4>,<1,3>},{3,4}>	deleted taken transition
<5,[e3,e,e2,e,e2]> ?	<5,{<5,1>, <2,4>,<1,3>,<3,2>},{2,4}>	extended green set at green state 3, no copy of sta
<5,[e3,e,e2,e,e2,e]> ?	<5,{<5,1>, <2,4>,<4,5>,<1,3>,<3,2>},{4,5}>	no copies of 5 and 4 – overrun of state 5
<5,[e,e2,e,e2,e]> ?	<5,{<5,1>, <2,4>,<4,5>,<1,3>,<3,2>},{4,5}>	discard steps have already been catered for
<5,[e2,e,e2,e]> ?	<5,{<5,1>, <2,4>,<4,5>,<1,3>,<3,2>},{4,5}>	discard steps have already been catered for
<1,[e,e2,e]> ?	<1,{<2,4>,<4,5>,<1,3>,<3,2>},{4,5}>	delete taken transition
<3,[e2,e]> ?	<3,{<3,2>,<2,4>,<4,5>},{4,5}>	eliminate isolated components
<2,[e]> ?	<2,{<2,4>,<4,5>},{4,5}>	delete taken transition
<4,[]> ?	<4,{<4,5>},{5}>	eliminate isolated green state

Fig. 5. The artificial example of Figure 2 revisited, assuming states *2,4,* and *5* to be relaxed.

As inspiration, we observe that in many protocols, it is possible to identify a certain subset of "important" control states in each protocol machine. These states represent stable situations, associated with certain functionality of the protocol, and typically represent knowledge about the global system state. We use the term *modes* to denote such "important" states of a machine. Furthermore, the occupancy of modes is typically synchronized between the machines, i.e., if at some point in time machine *M1* occupies a certain mode, then *M2* occupies a unique corresponding mode, except possibly during a mode-change. Mode-changes are then synchronized between protocol machines, typically by exchanging a pair of *request* and *grant* messages.

We consider, as previously, a system *S* consisting of protocol machines *M1* and *M2*. We will in addition assume that the message alphabet *E* is finite, and that there are no local actions or guards, i.e., transitions are labeled only by event emissions and consumptions. Moreover, we forbid any reception of events from the environment (i.e., there are no computation steps generated by rule *Env-i*). Let *D* be a subset of the messages exchanged between M1 and M2 (the intuition is that they should include request and grant messages used to synchronize mode changes). Let a *D-emission* be a transition which emits an event in *D*. Let a *D-reception* be a transition which consumes an event in *D*. Let a *D-transition* be a *D*-emission or a *D*-reception. The terms *non-D-emission, non-D-reception,* and *non-D-transition* are defined analogously.

Definition We say that a state machine *Mj* is *mode-separated* by a set *D* of messages if along any sequence of transitions from the initial state, the number of *D*-emissions is at most one more than the number of *D*-receptions.

The intuition is that the potentially extra $D.emession$ is a request for a mode change, which will be acknowledged by a grant message in the other direction.

In our first result, Theorem 3, we assume all states to be exact, implying that the symbolic semantics coincides with the actual semantics (by Theorem 1), and define conditions under which the symbolic semantics is finite-state.

Theorem 3

> Let the protocol machines M1 and M2 be mode-separated by the set D of messages. If each loop in any of the protocol machines M1 and M2 contains a D-transition, then there is a finite number of distinct reachable symbolic configurations.

Proof

> The proof relies on the observation that, due to mode-separation, any green-set in a symbolic configuration may not contain more than two subsequent D-receptions. By the condition in the theorem, this restriction gives a uniform bound on the size of any symbolic configuration.

The conditions in Theorem 3 are quite restrictive. They essentially entail that there is a uniform bound on the number of messages in the channels, implying that the entire protocol is finite-state. We will therefore, in Theorem 4, introduce a less restrictive condition, which allows control loops involving emission and reception of messages not in D, e.g., for the purpose of retransmission. To obtain a finite symbolic semantics, we must designate the control states in such loops as relaxed, since they otherwise run the risk of being copied unboundedly. This relaxation may induce an over-approximation of the behavior; hence we will state conditions under which such an over-approximation does not affect the core protocol, as defined by its D-transitions.

Definition Say that a protocol machine M is D-robust if whenever $(q, e?, q')$ is a non-D-reception in M, then
1. there is no path from q to q' which contains a D-transition,
2. there is a locally enabled path from q' to q in M without D-transitions
3. any path from q' reaches q without containing any D-transitions, using only locally enabled transitions.

Let us turn to the main result of this section. Let us lift the restriction that all states be exact, and assume that some partitioning of states into exact and relaxed states is performed.

Theorem 4

> Let D1 and D2 be sets of events with D1 $\subseteq$ D2. Let S be a system of two communicating D2-robust protocol machines M1 and M2., both mode-separated by D1, such that in both M1 and M2:
>
> (a)   each loop containing an exact state also contains a D1-transition,
> (b)   whenever there are two different paths from some state q to a relaxed state q', at least one of which contains a D2-transition, then one of the paths must contain at least 3 D1-receptions.

Then there is a finite number of distinct reachable symbolic configurations. Moreoever, the symbolic semantics generates the same sequences of D2-transitions as the exact semantics.

Proof

By induction over computation sequences of S, we prove that the potential over-approximation given by the green-sets is limited to loops that start by a non-$D2$-reception, and contain only non-$D2$-transitions. The proof of that depends on the following observations.

1. Any path in a green-set may contain at most two D1-receptions. Hence, the symbolic representation may not contain two different paths to a relaxed state, except for loops of non-$D2$-transitions.
2. Condition (a) implies that there is a bound on the number of exact states in any path in the induced symbolic representation, hence (as in Theorem 3) the symbolic semantics is finite.

5   Conclusions

We have considered the analysis of protocols, consisting of asynchronously communicating state+mahcines, as arising in UML based models of distributed real time systems. We have proposed a symbolic semantics, which replaces explicit representation of buffer contents by a representation of their effects on the receiving agent. The representation can be tuned to give a balance between succinctness and exactness. For certain classes of protocols, the representation is guaranteed to be both finite-state and exact.. Automatic verification of protocols governing coordination of autonomous systems can therefore be performed by constructing a finite state representation of the system using the techniques of this paper. A potential application of the ideas of the paper could be in code generation for multiple asynchronously communicating tasks allocated on the same processor, replacing event based communication by shared memory communication.

References

1. Euro-Interlocking Requirements, September 2001, see www.eurolock.org
2. W. Damm and J. Klose. Verification of a Radio-based Signaling System Using the Statemate Verification Environment. Formal Methods in System Design, Vol 19(2), 2001.
3. D. Harel and E. Gery. *Executable Object Modelling with Statecharts.* IEEE Computer, July 1997, 31-42
4. D. Brand and P. Zafiropulo. *On communicating finite-state machines.* Journal of the ACM, 2(5):323--342, April 1983.
5. A.P. Sistla and L.D. Zuck. *Automatic temporal verification of buffer systems.* in Larsen and Skou, editors, Proc.3rd Int. Conf. on Computer Aided Verification, volume 575 of Lecture Notes in Computer Science, Springer Verlag, 1991.
6. M.G. Gouda, E.M. Gurari, T.-H. Lai, and L.E. Rosier. *On deadlock detection in systems of communicating finite state machines.* Computers and Artificial Intelligence, 6(3):209-228, 1987.

7. J.K. Pachl. *Protocol description and analysis based on a state transition model with channel expressions.* In Protocol Specification, Testing, and Verification VII, May 1987.
8. P. A. Abdulla, A. Bouajjani, and B. Jonsson. *On-the-fly analysis of systems with unbounded, lossy FIFO channels.* In Proc. 10th Int. Conf. on Computer Aided Verification, volume 1427 of Lecture Notes in Computer Science, pages 305-318, 1998.
9. W. Peng and S. Purushothaman. *Data flow analysis of communicating finite state machines.* ACM Trans. on Progr. Languages and Systems 13(3):399-442, July 1991.
10. 10.   B. Boigelot and P. Godefroid. *Symbolic verification of communication protocols with infinite statespaces using QDDs.* In Alur and Henzinger, editors, Proc. 8th Int. Conf. on Computer Aided Verification, volume 1102 of Lecture Notes in Computer Science, pages 1-12. Springer Verlag, 1996.
11. B. Boigelot, P. Godefroid, B. Willems, and P. Wolper. *The power of QDDs.* In Proc. 4th Int. Static Analysis Symposium, Lecture Notes in Computer Science. Springer Verlag, 1997.
12. A. Bouajjani and P. Habermehl. *Symbolic reachability analysis of FIFO channel systems with nonregular sets of configurations.* in Proc. ICALP 97, volume 1256 of Lecture Notes in Computer Science, 1997.
13. 13.P.A. Abdulla and B. Jonsson. *Channel representations in protocol verification.* in Proc. CONCUR 2001, 12th int. Conf. on Concurrency Theory, volume 2154 of Lecture Notes in Computer Science, pages 1-15, 2001.
14. B. Westphal *Exploiting Object Symmetry in Verification of UML-Designs*, Diplomarbeit, Carl von Ossietzky Universität, 2001
15. W. Damm and A. Pnueli. *An Active Object Model.* Technical Report, OFFIS, Oldenburg, FRG, 2002.

Model Checking
Timed UML State Machines and Collaborations

Alexander Knapp[1], Stephan Merz[1], and Christopher Rauh[2]

http://www.pst.informatik.uni-muenchen.de/projekte/hugo/

[1] Institut für Informatik, Ludwig-Maximilians-Universität München
{knapp, merz}@informatik.uni-muenchen.de
[2] Institut für Informatik, Technische Universität München
rauh@in.tum.de

Abstract. We describe a prototype tool, HUGO/RT, that is designed to automatically verify whether the timed state machines in a UML model interact according to scenarios specified by time-annotated UML collaborations. Timed state machines are compiled into timed automata that exchange signals and operations via a network automaton. A collaboration with time constraints is translated into an observer timed automaton. The model checker UPPAAL is called upon to verify the timed automata representing the model against the observer timed automaton.

1   Introduction

Object-oriented methods are widely accepted for software development in the business application domain and have also been advertised for the design of embedded and real-time systems [20]. The standard object-oriented software modelling language UML (Unified Modeling Language [3]) accounts for the description of real-time systems by including timed versions of the diagrams used to specify dynamic behaviour [7,2]. Moreover, specialised, UML based real-time modelling tools like Rose RealTime[TM] or Rhapsody[TM] provide testing and code generation facilities to support the development process of object-oriented real-time systems, but they lack support for verification.

The UML offers mainly two complementary notations for the specification of dynamic system behaviour: the state/transition-based notion of state machines, and the notion of collaborations that is based on the exchange of messages. In practise, collaborations describe scenarios of desired or unwanted system behaviour and are used in the early phases of software development. The detailed design is later described by state machines. It should therefore be ensured that these two views of a system are indeed consistent by verifying that the state machines may exchange messages according to the test scenarios.

Several tools provide verification support for the state machine view of an untimed UML model via translation into the input languages of model checkers [14,16]. In previous work [19], we have reported on a tool that additionally addresses the problem of consistency between the state machine view and the collaboration view in the untimed fragment of UML.

W. Damm and E.-R. Olderog (Eds.): FTRTFT 2002, LNCS 2469, pp. 395–414, 2002.
© Springer-Verlag Berlin Heidelberg 2002

This paper describes a prototype tool, HUGO/RT, that is designed to automatically verify whether scenarios specified by UML collaborations with time constraints are indeed realised by a set of timed UML state machines. The timed state machines of a UML model are compiled into timed automata, as used by the model checker UPPAAL [13]. A time-annotated collaboration is translated into an observer UPPAAL timed automaton using basically the same techniques as described by Firley et al. [8]. The model checker UPPAAL is called upon to verify the timed automata representing the model against the observer timed automaton. We illustrate the translation and verification procedure by a benchmark case study in real-time systems, the "Generalised Railroad Crossing" (GRC) problem introduced by Heitmeyer et al. [12]. Although our translation is not based on a formal semantics for timed UML state machines, we attempt to be faithful to the informal specification of the UML [18] by following its semantic requirements as closely as possible.

Related work. The semantics of timed Harel-Statecharts, the main basis for UML state machines, has been investigated in detail by Damm et al. [5]. In the context of UML, Lavazza, Quaroni, and Venturelli [15] propose a translation of timed state machines into the real-time specification language TRIO, which, however, is not directly model checkable. The translation procedure is demonstrated for the GRC problem, using some extensions of the UML for testing the absence or presence of events, as is possible in Harel-Statecharts. However, compliance of their translation with the UML semantics for state machines, in particular regarding run-to-completion steps, is not obvious. Muthiayen [17] describes the verification of timed UML state machines with the theorem prover PVS. Again, the GRC problem serves as a case study. A translation of UML collaborations with time-constraints into UPPAAL timed automata has been presented by Firley et al. [8], though no implementation seems to be available. Also related is the translation of hierarchical timed automata into flat UPPAAL timed automata by David and Möller [6]. The direct use of this approach for the compilation of UML state machines is limited by the rather different notions of run-to-completion step.

Overview. The remainder of this paper is structured as follows: In Sect. 2 we briefly review the notation and semantics of timed automata as used by the model checker UPPAAL. In Sect. 3 we describe a case study, the GRC problem, and provide a UML solution, in passing explaining the UML notation and informal meaning of static structures, timed state machines, and collaborations with time constraints. A more detailed account of the semantics of timed UML state machines and, in particular, of our assumptions on the timing behaviour is given in Sect. 4. The translation of timed UML state machines into UPPAAL timed automata is explained in Sect. 5, the translation of UML collaborations with time constraints into observer UPPAAL timed automata is recapitulated in Sect. 6. We report on the verification results for the GRC case study in Sect. 7. We conclude with a discussion of some loose ends and of future developments.

2   Timed Automata

The framework of timed automata was originally defined by Alur and Dill [1].
The model checker UPPAAL that serves as the back end for HUGO/RT expects
models to be described as systems of timed automata, extended by primitives for
two-way synchronization. We briefly recall the main concepts of UPPAAL timed
automata.

A timed automaton is a non-deterministic finite state machine, extended by
finitely many real-valued clocks. States may be associated with invariants of
the form $x \sim c$ where x is a clock, c is an integer constant, and $\sim \in \{<, \leq\}$.
Transitions between states are labelled with triples (gd, sy, ac) where

– gd represents the guard of the transition, expressed as a conjunction of timing
  constraints $x \sim c$ or $x - y \sim c$ where x and y are clocks, c is an integer
  constant, and $\sim \in \{<, \leq, =, \geq, >\}$ is a binary relation,
– sy is a (possibly void) synchronization annotation of the form $a!$ or $a?$ that
  denotes an offer or an acceptance to synchronize over the channel a, and
– ac is a set of reset operations $x := c$ on clocks.

Moreover, UPPAAL allows integer variables as well as one-dimensional integer
arrays to be declared locally (i.e., for a single automaton) or globally. Transition
labels may include constraints on integer variables and array components in their
guards, similar to timing constraints, and may specify assignments to variables
in their actions, which are executed sequentially. However, clocks and integer
variables represent different, incomparable types. In particular, it is not possible
to compare the values of a clock and an integer variable, or to assign an integer
variable to a clock or vice versa.

The state of a system of timed automata consists of the control state for
each automaton, plus a valuation ν of the clocks and variables. Runs of timed
automata are infinite sequences of system states that satisfy the invariants, separated by actions that represent either the passage of time or the (instantaneous)
execution of transitions. A transition can be taken only if its guard evaluates
to true in the current system state. If the transition carries a synchronization
annotation of the form $a?$ or $a!$ then some corresponding transition (labelled
by $a!$ or $a?$) of some other timed automaton has to be taken simultaneously.
Finally, the resulting system state is obtained by updating the control states
of the timed automata involved in the transition, and by updating the valuation ν according to the action part of the transition label(s), i.e. by resetting
clocks and assigning values to variables. Note that the transition is not allowed
to occur if the resulting system state would violate the invariant associated with
the target location(s). In the case of a synchronization action, the assignments
specified by the "sending" automaton (whose transition is labelled by $a!$) are
performed before those of the "receiving" automaton. This allows synchronous
binary communication to be modelled with the help of global variables. Time
passage actions do not affect the control state or the values of the variables, but
increase the valuation of all clocks by the same amount, reflecting the assumption of perfect clocks. Again, the resulting system state is required to satisfy

all relevant state invariants. In particular, time-outs can be modelled by state invariants that disallow passage of time beyond the specified deadline.

As an additional modelling element, automata locations may be classified as either *committed* or *urgent*. Both of these annotations disallow the passage of time while the location is active. Additionally, committed locations require the next system action to involve a transition whose source state is the committed location. In this way, atomic transactions that involve more than a single transition can be modelled by labelling the intermediate locations as being committed. In particular, multiway synchronization can be modelled with the help of an atomic sequence of binary synchronizations. A channel can be declared *urgent* to disallow the passage of time as soon as synchronization over the channel is enabled.

3   GRC Case Study

We illustrate our translation of UML state machines and collaborations into UPPAAL timed automata by means of a UML model for the "Generalised Railroad Crossing" (GRC) case study [12].

The GRC problem asks for a system operating a gate at a railroad crossing: A gate for several railroad tracks lies in a critical section of the tracks, see Fig. 1(a). All trains pass the critical section in the same direction. The critical section is guarded by two sensors for each track indicating whether a train is entering or exiting the critical section. For every track at most one train passes the critical section, but trains on different tracks may pass at different speeds and overtake each other. Whenever the gate is occupied, i.e., some train is passing the gate, the gate must be closed (safety property). A utility property specifies that within certain tolerance intervals, prior and past being occupied the gate must be open; moreover, when the gate initiates opening, it must become fully open and must stay open for a certain period.

Timing annotations. We more concretely assume, see Fig. 1(b), that the minimal resp. maximal time a train may take to pass the distance between entering the critical section at A (the position of the entry sensor) and arriving at the gate at

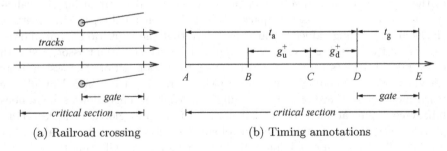

(a) Railroad crossing   (b) Timing annotations

Fig. 1. "Generalised Railroad Crossing" problem

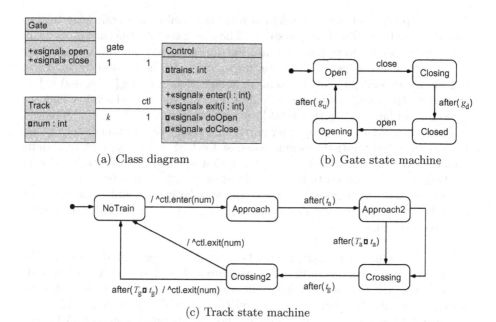

(a) Class diagram   (b) Gate state machine

(c) Track state machine

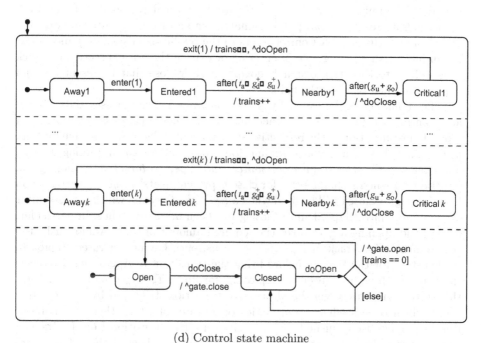

(d) Control state machine

Fig. 2. UML model of the Generalized Railroad Crossing.

D is t_a resp. T_a; and that the minimal resp. maximal time a train may take to pass the gate from D to E is t_g resp. T_g. The gate bars take the time g_u to go up from fully closed to fully open, and take the time g_d to go from fully open to fully closed. The minimal period the gate has to stay open is denoted by g_o. Thus, taking into account possible delays in communication, it is at $g_d^+ = g_d + \Delta$ before the fastest train may reach the gate after entering the critical section that the gate must initiate closing, that is, at location C determined by $t_a - g_d^+$. Moreover, in order to avoid the gate opening partly and then closing immediately again, the gate may only initiate opening when at least $g_u^+ = g_u + g_o + \Delta$ time units remain before the next closing is scheduled, that is, when the train that is closest to the gate is guaranteed to be before location B determined by $t_a - g_d^+ - g_u^+$. We assume that the thereby determined distance between A and B must at least allow for the communication delay, i.e. $t_a - g_d^+ - g_u^+ > \Delta$, in order to prevent premature openings.

UML model. Our UML model for the GRC problem is presented in Fig. 2. The *static structure* is set out in the class diagram in Fig. 2(a). Every (instance of) *class* Control refers to a single gate and, vice versa, every Gate is controlled by a single control. Moreover, every Control is connected to k instances of Track, each track knowing its control via ctl and holding its number in num. A Control records the number of trains currently in the critical region in the attribute trains. A Gate reacts to two public signals open and close by initiating opening and closing of the gate. A Control reacts to the public signals enter(i) and exit(i) for an integer i reporting a train entering or exiting the critical section on track i, as well as to the private signals doOpen and doClose that represent internal requests to open or close the gate.

The dynamics is described by *state machines* for the classes Gate, Track, and Control, see Fig. 2(b)–(d). Each instance of these classes is governed by a separate instantiation of the respective state machine. The state machine for Gate in Fig. 2(b) shows an *initial state* and four *simple states* Open, Closing, Closed, and Opening. The *transition* from *source state* Open to *target state* Closing can only be *fired* when a *signal event* for close is present as its *trigger*. The transition from Closing to Closed will be fired when a *time event* occurs, which is raised after g_d time units have elapsed since Closing has been *activated*. Thus, in particular, closing and opening a gate takes the required amount of time. Analogously, the state machine for Track in Fig. 2(c) sojourns, once having activated Approach, in this state for the time t_a before firing the transition to Approach2. However, the state machine may dwell in Approach2 for up to $T_a - t_a$ time units or leave this state prematurely via the alternative transition, triggered by a *completion event* which occurs when all activities of a state, of which there are none in this case, have been finished. In the same vein, the transition from NoTrain to Approach may be fired immediately after NoTrain has been activated, as there are again no activities; but this transition also shows an *effect*, viz., that signal enter(num) is raised for the instance of Control referred to as ctl. Hence, the state machines for the tracks simulate the entering and exiting of trains in the critical section; the minimal time a train may take for this distance is $t_a + t_g$,

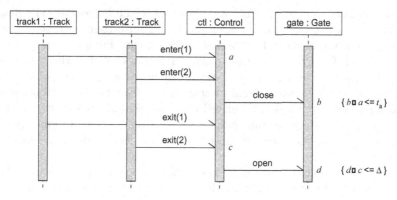

(a) Sequence diagram for the safety property

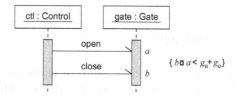

(b) Sequence diagram for the utility property

Fig. 3. UML model of the Generalized Railroad Crossing (cont'd.).

the maximal time is $T_a + T_g$. Finally, the state machine for Control in Fig. 2(b), shows a *concurrent composite state* consisting of several *orthogonal regions* which are again *composite*, though sequential, *states*. The upper k orthogonal regions, the ith region handling the entering and exiting of a train on the ith track, all provide the same behaviour, ensuring that when a train on track i has entered the critical region, an internal signal doClose requesting the closing of the gate is raised after $t_a - g_d^+ - \Delta$, and that when a train on track i leaves the critical region an internal signal doOpen requesting the opening of the gate is raised. The last orthogonal region actually handles closing and opening of the gate: When in Open and receiving a signal event for doClose, a signal event for close to the instance in gate is sent. However, when in Closed only a signal event for doOpen is reacted to—should a signal event for doClose arrive in this state it is discarded by the whole state machine as there is no other transition taking such an event as its trigger. The transition fired by a signal event for doOpen has two possible target states, linked by a *junction pseudo-state*: If the *guard* trains==0 is true on firing the transition indeed a signal event for open on gate is raised and Open is activated; otherwise the other branch is taken: Closed is first *deactivated* but becomes activated immediately again.

Finally, two test cases for the system behaviour are depicted in the *collaborations*, shown as sequence diagrams, in Fig. 3 that partially describe the safety and utility properties for the UML model.

The sequence diagram in Fig. 3(a) describes a safe behaviour. The diagram specifies that, given two tracks track1 and track2 for a control ctl surveying the gate gate, when a *stimulus* for the first *message*, carrying an enter(1) signal, is received by ctl from track1 at time point a it is possible that the gate receives a stimulus for the third message, carrying signal close, at time point b within t_a, independently of when a signal enter(2) is sent from track2 to ctl in-between. Analogously, after the last train exited the gate, as indicated by ctl receiving a signal exit(2) from track2 at time point c, the gate may receive a signal open from ctl at time point d such that at most the communication delay Δ has elapsed after c.

The sequence diagram in Fig. 3(b) describes a behaviour that is not allowed to occur: it must be impossible that after the gate received an open signal, a close signal arrives before at least time $g_u + g_o$ has elapsed, as this would contradict the second part of the utility property.

4   Model of Computation

The UML specification of the semantics of state machines [18, Ch. 2.12] can be summarized as follows: The actual state of a state machine is given by its *active state configuration* and by the contents of its *event queue*. The active state configuration is the tree of active states; in particular, for every concurrent composite state each of its orthogonal regions is active. The event queue holds the events that have not yet been handled by the machine. The *event dispatcher* dequeues the first event from the queue; the event is then processed in a *run-to-completion* (RTC) step. First, a maximal consistent set of enabled transitions is chosen: a transition is *enabled* if all of its source states are contained in the active state configuration, if its trigger is matched by the current event, and if its guard is true; two enabled transitions are *consistent* if they do not share a source state. For each transition in the set, its *least common ancestor* (LCA) is determined, i.e. the lowest composite state that contains all the transition's source and target states; the transition's main source state, that is the direct substate of the LCA containing the source states, is deactivated, the transition's actions are executed, and its target states are activated.

The UML semantics deliberately does not prescribe the timing assumptions that underly the computation of timed state machines. For example, it is left unspecified whether state transitions are instantaneous or durative, although the zero-time assumption adopted for Harel-Statecharts [10,11] is explicitly mentioned as a possible model [18, p. 2-161]. Similarly, arbitrary queueing delays are allowed to occur between the time an event is received by a state machine and the time it is dispatched for processing.

Because we are interested in a precise analysis of timed UML state machines, we have to assume a specific computational model. Following ideas from timed automata and synchronous languages, our basic assumption is that noticeable delays are only due to communication between objects whereas local computation is (infinitely) fast. Formally, we make the following assumptions:

1. The run-to-completion (RTC) step performed locally by a state machine takes no time. Similarly, the event queue is eager to dispatch events it has received.
2. The delay between the sending of an event and its reception at the target object is bounded by a constant Δ.
3. A state machine may delay arbitrarily before generating completion events, unless that delay is restricted by an explicit constraint.

Our basic tenet is that the specifier should have complete control over the behavior of the model. For example, the event queue is an implicit part of every state machine and is outside the control of the specifier. If we allowed the event queue to introduce arbitrary delays it would obviously be impossible to guarantee any lower bounds on the response time. We have therefore chosen to impose a zero-time assumption on the behavior of the queue. Should the specifier wish to allow for delays, these can always be modelled explicitly.

Assuming zero-time behavior of the event queue and the RTC step implies that usually, the times of reception, dispatch, and consumption of an event are the same. However, after sending a synchronous call event to another object, a state machine will be blocked until the notification about the dispatch of the event at the receiver machine has arrived at the sender. During this period, events may be received by the event queue, but they will be dispatched only after the synchronous call event has been handled.

Our second assumption is similar in spirit because, again, the mechanism for inter-object communication is an implicit part of the model and cannot be controlled by the specifier. Although we model inter-object communication as being time-consuming, we introduce a user-definable constant Δ to represent the maximum network latency. We assume, however, that messages that represent internal signals or operations are not sent over the network, and therefore do not incur any communication delay. Obviously, this model of communication could be refined, for example by imposing a minimum communication delay or by distinguishing several degrees of "remoteness" (e.g., faster communication within a single package etc.).

Finally, we do not restrict the delay before raising completion events because these concern a part of the model that is under the control of the modeller, using either time events or clock constraints. For example, the transition from NoTrain to Approach in the track state machine of Fig. 2(c) can be delayed arbitrarily. On the other hand, once the completion event has been raised, it will be inserted into the event queue without any further delay.

5   Representation of UML State Machines in uppaal

We now describe in detail our approach to compiling a system of UML state machines into a set of UPPAAL timed automata. For simplicity, the current version of HUGO/RT assumes that there is only a single instance of any class declared in the UML model, that the names of operations and signals are distinct, and that events do not carry parameters. These assumptions could be easily removed at the expense of a slightly more elaborate naming scheme.

5.1 State Configurations and Transitions

Although both UML state machines and timed automata describe state transition systems, the hierarchical state configurations of UML state machines have to be encoded as states of "flat" timed automata. The original implementation of HUGO described in [19] was based on a translation of untimed UML state machines to PROMELA, the input language of the SPIN LTL model checker, that represented each substate of a UML state machine by a separate process. The main benefit of that strategy was a high degree of modularity and flexibility, at the cost of an inefficient state representation, which was largely offset by the state-space compression techniques available in SPIN. Because UPPAAL offers neither compression nor structured data types beyond one-dimensional integer arrays, we decided to flatten the state configurations and to compile each UML state machine into only two timed automata that represent, respectively, the transitions of the state machine and its associated event queue. A state configuration of the UML state machine, described as a tree of states, is encoded by a single location of the first timed automaton, and any attributes that are declared in the UML class diagram are translated into local variables of the UPPAAL timed automaton.

Possible transitions of the UML state machine are represented in the UPPAAL model as sequences of transitions. Given a location of a timed automaton that represents a configuration tree of the UML state machine, we first determine the set of events (including time and completion events) that may trigger a transition, starting at the leaves of the configuration tree. Whenever a higher-level state may react to the same event as a lower-level state, the negation of the guard associated with the lower-level transition is added to the guard of the higher-level transition. This ensures that transitions originating from inner states take priority over outermost transitions, as prescribed by the UML semantics. For each event e, we compute the sets of transitions that may be triggered by e and successor configurations, by calculating the transition's main source and target states. In particular, we must consider the case that the same event is consumed by states in several orthogonal regions. All pertinent guards are copied to the first transition of the UPPAAL model, as is a synchronization that indicates consumption of the event.

We then consider the effects of the UML transition. First, we model the deactivation of states, beginning at the leaf states of the source configuration tree, and working upwards towards the main source state. Updates to instance variables are again copied verbatim as assignments to the corresponding local variables of the UPPAAL model. For every signal sent in the UML model, we generate an intermediate committed state to let the UPPAAL model synchronize over an appropriate channel (observe that UPPAAL transitions may carry at most one synchronization annotation). Next, we translate the effects that are explicitly given by the UML transition in a similar way. If the transition generates a

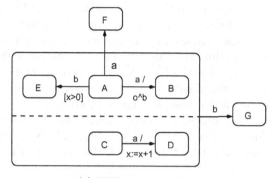

(a) UML state machine

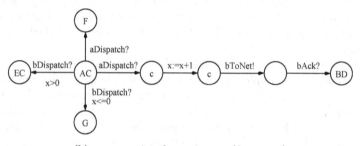

(b) UPPAAL timed automaton (fragment)

Fig. 4. Translation of UML transitions.

synchronous call the UPPAAL model enters a non-committed intermediate state, awaiting the notification of dispatch to arrive from the receiving machine. Our current prototype does not allow sequences of call actions to occur in a transition. Finally, target states are being activated, and any entry actions are translated to corresponding actions in the UPPAAL model. This part of the translation is symmetric to deactivation, but starting at the main target state and working downwards towards the leaves. The current version of HUGO/RT, unlike the untimed version, does not support "do" activities associated with states; this is partly offset by the possibility to delay, abstracting from changes of attribute values.

Finally, we add loops for all events that occur as input events of the state machine but do not trigger a transition from the current state configuration. These transitions correspond to situations where the current state configuration does not react to the current event; the UML semantics prescribes that the event should then be discarded. HUGO/RT does not currently handle deferred events.

Figures 4(a) and 4(b) show an excerpt of the translation of a hypothetical UML state machine into the corresponding UPPAAL timed automaton that exhibits some of the difficulties that can arise. In particular, event a may trigger two different transitions in the state configuration that consists of the states A and C that lead, respectively, to the target configurations BD and F. The first of these transitions is represented by a sequence of transitions in the UPPAAL model that involve consumption of the trigger event, updates of local variables, and network communication. For this example, we have assumed that b is a call event that should be sent to the object o. After sending the event over the network (cf. Sect. 5.3), the timed automaton waits in a non-committed intermediate state for the corresponding acknowledgement to arrive.

The same state configuration AC may react in two different ways to event b. The innermost transition (resulting in configuration EC) is prioritized; therefore, the outermost transition can be taken only if the guard x>0 is false.

Completion events. Transitions of a UML state machine for which no trigger event is shown are triggered by an implicit completion event. Simple states raise a completion event after all internal activity has terminated. Composite states raise a completion event when all orthogonal regions have reached a designated final state.

Since HUGO/RT does not consider "do" activities or non-atomic entry actions, we generate a completion event for any simple state with outgoing completion transitions via a transition to an intermediate "completion" state[1]. Similarly, a completion event for a composite state with outgoing completion transitions is generated whenever all its orthogonal regions have reached final states; this can be readily seen from the configuration. Consumption of completion events is similar to the consumption of regular events discussed above, except of course that the same completion event cannot be consumed by different states. Completion events are discarded if the state to which it corresponds is no longer active; this may occur if another (completion) event has caused some containing composite state to be deactivated. As explained in Sect. 5.2, the implementation of event queues ensures that completion events take priority over signal and call events.

Compound transitions. The UML allows several transitions to be connected by pseudo-states; in particular, the resulting compound transition may have several source or target states. The translation of fork and junction transitions poses no particular problems. Join transitions are required by the UML to be triggered by completion transitions from all of its source states. Our UPPAAL translation uses a similar technique as for the completion of composite states: for each source state *s* of a join transition, we add an auxiliary state that indicates that *s* has completed; completion of the last source state, which is again evident from the active state configuration, fires the join transition.

Time events. Transitions of timed UML state machines may be triggered by the elapse of time, indicated by an annotation of the form after(d) where d is

---

[1] One may be tempted to suppress the completion event altogether in such a simplified model, but note that a completion event should nevertheless be handled in a separate RTC step.

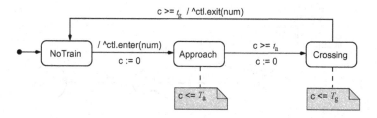

Fig. 5. Track state machine with clock.

a non-negative integer constant. HUGO/RT defines a clock c_s for every state s with an outgoing time transition. Every location of the timed automaton that corresponds to a state configuration containing s is required to satisfy the invariant $c_s \leq d$; incoming transitions to any such locations reset c_s to 0. A time event is raised during a transition from s to an intermediate state, guarded by the condition $c_s = d$. Consumption of time events is analogous to that of completion events.

The support UML offers for time annotations in state machines is rather limited, and it can be cumbersome to model real-time systems using only basic time events of the form after(d), which represent precise deadlines. For example, the track state machine shown in Fig. 2(c) combines time transitions and completion transitions to specify upper bounds on the occurrence of transitions, and introduces auxiliary states to specify lower bounds. We therefore extend the UML notation by allowing clocks to be declared explicitly in a UML class diagram. These clocks can be tested for in transition guards, and can be reset as the effect of transitions, in the same way as this is possible in UPPAAL timed automata. Similarly, clock invariants may be associated with the states of a UML state machine to model timeouts. For example, Fig. 5 shows an alternative presentation of the track state machine using an explicit clock c. This modest addition makes the notation more expressive because strict comparisons such as $x < c$ can not be expressed using triggers of the form after(d). Besides, time constraints become more localized, which should make the models easier to understand.

5.2 Representing the Event Queue

The second timed automaton that is generated for every state machine of the UML model represents its associated event queue. A local array variable of user-definable capacity holds the current contents of the queue such that the first array element represents the head of the queue (event types are encoded as integer constants). A local integer variable indicates the number of events in the queue. The queue reacts to incoming events by synchronizing on its input channel and appending the transmitted event to the current contents of queue. A possible overflow is indicated by moving to a distinguished overflow (sink) state. Completion events are enqueued similarly, but are prepended to the contents of the queue, shifting all array elements by one position towards the end. This

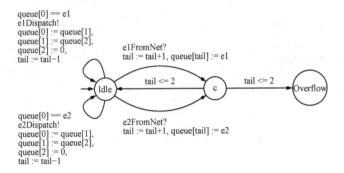

Fig. 6. Event queue with capacity two for two events.

ensures that completion events take precedence over regular events, as prescribed by the UML semantics. Observe that the event queue is always ready to accept a new event unless an overflow has occurred.

For every input event of the state machine, the UPPAAL model declares an urgent channel shared by the automata representing the event queue and the proper state machine. The queue communicates the event at the head of the queue to the associated state machine by offering a synchronization on the associated channel. The event is then dequeued by shifting all array elements one position towards the head of the queue, decrementing the length of the queue, and assigning a null value to the last array position. Because the channels representing input events are declared urgent and the state machine accepts synchronization on all these channels in every location where an RTC step can be started, no time is allowed to elapse whenever an RTC step is enabled. Figure 6 shows a sample event queue automaton with capacity two that can hold two types of events.

Our style of implementation of the event queue, which would be inefficient in a conventional programming language, ensures that identical configurations of a state machine are mapped to a unique system state of the UPPAAL model, and that state repetitions can therefore be reliably identified. If we used a more conventional implementation based on two index positions corresponding to the head and the tail of the queue, identical state configurations could be mapped to UPPAAL states that differ in the particular layout of the queue array.

5.3   Representing the Network

The final addition to complete the UPPAAL model associated with a system of state machines is a timed automaton that represents messages in transit between different state machines; recall from Sect. 4 that we consider remote communication to be time-consuming. The network automaton essentially consists of a user-defined number of buckets that may hold messages. For every event e it listens on a global channel eToNet for e being sent by the state machines and then places e in the lowest-numbered unused bucket. With every bucket we as-

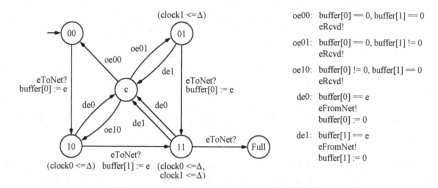

Fig. 7. Network with capacity two (transition annotations to the right).

sociate a clock that is reset when the bucket is filled, and times out after Δ time units have elapsed. If the bucket is full it may offer synchronization on the corresponding input channel of the receiving object's event queue, communicating the event to the receiving state machine. Notifications of dispatch of call events are handled slightly differently, as they are communicated directly to the state machine, bypassing the event queue.

For UML models that also specify a collaboration to be checked, the network also informs the observer timed automaton generated from the collaboration (cf. Sect. 6 below) whenever it communicates an event to the receiving state machine so that the observer automaton may react appropriately. Figure 7 presents a network with capacity two.

The network described above only imposes an upper bound on the communication delay, allowing messages to be reordered. We have also experimented with a more efficient, though perhaps less realistic, network model where every message is delayed by a fixed amount of time. Because both implementations offer the same external interface, they can be exchanged for each other easily.

6   Representation of UML Collaborations in UPPAAL

We briefly describe the translation of UML collaborations with time constraints into observer UPPAAL timed automata. The translation is similar to the construction by Firley et al. [8], but includes stuttering states, i.e., states that allow arbitrary stimuli to occur in-between the stimuli that are required by the messages of the UML collaboration. Following the UML, we thus view collaborations as incomplete specifications of possible system runs where arbitrary message exchange may occur between the explicitly specified messages.

We assume a total order on the messages in an interaction. Each message m is represented by an UPPAAL channel $m\text{Rcvd}$ over which the observer automaton learns of a stimulus for message m being received by an instance. A constraint of the form $v - u \sim c$ with $\sim \in \{<, \leq, \geq, >\}$ is associated with a clock x_{vu}.

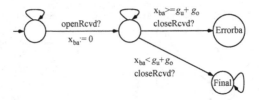

Fig. 8. Observer UPPAAL timed automaton for collaboration in Fig. 3(b)

Each state of the observer UPPAAL timed automaton checks either the occurrence of a reception of a stimulus according to the order of the collaboration or the violation of a timing constraint. The automaton registers the reception of a stimulus complying to message m by a transition accepting communication on channel mRcvd. Furthermore, if the reception of message m is annotated by u for a timing constraint $v - u \sim c$ the clock x_{vu} is initialised when a stimulus for m is successfully registered. Conversely, if the reception of message m is annotated by v for a timing constraint $v - u \sim c$, there are two transitions accepting communication on channel mRcvd: A transition guarded by $\neg(x_{vu} \sim c)$ leads to an error state, indicating that the timing constraint is violated; another transition guarded by $x_{vu} \sim c$ enables the remaining messages. Each state allows for an arbitrary stuttering of stimuli. Reaching the final state indicates the successful performance of the collaboration.

Figure 8 illustrates this construction for the GRC test case collaboration in Fig. 3(b) where each looping transition abbreviates arbitrary stuttering, i.e., offering synchronisation on every channel of the form mRcvd?.

The registering procedure for stimuli that we employ in our translation uses the assumption that the sender and receiver of a stimulus are uniquely determined by the stimulus. A more elaborate scheme checking the sender and receiver stored in additional global variables is easily devised [8]. Note, however, that Firley et al. [8] check the originator of a stimulus before communication is accepted which may become problematic when different instances send stimuli for the same signal to the same instance.

7   Verification

HUGO/RT analyzes a model by calling on UPPAAL to verify that the final state of the observer timed automaton is reachable in the model that consists of the timed automata representing the UML state machines and the observer automaton generated from the collaboration. For our case study, the feasibility of the collaboration shown in Fig. 3(a) is confirmed in a fraction of a second (all timings were taken on a Pentium III with 768MB of memory running UPPAAL 3.2.2 on Linux 2.2.16).

Some correctness properties of systems can be expressed by requiring certain executions to be impossible. For example, we can check the second part of the utility property that requires the gate never to open for less than g_o time units

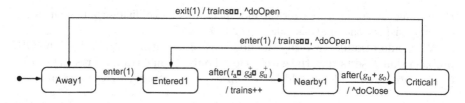

Fig. 9. Corrected control state machine for the GRC problem (representative region).

by verifying that the collaboration shown in Fig. 3(b) is not feasible. The verification of this property requires an exhaustive search of the model and takes approximately 11 seconds.

However, not all interesting properties are expressible using UML collaborations with time constraints. In particular, UML collaborations do not allow to check for the *absence* of signals as can be done, for example, using live sequence charts [4]. We have therefore resorted to model checking invariants to verify the safety and utility properties stated for the GRC case study. The basic safety property requires the gate to be down whenever a train is crossing, expressed as the formula

$$\forall\Box\big((\mathsf{Track1.Crossing} \vee \mathsf{Track2.Crossing}) \Rightarrow \mathsf{Gate.Closed}\big)$$

Our first attempt to verify this formula resulted in a counter-example where a train was crossing but the gate was closing, with precisely g_d time units elapsed since the Closing state was entered. Rather than adding some safety margins, we deemed this behavior acceptable and checked for a weaker invariant that also allowed for this boundary case.

Much to our surprise, UPPAAL again produced a counter-example: very briefly after a train had left the crossing, a second train entered on the same track (this is allowed by our model since a completion event for the NoTrain state may be generated immediately after the state has been activated). Because of variable network delays, the corresponding enter signal actually arrived at the controller before the preceding exit signal, that is, when the corresponding region of ctl was still in its Critical state. Because that state does not define a transition for the enter signal, it was discarded, and the gate was opened when the exit signal arrived, leaving the gate open while the second train was approaching and crossing.

This counter-example represents an actual error in our gate controller, which none of us had realized, and which would have been difficult to find by simulation alone. The error can be fixed by adding a transition from the Critical to the Entered states of the controller state machine of Fig. 2(d) that is triggered by an enter signal, decrements the attribute trains, and raises a doOpen signal, cf. Fig. 9. (Observe that the following exit signal will be discarded at the Entered state.) Another solution, which is not currently possible to analyze using HUGO/RT, would be to mark the enter signal as deferred in state Critical.

Rerunning the verification over the modified model establishes that the invariant is now satisfied; the analysis takes ca. 2.5 seconds.

We would also like to verify the first part of the utility property of the GRC problem that asserts that the gate is closed only if some train is crossing or close to the gate. A first idea would be to express this property by the formula

$$\forall\Box\left(\mathsf{Gate.Closed} \implies \bigvee_{i=1,2} \mathsf{Track}i.\mathsf{Crossing} \vee (\mathsf{Track}i.\mathsf{Approach} \wedge \mathsf{Track}i.\mathsf{c} \geq t_a)\right)$$

in terms of the track state machine shown in Fig. 5. Unfortunately, this property cannot hold because the gate will still be closed for a short while after the trains have left. A possible solution is to enhance the model by an additional clock measuring the time since a train has left the gate.

Finally, we want to establish the absence of deadlocks in our solution of the GRC problem. UPPAAL provides a designated state formula deadlock to identify deadlock states. Our translation, however, may introduce extra deadlocks: a full network cannot accept any further stimuli, the event queues may overflow, and the observer automaton may run into an error state. In all of these cases designated deadlock states (Full, Overflow, Errorvu) are entered. In fact, UPPAAL reports that these are the only deadlocks of the translated model, confirming the absence of deadlocks in the UML model.

8   Conclusions

We have described procedures for translating timed UML state machines and UML collaborations with time constraints into UPPAAL timed automata. The translation has been implemented in a prototype tool called HUGO/RT. The results of model checking the translation of scenarios given by UML collaborations with time constraints against timed UML state machines have been illustrated for the "Generalised Railroad Crossing" case study.

The current prototype shows several limitations: HUGO/RT by now only handles a subset of the possibilites of UML state machines. Most prominently, history pseudo-states and deferred events still need to be implemented, events cannot have parameters, and there can only be a single instance of any given class. Some optimizations for more efficient analysis should also be considered. For example, the number of clocks could be minimized by reusing clocks in different states. More importantly, the expressiveness of UML collaborations to describe correctness properties is rather limited. We therefore plan to integrate live sequence charts as a specification formalism into HUGO/RT. For specifying state-based properties on the level of state machines it would be useful to integrate constraints in UML's textual annotation language OCL.

Even so, HUGO/RT is a first step towards the application of model checking techniques "behind the scenes" to real-time object-oriented designs, even spanning several phases of software development. Both the design model and the properties of a system are described in the unifying framework of the UML. For seamless integration with existing tools, HUGO/RT imports state machines and collaborations from the XMI (XML metadata interchange) output produced by standard UML editors. The time overhead for compiling into UPPAAL models is tolerable and the time for verification is encouraging.

References

1. Rajeev Alur and David L. Dill. A Theory of Timed Automata. *Theo. Comp. Sci.*, 126:183–235, 1994.
2. Rodolphe Arthaud, Udo Brockmeyer, Werner Damm, Bruce P. Douglass, Francois Terrier, and Wang Yi, editors. *Proc. Wsh. Formal Design Techniques for Real-Time UML*, York, 2000. http://wooddes.intranet.gr/workshop.htm.
3. Grady Booch, James Rumbaugh, and Ivar Jacobson. *The Unified Modeling Language User Guide*. Addison–Wesley, Reading, Mass., &c., 1998.
4. Werner Damm and David Harel. LSCs: Breathing Life into Message Sequence Charts. *Formal Methods in System Design*, 19(1):45–80, 2001.
5. Werner Damm, Bernhard Josko, Hardi Hungar, and Amir Pnueli. A Compositional Real-Time Semantics of STATEMATE Designs. In Willem-Paul de Roever, Hans Langmaack, and Amir Pnueli, editors, *Proc. Int. Symp. Compositionality (Revised Lectures)*, volume 1536 of *Lect. Notes Comp. Sci.*, pages 186–238. Springer, Berlin, 1998.
6. Alexandre David and M. Oliver Möller. From HUPPAAL to UPPAAL — A Translation from Hierarchical Timed Automata to Flat Timed Automata. Technical Report BRICS RS-01-11, Department of Computer Science, Aarhus Universitet, 2001.
7. Bruce P. Douglass. *Real-Time UML*. Addison-Wesley, Reading, Mass., &c., 1998.
8. Thomas Firley, Michaela Huhn, Karsten Diethers, Thomas Gehrke, and Ursula Goltz. Timed Sequence Diagrams and Tool-Based Analysis — A Case Study. In France and Rumpe [9], pages 645–660.
9. Robert B. France and Bernhard Rumpe, editors. *Proc. 2nd Int. Conf. UML*, volume 1723 of *Lect. Notes Comp. Sci.* Springer, Berlin, 1999.
10. David Harel. Statecharts: A Visual Formalism for Complex Systems. *Sci. Comp. Program.*, 8(3):231–274, 1987.
11. David Harel and Eran Grey. Executable Object Modeling with Statecharts. *Computer*, July:31–42, 1997.
12. Constance L. Heitmeyer, Ralph D. Jeffords, and Bruce G. Labaw. Comparing Different Approaches for Specifying and Verifying Real-Time Systems. In *Proc. 10th IEEE Wsh. Real-Time Operating Systems and Software*, pages 122–129, New York, 1993.
13. Kim Guldstrand Larsen, Paul Pettersson, and Wang Yi. UPPAAL in a Nutshell. *Int. J. Softw. Tools for Techn. Transfer*, 1(1–2):134–152, 1997.
14. Diego Latella, Istvan Majzik, and Mieke Massink. Automatic Verification of a Behavioural Subset of UML Statechart Diagrams Using the SPIN Model-Checker. *Formal Aspects Comp.*, 11(6):637–664, 1999.
15. Luigi Lavazza, Gabriele Quaroni, and Matteo Venturelli. Combining UML and Formal Notations for Modelling Real-Time Systems. In *8th Europ. Conf. Software Engineering*, Wien, 2001.
16. Johan Lilius and Iván Porres Paltor. Formalising UML State Machines for Model Checking. In France and Rumpe [9], pages 430–445.

17. Darmalingum Muthiayen. *Real-Time Reactive System Development — A Formal Approach Based on UML and PVS*. PhD thesis, Concordia University, Montreal, Canada, 2000.
18. Object Management Group. Unified Modeling Language Specification, Version 1.4. Specification, OMG, 2001. http://cgi.omg.org/cgi-bin/doc?formal/01-09-67.
19. Timm Schäfer, Alexander Knapp, and Stephan Merz. Model Checking UML State Machines and Collaborations. In Scott Stoller and Willem Visser, editors, *Proc. Wsh. Software Model Checking*, volume 55(3) of *Elect. Notes Theo. Comp. Sci.*, Paris, 2001. 13 pages.
20. Bran Selic, Garth Gullekson, and Paul T. Ward. *Real-Time Object-Oriented Modeling*. John Wiley & Sons, New York, 1994.

Part VIII

Timed Automata II

Partial Order Path Technique
for Checking Parallel Timed Automata[*]

Jianhua Zhao, He Xu, Xuandong Li, Tao Zheng, and Guoliang Zheng

State Key Laboratory of Novel Software Technology
Dept. of Computer Sci. and Tech. Nanjing University
Nanjing, Jiangsu, P.R.China 210093
zhaojh@nju.edu.cn

Abstract. In a parallel composition of timed automata, some transitions are independent to others. Generally the basic method generates one successors for each of the legal permutations of the transitions. These successors may be combined into one bigger symbolic state. In other words, the basic algorithm slices one big symbolic state into pieces. The number of these pieces can be up to $n!$, where n is the number of independent transitions.

In this paper, we introduce a concept, 'partial order path', to avoid treating the permutations one by one. A partial order path includes a set of transitions and a partial order on this set. Our algorithm generates one symbolic successor w.r.t. each partial order path. This big symbolic successor is just the combination of the successors w.r.t. all the global paths which are consistent to this partial order path. It is shown by some case studies that this method may result in significant space reduction.

1 Introduction

Model checking is a formal technique for validating whether a system model holds for a specific property. The basic method of model checking is exhaustive exploration of the system state space. However, the state space increases explosively when the scale of the model increases. Many techniques have been introduced to attack this problem. Partial order technique is one of the most efficient ones.

Partial order technique is first introduced for temporal model checking, and get many successful results[8], [2]. However, the progress of applying such technique into timed automata is slow. The main reason is that the clocks in different automaton increase in same rate. Different transition orders will result in different successors. A partial order technique for checking real time systems has been proposed in [3]. In that paper, the authors let the time of each component

---

[*] This work is supported by the National Natural Science Foundation of China (No.60073031 and No.69703009), the National 863 High-Tech Programme of China (No.2001AA113203), Jiangsu Province Research Project (No.BK2001033), and by International Institute for Software Technology, United Nations University (UNU/IIST).

automaton evolves independently. The authors proved that there are equivalence relations which can divide the infinite number of unsynchronized states into finite number of equivalence classes. However, the proof is not constructive.

Some other partial order techniques for checking timed petri net can be found in [9][10][11]. These techniques remove orderings in the zone on sets of independent transitions, reducing the representation size of the timed state space, and also reducing the number of generated states. They yield significant reduction in the number of symbolic states at each un-timed state.

In [5], F.Panagi also presented a partial order technique for checking real-time system models. In that paper, she studied the dependence relation between transitions, and the cases when partial order reduction can be applied.

In this paper, we propose a so-called 'partial order path' technique for real-time reachablity analysis. Given a global symbolic state (l, D), this technique calculates the successors of (l, D) w.r.t. a set of global paths, instead of one global transition, starting from the location.

2   Background

2.1   Timed Automaton Networks

In this subsection, we will give an informal description of timed automata[1] and timed automaton network. The definition of global paths and executions are different from, but essentially equivalent to, the ones in the literate.

Give a clock set C, A *clock assignment* u over C of clocks is a map from C to real R. For $d \in R$, we use $u + d$ to denote the clock assignment which maps each clock x in C to the value $u(x) + d$ and for $r \subseteq C$, $[r \mapsto 0]u$ to denote the assignment for C which maps each clock in r to the value 0 and agrees with u on $C - r$. For a subset C' of C, we use $u \triangleright C'$ to denote the clock assignment over C' satisfying $\forall x \in C' \bullet u(x) = u'(x)$.

We use $\mathcal{B}(C)$ ranged over by $D, D_1, D_2, \ldots$ and $g, g_1, g_2, \ldots,$ to stand for the set of conjunctions of atomic formula of the form $x - y \sim n$ for $x, y \in C \cup \{0\}$, $\sim \in \{\leq, <, >, \geq\}$ and n being an integer. Notice that, a formula like $x \sim n$ can be expressed as $x - 0 \sim n$. Elements of $\mathcal{B}(C)$ are called clock constraints over C. We use $u \models D$ to denote that the clock assignment $u \in R^C$ satisfies the clock constraint $D \in \mathcal{B}(C)$.

A set $\mathcal{A}$ of actions includes finite number of labels such that if a is in $\mathcal{A}$, $\overline{a}$ is also in $\mathcal{A}$. For convenience, we let $\overline{\overline{a}} = a$.

A timed automaton A is a tuple $\ll N, l^0, \mathcal{A}, C, E, I \gg$, where N is a finite set of locations, $l^0 \in N$ is the start location; $\mathcal{A}$ is a set of actions; C is a finite set of clocks; $E \subseteq N \times (\mathcal{A} \cup \{\perp\}) \times \mathcal{B}(C) \times 2^C \times N$ is a set of transitions; I assigns each location in N a location invariant in $\mathcal{B}(C)$.

A *timed automaton network* is a parallel composition of finite set of timed automata $A_1, A_2, \ldots, A_n$. These automata share a same set $\mathcal{A}$ of actions.

A concrete *state* of timed automaton A is a tuple (l, u), where $l \in N$ and u is a clock assignment over C. A state can be viewed as a snapshot of A on a certain time point when A is evolving. A *state* of a network $A = A_1 \mid \ldots \mid A_n$ is a pair (l, u) where l, called *global location*, is a vector of control locations of each automaton and u is a clock assignment over $C = C_1 \cup \ldots \cup C_n$. A state of the network is essentially a combination of local states of the component automata.

In the rest part of this paper, for a transitions $e = (l_1, -, -, -, l_2)$, we use $\overleftarrow{e}$ to denote the source location l_1 of e and $\overrightarrow{e}$ to denote the target location l_2 of e.

A *global transition* e can be a single transition if $e = (-, \perp, -, -, -)$, or a pair of transition $e_1|e_2$, where $e_1 = (-, a, -, -, -)$ and $e_2 = (-, \overline{a}, -, -, -)$ are transitions of different automata. Given a global transition e, the projection of e on A_i, denoted e/A_i, is defined as follows.

$$e/A_i = \begin{cases} e & e \text{ is a single transition of } A_i \\ e_1 & e \text{ is } e_1|e_2 \text{ or } e_2|e_1, \text{ and } e_1 \text{ is a transition of } A_i \\ \delta & \text{else} \end{cases}$$

A *local path* of A starting from a location l is a sequence of transitions $e_1 \rightarrow e_2 \rightarrow \ldots \rightarrow e_n$ satisfying that $\overleftarrow{e_1} = l$ and $\overrightarrow{e_i} = \overleftarrow{e_{i+1}}$ $(1 \leq i \leq n - 1)$.

A *global path* of the network starting from a global location l is a sequence of transitions $e_1 \rightarrow e_2 \rightarrow \ldots \rightarrow e_n$ such that for each component automaton A_i, the sequence $e_1/A_i \rightarrow e_2/A_i \rightarrow \ldots \rightarrow e_n/A_i$ is a local path of A_i starting from $l[i]$ if all δ are ignored.

Suppose that on a specific time point, the state of $A_i(1 \leq i \leq n)$ is (l_i, u_i). A_i can stay on l_i as long as its local clock value satisfies $I_i(l_i)$, which is the location invariant of l_i. It can also change to a state (l_i', u_i') if there is a transition $(l_i, \perp, g, r, l_i')$ such that $u_i \models g$, $u_i' = [r \mapsto 0]u_i$ and $u_i' \models I_i'(l_i')$. If two timed automata, A_i and A_j, respectively stay on (l_i, u_i) and (l_j, u_j), they can change to new state (l_i', u_i') and (l_j', u_j') simultaneously if there are two transitions (l_i, a, g_i, r_i, l_i'), $(l_j, \overline{a}, g_j, r_j, l_j')$ such that $u_i \models g_i$, $u_j \models g_j$, $u_i' = [r_i \mapsto 0]u_i$, $u_j' = [r_j \mapsto 0]u_j$, $u_i' \models I_i(l_i')$ and $u_j' \models I_j(l_j')$.

We can use executions to record the evolution progress of the component automata and the network.

A *local execution* of A_i starting from a state (l, u) is a time stamped local path $(e_1, t_1) \rightarrow (e_2, t_2) \rightarrow \ldots \rightarrow (e_k, t_k) \rightarrow (\delta, t_{k+1})$, where t_i is a real number. Suppose A_i is on (l, u), if we don't consider the synchronization between transitions, A_i can evolve as follows. It stays on l for t_1 time, then e_1 take place, then stays on $\overrightarrow{e_1}$ for $t_2 - t_1$ time, then e_2 takes place, ..., then e_k takes place, stays on $\overrightarrow{e_k}$ for $t_{k+1} - t_k$ time. Because the synchronization is ignored here, a local execution is possibly illegal in the global environment.

A *global execution* of the network starting from a global state (l, u) is a time stamped global path $(e_1, t_1) \rightarrow (e_2, t_2) \rightarrow \ldots \rightarrow (e_k, t_k) \rightarrow (\delta, t_{k+1})$ such that the time stamped transition sequence $(e_1/A_i, t_1) \rightarrow (e_2/A_i, t_2) \rightarrow \ldots \rightarrow (e_k/A_i, t_k) \rightarrow (\delta, t_{k+1})$ is a local execution of A_i if all the time stamped δs, except (δ, t_{k+1}), are ignored.

2.2 Symbolic States and Their Reachablity Relationship

Because the value of clocks are real numbers, the state space of a timed automaton network is infinite. However, we can use *symbolic states* of the form (l, D), where $D \in \mathcal{B}(C)$, to express a set of concrete states. Intuitively, (l, D) represents the set of concrete states (l, u) such that $u \models D$. There is an equivalence relation to divide all the symbolic states into finite number of equivalence classes. We write $(l, u) \models (l', D)$ if $l = l'$ and $u \models D$.

We will use the following four operators on time constraints in this paper. Let C be a set of clocks, r and C' be subsets of C. For two time constraints $D \in \mathcal{B}(C)$ and $D' \in \mathcal{B}(C')$, the operators $D^\uparrow$, $r(D)$, $D \rhd C'$ and $D' \lhd C$ are defined as follows.

- for all $d \in R$, $u + d \models D^\uparrow$ iff $u \models D$.
- $u \models r(D)$ iff $\exists u' \bullet (u' \models D \wedge u = [r \mapsto 0]u')$.
- $D \rhd C' \in \mathcal{B}(C')$ and $u' \models D \rhd C'$ iff $\exists u \bullet (u \models D \wedge u' = u \rhd C')$.
- $D' \lhd C \in \mathcal{B}(C)$ and $u \models D' \lhd C$ iff $\exists u' \bullet (u' \models D' \wedge u' = u \rhd C')$.

It can be shown that $D^\uparrow$, $r(D)$ and $D' \lhd C$ are in $\mathcal{B}(C)$ and $D \rhd C'$ is in $\mathcal{B}(C')$.

We now define a strongest post-condition operator sp over the global state set of the three types of global evolutions.

- For global delay, $sp(\delta)(l, D) \overset{def}{=} (l, D^\uparrow \wedge I(l))$
- For a single transition $e = (l[i], \perp, g, r, l'_i)$ of A_i, $sp(e)(l, D) \overset{def}{=} (l', (r(g \wedge D)) \wedge I(l'))$, where $l' = l[l'_i/i]$.
- For a pair transitions $e = (l[i], a, g_i, r_i, l'_i) \in E_i$, and $e' = (l[j], \bar{a}, g_j, r_j, l'_j) \in E_j$, $sp(e|e')(l, D) \overset{def}{=} (l', ((r_i \cup r_j)(g_i \wedge g_j \wedge D)) \wedge I(l'))$, where $l' = l[l'_i/i][l'_j/j]$.

In this definition, $sp(\delta)(l, D)$ expresses all the set of state reachable from a state in (l, D) by only time advancement. $sp(e)(l, D)$ expresses the set of state reachable from a state in (l, D) through a single transition $e \in E_i$. $sp(e|e')(l, D)$ expresses the set of state reachable from a state in (l, D) through a pair of matched transitions.

Now we extend the operator sp to global paths. Let $p = e_1 \to e_2 \to \ldots \to e_n$ be a global path,

$$sp(p)(l, D) = \begin{cases} sp(\delta)(l, D) & \text{if } p \text{ is a empty path} \\ sp(\delta)(sp(e_n)(sp(p')(l, D))) & p' = e_1 \to e_2 \to \ldots \to e_{n-1} \end{cases}$$

Let p be a global path from l to l'. From the definition of sp, we have that, for any concrete state (l', u'), $(l', u') \models sp(p)(l, D)$ iff there is a state (l, u) such that $(l, u) \models (l, D)$ and there is a global execution from (l, u) to (l', u') corresponding to p.

For each automaton, the local strongest post-operator sp_l is similar to sp and defined as follows.

1. For time delay, $sp_l(\delta)(l, D) \overset{def}{=} (l, D^\uparrow \wedge I(l))$
2. For a transition $e = (l, -, g, r, l')$, $sp_l(e)(l, D) \overset{def}{=} (l', r(g \wedge D))$

This local operator does not consider the synchronizations. We can also similarly extend sp_l to local paths. For a local path p, for any concrete state (l', u'), $(l', u') \models sp_l(p)(l, D)$ iff there is a state (l, u) such that $(l, u) \models (l, D)$ and there is a local execution from (l, u) to (l', u') corresponding to p.

Definition 1. Symbolic reachablity *Given two global symbolic state* (l, D) *and* (l', D'), *we say that* (l', D') *is reachable from* (l, D) *iff there is a global path* p *such that* $sp(p)(l, D) = (l', D'')$ *for some* D'' *and* $D' \wedge D'' \neq FALSE$.

Using the operator sp, we can get a basic algorithm to check whether a global symbolic state (l', D') is reachable from another state (l, D). This algorithm, or its variants, is wildly used in different model checking tools[6][4][7]. The basic algorithm depicted in Fig 1 checks whether a global symbolic state (l_{tgt}, D_{tgt}) is reachable from (l_0, D_0). In the figure, for a global location l, we use $enable(l)$ to denote the set $\{(l[i], \perp, -, -)\} \cup \{(l[i], a, -, -)|(l[j], \overline{a}, -, -) \mid i \neq j\}$. This algorithm, or its variants, is wildly used in different model checking tools[6][4][7]. In this paper, we will present a method to improve this algorithm.

```
PASSED    := {}
WAITING := {(l₀, D₀)}
repeat       begin
             get an auxiliary state (l, D) from WAITING
             WAITING = WAITING - {(l, D)}.
             if D ⊈ D' for all (l, D') ∈PASSED then
                begin
                      add (l, D) to PASSED.
                      for each transition e in enabled(l) do
                      begin
                            let(l₁, D₁) = sp(δ)(sp(e)((l, D)))
                            if l₁ = l_tgt and D₁ ∩ D_tgt ≠ φ
                            return YES
                            else begin
                               if (l₁, D₁) is not contained by a state in WAITING∪PASSED
                                    WAITING:= WAITING ∪ {(l₁, D₁)}
                            end
                      end
                end
             end
until WAITING = {}
return NO.
```

Fig. 1. The basic reachability analysis algorithm

3   Basic Idea of Partial Order Path Technique

Let's take the system depicted in Fig 2 as an example to show our basic idea of real-time partial-order-path model-checking. Suppose the system stays on a symbolic state $(< l_{11}, l_{21}, l_{31} >, x_1 \geq 0 \wedge x_2 \geq 0 \wedge x_3 \geq 0)$. It evolves in the following way: A_1 evolves to l_{12} through e_{11}, A_2 evolves to l_{22} through e_{21}, and A_3 evolves to l_{32} through e_{31}. The basic algorithm calculates the successors in one-transition step-wise. So it will generally get many successors according to different global paths: $e_{11} \rightarrow e_{21} \rightarrow e_{31}$, $e_{11} \rightarrow e_{31} \rightarrow e_{21}$ and so on. If e_{11},

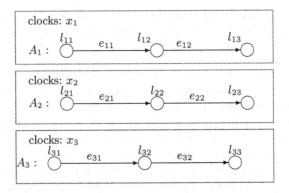

Fig. 2. Demo of partial order path model-checking

e_{21} and e_{31} respectively reset the clocks x_1, x_2 and x_3, the time constraints $x_3 - x_2 \leq 0$ and $x_2 - x_3 \leq 0$ will respectively appeared in the successors w.r.t. the first two paths. If e_{11}, e_{21}, e_{31} are not synchronizing transitions, the order of e_{11}, e_{21}, e_{31} in the paths is inessential. However, because the basic algorithm calculates the successors in a one-transition step, it generates a successor for each permutation of the transitions. So 6 successors will be generated in this cases. However, we know that, these symbolic states can be combined into one states $(< l_{12}, l_{22}, l_{32} >, x_1 \geq 0 \wedge x_2 \geq 0 \wedge x_3 \geq 0)$. Generally, if there are n independent transitions, the basic algorithm will generate $n!$ successors. In this paper, we will present a way to generate the combination of these successors as one symbolic state. So, the number of states generated by our algorithms is smaller.

3.1   Partial Order Path

However, the transitions of different automata are not always independent to each other. They interact with each other through some synchronization mechanisms. The orders of some transitions are essential. We use a partial order to express the essential orders and ignore the inessential ones.

Definition 2. Partial order path. *Given a set of global transitions $T = e_1, e_2, \ldots, e_m$ and a partial order $<$ over T. The tuple $(T, <)$ is a partial order path iff the following condition holds.*

1. *For any two transitions e_1, e_2 in T and a component automaton A_i, $e_1/A_i \neq \delta$ and $e_2/A_i \neq \delta$ implies that either $e_1 < e_2$ or $e_2 < e_1$.*
2. *For each permutation $p = e_{i_1} \to e_{i_2} \to \ldots \to e_{i_m}$ of T, p is a global path if for all k and l, $e_{i_k} < e_{i_l} \Rightarrow k < l$.*

We also say p is a global path consistent to $(T, <)$.

In the rest part of this paper, we will present a method to calculate the successor w.r.t. a partial order path, instead of a global transition.

From the definition of global paths, for a partial order path $(T, <)$ and a component automaton A_i, the local transition set $\{e/A_i \mid (e \in T) \wedge (e/A_i \neq \delta)\}$ should be able to form a local path of A_i. So a partial order path can be decomposed into a set of local paths.

Definition 3. Local path set. *Let l, l' be two global locations of a timed automaton network. Let $\mathcal{P} = \alpha_1, \alpha_2, \ldots, \alpha_n$ be a set of local paths. $\mathcal{P}$ is called a local path set from l to l' if for each i, $(1 \leq i \leq n)$, α_i is a local path of A_i from $l[i]$ to $l'[i]$.*

Example 1. $\{e_{11} \rightarrow e_{12}; e_{21} \rightarrow e_{22}; \phi\}$ is a local path set from $< l_{11}, l_{21}, l_{31} >$ to $< l_{13}, l_{23}, l_{31} >$

A local path set from l to l' describes a set of possible global paths from l to l'. The synchronizing transitions in different local paths can synchronize with each other in different ways.

Definition 4. Synchronization solution. *Let l, l' be two global locations. Let $\mathcal{P} = \alpha_1, \alpha_2, \ldots, \alpha_n$ be a local path set from l to l'. A synchronization solution $\mathcal{C}$ of $\mathcal{P}$ is a set of pairs of transitions satisfying the following conditions.*

1. *For each synchronizing transition $e = (-, a, -, -, -)$ in $\mathcal{P}$, there is one and only one pair of the form (e, e') or (e', e) in $\mathcal{C}$, where $e' = (-, \bar{a}, -, -, -)$.*
2. *Two transitions of each pair in $\mathcal{C}$ are of different component automata.*

A local path set $\mathcal{P}$ may have zero or many synchronization solutions.

For each synchronization solution $\mathcal{C}$, we can construct a global transition set T as $\{e \mid e$ is a non-synchronising transition in $\mathcal{P}\} \cup \{(e|e') \mid (e, e')$ is a pair in $\mathcal{C}\}$. We define a relation $<_{\mathcal{P}, \mathcal{C}}$ over T as follows.

Definition 5. *For any two global transition e and e', $e <_{\mathcal{P}, \mathcal{C}} e'$ if one of the following conditions holds.*

1. *There is an automaton A_i such that $e/A_i \neq \delta$, $e'/A_i \neq \delta$ and e/A_i takes place earlier than e'/A_i does in α_i.*
2. *There is a transition e'' in T such that $e <_{\mathcal{P}, \mathcal{C}} e''$ and $e'' <_{\mathcal{P}, \mathcal{C}} e'$.*

Proposition 1. *The tuple $(T, <_{\mathcal{P}, \mathcal{C}})$ is a partial order path if $<_{\mathcal{P}, \mathcal{C}}$ is a partial order relation.*

Proof. Let $T = \{e_1, e_2, \ldots, e_k\}$. Let $p = e_{i_1}, e_{i_2}, \ldots, e_{i_k}$ be an auxiliary permutation of T such that $e_{i_l} <_{\mathcal{P}, \mathcal{C}} e_{i_m}$ implies $l < m$. From the definition of $<_{\mathcal{P}, \mathcal{C}}$, we have that for any component automaton A_k, $e_{i_1}/A_k, e_{i_2}/A_k, \ldots, e_{i_k}/A_k$ is just α_k. That is, p is a global path. So $(T, <_{\mathcal{P}, \mathcal{C}})$ is a partial order path.

Example 2. Let's suppose that, in the example in Fig 2, $e_{11} = (-, a, -, -, -)$, $e_{12} = (-, a, -, -, -)$, $e_{21} = (-, \bar{a}, -, -, -)$ and $e_{31} = (-, \bar{a}, -, -, -)$ be synchronizing transitions. Let e_{22} and e_{32} be local transitions. For the local path set

$\mathcal{P} = \{e_{11} \rightarrow e_{12}; e_{21} \rightarrow e_{22}; e_{31} \rightarrow e_{32}\}$, both $\mathcal{C}_1 = \{(e_{11}, e_{21}), (e_{12}, e_{31})\}$ and $\mathcal{C}_2 = \{(e_{11}, e_{31}), (e_{12}, e_{21})\}$ are synchronization solutions of $\mathcal{P}$.

The global transition set w.r.t. $\mathcal{P}$ and $\mathcal{C}_1$ is $T = \{(e_{11}|e_{21}), (e_{12}|e_{31}), e_{22}, e_{32}\}$. The relation $<_{\mathcal{P},\mathcal{C}_1}$ over T is $\{ (e_{11}|e_{21}) <_{\mathcal{P},\mathcal{C}_1} e_{22}, (e_{11}|e_{21}) <_{\mathcal{P},\mathcal{C}_1} (e_{12}|e_{31}), (e_{11}|e_{21}) <_{\mathcal{P},\mathcal{C}_1} e_{32}, (e_{12}|e_{31}) <_{\mathcal{P},\mathcal{C}_1} e_{32} \}$. We can check that $(T, <_{\mathcal{P},\mathcal{C}_1})$ is a partial order path. The global transition sequences $(e_{11}|e_{21}) \rightarrow e_{22} \rightarrow (e_{12}|e_{31}) \rightarrow e_{32}$; $(e_{11}|e_{21}) \rightarrow (e_{12}|e_{31}) \rightarrow e_{22} \rightarrow e_{32}$ and $(e_{11}|e_{21}) \rightarrow (e_{12}|e_{31}) \rightarrow e_{32} \rightarrow e_{22}$ are global paths consistent to $(T, <_{\mathcal{P},\mathcal{C}_1})$.

3.2   Local Symbolic Successors

In this section, let (l, D) be a global symbolic state of the network. Let l' be a global location of the network. Let $\mathcal{P} = \alpha_1, \alpha_2, \ldots, \alpha_n$ be a local path set from l to l'. Let $\mathcal{C}$ be a synchronization solution of $\mathcal{P}$. Let $(T, <_{\mathcal{P},\mathcal{C}})$, as described above, be a partial order path w.r.t. $\mathcal{P}$ and $\mathcal{C}$. We will explain informally how to calculate the global symbolic successor w.r.t. such a partial order path. We will first calculate the local successors w.r.t. α_i in $\mathcal{P}$, then compose the local successors into one global successor.

Let (l, u) be a concrete state. Let $Exe_i (1 \le i \le n)$ be executions from $(l[i], u \triangleright C_i)$ to $(l'[i], u'_i)$ through α_i. Let u' be a clock assignment satisfying that for each i, $u' \triangleright C_i = u'_i$. Then $Exe_i (1 \le i \le n)$ can be composed into a global execution from (l, u) to (l', u') through a path consistent to $(T, <_{\mathcal{P},\mathcal{C}})$ if the following conditions hold.

1. The executions $Exe_i (1 \le i \le n)$ have same time length.
2. For each transition pair (e, e') in $\mathcal{C}$, e and e' have same time stamp.
3. For any two transitions e and e' in T satisfying that $e <_{\mathcal{P},\mathcal{C}} e'$, the time stamp of e(or its component transition) must be non-greater than that of e'(or its component transition).

Notice that, for any global transition $e|e'$ in T, the time stamp of e and e' in their local executions are same, so we can construct the global execution as follows. For each transition e in T, the time stamp of e is that of e/A_i in α_i if $e/A_i \ne \delta$. From the definition of $<_{\mathcal{P},\mathcal{C}}$, the condition 3 holds if the condition 2 holds. So we get a global execution corresponding to a path consistent to $(T, <_{\mathcal{P},\mathcal{C}})$.

We must present a way to check the above conditions in a symbolic way because the algorithm operates on symbolic states. To do this, when calculating a local successor w.r.t a local path α_i, we introduce a set of auxiliary clocks for each component automata. The auxiliary clock set $\overline{C}$ includes the following clocks.

1. A clock t is introduced to record the time length of local execution. When the local execution starts, the initial value of t is 0 and no transition resets t.
2. For each clock c of the network, a shadow clock $\bar{c}$ is introduced. Each $\bar{c}$ has the same value as c at the start point, and it will never be reset. At the end of any local executions, the value of $\bar{c} - t$ is the initial value of c.

3. For each synchronizing transition e in α_i, a clock c_e is introduced to record at what time e takes place. This clock c_e will only be reset by e. So if e is in α_i, the ending value of $t - c_e$ is the time point at which e take places. (Two occurrence of one transition in α will be treated as two different ones.)

For each synchronizing transition $e = (-, -, r, -, -)$, it will also reset c_e when it takes place. So e is modified to $(-, -, r \cup \{c_e\}, -, -)$ when our algorithm calculates the local successors.

Definition 6. Extended local clock set. *Let $A = A_1 \mid A_2 \mid ... \mid A_n$ be a timed automaton network. The extended local clock set of A_i is $C_i \cup \overline{C}$, where C_i is the clock set of A_i and $\overline{C}$ is the auxiliary clock set as described above.*

In our algorithm, the local operator sp_l of A_i will operate on $N_i \times \mathcal{B}(C_i \cup \overline{C})$. The clocks in $\overline{C}$ is somehow 'global' because they appear in different extended local symbolic state. When we combine local successors into a global successor, it is required that the value of each auxiliary clock x in $\overline{C}$ are same in different local successors. However these clocks are never tested when we calculate the local successors.

Example 3. For the network depicted in Fig 2, the extended local clock set of A_1 is $\{x_1, x_2, t, \overline{x}_1, \overline{x}_2, \overline{x}_3, \overline{x}_4, c_{e_{11}}, c_{e_{12}}, c_{e_{21}}, c_{e_{32}}\}$.

To calculate the successor of a global symbolic state (l, D), the initial extended local symbolic state of A_i is the start state of the local executions. From the definition of auxiliary clocks, we should assign some time constraints to them as follows.

Definition 7. Shadow extended local symbolic state. *Let (l, D) be a global symbolic state. Let A_i be a component timed automaton. Let D' be a conjunction of following atomic formula.*

1. $t = 0$.
2. *For any clock constraint $x - y \sim n$ (or $x \sim n$) in D, $\overline{x} - \overline{y} \sim n$ (or $x \sim n$).*
3. *For each clock $x \in C_i$, $\overline{x} = x$.*

The symbolic state $(l[i], D')$ is called the shadow extended local symbolic state of (l, D) w.r.t. A_i.

From this definition, for each concrete state $(l[i], u')$ in $(l[i], D')$, we have that $u(t) = 0, \forall x \in C_i \bullet u'(x) = u'(\overline{x})$. For a clock assignment u over the clock set C of the network, we have that $u \models D$ if there is a $u' \models D'$ such that $\forall x \in C \bullet u(x) = u'(\overline{x})$.

Example 4. Let $(< l_{11}, l_{21}, l_{31} >, (x_1 - x_2 \leq 0) \wedge (x_3 = 0) \wedge (x_4 = 0))$ be a global symbolic state. Then the shadow extended local symbolic state of this state w.r.t. A_1 is $(l_{11}, \overline{x}_1 = x_1 \wedge \overline{x}_2 = x_2 \wedge t = 0 \wedge \overline{x}_1 - \overline{x}_2 \leq 0 \wedge \overline{x}_3 = 0 \wedge \overline{x}_4 = 0)$.

Notice that, the clock $\overline{x}$ will never be reset and the clock c_e for each synchronizing transitions will only be reset by e. The value t record the time length from the start point. From the definition of auxiliary clocks and sp_l, we have the following proposition.

Proposition 2. *Let $(l[i], D)$ be an extended local symbolic state of A_i. Let α be a local path from $l[i]$ to $l'[i]$. Let $(l'[i], D') = sp_l(\alpha)(l[i], D)$. Then for each concrete state $(l'[i], u'_i)$ such that $u'_i \models D'$, the following conditions hold.*

1. *The concrete state $(l'[i], u'_i)$ is reachable from a state $(l[i], u_i)$ in $(l[i], D)$ through α, and $u_i[x] = u_i[\overline{x}] = u'_i[\overline{x}] - u'_i[t]$, $u_i[t] = 0$, and*
2. *the value $u'_i[t]$ is the time length of the local execution from $(l[i], u_i)$ to $(l'[i], u'_i)$.*
3. *Of each synchronizing transition e in the local execution, the time stamp is $u'_i[t] - u'_i[c_e]$.*

From this proposition, for each concrete state in the local extended symbolic successor, we can decide the time length of the local execution, the time stamp of each synchronizing transition, and from which concrete state the execution starts. So we can compose these local successors into one global successor.

3.3   Composing the Extended Local Symbolic States

In the above subsection, we present a way to calculate local successors. Some information are incorporated into the local successors. Give a concrete state in a local successor, we can know from which concrete state this one evolves, the time length of the corresponding local execution, and when the synchronizing transitions take place in this execution.

Let (l, D) be a global symbolic state of $A = A_0 \mid A_1 \mid \ldots A_n$. Let $(l[i], D_i)$ be the shadow extended local symbolic states of (l, D) w.r.t. A_i. Let $\mathcal{P} = \alpha_1, \ldots, \alpha_n$ be a local path set from l to l'. Let $\mathcal{C}$ be a synchronization solution of $\mathcal{P}$. Let T be the global transition set w.r.t. $\mathcal{P}$ and $\mathcal{C}$. If $(T, <_{\mathcal{P},\mathcal{C}})$ is a partial order path, we can get the global successor of (l, D) w.r.t. $(T, <_{\mathcal{P},\mathcal{C}})$ by the operator defined below.

Definition 8.   Global successors. *Using the above denotations, we can define a global successor operator $\overline{sp}$ as follows. Let $(l'[i], D'_i) = sp_l(\alpha_i)(l[i], D_i)$ where $1 \le i \le n$, and $D_{\mathcal{C}} = \wedge_{(e,e') \in \mathcal{C}}(c_e = c_{e'})$. Let $D' = D_{\mathcal{C}} \wedge (\wedge_{1 \le i \le n}(D'_i \lhd (C \cup \overline{C})))$.*

$$\overline{sp}(T, <_{\mathcal{P},\mathcal{C}})(l, D) = (l', D' \rhd C)$$

where C is the clock set of the network, and $\overline{C}$ is the set of all auxiliary clocks.

Notice that, if we use $\overline{sp}$ to compose the local successors, for any global transition $e|e'$ in T, it requires that $c_e = c'_e$. That is, $t - c_e = t - c'_e$, so the time stamps of e and e' in their local executions are equal. In each local execution Exe_i, if e_1 takes place earlier than e_2 does, the time stamp of e_1 is not greater than that of e_2. From the definition of $<_{\mathcal{P},\mathcal{C}}$, for any two global transitions e and e' in T, $e <_{\mathcal{P},\mathcal{C}} e'$ implies the time stamp of e is not greater than that of e'. In this case, we do not explicitly require that the time stamp e should not be greater than that of e' if $e <_{\mathcal{P},\mathcal{C}} e'$.

Lemma 1. *Using the above denotations, the symbolic state $\overline{sp}(T, <_{\mathcal{P},\mathcal{C}})(l, D)$ is just the set of concrete states reachable from a concrete state in (l, D) through a global path p, which is consistent to the partial order path $(T, <_{\mathcal{P},\mathcal{C}})$.*

Proof. From the definition of $\triangleright$, for each concrete state (l', u') in $\overline{sp}(\mathcal{P})(\mathcal{C})(l, D)$, there is a concrete state (l', u'') in (l', D') such that $u' = u'' \triangleright C$. From the definition of D', y we have that for each i, $(l', u'' \triangleright (C_i \cup \overline{C}))$ is in $sp_l(\alpha_i)(l[i], D_i)$. From proposition 2, we have that there is a local execution $Exe_i (1 \leq i \leq n)$ from $(l[i], v_i)$ to $(l'[i], u'' \triangleright (C_i \cup \overline{C}))$. For each clock x in C_i, $v_i(x) = v_i(\overline{x}) = u''(\overline{x}) - u''(t)$. The time length of Exe_i is $u''(t)$. And each synchronizing transition e in Exe_i takes place at the time point $u''[t] - u''[c_e]$. We can construct a sequence of time-stamped transitions based on the local executions as follows.

1. The global transition set of this execution is T.
2. The time stamp of a transition e in T is just that of e, or its projection, in its local execution.
3. The take-place order is as follows, e takes place previously to e' either if the stamp of e is less than that of e', or if the time stamp of e is equal to e' and $e <_{\mathcal{P},\mathcal{C}} e'$.

From the definition of $\overline{sp}$ and $<_{\mathcal{P},\mathcal{C}}$, the transition sequence is a path consistent to $(T, <_{\mathcal{P},\mathcal{C}})$. The time constraints of timed automata are satisfied because the time stamps of local executions satisfy the time constraints. So this sequence of time-stamped transitions is a global execution from (l, u) to (l', u'), where for each clock x in C, $u(x) = v_i(x) = u''(\overline{x}) - u''(t)$. So $(l, u \triangleright C)$ is a concrete state in (l, D). Thus we prove that each concrete state in $\overline{sp}(T, <_{\mathcal{P},\mathcal{C}})(l, D)$ is reachable from a concrete state in (l, D).

Now we prove another direction of this lemma. Let (l', u') be a concrete state which is reachable from a state (l, u) in (l, D) through a global path consistent to $(T, <_{\mathcal{P},\mathcal{C}})$. So we have a global execution Exe from (l, u) to (l', u'). Let $Exe_i = Exe/A_i$, $1 \leq i \leq n$, be the projections of Exe on A_i. From the definitions of sp_l and $\overline{sp}$ and the auxiliary clock set, (l', u') is in $\overline{sp}(T, <_{\mathcal{P},\mathcal{C}})(l, D)$.

4   The Algorithms

In the previous sections, we present a method to generate the successors of a symbolic state w.r.t. a partial order path. However, the number of partial order paths leaving from a state is infinite. And we can not find an equivalence relation over the set of extended local symbolic states. So in our algorithm, we limit the number of local successors by limit the length local pathes. We count only the partial order path of which the local paths have at most M transitions. In the algorithm, for an un-timed state l, we use $\mathbf{P}_M(l)$ to denote the local path set, of which all local paths has no more than M transitions.

$$\mathbf{P}_M(l) = \{\mathcal{P} \mid (\text{the length of each local path in } \mathcal{P} \text{ is not greater than } M)\}.$$

We use $\mathcal{T}_M(l)$ to denote the set of partial order paths of which the length of local paths are no more than M.

$$\mathcal{T}_M(l) = \{(\mathcal{P}, <_{\mathcal{P},\mathcal{C}}) \mid \mathcal{P} \in \mathbf{P}_M(l) \wedge (<_{\mathcal{P},\mathcal{C}} \text{ is a partial order})\}$$

The improved algorithm is depicted in Fig 3. The improved one is same as the basic one except the part used to calculate successors.

```
Passed   := {}
Waiting  := {(l₀, D₀)}
repeat    begin
          get an auxiliary state (l, D) from WAITING
          WAITING = WAITING - (l, D)
          if D ⊈ D' for all (l, D') ∈ PASSED then
             begin
                    add (l, D) to PASSED.
                    For each p in 𝒯_M(l) do
                    begin
                           let (l₁, D₁) = s̄p̄(p)(l, D)
                           if l₁ = l_{tgt} and D₁ ∩ D_{tgt} ≠ φ
                             return YES
                           else begin
                             if (l₁, D₁) is not contained by a state in WAITING∪PASSED
                                WAITING:= WAITING ∪ {(l₁, D₁)}
                           end
                    end
             end
          end
until WAITING = {}
return NO.
```

Fig. 3. The improved algorithm

5   Checking Systems Using Shared Variables

We have presented an algorithm to checking parallel timed automata using synchronizing labels. The technique presented in this paper can also be applied to parallel systems using shared variables.

Notice that, we can record the time point at which a transition takes place. So for each transition e which testing or setting shared variables, we can introduce an auxiliary clock c_e to record when e takes place. When we try to combine the local successors, we can give such a partial order over the local transitions that each transition sequence which is consistent to the partial order is a global path. For any two transitions e and e' such that e must take place later that e', we can add the constraint $c_e \leq c_{e'}$ in to the combined extended global successor.

6   Performance Analysis and Case Studies

Let (l, D) be a global symbolic state, and p_1, p_2 be two global paths from l to l'. In the basic algorithm, two successors(if exist) $sp(p_1)(l, D)$ and $sp(p_2)(l, D)$ will be generated. However, in the improved algorithm, these two successors will be included by a generated symbolic state if p_1 and p_2 are consistent to same partial order path. So the improved algorithm will generate less symbolic states when it checks a timed automaton network. The technique used in this algorithm improve the memory efficiency by generating bigger symbolic states.

We enumerate the partial order paths starting from l by enumerating the local path sets from l and the corresponding synchronization solutions. However, we don't have to calculate the local successors for each partial order path. Notice that a local path may be of many partial order paths, we can first calculate the local successors for local paths. The global successor $\overline{sp}(p)(l, D)$ is generated by just combining the local successors, which are calculated previously.

A handicap of this technique is that some auxiliary clocks are introduced to record extra information. More clocks means that more memory space are need for each symbolic state. More CPU time is also required for operations on these symbolic states. However, these auxiliary clocks are only used when the algorithm calculates $\overline{sp}(p)(l, D)$, where $p \in T_M(l)$. The number of local symbolic successors are decide only by the number of the leaving local paths. Additional clocks will not increase the number of local successors. As soon as all successors of (l, D) w.r.t. the leaving partial order paths are generated, the local successors can be removed. The symbolic states in WAITING and PASSED are over the original clock set C. So the extra space requirement because of the auxiliary clock set is limited.

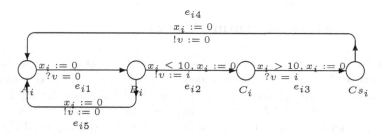

Shared Variable: v; Clock x_i;

Fig. 4. The ith process of Fischer's exclusive protocol

We have incorporated this technique into our experimental tool. We applied this technique to several examples. The following tables are the performance data of our tool when it is used to check CSMA protocol and Fischer's protocol.

Fischer's protocol ensures mutex access to criteral regions using one shared variable and local clocks. Our tool checks the Fischer's protocol(as depicted in Fig 4) of 10 processes by exact and exhaustive exploration, using about 17 hours

Number of process	2	3	4	5	6	7	8	9	10
States generated	22	104	494	2392	11694	57220	278782	1291337	6347930
TIME	< 1 S.	< 1 S.	< 1 S.	3 S.	15 S.	157 S.	26.6 M.	2.2 H.	17.1 H.

Fig. 5. Space performance when checking Fischer's Protocol

Number of process	2	3	4	5	6	7	8
States generated(POP)	15	84	527	2877	13561	56836	218007
Time(POP)	< 1 S	< 1 S	3 S	21 S	5.0 M	31.6 M	3.7 H
States generated(w/o POP)	15	93	675	4794	34507	N/A	N/A

Fig. 6. Space performance when checking CSMA Protocol

in a Pentium4/1G memory computer. The total memory used by the algorithm is about 800M. As reported in the web page 'http://www.docs.uu.se/rtmv/ uppaal/benchmarks', the tool UPPAAL check's this protocol of 7 processes by exact exhaustive exploration. It can check this protocol of 11 processes using 'convex hull' approximation technique.

The CSMA/CD protocol is a protocol used in a broadcast network with a multi-access bus. This protocol is first checked by Kronos[12]. In Fig 6, we can see that when checking CSMA protocol, our technique also result in noticeable space reduction.

The above case studies show that this technique is effective in some cases. However, the technique may result in little space reduction in some other cases. The perform becomes worse because this technique needs extra space and CPU time for calculating partial order paths.

7   Conclusions and Future Works

In this paper, we proposed a so-called 'partial order path' technique for real-time reachablity analysis. Given a global symbolic state (l, D), this technique calculates the successors of (l, D) w.r.t. a set of global paths starting from the location. This set of global paths is expressed as a partial order path. Each successor can be expressed by one symbolic state. So the improved algorithm can have a better space efficiency.

This technique first suppose that each component timed automaton evolves independently to each others. The local successors are calculated without considering synchronization between different automata. After the local successors are calculated, this technique can combine these local successors into global successors w.r.t. the partial order over the transitions. However, combining these local successors needs some additional information. Some auxiliary clocks are introduced to record these information.

In [3], the authors let the time of each component automaton evolves independently. However, they did not give a constructive equivalence relation over the set of un-synchronized states. Our technique also calculate the local successors independently. But these successors are combined into global states immediately. So we avoid checking the equivalence between two un-synchronized states.

This technique has been incorporated into an experimental tool. By applying these tool to several cases, we show that this technique may result in an improvement in time- and space- efficiency.

The primitive algorithm generates a reachability graph of the model being checked. The nodes of this graph is the generated symbolic states. Each edge is labeled by a global transitions. There is a edge labeled e from s to s' if and only if the successor of s w.r.t. e is included by s'. Our technique also generates a similar graph except that the edges are labeled by partial order paths. Notice that, a transition can be viewed as a special partial order path. Most properties which can be verified based on the basic graph can also be verified based on the graph generated by our algorithm.

Acknowledgement

The timed automaton model of Fischer's protocol and CSMA protocol used in this paper are downloaded from homepage of UPPAAL(http://www.docs.uu.se/rtmv/uppaal).

References

1. R. Alur and D. Dill. Automata for Modelling Real-Time Systems. In *Proc. of ICALP'90*, LNCS 443, 1990.
2. Rajeev Alur, Robert K. Brayton, Thomas A. Henzinger, Shaz Qadeer, and Sriram K. Rajamani. Partial-order reduction in symbolic state-space exploration. In *Proceedings of the Ninth International Conference on Computer-aided Verification (CAV 1997), LNCS 1254*, pages 340–351. Springer-Verlag, 1997.
3. Johan Bengtsson, Bengt Jonsson, Johan Lilius, and Wang Yi. Partial Order Reductions for Timed Systems. In *Proc. of the 9th International Conference on Concurrency Theory*, September 1998.
4. C.Daws, A.Olivero, S.Tripakis, and S.Yovine. The tool kronos. In *DIMACS Workshop on Verification and Control of Hybrid Systems*, LNCS 1066. Springer-Verlag, October 1995.
5. F.Pagani. Partial orders and verification of real-time systems. In B. Jonsson and J. Parrow, editors, *Proc. of Formal Techniques in Real-Time and Fault-Tolerant Systems*, LNCS 1135, pages 327–346. Springer-Verlag, 1996.
6. Kim G Larsen and Paul Pettersson Wang Yi. UPPAAL: Status & Developments. In Orna Grumberg, editor, *Proceedings of the 9th International Conference on Computer-Aided Verification. Haifa, Israel,*, LNCS 1254, pages 456–459. Springer-Verlag, June 1997.
7. T.A.Henzinger and P.-H. Ho. Hytech: The cornell hybrid technology tool. In *Proc. of Workshop on Tools and Algorithms for the Construction and Analysis of Systems*, 1995. BRICS report series NS-95-2.
8. Hans van der Schoot. Partial-order verification in spin can be more efficient, http://citeseer.nj.nec.com/vanderschoot97partialorder.html.

9. T.G.Rokicki. Representing and Modeling Circuits, 1993. PhD thesis, Standford University.

10. C.J. Myers, T.G.Rokicki, and T.H.Y.Meng. POSEET timing and its application to the synthesis and verification of gate-level timed circuits. *IEEE Transactions on Computer-Aided Design of Integrated Circuits* 18(6):769-786, June 1999.

11. W. Belluomini and C. J. Myers. Timed state space exploration using POSETs. *IEEE Transactions on Computer-Aided Design of Integrated Circuits*, 19(5), May 2000.

12. Sergio Yovine. Kronos: A verification Tool for Real-Time Systems. *Springer International Journal of Software Toolls for Technology Transfer* 1(1/2), Oct 1997.

Constructing Test Automata
from Graphical Real-Time Requirements

Henning Dierks[1] and Marc Lettrari[2]

[1] University of Oldenburg, Department of Computer Science,
P.O.Box 2503, 26111 Oldenburg, Germany
dierks@informatik.uni-oldenburg.de
[2] OFFIS, Escherweg 2, D-26121 Oldenburg, Germany
lettrari@informatik.uni-oldenburg.de

Abstract. A semantics for a graphical specification language of real-time properties (Constraint Diagrams) is presented. The new semantics is given in terms of Timed Automata. A model in terms of Timed Automata satisfies the property given by a Constraint Diagram if the model in parallel composition with the semantics of the Constraint Diagram can reach a certain state. This kind of question can be checked by all model-checkers for Timed Automata. A prototype of a tool is presented that automatically translates an appropriate Constraint Diagram into the input language of the tool Uppaal.

1 Introduction

Whenever continuous time is necessary to model a real-time system, Timed Automata [AD90,AD94] are usually applied. The advantage of this model is the existence of decision procedures which have been successfully implemented by model-checking tools like Uppaal [LPW97] and Kronos [Yov97]. In principle, it is decidable whether a system of Timed Automata satisfies a formula given in TCTL (timed computation tree logic, [ACD90,HNSY94]). However, reachability properties can be verified more efficiently.

One of the main obstacles to verify formally a real-time system is to specify the desired properties correctly. In the case of reachability this task is not difficult. However, many properties of interest are not simple reachability questions. Then the user has the choice between these possibilities:

- To express the property in TCTL formulas or
- to build a *test automaton* that serves as a wrapper for the property, i.e. the test automaton reaches a certain state if and only if the property is (is not resp.) satisfied.

The disadvantage of the first method is that it is error-prone in the sense of a mismatch between the property expressed by the formula and the property in mind of the specifier. The disadvantage of the second method is that the construction of a test automaton is also error-prone.

W. Damm and E.-R. Olderog (Eds.): FTRTFT 2002, LNCS 2469, pp. 433–453, 2002.

In this paper we propose the following approach. So-called "Constraint Diagrams" (CDs for short) have been proposed in [Die96,Kle00] as a graphical specification language for real-time properties. We present a *test automaton semantics* for CDs that is equivalent (in an appropriate sense) to the semantics given by [Die96,Kle00] in terms of Duration Calculus [ZHR91,HZ97]. All details about this equivalence including the proof can be found in [Let00][1]. The reasons for choosing CDs are

- the graphical oriented syntax (in assumption/commitment style) which employs sequences of phases to specify the behaviour and
- the formal semantics which is tailored to meet the human intuition.

The decision to construct test automata from CDs is driven by the demand for wide range of applicability. This is guaranteed by test automata because reachability tests are implemented in all available tools for Timed Automata.

The test automaton T that is the semantics of a Constraint Diagram C has a particular state q_{bad}. A model M in terms of Timed Automata satisfies the property expressed by C if and only if q_{bad} is not reachable for $M \parallel T$.

Related Work: A similar graphical language for requirements' capture are Symbolic Timing Diagrams [Sch01] (STD) and its real-time extension RTSTD [FJ97]. One of the main differences between CDs and (RT)STDs is that the latter do not allow commitments in the past.

Constructing test automata is not a new idea (e.g. [HLR93]) and has also been applied to Timed Automata [ABL98,LPW98]. The latter approaches construct test automata from formulas in temporal logics to overcome the lack of full TCTL in Uppaal. As discussed above these approaches still have the risk of a mismatch between the property in mind and the property written as formula. Our approach tries to minimise this risk by choosing CDs which are designed to be more readable and accessible for non-experts in temporal logics.

Structure: The paper is organised as follows: In Sect. 2 we introduce a running example, the well-known case study "Generalised Railroad Crossing". Properties of this case study are specified by CDs in Sect. 3 in order to explain the syntax and semantics briefly. In Sect. 4 we present the main contribution of this paper, namely the test automaton semantics for a subset of CDs. The prototypic implementation of a tool is explained in Sect. 5. Before we conclude we apply our result again to the running example in Sect. 6. Note that this paper concentrates on the description of the test automaton semantics and its application. Another issue is to establish the correspondence between this new semantics and the Duration Calculus semantics given in [Kle00]. This problem requires a relation between the semantical basis of Timed Automata (ie. timed traces) and the semantical basis of Duration Calculus (ie. function with domain $\mathbb{R}_{\geq 0}$. In [Die99,DFMV98a] such a relation can be found. On the basis of this relation equivalence proofs were worked out in [Let00] and cannot be presented here due to space limitations.

---

[1] Appendix A contains brief introductions to both DC and the DC semantics for CDs.

2   The Generalised Railroad Crossing

Our approach is illustrated by a case study. The problem of specifying a generalised railroad crossing (GRC) and verifying its properties was posed in [HL94] and suggested as a benchmark problem in comparing the suitability of different formal methods in [HM96], where many solutions are given. In [DD97] both the behaviour of the system and its properties were specified by CDs and an implementation was given in terms of PLC-Automata [Die99]. The question whether the implementation meets the specification was answered by semantical arguments on the basis of the temporal logic Duration Calculus [HZ97,ZHR91]. With the approach presented in this paper, the verification of CDs can be done automatically.

The description of the GRC in [HL94] is:

> The system to be developed operates a gate at a railroad crossing. The railroad crossing I lies in a region of interest R, i.e. $I \subseteq R$. A set of trains travels through R on multiple tracks in both directions. A sensor system determines when each train enters and exits region R. To describe the system formally, we define a gate function $g(t) \in [0, 90]$, where $g(t) = 0$ means the gate is down and $g(t) = 90$ means the gate is up. We define a set λ_i of *occupancy intervals*, where each occupancy interval is a time interval during which one or more trains are in I. The ith occupancy interval is represented as $\lambda_i = [\tau_i, \nu_i]$, where τ_i is the time of the ith entry of a train into the crossing when no other train is in the crossing and ν_i is the first time since τ_i that no train is in the crossing (i.e., the train that entered at τ_i has exited as have trains that entered the crossing after τ_i).

> Given two constants ξ_1 and ξ_2, the problem is to develop a system to operate the crossing gate that satisfies the following two properties:

> **Safety Property:** $t \in \cup_i \lambda_i \implies g(t) = 0$ (The gate is down during all occupancy intervals.)

> **Utility Property:** $t \notin [\tau_i - \xi_1, \nu_i + \xi_2] \implies g(t) = 90$ (The gate is up when no train is in the crossing.)

3   Constraint Diagrams

Constraint Diagrams (CDs for short) have been introduced in [Die96] as a graphical description language for real-time requirements. The motivation stems from the graphical notion of timing diagrams that are often used to specify properties of hardware designs. The idea of CDs is a representation of intervals in an assumption/commitment style. In Fig. 1 an example of a simple CD is given.

This CD can be read as follows: It constrains the behaviour of two Boolean variables called S and A. For all (prefixes of infinite) computations that satisfy the assumptions the commitments have to be fulfilled. The assumptions are the unboxed entities in Fig. 1. They specify that there is an interval with a length of 10 time units where the Boolean variable S is false. The commitments are

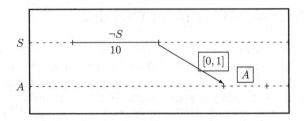

Fig. 1. Specification of a watchdog.

the boxed entities which require the Boolean variable A to be true after the $\neg S$ interval within 1 time unit. Hence, the CD in Fig. 1 specifies that whenever we observe an interval of length 10 where $\neg S$ holds, then the variable A ("alarm") should become true within at most one time unit.

The benefit of CDs are both the accessibility and the readability for non-experts in comparison to formulas given in temporal logic. The following examples of CDs specify the behaviour of trains in the case study GRC. The track under consideration in this case study (i.e. region R) can be empty ("E" for empty), at least one train is approaching the crossing and no train is crossing (i.e. no train is in I) ("A" for approaching), or at least one train is crossing (Cr for "crossing"). The CDs in Fig. 2 specify the following properties of the track:

a) Initially the track is empty;
b) if the track is empty, a train may approach; approaching trains need at least ε_1 time units to reach the crossing;
c) if A holds, a train may cross (Cr).

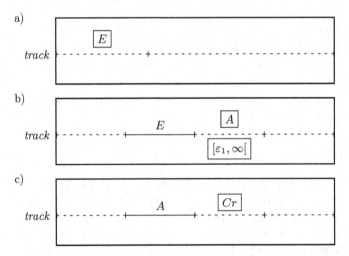

Fig. 2. Specification of track behaviour.

The first CD of Fig. 2 consists of two intervals with no assumptions at all which is indicated by the dashed lines. The commitment is that during the first

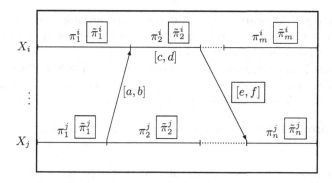

Fig. 3. General syntax of CDs.

interval the track has to be empty. The semantics of this CD basically requires the following: "Each finite prefix of an observation of the track which can be split into two intervals, can be split into two intervals with an empty track during the first interval."

The second CD of Fig. 2 assumes four intervals with the assumption that the track is in E during the second period. The commitment requires state A during the third interval if the track leaves state E. This has to hold for at least ε_1 time units if the track leaves state E. Note that the semantics of CDs always require just a *prefix* of the commitments[2]. In the case of the second CD this would also allow the track to remain E forever.

The last CD of Fig. 2 requires all A phases to be succeeded by Cr phases.

We discuss the CD of Fig. 3 to explain more generally syntax and semantics of CDs. Note that the CDs presented above contain some notational abbreviations which are explained later in this chapter. Figure 3 presents the general syntax of CDs.

A CD consists of a number of lines where each line symbolises the behaviour of a finitely typed variable. Each line is split into some phases[3]. Each phase carries two annotations:

---

[2] The idea of accepting also prefixes of commitments does not seem to be natural at first sight. However, without those prefixes the semantics of CD would not meet the intuitive meaning of the drawings. Consider the watchdog in Fig. 1 again. If a prefix of a computation with length 11 is observed where $\neg S$ was true within the interval $[0.5, 10.5]$, then we would not expected that this computation violates the CD because the alarm still might happen in time, namely within $]11, 11.5]$. Hence, as long as a computation τ can be *extended* in such a way that the extended computation satisfies the commitments of a CD, then τ satisfies the CD.

[3] If the duration of a phase is not specified, it is possible that the duration is 0. This fits to the Timed Automaton model where several transitions may happen at the same time point. This is sometimes called "two-dimensional time". If this is not desired, it is possible for all CDs presented in this paper to specify explictly that the duration of a phase is greater than 0 (cf. Subsect. 4.5).

- The unboxed annotation is a state assertion speaking about the variable of that line. This assertion represents the *assumption* for that phase. E.g. we assume that X_i satisfies initially π_1^i.
- The boxed annotation is a state assertion speaking about the variable of that line. This assertion represents the *commitment* for that phase. E.g. we require that X_j satisfies initially $\tilde{\pi}_1^j$.

Moreover, arrows between borders of phases are allowed which carry also two annotations:

- The unboxed annotation is an interval that represents the *assumed* time distance between the given events. E.g. we assume that the initial phase of X_i holds longer than the initial phase of X_j. The time difference is in $[a, b]$.
- The boxed annotation is an interval that represents the *required* time distance between the given events. E.g. we require that the second phase of X_i ends earlier than the beginning of the last phase of X_j. The time difference has to be in $[e, f]$.

The meaning of the CD is: For all computations and for all $t \in \mathbb{R}_{\geq 0}$ holds: Whenever the computation behaves within period $[0, t]$ in a way such that the variables evolve as given by the π_k^i assertions and the unboxed intervals, then it is possible to find a partition of $[0, t]$ such that a prefix of the commitments ($\tilde{\pi}_k^i$ and the boxed intervals) is satisfied. An introduction of the formal semantics employing Duration Calculus can be found in App. A.

Several abbreviations have been introduced for notational convenience. Those we need in this paper are the following: If a state assertion π_k^i is equivalent to true, then π_k^i is omitted and a dashed line is drawn instead of a solid line. If a state assertion $\tilde{\pi}_k^i$ is equivalent to true, it can be omitted. If an interval annotation of an arrow is $[0, \infty[$, it can be omitted. Intervals of the form $[r, r]$ are abbreviated by r. If an arrow restricts the beginning and the end of the same phase, the arrow itself is not drawn and the interval annotations are given as additional annotations of the phase. E.g. the $\neg S$ phase in Fig. 1 is assumed to last 10 time units. The arrow starting at the beginning and ending at the end of the $\neg S$ phase is not drawn. The time interval $[10, 10]$ is written as 10 and annotated to the phase instead of the arrow.

4   Test Automaton Semantics for Constraint Diagrams

Due to the expressiveness of Constraint Diagrams we cannot expect to be able to assign a test automaton semantics for all CDs[4]. Hence, we look for interesting subsets of CDs for which a test automaton semantics can be assigned. In [Let00] several subsets of CDs have been identified for which a test automaton semantics can be given.

---

[4] Appendix C presents an example for which no test automaton semantics can be found that uses only finitely many clocks.

4.1 Requirements for the Model

The test automaton semantics $\mathcal{T}(\mathcal{C})$ for a CD $\mathcal{C}$ is constructed such that a model M in terms of Timed Automata satisfies the property expressed by $\mathcal{C}$ if and only if state q_{bad} of $\mathcal{T}(\mathcal{C})$ is not reachable for $M \parallel \mathcal{T}(\mathcal{C})^5$. However, this holds only if the model M satisfies the following requirements:

- Initially M sets all information, i.e. at time 0 a synchronisation with the test automaton happens that signals the initial values.
- All changes of the relevant variables for the CD have to be signalled to the test automaton via synchronisation. Due to the construction of the latter it is allowed to execute stutter synchronisations, i.e. to signal the same values subsequently.

By this it is clear what it means that a system satisfies a given state assertion π over a variable X: If the last synchronisation of M for variable X signals a change of the value of X to the value σ, then the system satisfies currently π iff σ satisfies π (in symbols: $\sigma \models \pi$).

4.2 Future Commitments

The following kind of CDs requires the system to ensure a sequence of C_i phases after the occurrence of a sequence of A_j phases. In other words: When the system is engaged in a computation that satisfies the assertions $A_1, A_2, \ldots, A_n$ in this order, then the system should continue the computation such that it will also satisfy the commitments $C_1, C_2, \ldots, C_m$ in this order. The corresponding CD is given below.

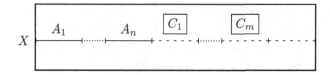

where $n, m \geq 1$, $A_n \neq$ true, $C_i \neq$ true for all $1 \leq i \leq m$, A_n and C_1 are disjoint ($A_n \implies \neg C_1$), and all neighbouring commitments are disjoint ($C_i \implies \neg C_{i+1}$ with $1 \leq i < m$). We call the set of all CDs of this kind CD_1.

The ideas of the construction of this test automaton are simple. We expect the system to keep the test automaton informed about all relevant changes of the variable X. The test automaton has a certain state q_{bad} that is only reachable when the system violates the property specified by the CD $\mathcal{C} \in CD_1$. That means, the question whether $\mathcal{C}$ is satisfied boils down to the question whether q_{bad} is not reachable. The construction of $\mathcal{T}(\mathcal{C})$ is designed in a way that the

---

[5] In the literature are several variants of both Timed Automata and parallel composition of them. In this paper we use basically the model of [AD94] and their notion of parallel composition. That means that a σ-labelled transition can only be executed iff each automaton in the system that uses label σ executes a σ-labelled transition.

test automaton never blocks a synchronisation since it can always switch into a special state q_{good} to stop looking for a violation of the property. In the case of CD_1 a violating computation has to satisfy the assumptions $A_1, \ldots, A_n$ in that order. Then it has to change the value of X such that A_n is not satisfied anymore. Then the value should satisfy C_1. If not, C is already violated. Otherwise, it can only be violated by a change of X to a value that satisfies neither C_1 nor C_2. If the value changes to C_2 the system has to satisfy C_2 further on or C_3 and so on.

Let $C \in CD_1$ be a CD that speaks about the variable X with type Σ. A test automaton $\mathcal{T}(C)$ for C is formally defined as follows: (We assume that $\varepsilon \notin \Sigma$ is a fresh synchronisation label.)

$$\mathcal{T}(C) = (\mathcal{S}, \mathcal{X}, \mathcal{L}, \mathcal{E}, \mathcal{IV}, S_0) \text{ with}$$

$$\mathcal{S} = \{q_0, q_{n+1}, \ldots, q_{n+m}, q_{bad}, q_{good}\} \cup \{q_{i,\sigma} | 1 \leq i \leq n, \sigma \models A_i\}$$

$$\mathcal{X} = \{x\}$$

$$\mathcal{L} = \Sigma \cup \{\varepsilon\}$$

$$\mathcal{IV}(q) = \text{true for all } q \in \mathcal{S}$$

$$S_0 = \{q_0\}$$

$$\mathcal{E} = \{(q_0, \sigma, x = 0, \emptyset, q_{1,\sigma}) \mid \sigma \models A_1\} \tag{1}$$

$$\cup \{(q, \sigma, \text{true}, \emptyset, q_{good}) \mid q \in \mathcal{S}, q \neq q_{bad}, \sigma \in \Sigma\} \tag{2}$$

$$\cup \{(q_{i,\sigma}, \sigma', \text{true}, \emptyset, q_{i,\sigma'}) \mid 1 \leq i \leq n, \sigma, \sigma' \models A_i\} \tag{3}$$

$$\cup \{(q_{i,\sigma}, \sigma', \text{true}, \emptyset, q_{i+1,\sigma'}) \mid 1 \leq i < n, \sigma \models A_i, \sigma' \models A_{i+1}\} \tag{4}$$

$$\cup \{(q_{i,\sigma}, \varepsilon, \text{true}, \emptyset, q_{i+1,\sigma}) \mid 1 \leq i < n, \sigma \models A_i \wedge A_{i+1}\} \tag{5}$$

$$\cup \{(q_{n,\sigma}, \sigma', \text{true}, \emptyset, q_{n+1}) \mid \sigma \models A_n, \sigma' \models C_1\} \tag{6}$$

$$\cup \{(q_{n,\sigma}, \sigma', \text{true}, \emptyset, q_{bad}) \mid \sigma \models A_n, \sigma' \not\models A_n \vee C_1\} \tag{7}$$

$$\cup \{(q_{n+i}, \sigma, \text{true}, \emptyset, q_{n+i}) \mid 1 \leq i \leq m, \sigma \models C_i\} \tag{8}$$

$$\cup \{(q_{n+i}, \sigma, \text{true}, \emptyset, q_{n+i+1}) \mid 1 \leq i < m, \sigma \models C_{i+1}\} \tag{9}$$

$$\cup \{(q_{n+i}, \sigma, \text{true}, \emptyset, q_{bad}) \mid 1 \leq i < m, \sigma \not\models C_i \vee C_{i+1}\} \tag{10}$$

$$\cup \{(q_{bad}, \sigma, \text{true}, \emptyset, q_{bad}) \mid \sigma \in \Sigma\} \tag{11}$$

The state space includes an initial state q_0, states $q_{i,\sigma}$ for each assumption A_i and each $\sigma \models A_i$, states q_{n+j} for each commitment phase C_j, and special states q_{bad} and q_{good}. The idea of q_{bad} is that this state is reachable iff the given CD is not satisfied. State q_{good} is always reachable from all states with all synchronisations. That ensures that the test automata cannot block any behaviour of the system under consideration. Hence, all traces that are admissible *without* the test automaton remain admissible.

We need only one clock x and the set of synchronisation labels is given by the type Σ of the variable X together with the fresh label ε. Moreover, the test automaton does not need invariants. The transitions are defined as follows: Initially we expect that A_1 holds when the system starts its computation (1). In (2) we add transitions from all states to q_{good} to avoid blocking. In (3) we handle stuttering steps of assumption phases. In cases where a synchronisation happens

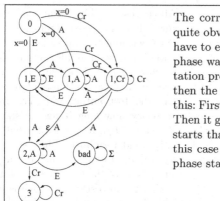

The correctness of this test automaton is quite obvious. All paths to reach state q_{bad} have to ensure that after an A-phase an E-phase was observed. Moreover, if a computation produces such a wrong state change, then the test automaton is able to observe this: First, it may stay in $\{q_{1,E}, q_{1,A}, q_{1,Cr}\}$. Then it guesses correctly when the A-phase starts that is succeeded by an E-phase. In this case it changes to $q_{2,A}$. When the E-phase starts it changes into q_{bad}.

Fig. 4. Test automaton for Fig. 2 c).

which allows us to proceed in the assumptions we can apply transitions in (4). If the last synchronisation belongs to both the current and the following assumption, then (5) allows us to proceed spontaneously in the assumptions. When all assumptions are given we apply (6) if a synchronisation is given that satisfies the first commitment. If a synchronisation is given that neither belongs to the last assumption nor to the first commitment, then we have seen a counterexample for the CD and enter q_{bad} (7). In (8) we allow stuttering steps in commitments whereas (9) allows us to proceed in the commitments provided that an appropriate synchronisation happens. If during a commitment a synchronisation occurs that neither belongs to the current nor to the following commitment, then we have seen a counterexample (10). Finally, (11) introduces idle transitions for q_{bad}.

The automaton $\mathcal{T}(\mathcal{C})$ is basically a nondeterministic finite automaton that accepts a regular language, because CDs in CD_1 have no time requirements. Hence, an equivalent minimal deterministic automaton could be constructed. We refrain from that here, since introducing time assumptions and time commitments is easier with the given structure.

The CD in Fig 2 c) is in CD_1 with $A_1 = \text{true}$, $A_2 = A$, and $C_1 = Cr$. The type of the variable $X = track$ is $\{E, A, Cr\}$. The corresponding test automaton is given in Fig. 4. Note that for sake of readability we omitted state q_{good} and all transitions to this state.

4.3   Past Commitments

The following kind of CDs requires the system to ensure a sequence of C_i phases before the occurrence of a sequence of A_j phases.

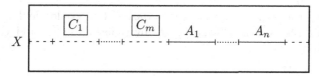

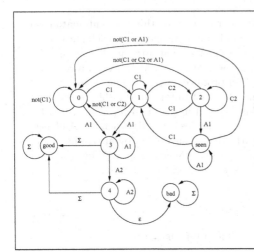

All paths reaching state q_{bad} ensure that an A_1-A_2-sequence happens without a preceeding C_1-C_2-sequence. Therefore all computations reaching q_{bad} violate the CD. Moreover, if a computation violates the CD the test automaton may guess correctly how long it has to stay in the states $\{q_0, q_1, q_2\}$. Note that the only nondeterministic choices are in q_0 and q_1 for A_1-signals. If the assumptions of the CD have to be met it changes into state q_3 which is possible because the preceeding phases are not a C_1-C_2-sequence. Hence, all violating computation can reach q_{bad}.

Fig. 5. Test automaton for a CD $\mathcal{C} \in CD_2$.

where $n, m \geq 1$, $C_i \neq$ true for all $1 \leq i \leq m$, and $A_1, C_1, \ldots, C_m$ are *pairwise disjoint*. We call the set of all CDs of this kind CD_2.

The additional requirements for the commitments C_j allow us to construct a test automaton for these CDs as follows: The test automaton can deterministically check whether all commitments have occurred before the first assumption A_1 is visible. After the recognition of A_1 the automaton searches nondeterministically for the successive assumptions. If it is successful after an incorrect past a counterexample for the property was found. A formal description of the semantics of diagrams in CD_2 is given in App. B. The automaton $\mathcal{T}(\mathcal{C})$ with $m = n = 2$ is shown in Fig. 5 where we assume for simplicity that A_1 and A_2 are singletons.

4.4   Mixed Assumptions and Commitments

In [Let00] it is shown that it is possible to assign a test automaton for the following patterns of CDs:

$$X \quad \begin{array}{c} A_1 \qquad A_n \quad \boxed{C_1} \qquad \boxed{C_m} \; A_{n+1} \quad A_{n+k} \end{array}$$

with the following assumptions:

- $n, m, k > 0$,
- replacing the $A_1, \ldots, A_n$ phases by a dashed line would yield a CD in CD_2,
- replacing the $A_{n+1}, \ldots, A_{n+k}$ phases by a dashed line would yield a CD in CD_1, and
- $A_n \Longrightarrow \neg A_{n+1}$.

4.5   Time Requirements

The time requirements which are allowed in our approach are

- time assumptions for assumption phases A_i and
- time commitment for commitment phases C_j.

Due to the construction of $T(C)$ for a CD C in a form of the previous sections it is simple to add those time requirements. Instead of a formal treatment we will discuss the following example:

The CD without time requirements belongs to CD_1 with $A_1 = \text{true}$, $A_2 = A \vee B$, $A_3 = A$, $C_1 = C$, and $C_2 = B$. The test automaton semantics of this example is given in Fig. 6. This test automaton is a convincing example that it is non-trivial to construct correct test automata by hand. It is far too easy to introduce a misleading edge or typo such that a verification would lead to wrong conclusions. Thus, tool support is needed.

Figure 6 omits state q_{good} again; the horizontal lines indicate the following: The first horizontal line annotated with $x := 0$ indicates that all crossing edges carry this annotation. Similarly the second horizontal line with $b_1 \leq x \leq e_1$ and $x := 0$ as annotations. Due to the construction of this test automaton a computation that leads into state q_{bad} has to ensure a phase where $A \vee B$ holds (states $q_{2,A}$, $q_{2,B}$) for a duration in $[b_1, e_1[$. After that it can reach state $q_{3,A}$ where it has to remain for a duration in $[b_2, e_2]$. If the system signals a change of the variable X to B before b_2 time units have elapsed, then the assumptions of the CD are not fulfilled. In this case the omitted transition to q_{good} is applicable. If B happens after b_2 and before e_2 time units, the assumptions are fulfilled, but the system does not satisfy the property since C was required. If the system fails to change X before e_2 time units are elapsed, the test automaton may also change to q_{bad} with an ε-transition. If the expected transition to C happens in time, the test automaton may change to q_4 to check the remaining commitments.

When the test automaton changes to q_4 it knows that all assumptions of the CD have occurred. It has to find all commitments now. The required change to C has also occurred. The CD requires that C holds for a duration in $]b_3, e_3[$ and then the system has to change to B and remain there for at least b_4 time units. Hence, in state q_4 a change to A is wrong, a change to B too early is wrong, and keeping the state for e_3 time units is wrong. If B arrives in time the system has met the commitment C_1 and now has to check whether C_2 is satisfied, too. The only way to violate this commitment is the arrival of A or C too early.

4.6   More Variables

In Constraint Diagrams it is allowed to constrain the behaviour of several variables (cf. Fig. 1). The approach described in the previous sections can be generalised for several variables as long as *commitments* are given for only one

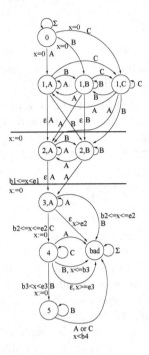

Fig. 6. Test automaton with time requirements.

variable.[6] We construct basically the test automaton for the Constraint Diagram that we get by omitting all variables without commitments. This is described above. The remaining assumptions about all other variables are checked by auxiliary automata which are synchronised appropriately with the main test automaton. Each of those automata has to reach a certain state which is only possible if all corresponding assumptions for the variable were seen.

5   Implementation

A prototypic implementation of the presented test automaton semantics was developed for the model-checker Uppaal [LPW97]. The tool Moby/CD allows the graphical development of Constraint Diagrams. The constructed CDs are translated into a textual representation which serves as the input language for the test automaton compiler. Applied to a textual description cd of a CD C the compiler generates three output files cd.ta, cd.v and cd.q. The file cd.ta contains the generated test automata and an additional timed automaton which

---

[6] If commitments for two or more variables are independent, this is no restriction, because the CD can be split into an equivalent conjunction of CDs which meet the restriction. Otherwise, there is no test automaton semantics possible in the general case (cf. the CD given in App. C).

we denote *demultiplexer*. This automaton serves as an interface to the test automata and interacts with the considered system via a simple protocol. The need for this additional automaton is given by the restricted synchronisation mechanisms in Uppaal. In contrast to the definition of [AD94] there are no direct ways to synchronise more than two automaton simultaneously. The workaround for this problem is as follows: Whenever there are changes of system variables referenced in $\mathcal{C}$ the system signals this via a certain synchronisation CHANGE_SYNC to the demultiplexer. Then the demultiplexer controls the values of all relevant system variables and sends to each test automaton synchronisations which indicate the actual values of the variables. Using such an interface decouples the test automata from the target system and allows an easy application because introducing the synchronisation CHANGE_SYNC can be done easily for many systems.

The file cd.v contains declarations of variables and clocks for the generated test automata. The files cd.ta, cd.v and the description of the considered system in terms of timed automata must be merged beforehand in order to build the complete system for the model checker. The other necessary input is a suitable reachability question (is q_{bad} reachable) which is contained in cd.q. If the Uppaal model checker negates this question the considered system fulfils the property described in $\mathcal{C}$. Otherwise Uppaal generates a trace which is a counterexample to the property in $\mathcal{C}$.

The sizes of the test automata produced from a CD are as follows: For each line of the CD we introduce a clock and an automaton (slightly optimised) with at most $2n + 3$ states where n is the number of phases in the line. For each arrow we need an additional clock. The demultiplexer consists of two states plus a state for each line of the CD.

6   GRC Revisited

Consider the CDs in Fig. 2 again. It is obvious that b) and c) belong to the set of CDs for which a test automaton semantics was assigned. Constraint Diagram a) restricts the initial phase of the system, but it does belong neither to CD_1 nor to CD_2 nor to any of the extensions. In [Let00] some particular patterns[7] of CDs were considered and a test automaton semantics for these patterns was defined. Fortunately, Fig. 2 a) belongs to this set of patterns such that we have defined a test automaton semantics for all the CDs given in Sect. 3. Hence, given a Timed Automaton model of the track we would be able to verify with our approach whether this model satisfies the assumptions about the track.

When we consider an implementation of a controller for the GRC we are interested whether the controller satisfies the properties **Safety** and **Utility** given in Sect. 2. Due to the assumption that trains need at least ε_1 time units to approach the crossing (Fig. 2 b)) it is safe when the controller satisfies the

---

[7] These patterns stem from a sublanguage of Duration Calculus [ZHR91,HZ97] called "Implementables" [Rav95]. This sublanguage consists of frequently used specification patterns for real-time systems.

following property. It requires the gate to become closed whenever the track is not empty for ε_1 time units:

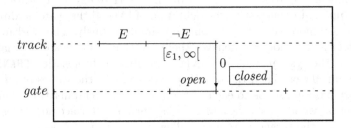

This CD belongs to CD_1 with time extension and the extension for several variables. Hence, a test automaton can be constructed for **Safety**. Similarly, a CD can be found to specify a property of both gate and track to ensure **Utility**:

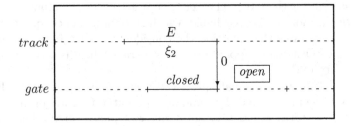

It requires the gate to open when the track is empty for more than ξ_2 time units. In [DD97] it is shown why these properties in conjunction with the assumptions about the track behaviour meet **Safety** and **Utility**.

7   Related Work Revisited

In this we discuss the similar approaches [ABL98,LPW98] in more detail.

[**LPW98**]: In this paper two kinds of formulas are introduced for which test automata are produced. The authors comment the expressiveness as follows:

> "We also noticed that though the logic is so simple, it characterizes the class of logical properties verified in all previous case studies where Uppaal is applied [...]."

The formulas are either invariants (syntax: $Inv(f)$) where f is a boolean formula over atomic propositions or bounded response formulas (syntax: $f_1 \rightsquigarrow_{\leq T} f_2$) where T is a natural number.[8] Both kinds are expressible by CDs. An invariant $Inv(f)$ is equivalent to

---

[8] Note that [LPW98] allowed boolean formulas over atomic propositions *and* clock constraints. The clock constraints can be replaced by auxiliary atomic propositions.

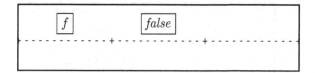

This CD belongs to the set of patterns mentioned in the previous section. Thus, it has a test automaton semantics. The meaning is that the system has to fulfill f initially and *false* afterwards. Hence, f must hold forever.

The bounded response formula $f_1 \leadsto_{\leq T} f_2$ requires the system to ensure the property f_2 within at most T time units when the property f_1 becomes true. This is stronger than the classical until-operator where f_1 has to hold until f_2 becomes true. The bounded response can be expressed by the following CD that belongs to CD_1 (with extensions):

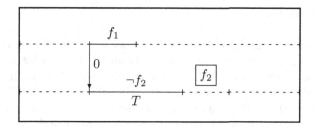

[**ABL98**]: The approach in this paper is more general and difficult to compare to our approach. The reason is that in [ABL98] a logic called SBLL (safety and bounded liveness) is introduced for which a translation into a test automaton is presented. Instead of discussing the details of SBLL we discuss a SBLL formula in [ABL98]:

$$inv([\mathsf{send}_1!]\ s\ \underline{\mathsf{in}}\ \mathbb{W}([\mathsf{recv}_2!](s < 4) \wedge [\mathsf{recv}_3!](s < 4))) \tag{12}$$

This describes a requirement for the CSMA/CD protocol. The informal meaning is that whenever node 1 sends a message then nodes 2 and 3 receive the message within less than 4 time units. Note that SBLL formulas speak about synchronisation labels whereas CDs speak about the states and variables. Assuming appropriate variables s_1, r_2, r_3 we can represent this property by

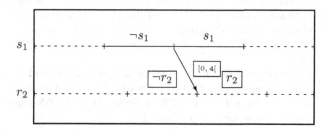

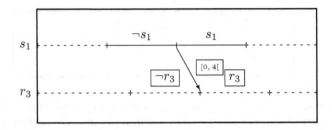

Note that CDs allow to represent this property by a single CD but the given representation is equivalent and uses commitments only for a single observable. Hence, there is a test automaton semantics available (cf. Sect. 4.6). It depends on the individual skills, experiences and education which representation is more accessible: The formula (12) or the CDs above.

8   Conclusion

Constraint Diagrams have been designed as a graphical language for the requirements capture of real-time system. From the CD's point of view the main contribution of this paper is the new applicability of this specification language as temporal logic for automatic formal verification. From the Timed Automata point of view the main contribution of this paper is the new availability of a graphical temporal logic in assumption/commitment-style for which test automata can be constructed automatically.

Acknowledgements

The authors thank E.-R. Olderog and the members of the "semantics group" in Oldenburg for fruitful discussions on the subject of this paper.

References

ABL98.   L. Aceto, A. Burgueño, and K. Larsen. Model Checking via Reachability Testing for Timed Automata. In Steffen [Ste98], pages 263–280.

ACD90.   R. Alur, C. Courcoubetis, and D. Dill. Model-Checking for Real-Time Systems. In *Fifth Annual IEEE Symp. on Logic in Computer Science*, pages 414–425. IEEE Press, 1990.

AD90.   R. Alur and D.L. Dill. Automata for modeling real-time systems. In M.S. Paterson, editor, *ICALP 90: Automata, Languages, and Programming*, volume 443 of *LNCS*, pages 322–335. Springer, 1990.

AD94.   R. Alur and D.L. Dill. A theory of timed automata. *TCS*, 126:183–235, 1994.

DD97.   H. Dierks and C. Dietz. Graphical Specification and Reasoning: Case Study "Generalized Railroad Crossing". In J. Fitzgerald, C.B. Jones, and P. Lucas, editors, *FME'97*, volume 1313 of *LNCS*, pages 20–39, Graz, Austria, September 1997. Springer.

DFMV98a.   H. Dierks, A. Fehnker, A. Mader, and F.W. Vaandrager. Operational
           and Logical Semantics for Polling Real-Time Systems. In A.P. Ravn
           and H. Rischel, editors, *FTRTFT'98*, volume 1486 of *LNCS*, pages
           29–40, Lyngby, Denmark, September 1998. Springer. short version of
           [DFMV98b].

DFMV98b.   H. Dierks, A. Fehnker, A. Mader, and F.W. Vaandrager. Operational and
           Logical Semantics for Polling Real-Time Systems. Technical Report CSI-
           R9813, Computer Science Institute Nijmegen, Faculty of Mathematics
           and Informatics, Catholic University of Nijmegen, April 1998. full paper
           of [DFMV98a].

Die96.   C. Dietz. Graphical Formalization of Real-Time Requirements. In B. Jon-
           sson and J. Parrow, editors, *Formal Techniques in Real-Time and Fault-
           Tolerant Systems*, volume 1135 of *LNCS*, pages 366–385, Uppsala, Swe-
           den, September 1996. Springer.

Die99.   H. Dierks. *Specification and Verification of Polling Real-Time Systems*.
           PhD thesis, University of Oldenburg, July 1999.

FJ97.   K. Feyerabend and B. Josko. A Visual Formalism for Real-Time Require-
           ments Specifications. In M. Bertran and T. Rus, editors, *ARTS'97*, vol-
           ume 1231 of *LNCS*, pages 156–168, Mallorca, Spain, May 1997. Springer.

HL94.   C. Heitmeyer and N. Lynch. The Generalized Railroad Crossing. In *IEEE
           Real-Time Systems Symposium*, 1994.

HLR93.   N. Halbwachs, F. Lagnier, and P. Raymond. Synchronous observers and
           the verification of reactive systems. In M. Nivat, C. Rattray, T. Rus,
           and G. Scollo, editors, *Third Int. Conf. on Algebraic Methodology and
           Software Technology, AMAST'93*, Workshops in Computing. Springer,
           June 1993.

HM96.   C. Heitmeyer and D. Mandrioli, editors. *Formal Methods for Real-Time
           Computing*, volume 5 of *Trends in Software*. Wiley, 1996.

HNSY94.   T. Henzinger, X. Nicollin, J. Sifakis, and S. Yovine. Symbolic Model
           Checking for Real-Time Systems. *Information and Computation*,
           111:193–244, 1994.

HZ97.   M.R. Hansen and Zhou Chaochen. Duration Calculus: Logical Founda-
           tions. *Formal Aspects of Computing*, 9:283–330, 1997.

Kle00.   C. Kleuker. *Constraint Diagrams*. PhD thesis, University of Oldenburg,
           December 2000.

Let00.   M. Lettrari. Eine Testautomatensemantik für Constraint Diagrams und
           ihre Anwendung. Master's thesis, University of Oldenburg, Department
           of Computer Science, Oldenburg, Germany, April 2000.

LPW97.   K.G. Larsen, P. Petterson, and Wang Yi. Uppaal in a nutshell. *Software
           Tools for Technology Transfer*, 1(1+2):134–152, December 1997.

LPW98.   M. Lindahl, P. Pettersson, and Wang Yi. Formal Design and Analysis of
           a Gear Controller. In Steffen [Ste98], pages 281–297.

Mos85.   B. Moszkowski. A Temporal Logic for Multilevel Reasoning about Hard-
           ware. *IEEE Computer*, 18(2):10–19, 1985.

Rav95.   A.P. Ravn. Design of Embedded Real-Time Computing Systems. Tech-
           nical Report 1995-170, Technical University of Denmark, 1995.

Sch01.   R. Schlör. *Symbolic Timing Diagrams: A Visual Formalism for Model
           Verification*. PhD thesis, University of Oldenburg, Department of Com-
           puter Science, Oldenburg, Germany, 2001.

Ste98.   B. Steffen, editor. *Tools and Algorithms for the Construction and Anal-
           ysis of Systems*, volume 1384 of *LNCS*. Springer, 1998.

Yov97.   S. Yovine. Kronos: a verification tool for real-time systems. *Software Tools for Technology Transfer*, 1(1+2):123–133, December 1997.

Zho93.   Zhou Chaochen. Duration Calculi: An overview. In D. Bjørner, M. Broy, and I.V. Pottosin, editors, *Formal Methods in Programming and Their Application*, volume 735 of *LNCS*, pages 256–266. Springer, 1993.

ZHR91.   Zhou Chaochen, C.A.R. Hoare, and A.P. Ravn. A Calculus of Durations. *IPL*, 40/5:269–276, 1991.

A   Duration Calculus Semantics for CDs

In this appendix first we introduce briefly Duration Calculus , a formalism in which the semantics of CDs is given in [Kle00]. After this we explain briefly the ideas of the semantics of CDs in Duration Calculus. A full treatment of the semantics can be found in [Kle00].

Duration Calculus [ZHR91,Zho93,HZ97] (DC for short) is a real-time interval temporal logic extending earlier work on discrete interval temporal logic of [Mos85]. A formal description of a real-time system using DC starts by choosing a number of time-dependent state variables (called "observables") *obs* of a certain type. An interpretation I assigns to each observable a function $obs_I : \mathsf{Time} \longrightarrow D$ where Time is the time domain, here the non-negative reals, and D is the type of *obs*. If D is finite, these functions obs_I are required to be *finitely variable*, which means that any interval $[b, e] \subseteq \mathsf{Time}$ can be divided into finitely many subintervals such that obs_I is constant on the open subintervals.

State assertions P are obtained by applying propositional connectives to elementary assertions of the form $obs = v$ (v for short if *obs* is clear) for a $v \in D$. For a given interpretation I state assertions denote functions $P_I : \mathsf{Time} \longrightarrow \{0, 1\}$.

Duration terms are of type real and their values depend on a given time interval $[b, e]$. The simplest duration term is the symbol ℓ denoting the length $e - b$ of $[b, e]$. For each state assertion P there is a duration term $\int P$ measuring the duration of P, i.e. the accumulated time P holds in the given interval. Semantically, $\int P$ denotes $\int_b^e P_I(t)dt$ on the interval $[b, e]$.

Duration formulas are built from arithmetical relations applied to duration terms, the special symbols true and false, and other terms of type real, and they are closed under propositional connectives and quantification over rigid variables. Their truth values depend on a given interval. We use F for a typical duration formula. true and false evaluate to true resp. false on every given interval. Further basic duration formulas are:

Relation over Durations: For example, $\int P = k$ expresses that the *duration* of the state assertion P in $[b, e]$ is k.

Chop: The composite duration formula $F_1; F_2$ (read as F_1 *chop* F_2) holds in $[b, e]$ if this interval can be divided into an initial subinterval $[b, m]$ where F_1 holds and a final subinterval $[m, e]$ where F_2 holds.

Besides this basic syntax various abbreviations are used:

$$\text{point interval: } \lceil\rceil \stackrel{\text{df}}{=} \ell = 0$$
$$\text{everywhere: } \lceil P\rceil \stackrel{\text{df}}{=} \int P = \ell \wedge \ell > 0$$
$$\text{somewhere: } \Diamond F \stackrel{\text{df}}{=} \text{true}; F; \text{true}$$
$$\text{always: } \Box F \stackrel{\text{df}}{=} \neg\Diamond\neg F$$

A duration formula F *holds* in an interpretation I if F evaluates to true in I and every interval of the form $[0, t]$ with $t \in$ Time. If convenient, we use F to describe a set of interpretations namely all interpretations in which F holds.

Semantically, Constraint Diagrams denote an implication between assumptions and commitments of the form

$$\forall\epsilon_1, \ldots, \epsilon_k. \ (\ Assm(\epsilon_1, \ldots, \epsilon_k) \implies \exists\delta_1, \ldots, \delta_l. \ Comm(\epsilon_1, \ldots, \epsilon_k, \delta_1, \ldots, \delta_l))$$

for real variables ϵ_i, δ_j with $i \leq k, j \leq l, k, l \in \mathbb{N}$. Assumptions as well as commitments characterising lines are conjunctions of sequence formulae like

$$(\lceil P_1\rceil \wedge \ell = \epsilon_1); \ldots; (\lceil P_n\rceil \wedge \ell = \epsilon_n)$$

for state assertions P_i and real variables $\epsilon_i, i \leq n, n \in \mathbb{N}$. Difference formulae characterising arrows have the form

$$\left(\sum_{i=1}^{n}\epsilon_i - \sum_{j=1}^{m}\delta_j\right) \in Intv$$

for real variables $\epsilon_i, \delta_j, \ i \leq n, j \leq m, n, m \in \mathbb{N}$ and an interval $Intv$. They are also needed in length requirements between lengths of phases in assumptions and commitments to assure that they concern the same subintervals.

Consider the CD for the watchdog (Fig. 1). The DC semantics is equivalent to this formula:

$$\forall\epsilon_1, \epsilon_2 : \ell = \epsilon_1; (\lceil\neg S\rceil \wedge \ell = 10); \ell = \epsilon_2$$
$$\implies \exists\delta_1, \delta_2, \delta_3 : \ell \geq \epsilon_1 + \epsilon_2 + 1$$
$$\implies \ell = \delta_1; (\lceil A\rceil \wedge \ell = \delta_2); \ell = \delta_3 \wedge$$
$$\delta_1 - (\epsilon_1 + \epsilon_2) \in [0, 1]$$

Detailed definitions and discussions of the semantics are found in [Kle00].

B   Test Automaton Semantics for CD_2

Formally we define the test automaton $\mathcal{T}(\mathcal{C})$ for a CD $\mathcal{C} \in CD_2$ in this way:

$$\mathcal{T}(\mathcal{C}) = (\mathcal{S}, \mathcal{X}, \mathcal{L}, \mathcal{E}, \mathcal{IV}, S_0) \text{ with}$$
$$\mathcal{S} = \{q_0, q_{bad}, q_{good}, q_{seen}, q_1, \ldots, q_m\} \cup \{q_{m+i,\sigma} | 1 \leq i \leq n, \sigma \models A_i\}$$
$$\mathcal{X} = \{x\}$$
$$\mathcal{L} = \Sigma \cup \{\varepsilon\}$$
$$\mathcal{IV}(q) = \text{true for all } q \in \mathcal{S}$$
$$S_0 = \{q_0\}$$

The transitions $\mathcal{E}$ are defined in Figure 7.

$$\mathcal{E} = \{(q, \sigma, \text{true}, \emptyset, q_{good}) \mid q \in \mathcal{S}, q \neq q_{bad}, \sigma \in \Sigma\} \tag{13}$$
$$\cup \{(q_i, \sigma, \text{true}, \emptyset, q_{i+1}) \mid 0 \leq i < m, \sigma \models C_{i+1}\} \tag{14}$$
$$\cup \{(q_0, \sigma, \text{true}, \emptyset, q_0) \mid \sigma \not\models C_1\} \tag{15}$$
$$\cup \{(q_i, \sigma, \text{true}, \emptyset, q_i) \mid 1 \leq i \leq m, \sigma \models C_i\} \tag{16}$$
$$\cup \{(q_i, \sigma, \text{true}, \emptyset, q_1) \mid 1 \leq i \leq m, \sigma \models C_1\} \tag{17}$$
$$\cup \{(q_i, \sigma, \text{true}, \emptyset, q_0) \mid 1 \leq i < m, \sigma \not\models C_1 \cup C_i \cup C_{i+1}\} \tag{18}$$
$$\cup \{(q_i, \sigma, \text{true}, \emptyset, q_{m+1,\sigma}) \mid 0 \leq i < m, \sigma \models A_1\} \tag{19}$$
$$\cup \{(q_m, \sigma, \text{true}, \emptyset, q_0) \mid \sigma \not\models C_1 \cup C_m \cup A_1\} \tag{20}$$
$$\cup \{(q_m, \sigma, \text{true}, \emptyset, q_{seen}) \mid \sigma \models A_1\} \tag{21}$$
$$\cup \{(q_{seen}, \sigma, \text{true}, \emptyset, q_{seen}) \mid \sigma \models A_1\} \tag{22}$$
$$\cup \{(q_{seen}, \sigma, \text{true}, \emptyset, q_1) \mid \sigma \models C_1\} \tag{23}$$
$$\cup \{(q_{seen}, \sigma, \text{true}, \emptyset, q_0) \mid \sigma \not\models A_1 \vee C_1\} \tag{24}$$
$$\cup \{(q_{m+i,\sigma}, \sigma', \text{true}, \emptyset, q_{m+i,\sigma'}) \mid 1 \leq i \leq n, \sigma, \sigma' \models A_i\} \tag{25}$$
$$\cup \{(q_{m+i,\sigma}, \sigma', \text{true}, \emptyset, q_{m+i+1,\sigma'}) \mid 1 \leq i < n, \sigma \models A_i, \sigma' \models A_{i+1}\} \tag{26}$$
$$\cup \{(q_{m+i,\sigma}, \varepsilon, \text{true}, \emptyset, q_{m+i+1,\sigma}) \mid 1 \leq i < n, \sigma \models A_i \wedge A_{i+1}\} \tag{27}$$
$$\cup \{(q_{m+n,\sigma}, \varepsilon, \text{true}, \emptyset, q_{bad}) \mid \sigma \models A_n\} \tag{28}$$
$$\cup \{(q_{bad}, \sigma, \text{true}, \emptyset, q_{bad}) \mid \sigma \in \Sigma\} \tag{29}$$

Fig. 7. Definition of $\mathcal{E}$.

The idea of the state space is that $q_0, \ldots, q_m$ represent the number of fulfilled commitments at the moment. Hence, if we are not in state q_m and the assumption can be match, then a counterexample was found. If we are in state q_m and the first assumption is fulfilled, we switch into the special state q_{seen} in order to avoid the detection of a wrong counterexample. All other states have a similar meaning as in the semantics for CD_1.

(13): Transitions to q_{good} are always possible to avoid blocking. (14): In state q_i the next commitment was observed, thus the successor state is q_{i+1}. (15): Idling is possible for q_0 as long the first commitment was not seen. (16)–(19): Transitions for q_i ($1 \leq i < m$). If C_i holds, it idles (16); if C_1 holds, the first commitment was seen and q_1 is the successor state (17); if C_{i+1} holds, (14) is applicable to proceed in the sequence of the commitments; in all other cases a change to q_0 is allowed (18); if the first assumption is observed it may change to the assumption states (19). Transitions for q_m are similar except for the case of A_1 where it changes into q_{seen} in order to avoid wrong counterexamples (21). Transitions for q_{seen} hold the state as long as A_1 is true (22) and changes otherwise to q_0 or q_1 respectively (23),(24). (25)–(27): Similar to (3)–(5). (28): If all assumptions were seen a counterexample was found. (28): Idling of sink states.

C   A CD without TA Semantics

For the following CD it is not possible to find a test automaton semantics, because it would need infinitely many clocks:

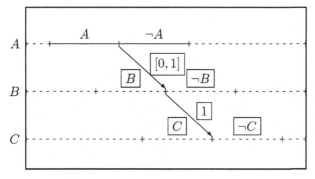

The meaning of this CD is that whenever we observe a change from A to $\neg A$ at time t_A the system has to produce a change from B to $\neg B$ at time $t_B \in [t_A, t_A + 1]$ and a change from C to $\neg C$ at time $t_B + 1$. In order to detect a counterexample the test automaton has to verify that all possible instances of t_B do not satisfy the commitment. However, the decision whether an instance of t_B satisfies the commitments depends on the future. Therefore the test automaton has to remember all possible candidates for t_B, i.e. all time points when the system changes from B to $\neg B$. However, this is not possible with a static number of clocks because it is possible that more changes happen as clocks are available.

Author Index

Lecture Notes in Computer Science

For information about Vols. 1–2371
please contact your bookseller or Springer-Verlag

Vol. 2407: A.C. Kakas, F. Sadri (Eds.), Computational Logic: Logic Programming and Beyond. Part I. XII, 678 pages. 2002. (Subseries LNAI).

Vol. 2408: A.C. Kakas, F. Sadri (Eds.), Computational Logic: Logic Programming and Beyond. Part II. XII, 628 pages. 2002. (Subseries LNAI).

Vol. 2409: D.M. Mount, C. Stein (Eds.), Algorithm Engineering and Experiments. Proceedings, 2002. VIII, 207 pages. 2002.

Vol. 2410: V.A. Carreño, C.A. Muñoz, S. Tahar (Eds.), Theorem Proving in Higher Order Logics. Proceedings, 2002. X, 349 pages. 2002.

Vol. 2412: H. Yin, N. Allinson, R. Freeman, J. Keane, S. Hubbard (Eds.), Intelligent Data Engineering and Automated Learning – IDEAL 2002. Proceedings, 2002. XV, 597 pages. 2002.

Vol. 2413: K. Kuwabara, J. Lee (Eds.), Intelligent Agents and Multi-Agent Systems. Proceedings, 2002. X, 221 pages. 2002. (Subseries LNAI).

Vol. 2414: F. Mattern, M. Naghshineh (Eds.), Pervasive Computing. Proceedings, 2002. XI, 298 pages. 2002.

Vol. 2415: J.R. Dorronsoro (Ed.), Artificial Neural Networks – ICANN 2002. Proceedings, 2002. XXVIII, 1382 pages. 2002.

Vol. 2416: S. Craw, A. Preece (Eds.), Advances in Case-Based Reasoning. Proceedings, 2002. XII, 656 pages. 2002. (Subseries LNAI).

Vol. 2417: M. Ishizuka, A. Sattar (Eds.), PRICAI 2002: Trends in Artificial Intelligence. Proceedings, 2002. XX, 623 pages. 2002. (Subseries LNAI).

Vol. 2418: D. Wells, L. Williams (Eds.), Extreme Programming and Agile Methods – XP/Agile Universe 2002. Proceedings, 2002. XII, 292 pages. 2002.

Vol. 2419: X. Meng, J. Su, Y. Wang (Eds.), Advances in Web-Age Information Management. Proceedings, 2002. XV, 446 pages. 2002.

Vol. 2420: K. Diks, W. Rytter (Eds.), Mathematical Foundations of Computer Science 2002. Proceedings, 2002. XII, 652 pages. 2002.

Vol. 2421: L. Brim, P. Jančar, M. Křetínský, A. Kučera (Eds.), CONCUR 2002 – Concurrency Theory. Proceedings, 2002. XII, 611 pages. 2002.

Vol. 2422: H. Kirchner, Ch. Ringeissen (Eds.), Algebraic Methodology and Software Technology. Proceedings, 2002. XI, 503 pages. 2002.

Vol. 2423: D. Lopresti, J. Hu, R. Kashi (Eds.), Document Analysis Systems V. Proceedings, 2002. XIII, 570 pages. 2002.

Vol. 2425: Z. Bellahsène, D. Patel, C. Rolland (Eds.), Object-Oriented Information Systems. Proceedings, 2002. XIII, 550 pages. 2002.

Vol. 2426: J.-M. Bruel, Z. Bellahsène (Eds.), Advances in Object-Oriented Information Systems.Proceedings, 2002. IX, 314 pages. 2002.

Vol. 2430: T. Elomaa, H. Mannila, H. Toivonen (Eds.), Machine Learning: ECML 2002. Proceedings, 2002. XIII, 532 pages. 2002. (Subseries LNAI).

Vol. 2431: T. Elomaa, H. Mannila, H. Toivonen (Eds.), Principles of Data Mining and Knowledge Discovery. Proceedings, 2002. XIV, 514 pages. 2002. (Subseries LNAI).

Vol. 2435: Y. Manolopoulos, P. Návrat (Eds.), Advances in Databases and Information Systems. Proceedings, 2002. XIII, 415 pages. 2002.

Vol. 2436: J. Fong, C.T. Cheung, H.V. Leong, Q. Li (Eds.), Advances in Web-Based Learning. Proceedings, 2002. XIII, 434 pages. 2002.

Vol. 2438: M. Glesner, P. Zipf, M. Renovell (Eds.), Field-Programmable Logic and Applications. Proceedings, 2002. XXII, 1187 pages. 2002.

Vol. 2439: J.J. Merelo Guervós, P. Adamidis, H.-G. Beyer, J.-L. Fernández-Villacañas, H.-P. Schwefel (Eds.), Parallel Problem Solving from Nature – PPSN VII. Proceedings, 2002. XXII, 947 pages. 2002.

Vol. 2440: J.M. Haake, J.A. Pino (Eds.), Groupware: Design, Implementation and Use. Proceedings, 2002. XII, 285 pages. 2002.

Vol. 2442: M. Yung (Ed.), Advances in Cryptology – CRYPTO 2002. Proceedings, 2002. XIV, 627 pages. 2002.

Vol. 2443: D. Scott (Ed.), Artificial Intelligence: Methodology, Systems, and Applications. Proceedings, 2002. X, 279 pages. 2002. (Subseries LNAI).

Vol. 2444: A. Buchmann, F. Casati, L. Fiege, M.-C. Hsu, M.-C. Shan (Eds.), Technologies for E-Services. Proceedings, 2002. X, 171 pages. 2002.

Vol. 2445: C. Anagnostopoulou, M. Ferrand, A. Smaill (Eds.), Music and Artificial Intelligence. Proceedings, 2002. VIII, 207 pages. 2002. (Subseries LNAI).

Vol. 2446: M. Klusch, S. Ossowski, O. Shehory (Eds.), Cooperative Information Agents VI. Proceedings, 2002. XI, 321 pages. 2002. (Subseries LNAI).

Vol. 2447: D.J. Hand, N.M. Adams, R.J. Bolton (Eds.), Pattern Detection and Discovery. Proceedings, 2002. XII, 227 pages. 2002. (Subseries LNAI).

Vol. 2448: P. Sojka, I. Kopeček, K. Pala (Eds.), Text, Speech and Dialogue. Proceedings, 2002. XII, 481 pages. 2002. (Subseries LNAI).

Vol. 2451: B. Hochet, A.J. Acosta, M.J. Bellido (Eds.), Integrated Circuit Design. Proceedings, 2002. XVI, 496 pages. 2002.

Vol. 2453: A. Hameurlain, R. Cicchetti, R. Traunmüller (Eds.), Database and Expert Systems Applications. Proceedings, 2002. XVIII, 951 pages. 2002.

Vol. 2454: Y. Kambayashi, W. Winiwarter, M. Arikawa (Eds.), Data Warehousing and Knowledge Discovery. Proceedings, 2002. XIII, 339 pages. 2002.

Vol. 2455: K. Bauknecht, A M. Tjoa, G. Quirchmayr (Eds.), E-Commerce and Web Technologies. Proceedings, 2002. XIV, 414 pages. 2002.

Vol. 2456: R. Traunmüller, K. Lenk (Eds.), Electronic Government. Proceedings, 2002. XIII, 486 pages. 2002.

Vol. 2469: W. Damm, E.-R. Olderog (Eds.), Formal Techniques in Real-Time and Fault-Tolerant Systems. Proceedings, 2002. X, 455 pages. 2002.

Vol. 2470: P. Van Hentenryck (Ed.), Principles and Practice of Constraint Programming – CP 2002. Proceedings, 2002. XVI, 794 pages. 2002.

Vol. 2483: J.D.P. Rolim, S. Vadhan (Eds.), Randomization and Approximation Techniques in Computer Science. Proceedings, 2002. VIII, 275 pages. 2002.